THE NEW

ABOLITION

W. E. B. Du Bois and the Black Social Gospel

Gary Dorrien

Yale

UNIVERSITY

PRESS

New Haven & London

Published with assistance from the Louis Stern Memorial Fund

Yale University Press books may be purchased in quantity for educational, business,
or promotional use. For information, please e-mail sales.press@yale.edu (U.S. office) or
sales@yaleup.co.uk (U.K. office).

Set in PostScript Electra type by IDS Infotech, Ltd.
Printed in the United States of America.

Library of Congress Control Number: 2015933802
ISBN: 978-0-300-20560-2

A catalogue record for this book is available from the British Library.

This paper meets the requirements of ANSI/NISO Z39.48–1992 (Permanence of Paper).

10 9 8 7 6 5 4 3 2 1

For Professor Romeo Phillips,
treasured friend and educator extraordinary

CONTENTS

PREFACE

This book comes from a deep wellspring of feeling and years of imploring colleagues, students, and lecture audiences that we need a book on the black social gospel tradition. There is a growing literature on parts of this subject, but there is no book on the black social gospel as a whole.

There came a point when I stopped complaining about this situation and applied the imploring to myself. My work operates on two tracks, ranging across social ethics and politics on one side, and modern theology and religious philosophy on the other. As a social ethicist I work mostly at the intersections of ethics, social theory, and politics, and as a historical theologian I work mostly at the intersections of modern religious and philosophical thought. Friends have noted pointedly, when I start up about the book that we need, that I have analyzed aspects of the black social gospel on both sides of my work. Surely, they reasoned, I was ready to see this subject through.

Surely I care about it too much *not* to see it through; whether I am ready is hard to say. This book's subject is distinctly important to me and is long abiding in me. I was an aspiring four-sport athlete in a semirural, lower-class area in mid–Michigan Bay County when the civil rights movement exploded into its climactic phase in the early 1960s. My parents, Jack and Virginia Dorrien, had come from similarly poor areas in Michigan's Upper Peninsula, where my father's Cree heritage made him a target of racial abuse. He became passably white by moving away, and raised his five sons as definitely white, never mind that we had obviously Native American relatives.

All my life I have been a jock with a mystical streak and autodidactic intellectual tendencies. In my youth I was a voracious reader, though never of schoolbooks. Fortunately I played sports year-round, which forced me to earn passing grades at school. My family, though not religious, got to Catholic Mass just enough for me to be caught by the image of the suffering God on a cross. Christ crucified broke through my everyday horizon of lower-class culture, the next game, and a bruised psyche. Then the stunning witness of Martin Luther King Jr. and the civil rights movement similarly broke through, eventually melding in my thought and feeling with the cross of Christ.

The images of police violence against African Americans during the great demonstrations in Birmingham and Selma made a searing impression on me. What was behind the vicious racial hostility on display? My schoolteachers said the United States was the world's greatest nation in every way that mattered, and the greatest ever. But the civil rights movement taught a different lesson.

My lowly school system fell to a half-day schedule, causing my parents to move three miles west, to Midland, where I consumed library books about the civil rights and antiwar movements. Later I became a high-profile athlete in a large sports-obsessed high school, where my politics and autodidactic intellectualism eventually alienated me from my gang of jock friends. Long before I understood very much about politics or religion, King was the formative figure for me, the exemplar of the peacemaking and justice-making way of Christ. That was the sum total of my religious worldview when I squeaked into college, mostly to play sports. Forty-plus years later it is still my touchstone.

In college I plunged into social activism and discovered that school could be interesting. Kant and Hegel put me on track to an unexpected academic career, although I resisted it, feeling called to ministry. In graduate school and seminary I studied for the Episcopal priesthood and joined solidarity organizations working on anti-imperialist and antipoverty issues. Then I worked for eight years as a pastor, community organizer, and activist in Albany, New York, writing books that led to a belated academic career.

I am grateful for the immense privilege that I hold in being able to teach and write for a living. No one in my Bay County neighborhood talked about going to college or having a "career." My neighbors and relatives would have repudiated the notion that being white conferred any cultural privileges upon them—even as they struggled intently to secure whatever white privilege they could get and passed it to me. Interrogating one's racial bias is exceedingly difficult. Interrogating one's complicity in white supremacy—a structure of power based on privilege that presumes to define what is normal—is harder yet. I am torn between knowing that I am terribly limited as an interpreter of African American social Christianity and believing that it deserves all the books it can get, even from me.

Many of the leading figures in this book were full-time ministers, and some were every-week preachers despite holding day jobs elsewhere. Nearly all were products of black churches in which the bedrock doctrine was that all human beings are brothers and sisters under the Providence of a personal God. On Sundays they preached in congregations for which the morning worship service routinely stretched long into the afternoon. A three-hour service of prayer, testimony, spectacular singing, preaching, and call-and-response was customary, because where else would you rather be? This was where the Spirit blew freely. This was where the world was differently construed. This was where a better world was prayed and preached and sung and shouted into being.

This book employs the terms "black," "African American," and "Afro-American" interchangeably, interpreting a protest tradition that prefigured and influenced contemporary usage. In the 1890s, when the National Afro-American League and the National Association of Colored Women were founded, these organizations chose names that were favored, respectively, by the protest-nationalist and accommodative-integrationist camps. The protest tradition usually preferred "Afro-American," while the accommodation camp preferred "colored" or "Negro." These were mere tendencies, however. Eminent black journalist T. Thomas Fortune gave currency to "Afro-American" in the 1880s and continued to use it during his Booker Washington phase, while W. E. B. Du Bois usually used the term "Negro." Moreover, Du Bois favored the term "colored" to mark his concern for all people on the nonwhite side of the color line. On that ground he prevailed on what the National Association for the Advancement of Colored People should be called, yielding years of in-house debates as to whether this was truly the best name for the new abolition movement. A decade later the "New Negro" movement renewed the term "Negro" for many who belonged to the protest tradition—some of whom lived to see usage change again with the rise of the Black Power movement of the 1960s. I will also employ the term "U.S. American" frequently, when such usage does not misrepresent the history I am recounting, as a protest against the presumed ownership of "America" and "American" by citizens of the United States.

This book describes four streams of black social Christianity that led to a full-fledged social gospel tradition that led to King. It puts Du Bois at the center of the story, describes founding figures who were wrongly forgotten, examines their relationships to Du Bois, and argues that the black social gospel itself was wrongly forgotten. A succeeding book will similarly revolve around King, beginning with two figures who directly influenced him—Mordecai W. Johnson and Benjamin E. Mays. For me, the tricky part in these books is to give Du Bois and King their due without letting them overwhelm the subject. Both books are primarily about the black social gospel and its call for a new abolitionist movement, not primarily about Du Bois or King. But Du Bois is central to almost everything that the black social gospel became, and King is even more so. I do not claim that Du Bois was a social gospeler, since Du Bois had only one foot in Christianity and he declined to self-identify as Christian. But I do claim that Du Bois inspired and influenced, more than anyone until King, the black social gospel tradition and its call for a new abolition.

Since there is no literature on the black social gospel as a whole, one might expect that I have few scholarly debts to acknowledge. The opposite is the case. I am indebted to countless scholars that have enriched our understanding of social, historical, religious, and political topics related to this book. I meant to name them here, but the list grew impossibly long, so the endnotes will have to suffice, with three categories of exceptions.

The first exception consists of the ever-growing scholarship on Du Bois. The classic works by Francis L. Broderick, Arnold Rampersad, and Manning Marable remain admirable and valuable, in my view, despite being overtaken by the massive scholarship of David Levering Lewis. Lewis is the towering scholar that all Du Bois scholars have to deal with, to our benefit. But Lewis is tone-deaf to the vibrant, yearning, heterodox spirituality that surged through Du Bois's work, refusing to see it as religious, much less as Christian.

For years it frustrated me that scholars routinely recycled this religion-unfriendly reading, although Marable and Cornel West dissented from it. Recently Edward J. Blum and Jonathon S. Kahn helpfully weighed in, taking seriously that Du Bois did not stop referring to his spiritual strivings after he wrote *The Souls of Black Folk*. Blum fits Du Bois too securely into the tradition of black radical Christianity and Kahn fits him too securely into the tradition of pragmatic religious naturalism. I believe that Du Bois was double-minded and purposely elusive about his personal relationship to Christianity.

But Blum and Kahn rightly insist that Du Bois had a passionate religious spirit. There are similar debates about Du Bois and double-consciousness, political theory, and social theory, on which West, Robert Gooding-Williams, Joel Williamson, Paul Gilroy, and Lawrie Balfour are especially helpful to me. Moreover, although I disagree with Adolph Reed Jr. about other things, I appreciate his emphasis that Du Bois cared above all about social justice politics opposing racial oppression. Any reading of Du Bois that depoliticizes him is not in his spirit.

My emphasis in this book is decidedly sociopolitical, not just in the Du Bois sections. The black social gospelers had differing theologies and philosophies, to which I pay ample attention. But Du Bois versus Washington was primarily an argument about social justice politics, and the black social gospelers self-identified and argued with each other primarily over things related to this matter, even after Washington was gone. They could live with a variety of theologies, especially in ecclesiology and biblical interpretation, but the crucial thing was to build strong black institutions through which religious commitments effected social change. This was a subject of dispute and accountability, one that grounded the hope of making a difference.

The second exception is a distinct category of two scholars, Ralph E. Luker and Ronald C. White Jr., who compelled scholars to stop saying that white social gospel leaders of the late nineteenth and early twentieth centuries ignored racial justice issues. Since this is a book about the development of the black social gospel tradition, I have kept discussion of the white social gospel to a minimum. The black social gospel is a distinct tradition with its own problems, figures, history, and integrity. But it was always in conversation with, and played a role within, the white social gospel movement that created ecumenical institutions and, to some degree, crossed racial lines. Luker and White refuted decades of scholarship that portrayed the white social gospel as a movement lacking any concern about racial reform. Luker, in particular, did so in a way that drew attention to black social gospel leaders. I am in his debt for that, as are many scholars in the third category.

Category three consists of scholars that have begun to provide works on black social gospel figures and contexts. Most are black religious historians. On figures and issues featured in this book I am deeply grateful for and indebted to the work of Stephen Angell, Wallace D. Best, James H. Cone, Philip S. Foner, Paula J. Giddings, Cheryl Townsend Gilkes, Anetta L. Gomez-Jefferson, Louis R. Harlan, Evelyn Brooks Higginbotham, Andre E. Johnson, John W. Kinney, Linda O. McMurry, George M. Miller, Calvin Morris, Wilson Jeremiah Moses, Robert J. Norrell, Anthony Pinn, Barbara Dianne Savage, William Welty, Cornel West, David W. Wills, and Gayraud S. Wilmore. There will be a similar list of figures in the succeeding work on the black social gospel in the King era.

I am deeply grateful to Sarah Azaransky, James Cone, Juan Floyd-Thomas, Anthony Pinn, Eboni Marshall Turman, and Cornel West for reading parts of the manuscript and giving me their expert advice. Some of this help began before there was a book, as I worked on Reverdy Ransom and pondered the idea of a book. As always I am grateful to my doctoral students for the distinct privilege of being their friend and learning with them. A few have recently graduated: Malinda Berry, Ian Doescher, Christine Pae, Eboni Marshall Turman, Rima Vesely-Flad, and Demian Wheeler. Others are en route: Nkosi Anderson, Chloe Breyer, Jeremy Kirk, David Orr, Dan Rohrer, Isaac Sharp, Charlene Sinclair, Aaron Stauffer, Joe Strife, Colleen Wessel-McCoy, Todd Willison, Jason Wyman, and Tracy Riggle Young. I am grateful to Nkosi, Todd, and Andrew Jungclaus for running down some references, and to Jason for helping me with the photo gallery.

As much as possible I have relied on lectures, sermons, and published writings as source material for this book, because the black social gospel was a public enterprise. It was carried out in a counterpublic black sphere that had to be invented, and in interracial forums more readily invented, in which African Americans struggled against the contempt and invisibility rendered to them by the dominant society. The black social gospel has been ignored until recently, but not because its advocates did not try to reach public audiences. The story that matters was out there in the literature of the black press, the witness of religious communities, and the writings of black intellectuals.

For the rights of access to materials in special collections, I am grateful to the Schomburg Center for Research in Black Culture, New York Public Library, in New York City; the W. E. B. Du Bois Library of the University of Massachusetts in Amherst, Massachusetts; the Rembert E. Stokes Library of Wilberforce University in Wilberforce, Ohio; Houghton Library of Harvard University in Cambridge, Massachusetts; and the Ohio Historical Society in Columbus, Ohio. For daily access to materials not in special collections, and for unfailing courtesy and support, I am grateful to the staff of Burke Library of Columbia University. I am grateful for permission to adapt previously published material from my *Social Ethics in the Making: Interpreting an American Tradition* (Oxford: Wiley-Blackwell, 2009).

Many thanks to my editors at Yale University Press for their skillful work, especially the executive editor Jennifer Banks, copy editor Kate Davis, and senior manuscript editor Susan Laity. And thanks to my longtime indexer Diana Witt for another excellent index.

Lastly I thank Eris McClure and Sara Biggs Dorrien for living with this book as it claimed a place in our lives and occasioned countless conversations. I have written and lectured about this topic for many years, but the book was launched at the Chautauqua Institution in July 2011, where I provided afternoon counterpoint to morning lectures on espionage. Eris and Sara could hear a new book coming, and my friend Joan Brown Campbell regaled us with stories about King, Benjamin Mays, Andrew Young, and Otis Moss Jr.—a week to savor for years to come.

Alexander Crummell   Henry McNeal Turner

William J. Simmons

Booker T. Washington

Ida B. Wells

Alexander Walters

W. E. B. Du Bois

Reverdy C. Ransom

Nannie H. Burroughs   Adam Clayton Powell Sr.

George W. Woodbey   Richard R. Wright Jr.

THE NEW ABOLITION

Recovering the Black Social Gospel

The black social gospel is wrongly and strangely overlooked. One might expect there to be dozens of books on a tradition of thought and activism that began in the 1870s, that included the mentors and allies of Martin Luther King Jr., plus King himself, and that remains relevant today. Instead there are none. Few books even refer to the black social gospel, and there are no books that deal with this tradition as a whole. In recent years scholars have begun to rectify the former situation, but it is no easy task to overcome decades of stereotypes about a tradition that supposedly had few proponents and was best left for dead for other reasons too.

The civil rights movement began in 1884 with a call for what became the National Afro-American League in 1890, and it had a brilliant moment of hope in the Niagara Movement of 1905 to 1909. It entered a second phase of activism in 1909 with the founding of what became the National Association for the Advancement of Colored People (NAACP). It entered a third phase in December 1955 by exploding into a historic mass movement. In every phase it had leaders who espoused the social ethical religion and politics of modern social Christianity.

But the name "civil rights movement" is usually reserved for the movement of the 1950s and 1960s, and most scholars have ignored the black social gospel that supported civil rights activism in all three of its historic phases, struggled for a place in the black churches, and provided the neo-abolitionist theology of social justice that the civil rights movement proclaimed and sang. This book describes the tradition of black social Christianity that arose in the Progressive Era, gave leaders and ballast to the civil rights movement, provided much of the movement's intellectual underpinning, and remains a vital perspective.

The white social gospel movement is renowned and heavily chronicled. It arose during the Progressive Era and was already a movement by the mid-1880s, with national organizations and a movement agenda linked with Progressivism. It had its heyday from 1900 to 1917, and by the 1930s it was mostly a peace and ecumenical movement. The black social gospel arose during the same period and had its heyday in the King years. It lacked movement organizations during the early struggle for civil rights, but the black social gospel gave church leaders, intellectuals, and activists to the civil rights movement, advocating protest activism within reluctant religious communities and helping to create an alternative public sphere of excluded voices. Later, as a succeeding book will recount, black social gospelers Mordecai Wyatt Johnson, Benjamin E. Mays, and Howard Thurman influenced King and other leaders of the Southern Christian Leadership Conference. Still later, the black social gospel influenced the development of liberation theology and progressive black theology. But most of its founders are forgotten, and the work of remembrance is strewn with obstacles.[1]

The black social gospel arose during the trauma and abandonment of Reconstruction, resuming the struggle for black freedom in America. Like the white social gospel and Progressive movements, it espoused principles of social justice, conceived the federal government as an indispensable guarantor of constitutional rights, struggled with industrialization and economic injustice, and grappled with the Great Migration. Like the white social gospel, it also wrestled with modern challenges to religious belief. But the black social gospel addressed these things very differently than white progressives did, for racial oppression trumped everything in the African American context *and* refigured how other problems were experienced.

The black social gospel affirmed the dignity, sacred personhood, creativity, and moral agency of African Americans and responded to racial oppression. It asked what a new abolitionism should be and what role the churches should play within it. Like the white social gospel, it had numerous ideologies and theologies, but here the trump concern was distinctly given, obvious, and a survival issue: upholding black dignity in the face of racial tyranny. Here the belief in a divine ground of human selfhood powered struggles for black self-determination and campaigns of resistance to white oppression.

The early social gospel heralded the growing prosperity and democracy of U.S. American society during the very period when black Americans were stripped of their constitutional rights in much of the nation and terrorized by an epidemic of racial lynching. This contradiction did not stop black social gospel leaders from employing the rhetoric of progress and idealism, but it shaped their understanding of how the church should struggle for social justice. White social gospel theologians took for granted their access to the general public. Black social gospel theologians could barely imagine what it felt like to address the general public. They had to create a counterpublic sphere merely to have a public. White social gospel theologians sought to be stewards of a good society and usually preached a moral influence theory of the cross. Otherwise they played down the cross of Jesus as problematic for modern Christianity. The black social gospel arose from churches where preaching about the cross was not optional, because black Americans experienced it every day as a persecuted, crucified people.[2]

Like any tradition, the black social gospel can be defined broadly or narrowly. I will do both, describing four streams of black social Christianity and a full-fledged progressive black social gospel that emerged mostly from the third stream. All four of these traditions have rich legacies, but the black social gospel that led to King came mostly from the protest group aligned with Du Bois and some figures in the fourth stream, plus a tiny Socialist flank. The full-fledged black social gospel combined an emphasis on black dignity and personhood with protest activism for racial justice, a comprehensive social justice agenda, an insistence that authentic Christian faith is incompatible with racial prejudice, an emphasis on the social ethical teaching of Jesus, and an acceptance of modern scholarship and social consciousness. Reverdy Ransom, Alexander Walters, Adam Clayton Powell Sr., Richard R. Wright Jr., Mordecai Wyatt Johnson, Howard Thurman, Benjamin E. Mays, Pauli Murray, and Martin Luther King Jr. were exemplars of it, comprising an ample tradition by themselves.

I could have made things easier by restricting my focus to this line of figures, plus Du Bois. But to confine this work to the figures that joined Du Bois in the Niagara Movement and the NAACP, espoused liberal theology, and led to Mays and King would miss nearly half the story. Du Bois himself had an ambiguous religious standpoint, though he had a huge influence on what became the black social gospel. The same thing is true, very differently, of Booker T. Washington, who epitomized the social gospel to a vast audience. Moreover, Henry McNeal Turner dismissed the black social gospel, but he and William J. Simmons paved the way to it. Ida B. Wells took no interest in modern theological scholarship, but she gave the black social gospel an unsurpassed example of righteous Christian militancy. Thus, this book begins with a broad rendering of black social Christianity before narrowing to the specific version of it that fired America's greatest liberation movement.

Certain things that define the category "social gospel" apply across racial and denominational lines. The social gospel was fundamentally a movement, not a doctrine, featuring a social ethical understanding of the Christian faith. It taught that Christianity has a mission to transform the structures of society in the direction of social justice. This idea was rooted in the commands of the Bible to lift the yoke of oppression and to build a just order. At its best it refashioned the demand of antebellum abolitionism to break the chains of racial caste. The social gospel, however, had something that previous socially oriented forms of Christianity lacked—modern social consciousness, especially the idea that there is such a thing as social structure. The concepts of "social structure" and "social justice" came into being in the 1880s with the rise of the Socialist, trade union, and Progressive movements. Not coincidentally, so did the social gospel, the fields of sociology and social ethics, the idea of social salvation, and the idea that theology had to be modernized to deal with social salvation and the modern world. Only with the rise of modern social Christianity did Christian thinkers begin to say that salvation had to be personal *and* social to be saving. If there was such a thing as social structure, salvation had to be reconceptualized to take account of it.

In Europe this idea was called Christian Socialism, a movement radiating out of England and Germany. In the United States it had to be called something else. Until 1910 it was usually called "applied Christianity" or "social Christianity." Afterward it was called the social gospel. In the social gospel, society became a subject of redemption. Christianity had a mission to transform society as a whole, building the kingdom of God on earth. Ransom, Wright, Walters, Powell Sr., and George Washington Woodbey spoke this language with full self-consciousness and conviction. In the succeeding generation, so did Johnson, Mays, Thurman, Murray, King, Adam Clayton Powell Jr., and many others. These black Christian leaders spoke of "Christianizing" American society, calling America to fulfill the Declaration of Independence and the Reconstruction Amendments. Many of them believed that "advanced" societies got to be advanced by submitting to supposedly universal laws of civilization, attaining the inevitable social progress that came with submitting to the laws. Much of black social Christianity was procapitalist, equating capitalism with freedom and economic self-determination, but the full-fledged black social gospel stream was usually critical of capitalism, holding out for equality and economic democracy. The black social gospel had radical wings that espoused democratic Socialism and/or anti-imperialism, and it had accomplished proponents that were wrongly forgotten.

The founders of Afro-American social Christianity were products of the bitter defeat of Radical Reconstruction, who were forced to imagine a new abolitionist politics and Christianity. For them, Christianity had no social relevance if it did not lift the struggle for racial justice above everything else. It was not simply a matter of reclaiming the abolitionist religion of David Walker and Sojourner Truth, for the new struggle for racial justice took place amid the turmoil of the modern social problem. The legacy of abolitionist "radical religion" was foundational for black social gospelers, but they lived in a time of new problems, ministering in churches that for the most part did not support the idea of social justice ministry.

Turner and Simmons lived through the drama of Reconstruction and went on to pioneer forms of social Christianity in the African Methodist Episcopal Church (AME) and the American National Baptist Convention. Turner is usually understood, rightly, as the last of the nineteenth-century black religious radicals, a throwback to the abolitionist era who found himself living in a time of Gilded Age smallness, the evisceration of the Fourteenth Amendment's "privileges or immunities" of citizenship, and the betrayal of the Fifteenth Amendment's right to vote. But to view him only as the symbol of a shattered liberationist or nationalist dream is to perpetuate the misreading that there was no black social gospel. Turner also marked the beginning of something, as did his Baptist peer, Simmons.

The racial crisis of the 1890s yielded four versions of black social Christianity, plus a tiny Socialist flank, before and after Du Bois rose to prominence. Booker T. Washington became a colossal figure in American life by bargaining with white elites for a season of peace and economic opportunity for blacks. He had a vast national following among blacks and whites, counting black and white social gospel leaders among his strongest allies. For a while, the Washington group was so dominant that many Bookerites believed there was no such thing as a legitimate alternative or opposition; Washington believed it adamantly. His black supporters included powerful denominational leaders such as AME bishops Wesley J. Gaines and Abram Grant, African Methodist Episcopal Zion (hereafter AME Zion) bishop George W. Clinton, and Baptist officials E. C. Morris and R. H. Boyd.[3]

The second group of socially active black Christians took the Turner path of nationalist separation and/or African emigration. The only hope for African Americans was to have their own nation. This group had a distinguished leader in Episcopal missionary and intellectual Alexander Crummell, an equally Anglophile leader in Episcopal bishop and missionary James T. Holly, and a loyal follower of Turner in AME missionary Alfred L. Ridgel. Then as now, there were different kinds of black nationalism. Broadly defined, black nationalism is the view that all people of African descent share something as a nation or people. In the nineteenth and twentieth centuries, the posited basis for national belonging was sometimes biological, rendering the nation as analogous to a biological organism; and/or ontological, making a claim about the distinct being of blackness; and/or cultural or sociohistorical, making a claim about black cultural authenticity or distinctiveness. Defined broadly, however, there were nationalists in all four streams of black social Christianity. The second group espoused stricter and more emphatic forms of nationalism, contending that blacks were a distinct people that needed to create a sovereign nation-state and, even if the statehood project failed, a black civilization.

Some nationalists devoted themselves to the hope of colonizing West Africa, following Turner, or Haiti, following Holly, but many eventually gave up on emigration, following Crummell. Much of the nationalist tradition shared the emphases of Crummell and Turner on moral uplift, authority, elite leadership, and the shortcomings of ordinary black Americans. Despite its rhetoric of sepa-ration, the nationalist tradition ironically played a major role in transmitting assimilationist values into African American culture. Most black nationalists were politically and culturally conservative, and most had a conflicted relation-ship with Washington after he rose to prominence. But some combined protest egalitarianism and separatist politics. Baptist minister Sutton Griggs and Congregational minister William Henry Ferris, for example, each had one foot in the Niagara Movement. Black nationalism had an electrifying moment after World War I, with the rise of Marcus Garvey and his movement. A generation earlier, Crummell and Turner clashed over the question of whether nationalists should continue to strive for a separate nation-state. Turner became the domi-nant figure in this school of thought and activism by saying yes.[4]

The third group vehemently opposed Washington's strategy and his "Tuskegee Machine," calling for a new abolitionist politics of racial and social justice. Boston journalist William Monroe Trotter had church-based allies in this cause before Du Bois emerged, notably AME minister Reverdy Ransom, AME journalist Ida B. Wells (later, Wells-Barnett), and Baptist ministers J. Milton Waldron and William Henry Scott. After Du Bois emerged and cofounded the Niagara Movement, there were numerous black social gospelers that identified with Niagara protest activism, notably Ransom, Wells-Barnett, Waldron, AME minister Richard R. Wright Jr., Baptist ministers James R. L. Diggs and Peter James Bryant, Congregational minister Byron Gunner, Episcopal rectors Robert W. Bagnall and George Frazier Miller, and Baptist layman and historian Carter G. Woodson. Eminent Presbyterian minister Francis J. Grimké was an ally of this group, as was his brother Archibald Grimké, a prominent attorney with ties to Trotter. Diggs, while serving as president of

State University in 1906, boasted to Du Bois, "I am indoctrinating our students with the Niagara spirit."[5]

The fourth group was equally important for what became the black social gospel. These figures advocated civil rights activism while relating more diplomatically to Booker Washington and Bookerism. In the heyday of the battle between the protest and accommodation parties, nearly every public gathering of one party evoked a name-calling riposte from the other. The Bookerite *New York Age* called the Niagarites "an aggregation of soreheads" that selfishly prized notoriety over the interests of black Americans. Both sides, however, alienated people that disliked ideological bickering, a fact that each side ruefully acknowledged. Religious communities naturally brought together the rival camps and the nonaligned. At church, ministers appealed to Christian fellowship and racial solidarity; moreover, many ministers had friends on both sides of the partisan divide. The fourth group conceived the social gospel as a both/and enterprise, contending that Du Bois–style militancy and Washington-style realism were both indispensable to the civil rights movement that was needed. AME Zion bishop Alexander Walters, Baptist educator Nannie H. Burroughs, Howard University dean Kelly Miller, and Baptist minister Adam Clayton Powell Sr. were leading figures in this group. Others included sociologists Monroe Work and George Edmund Haynes, Methodist Episcopal minister William Henry Brooks, Baptist feminists Lucy Wilmot Smith and Sarah Willie Layten, Congregational ministers Henry Hugh Proctor and William N. DeBerry, and Gammon Theological Seminary theologian J. W. E. Bowen.[6]

Meanwhile, Baptist ministers George W. Woodbey and George W. Slater Jr. tried to shift the debate to the ravages of capitalism, espousing a Marxian socialist version of the social gospel. Woodbey had a long career as a Socialist Party organizer and was also active in the Industrial Workers of the World (IWW). There were black Socialists besides Du Bois and Ransom in the mainstream of the NAACP, notably Bagnall and George Frazier Miller, who served Episcopal parishes in Detroit and Brooklyn, respectively. Bagnall and Miller wrote for A. Philip Randolph's Harlem Socialist magazine the *Messenger*; Bagnall served as director of branches of the NAACP; and Miller led Howard University's alumni association. But Socialist activism had a lot going against it in black communities: a fantasized solidarity with a racist white proletariat, the specter of appearing to be anti-American, and the desire of African Americans to own property and succeed in the existing system. These factors suppressed Du Bois's Socialism for twenty years.[7]

These four groups, plus the Socialists, constituted the orbit of black social Christianity in the early twentieth century. Some of the figures I have named were full-fledged social gospel progressives, and some were not progressive about anything. But all had some connection to social Christian intellectualism or activism. The borderline cases were sufficiently prominent as activist ministers, church workers, or religious intellectuals that excluding them is harder to justify than naming them. Washington is the towering example of a mostly conservative black social Christian leader. Kelly Miller was equally conservative on many issues, but he was an important player in the development of social Christian intellectualism. Monroe Work, despite moving into a secular career, had a background in the ministry and belonged to the social gospel network of ministers and intellectuals, as did George Edmund Haynes, a longtime associate of the Federal Council of Churches. These figures contributed to the defining social gospel discussion of how to make Christianity relevant to modern life and the struggle for civil rights. There were enough of them to make a difference and to launch a tradition that bloomed into something historic.

For some in the fourth group, the founding of the NAACP in 1909 and the subsequent fading of Washington nullified the necessity of making a both/and argument, while others stuck to it for the rest of their lives. The black social gospel brought ordinary church members into the civil rights movement, though never as many as Du Bois and Woodson envisioned, which prompted both to sharply criticize the churches. The founders called for a second great movement of abolition, passing this cause to Mordecai Wyatt Johnson, Vernon Johns, Adam Clayton Powell Jr., Benjamin E. Mays, Howard Thurman, Pauli Murray, Martin Luther King Jr., Ralph Abernathy, James Lawson, Wyatt Tee Walker, Andrew Young, Gardner Taylor, Samuel Proctor, Jesse Jackson, and many other leaders of the civil rights movement of the 1950s and '6os. This roll of black social gospel leaders is vastly more accomplished and interesting than its white counterpart, and is every bit as variegated theologically. Yet most of the founders are long forgotten, and even the familiar figures often are not identified with the social gospel.

Numerous conventions have long kept the black social gospel from being remembered, and they remain obstacles to recovering it today. It is often assumed that the orbit of early black social Christianity was very small, numbering only a handful of ministers; thus I have begun by refuting the deadliest assumption. For decades scholars claimed that the social gospel was an overwhelmingly white phenomenon that ignored racial justice issues. This twofold claim misleadingly generalized from a few social gospel leaders, obscuring the complex and conflicted debates that white Christian progressives held about racial justice, and it obscured the existence of black social gospelers.

In addition, Washington and Du Bois are usually read out of social Christianity, notwithstanding that both influenced it enormously. Many scholars have recycled the convention that black churches were too self-centered and preoccupied with survival to advocate a social justice agenda, never mind that the black social gospel leaders that were thus ignored addressed this issue constantly.[8]

A broader convention of American historiography has applied with particular vengeance to black social gospel leaders. The convention is that religious intellectuals no longer mattered by the end of the nineteenth century. In that case, black religious intellectuals did not matter whether or not they existed. Both verdicts got ballast from black academics of the early twentieth century that historians tend to favor—Ralph Bunche, Alain Locke, Abram Harris, E. Franklin Frazier, and Rayford Logan. All shared the customary academic prejudice against religion and religious intellectuals, contending that the black church was hopelessly provincial and conservative. So black social gospel intellectuals such as Ransom, Wright, and Johnson had no chance of being remembered, and even Thurman and Mays were overlooked for decades.[9]

Another kind of dismissal flips the "unimportant" or "didn't exist" rationales, reasoning that the category "social gospel" does not name anything worth distinguishing in African American Christianity. This objection comports with the image of a singular, politically active "black church" that many people hold. But black churches have always been widely diverse theologically, politically, culturally, and socially. There has never been a dominant or singular black church in the mold of the usual stereotype, which, ironically, is a social gospel construct. The very influence of the social gospel idea of what the black church is, or should be, has obscured that it is a social gospel idea, which many black religious communities reject. The leading architects of this quite particular idea were Simmons, Ransom, Walters, Wells-Barnett, Du Bois, Wright, Powell, Woodson, Johnson, Mays, and King. They realized it was a modern social Christian idea, and said so.

The black social gospel produced significant religious intellectuals and activists, and not only during the King era. The Progressive Era was an emergency for African Americans that posed new problems that became defining for black religion. For fifty years black religion had fixed on the dream of abolition. Then came Emancipation—a veritable "Coming of the Lord," as Du Bois put it—only to be followed by the terrible necessity of imagining a new abolition. Black churches in the late nineteenth and early twentieth centuries had much at stake in the question of whether they should support efforts to fuse social justice politics with progressive theology. Subsequently the black social gospel paved the way to the civil rights explosion of the 1950s, and it continues to be espoused wherever religious leaders carry on the legacies of Ransom, Walters, Mays, Murray, and King.

The civil rights movement of the 1950s and '60s was sufficiently profuse, unwieldy, and many-layered to yield vastly different accounts of what it was, how it came together, and where it went. Undeniably, the movement had a religious dimension, but scholars debate almost every aspect of this influence, pushing back against interpretations that attribute too much importance to religion or too little, or too much or too little emphasis on charismatic leaders, community organizations, or anything not at the local level. Much of the best scholarship of the past generation has restored due credit to black churches for helping to spark and sustain the movement, serving as the sites at which most of it took place. Other important works have pushed back against too much religion, usually by playing up community organizing. But religion versus community organizing is a strange debate, revealing more about interpretive fashions than about what happened. "Religion" goes hand in hand, in the case of the civil rights movement, with local communities, activist organizing, and public intellectual discourse. We need to take the story back to the black social gospel tradition that pressed the issue of social justice, organized at the community and denominational levels, and created public intellectuals. King did not come from nowhere, and neither did the civil rights explosion of the 1950s.[10]

Throughout the first and second phases of the civil rights movement, and even in its heyday third phase, only a minority of Afro-American congregations supported social justice preaching and activism. Turner and Simmons were accused throughout their careers of replacing religion with politics, notwithstanding that Turner was a powerful revival preacher and Simmons preached about the saving grace of sincere piety. Ransom's clerical colleagues in Chicago and Boston were so offended by his advocacy of the social gospel that they drove him out of both cities. This, despite the facts that Ransom belonged to an abolitionist denomination and he ministered in the two cities that seemed best suited to support social gospel activism. Ransom and Wright, after years of being thwarted by bishops, reluctantly concluded that they had to become bishops, after which they vied with bishops that wanted nothing to do with protest movements. Woodson, writing the first comprehensive history of black Christianity in 1921, organized his account around the battle between a minority tradition of progressives linked to abolitionism and the social gospel and a dominant tradition of conservatives that resisted modernity and social religion. A decade later, Mays documented that most black churches did not preach or practice anything like his concept of social gospel religion. A generation later, King had ample experience with this problem, as his own denomination opposed the civil rights movement and only a minority of black congregations supported it during his lifetime.[11]

The founders of black social Christianity were distinct and marginalized in their interactions with the white social gospel movement and within Afro-American Christianity. They were marginalized ecumenically because white American Protestantism was as segregated and as prone to white supremacism as the rest of American society. They were marginalized in black churches for pressing a national social justice agenda and for adopting social gospel theology. Some of them succeeded sufficiently to win denominational leadership positions, take over the publishing houses, and change the mainstream. But the founders' long two-sided struggle for legitimacy and recognition kept them from being remembered after they were gone. Turner, Simmons, Ransom, Wells-Barnett, Burroughs, Walters, Woodbey, Johnson, and Wright would not have been forgotten had scholars and journalists paid attention to the black social gospel. As it is, Wells-Barnett had to wait until the 1970s to be remembered, and the others, until recently, have been confined to histories of the black Methodist and Baptist Churches.

The black social gospel had a distinct integrity *and* much of it had significant dealings with white social gospelers and progressives. Some black social gospel leaders became public figures by bridging both worlds, providing rare evidence that such a thing was possible in Jim Crow America. Walters, Johnson, Mays, and Thurman had sparkling careers on the lecture circuits of ecumenical organizations, especially the Student Christian Movement. Some black social gospel leaders had dual memberships in black and white Baptist denominations. Some belonged to black denominations that were deeply involved in the ecumenical movement. Some operated in predominantly white denominations, especially the Episcopal and Congregational Churches, while Egbert Ethelred Brown carried out a pioneering ministry at Harlem Unitarian Church. Ransom, Walters, Haynes, and Mays were important players in the Federal Council of Churches, and Woodbey was the Socialist Party's leading black organizer and author. But these relationships were not reciprocal. White church leaders did not treat their Afro-American colleagues as leaders of a social gospel tradition or as equal counterparts in the development of ecumenical social Christianity, and the Socialist movement made little attempt to recruit black members.[12]

I confess to admiring the black apostles that dreamed of abolishing America's system of racial caste. They resisted with shimmering dignity, even as some were deeply wounded by racism. They wrung a liberating message from the Christianity of their time. They did not settle for making segregation more tolerable. They rebelled and endured, taking the long view, laying the ground-work for something better than the regime of oppression and exclusion they inherited. They conceived what social salvation meant in post-Reconstruction black religion. Sometimes they played into the hands of white racists, advo-cating a "politics of respectability" that recycled harmful stereotypes about Afro-American culture and manners. The nationalist tradition, in particular, sometimes folded ugly denigrations of black humanity into its message of racial solidarity. Some social gospel preaching about family life caused particular harm to women in perpetuating stereotypes. Many social gospel ministers exhorted women to keep the churches going with no chance of becoming church leaders or public leaders of any kind. Whenever they preached about gay and lesbian sexuality, it was in condemnation. Sometimes they exaggerated the conservatism of their black church opponents, which undercut the very moral agency they sought to mobilize. But the problem of transcending "compensatory religion" was terribly real for black social gospel leaders, and without their witness the radical social gospel theology and activism of King are inexplicable.[13]

NEW ABOLITION FOUNDERS

Turner and Simmons were pioneers of black social Christianity, bridging the Civil War and Progressive Era generations, in different ways clearing a path for the social gospel. Turner enabled new abolition movements that he did not join, as he believed that America was hopelessly hostile territory for blacks. He was singly responsible for much of the explosive growth of the AME Church in Georgia during Reconstruction. He roared for equal rights and the dream of African emigration. He preached a gospel of Christian revival and personal responsibility, teaching that God is black. He defied white terrorists fearlessly. He railed against enemies but was rough on underachievers and whiners too, blistering what he called "scullions." Having worked hard for the Republican Party, Turner wanted to love it, but he despised it after the party sold out Reconstruction. Turner's rough edges and his fixation with colonizing West Africa caused him to fade in later life, but he was a giant figure in the black church struggle against white racism who distinctly prefigured liberation theology.

Simmons had a similar generational experience, although he died young, and his modernism was stronger. Like Turner, Simmons worked hard for Radical Reconstruction, he treasured the abolitionists, and, like them, he conceived the God of the Bible as a partisan, liberating friend of the poor and oppressed. As a journalist, author, educator, and minister, Simmons kept alive the witness and lore of David Walker, Sojourner Truth, Nat Turner, Henry Highland Garnet, Alexander Crummell, Frederick Douglass, and other black abolitionists. He stood up for the rights and empowerment of women, insisting that feminism had an important role to play in the new Christian abolition. He mediated the debate among black Baptists over assimilation versus separatism, taking a middling position that did not prevail in the National Baptist Convention. He was the person most responsible for getting black Baptists to pull together in a national convention. He also mediated, before Du Bois entered the picture, an intense debate among black Baptists about the priority of higher education. Had Simmons lived to see the issue become Du Bois versus Washington, he undoubtedly would have kept saying that higher education and vocational education were equally important and should not be set against each other. At least, he would have kept saying it until this question was no longer a defining issue for the new abolition.

Ransom, Wells, and Walters played major roles in early black social Christianity. Ransom advocated liberal social gospel theology and radical social gospel Socialism. He personified the spirit of the Niagara Movement. He pioneered the cause of black Christian Socialism and cut his teeth in politics by joining Wells's anti-lynching crusade. Wells, more than anyone, established that the struggle against lynching had to be defining for the new abolition. She inspired, implored, and shamed such a movement into being. For a while, in the early 1890s, she generated more publicity and controversy than any black American, seizing the years that fell between a fading Frederick Douglass and an ascending Booker Washington. Then she married Frederick Barnett, just as Washington skyrocketed to eminence and Walters emerged as a civil rights leader. Walters espoused social gospel theology, political independence, Pan-African consciousness, civil rights agitation, and, most important, united-front activism for civil rights. He symbolized the volatile racial politics of the early twentieth century by leading an organization that featured pro-Washington and anti-Washington flanks. In Walters's case the usual story of embattlement with the church did not occur, as the AME Zion Church took pride in his leadership and accomplishments. But he had his hands full trying to hold together and sustain a civil rights protest movement.

In different ways these figures made society a subject of redemption, and all made a mark before Du Bois versus Washington became the issue. A black tradition of the social gospel was already coming when Du Bois dramatically entered the picture. It already had four ideological tendencies when Du Bois burst into prominence, which cut to a famous dualism shortly afterward. Kelly

Miller introduced the distinction that has ruled the field ever since, identifying Du Bois with black radicalism and Washington with black conservatism. Miller was a Howard University dean and sociologist, socially conservative, antifeminist, strongly procapitalist, thoroughly middle-class, and imbued with indignation that white America violated his rights as a human being and a citizen. His binary had an unintended upshot, as he tried to keep the two groups from breaking apart. Miller stressed that even black conservatives opposed racism and the Du Bois faction was vastly outnumbered. Many black social gospel ministers implored against breaking apart; Adam Clayton Powell Sr. put it poignantly many times. There are no black conservatives, Powell would say, so why are we fighting over radical versus conservative?[14]

Liberationist historian Gayraud S. Wilmore, in his landmark work *Black Religion and Black Radicalism* (1973), offered an answer that built upon Miller's historic distinction. First, there was definitely such a thing as black conservatism, contrary to integrationist liberals like Powell. Second, what mattered was to define and defend black radicalism. Wilmore offered a three-factor definition, explaining that the radical tradition in black religion sought to be liberated from white domination, commended respect for Africa, and used protest and agitation in the struggle for liberation. Wilmore noted that black radicalism, thus defined, tended to be "less political" and "less obsessed with ideology on the grand scale" than other forms of radical politics, such as social democracy, Marxist syndicalism, Communism, or Progressivism. In black radicalism, "race and color are at the root of the problems of Western civilization." Black radicalism perceived the soul sickness of white society—something deeper than mere racism. Thus it did not sing the liberal song of racial integration.[15]

Wilmore cogently explicated much of the religious contribution to black radicalism, an intellectual tradition analyzed by political scientist Cedric J. Robinson in his classic work, *Black Marxism* (1983), and developed theologically in the seminal works of James Cone, *A Black Theology of Liberation* (1970) and *Martin & Malcolm & America* (1991). Though Robinson did not mention Wilmore or Cone, he developed a similar critique of Western religiosity as a structure of domination, emphasizing the unique experiences of blacks in Western contexts. Robinson described Du Bois, Trinidadian cultural critic C. L. R. James, and novelist Richard Wright as the major exemplars of this tradition. For Wilmore, the exemplary black radical was Turner, who towered above others "without peer in the early twentieth century." Turner was deeply alienated from white society, Wilmore explained, and he called for reparations to finance black emigration to West Africa, whereas social gospel liberals (like Powell) complained about fighting because they lacked the will to fight white supremacy. On this basis,

Wilmore ignored black social gospel leaders of the early twentieth century—barely mentioning any—in his otherwise outstanding account of black religion, a textbook that dominated black religious historiography for four decades. Wilmore argued that Turner should have challenged Washington for national leadership after Douglass died, but Turner failed to try, and afterward black Christianity got a generation of leaders not worth mentioning, except Ransom and Walters, whom Wilmore mentioned only in passing.[16]

The black social gospel founders deserved greater credit for advocating social justice causes that Turner spurned, and many of them were equally or more radical than Douglass, who advocated progressive assimilation to the end of his days. There were three large reasons why Turner did not challenge Washington in the late 1890s: He lost influence by insulting the majority of African Americans with harshly demeaning statements. He lost followers by insisting on back-to-Africa. And he shared most of Washington's ideology. Had Turner felt compelled to choose between Washington and Du Bois, he would have chosen Washington, for whom he had greater respect. As it was, Turner believed that Du Bois versus Washington was about the wrong things, so he looked away in disgust.

Afro-Americans had to have their own nation. For Turner, everything else was a sideshow, a waste of time. The Du Bois group had a better idea, even if it eventually required cutting a deal with white liberals, something that black social gospel progressives were willing to do, with no lack of commitment to abolishing white oppression. Ransom, Wells, Walters, Waldron, and Wright were leading examples. All were already adamant, when Du Bois came along, that Washington did not epitomize black social Christianity. Many others said it more gently, fashioning a Booker-yes, Booker-no dialectic. The founders established a tradition of black social Christianity that was as radical as Du Bois on one flank and nearly as conservative as Washington, for a while, on the other flank. Put differently, there were black social gospel founders that fully belonged to the tradition of black religious radicalism, there were others that did not, and both things were already true before Du Bois came out against Washington.[17]

But Du Bois is central to this story because he changed the conversation and made everybody deal with him. He did not merely take up an existing critique of Washington's strategy, putting it more colorfully and memorably. He inspired a revolution of consciousness that defined the problem of the twentieth century and provided a language for it. He helped to launch the Pan-African movement, the Niagara Movement, and the NAACP, and helped to radicalize the black social gospel through his influence on Ransom, Wright, Walters, Waldron, Powell, Johnson, Mays, and others. The double-consciousness that Du Bois projected onto all African Americans was deeply and powerfully true for him and a source of creativity in him. He was simultaneously black and American. He grew up with little experience of racial abuse but became an unsurpassed critic of the color line. He railed against the evils of white civilization while affirming the intellectualism and progressive social ideals that he internalized from white civilization. Du Bois fashioned an alternative to the draining debate between nationalists and integrationists by affirming his own tortured double-consciousness. Black Americans had to stop taking sides about which of their selves to give up, opting for a richer, contentious, full-bodied struggle for liberation and radical democracy.

Eventually, Du Bois tempered his emphasis on moral failings and uplift elitism, dropped neo-Lamarckian theory and his early Social Darwinist tropes, let go of romantic imperialism, pulled back from his neo-Hegelian idealism, absorbed Freud and Marx, and dropped the too-simple, idealistic, dualistic idea of double-consciousness. But through all his shifts and phases, Du Bois fixed on exemplary individuality—the character, status, personhood, and circumstances of personal examples. He construed his life as an example through which he fashioned his ideas about race.

Though he began as a Crummell-style elitist and neo-Lamarckian, Du Bois later adopted what he called a "vaster and far more intricate jungle of ideas conditioned on unconscious and subconscious reflexes of living things." Political theorist Lawrie Balfour aptly cautions that Du Bois traded on his readers' awareness that he was too important to be a "mere example." Du Bois mined the fissure between his status as a member of a denigrated caste and his role as a race leader, and he stuck to his focus on exemplary individuality long after he mitigated its elitist drawbacks by embracing radical democratic Socialism. For many years Du Bois had to live down the charge that he cared about elite performers while Washington cared about ordinary workers. There was always something ridiculous about this comparison, yet Du Bois provided grist for it by insisting, in the spirit of Crummell, "The Negro race, like all races, is going to be saved by its exceptional men." This trope provided quotable material for countless sermons, editorials, church bulletins, and commencement addresses. Gradually, Du Bois bridled at hearing it from speakers lacking his commitment to radical democracy. He got increasingly forthright, in response, about economic justice and the structural ravages of global capitalism. But that did not dissuade him from focusing on what it meant to be an exemplar in a wretched time.[18]

For two decades that question overwhelmingly favored Washington. Du Bois grew up in a quiet New England town where white men took pride in having fought to free blacks from slavery; Washington was born into slavery and schooled in oppression. Du Bois was encouraged by admiring teachers to fill his head with Hegel and social theory; Washington had to claw his way to a vocational school, where he was trained in survival education. Washington achieved a level of national renown and esteem that few Americans have experienced, widely regarded as a paragon of virtue, but Du Bois brilliantly challenged Washington over the future of black Americans. Washington lived to see the argument turn in Du Bois's favor, but the upshot was only beginning to appear when Washington passed from the scene.

Today Washington is remembered chiefly as the symbol of a demoralizing strategy that sold out black Americans and failed on its own terms. With so much counting against him, it has become difficult to fathom why he was widely revered across racial lines and remained so for decades after he lost the argument and passed on. Booker Washington was complex, wily, and awesomely accomplished at a time when the constraints on what most black Americans were allowed to accomplish were horrendous. In the face of Klan terrorism, an upsurge of lynching, a southern civil religion of "Lost Cause" propaganda, and a suffocating plague of disenfranchisement and Jim Crow abuse, Washington built a powerhouse institution in Alabama—Tuskegee Institute. He cultivated an image of simple altruism while fighting in a savvy, calculated fashion for as much power as he could get, fulfilling the American fantasy of ascending from poverty and disadvantage to greatness.

Washington accommodated disenfranchisement and segregation while organizing legal efforts to thwart both. He told African Americans to stay out of politics even after he became the nation's leading black patronage broker. He denied that he made federal patronage appointments for blacks long after he routinely made all of them. He implored blacks to stay in the South even as he spent half of each year fund-raising in the North. He hobnobbed with the high and mighty but stayed in touch with the everyday struggles of ordinary people. He attracted wealthy benefactors, became an advisor to four U.S. presidents, launched hundreds of community schools, and amassed a powerful political machine. He bought black newspapers and controlled them, denying that too. He controlled college presidents and professors through his influence with philanthropists, and hired spies to infiltrate rival organizations. Had Washington not been a great organizer and fund-raiser, Tuskegee Institute would not have survived any of its first twenty years. But he monopolized racial philanthropy and bullied his competitors, which fueled a backlash against him.

Washington keenly understood that most white southerners did not want black Americans to succeed at anything besides picking cotton. Any black success at anything else raised the frightening specter of "Negro rule." A black postmaster represented Negro rule. A black shopkeeper, a black teacher, or a black lawyer represented Negro rule. But to give African Americans a glimmer of opportunity in a brutally hostile context, Washington pretended not to know it. He got to be Number One by bartering the civil and political rights of black Americans for a season of interracial peace and economic opportunity. On the few occasions that he plainly expressed his strategy, he wrote quintessential descriptions of political realism. But everything got worse for African Americans during this ostensible season, while Washington ascended to national eminence, setting him up for the devastating objection that black Americans had not appointed him to be Number One. Booker Washington was the first black leader to be selected by white Americans, an arrangement that he lived to see unravel. For the "race problem" in America was white racism, and the antidote to it had no chance of coming out of Alabama.

Washington epitomized an influential version of the social gospel. Here the ties between black and white versions of social Christianity were strong, because Washington owed much of his fame to Lyman Abbott and other leaders in the right-assimilation wing of the social gospel. Abbott serialized Washington's memoir *Up from Slavery* to his vast audience in *Outlook* magazine and published articles lauding Washington as the embodiment of the social Christian ideal. The very term "social gospel" gained currency in the 1890s as the title of a journal by a white Christian Socialist community in Georgia that sought to build a school modeled on Tuskegee's trinity of work, education, and Christianity. Washington contended that black church religion, especially in the South, wrongly separated religion from morality—exactly as northern social gospel missionaries said. For Washington, Christianity was a practical faith, it nurtured the correct moral virtues, and it helped to build a good society— exactly as white social gospel leaders said.[19]

Many of these leaders were Washington's personal friends, especially Abbott and white social gospel founder Washington Gladden. Gladden and Washington implored that black churches needed to become more ethical, caring about righteousness, and less emotional, caring about rapture. Gladden preached on personal faith every Sunday morning and on social issues every Sunday night, contending that Christianity was a social ethical religion linking personal and social redemption. On the first Sunday of every year he preached about how America and the world had improved over the past year. These practices fit Washington's idea of how Christianity should be espoused in a modern, progressing world, though he and Gladden agreed to disagree about trade unions and corporate capitalism.[20]

The deepest commonality between the white church and black church traditions of the social gospel is that both responded to the charge that the church did not care about society's poorest and most vulnerable people. The social gospel arose as a response to the corruption of the Gilded Age, the end of Reconstruction, the rise of industrialization and urbanization, and the challenge of what became the Great Migration. Gilded Age capitalism was structurally similar in America's major northern cities, notably Boston, Chicago, Cleveland, New York, Philadelphia, and St. Louis. A machine ran the municipal government, which served the capitalist class while distributing patronage to working class allies. Meanwhile, the U.S. Supreme Court ruled in 1886 that corporations were legal persons under the Fourteenth Amendment and that states could not regulate interstate commerce passing through their borders, thus annulling the legal powers of states over powerful trusts, railroads, and holding companies.

This was the political-economic context that gave rise to Progressivism, Populism, and the social gospel. All espoused reforms on behalf of economic equality and opportunity. The Progressive and white social gospel movements sought to clean up government, especially at the federal and city levels. To many white reformers, the domination of urban politics by capital made political rights seem useless, so they turned urban corruption and labor reform into moral issues. This agenda lifted urban and labor reforms above political rights at the very time that African Americans were stripped of their rights under the Fourteenth and Fifteenth Amendments. The Progressive and white social gospel movements, at their worst, consented to this trade-off, or simply ignored African Americans. At their best, these movements urged that America only worked as a multiracial, multiethnic democracy that fulfilled its constitutional pledge to African Americans. Usually they sought to democratize American society on decidedly middle-class terms, except when they fused with Socialist or Populist movements.

In the South the Populist factor loomed larger and the social gospel was usually a form of Populism. Many southern states had a Populist movement, dominated by white farmers, that sought to wrest control from the planter class and the Rockefeller-Vanderbilt-Harriman class of capitalists. In the South and Midwest the movement generally took on political form as a farmers' alliance or a farm and labor party. At the national level, the People's Party of 1892 nominated James B. Weaver for president, calling for government ownership and control of the railroad, telephone, and telegraph systems. In some places, Populist movements injected vile racist demagoguery into their polemics against bankers, railroad barons, and the plantation class; white nationalism readily took on an aggrieved Populist hue. In other locales Populists took a different tack, appealing for black votes.

Disenfranchisement was a brutally direct method of preventing African Americans from voting for Populists, white Republicans, or themselves. Lynching was another. Lynching had been a feature of southern culture long before the Civil War. Between 1840 and 1860, three hundred people were hanged or burned by southern mobs, and 90 percent of the victims were white. Lynching did not become an instrument of racial terror until Reconstruction. Blacks were brutalized long before racist lynching erupted in the 1880s and 1890s, a fact that the C. Vann Woodward school of southern historiography underplayed in its emphasis on the novelty of white nationalist hostility. Still, the unleashed hatred of white nationalists *was* even worse than the commonplace white American racism that denigrated blacks for their supposed inferiority. With the ascendancy of white nationalism in the 1880s, the stereotype of the dim-witted inferior was recast as a predator and enemy. South Carolina governor and U.S. senator Ben Tillman described black men as beastly rapists. Georgia Populist Tom Watson, running for the presidency in 1904, excoriated the Democratic Party for basing its southern existence on race hatred. The following year he smoothed his return to the Democrats by giving racist speeches. Many voters that Watson tried to woo said that Tillman was right about black barbarism. But the barbaric spectacle in this story was the lynching mania that swept the American South.[21]

In northern cities the social gospel, black and white, forged alliances with the Progressive movement, which was usually averse to Populist rhetoric and leaders. The site of fusion was usually a settlement house modeled on Toynbee Hall in London's East End. The settlement houses, in the North and South, provided care for infants and toddlers, nursed the sick, organized garbage removal, and offered lecture programs, concerts, reading groups, and discussion groups. The lodestar American settlement, Hull House in Chicago, founded by Jane Addams, was a pillar of the national College Settlement Association. In the black Methodist and Baptist denominations, where settlements were called "institutional" churches, the pioneers of settlement ministry were Ransom and Waldron—figures who welcomed the Great Migration as a potential game changer for Afro-Americans and American politics.[22]

Most black congregations were too small and embattled to become social welfare agencies, but nearly every U.S. American city with a sizable black population had a few large, socially conscious congregations that developed programs offering child care, health care, garbage removal, and employment counseling. These congregations were anchors of the black social gospel. Waldron's Shiloh

Baptist Church in Washington, DC, was a prototype. Other leading black insti-
tutional churches included Powell's Abyssinian Baptist Church in Harlem,
Henry Hugh Proctor's First Congregational Church in Atlanta, George
Freeman Bragg's African Episcopal Church in Baltimore, William N. DeBerry's
St. John's Congregational Church in Springfield (Massachusetts), Lacey Kirk
Williams's Olivet Baptist Church in Chicago, W. W. Browne's Metropolitan
Baptist Church in Harlem, Walter H. Brooks's Nineteenth Street Baptist
Church in Washington, DC, Charles T. Walker's Tabernacle Baptist Church
in Augusta, and J. E. Ford's Bethel Baptist Church in Jacksonville (Florida),
where Waldron established social welfare programs.[23]

These congregations established or cofounded literary societies sponsoring
debates, lectures, discussion forums, recitals, and elocution contests. Literary
societies flourished in some cities where social welfare ministries lagged. For
example, Brooklyn had the gold-standard black literary society—the Brooklyn
Literary Union, founded by Siloam Presbyterian Church in 1886. T. Thomas
Fortune and many of Brooklyn's black elites played active roles in this organization, and it spawned other Brooklyn literary societies in which Fortune usually
played a role, notably the Concord Literary Circle of Concord Baptist Church,
the Nazarene Literary Society of Nazarene Congregational Church, the Young
People's Literary Society of Union Bethel AME Church, and the Progressive
Literary Union of Fleet Street AME Zion Church.[24]

The literary societies were devoted to cultural literacy and building a
cultured black public, and the settlement movement was the usual point of
intersection for social welfare ministries that crossed racial lines. The white
settlement leaders were usually female and socioeconomically privileged. They
struggled with how they should relate to black communities and questioned
whether their houses should be located in predominantly black communities.
Waldron and Nannie Burroughs replied that the movement needed as many
black social workers as it could find; otherwise white settlements merely reinforced white domination.

The settlement movement reinforced the social gospel predisposition to
keep sectarian theology to a minimum, because settlement houses served a
variety of ethnic and racial groups. The social gospel and liberal theology did
not necessarily go together. It was possible to embrace the social gospel without
accepting biblical criticism or Darwinian evolution, and it was possible to
embrace liberal theology without adopting the progressive or radical politics of
the social gospel. For many black ministers, the social gospel was more palat-
able than liberal theology because the latter seemed to disavow biblical authority
and evangelical doctrine. But in the early twentieth century the social gospel

swept the elite northern seminaries and divinity schools, where it was deeply intertwined with liberal theology. Many Christian leaders judged that the social gospel and liberal theology arose together and fit together because they were the same thing. This reading acquired taken-for-granted status across most of the theological spectrum, which increased the difficulty of making inroads for the social gospel in black churches.

The leading black social gospel ministers, activists, and academics did not back down on the need for a modernized theology. They pressed the case for it forcefully, even as they struggled with problems of greater magnitude. They built a tradition of their own that drew mostly on black Christian experience and operated mostly in segregated black space while also drawing upon their connections to religious and political white Progressivism. This dialectical consciousness already pervaded black social gospel rhetoric before Du Bois offered a famous description of it. The black social gospel founders were influenced by the same debates over social science, social ethics, Social Darwinism, and Socialism that shaped the white social gospel, and at the popular level, Charles M. Sheldon's best-selling social gospel novel, *In His Steps* (1897), readily crossed racial lines, urging readers to ask themselves, "What would Jesus do?" But Du Bois's description of double-consciousness was brilliantly illuminating for describing the differences drawn by the color line, which made all things different.[25]

DU BOIS AND THE BLACK SOCIAL GOSPEL

Du Bois was enormously important for the black social gospel, and not only because he said that the black church was enormously important. He loathed every kind of religious orthodoxy, which, in his view, yielded stunted and provincial souls. Du Bois could be blistering on this theme. In 1940, speaking at Wilberforce University's commencement, he excoriated the school's Christian legacy as "childish belief in fairy tales, a word-of-mouth adherence to dogma, and a certain sectarian exclusiveness." Wilberforce's tradition of religious orthodoxy, he charged, was "a miserable apprehension of the teaching of Christ." Du Bois, however, had a spiritual wellspring of his own, a keen appreciation of Jesus, and a lover's quarrel with the black church. His writings were strewn with religious images and references throughout his career, even after he supposedly dropped religion for Marxism. *The Souls of Black Folk* famously invoked "Our Spiritual Strivings" and lauded the spirituals. *Darkwater* began with his social gospel "Credo," conjured a black baby Jesus in "The Second Coming," conjured an adult black Jesus in the scathing "Jesus Christ in Texas," and ended with "A Hymn to the Peoples," in which the Buddha walked with Christ. As late as the 1950s Du Bois was still writing about saving "the tattered shreds of God."[26]

His passionate, unorthodox spiritual sensibility came through to many readers. They caught that a religious, arguably Christian passion lay behind Du Bois's furious attacks on unworthy ministers and church dogmatism. Religious studies scholar Jonathan S. Kahn notes that Du Bois gave expression to his religious longing by attacking forms of religion that he considered to be backward, reactionary, and/or oppressive: "At these moments, his irreligion itself turns religious." Historian Edward J. Blum cautions that even the language of "irreligion" or "anti-religion" should be used carefully when applied to Du Bois, because he had religious feelings that many of his secular protégés and interpreters did not fathom: "Du Bois was not anti-religious; he was against faith used for fraud, belief used to bully, and Christianity when used to control." Even at Wilberforce, lashing the university for hiding behind mediocre religion, Du Bois stumped for social gospel religion: "Christianity means sympathy; the realization of what it costs a human being to live and support a family in decency. . . . Christianity means unselfishness; the willingness to forgo in part one's personal advantage and give up some personal desires for the sake of a larger end which will be for the advantage of a greater number of people."[27]

By 1940 that was an echo of what the younger Du Bois had hoped the church would become under the sway of the social gospel. In the early twentieth century he was a critical booster, taking for granted that the movement for black liberation had to be religion-friendly. Nothing compared to the black church as a source of inspiration, hope, solidarity, identity, belonging, moral language, and transcendent meaning. Du Bois stressed that it was the only institution that black Americans owned outright. Any movement worth building in the black community had to share in the life of the black church, speaking its language of hope and redemption. Bookerism, as Du Bois realized, was strong in this area, equating its bootstrap ethic with good religion, although some complained when Washington sermonized in pulpits about carpentry and bricklaying. The early anti-Booker party was long on secular professionals; thus, so was the Niagara Movement. But to reach beyond its limited circle of urban intellectuals and professionals, the Niagara Movement and the NAACP had to have religious leaders. When Du Bois called for an anti-Washington uprising, three of the four figures he called out—Kelly Miller, J. W. E. Bowen, and Francis Grimké—were religious intellectuals. Then he found a firebrand in Ransom, who prized his standing as the Du Bois figure in black Christianity.[28]

Ransom gained a national following and won a bishop's chair. But he lacked a movement vehicle, the tasks of the episcopacy wore him down, and the unrelenting hostility of white society bruised and exhausted him. Moreover, Ransom lived to see his social gospel rhetoric of progress and ideals become quaint under the devastation of the Great Depression. Union Theological Seminary theologian Reinhold Niebuhr led the Depression Era attack on social gospel idealism. In the 1920s Niebuhr was a social gospel progressive and paci- fist. In the 1930s he repudiated social gospel idealism and pacifism as a radical Socialist. In the 1940s he blasted the social gospel from a theologically neo- Reformation and politically liberal-centrist Democratic Party perspective, which he called Christian realism. The social gospel, Niebuhr claimed, failed to take seriously the realities of sin, evil, and power politics.[29]

This did not mean that Niebuhr repudiated modern social Christianity. Throughout his career he assumed the core of the social gospel—that Christianity has a social ethical obligation to support movements for social justice. The field in which Niebuhr taught—social ethics—had no history and no basis apart from this assumption. Niebuhr shared most of the modernizing theology that went along with the social gospel, especially its recognition that biblical myths are myths. But he heaped powerful ridicule on the social gospel attempt to fashion a social ethic from the teaching of Jesus and modern humanism. Niebuhr's neo-Reformation theology of sin and grace featured an existential rendering of the doctrine of original sin. He taught his readers to view the world as a theater of perpetual struggles for power among selfish competing interests. He forged a dialectical, ironic, paradoxical approach to social ethics, which both fired and limited his own involvement in the civil rights movement of the 1950s, and he symbolized the adjustment of ecumenical churches to the global traumas of his time.[30]

Everything that Niebuhr wrote was a form of public apologetics for his version of modern, realistic, social Christianity. And everything that he wrote was of deep interest to King, especially Niebuhr's analysis of nonviolence as a stratagem of power. But with Niebuhr there is always an irony, his favorite trope. Two ironies stand out in the present case. One, the foremost critic of the social gospel played a major role in advancing the causes and legacy of the social gospel. But, two, Niebuhr's influence also played a significant role in obscuring the black social gospel. If the social gospel was a bad idea, as Niebuhr was repeatedly, simplistically claimed to have said, better not linger with the social gospel. If Niebuhr was the hero of twentieth-century American theology, the black tradition of the social gospel was better left for dead, along with Gladden and Rauschenbusch. King grappled intently with that possibility as a student in seminary and graduate school, writing papers that compared Niebuhr to the unreconstructed liberals favored by King's teachers. Niebuhr said things about power and social evil that rang true to King. He also said things about theological and political realism that were off-kilter for King, undercutting the hope that kept black Americans from falling into cynicism and despair.

The importance of keeping hope alive outstripped everything else. Here the black social gospelers who succeeded Niebuhr held the same conviction as the black social gospelers who preceded Niebuhr. They did not believe that the biggest problem with the social gospel was that it dreamed too wildly. They never thought that the social gospel erred by projecting its ethical idealism into the public realm, and they did not have the cultural privilege that allowed Niebuhr to dichotomize between the religious and political spheres. They believed the problem with the white social gospel was that it gave low priority to the struggle against racism. The black social gospel leaders who directly influenced King—Johnson, Mays, and Howard Thurman—acquired their social agency on the social gospel conference circuit sponsored by the YMCA, the YWCA, and the Fellowship of Reconciliation. They came up through the Student Christian Movement, an international social gospel organization blending YMCA and YWCA activists, as did black social gospel colleagues Channing Tobias, Juliette Derricotte, Frank Wilson, Marion Cuthbert, Max Yergan, and Sue Bailey Thurman.[31]

For these ecumenical leaders and activists, the social gospel was indispensable and still in an early phase. They wanted church leaders to stir up their courage and idealism, advocating racial justice with the same ethical passion that the white social gospel devoted to peace, temperance, and economic cooperation. If Christianity had *any* moral meaning in the U.S. American situation, the churches had to confront the evils that oppressed black Americans. Black social gospel leaders vehemently denied that the social gospel exaggerated the kingdom of God as a spiritual and social ethical ideal. How was that possible, if the teaching of Jesus centered on the kingdom of God?

I have long argued that "black social gospel" is the category that best describes King, his mentors, many of his movement allies, and the founders of black social Christianity. Twenty years ago there were not many of us; now there are many more, mainly because black scholars have entered the academy in significant numbers. Historian Clayborne Carson, religious historian Calvin S. Morris, religious studies scholar Anthony Pinn, religious historian Randal M. Jelks, social ethicist and religious historian Walter E. Fluker, and religious studies scholars Quinton Dixie and Peter Eisenstadt, among others, have played leading roles in recovering the language and history of the black social gospel. For all my stumping for an overlooked tradition, however, I am careful not to exaggerate the influence of early black social Christian leaders, who played only supportive roles in the Niagara Movement and the NAACP.[32]

My relationship to a related scholarly trend is more qualified. Today many scholars push hard against "spotlight" history, contending that Du Bois and King get too many books to the exclusion of others. Historian Angela Jones says it forcefully in her valuable work *African American Civil Rights*, adding that spotlight history produces accounts of the civil rights movement that give too much attention to religion. Historian Shawn Leigh Alexander, in his excellent history of the Afro-American Council, *An Army of Lions*, contends that scholars give short shrift to the council because they habitually exaggerate the importance of Du Bois. In his words: "Du Bois has mistakenly become central to our understanding of this period of African American history." Alexander gives the Afro-American Council its long-denied due by "shifting attention away from Du Bois and his leadership of the Niagara Movement."[33]

Here I am emphatically two-handed. I agree with Jones, Alexander, and others that we must recover the forgotten or overlooked players in this story. And I agree with Alexander that the Afro-American Council deserves greater consideration than it has long received. But I do not agree that doing so should make Du Bois less central to the story, and I have similar convictions about King. Du Bois shined too brightly not to be at the center. Even his political rivals, plus many who just didn't like him, called him the breakthrough genius of his time. He was deeply learned, exceedingly brilliant, and historic. He was a warrior for humanity and human culture, exactly as he thought, and a prickly egotist who could be abusive to allies that deserved better, as he knew. Near the end of his first major work, *The Philadelphia Negro*, Du Bois wrote a stunning sentence that explained what it meant to fight for humanity and where he was headed: "If in the heyday of the greatest of the world's civilizations, it is possible for one people ruthlessly to steal another, drag them helpless across the water, enslave them, debauch them, and then slowly murder them by economic and social exclusion until they disappear from the face of the earth—if the consummation of such a crime be possible in the twentieth century, then our civilization is vain and the republic is a mockery and a farce." Nobody else wrote like that.[34]

Du Bois had warm and jovial relationships with a small circle of friends, and he gave brusque treatment to pretty much everyone else, in the manner of many withholding male hero types. At least he was reflective about the gender factor. Du Bois grasped and acknowledged that churches, male intellectuals, and activist organizations lived off the labor of women, taking credit for their achievements. Here, prophetic brilliance, personal foibles, sexist presuppositions, and feminist insight meshed together. Du Bois handed out shabby treatment to his wife, Nina, humiliated her with numerous long-running affairs, and excluded black women who threatened to steal attention from him. Ida

Wells-Barnett, Anna Julia Cooper, and Mary Church Terrell got icy put-downs from him, and he went out of his way to marginalize Mary McLeod Bethune too. His early writings on the "degradation" of black family life helped to fuel a pernicious tradition of attacks on the character and culture of black women, and black studies scholar Hazel Carby exaggerates only slightly in censuring Du Bois for his "complete failure to imagine black women as intellectuals and race leaders."[35]

My caveat on "complete" is that Du Bois played a role in lifting up black female writers during the Harlem Renaissance, and he commended the social activism of black women, which implied something about leadership. Sociologist and black studies scholar Cheryl Townsend Gilkes notes that Du Bois offered the first "self-consciously sociological interpretation of the role of African American women as agents of social change." Despite his personal chauvinism and his conflicted record concerning women's agency, Du Bois passionately defended the dignity and rights of black women, offering a feminist critique of male domination, with a pinch of idealistic chivalry. In *Darkwater* he wrote a perfect comeuppance to churches (nearly all of them, of every denomination) that depended on women they put down: "As I look about me in this veiled world of mine, despite the noisier and more spectacular advance of my brothers, I instinctively feel and know that it is the five million women of my race who really count. Black women (and women whose grandmothers were black) are today furnishing our teachers; they are the main pillars of those social settlements which we call churches; and they have with small doubt raised three-fourths of our church property."[36]

The women in this story that broke the grip of male domination and presumption were usually good at working with others and building new organizations. Burroughs, Lucy Wilmot Smith, S. Willie Layten, Mary Cook, and Virginia Broughton were backed by the power of a national organization they created, the Woman's Convention of the National Baptist Convention. Terrell, Lucy Thurman, Mary B. Talbert, and others similarly derived much of their social agency from the National Association of Colored Women (NACW), which originated with Victorian calls to true womanhood and purified homes, but went on to become deeply involved in suffrage, anti-lynching, and antisegregation activism. For the NACW's founding leaders—Terrell and Josephine St. Pierre Ruffin—and for many others, the coming of the NACW was a godsend precisely because it offered Afro-American women an opportunity to work together outside the church. Mary McLeod Bethune, an NACW president in the mid-1920s, similarly won renown as a school founder in Daytona, Florida, before winning renown as a New Deal leader. Even Wells-Barnett, who had trouble working with others, at least recognized the importance of organizations and played a role in cofounding several of them. These figures had to be as creative and stubborn as they were tough, working with religious communities that denied women the right to lead.[37]

Some women found greater opportunity and enrichment in the Wesleyan/ Holiness movements of the nineteenth and twentieth centuries or the Pentecostal movement that emerged in the early twentieth century. Holiness congregations claimed to restore the emphasis of Methodist founder John Wesley on the necessity of born-again conversion as evidenced by a holy life. Hundreds of white Holiness communities, such as the Church of the Nazarene, and black communities, such as the Evening Light Saints, taught that sanctification was a second part of the conversion experience. To be sanctified was to be freed from all sinfulness of the heart, something necessary for total salvation. The Pentecostal movement grew out of Holiness religion, originating at a revival in 1906 at the Azusa Street Mission in Los Angeles led by former Evening Light Saints preacher William J. Seymour, who taught that sanctified living was not sufficient proof that one had received the Holy Spirit. Seymour preached about the gift of ecstatic speech in an unknown tongue—Pentecostal experience.[38]

The "Sanctified Church"—the collective term for the Holiness and Pentecostal Churches—rejected the regularization of worship in the Baptist and Methodist Churches and the tendency of these churches to assimilate culturally. Black Holiness groups restored the oral music and ecstatic praise traditions of slave religion, sometimes with female leadership. Seymour spoke at the front of the congregation without a pulpit or platform, encouraging congregants to speak in tongues. The Pentecostal movement featured singing, dance, shaking, trances, dreams, and healing. It spread immediately at a phenomenal rate, for a while as an interracial movement, until white Pentecostals came up with doctrinal reasons to dissociate themselves from blacks, forming the Assemblies of God denomination in 1914. From the beginnings of the black Holiness and, especially, Pentecostal movements, women in disproportionate numbers flocked to the participatory testimony, music, rhythm, and holistic worldview of the Sanctified Church.[39]

Traditional black denominations already featured, as Du Bois famously observed, the "frenzy" of shouting, the personality of the preacher, and the beauty and longing of black music. Most northern black churches spurned gospel music until the southern migrants came along and refused to be denied, infusing urban congregations with their expressive music. But long before gospel music surged into the North, black churches North and South worshipped buoyantly around "a king in a private kingdom," as civil rights icon James Farmer vividly described the black (especially Baptist) preacher. This commanding figure was "both oracle and soothsayer, showman and pontiff, father image to all and husband-by-proxy to the unattached women in the church and others whose mates are either inadequate or missing. More than a priest, he is less only than God." Farmer, having grown up as a preacher's kid (PK), stressed that preachers had a tendency to overwhelm: "The old thesis about maternal dominance in the black family has no validity here whatever. The PK lives with a dominant male image." For many women and some men, the historic churches had too much of that, plus they were too formal and assimilated. Many were migrants who took up storefront religion after feeling unwelcomed by northern congregations. Some found their way to large sanctification churches such as Chicago's All Nations Pentecostal Church, headed by Elder Lucy Smith. A few found refuge in scattered community churches. Gilkes puts it bluntly, observing that for these reasons the sanctification churches became "overwhelmingly female," leading some to permit female leadership.[40]

The feminist irony of Sanctification Christianity cuts across racial lines. Traditional black churches, with the partial exception of the AME Zion Church, were like most traditional white churches in excluding women from ordained ministries. But these were the churches where the social gospel made the deepest inroads. Meanwhile, the churches that allowed women to preach were not the ones that produced social gospel ministers. Historian Barbara Dianne Savage, in her luminous reflection on the politics of black religion, *Your Spirits Walk Beside Us*, notes that three scholars had the greatest influence on the historiography of nineteenth- and early-twentieth-century black American Christianity: Du Bois, Woodson, and Mays. All were unsettled by the emotional fervor of rural black worship and the sanctification churches. All expressed appreciation for the emotional vitality of black religion while calling for modernized churches committed to social justice theology. All said sympathetic things about the women that comprised and sustained the black churches. And all three perpetuated the view that the black churches needed strong and progressive male ministers more than they needed anything else. Savage aptly observes that Du Bois, Woodson, and Mays, by giving highest priority to developing a male clerical elite, silenced the two largest groups in this picture: "The majority of church members, who were women, and the majority of men, who remained outside the churches."[41]

Black America needed an elite of male ministers because it had a dearth of male leadership in general and the church was the most important institution in African American life. Du Bois said it as a sympathetic fellow traveler who rarely went to church. Mays said it as a Baptist minister and theologian who mentored students as a college president. Woodson said it as a Baptist layman who founded the *Journal of Negro History,* the Association for the Study of Negro Life and History, and what became Black History Month. In Woodson's telling, he had two reasons for belonging to Shiloh Baptist Church in Washington, DC: (1) "I find there better people than I do on the outside fighting the institution," and (2) "I find my people there, and I cannot help them unless I remain among them." That was a decidedly social gospel rationale for belonging to a church, a form of religious pragmatism. Woodson readily acknowledged that women made the best Christians and kept the black churches going. But his only word for them was to carry on as they were. He had a bold vision of the church's future, urging black Christians to discard their denominations and form a united black church. But Woodson envisioned no expanded role for female leaders in the black superchurch. The wing of black Christianity that talked about being progressive and modern pulled back when it came to women; among the male founders, the leading exceptions were Turner, Simmons, and Ransom. For similar reasons it had no progressive inklings concerning gay and lesbian sexuality, a subject on which Powell Sr. and Powell Jr. spoke vehemently from the pulpit.[42]

The founders of black social Christianity had to modernize their theology without losing their homes in embattled churches. Significant Christianization of America's slave population did not begin until the 1760s. It did not come into full swing until the 1830s. The great revival movements of the eighteenth and early nineteenth centuries — the so-called First and Second Awakenings — sent most black American Christians into the Baptist and Methodist camps. These two religious groups became the primary keepers of the dream that religion might bridge America's racial chasm and thereby bring relief to oppressed black Americans. From the beginning it was an evangelical dream. Black ministers kept it alive even after they were driven by white racism to form their own denominations. The early black social gospel leaders, in order to make inroads into denominations to which they belonged, had to be convincingly evangelical, even as they introduced critical perspectives on the Bible and Christian teaching that challenged the folk traditions of many congregations.

The social gospel *was* essentially evangelical, in the sense of being centered on the life, teaching, and cross of Jesus, in its black and white Protestant forms. Otherwise it would have gotten nowhere. But modern theology had a demythologizing spirit that introduced the way of doubt and negation wherever it entered. The black social gospel, though always embattled for purveying a modern critical consciousness, did better at restraining the way of doubt, because existential life-and-death issues were palpable in black churches and the black social gospel held fast to gospel norms about the sacred personality of God and all human beings.

Most black social gospel leaders preached in pulpits about a personal God who demanded justice and loved all the children. They welcomed pragmatists like Woodson and drew strength from Du Bois, whatever they made of his personal beliefs. Today scholars vigorously debate the latter point, variously contending that Du Bois was a radical Christian theist, an atheistic Marxist, a skeptical Deist, a Hegelian idealist, or a pragmatic religious naturalist. I believe that Du Bois carved a place for pragmatic heterodox religion within the black radical Christian tradition. He drew upon and employed the language of Christian prophecy, declaring that his work expressed "divine discontent with the imperfect," but he declined to call himself a Christian. He wrote moving prayers during his teaching career at Atlanta University but questioned "whether they were orthodox or reached heaven." Du Bois believed that religion is rightly about struggling with religious meaning and sacrificing for it, and he had a definite exemplar of good religion—the social gospel Jesus, who befriended the marginalized, prayed to a God of the oppressed, and taught that God was present in the poor and oppressed. That was enough for Du Bois, even as he variously mediated Marx, Hegel, Crummell, Turner, William James, and a host of others in thinking about religion.[43]

The black social gospel had debates about dual identities and permeable boundaries, it identified with the NAACP as soon as the NAACP existed, and it had a small flank that fused NAACP liberalism with social gospel Socialism. Moreover, the NAACP was more religious on the ground than it advertised, like the NACW. For decades the NAACP routinely convened in church sanctuaries, welcomed ministerial leaders, and opened and closed its meetings with prayers. Often it sang a hymn or two. Du Bois, blasting NAACP leaders during his stormy farewell in 1934, noted that the staunchly antisegregationist NAACP would have no place to exist or meet without its twenty thousand segregated black churches. The issue of segregation, he said, was not as simple as the NAACP pretended to believe. Many black ministers boasted that the church was the one place that African Americans *chose* to be segregated. Black social gospel leaders negotiated this complex reality long before Du Bois made a ruckus about it, adopting simple, conflicted, and complex views in dealing with it.[44]

Today theorists debate what to make of Du Bois's assertion that he was doubly conscious as a black and American. Literary theorist Henry Louis Gates Jr. describes this expression as a singularly illuminating metaphor for "the Afro-American's peculiar psychology of citizenship." Lawrie Balfour describes it as

Du Bois's trademark rhetorical device marking his own experience as a symbol of uplift and a member of an oppressed caste. Political theorist Robert Gooding-Williams says that Du Bois employed this idea chiefly to criticize the failings of black political leaders. Historian Joel Williamson says that Du Bois took this idea from Hegel and refashioned it brilliantly as the spirit of freedom realizing itself behind the veil of color. Cornel West says that Du Bois rightly fixed on the in-but-not-of dialectic of black self-recognition but oversimplified the cultural predicament of black Americans. Sociologist Lawrence Bobo and political scientist Adolph L. Reed Jr. counter that Du Bois was too committed to being an empirical social scientist to stick with a trope that didn't explain anything (Bobo) or that smacked of late-nineteenth-century neo-Lamarckian social science (Reed). Historian Ernest Allen Jr. says that Du Bois used this idea merely as a tactic, a "double sleight of hand" to ease the fears of "Talented Tenth" achievers that their success in the white world would be discredited. Social ethicist Eboni Marshall Turman says that Du Bois left a problematic legacy for black moral agency by pathologizing black embodiment. Cultural theorist Paul Gilroy, in his early career, employed Du Boisian double-consciousness as a precursor of Gilroy's dialectic of fulfillment and transfigura-tion, but later Gilroy judged that this idea belongs too much to the nineteenth century to handle the postmodern experience of cultural multiplicity and hybrid identities.[45]

Double-consciousness, though variously conceived and historicized, remains the subject of profuse contention, and not solely on account of Du Bois. For nearly all of us involved in social theoretical discussions of "race" assume a baseline smacking of Du Boisian double-consciousness: Race is a social inven-tion, yet it is terribly real and embedded in psyches, social structures, and communal legacies. Black social gospel theologians were familiar with the complexities of these claims. They debated varieties of integration, cultural distinction and interchange, equality, and theological pluralism while giving priority to the political struggle for justice. Thus the two leading denominations in this story, the African Methodist Episcopal Church and the National Baptist Convention, though operating very differently, advocated essentially the same social ethic of moral responsibility, equal rights, and human brotherhood/sister-hood under the sovereignty of a personal God—as social ethicist Peter J. Paris showed in his seminal study *The Social Teaching of the Black Churches*.[46]

The black Methodists had major pioneering roles, but they belonged to small denominations. One black denomination, the National Baptist Convention, dwarfed all others, boasting over two million members by 1905. But it did not exist until 1895, partly because black Baptists struggled more than any other group with the separatism-versus-assimilation issue. The black Baptists, being Baptists, had special problems creating a denominational struc-ture beyond congregational and regional levels. More important, they debated separatism versus assimilation for decades before they assembled a huge denomination. By the time that black Baptists founded the National Baptist Convention, the separatist party prevailed, usually with Booker Washington politics, conceiving the church as a refuge from a hostile white society. But that did not settle any aspect of the separatist issue, for black Baptists wanted two things that did not go well together: a separate identity and an important role in changing American politics and society. Neither of these things comported well with a fading Bookerism.

Black Baptist churches used the philosophy of self-help to survive America's racial caste system, which continually raised the question of how separate they should want to be. Northern Baptists had the same debates as Northern Methodists about whether they owed special obligations to southern migrants and whether they needed to sing the migrants' gospel music. But Northern Baptists got to yes more often, which put them in the forefront of the black social gospel, which forced them to decide how modernist they wanted to be. Always there was a diversity of views about what worked and how one should think about the separatist issue. But black social gospelers tended to converge on the pragmatic verdict that the best way to overcome the pernicious doctrine of racial inferiority was to build strong black institutions.

APOSTLES OF NEW ABOLITION

Two of the greatest contributors to nineteenth-century black social Christianity belonged to different generations of it. Henry McNeal Turner was already a hard-charging AME minister in Washington, DC, when Ida B. Wells was born in July 1862—two months after Turner converted to African homeland nationalism. Both were powerful speakers and influential journalists. Both were icons of militant bravery in repressive contexts, although Wells had to flee the South to save her life and career, while Turner spent most of his life in the Deep South. And both lived in the shadow of Frederick Douglass.

Turner was freeborn and autodidactic. He made his early mark as a revival preacher and pastor, served as a chaplain in a Union Army regiment that he founded, and came early to the vision of exodus and West African homecoming, having come to it by way of another formidable nationalist and cleric, Alexander Crummell. Then Turner poured himself out for something that was not to be—black American freedom and self-determination in the aftermath of American slavery. Then he fell back on the hope of West Africa and his enormous devotion to the AME Church. Along the way he founded three newspapers, and throughout his career Turner delivered powerful oratory ranging over many subjects, sometimes in a single address.

Ida Bell Wells was a different kind of speaker, a messenger about one thing—the evil of lynching. She was born into slavery, educated by white missionaries from the North, and driven by a vision of emancipation that consumed her life. She had a fiery temperament that contrasted with Booker T. Washington's opaque, calculating, accommodating temperament, and her politics reflected the difference. She attacked Jim Crow and the epidemic of lynching with blistering rage. She ripped apart Victorian conventions about helpless women and female sexuality, even as she deeply internalized Victorian Christian morality and prayed to be a faithful AME Christian. Her militancy made most black leaders of her time look timid, with the foremost exception of Turner. Wells might have become the successor to Douglass had she not been female, a loner, and in some way threatening to nearly everyone who knew her. Turner was among the few to feel only admiration.

Turner paved the way for new abolition movements that he did not join, as he believed that African Americans had no future worth discussing in America. The power and limitations of the nationalist idea were fully manifest in his extraordinary career. After white America trampled the rights of black Americans, Turner became too alienated from the United States to take seriously the next wave of abolitionist visions for America. Many dismissed him as a raging extremist, but he was a giant figure who distinctly bridged the old and new abolitionism. He was historic, influential, incomparable, and literally large and forceful. Wells was not inclined to look up to others, and Turner did not fulfill all her requirements of what a minister should be. But Wells knew from Turner what fearless leadership looked like, and she appreciated that he had the rare courage to defend her.

The prominence of the AME Church in the founding of black social Christianity confirms Du Bois's description of this abolitionist denomination as "the greatest voluntary organization of Negroes in the world" and his remark that the AME story bears, from its beginning, "a tinge of romance." The African Methodist Episcopal Church germinated in 1792 when Richard Allen and Absalom Jones were pulled off their knees at prayer at St. George's Methodist Church in Philadelphia and directed to the colored section. Allen and Jones had bought their freedom in Delaware after learning trades. They had established a quasi-religious Free African Society in 1787, a mutual aid group working with the local Abolition Society. Upon being insulted at prayer, they walked out of St. George's, followed by other members of the group.[1]

For a while they held Quaker-style meetings, but that didn't work. The majority opted for Anglicanism, as Jones became the first black American Episcopal priest, organizing the African Episcopal Church of St. Thomas in the building previously used by the Free African Society. The others started Bethel Church, a Philadelphia Methodist congregation, in 1794. Bishop Francis Asbury ordained Allen to the diaconate in 1799, and in 1807 and 1815 Allen had to sue in Pennsylvania courts to establish the right of his congregation to exist as an independent institution. In 1816 black Methodists from four states held the founding General Conference of the AME Church, where Allen was consecrated as its first bishop.

Evangelists William Quinn and Jarena Lee spread the AME faith. Lee, freeborn in Cape May, New Jersey, in 1783, felt called to preach by an instant experience of sanctification. In 1811 Allen rejected her petition to preach, declaring that her sex disqualified her, but eight years later Allen reversed his position upon hearing Lee spontaneously sermonize during a visiting minister's sermon. She traveled thousands of miles per year, preaching on the itinerant circuit. Lee had to live down constant criticism for presuming to preach and, later, for holding prayer meetings in her home. Later she became a symbol of something not allowed in the AME Church—female preachers. Morris Brown, a former slave who fled the aftermath of the Vesey revolt in Charleston, South Carolina, became the church's second bishop. By 1860 the AME Church had 20,000 members, nearly all in the North. By 1895 it had 450,000 members— 355,000 of them in the eleven states of the former Confederacy. The explosive growth of this denomination in the South after the Civil War owed much to one person—Henry McNeal Turner, who had conflicted feelings about the social gospel after it arose, but whose contribution to it was immense.[2]

BLACK METHODISM AND THE AMERICAN NATION

Turner was born to free parents, Hardy and Sarah Turner, in rural Newberry Court House, South Carolina, in 1834. His paternal grandmother was a white female plantation owner, Julia Turner, whose son Hardy never learned the name of his father, a black superintendent on the plantation. Hardy Turner died when Henry was young, leaving him to be raised by his teenaged mother, Sarah, and her mother, Hannah Greer. Free blacks were a tiny minority in the antebellum South lacking any civil, social, or political rights aside from the right not to be legally reduced to slavery and, thus, not to be whipped by over- seers. As a child Turner labored under cruel overseers picking cotton, and he believed deeply in Hannah Greer's story that her husband's father had been the son of an African king whose royal blood got him released from American slavery. Turner claimed, overlooking his paternal grandmother, that he was freeborn because his maternal grandfather was a prince. On stronger ground he attributed his early pride in his African heritage to Hannah Greer's story.[3]

At age twelve he had a dream in which he stood on a mountain giving instruction to millions. Later this dream played a central role in his call story. Turner willed himself to literacy in his youth and caught a break when he was fifteen by landing a janitorial position at a law firm in Abbeville, South Carolina. His employers, struck by Turner's intellectual curiosity and his memorization of Scripture passages, violated state law by teaching him arithmetic, astronomy, geography, history, law, and theology. At the same time Turner accompanied his mother at Methodist and Baptist revivals in the Abbeville area, where he selectively appropriated white preaching about Jesus and slavery. Turner heard a South Carolina presiding elder implore God to drown every abolitionist in the sea of divine wrath. He also met white and black ministers who took a personal interest in him, befriending him and praying for his salvation. That was enough to launch him as a riveting teenaged revival preacher. At age seventeen Turner was licensed as an exhorter in the Methodist Episcopal Church (ME), South; two years later he was licensed to preach.[4]

The Northern and Southern Methodist Churches had split over slavery in 1844. The southern church called itself the Methodist Episcopal Church, South, while the northern church called itself the Methodist Episcopal Church. In the 1850s southern churches were still mostly biracial, especially in rural areas, with blacks confined to the gallery. The church was the only place at which Turner or any black person had a chance to address white people from a position of nominal respect. Few antebellum black preachers in any denomination were ordained, and the black ministers that Turner met on the revival trail preached standard come-to-Jesus evangelicalism with a distinct emphasis on the equality of all people in heaven.

Turner preached that gospel, warning of hellfire, assuming biblical inerrancy, stressing divine Providence, and dwelling on the righteous egalitarianism of heaven. White and black churchgoers tended to hear the heaven part differently. The black preacher daring to speak to biracial congregations had to connect with the oppressed audience in the gallery without getting anyone into trouble. Turner became highly skilled at doing so, earning a reputation as an evangelical spellbinder, calling individuals to come forward, confess their sins, and accept Christ as their savior. As an itinerant preacher he spoke mostly to segregated congregations of Methodists and Baptists, segregated crowds at revivals, and all-black congregations of Methodists, Baptists, and Presbyterians, always preaching to an area's best educated black Methodist congregation whenever possible. In 1856 he married a South Carolina carpenter's daughter, Eliza Ann Peacher; the following year Turner learned there was such a thing as a black Methodist denomination.[5]

Willis H. Revels, pastor of an AME congregation of free blacks in New Orleans, told Turner the story of the AME Church. Turner was surprised to learn that black Methodists had a fully connectional denomination with deacons, elders, and bishops, just like the ME and ME, South Churches. In Turner's later telling he promptly joined the AME Church. In fact it took him a year to do so, as he conducted successful revivals in Atlanta and Athens, Georgia, in 1858 as an ME Church, South, preacher. Turner had collegial relationships with white preachers that shared his commitments to saving souls and building a peaceable social order. He did not kid himself, however, that his growing stature in the church protected him from harm, and he could not feel at home in a slaveholding church.

The Supreme Court's *Dred Scott* decision of 1857 decreed that no black American was protected by the Constitution, which gave ballast to political movements in the South seeking to enslave free blacks. Turner joined a wave of African Americans out of the South in 1858, preaching a trial sermon at the AME annual conference in St. Louis. The AME Church featured Episcopal districts presided over by a bishop elected by the General Conference, and each district held as many annual conferences as its size required. In St. Louis, delegates hazed Turner with wary questions until Bishop Daniel A. Payne, the AME Church's spiritual leader, welcomed him to the denomination. Turner served two small congregations in Baltimore, for two years each; read assiduously in philosophy, classics, and physiology; and watched medical students dissect cadavers. By 1860 he could read Latin, Greek, and Hebrew "with facility." Turner later recalled that he shot up in Payne's estimation after Payne inspected his impressive library, although Turner scrambled the chronology in his telling. Payne assigned him in 1862 to a "very much dilapidated" but very desirably located congregation in Washington, DC—Israel Church, a few blocks from the U.S. Capitol, where Turner would have stayed longer had the Union Army not opened other possibilities.[6]

In Washington Turner befriended the foremost Radical Republican leaders in the U.S. Congress, Massachusetts senator Charles Sumner and Pennsylvania House representative Thaddeus Stevens, plus Treasury secretary Salmon Chase and U.S. senator Benjamin Wade (Ohio). He admired Sumner above all politicians for his passionate abolitionism. Turner joined the Freemasons to strengthen his network of powerful friends, gambling that Payne would not find out, as Payne condemned Masonic secrecy. When the Civil War broke out, Turner grieved at the prospect of brothers killing each other. As soon as Union soldiers were killed at Bull Run, he began to say that the war was about the evil of slavery, but he continued to preach against the hatred and violence of war: "We must love our enemies. There is too much hatred in this land, and God will never deliver us while we cherish such hellish feelings." For two years, Turner and his Radical Republican allies implored Lincoln to issue the Emancipation Proclamation. After Lincoln did so, Turner did not begrudge him for waiting too long or for saying that he only wanted to save the Union. For the rest of his life Turner revered Lincoln as a savior figure. On October 4, 1862, Turner declared in the *Christian Recorder*: "Mr. Lincoln loves freedom as well as anyone on earth, and if he carries out the spirit of the proclamation he need never fear hell. GOD GRANT HIM A HIGH SEAT IN GLORY." Fifty years later, Turner waved off trying to express what he felt on September 22, 1862: "Such a time I never expect to witness on earth in the future. I may witness such a time again in heaven, but not in the flesh."[7]

By comparison to America's most famous preacher, Henry Ward Beecher, Turner came slowly and a bit hesitantly to the theme that God's providential redemption was unfolding in the carnage of the nation's suffering for its sins. In northern versions pioneered by Beecher, the Civil War was a bloody atonement for disunity and moral failing that facilitated the rebirth of the nation as a unified country. The United States would no longer be a loose collection of states divided by slavery; it would become a unified nation based on the promise of freedom for all Americans. Beecher put it dramatically at the outset of the war, declaring that the social order of the North was organized as a regime of liberty, while southern society was based on slavery—"a rotten core." Under this circumstance, "I hold that it is ten thousand times better to have war than to have slavery. I hold that to be corrupted silently by giving up manhood, by degenerating, by becoming cravens, by yielding one right after another, is infinitely worse than war."[8]

America would become itself through war and assimilation. Turner admired the Beecher of the war years that thundered for equal rights for African Americans, spoke at recruiting meetings, raised money for Union regiments, and demanded that Lincoln make the war about slavery. In 1856 Beecher had given antislavery speeches across Kansas and raised the abolitionist ante by donating Sharp's rifles to the antislavery cause there. Beecher, however, could thunder about the moral meaning of the war because his privileged standing in American society was never in question. He took for granted his right to expound on the kind of nation that America should be. Turner had to assert and defend his right even to address the issue, even before friendly audiences. He believed that God used slavery to bring blacks to Christ and civilization, and by 1863 Turner preached emphatically that the Civil War was God's deliverance from slavery. For a while he preached the full-bore American Creed about America as God's vehicle of freedom. But Turner had already taken his first pass at colonization activism, which provided a fallback after postwar America proved to be savagely disappointing.

The idea that black Americans might find a better life in West Africa or perhaps Haiti had spiked in the 1850s. This idea gained currency in the 1780s, it got real in 1821 when the white American Colonization Society founded Liberia, it declined among black Americans in the 1830s, and it surged in the 1850s after Congress passed the Fugitive Slave Law (1850) and the *Dred Scott* decision left African Americans defenseless before the law. The 1850s were so disastrous and desperate that even Frederick Douglass flirted with the colonization idea. Turner was already drawn to it when the Civil War began. Until that time, homeland dreamers usually fixed on Liberia or Haiti as a destination. But Liberia was far away, and it smacked of white Americans forcibly evicting black Americans. Radical journalist James Redpath founded the Haitian Emigration Bureau in 1860 to help free blacks move to Haiti. In two years over two thousand blacks did so, but that did not go well. Thus many advocates of a separate homeland fixed on Central America as a destination site, especially the Chiriquí region later renamed Panama. Turner supported these initiatives while urging African Americans to hold out for a homeland on the North American continent, preferably in the South. West Africa and Central America were important options, but the separatist movement needed more than one option.

On May 6, 1862, Alexander Crummell spoke at Israel Church, urging Afro-Americans to commit themselves to "race love" and to "civilizing Africa." Crummell, a black Episcopal priest and missionary to Liberia who will be discussed in the next chapter, had graduated from Queen's College, Cambridge, in 1853 and had served for nine years, thus far, in Liberia. Crummell's idea of race love was a forerunner of Pan-Africanism, his idea of civilizing Africa was a straightforward missionary and colonizing project, and in 1862 he believed that the "best" black American Christians should build a homeland in Liberia to civilize West Africa. Turner converted wholly to the homeland idea upon hearing Crummell speak. Black nationalist feeling was running high, as in the previous month Lincoln had emancipated all slaves in the District of Columbia, the first time that the federal government abolished slavery anywhere. The law that Lincoln signed appropriated one hundred thousand dollars to assist any blacks from the District of Columbia who wanted to emigrate to Haiti, Liberia, or any other country outside the United States. Forty black men petitioned Congress to support their resettlement in Central America. Liberia, they reasoned, was too far away and foreign for them. Haiti was a bad option because its civilization originated in Africa, it was degraded by "abject slavery under Spanish and French greed," and it was further brutalized by "unrestrained and licentious liberty." The same thing went for the West Indian islands. The group asked for a chance to export the superior republican ideals of the United States to "part of your own continent," in an uninhabited region of Central America.[9]

Turner signed this statement with no intention of personally moving to Central America, confirming local impressions that he was the ringleader of the homeland movement. Lincoln endorsed the Panama idea and Turner strongly commended the president for doing so. Many Radical Republicans were appalled, contending that colonization and/or paying for a mass exodus was a morally pathetic, if not perverted form of abolition. It could not be that the Civil War was being fought to colonize Afro-Americans in Central America or otherwise get rid of them. Insiders rumored that Turner was the chief player in getting Lincoln to take this path, which he denied, adding that he supported the right to voluntarily emigrate and absolutely opposed "compulsory colonization." Turner shook his head at acquaintances claiming to believe "that it was in the voluntary power of the president to transport at his option all the colored people out of the country." The following year, however, after Napoleon III invaded Mexico, Turner bizarrely urged Lincoln to dispatch an all-black army to Mexico to defeat the French and "take" Mexico as the black American homeland. He assured that conquering Mexico would be easy, popular, and good for all parties: "For every man, white or colored, who loves republican institutions would lend us aid; besides we would take one of the richest nations for its minerals on earth."[10]

Black regiments had existed for only five months when Turner issued this proposal in October 1863. He was soon diverted from colonizing ambitions by the carnage of the war at hand. Turner organized the First Regiment of the United States Colored Troops in Washington, DC, which fought in nine battles in the Virginia theater. He supported legislation that made African Americans eligible for the draft, which infuriated members of his congregation that did not want to fight for the Union. Some blamed Turner for the new draft law. He told them to get a grip on reality: "Am I the President of the United States? Can I go to the War Department and give orders? Or perhaps I went to Congress and they passed the enrollment act just to please me." Israel Church, he admonished, needed to stop cheering the war and start helping the Union: "The war has gone on for nearly three years and our people have been enjoying it. . . . Just as our prayers are being answered, just as victory is dawning, just as God is about to deliver us, we hear the hoarse voice of murmuring and complaint." Turner told his congregants they were exactly like the Hebrews that complained while being liberated from Egyptian bondage, and they needed to show some respect for people dying on their behalf: "We have been rejoicing while the whole land has been mourning."[11]

In November 1863 he became the second African American to receive a commission as an army chaplain, joining the regiment he had organized. Turner's evangelical faith and his hatred of slavery carried him through fierce fighting, smallpox, and the trauma of witnessing grisly amputations. For nearly three months in 1864 he struggled on the verge of death after contracting smallpox. Turner took a leave for three months and nursed himself to health.

Historian Stephen Ward Angell, in his excellent biography of Turner, notes that Turner returned to his regiment bearing facial scars, and he told soldiers that the side that prayed harder was likely to prevail. At the end of the war, Turner's regiment was in North Carolina, where he witnessed the genocidal destructiveness of General William T. Sherman's army, to his horror. He also reeled at the racism of Union soldiers. Sherman recouped a bit of moral credit with some by issuing Special Field Order Number Fifteen, setting aside the coastal lands of Georgia and South Carolina for African Americans. Turner, however, thought that was wrongheaded, too. He believed in thrift and hard work; giveaways were corrupting, misguided, and impractical. As it was, President Andrew Johnson soon remanded "forty acres and a mule" anyway.[12]

Turner served briefly as a regular army chaplain assigned to the Freedmen's Bureau in Georgia. But the tasks of army chaplaincy were confining, even boring, compared to the opportunity to build up the AME Church in the South through missionary evangelism, or politics, or better—both. Here the AME Church's competition with the AME Zion Church loomed large.

SOUTHERN BLACK RELIGION AND RECONSTRUCTION

The AME Zion Church was basically a New York version of the AME secession story, with less drama. In the mid-eighteenth century the evangelical religion of the early Methodist societies and their opposition to slavery attracted blacks to the Methodist denominations. By the 1790s, some Methodist congregations had black memberships ranging up to 50 percent, which set off white anxieties about losing control. These churches refused to fully ordain black preachers, which fueled secessionist feeling. John Street Methodist Episcopal Church in New York City was a prototype on both counts.

Peter Williams, a former slave employed at John Street Church, organized an African chapel in 1796 at a local cabinetmaker's shop for black members of John Street Church seeking a break from white prejudice. The group built a new house of worship in 1800, Zion Church, incorporating it the following year as the African Methodist Episcopal Church of the City of New York. Zion Church's board of trustees owned the church property. Only trustees of African descent were permitted to act for the corporation, and the New York Methodist Episcopal Conference continued to provide the church's ministers. For twenty years Zion Church continued to operate under the jurisdiction of the Methodist Episcopal Church, more or less agreeably. In 1820 the congregation joined another black congregation, Asbury African Methodist Episcopal Church, to form an independent conference, mainly to control their own money and to call their own pastors. The two black congregations refused to join the AME Church because Bishop Allen had used a former member of Zion Church, William Lambert, to recruit members in New York City for the AME Church. Allen's poaching offended the territorial feeling of New York African Methodists, who convened a conference in 1821 with representatives from six congregations in New York, Pennsylvania, and Connecticut. The following year Zion Church pastor James Varick was elected as the new denomination's first bishop, and in 1824 the AME Zion Church formally separated from the General Conference of the Methodist Episcopal Church, although it did not formally adopt the name "Zion" until 1848.[13]

The new denomination tried to win support from white Methodist and Episcopal bodies for its selection of Varick as a bishop, hoping to avert the AME precedent of ordaining its own bishop, but the white churches begged off. Frederick Douglass and Underground Railroad leader Harriet Tubman were AME Zion luminaries. In the aftermath of the Civil War, the AME Zion Church pushed aggressively into the same opening in the South that Turner saw. James Walker Hood was the leading AME Zion missionary. The son of a Pennsylvania Methodist preacher who converted to the AME Zion Church, Hood persuaded black Southern Methodist congregations in New Bern and Beaufort, North Carolina, to join the AME Zion Church in 1864, establishing the first conference of his denomination in that state, which set off alarms in the AME Church.

Turner implored the bishops of both denominations to work together. In 1864 he convened a unity conference in Philadelphia, which yielded lip service to unity and no agreements. Turner's faction of the AME Church wanted to unify the independent black Methodist churches. Others, led by AME missionary James Lynch, wanted to unify all black and white American Methodists; various black Baptist missionary societies had similar debates; and the AME Zion Church sought and failed to unite with the AME Church and the ME Church. Thus the two northern-based black Methodist churches competed for converts in the South, especially in North Carolina and Georgia. Hood and the AME Zion Church prevailed in most of North Carolina, frustrating Turner, who quit the Freedmen's Bureau, giving himself wholly to AME evangelism in Georgia. Turner's official title was "superintendent" (presiding elder) of the North Georgia mission. In effect he served as an unpaid bishop from 1866 to 1871, preaching every weeknight and three times on Sunday, planting new churches across the state and supervising existing churches.

After the Thirteenth Amendment was passed by the House of Representatives on January 31, 1865, and formally adopted on December 6, 1865, January 1 became the festival day for celebrating Emancipation. On January 1, 1866, Turner urged an Emancipation Day celebration in Augusta, Georgia, to be grateful for the privilege of meeting, grateful for the destruction of slavery, and grateful for the freedom of schools, the mind, matrimony, labor, and the gospel. He registered a realistic note—"The fact is, we have a better heart than the white people"—but he was determinately optimistic and conciliatory: "Let us love the whites, and let by-gones be by-gones, neither taunt nor insult them for past grievances; respect them; honor them; work for them; but still let us be men. Let us show them we can be a people, respectable, virtuous, honest, and industrious, and soon their prejudice will melt away, and with God for our father, we will all be brothers."[14]

A new day had come for America, Turner preached. Black Americans were grateful to be Christians and Americans, and they looked forward to building a Christian America worthy of the name. The yield from Turner's tireless preaching of this message, aided by similar preaching from Lynch and Georgia native William Gaines, was enormous. Turner built a huge personal following that made possible his subsequent political and ecclesiastical career. He struggled to find preachers for the many churches he planted, issuing certificates to aspiring preachers lacking any training or even literacy. Many critics, especially in the North, chastised him for filling the church with uneducated ministers. Turner replied that emergency circumstances left him no alternative and that the AME Church had to build its own supply of black preachers; otherwise it would fall into a dependent relationship on the ME Church, South. He facilitated reasonably cooperative relationships with white Southern Methodists while imploring his ministers to hold fast to their independence. Lynch played a similar role for the AME Church in Mississippi, as did Richard Cain in South Carolina and Charles Pearce in Florida. All were on the front lines of the cultural-religious struggle to establish black families after surviving a slave system that savaged the father role. All did whatever they could to promote literacy for former slaves and free blacks. And most were swept into Reconstruction politics.

Turner plunged into political activism during the same period that he planted AME churches across Georgia. He launched Union Leagues across the state and helped to organize the Republican Party in Georgia, which were variations on the same thing, as the Union Leagues were oath-bound societies dedicated to building up a Republican Party and promoting civic education. White Union Army officers founded the first Union Leagues; soon afterward, black Reconstruction activists dominated the movement and greatly expanded it. Turner's Union League meetings featured a call-and-response catechism in which he called out the questions and the entire gathering roared the answers:

Q. Who freed the slaves of the South?

A. Abraham Lincoln, the Republican President, by proclamation.

Q. Who passed the Freedman's Bureau Bill?

A. A Republican Congress by more than a two-thirds vote over the veto of Andrew Johnson, the leader of the Democratic or conservative party.

Q. Who gave us the Civil Rights Bill?

A. The same Republican Congress.

Q. What party gave us the right to vote?

A. The Republican Party.

Q. With whom do the disloyal white men of the South desire the colored men to vote?

A. With the Democratic Party.

Q. Would not the Democrats take away all the negro's rights?

A. They would.[15]

Turner was the gold standard Union League organizer. Politically, his Union League activism was temperate and conciliatory to a fault, urging audiences that race should mean nothing in politics. There were no differences between whites and blacks as human beings or as citizens: "The interests of white and black are one and the same—all are citizens in common. It therefore behooves both colors to cooperate, to join hands and to strive to the same goal." That was in April 1867, in Columbia, South Carolina. Four years later Turner summarized his recent experiences in this work:

My labors have not stopped in the religious sphere; but it is well known to everyone that I have done more work in the political field than any five men in the State, if you will take out Colonel Bryant [white Georgia Republican politician John E. Bryant]. I first organized the Republican Party in this State, and have worked for its maintenance and perpetuity as no other man in the State has. I have put more men in the field, made more speeches, organized more Union Leagues, political associations, clubs, and have written more campaign documents that received large recirculation than any other man in the State. Why, one campaign document I wrote alone was so acceptable that it took four million copies to satisfy the public.

On the other hand, Turner had just been driven from office, which forced him to resign as the AME Church's presiding elder in Georgia, since he needed a job that paid a salary, and he incurred vicious treatment for trying to establish Reconstruction in Georgia: "I have been the constant target of Democratic abuse and venom and white Republican jealousy. The newspapers have teemed with all kinds of slander, accusing me of every crime in the catalogue of villainy; I have even been arrested and tried on some of the wildest charges and most groundless accusations ever distilled from the laboratory of hell."[16]

Specifically, in 1867 Republicans in the U.S. Congress wrested control of Reconstruction away from President Johnson and forced Southern states to elect new governments open to white and black participation. To secure readmission to the Union on the conditions of the Reconstruction Acts, Southern states had to form new governments that allowed suffrage for black males and secured ratification of the Fourteenth Amendment. Seven states had done so by mid-summer 1868. In April 1868 Turner won a seat in Georgia's state house of representatives, along with twenty-three other black legislators, most of them ministers. All were expelled in September by a vote of eighty-three to twenty-three for being black. This vote took place shortly after federal troops were withdrawn from Georgia, with the black legislators abstaining. On their way out, the unseated African American legislators were vilified for presuming to govern Georgia. The following March the state legislature rejected the Fifteenth Amendment and Congress reluctantly put Georgia under military rule again. In May 1869 Turner got a patronage plum via Sumner and other Washington friends—postmaster in Macon—but that escalated the attacks upon him, featuring fabrications, slander, political fratricide, and a sexual scandal, plus a spike in death threats. The following year Congress ordered Georgia to restore its elected black officers, and Turner returned to office. But the Democratic Party, the Conservative Union Party, and the Ku Klux Klan ramped up their violence, and Turner was unseated by a dubious Democratic election recount that negated his victory.[17]

The core issue was always white outrage at finding black people in positions of authority. Many white southerners that appreciated Turner's evangelical labors were appalled when he turned out to be a political organizer too. It didn't matter that his politics were conciliatory and generally conservative, though he stepped out by supporting suffrage for women. Most African American officials advocated reconciliation during Reconstruction, contrary to decades of propaganda about "vindictive Negro misrule." Turner supported a full pardon for Jefferson Davis and the removal of suffrage restrictions on former Confederates. He preached the gospel of entrepreneurial self-help to black and white audiences. He went to extraordinary lengths to support white economic interests, pushing a bank-relief bill through the Georgia convention and a bill that protected property owners unable to pay their taxes from losing their homes and businesses. As a member of the state education committee he advocated literacy restrictions on suffrage, sponsoring legislation that within five years of establishing a common school system, no persons on becoming twenty-one years of age would be allowed to vote if they lacked a basic education. Turner tried to show that he could work with Democrats, which angered white Republicans, who also resented his quest for power at their expense. In *Black Reconstruction in America*, Du Bois put it tartly: "He desired civil rights, but did not wish the downfall of the aristocracy. There was enthusiasm in his efforts to secure pardon for Jefferson Davis."[18]

Upon being ousted from the Georgia legislature in 1868, Turner delivered the mother lode of all Reconstruction speeches to the assembly that had just expelled him and all others of his race. He asked the legislators to remember that the very state government they constituted was called into being by the hope and idealism of downtrodden African Americans and "the few humanitarian-hearted white men who came to our assistance." He implored them to deal with the rule of law and his humanity: "The great question, sir, is this: Am I a man? If I am such, I claim the rights of a man. Am I not a man, because I happen to be of a darker hue than honorable gentlemen around me?" Turner gave a lesson in physiology, noting that he had helped to dissect over fifty men. Human brains and bones are the same regardless of skin color, he reported. So what was the claim? That he had no soul? Turner declared: "Because God saw fit to make some red, and some white, and some black, and some brown, are we to sit here in judgment upon what God has seen fit to do? As well might one play with the thunderbolts of heaven as with that creature that bears God's image."[19]

It was said, Turner observed, that blacks were unworthy of holding office in the state legislature—"They want to turn the 'nigger' out." But if Afro-Americans could be appointed as lieutenants, captains, majors, surgeons, and even chaplains serving the U.S. government, how could being black disqualify anyone from holding a mere state office? Turner acknowledged that many legislators still operated under the idea that Georgia was supposed to be a slave state in which blacks had no rights. They did not believe in the Reconstruction Acts; they believed in the U.S. Constitution. Turner replied that chattel slavery violated the "spirit and letter" of the Constitution and the beliefs of the American Fathers. He quoted Benjamin Rush, Samuel Adams, John Adams, George Washington, and Thomas Jefferson to this effect, plus General Lafayette, who said that he never would have lifted his sword on America's behalf had he thought he was fighting to perpetuate slavery. The Georgia legislators routinely denied that African Americans contributed anything of importance to American civilization. Turner replied, "We have pioneered civilization here; we have built up your country; we have worked in your fields, and garnered your harvests, for two hundred and fifty years! And what do we ask of you in return? Do we ask you for compensation for the sweat our fathers bore for you—for the tears you have caused, and the hearts you have broken, and the lives you have curtailed, and the blood you have spilled? Do we ask retaliation? We ask it not. We are willing to let the dead past bury its dead; but we ask you, now, for our RIGHTS."[20]

White southerners already owned and controlled everything of value in the South, Turner admonished. They had no reason to be hysterical about the rise of black people: "You have our money and your own; you have our education and your own; and you have our land and your own, too. We, who number hundreds of thousands in Georgia, including our wives and families, with not a foot of land to call our own—strangers in the land of our birth; without money, without education, without aid, without a roof to cover us while we live, nor sufficient clay to cover us when we die!" Turner urged his expellers to stir up some Christian moral dignity: "It is extraordinary that a race such as yours, professing gallantry, and chivalry, and education, and superiority, living in a land where ringing chimes call child and sire to the Church of God—a land where Bibles are read and Gospel truths are spoken, and where courts of justice are presumed to exist; it is extraordinary, I say, that, with all these advantages on your side, you can make war upon the poor defenseless black man. You know we have no money, no railroads, no telegraphs, no advantages of any sort, and yet all manner of injustice is placed upon us."[21]

African American studies scholar Andre E. Johnson notes that Turner shrewdly appealed to the spirit of "the Reconstruction measures" instead of getting bogged down in legal arguments about particular laws. Georgia legislators claimed that Congress never granted to black Americans the right to hold office. Turner was sure that Congress would confirm his interpretation of its work. Meanwhile, Georgia Republicans appealed the ouster to the state supreme court, which ruled in their favor; the state legislature silently defied the ruling; and Turner watched for the Klan. Two years previously, Turner had barely averted a lynch mob at the Opelika, Georgia, train station. In 1868, white Republican politician George Ashburn was killed by a mob shortly after he and Turner shared a platform at a public rally in Columbus, Georgia; Turner probably survived only because the mob could not find him. The following year, after the Klan killed two white Republican politicians—Benjamin Ayer and Joseph Adkins—Turner declared that they would not have been murdered had they betrayed Republican principles like other Republicans. Ayer and Adkins were cut down for being true Republicans. The ouster speech took place between the Ashburn and double killings. The *Columbus Weekly Sun* editorialized that if Turner were to be lynched, "we should neither be seized with astonishment or regret." Six months later Turner received a letter from the Macon Klan: "Radical H.M. Turner: Your course of conduct is being closely watched by the owls of the night; do not be surprised if you should be aroused from slumber ere long by a boo hoo, boo hoo." Turner released the letter to the *Macon American Union* and replied: "I have been in readiness for you brutes for some time, and you will always find me prepared to give the reception."[22]

Turner survived physically, but not politically, the failure of the Radical Republicans to take control of Reconstruction in Georgia. By the time that the Afro-American legislators were reseated, Reconstruction had been fatally undermined in Georgia. Republican governor Rufus Bullock fled the governor's seat and the state, confirming that Reconstruction was going nowhere. Turner's feud with his former closest ally, *Macon American Union* editor J. C. Swayze, also hurt the cause and Turner's reputation. Swayze was a white Radical Republican militant. A native Georgian and former Unionist, he railed fearlessly against the Klan, publishing numerous articles about its crimes against blacks. Swayze also had a high sense of entitlement, seething that Turner pushed him aside to win the postmaster position that should have gone to him. In some versions of this story, Turner promised to support Swayze for the lucrative postmaster job before promoting himself for it. In Turner's version, Swayze demanded to control the post office and its salary after Turner won the appointment. Whatever happened, most of Macon's white citizens were outraged to have a black postmaster, and Swayze knew how to hurt Turner.[23]

In June 1869 Turner traveled to Washington to defend the postmaster appointment he had just received and to plead for federal intervention in Georgia. He returned to Georgia with a prostitute, Marian Harris, with whom he had maintained a relationship in at least three cities—Atlanta, Philadelphia, and Washington. In Augusta Harris was arrested carrying eighteen hundred dollars of fraudulent Bank of New Jersey notes, and Turner appealed to Swayze for legal help for himself. Swayze judged that the real story was that Turner tried to pass counterfeit money and got his prostitute girlfriend to be his accomplice and/or take the fall. The case against Harris went to Macon's U.S. commissioner, William Morrill of Maine. Harris testified that the bad money belonged to her, Swayze testified against Turner, and Morrill ruled that the evidence against Turner was insufficient to make him stand trial. The publicity was sensational, focusing on sex. The Grant administration pressured Turner to resign from the post office, which he did. Daniel Payne, mortified at the sexual aspect, wrote off Turner as an embarrassment to the church. Until now,

Payne had supported the two-track ministries of Turner and other politically engaged Reconstruction ministers in the South. With Turner's moral lapse, Payne began to say that politics was too corrupting for ministers to be involved in it.[24]

Turner was too important to black Methodists to be tarnished by this episode, although he had to deflect aftershocks for years to come. Many critics rang him up as the epitome of corrupted political religion, folding his moral lapse and a presumption about his guilt for fraud into a story about pervasive Negro misrule. This was a perverse fate for someone that poured himself out for causes that paid nothing. Turner was persecuted and impoverished, and the trope about Negro misrule was a useful fiction for white supremacists. At no time anywhere in the South did African Americans control a state government. In North Carolina blacks never held more than one-seventh of the legislature. James Walker Hood was the only black official of any consequence in North Carolina—serving as assistant superintendent of public instruction. In Florida blacks were outnumbered in the state legislature by seventy-six to nineteen and boasted a single high-ranking official. In Arkansas and Texas there were almost no black officials, high-ranking or otherwise. In South Carolina and Mississippi blacks had strong Reconstruction majorities but never controlled the government, and in Louisiana they had numerous high officials but never held a majority in the legislature. Historian John Hope Franklin summarized aptly: "The 'horrors of Negro domination' from which Alabamans prayed deliverance simply did not exist."[25]

Moreover, the black ministers that flocked into politics during Reconstruction did so almost entirely at the local and state levels, where there was little glamour. Mostly there was survival work to keep from being crushed. At the federal level sixteen African Americans were elected to Congress between 1869 and 1880, all Republicans. Fourteen were elected to the House, two of them ministers, notably AME minister Richard Cain, who represented South Carolina in the Forty-third and Forty-fifth Congresses with eloquence and distinction. There were two black U.S. senators from Mississippi, Blanche K. Bruce and Hiram R. Revels, the latter an AME minister. Turner appreciated that his friend Revels held the Senate seat previously occupied by Jefferson Davis. But successes of this sort were rare. Turner had tasted political power only to have it snatched away by racism. The hatred inflicted on him took its toll, and he stopped preaching about Christian America fulfilling its divine promise. He returned to his Afro-American denomination to make a case for getting the hell out of America. In 1871 Turner told the Georgia annual conference in Savannah, where he had gone to serve as a pastor: "I have had to pass through blood and fire. No man can imagine what I have had to endure but one who has gone through it."[26]

EXODUS AND EXILE IN QUESTION

For the rest of his life, Turner devoted himself to the work of the church and the cause of a black homeland. He advocated merger talks with the AME Zion Church but lost the argument to conservative opponents in the North and to Cain, who chafed at rewarding AME Zion bishops and poachers. The AME cause in the South took a greater blow in 1869 when the Colored Methodist Episcopal Church (CME) broke off from the ME Church, South, to form its own denomination. The new black Methodist denomination was submissive and culturally southern. It sustained a friendly relationship with the ME Church, South. It decidedly favored light-colored blacks. And it slowed the growth of the AME Church, embroiling the AME Church in draining church property disputes, as the ME Church, South, still held the titles to many AME buildings that it now sought to transfer to the CME Church. Turner gasped and railed at AME ministerial colleagues who joined the new denomination. The ME Church, AME Church, and most black Baptists strongly supported Reconstruction and the Republican Party, while the ME Church, South, and most white Baptists supported Democrats, usually while saying that the church, and especially blacks, should stay out of politics. The CME Church won favor with white Southern Methodists by pledging to do so.[27]

Turner defended his beleaguered but growing denomination and tried not to feel completely driven out of politics. He grieved at Sumner's death in 1874, losing a treasured friend and political ally. In Turner's telling, Sumner was the single figure most responsible for the abolition of slavery, having pressed for equality and having exhorted Lincoln about abolition until Lincoln relented. At the time of his death, Sumner had pushed a civil rights bill through the Senate and was trying to get it before the House. Turner had misgivings about the bill, because white Americans North and South despised blacks as subhuman. Why bother with civil rights laws if white America felt entitled to ignore the laws? The Civil Rights Act of 1866, a federal statute, had required strenuous political struggle. It established the rights of blacks to make and enforce contracts, give evidence in court, sue and be sued, and own property — yet these rights were routinely violated. Turner usually caught himself and pulled back, however, upon warming to this theme, since he did believe in trying, and black Christians looked to him for leadership and hope. The Civil Rights Act of 1875 prohibited discrimination by owners of hotels, theaters, restaurants, and other public accommodations. When it passed into law on March 1, Turner tried to be optimistic, or at least to appear so.

At the same time he recommitted to homeland activism. In April 1875 Turner declared in the American Colonization Society's *African Repository and Colonial Journal* that he believed with equal certainty in the existence of God and the necessity of blacks returning to Africa: "And the sooner we begin to recognize that fact and prepare for it, the better it will be for us as a people." For black Americans, Turner reasoned, America was a school where blacks learned Christian theology and the workings of civil government. Slavery had a role in God's plan to raise up the children of Africa, and thus so did America. As soon as black Americans were "educated sufficiently to assume control of our vast ancestral domain," God would call them back to Africa.[28]

The American Colonization Society was founded in 1816 by a coalition of planter-class patricians led by Henry Clay and John Randolph of Roanoke, Quaker abolitionists, and evangelical antislavery activists. It was always an odd assortment, although the group's abolitionist faction thinned out by the 1850s. By 1870 the society had helped more than thirteen thousand Afro-Americans move to Liberia, and in 1876 it appointed Turner as an honorary vice president. He was deeply moved: "I am at a loss for language to express my deep sense of the honor conferred." Turner's separatism was a factor. After Sumner died and Reconstruction was killed off, Turner tended to get along better with white paternalists who supported emigration than with liberals who believed in racial integration. He contended, however, that the society's white leaders were motivated by "pure impulses and Christian desires," not by racism. The society realized that blacks had to have their own nation and government; otherwise they would never grow into "manhood." Turner put it sharply, in the tradition of Crummell. It was pointless to go on complaining of bad treatment, passing resolutions, voting for white men, serving as caterers and barbers, and sending their wives and daughters to work as servants: "No—a government and nationality of our own can alone cure the evils under which we now labor, and are likely yet the more to suffer in this country."[29]

This was a missionary enterprise, Turner stressed. American blacks needed to civilize and Christianize Africa, not just save themselves by going there. In the early going, Turner did not envision mass emigration. The American Colonization Society had been working on this issue for decades, with modest but solid results, and for Christians the missionary model was familiar and workable. Turner encouraged black missionaries to settle permanently among the Africans they sought to convert: "The only way to civilize a people is to move into their midst and live among them." In 1879 he offered a fourfold case for doing so: African Americans had every reason to take pride in their home-land; Africa's land and climate were good for planting and farming; Africa offered a safe haven for oppressed black Americans; and things were likely to get worse for black Americans.[30]

Benjamin T. Tanner, editor of the AME journal the *Christian Recorder*, was dismayed and offended that Turner changed the subject. The debate between Tanner and Turner began in 1874 and carried on for over fifteen years—before and after Turner was elected bishop in 1880 and Tanner was elected bishop in 1888. Tanner pleaded with AME readers to ignore Turner's counsel of despair. It was cowardly to run from white people, Tanner admonished. Blacks needed to stand their ground against white abuse. Turner needed to take more pride in his own accomplishments, all of which occurred in the United States. He espe-cially had to stop stealing the hope of young people. If things were impossibly bad in America, Tanner urged, why did people everywhere clamor to get into America? Why did African students studying in the United States do everything they could to remain in the United States?[31]

Turner shrugged off the charge of cowardice and the questions about people trying to immigrate to the United States. Things were so terrible for black Americans that fleeing was honorable and blacks needed a place of refuge; he would not speak for others. In the 1880s, after Turner was elected bishop but before Tanner was elected, Turner commended Tanner as the AME Church's leading scholar. He envied Tanner's perch at the *Christian Recorder*, where Tanner commanded the attention of the entire denomination. Turner only wished there were some evidence that Tanner cared about the redemption of Africans and Africa: "Did you ever sit down and write an article presenting the claims of Africa upon our church and our religion by giving the people a knowl-edge of the millions who are there in moral darkness, and the people their duty in the premises?" Tanner, though writing extensively about many things, had almost nothing to say about Africa. This was incomprehensible to Turner; he was not the one that needed to explain himself. How could a black American Christian not care about the salvation of Africans and the fate of Africa? "Such a Christianity to my judgment is hypocrisy of the meaner sort, or to use the pertinent language of Bishop Payne, is the 'lopsided Christianity of an igno-ramus.'" Admittedly, Turner had not gone to Africa, despite writing about it constantly. But Tanner needed to stop sneering about that, because Turner had every intention of getting to Africa as soon as he was in a position to take African Americans with him.[32]

By then Turner had taken leave of the Republican Party, because there was nothing left of Reconstruction. The last presidential election that he really cared about was in 1876, although Turner usually made lesser-evil judgments about subsequent elections, and he had family patronage interests at stake. In 1876 Ohio Republican Rutherford B. Hayes won 166 undisputed electoral votes, and New York Democrat Samuel Tilden won 184 undisputed votes—one less than Tilden needed to become president. A 15-member electoral commission bargained over the outcome, concluding that Hayes could have the White House in exchange for abolishing Reconstruction. Hayes secretly promised to remove federal troops from the South, and in April 1877 he shut down the army in South Carolina and Louisiana, where Republican governments fell immediately.

Turner wrote a bitter obituary for the Republican Party, "slaughtered in the house of its friends, April 24, 1877," alarming the new president. Hayes met with Turner, imploring him not to bail out. He cared about black Americans; that was why he was a Republican. He had worked for the antislavery cause since 1853, and Grant had advised him to remove the army from the South. Turner admired Grant, so this disclosure carried some weight. For seven months Turner pulled back from criticizing Hayes, giving his policy a fair trial. But life in the South became intolerable, and in December Hayes appointed a white Democrat as U.S. marshal in Savannah. That was the end of the line for Turner. Republicans had capitulated to white Democratic rule in the South, and he could not bear to defend what remained of the party of Sumner, Stevens, and Douglass, even as Douglass sacrificed his dignity by serving as marshal of the District of Columbia under Hayes.[33]

By 1880 Turner had no qualms about saying that James A. Garfield versus Winfield Scott Hancock meant nothing to him. The presidential candidates were reduced to small arguments about tariffs, and it did not matter who won. White progressives were aroused about coal-mine and railroad strikes, but Turner opposed trade unions and felt no affinity with working-class whites. He declared, "I have thought it prudent to keep out of the Presidential agitation for the reason that I am down upon the whole nation. I think my race has been treated by it with the kindness that a hungry snake treats a helpless frog." He noted that he had no particular region of the country in mind. He traveled in every region and had "been made sick a thousand times—wished I had never been born, so that I might not have been a witness to the deviltry perpetrated upon my people by a so-called civilized country." Many people told him to get out of politics and stick with church work; Turner assured them he was done with politics, although only for bad reasons: "My race has been treated with so much treachery, vile contempt and diabolical meanness, that I have but little in the country anyway, except to eke out my existence and get out of this world with a prospect of finding a better."[34]

Two months later the AME Church convened in St. Louis to elect three more bishops. There were six at the time—two at Wilberforce, two in Washington, DC, and one each in Philadelphia and Baltimore. The preeminent bishop, Payne, had shrewdly organized AME missionary support in the South after the Civil War and founded Wilberforce University as an AME institution in 1863. Payne was born free in Charleston, South Carolina, in 1811 of African, European, and Native American descent. In the mid-1830s he studied at Lutheran Theological Seminary in Gettysburg, Pennsylvania, and in 1842 he joined the AME Church. Ten years later he was elected as the church's sixth bishop. Intensely pious, disciplined, scholarly, theologically conservative, and frail, Payne never weighed more than ninety-six pounds. He inveighed against emotional religion, the spirituals, and disrespect for church law. He took a stringent view of Episcopal authority, especially his own. His favorite theologian was Charles Hodge, Princeton Theological Seminary's guardian of Reformed orthodoxy. On the other hand, unlike Princeton Seminary, Payne's university reverberated with the language of racial equality and black progress. Heading into the General Conference, Payne stressed repeatedly that he wanted only godly bishops. Everyone knew what that meant for this conference.

The AME Church did not ordain anyone that used tobacco products, yet Turner was addicted to snuff. Payne was zealous about sexual morality, yet Turner had embarrassed the church by consorting with a prostitute, and there were rumors of other affairs. At the General Conference Payne was blistering and indignant, condemning any delegate who voted for a candidate that had "a concubine following him behind as he goes through the country." A bishop must be morally blameless, Payne thundered: "Anathema be the man, anathema be the man, I say *thrice*, anathema be the man who votes otherwise." The delegates were stricken silent. A Payne operative, C. C. Felts, began to read a list of charges against Turner, but the delegates exploded in response, drowning out Felts with foot stomping and shouts of "No, no, can't allow that." Payne tried to quiet the crowd, urging that certain things had to be said before anyone voted, but the crowd drowned out Payne too. He likened the tumult to a hurricane sweeping over the Atlantic. An immediate vote by secret ballot was ordered, and Turner won on the first ballot. Richard Cain and a minister closer to Payne's mold, William F. Dickerson, were elected subsequently. Payne was stunned and appalled by the gathering; he later recalled that it was packed with young delegates from Georgia and both Carolinas who disrespected their elders and all forms of authority, including—incredibly to him—the Bible.[35]

The formal authority of the Bible was not really an issue in 1880, as Turner held near-fundamentalist beliefs at the time about biblical inspiration and infallibility. Payne believed that Turner lacked essential Christian virtues and that the election of Turner and Cain represented a victory for baleful things— political religion, African emigration, a southern cultural ethos, and Southern AME colleges. The AME Church battled over these things throughout the 1880s, adding questions about the Bible, too. In 1881 Allen University (formerly Payne Institute) was established in Columbia, South Carolina. In 1882 Paul Quinn College was founded in Waco, Texas. In 1882 Turner College was founded in Hernando, Mississippi; five years later it was absorbed into a new institution, Campbell College. In 1882 the Ward Normal and Collegiate Institute was founded in Huntsville, Texas. In 1883 the Scientific, Normal and Divinity Institute (later, Edward Waters College) was founded in Jacksonville, Florida. In 1885 Morris Brown College was founded in Atlanta. Southern AME ministers exulted that Payne's vision of an educated church and clergy was realized in the establishment of new AME schools. Payne replied, acidly: "The founding of a college requires a great deal of forethought and preparation." Nearly every new college came from "the thought of a single head." Payne wanted the AME Church to build Wilberforce into an educational powerhouse. He protested that instead it threw away money on weak schools it could not afford.[36]

The balance of power in the AME Church shifted dramatically with the rise of Turner and Cain. Turner worked hard at growing the church, devoting his extraordinary energy to evangelizing and managing his district, comprising Mississippi, Arkansas, and Oklahoma. He urged blacks to take pride in their race and exhorted ministers to organize literary associations. He also ramped up his homeland activism, folding emigration into his sermons and lectures, befriending Liberian emigration activist Edward W. Blyden, and debating AME critics, especially Tanner. Critics charged that he was too rough on white people and the North. Turner replied that the North was every bit as guilty as the South in originating and perpetuating slavery; it deserved no moral medals for belatedly destroying slavery, and in some ways the South was better than the North, because at least southerners were honest about their racism. He was grateful "for the services of a few individuals," but in the aggregate he had no thanks for white northerners or white southerners. Critics objected that Africa's climate was too harsh; Turner asked these "simply ridiculous" people to learn about the settlement of Roanoke, Annapolis, Plymouth Rock, Baltimore, Philadelphia, Charleston, and Louisville. If white people were brave enough to deal with pioneer adversity, what was wrong with American blacks?[37]

The bane of this debate, for Turner, was the misconception that he wanted all black Americans to move to Africa. Repeatedly he replied that he wanted only the proud and resourceful to try it. Between five and ten thousand per year would be enough; a half million per year would be lunacy: "The truth is, two-thirds of our race have no faith in themselves individually; they do not have any in each other." Turner did not want anyone in that group to emigrate: "The whole tendency of our ignoble status in this country is to develop in the Negro mean, sordid, selfish, treacherous, deceitful and cranksided characteristics. There isn't much real manhood in the negro in this country today." He allowed that more Afro-Americans were educated than previously, but "the American negro does not possess half the respect for himself today he did fifteen years ago, and it only requires a little sober sense to see it." Turner was routinely rough and insulting on this topic, blasting "all the riffraff white-men worshippers, aimless, objectless, selfish, little-souled and would-be-white Negroes of this country." He chafed at having to say it repeatedly to people who kept repeating the same objection: "All this jargon about 'Bishop Turner trying to get all us colored people out of the United States' is not only nonsense, but absolutely false, for two-thirds of the American Negroes would be of no help to anyone anywhere."[38]

The people that he wanted would have to relinquish their standing and achievements. Turner appealed to their heroism and race pride: "We must raise a symbol somewhere. We are bitten, we are poisoned, we are sick and we are dying. We need a remedy. Oh for some Moses to lift a brazen serpent, some goal for our ambition, some object to induce us to look up." Blacks needed to see, upon looking up, "black men in the seat of power, respected, honored, beloved, feared, hated and reverenced." It would never happen in America, Turner insisted. He leveraged his ecclesiastical authority to implore young people to make a new world somewhere else. No race deserved to be respected that did not found a respectable nation, he urged: "This has not been done creditably yet by the civilized negro, and till it is done he will be a mere scullion in the eyes of the world." A beginning had been made in Liberia. The leaders of the American Colonization Society, by helping Afro-Americans build up Liberia, proved that they were "our best friends and greatest benefactors."[39]

In October 1883 the U.S. Supreme Court struck down the Civil Rights Act of 1875, contending by a vote of eight to one that the federal government lacked any authority to prohibit private businesses from practicing racial discrimination. Only state governments could enforce the Fourteenth Amendment's principle of equal protection under the law. Kentucky Justice John M. Harlan cast the dissenting vote, arguing that the Constitution's interstate commerce clause, the Thirteenth Amendment, and the Fourteenth Amendment provided ample authority for Congress to pass civil rights laws. Turner blasted the decision as a monstrosity that turned the American flag into "a rag of contempt instead of a symbol of liberty." This barbaric decision, Turner said, reopened the issues over which the Civil War was fought. It revived the recently fading Klan and "literally unties the devil." Turner denied that he expected the federal government to ignore the Constitution, "but everybody knows that the recent amendments put the status of the negro race in the hands of Congress. They were ratified by the states with that distinct understanding."[40]

The plain meaning of the Fourteenth Amendment had been distorted by "wicked ingeniousness, superinduced by color-phobism." Turner expected most white Americans to ignore the civil rights laws, but he did not expect this "farce" of a ruling by justices placed in power by Republican presidents, which undermined the civil status of every black American. He predicted that the fallout would be staggering; *Dred Scott* was a "molehill" by comparison. This "barbarous" decision merited "no moderate talk," Turner declared: "It should be branded, battle-axed, sawed, and cut with the most bitter epithets and blistering denunciations that words can express. We want fire-eaters now."[41]

A year after the Supreme Court struck down civil rights for African Americans, America elected its first Democratic president since before the Civil War, Grover Cleveland. Many Afro-Americans were alarmed that Cleveland might reinstate slavery. Southern congressmen in the nation's capital carried on obnoxiously in restaurants, debating about which waiters they should take for slaves. *Washington Bee* editor W. Calvin Chase, indulging his hyperbolic tendency, predicted that millions of blacks would be killed, especially helpless virgins and babies. Turner told *A.M.E. Church Review* readers that things were worse and not as bad as they thought.

Yes, the Supreme Court had "wickedly, cruelly and infernally turned us over to the merciless vengeance of the white rabble of the country." And yes, Turner had given up on America: "I care nothing about it, wish it nothing but ill and endless misfortune, which I could only live to see it go down to ruin and its memory blotted from the pages of history." On the other hand, he doubted that Cleveland would be worse for African Americans than the recent Republican administrations. Now that southern whites had a Democrat in the White House, they were unlikely to "hazard very many outrages," and on the issue that consumed the two political parties—free trade versus tariffs—the Democrats were better. In the South, Turner observed, blacks were cotton producers; in the North, they were waiters; in both cases they were better off under a free-trade regime. Turner ended in his usual way: "Nothing will remedy the evils of the Negro but a great Christian nation upon the continent of Africa." Then he reached for a larger way of saying it: "White is God in this country and black is the Devil. White is perfection, greatness, wisdom, industry, and all that is high and holy. Black is ignorance, degradation, indolence, and all that is low and vile, and three-fourths of the colored people of the land do nothing day and night but cry: 'Glory, honor, dominion, and greatness to White.'" Turner had a two-word admonition for all: "Respect black."[42]

This ringing black nationalist proclamation and Turner's let's-see approach to Cleveland yielded a delicate dance with the new president. Turner had received patronage favors from every Republican president of the 1870s and 1880s, winning jobs for one or both of his sons, but the Republican nominee of 1884, James Blaine, refused to meet with Turner, embittering their relationship. Turner asked Cleveland to resume the family patronage he had received from Republicans, and Cleveland obliged him. Cleveland also appointed six blacks to federal offices, something that Republicans had never done. No black American held a federal office under the Grant and Hayes administrations; James Garfield broke the mold by appointing Douglass as recorder of deeds, who served under Garfield and Chester Arthur; now Cleveland rewarded six black Democrats with federal offices, replacing Douglass with James Monroe Trotter, the father of William Monroe Trotter. A surprised Turner urged his readers to give Cleveland a fair trial. Stephen Angell judges that Turner subsequently enjoyed a closer relationship to Cleveland than to any other president of the 1880s and 1890s. Turner claimed that ordinary white southerners were becoming more friendly to blacks than the hypocritical whites of the North: "I believe the Negro will receive more personal kindness throughout the South, than has been accorded to him since the war. The southern Whites are determined to make the black man feel, if possible, that they are better friends of the Negro race, than the northern Whites; therefore I look for a general reform in the treatment of the Negro South."[43]

Turner stuck to that line through Cleveland's term in office, defying the Republican sentimentality of his readers and, at times, their experience of heightened hostility in the South. Cleveland versus Benjamin Harrison in 1888 recycled the free-trade debate, with Cleveland opposing tariffs as unfair to consumers, and Harrison defending the interests of industrialists and factory workers. Harrison's Des Moines, Iowa, operative James S. Clarkson, a former associate of John Brown, rallied black support for Harrison, but Turner spurned Harrison, even after he won the presidency. Harrison appointed Clarkson as postmaster general, who appointed sixteen thousand blacks to federal jobs, and Harrison replaced the six black Democrats with six black Republicans.

Turner still said no, contending that Harrison ignored the "wails and dying groans" of African Americans in the South. That worsened the usual grumbling that Turner insulted his readers, told them to leave America, and abandoned the Republican Party. Moreover, Turner nettled critics and friends alike by making off-key statements about getting along in the South. Turner was doubly disqualified from traveling in polite society and doubly disinclined from doing so. Being black disqualified him from traveling on first-class train cars, but Turner was a nationalist who didn't care to associate with whites anyway, and as a smoker he was disqualified from first-class train cars. He was accustomed to the dirty train cars to which his smoking habit consigned him. In 1889 he told a reporter that he had little difficulty traveling in the South, as he took no interest in going where he was not wanted. That offended many black readers. Georgia AME pastor C. Max Manning blasted Turner for trivializing the issue, as did Ida B. Wells, who protested that being excluded from decent train cars went hand in hand with being excluded from good colleges.[44]

In 1890 the Reconstruction Era took its last gasp of breath. The Federal Elections Bill of 1890, drafted by Massachusetts representative Henry Cabot Lodge, forced Republicans to consider whether they were willing to risk anything to protect the rights of blacks in the South. The bill called for federal supervision of elections in the South. Opponents dubbed it the "Force Bill" because it forced southern states to allow African Americans to vote. For certain groups on both sides of the issue, this was a do-or-die moment. It was a catalyzing moment for white nationalists, who wailed that the Force Bill would institute a second Reconstruction. It was a defining moment for white social gospelers that cared about the future of African Americans. It was a depressing and frustrating moment for legendary black journalist Timothy Thomas Fortune, who had just launched a black civil rights organization to take on this issue. And it was a puzzling moment for Turner, who was caught between what he believed and what he should say.

THE BLACK IMAGE IN THE WHITE MIND

The white social gospel movement had four ideological traditions concerning racial justice. One was straightforwardly racist and hateful, though virtually all social gospel leaders denied that one could be a true social gospeler and belong to this group. The second group, the right-leaning assimilationists, advocated black assimilation to an Anglo-Saxon ideal and deferred the issue of rights. The third group, the left-leaning assimilationists, advocated assimilation with a stronger recognition that Afro-Americans were wrongly cheated of their rights. The fourth group, the neo-abolitionists, strongly defended the dignity and rights of African Americans. But there were never enough of them.

The right-leaning assimilationists espoused missionary idealism and a gradual, usually qualified path to assimilation, taking pride in their high-minded tone. They contended that in much of the nation it was premature to raise issues about civil rights for blacks. African Americans needed to make themselves worthy of the rights of citizenship, mostly by getting trained for a job, embracing Christianity, and behaving better, exactly as Booker Washington prescribed. Prominent northern ministers Lyman Abbott, Josiah Strong, and Francis Greenwood Peabody were leading figures in this group, as were Southern Episcopal rector Edgar Gardner Murphy and, in some contexts, Southern Methodist bishop Atticus G. Haygood. All were patronizing without apology, taking white supremacy for granted. All considered themselves to be righteous on the race issue. Accusing them of racism would have seemed ludicrous to them, for they preached against bigotry and tried to help black Americans move up.[45]

Murphy was a romantic racialist with a full-blown theory of white soul, who urged Washington to support the appeal of the Fifteenth Amendment so that white southerners could stop fearing that Afro-Americans would regain political power. Abbott told a gathering of white paternalists in 1890 that they did not need to hear from any blacks concerning the Negro situation, for the assembled white leaders were like doctors, and American blacks were their patients. Abbott opposed the Lodge Bill, but he favored federal aid for education. He had opposed slavery when that was the issue, but he had recoiled at abolitionists too. In the 1890s Abbott declared that he still disliked abolitionists, although he put up with a few neo-abolitionist colleagues at the *Christian Union* (later renamed the *Outlook*). There he specialized in patronizing racial put-downs, further corrupting the atmosphere in which his less-quotable friends purveyed a similar attitude. Sometimes they rationalized that a bit of racist pandering helped them to influence the white audiences that they sought, more or less, to liberalize.[46]

The left-leaning assimilationists also lionized Washington and the vocational path to progress, but they supported higher education for high achievers and were willing to offend white audiences concerning the rights and abilities of African Americans. Some figures in this school wanted to be neo-abolitionists but were chastened by a dire sense of the regional politics, the national politics, and/or the failures of Reconstruction. They clung to a missionary belief in the liberating and civilizing role of higher education. This school espoused the "talented tenth" idea later championed by Du Bois, building on Henry Morehouse's call in 1896 for "the high education of the talented tenth man." Morehouse, a white Baptist mission executive (secretary of the American Baptist Home Mission Society), grudgingly accepted that white America was not going to invest in mass public education for blacks. Industrial education was "fine for the nine," he reasoned, but "that tenth man ought to have the best opportunities for making the most of himself for humanity and God." Morehouse urged that in every age, "the mighty impulses that have propelled a people onward in their progressive career have proceeded from a few gifted souls."[47]

The chief vehicles of left-assimilation were the Congregational and Baptist missionary societies—the American Missionary Association (AMA) and the American Baptist Home Mission Society (ABHMS). The AMA was a consolidation of several Congregational antislavery missionary societies, founded in 1846. Before the Civil War it worked entirely among northern blacks. After the war, it moved into the South and established numerous colleges for African Americans, as well as scores of primary and secondary schools. The colleges included Hampton Institute, Fisk University, Berea College, Tillotson Institute, Atlanta University, Howard University, Tougaloo University, Straight University, and Talladega College. The AMA fought against segregation in the South but gradually acquiesced to local governance after Reconstruction. Many AMA leaders were left-assimilationists, notably Amory Bradford, Washington Gladden, Charles Cuthbert Hall, and Henry Churchill King.[48]

Their counterparts in the ABHMS included Morehouse, T. J. Morgan, George Sale, and Malcolm MacVicar. Morehouse's "talented tenth man" prescription was not as male as it sounded, as most of the ABHMS schools were coeducational. By 1880 the ABHMS had built and supported eight schools of higher education for African Americans—Shaw University in Raleigh, North Carolina; Benedict Institute in Columbia, South Carolina; Nashville Institute in Nashville, Tennessee; Natchez Seminary in Natchez, Mississippi; Leland University in New Orleans, Louisiana; Wayland Seminary in Washington, DC; Richmond Institute in Richmond, Virginia; and Atlanta Baptist College in Atlanta, Georgia, later renamed Morehouse College. Only the last two were exclusively male. AMA schools were similarly mixed, emphatic that high-achieving women deserved an advanced education and that successful assimilation demanded it. In addition to the mission specialists and educators, the left-assimilationists included *Our Day* editor Joseph Cook and *Independent* editors Henry Bowen and William Hayes Ward. The Congregational *Independent*, reflecting its antislavery past under Henry Ward Beecher and Theodore Tilton, was the chief venue of left-assimilation and neo-abolitionist opinion in the 1890s.[49]

In the South, left-assimilation was the most radical possibility, and usually not possible; thus only a handful of white southerners took a stand against racial injustice or lynching during the heyday of white nationalism. Haygood,

Louisiana/Mississippi Episcopal rector Quincey Ewing, and Louisiana novelist George Washington Cable were the leading figures. Haygood straddled the line between the two assimilation camps, dispensed Slater Fund money on behalf of ex-president Hayes, and preached that all races were one in humanity. Ewing daringly compared the cross of Jesus to the lynching poles of the South. Cable, the South's leading writer, was a devout Presbyterian/Congregational layman who fought with the Confederate cavalry. He later reflected that he was in his thirties before he began to think, which led him to writing and social activism. His first and greatest novel, *The Grandissimes: A Story of Creole Life* (1880), portrayed mixed-race families of the early nineteenth century shortly after the Louisiana Purchase. It made Cable famous, qualifying him for the pinnacle of the lecture circuit—a two-man show with Samuel Clemens (Mark Twain). In 1885 Cable opted for direct communication, writing an article, "The Freedman's Case in Equity," which advocated equality of opportunity in public places, and another, "The Silent South," which appealed to the humanity of decent white southerners. Both were published in a national venue, the *Century Magazine*. Cable pioneered the evocative, distinctly southern genre of racial description later fashioned by William Faulkner and Robert Penn Warren, and he kept writing to spark a movement for racial equality, appealing to silent southerners that he said were out there. But he had to do it from the safer climes of Northampton, Massachusetts, because in 1885 he fled from the racial fury of his Louisiana neighbors.[50]

The neo-abolitionists were spiritual descendants of the abolitionists and Radical Republicans. They protested that white American racism was oppressive and indefensible. The social gospel had to stand up for racial equality and the abolition of lynching; otherwise it betrayed the spirit of Jesus. Congregationalists were the strongest party in this school, as in both schools of assimilation. Methodists, Baptists, Episcopalians, Unitarians, Quakers, Disciples, and Presbyterians lagged behind the Congregationalists on the activist front. The leading white neo-abolitionist was Albion Tourgée, a best-selling author and former judge in Greensboro, North Carolina. During Reconstruction, Tourgée's judicial circuit was a hub of Klan terrorism. Often called the most hated man in North Carolina, Tourgée was a superb courtroom judge and legal reformer. In 1876 he moved to Raleigh as a federal pension agent; three years later, having survived fourteen years of death threats and constant hostility, Tourgée moved to Denver, Colorado, reluctantly acknowledging that he had no future in the post-Reconstruction South.[51]

Other white neo-abolitionists included Cincinnati Congregational minister Herbert Seeley Bigelow, Rochester Episcopal rector Algernon Crapsey,

Brooklyn Congregational minister Newell Dwight Hillis (Abbott's successor at Plymouth Church), *Outlook* editor Charles B. Spahr, New York Unitarian minister John Haynes Holmes, and AMA superintendent of education Harlan Paul Douglass. The flagship of Radical Republicanism, the *Independent*, tacked in a neo-abolitionist direction after Ward became editor in 1896 and the magazine resisted a gusher of pro-Washington fare. There were important neo-abolitionist bases at Oberlin College, where abolitionism was a tradition and where Henry Churchill King taught, and at Grinnell College, where George Herron, George A. Gates, and Herron's successor, Edward A. Steiner, espoused a radical social gospel.[52]

The differences between the left-assimilation and neo-abolitionist positions replayed, to some degree, the distinction between the antislavery and abolitionist camps of the 1830s to 1850s. The crucial difference in both cases was dispositional militancy. In the 1840s one could be an antislavery activist in northern polite society, but not an abolitionist. Abolitionists were abhorred in respectable circles for condemning slaveholders and for demanding the immediate eradication of slavery. Sixty years later, left-assimilationists put off issues about civil and social equality, always in the name of gradual progress. Neo-abolitionists refused to be put off: The Reconstruction Amendments had to be defended, public education for blacks and all others had to be provided, and lynching had to be abolished.

The neo-abolitionists supported the Lodge Bill but objected that it was too weak. Tourgée said it was barely worth supporting. The left-assimilationists rallied passionately behind the bill. Cable said it was a force bill only "to those who cannot be kept from fraud except by force." The *Independent* and *Our Day* implored that the soul of the Republican Party and the existence of a decent society were at stake. Bowen and Cook editorialized that America was not a decent society if it could not manage to conduct free and honest elections. Even if the franchise was not a natural right, it was inalienable once conferred, and no section of the nation had a right to nullify the Fifteenth Amendment. Opponents warned that honest elections would yield black mayors and governors. The *Independent* replied, "As between a government which is based on fraud and intimidation and a government in the hands of Negroes there should not be a moment's hesitation."[53]

But hesitation and lukewarm feeling prevailed in key places, especially the swing vote section of the Senate. The Lodge Bill passed the House and stalled in the Republican-controlled Senate, where Republicans and Democrats bargained over the Tariff Act and Silver Act. Booker Washington predictably opposed the bill, fearing a bloodbath in the South. Atticus Haygood warned that his fellow white southerners would destroy the public schools before they accepted federally monitored elections. That gave pause to nervous accommodationists on both sides of the color line.[54]

In 1884 Fortune had issued a call for a black civil rights organization. The old abolitionist convention movement, still creaking along, was wholly inadequate, merely a forum for speeches. Douglass gave speeches urging blacks not to form their own organizations. Fortune was done with that, because blacks needed an activist vehicle that agitated for a new abolition. A local branch of what became the National Afro-American League was founded in 1887, and Fortune organized a national organization in 1890, the same year that Tourgée launched a national interracial organization, the Citizens' Equal Rights Association. But the Afro-American League declined to take a position on the Lodge Bill and the organization withered from lack of support, raising the question of whether African Americans were too beaten down to resist their own oppression. Fortune worked himself into a depressive spiral and a fateful alliance with Washington on the way to concluding that the answer was yes.[55]

Fortune despaired that he could not get African Americans to mobilize or even to support him. For a while Turner puzzled over what he should say, giving mixed messages. He had written off Republicans and white America, so how could he pretend that anything important was at stake? But that suggested that he opposed the bill, giving aid to reactionaries, which Turner denied when AME ministers pressed him on the subject. He set the record straight in the *Christian Recorder,* announcing his support. If the Senate passed the Lodge Bill and Harrison signed it, Turner allowed, there was still a chance for African Americans to be "a small political factor" in America. If the bill failed, "the Republican party will be as dead as a mummy, nor will it ever be resurrected nor will it deserve to be. I thank God from my heart that the Republican party has at last got where it will be death to retreat from the interests of the Negro." Turner reasoned that losing the White House to Cleveland had reminded Republicans they were supposed to care about black Americans. It was nice, and not meaningless, that Republicans had returned to a somewhat decent posture. But if they failed to pass the election bill, "their failure will be their lasting overthrow."[56]

As it was, the bill died in the Senate and the onslaught of disenfranchisement and expanded segregation commenced. That summer, still in 1890, the leaders of the right-assimilation and left-assimilation camps held a conference on "The Negro Question" at Lake Mohonk, New York. Former U.S. president Rutherford B. Hayes presided, and eighty religious and civic leaders attended. Several speakers noted that political leaders no longer paid much attention to the Negro

question. Many patronizing things were said, and no Afro-American participants were invited, as the organizers opted for southern participants over blacks;
this was where Abbott made the doctors-and-patients analogy. Nearly all the
delegates took for granted that Reconstruction had been a tragic disaster.
Tourgée had contempt for the conference before it began, but he showed up
anyway to make sure that certain things got said.

Tourgée's first novel, *A Fool's Errand, by One of the Fools* (1879), fictional-
ized his experience as a Union League organizer. The story line featured clashes
between Radical Republicans and racist southerners, while the hero, Comfort
Servosse, of French Huguenot background like Tourgée, explained that slavery
corrupted the slaveholders and their civilization. The book was a huge commercial success, launching a new career for Tourgée. The following year, in *Bricks
Without Straw,* he told a similar story from the standpoint of two former slaves,
stressing that former slaves entered freedom lacking a father, money, literacy,
land, tools, seeds, or a legal family name. In 1884 Tourgée's nonfictional *An
Appeal to Caesar* asked the "Caesar" of American democracy—its citizenry—to
recompense for slavery with a program of massive federal aid. In 1890 Tourgée
published a novel supporting black education and economic progress (*Pactolus
Prime*) and a novel advocating Christian Socialism (*Murvale Eastman: Christian
Socialist*). At the Mohonk Conference he heard some respected white civic
leaders contend that black Americans needed the same kind of education that
white Americans received and others contend that blacks should settle for vocational education.[57]

The group debated that question for three days, voting eventually to increase
expenditures for vocational education and to allow, in principle, that higher
education should be open to the most able blacks. Hayes had devoted his post-
presidential career to black education. He noted that the U.S. Senate had
become openly hostile to black Americans. He urged the delegates to fill the
void left by the withdrawal of government aid: "Having deprived them of their
labor, liberty, and manhood, and grown rich and strong while doing it, we have
no excuse for neglecting them." That put it aptly, but this was the very person
that abolished Reconstruction. Tourgée, speaking on the third day, made two
points. First, in twenty-five years Afro-Americans had accomplished greater
educational and economic progress "than any people on the face of the earth
ever before achieved under anything like such unfavorable conditions." Second,
the race problem was a white problem. Tourgée told the religious and civic
leaders that they should be ashamed of themselves for pretending otherwise:
"Indeed, I am inclined to think that the only education required is that of the
white race. The hate, the oppression, the injustice are all on our side. Even we

who are met here to discuss the Negro, to deplore his infirmities, to magnify our charity, to extol our own excellences and determine what ought to be done with and for him do not regard his opinion about the matter as at all important. We do not ask him what he thinks of his own condition."[58]

That year Tourgée founded the National Citizens' Equal Rights Association; the following year he refused to attend the second Mohonk Conference. But his organization withered from the same financial strains that sank the Afro-American League, and in 1892 a citizens' alliance from New Orleans enlisted Tourgée to challenge Louisiana's 1890 segregation law, fatefully. The law required state railway companies to provide separate accommodations for white and black passengers. The group's black members knew Tourgée mainly through his syndicated weekly newspaper column. On his recommendation the alliance enlisted a "nearly white" volunteer, Homer A. Plessy, an octoroon, to break the law. Plessy bought a train ticket in New Orleans and was arrested upon refusing to move from a white car to the Jim Crow section.

The case moved to the Supreme Court, where Tourgée contended that segregation was incompatible with the Thirteenth and Fourteenth Amendments. Segregationists argued that compelling white Americans to share any public venue with people of dark skin was un-American and repugnant. Insufferable presence was the key issue. Since blacks were obviously odious, social equality was unthinkable and so was civil equality. Tourgée replied that white Americans had no trouble suffering the presence of black nurses who cared for their children. Segregation was really about something else, an enforced relation of superiority and inferiority. White segregationists were determined to keep their unjust privileges, Tourgée contended, but American justice was supposed to be blind. Thus, the law was supposed to be color-blind.[59]

The Court ruled that Jim Crow was perfectly just on a "separate but equal" basis, pretending to keep the Fourteenth Amendment's equality principle in play. There was very little public opposition to this verdict. Most American newspapers nodded approvingly; highbrow journals and lowbrow mass-circulation magazines said nothing or assented. Trade unions were fine with it, too. Even freethinking and left-wing journals registered very little dissent. The exception was the religious press, where middlebrow religious sensibilities prevailed: public-spirited, morally reflective, book-oriented, and influenced by the social gospel. The leading journals of the Congregational Church (*Independent, Advance,* and *Congregationalist*), Northern Methodism (*Zion's Herald, California Christian Advocate, Northwestern Christian Advocate, Southwestern Christian Advocate,* and *Western Christian Advocate*), the African Methodist Episcopal Church (*A.M.E. Church Review* and *Voice of Missions*), the Unitarian Fellowship (*Christian Register*), the Northern Presbyterian Church (*United Presbyterian*), and a Roman Catholic journal (*Catholic Globe*) decried the Court's ruling, to no effect.[60]

It mattered to black Christian leaders that the ecumenical religious press howled against the Court's ruling. Here was the place to find white allies against America's official regime of racial denigration and abuse. But segregation prevailed and even the churches associated with the social gospel mostly submitted to it, even as they claimed a rebirth of kingdom-building Christianity. If the social gospel rhetoric of progress was to mean anything for black Americans struggling to survive American racism, it had to let go of the rights before educa- tion debate, and even education before rights, because the vote was hopelessly gone for most black Americans and so was the right to be schooled for anything not considered menial. Meanwhile, Tourgée accepted a consolation prize from President William McKinley, serving as U.S. consul to France, where he died in 1905, defeated and disgusted.

Historians, following Howard University historian Rayford Logan, have long debated when, exactly, the "nadir" occurred—the low point of white America's "betrayal of the Negro." Not a single African American served in Congress from 1901 to 1929, and there are numerous candidates for the lowest point during this period. The nadir among white social gospel leaders, however, is more definite. It occurred in the early years of the twentieth century before there was a vital civil rights organization to counteract the escalating attacks on African Americans. Respected northern white church leaders, the descendants of aboli- tionists, straddled the line between contempt and pity while indulging their society's contempt for black Americans. Peabody considered it dangerous for blacks to aim beyond the Hampton Institute and manual labor. Murphy, working as an author and rector in Texas, Ohio, New York, and Alabama, lectured that southern white men were the authorities on race and needed to be respected as such. Feminist leader Anna Howard Shaw, a Methodist minister, laced her speeches with racial epithets while campaigning for women's suffrage. All accommodated the white southern fear of Negro rule, stressing that white liberals had to take responsibility for the backlash against Reconstruction.[61]

GOD IS BLACK

Turner absorbed this outcome more readily and expectedly than the congre- gations to which he spoke. The benchmarks that really mattered to him were 1868, 1877, and 1883. The Lodge Bill was a last-ditch gesture, and *Plessy v. Ferguson* merely backstopped what white Americans were determined to do. After the Lodge Bill failed, Turner gave up hoping that he would ever vote again. He gave himself to the hope of an African refuge and the work of expanding the AME Church—supporting the temperance movement, urging the church to ordain women, and generally defending the AME Church's historic basis in conservative revival religion, though his theology turned liberal. Turner was a longtime advocate of women's suffrage in American politics and of women's leadership in the church. In 1870 he supported women's suffrage as a state legislator, and, like many feminists, he viewed temperance as a feminist issue in addition to being a moral one. In 1885, shortly after he became presiding bishop over the North Carolina annual conference, Turner ordained Sarah Ann Hughes to the diaconate, inaccurately boasting that she was the first woman to be ordained within Christendom in fifteen hundred years.

Many AME ministers and lay members protested that Turner lacked any biblical or ecclesiastical authority to perpetrate such a novelty. Turner backed off temporarily, declining to assign Hughes to a pastorate, but the issue went to the 1888 General Conference. Supporters appealed to the liberationist spirit of the Bible and the AME Church. They urged the conference not to disown Jarena Lee. If Richard Allen himself authorized Lee to preach, and if she could travel hundreds of miles per year by foot to build up the AME Church, how could the church forbid women to be ministers? Opponents cited biblical texts and church tradition about female subordination, waiting for a vote that was never in question, as the AME Church formally repudiated Hughes's ordination. Turner retreated without agreeing. He felt drowned out by weak arguments about the authority of Scripture and church tradition, believing that a black church born in abolitionism should be more wary of biblical literalism. Yet he had preached a very conservative theology up to that time. Turner's rebuke at the General Conference drove him to reflect more critically on the biblicism he had preached and indulged, which took a decade to think through.[62]

In 1891 the AME Church sent him to Sierra Leone and Liberia to assess its mission congregations. Turner mostly enjoyed Sierra Leone, though he chafed at the gusher of white American missionaries arriving there, and at African slavery. It surprised him that the British Empire was an abolitionist force in West Africa, emancipating slaves wherever it advanced, whereas the Germans and French returned slaves to their owners: "God save old England, is my prayer!" Liberia, a free republic with a black president and government, exceeded Turner's fondest imagining: "Liberia is one of the most paradisical portions of earth my eyes ever beheld. Any person who cannot live here with reasonable health cannot exist anywhere." Congo blacks, as Turner expected, were "the lowest of the African races," because they were weak, then sold into American slavery, and later planted by the U.S. Navy in Liberia. Turner judged that they were much lower than the Mandingo, Vey, Pessa, and Gullah tribes. He stressed that Liberia overflowed with natural resources that Liberians would have preferred to share with Americans if only the stupid Americans would get in the game: "Oh! How the people of Liberia want a steamship directly to America. England, France, Spain and Germany all have scores of steamships laden with goods and whiskey at fabulous prices." White Americans were missing a bonanza, somehow overlooking that Liberians had fond feelings for Americans. Turner's commercial fantasy focused on black Americans. If only the "moneyed colored men of America" would band together, go to England, and buy a secondhand steamship, "they would be worth millions in a few years." The Liberian government was equally lacking in capitalist initiative, he lamented: "She is so American in her ideas; she thinks it beneath her national dignity to engage in commercial enterprise, and here we are fools together, while England, France, Spain and Germany are reaping untold millions that the black man ought to have."[63]

In Monrovia Turner visited the unmarked grave of Henry Highland Garnet and was ashamed. Garnet, born on a slave plantation in Maryland in 1815, had ended his distinguished career as a Presbyterian minister, abolitionist, and president of the African Civilization Society by serving as minister to Liberia in January 1882, only to fall ill and die a month after arriving in Liberia. He was given a state burial and was revered by Liberians. Turner, standing at Garnet's grave overlooking the Atlantic Ocean, wept bitter tears, asking God if there was any hope for black Americans: "If we do not send a tombstone here to mark this grave, the whole Negro race in America deserves the contempt of perdition, to say nothing of heaven."[64]

Turner visited immigrant settlements, mission stations, and native villages, speculated on the promise of coffee plantations and coal mines, and exulted that Liberia was not a colony. Blacks were self-determined human beings in Liberia: "One thing the black man has here—that is, manhood, freedom, and the fullest liberty; he feels as a lord, and walks and talks the same way." If that sounded good, he had one caution—Do not come with less than a hundred dollars: "This is not the place for anyone to come with no money." A trained carpenter, blacksmith, or watchmaker might do all right lacking a stash of savings, Turner advised, "but a mere laborer should bring some money, for the native African stands ready, ten thousand strong, to snatch up all the mere common labor to be done." At the end he made a terminological note. Turner noticed that when the English "or even the cultured Africans" referred to black

Americans arriving in Liberia, they did not use the word "emigration." They used the word "repatriation," and they spoke of "coming home," as when they asked him: "When are you coming home?"[65]

These letters were powerful stuff for many, some of whom overlooked Turner's advice about financial preparation. Turner returned from West Africa in February 1892. The following month three hundred African Americans showed up unexpectedly in New York, hoping to get on the American Colonization Society's next ship to Liberia. Most were penniless refugees from Arkansas and Oklahoma. They were terrified of New York and stranded there, as the ship held only fifty people. Neither the society nor Turner had any idea this was coming, but both were excoriated in the press for causing a human disaster. In addition, Turner was identified as an agent of the society. Turner hotly denied the accusations and turned the humanitarian table on his accusers. He was not an agent for the society, he had never received a dime from it, he had never advised anyone to move to Africa, and he doubted that his accusers were moved by humanitarian sympathy. Otherwise they would not be so keen to return the stranded victims "to the devil-ridden region of the country from whence they came," a banishment to "the jaws of slaughter and death." Turner built up to his customary conclusion: "I have said and I will say again that we will never be anything in this country but scullions and lick-spittles. The man must be very blind who cannot see that the chasm between white and black is widening and deepening."[66]

Turner's bitterness deepened as a consequence, also his grumpiness. In 1893 he organized a national convention of African Americans in Cincinnati to discuss the homeland idea. Douglass sent a friendly response, affirming that he stood for integration and civil rights, supported emigration for those that chose it, and opposed calls for colonization or a mass exodus. The Indianapolis *Freeman* polled black leaders on emigration. Twenty-two were strongly opposed, two said yes, and the other fifteen took the Douglass position. Turner could feel his convention turning into a crushing disappointment before it began. Approximately eight hundred delegates joined approximately two hundred local observers in Cincinnati. Turner gave an opening keynote address calling for a massive investment in emigration. A long letter from Tourgée was read aloud, which took the Douglass position. Many delegates railed against lynching, but the group proposed no plan of action; meanwhile, Turner's resolutions calling for black emigration to Africa, Mexico, or somewhere were decisively defeated. Turner acknowledged, "Some of you may think I am over-gloomy, too despondent, that I have reached the plane of despair." He did not claim they were wrong; instead he told them: "I have seen so much and know so much about American prejudice that I have no hope in the future success of my race in our present situation."[67]

The same thing happened in the church, where Turner tired of dealing with clerical complaints, often admonishing young ministers that they were spoiled and needy compared to the older generation that built up the AME Church from nothing. Turner was inclined to romanticize the rough-hewn preachers of earlier decades who conducted every-night revivals lasting several months. He believed that revival preaching was still the mainstay of the church and that "any preacher who is opposed to revivals does not deserve a horse stable to preach in." He exhorted his ministers to keep their churches open every night of the week. A minister who was too lazy to preach on Wednesday or Thursday night was too lazy to be a minister.[68]

Turner preached and required evangelical vibrancy to the end of his days. Theologically, however, he let go of fundamentalist doctrine, acknowledging the legitimacy of theological pluralism in the church. Biblical scholar John William Colenso was a benchmark figure for Turner. Colenso was the first English Anglican bishop of Natal, South Africa. In the 1850s he began to translate the Bible into Zulu, often struggling to explain biblical passages to his Zulu assistants. In 1862 he published a commentary on the Pentateuch and Joshua that did the math on numerous problem texts. If Israel had six hundred thousand men, as Numbers 2:32 attests, how did the whole of Israel fit into a courtyard (Lev. 8:14) with a capacity of five thousand? How did Israel grow from seventy persons (Gen. 46:26, Exod. 1:5) to over two million in merely four generations? Colenso showed that the Pentateuch made numerous claims about the size of the nation, its battles, its traveling equipment, its ritual ceremonies, and the like that were impossible.[69]

English bishops, clergy, and reviewers were horrified by Colenso's appropriation of German historical criticism and his pursuit of factual problems that poked many small holes in inerrancy doctrine. In February 1863, forty English bishops urged Colenso to resign his office. Later that year Colenso was tried and convicted before the Synod of South African Bishops, but he appealed to the Privy Council, which ruled in his favor on jurisdictional grounds that Colenso was wronged as a citizen of the empire. Whether or not he was a heretic was another matter. Years of legal wrangling followed. Colenso wrote more books, and he established his legal right to continue as bishop of Natal, which gave rise to a rival bishop and a diocesan schism. In his lifetime and for twenty years after his death in 1883, Colenso introduced more English-language readers to biblical criticism than any other scholar. He was protected somewhat by location and appointment, which infuriated the English church establishment. He also incurred hostility by defending the Zulu people, contending that they were oppressed by British and colonial authorities.[70]

Colenso spent his career battling a reactionary tide, as the spectacular backlash against a liberal book in England, *Essays and Reviews*, delayed the acceptance of biblical criticism in English theology by thirty years. In the United States it was much the same; in 1863 Turner had been appalled that anyone, let alone an Anglican bishop, should write the terrible things that Colenso published. "The bold and daring attack of Bishop Colenso is highly criminal," Turner charged. The Bible contained no contradictions or errors, although God accommodated the limited understanding of the biblical writers in verbally inspiring the Bible. Turner implored that if the Bible was God's Word, it was sacrilegious to correct the Bible in Colenso's fashion: "With the Pentateuch the whole Bible stands or falls." But Colenso-style questions were not so easily dismissed. The harder that Turner tried to solve problems of this kind, the more problems he discovered. His regress of concessions began in the early 1870s, letting go of literal interpretations. In the 1880s he was still blasting liberal theologians like Beecher for undermining the doctrines of biblical authority and inspiration, but by the 1890s Turner stopped saying that liberal theologians specialized in illegitimate questions: "The Bible is an extremely human book. It is full of man as well as of God." In his later career Turner reasoned that the Bible is inspired in the way it is inspired, not in the way of a prior dogmatic claim about the Bible. Doctrines were human constructions of limited usefulness and variable meaning. By the turn of the twentieth century his model of a great biblical scholar was J. W. Colenso.[71]

Elizabeth Cady Stanton's multiauthored commentary of 1895, *The Woman's Bible,* was doubly influential for Turner. Cady Stanton relied on Colenso for her understanding of biblical criticism, which helped to bring Turner back to Colenso. More important, Cady Stanton found herself struggling with the Bible because religion played a reactionary role in American life. Most of the religion that Cady Stanton encountered on the Lyceum lecture circuit was insistently Bible-quoting, authoritarian, and inimical to feminism. She conceived *The Woman's Bible* as an antidote—a feminist commentary on the Bible, focusing on passages that referred to women and to passages in which the absence of reference to women was especially notable. Cady Stanton and, to a lesser extent, her fellow authors, criticized aspects of biblical teaching that were harmful to women. Turner, reading her brave work, imagined an analogous project: "The white man's digest of Christianity or Bible doctrines are not suited to the wants, manhood growth, and progress of the Negro. Indeed he has colored the Bible in his translation to suit the white man, and made it, in many respects, objectionable to the Negro. And until a company of learned black men shall rise up and retranslate the Bible, it will not be wholly acceptable and in keeping with the higher conceptions of the black man." Turner did not feel qualified to organize a scholarly critique of the Bible from a black perspective, but he knew it was needed.[72]

For years he had admonished young ministers against pining for racial integration and worshipping white gods. In February 1895, speaking at the founding meeting of the National Baptist Convention, Turner put his credo in four words: "God is a Negro." This utterance startled and excited many delegates at the predominantly separatist convention. Others found it the most ridiculous thing they had ever heard; the *Observer* called it "demented." Henry Lyman Morehouse followed Turner to the podium. Morehouse grieved that black Baptists were taking the separatist path. Imploring them to turn back, he replied to Turner's credo: "Talk of this sort is the race spirit gone mad." Three years later, Turner elaborated on the blackness of God. Black people had as much right to conceive God as black as white people had to assume and project onto everyone else a white God, he argued: "For the bulk of you, and all the fool Negroes of the country, believe that God is a white-skinned, blue-eyed, straight-haired, projecting-nosed, compressed-lipped and finely-robed *white* gentleman, sitting upon a throne somewhere in the heavens." No self-respecting race of people worships a God that resembles a different race, Turner contended: "We had rather be an atheist and believe in no God, or a pantheist and believe that all nature is God, than to believe in the personality of a God and not to believe that He is a Negro." Turner did not believe in the eternity of matter, but he did believe that chaos floated "in infinite darkness" for billions of years before God said, "Let there be light." He was no "stickler" about God's literal color, but Turner could not abide a white God. This was why he harped about a black homeland, "for as long as we remain among the whites, the Negro will believe that the devil is black and that he (the Negro) favors the devil, and that God is white." To be black and yet believe that God bears no relation to blackness "is contemptuous and degrading."[73]

Turner's arguments about Godly blackness and black identity had greater carrying power than his emigration activism. In his later career he coped with an influx of young ministers who were seminary educated and thus steeped in the social gospel. Not coincidentally, Turner gave up trying to interest them in West Africa. He had built up the church by recruiting unlettered preachers possessed by a spiritual fire for mission. In the 1890s the AME Church attracted an oversupply of young men wanting to be ministers. Fresh out of theological training, sometimes at a graduate seminary, they plied Turner for appointments and protested that he favored older types who reminded him of himself. Turner sent many young ministers to tiny congregations lacking the means to pay a salary. He tried to be sympathetic but could not resist admonishing them: Stop complaining, preach more revivals, build up your church like we did, plant a garden, be your own janitor, respect your elders. He yearned for ministers who would help him set off an inspired exodus to West Africa. But most of the ministers that Turner got, while respecting him personally, did not embrace his hopelessness about America or his rejection of racial integration. Thus his homeland mission work fizzled.

For years Turner feuded with the AME Church's founding missionary pastor in Sierra Leone, John R. Frederick, over issues that cut to the heart of the church's work in West Africa. Frederick contended that Turner was prejudiced against pure blacks like him and that Turner had a chauvinistic idea of mission. Turner hotly denied the racial charge and countered that Frederick lacked the requisite commitment to convert West Africans to AME Christianity. This feud had a backstory—the separate founding of the AME mission in Sierra Leone from the issue of African emigration. In 1885 a congregation in Freetown, Sierra Leone, asked to become part of the AME Church. The following year the AME Church sent Frederick, a minister in New England, to the Freetown congregation to be its pastor. Frederick owed his presence in West Africa to Bishop Payne, who supported conventional mission work but not homeland activism. From the beginning there were tensions between Turner and Frederick as to what Frederick should do in Sierra Leone, which magnified as Frederick became more African culturally. As long as Payne was alive and controlled the church's mission fund, Turner was no threat to Frederick, who lobbied to prevent Turner from making appointments in Sierra Leone. As soon as Payne died, in November 1893, Frederick became vulnerable. Turner became the church's dominant figure and cut off its mission support for Frederick.[74]

The ideological dimension of their feud reverberated beyond the personal issues. Frederick lauded traditional African cultures, exhorted middle-class members of his congregation not to disparage traditional styles of dress, and argued (following Blyden) that Islam was superior to Christianity in two crucial respects. One, Islam had almost no history of racial prejudice; two, Islam had a better history than Christianity of coexisting peacefully with indigenous cultures. Muslims, Frederick contended, did not shred or put down cultures they entered, while Christianity had a long history of shredding and putting down. Turner's missionary protégé in Liberia, Alfred L. Ridgel, clashed with Frederick on these issues, conceding nothing: Islam was a false religion, and American Christians had nothing to learn from West African culture. Turner supported his protégé when it mattered, albeit with more cultural sensitivity. Turner did not brandish the term "heathen" exclusively as an epithet. He admired the moral seriousness and dignity of Islam. He respected that Islam had a better record than modern Christianity on racial prejudice. And he contended that native Africans were miles ahead of black Americans in "manhood" and self-reliance. But the former issues were civility matters, and the latter issue did not impede Turner from saying that Africans were heathens in need of salvation and Christian civilization. Missionary work was about converting everyone to the true religion, and black American Christians had a mission to bring their superior religion and civilization to Africa.[75]

Turner believed that slavery was a providential institution because God brought blacks to Christ and civilization through slavery. Slavery was a "trust from God," he said. God placed upon whites the responsibility to teach, train, evangelize, and civilize the enslaved. Turner said it plainly throughout his career. He said it in his Emancipation speech of 1866, appropriating the boilerplate proslavery claim that slavery should be credited for bringing Christianity to the slaves. He said it repeatedly in sermons, and emphatically in 1883 as an argument for emigration activism: "I do not believe that American slavery was a divine institution, but I do believe it was a providential institution and that God intends to make it the primal factor in the civilization and Christianization of that dark continent, and that any person whomsoever opposes the return of a sufficient number of her descendants to begin the grand work, which in the near future will be consummated, is fighting the God of the universe face to face." For most of his career Turner said that slavery failed in the United States because whites betrayed their responsibility, but in 1895 he revised this argument, influenced by black historian George Washington Williams. Now he stressed that African slavery long preceded the American slave trade, that the first American slaves were the children of African slaves, and that slavery ended in the United States because its providential work had been accomplished. Turner felt, and resisted, where his longtime argument about Providence, slavery, and African mission was taking him, until 1895, when he saw it through, proposing that the African slave trade should be renewed for a limited time. If slavery were reestablished, he contended, the lost African "heathen" would be brought into the arms of Christian civilization. Turner's followers replied that that was insane. They had indulged his missionary sermonizing about slavery past, but reestablishing slavery was beyond the pale. Even Ridgel rebuked his hero, admonishing him to write no more on this subject.[76]

By then Turner's West African dream was undeniably not working out. Ridgel committed suicide in 1896; Frederick left the AME Church, taking members with him; and the West Africans did not respond favorably to other missionaries whom Turner sent, with the partial exception of C. Max Manning. Turner's friendship with Blyden ended, too, although Blyden exaggerated the downfall of the AME Church in Liberia. By 1899 the AME presence in Liberia had plateaued at twenty-five ministers and fifteen hundred members—a significant mission commitment, though nothing like the homeland that Turner envisioned. In 1898 Turner visited South Africa, helping to launch an AME Church there—a story for a later chapter. He got a tumultuous welcome from South Africans who had never seen a black bishop, and he planted something that lasted, enduring a firestorm of controversy that he overreached his legal authority in doing so. But Turner realized that South Africa was nothing like a candidate for black American emigration. South Africa was too much like the U.S. American South.[77]

Turner made a final push for emigration in 1903, helping to found the Colored National Emigration Association, which tried to raise $125,000 to buy a ship. His call letter was abusive: "We very much fear that the Negro is an 'inferior animal' at best, and but very little account when it comes to helping himself. If you want any dirt-eating done, any foot-kissing, any humiliation, any condescension, any dog-fawning, he is ready to do it; but to be a man, a whole man, and to play the part of a gentleman in the full sense of the term, he is not there. Help yourself is not a characteristic of the American Negro. . . . We are fast coming to the conclusion that the white man is right when he represents the Negro as an 'inferior creature,' animal, or failure, to say the least." This call for financial support fell $124,000 short of its goal, and Turner gave up, just as the issue became Du Bois versus Washington. Angell notes that Turner "did little or nothing" after 1904 to advance the cause of emigration. The back-to-Africa cause had to wait for a more propitious moment, the end of World War I, and a more charismatic champion, Marcus Garvey.[78]

Had Turner not so deeply despaired of things American he might have recognized that he had more important things in common with Du Bois than with Washington. As it was, he did not see it, so he said that he was closer to Washington. Turner abhorred trade unions and Socialism, he heard the nationalist undertones in Bookerism, and he admired Washington's advocacy of hard-working self-reliance and entrepreneurship. Moreover, he disliked Du Bois's smart-aleck intellectualism. Du Bois got little credit, with Turner, for radicalism and Pan-Africanism, because he channeled both into a left politics that tried to make alliances with white liberals. After Washington set off a hysterical uproar in the South by dining with President Theodore Roosevelt in the White House, Turner told him, "You are about to be the great representative and hero of the Negro race, notwithstanding you have been very conservative." After Monroe

Trotter helped to set off a brawl in 1903 at Washington's speaking engagement in Boston, Turner said that Washington's strategy was worthless and the Trotter radicals were no better, because both sides evaded the only thing that mattered: blacks owning and controlling their own nation. After the issue became Du Bois versus Washington, Turner said that he liked Washington, but the new debate among black Americans was not "worth a pinch of snuff" because it evaded the separatist imperative: "Anything less than separation and the black man relying on himself is absolute nonsense."[79]

Turner usually gave the impression of being ferociously candid and bull-dozing. Alexander Crummell, though notorious for his own truculence and put-downs, judged that Turner went overboard in both areas. Crummell told journalist John E. Bruce that Turner was a "truculent screeching and screaming creature" that wrongly "sneered" contemptuously at "the good for nothing Negroes." Turner, in turn, resented that Crummell gave up on West Africa, although upon returning there in 1893 Turner repeated Crummell's lament that white people pouring into West Africa were ruining "the only spot upon the face of the globe where the black man can ever hope to be in power and demonstrate the ability of self-government." Turner ramped up his forceful editorializing in his last years. In 1897 he headlined in the *Voice of Missions*: "Negroes Get Guns." In 1899 he was equally blunt: "The Negro Should Not Enter the Army." In 1900 he described President McKinley as "the God of Fool Negroes." In 1902 he editorialized on "The Afro-American Future" very grimly: "I see nothing for the Negro to attain unto in this country. . . . I see nothing here for him to aspire after. . . . There is nothing in the United States for the Negro to learn or try to attain to." Even Turner's more hopeful statements about the future had a truculent quality. He was fond of saying, "The Indian represents the past, the white man the present, but the Negro the future. The Indian is old, decayed and worn out; the whites are in the prime of life and vigor; but the Negro is a boy, a youth at school, a mere apprentice learning his trade. When the white race reaches decrepitude, as races are periodical as well as worlds, the Negro will have reached his prime."[80]

He was equally bulldozing toward himself and his family. Turner had four-teen children with his first wife, Eliza, plus three more wives after Eliza died. Only two of his children survived into adulthood, one becoming a physician. Turner never wrote about any of them except in his diary. His many readers knew nothing of his children, let alone the colossal grief he must have suffered at losing so many of them, except for one notice. In 1890, commemorating the anniversary of Eliza's death, Turner mentioned "the babes who went a little before her to the heavenly land." That was it, by a prolific newspaper editorialist and preacher. Stephen Angell and Andre Johnson did not try to explain Turner's silence about his children and grief, and both relegated this subject to an endnote, not knowing what to say. Mungo Ponton, a Turner disciple, knew him well enough to fill the blanks, but he did not. Turner had no close friends, and the friends that knew him best did not see him as a spiritual figure. Ponton regretted both things, as Ponton fervently admired Turner. He noted that Turner "hungered and thirsted more for political power and civil authority" than he did for ecclesiastical leadership; becoming a bishop was something of a fallback, as Turner's mind "was more of a legal turn and a civil cast than of a religious turn." Ponton did not mean that Turner was not religious; he was deeply religious in his way. Ponton lamented, however, that Turner's friends "regarded him as the greatest political trickster of his time," an impression that plagued Turner before and especially after he became a bishop.[81]

Payne was like Turner's friends in this respect, unable to imagine Turner as a bishop, until it happened. Afterward, bullishness aside, Turner tried not to offend Payne, while Payne, writing the history of the AME Church in 1891, managed to confine Turner to one paragraph. Payne acknowledged that Turner spread the AME faith in Georgia with "self-denial and energy." In Payne's telling, however, Turner and Cain damaged their usefulness as ambassadors of the cross by allowing politics to lay hold of them. Turner, by contrast, was assiduously respectful toward Payne, and he could be lighthearted and expansive with friends, passing from jocularity to rage to jocularity. Turner was one of the great talkers, bantering with zest, always ready with a joke or an apt story, until something made him angry. Ponton recalled, "But out of that jocular mood and period of story-telling he would become as ugly and as furious as a prowling hyena. . . . He urged his people not to be scullions and cowards and crouch and crawl like 'belabored hounds beneath their master's leash.'"[82]

Some of Turner's disapproving eruptions passed into black Methodist lore. In 1883, crossing Kansas by railroad, Turner peered out his train window at a woman sitting outside her home. He told *Christian Recorder* readers that he was repulsed by the woman's "dirty face, knotted hair, filthy children, nasty door steps, no fence around the hut, no garden, no flowers, even the weeds trampled down, no chickens, geese, turkeys, ducks, and hogs." He had a solution, a variation on a stock sermon theme: "I felt like I would have given a hundred dollars for the privilege of using a bull whip at each one of those houses. I am in favor of forming vigilance committees whose business it will be to flog all such specimens of our race."[83]

Turner lacked a filter for realizing when his righteous rage passed into cruelty. He made adjustments and occasionally backed off in other areas, but not this one. His readers told him numerous times that his "scullion" rhetoric was cruel and demeaning, but that did not stop him from using it like a bull-whip. He did not believe that his rhetoric in this area was ethically objection-able and he never doubted that his middle-class absolutes were absolute. Thus, his railroad-car purview was an appropriate seat of judgment on the humanity of someone he did not know. In his early career he wrote mostly for AME publi-cations, but in 1887 he launched his own newspaper, *Southern Recorder*, which lasted two years; in 1893 he launched the *Voice of Missions*, which lasted seven years; and in 1901 he launched the *Voice of the People*, which lasted three years. Writing for his own newspapers further unleashed Turner from churchly decorum.

A few people knew that he had a tender side. Ponton observed: "Bishop Turner was not as sour and morose as the exterior of his nature seemed to indi-cate; but rather, behind that coarse and rough exterior, was a soul as sweet and serenely gentle as the zephyrs at eventide." Ponton saw Turner's gentle side on leisurely occasions when the bishop let himself be frivolous and teasing with a younger colleague who admired him. J. W. E. Bowen had a similar experience of Turner: "To those who did not know him, he appeared difficult of approach and a man of iron. His sternness was not in his heart or in his treatment of men. His roughness was all on the outside. He loved men and he was a simple brother at heart. His kind is no more—for his times are no more." Alexander Walters said the same thing more concisely: "Many considered him eccentric. He was a man with a rough exterior, but with a heart as tender and kind as a child. A splendid man, with a fine physique, strong in intellect, remarkable for his courage."[84]

Turner's fourth wife, Laura Pearl Lemon, knew the gentle Turner best. By 1907 Turner was seventy-three years old; he had been a widower three times; he was fond of his twenty-seven-year-old personal secretary, Lemon, who had worked for him for ten years; and shortly after Turner's third wife died, he announced that he would marry Lemon. Many ministers and laity were not happy for him. Lemon had almost married an AME minister when she was sixteen. Bishop William Gaines led the opposition, crying scandal. Critics protested that Turner had no business marrying a much younger woman who had divorced an AME minister. The facts about her previous non-marriage did not seem to matter, as Turner had enemies. The wedding took place, and Gaines threatened to hit Turner with a chair at the next bishops' council. There was a lot of talk about stripping Turner of his episcopal status, which did not happen, although he was not reappointed to the Georgia district or assigned to supervise any district. The General Conference of 1908 made Turner the denomination's historiographer, a poor fit for his skills. He went on to enjoy with Lemon the most closely affectionate relationship of his life, regretting nothing. They traveled together to speaking engagements, and sometimes she gave the address, to conserve his strength. In 1912 the General Conference restored Turner to full functioning status, placing the AME churches in Michigan and Canada under his supervision. Three years later he died of a massive stroke on a ferry to Windsor, Ontario. Laura Lemon Turner was heart-broken when he died, and she died only five months later in his empty house. Turner's body was transported back to Atlanta, where over twenty-five thousand people viewed him in state and where he was buried in South View Cemetery.[85]

Turner became the leading figure in AME history and the major forerunner of the black social gospel by building up the AME Church and by projecting far beyond its churchly confines. He was a historic figure, yet soon forgotten. He towered above his contemporaries because he was unfailingly strong and powerful, a bulwark against racist oppression. He had a driven, charismatic personality that carried him to outreaching accomplishments, and he always had an aim. His sizable faults contributed to his hugeness but also made him easy to forget after he was gone, even by scholars of black American history and religion. John Hope Franklin mentioned Turner only in passing. Rayford Logan and Vincent Harding barely mentioned him, once each. Benjamin Quarles did not mention him. James M. McPherson referred to him zero times in one book and once in another. E. Franklin Frazier reduced Turner to a page on Reconstructionist political religion. Carter G. Woodson did the same thing as Frazier, except Woodson called Turner "one of the outstanding men of the Negro race." After black liberation theology arose in the 1970s, Turner was rediscovered as a forerunner, but even that developed slowly, as the definitive work of C. Eric Lincoln and Lawrence H. Mamiya mentioned Turner only in passing.[86]

That was not what his contemporaries expected. Turner's critics and admirers in the AME Church debated whether he ranked ahead of Payne as a church leader, but hardly anyone disputed that Turner, Payne, and Richard Allen were the lodestar figures in AME history. In 1905, when Turner still had ten years of life and ministry ahead of him, the AME Church commemorated his twenty-five years as a bishop with a three-day festival in St. Louis. The singing was sensational, the speeches were laudatory, ongoing feuds were set aside, greet-ings were read from leaders of other denominations, and everyone said that Turner was a giant figure. H. B. Parks, who later became a bishop, described Turner as "the first Negro missionary to the Negro race" and "the spiritual father from whom has sprung a prolific progeny of missionary children." W. D.

Chappelle, also subsequently a bishop, highlighted Turner's missionary legacy: "We would place the name of Henry McNeal Turner above that of Daniel Alexander Payne." Turner was not holy like Payne, Chappelle allowed, "but we do mean to say that the life and work of Henry McNeal Turner touched all shores and spheres of human existence, and will shine forth forever in the characters who are to follow him."[87]

H. F. Kealing, an academic and lay leader, put it more personally, noting that Turner was a powerful figure outside the AME Church (unlike Payne) and that he led the church into broad new areas of social engagement, engrafting in the church "the cosmopolitan sweep of his sympathies." It was possible to clash with Turner without losing his regard, Kealing reflected. In fact, Turner only respected those who were strong and forceful. He thrived on the give and take with those who gave it back to him; whiners, on the other hand, repulsed him. If a critic "whined when Bishop Turner whacked, his place would be found among the scullions, and cowards and traitors to his race." *A.M.E. Church Review* literary editor George W. Forbes called Turner "the Grandest Old Roman of Them All," who roared for black dignity, "always fearless and forceful." J. D. Barksdale, a physician and lay leader, judged that Turner stood alone, like Napoleon: "Nobly and majestically stands this grand old hero, overtopping the forest of great men around him. And of him it might be said, as of Napoleon, that 'Alone he stands, wrapped in the solitude of his own grandeur.'"[88]

Bishop J. S. Flipper gave the eulogy at Turner's funeral, declaring that Turner made the arduous trip to Canada because he had a premonition of his death. Turner did not want to die under the U.S. American flag, Flipper explained: "He felt that he was going to die, and he did not want to die on a soil where the American flag waved." That was a clue to Turner's influence, his blunt capacity to say things that others felt in silence. Angell notes that Turner regularly expounded on who was in hell and who was bound to end up there; numerous Supreme Court justices were high on the list. As Turner's alienation from America deepened, he struggled to find words that conveyed it. Bryan versus McKinley, in 1896, stirred the public like no presidential election since 1860, as Democrats and Republicans fought over gold, silver, and a depressed economy. Turner, confronting a campaign that ignited strong feelings and ignored the catastrophe occurring to black Americans, told black readers they were on their own. Why bother about gold versus silver when they were being lynched, burned, and excluded? "Vote any way in your power to overthrow, destroy, ruin, blot out, divide, crush, dissolve, wreck, consume, demolish, disorganize, suppress, subvert, smash, shipwreck, crumble, nullify, upset, uproot, expunge, and fragmentize this nation, until it learns to deal justly with the black man. This is all the advice we have to give."[89]

This torrent of metaphors for smashing coexisted uneasily with Turner's image of a holy and nonviolent Jesus. Routinely Turner described Jesus as pure, peaceable, loving, and righteous. He never preached a sermon on the pacifist sayings of Jesus, and he let pass Payne's contention that a minister should be a holy follower of the way of the cross. But Turner evinced burning evangelical sincerity about renouncing Satan, alcohol, sloth, cowardice, injustice, and smallness. He felt the connection between the cross and the lynching tree. He believed that no power on earth came close to the saving power of Christ cruci- fied and resurrected. His sermons on these topics reached more people than Payne's appeals to sanctity and orthodoxy. *Atlanta Independent* columnist Henry Lincoln Johnson lauded Turner for pouring "his great learning, research, heart, and soul" into his sermons and activism. CME Bishop L. H. Holsey, speaking for many at Turner's funeral, recalled that one of Turner's sermons converted him to Christianity: "Away across this span of fifty-six years, I still hear his sounding, clarion voice calling sinners to repentance and the wicked to forsake his way." To Holsey, no one compared to Turner: "The name of Henry McNeal Turner presents to our consideration the greatest and most remarkable personality that the Negro race has ever produced." He could not imagine that Turner would be forgotten: "He cannot be forgotten. His earnest and honest voice still rings, re-echoes and vibrates in hall and chamber, and in ancient, fiery stream of eloquence and matchless defense for manhood's rights, and will long live and glow in the hearts of his people and ring in the annals of his race and nation."[90]

Five notable others felt compelled to say what made Turner a towering figure not to be forgotten. Richard R. Wright Jr. observed that Turner obviously had many faults, "but his faults pale into insignificance when his achievements are put beside them. And the world might well bear with them for the profit of his character." Forty-eight years later Wright added that Turner was "commanding in appearance, frank and blunt in expression, and terrible in debate." Booker Washington judged that Turner's greatest achievement was to establish the first centers of black social activity in Georgia, which by 1874 were worth over six million dollars: "The very large part which Bishop Turner had in laying these foundations makes him worthy of being classed as an useful citizen in its largest sense." Tanner noted that his longtime rival prized earnestness higher than manners, he was the first clean-shaven AME bishop, and he commanded respect by fearing only God. Du Bois lauded Turner as "a man of tremendous force and indomitable courage" who refused to be beaten down:

"In a sense Turner was the last of his clan: mighty men, physically and mentally, men who started at the bottom and hammered their way to the top by sheer brute strength; they were the spiritual progeny of American chieftains and they built the African church in America." Du Bois admired the "prouder and more independent type of Negro" that Turner epitomized—the type that refused to beg for justice. But Turner dropped out of Du Bois's later purview, a casualty of the Garvey phenomenon. Had the Garvey movement not soared after World War I, Du Bois might have ranked Turner higher in his later reflections. As it was, Du Bois took on the bitterest fight of his career and Turner became a footnote to "the crazy scheme of Marcus Garvey." In the meantime a massive African American exodus did occur—to the industrial cities of the North.[91]

The fifth witness was Reverdy Ransom. By the time of Turner's death, Ransom had long established the crucial differences between Turner radicalism and his own, and he had recently taken over the *A.M.E. Church Review*, which he used to build up a social gospel flank in the AME Church. Turner, Ransom declared, was the "staunch defender of his race" of his time in the black church: "To the doctrines of manhood, justice, equality, he was faithful to death." Ransom praised Turner's "flaming wrath against traitors, trimmers, sycophants, and cowards among his people." He lauded Turner's penchant for "dramatic and picturesque" language, which expressed "the long-restrained aspirations and ideals of the great silent mass." But Ransom observed that Turner had an ambiguous legacy, having been extremely controversial for good reasons and equally controversial for bad ones: "How strange it is that epoch-making men, who seem to have the stamp of divine approval, are so full of imperfections and inconsistencies. But our Jacobs and Davids, Luthers and Turners are of this mold."[92]

By 1915 Ransom was well on his way to having the same thing said about him, accompanied by similar impressions that he was unforgettable. In his early career he and Turner were the two strongest American clerical supporters that Ida Wells had in her crusade against lynching. Then Ransom became Wells-Barnett's pastor at Bethel Church in Chicago and dreamed with her of a national civil rights organization that fought against lynching, segregation, and disenfranchisement. The first attempt to build one, the Afro-American League, had already come and gone. Timothy Fortune, having failed with the Afro-American League, was not eager to try again. Ransom and Wells-Barnett became friends at the crossroads of their lives, which was also a crossroads for what became the new abolition movement. She was trying to pull back to a life of marriage and family; he was just getting started in social justice activism. Between them, though only briefly together, they showed what black social Christianity needed to be to advance black self-determination and resist white oppression.

BECOMING IDA B. WELLS

Ida Bell Wells was born into slavery, which she did not remember, to parents whom she lost early in life, in Holly Springs, Mississippi. Her parents married during slavery and married again after freedom came. Wells's owner at birth, Spires Boling, was an architect and builder who treated his nine slaves with as much decency as existed under slavery. Her mother, Lizzie Wells, cooked for Boling and appreciated his kindly treatment, which contrasted with the beatings she had taken from a previous master. Lizzie told her children that their maternal grandfather was half Native American. Ida's father, Jim Wells, was a slave owned by his father, a prosperous white farmer named Morgan Wells. Jim Wells got fatherly treatment from his father/owner, and at the age of eighteen he was apprenticed to Boling to become a carpenter, where he and Lizzie united.

In 1862, when Ida was born, Union general Ulysses S. Grant marched into Holly Springs, a town of fewer than four thousand people, forty miles from Memphis, with forty-five thousand troops. Most of the troops kept moving, as Holly Springs changed hands over sixty times during the war. But Grant hunkered down in a spacious home built by Boling, planning the assault on Vicksburg. Grant turned Holly Springs into a depot for Union supplies; by one account his wife brought along her personal slave. After the war, Jim Wells continued to work for Boling until November 1867, when Boling wanted Wells to vote Democratic and Wells refused. Jim Wells returned from voting to find Boling's shop padlocked. He quietly walked downtown, bought his own tools, gathered the family's belongings, and rented a house across the street from Boling, all before Boling returned home. Then he launched a successful career as an independent carpenter. Jim Wells would work and vote on his own, plus give generous care to his family, including his white father.[93]

Whites had flocked to Holly Springs in the late 1830s after President Andrew Jackson dispatched the native Chickasaw inhabitants to what became Oklahoma. Incorporated in 1837, the town attracted Episcopalians, Virginians, Whigs, land speculators, bankers, lawyers, and builders; Boling had moved there in the 1840s from Arkansas with his Virginia-born wife. During the war Union officers planted the seeds of a local Union League—then called Lincoln's Legal Loyal League. When the war ended, federal soldiers turned Holly Springs into the regional headquarters of the Freedmen's Bureau. Former Union officer Nelson Gill, a white captain from Illinois, was the leading Radical Republican in Holly Springs, surviving death threats, a mob attack, and a stabbing. He led torchlight parades of Union League marchers—thrilling spectacles in a region where whites had owned the night and blacks risked their lives by venturing into it.

Radical Republicans in Holly Springs founded Asbury Methodist Episcopal Church, which the Wells family joined. The same group enlisted the Freedmen's Aid Society of the Methodist Episcopal Church to launch a school, Shaw University (later named Rust College), which began as an elementary school and built upward with its student body. The school was located on the former site of Grant's campground. It originated when a northern white minister, Albert Collier McDonald, an outspoken abolitionist, discovered that no one attending a church meeting could read or write; the group included Ida's parents. Lizzie Wells learned how to read the Bible while attending school alongside Ida. For the rest of her life, Ida Wells was unequivocal about the church workers and teachers who came south after the war to support abolition. She hated and resented the carpetbag-invader myth "about which the white South has published so much that is false." Her teachers, in her telling, were "the consecrated men and women from the North who came into the South to teach immediately after the end of the war. It was they who brought us the light of knowledge and their splendid example of Christian courage."[94]

She grew up happy and secure as the oldest of eight children, two of whom died in infancy. Wells later recalled poignantly that when her parents married for a second time in 1869, her mother officially became a Wells. There was one messy slavery-aftermath situation in the family. Jim Wells's mother was a slave named Peggy who worked for Morgan Wells and whom Morgan Wells favored over his wife, Polly. Ida's earliest troubling memory, aside from hearing about the Klan, had to do with hearing that Polly had beaten her grandmother Peggy, apparently out of jealousy. Otherwise, Ida grew up happy; Lizzie Wells pressed her to excel at school, Ida adored her mother, and she adored her teachers. Yet she was a mediocre student. Ida allowed that she felt jealous of a light-skinned classmate whom the school's president favored, and she had a rebellious temperament. Otherwise she did not explain why she did not perform up to her ability, besides acknowledging that she regretted it. Probably the instruction was aimed too low to engage her, as Ida Wells was a voracious reader of Shakespeare, Charles Dickens, Louisa May Alcott, and Charlotte Brontë. She "formed her ideals," as she later put it, by reading these authors. Then tragedy struck, and Wells needed Dickens, Alcott, and Brontë more than ever.[95]

Holly Springs was a thousand feet above sea level and known for its refreshing springs, which were said to have healing properties, which attracted the resort class. The town had a history of avoiding epidemics that ravaged port cities and boggy villages. In 1878 Wells was visiting Peggy in Tippah County when a devastating yellow fever consumed New Orleans, spread to Grenada, Mississippi, and moved to Memphis. Holly Springs opened its doors to refugees from other parts of the Mississippi Valley, feeling protected by its legacy of health. In August, however, one of the refugees fell ill and died. Several people died shortly thereafter, including the mayor, and the town was seized with terror. More than half the population fled in panic; most of the fifteen hundred that remained in Holly Springs were black. Nobody knew in 1878 that yellow fever was spread by a mosquito-borne viral infection, but all locals knew that mortality rates were nearly ten times higher for whites. In nearby Memphis, half the city's population fled in panic. The twenty thousand that remained were mostly blacks and Irish; nearly eighteen thousand caught the disease, and more than five thousand died from it. The mortality rate among whites was 75 percent; among blacks it was 7 percent.[96]

Wells took for granted that her family would be all right once the epidemic had passed. In late September she was sweating out the malarial-like chill that nearly everyone had, when three neighbors from Holly Springs appeared at the door, announcing that her parents had died of the fever. Wells was sixteen years old, though in her later memory, she was fourteen. It took her three days to convince Peggy to let her return to Holly Springs. By then the passenger trains had stopped running, so she climbed aboard the caboose of a freight train to get home. Everyone told Wells it was crazy to enter Holly Springs; she replied that she had three younger sisters and three younger brothers. Upon arriving at home, Wells learned that all but one of her siblings had been ill and that the baby, Stanley, had died. The children had been stranded alone for two weeks. In his last days at a makeshift hospital, Jim Wells had built coffins for others and himself. He also asked his northern white physician, a trusted friend, to give his life savings to Ida. In mid-October Ida met the doctor in the town square to receive the money—three hundred dollars. Passersby, seeing the transaction, launched a sex rumor that plagued and enraged Ida for decades. An act of simple kindness and trust between two innocent parties was turned into an object of vicious gossip. According to the rumormongers, Ida confirmed her guilt by insisting on caring for her siblings.[97]

Jim Wells had been a Mason, so the Masonic brothers showed up after the epidemic ended. They pored over the situation for an entire Sunday afternoon, coming to a consensus: The two youngest girls, Annie and Lily, would be placed with separate families; the two boys, Alfred and George, would be apprenticed to carpenters; fourteen-year-old Eugenia, paralyzed from spinal meningitis, would have to go to a poorhouse; and Ida was old enough to fend for herself. Ida was appalled, telling the Masons that breaking up the family was not an option. If they wanted to be helpful they could secure a teaching position for her so she could take care of her siblings.

Ida Wells got a job at a country school, and Peggy came in from the country to live with the youngsters. On Sunday afternoons Wells rode a mule six miles into the country, to be ready for class on Monday in a one-room school; on Fridays she returned home to Peggy and the children, until Peggy was felled by a stroke. Reluctantly, while learning how to teach, Ida sent the boys and Eugenia to live with Lizzie's sister Belle in Memphis, but Eugenia died shortly afterward. Losing Eugenia must have cut Ida, who never wrote about it. When summer came Wells tried to complete her degree at Shaw but was expelled for reasons that remained, years later, too painful to recount, except to say in her diary, "My own experience as a teacher enables me to see more clearly and I know that I was to blame." That helped her cope with what she really believed, that she was more rebellious and darker than the favored classmates. In 1881 Wells moved to Memphis to live with her father's stepsister Fannie, keeping Lily and Annie with her, while teaching at a school in Woodstock, a small town ten miles north of Memphis in Shelby County. By this time her brothers had apprenticed themselves to carpenters. Throughout her years of mothering her young sisters, Wells was sustained by novels that talked about surviving epidemics, being orphaned, willing one's fate, and struggling with the sins of pride, envy, guilt, and anger.[98]

Memphis was her first experience of living in an urban black community. There were new forms of racial insult to learn; moreover, some were just being invented when Wells got there in 1880. Railroads were enormously important to Memphis, especially for shipping cotton to the north. Tennessee had a state law permitting racial discrimination on the trains, but the Civil Rights Act of 1875 was still operative at the federal level, permitting blacks to sue in state courts if they experienced discrimination in public accommodations. In October 1880 a black courtesan named Jane Brown beat the Memphis and Charleston Railroad in federal circuit court on a discrimination charge, winning a stunning sum of three thousand dollars for damages, which rocked the railroad industry. If the rail companies could not discriminate against a poor black woman of dubious morals, how were they to keep their white customers? For a while white passengers on interstate railways had to flee to vacant cars, locking the door behind them, to avoid the unbearable burden of sitting near black people.

It was hard to say where this situation was going. Wells avoided the smoking cars, which had the cheapest seats and the roughest crowds. Usually she bought a first-class ticket for the ladies car, which had upholstered seating and carpets on the floor. She was emphatically a lady and a nonsmoker, seeing no reason why she should put up with the coarse behavior that prevailed elsewhere on trains. The railroads enforced their discrimination policy inconsistently, depending on the conductor, the fullness of the ladies car, and the mood of the white passengers. Wells put up with this situation for three years, never knowing whether she would travel in peace or be insulted for trying. Then on a Saturday evening in September 1883, she snapped, lacking any plan. She took her usual seat in the ladies coach, and the conductor told her to move. She protested, he tried to dislodge her, she scratched and bit his hands, two passengers came to his aid, and Wells was dragged off the coach as the white passengers cheered. She filed suit in Shelby County Circuit Court against the Chesapeake & Ohio Railway, hiring an African American legislator, Thomas Cassels, who belonged to her church. Shortly afterward Wells had a similar experience on the same railway and sued again. The second case attracted national press attention, because between the two incidents the U.S. Supreme Court nullified the Civil Rights Act of 1875.

Now the stakes were higher. In both cases Wells was lucky to get one of the few local judges, James O. Pierce, a Union veteran from Minnesota, who was sympathetic to civil rights claims. The conductor in the first case claimed that smoking and drinking were not allowed in the colored car, so the company had not violated the principle of "separate but equal." Cassels assembled a parade of witnesses who testified that the colored car was, in fact, a very rough place, certainly no place for a lady as impeccably dressed, groomed, and mannered as the churchgoing teacher in question. That argument won the first case and eventually the second one, although Wells had to fire Cassels in the interim, as he advised her not to fight the company's appeal of the first verdict and she judged that he cut a political deal to sell her out. There was additional dirty dealing to follow, and she wrote in her diary, "A tried friend of mine has unfolded a conspiracy to me that is on foot to quash the case. . . . It is a painful fact that white men choose men of the race to accomplish the ruin of any young girl." After Wells won the second case with a white lawyer, the *Memphis Daily Appeal* headlined: "Darky Damsel Obtains a Verdict for Damages," and Timothy Fortune gave the story national publicity in the *New York Freeman*. Her victory was short-lived, however, as the state supreme court overturned the second verdict, opining: "We think it is evident that the purpose of the defendant in error was to harass with a view to this suit, and that her persistence was not in good faith to obtain a comfortable seat for the short ride." Wells was compelled to pay court costs. Years later she recalled: "None of my people had ever seemed to feel that it was a race matter and that they should help me with the fight. So I trod the winepress alone."[99]

Already Wells thought of herself as a loner who lived by the moral ideals of Dickens, Alcott, Brontë, and the Bible. Ministers provided her examples of living by the ideals. She later recalled, "The bishops I had known were scholarly, saintly men in the Methodist Episcopal church and most of the pastors we had were the same." In Memphis, Wells taught Sunday school to young men at an AME congregation, Avery Chapel, which black soldiers had founded during the Civil War. Avery Chapel, however, was merely a home base for her religiously, as Wells also attended Vance Street Christian Church, Beale Street Baptist Church, Immanuel Episcopal Church, and Collins Chapel, a branch of the CME Church. Sometimes she attended services at four congregations on a single Sunday, always with a critical eye. Wells lamented that the Memphis ministers failed to provide "needed guidance in everyday life," unlike the ministers she had known in Holly Springs. The bookish, prematurely grown-up Wells yearned for guidance and cultural literacy: "I had never read a Negro book or anything about Negroes." She grieved the loss of her beloved parents and two infant siblings and regretted that her formal education had been cut short. In her diary she reproached herself for being headstrong, volatile, and proud, vowing repeatedly to get control of her feelings. Her first diary entry prayed that God would "exorcise the spirit that haunts me." Wells reasoned that God saw fit "to send these trials & to fit me for His kingdom." She whipsawed between angrily vowing never to forget the injustice done to her and vowing to be a good Christian: "O My Father, forgive me, forgive me & take away the remembrance of those hateful words, uttered for the satisfaction of self. Humble the pride exhibited and make me Thy child."[100]

Though she made her living as a teacher, Wells tired of its "confinement and monotony," rarely writing in her diary about teaching. Historian Linda O. McMurry puts it bluntly: "She hated teaching and thought of it as a way to earn a paycheck rather than a calling." Teaching Sunday school was an important ministry for Wells, but that was confined to the realm and piety of the church. She found her calling by taking up freelance journalism, using a pen name, "Iola," though Wells worried that journalism would never pay enough to allow her to quit teaching. She started with letters and personal essays to local newspapers, which Fortune reprinted in the *New York Freeman*, helping her reach a national audience. From the beginning she had an edgy, moralistic, critical voice, often laced with sarcasm. An early article on black leaders excoriated the unnamed Blanche Bruce (Mississippi's U.S. senator from 1875 to 1881) and others for piling up wealth and celebrity without doing much for the less fortunate. Wells protested that privileged blacks floated above the struggles of ordinary people, paying for Pullman berths, while others were subjected to degrading treatment: "Tell me what material benefit is a 'leader' if he does not, to some extent, devote his time, talent and wealth to the alleviation of the poverty and misery, and elevation of his people?"[101]

Most female journalists wrote about motherhood and managing a household. Wells wrote about "women's issues," too, but differently, contending that black women were just beginning to realize their power and influence. She traced her subject to Genesis, noting that Eve, having caused the human race to fall into sin, with a "curse on all succeeding generations," certainly exercised immense influence of some kind. More recently, Wells argued, a woman wrote *Uncle Tom's Cabin*, helping to bring down slavery, and women inspired many great artists. Women had far more influence than they usually realized, especially black women: "The masses of the women of our race have not awakened to a true sense of the responsibilities that devolve on them, of the influence they exert; they have not yet realized the necessity for erecting a standard of earnest, thoughtful, pure, noble womanhood, rather than one of fashion, idleness, and uselessness."[102]

That was the standard to which Wells aspired, though her career ambitions and dalliances with various suitors above her social station yielded accusations that she was a ruthless climber and heartless flirt. Wells filled her diary with assessments of gentlemen callers and other prospective boyfriends. There were over a dozen of them during her Memphis years. She told herself that she was not looking for a husband, but a good-enough boyfriend would be nice. Wells held out for one that showed no weakness, liked strong women, conducted winsome banter, was going somewhere, and excited her. Only the strong need apply, because for Wells, finding a partner who would protect her from a hostile society was the crucial thing. She preferred to have no partner than to have one that would not protect her.

Wells got through her twenties without finding a candidate who met her requirements, which gave rise to complaints that she was full of herself and not a nice lady. Louis M. Brown, a leading candidate, wrote a feature about Wells in the *Washington Bee*, jauntily describing her as brainy, assertive, "about four and a half feet high," about twenty years old, "tolerably well-proportioned," ambitious, and pretentious: "We do not advise her to take to the stage." Wells, in her diary, reflected that Brown was a worldly type with a varied experience, which was interesting to a point. Brown came the closest to winning her, based on the excitement factor. On the other hand, he was "a blasé man of the world with no new worlds to conquer," so he reveled in petty battles: "With all his accomplishments and advantages there seems to be no depth to him." I. J. Graham, a fellow teacher, was briefly in the running, mainly because he adored Wells. But he was too shy, and overwhelmed by Wells, to win her over. For a while she considered Charles S. Morris, a Howard University divinity student from a prominent family. Wells appreciated that Morris always used "chaste and apt language" with her, a contrast to Brown's sexual innuendo, and he made her laugh. On the other hand, Morris was too boyish to inspire confidence, and he was headed for the confining decorum of church ministry, so Wells went back to favoring Brown, until she tired of his entreaties. Brown and another suitor, A. A. Mosely (a minister) both questioned angrily whether Wells was capable of loving anyone; she confessed to her diary that perhaps she was not.[103]

Fortune encouraged and promoted Wells during her early journalistic career, opening doors for her. Born a slave in Florida, Fortune had watched his Republican father struggle with the southern backlash against Reconstruction. After Hayes was elected and Reconstruction was sacrificed, Fortune moved to New York, where he founded the New York *Globe*. Quickly it became America's leading black paper, as Fortune was gifted, devoted to race pride, and a powerful advocate of civil and political rights. By the time that Wells began to write for him, Fortune had renamed his paper the *New York Freeman*; later he called it the *New York Age*. Wells also tried to write for the *Washington Bee*, an ardently Republican paper edited by the cantankerous, cheeky, sometimes erratic W. Calvin Chase, but that did not go well. The *Bee*'s slogan was "Honey for friends, stings for enemies." Chase stung Wells, telling readers that she was a bad writer who needed to stop publishing her half-baked thoughts. Since Iola "offered her effusions to a number of papers," Chase could only hope that no paper paid for her "pratting," as that would be embarrassing for the black press: "Of all the exchanges that come to our office, Iola's trenchant pen is the most conspicuous for grammatical and typographical errors." Wells recoiled at being ridiculed in public, writing in her diary that Chase accused everyone who did not agree with him of not knowing what they were talking about: "He is contemptible & juvenile in the extreme and knows as much about what constitutes journalism as—as—Louis Brown! I would not write for him for great pay & I will write something someday that will make him wince."[104]

For a while she floundered instead, dismayed with her love life and the harsh things that people said about her, regretting her academic shortcomings and lamenting her out-of-control emotions. Being a teacher made Wells think about her student years; had she been a better student, she reasoned, she might have been a better teacher. Her aunt Fannie moved to Visalia, California, taking Annie and Lily with her, which tortured Wells: Should she give up her life in Memphis to join her sisters and aunt in faraway California? Wells mused that she was a mystery to herself and to others. She was prone to angry outbursts, and people didn't like her: "I don't know what's the matter with me, I feel so dissatisfied with my life, so isolated from all my kind. I cannot or do not make friends & these fits of loneliness will come & I tire of everything. My life seems awry, the machinery out of gear & I feel there is something wrong."[105]

She worried so much about her fiery temperament that sometimes she overcompensated. In August 1886 Eliza Woods, a cook, was lynched in Jackson, Tennessee, for poisoning her employer, a white woman. The evidence against Woods was purely circumstantial: She had a box of "Rough on Rats" in her house, and the dead woman's stomach contained arsenic. That was proof enough for a lynch mob exceeding one thousand people that stormed the county jail, stripped Woods naked, called her a "black female devil" and similar fare, and hung her on the courthouse yard. The mob finished its business by riddling Woods's body with bullets and leaving her exposed to view. The story shook Wells to her core. She wrote about Woods for the *Gate City Press* so angrily that it scared her. In her diary she wrote, "O my God! Can such things be and no justice for it?" In the next breath she admonished herself to restrain her anger and uphold her faith. It could not be Christian, or safe, to rage at the world: "It may be unwise to express myself so strongly but I cannot help it & I know not if capital may not be made of it against me but I trust in God."[106]

Wells opted for journalism, Memphis, and taking back Lily, while Annie stayed in California. For the next three years Wells wrote often about ministers and rarely about lynching. She contended that ministers were more important to society than politicians, and also more corrupt. The Baptist and Methodist denominations, in her view, were riddled with the "most corrupt, immoral and incompetent" ministers, squandering their opportunities to witness to Christ. Wells grieved that the AME Church elected Wesley J. Gaines and Abram Grant to bishops' chairs, as both were too "uncultivated" to be church leaders. Then the Woods lynching made the newspapers again.[107]

The husband of Woods's employer had belatedly broken down, confessing that he killed his wife. Wells let the full horror of the story sink into her soul. This time she unleashed her rage without equivocating, publicly blasting Jackson's black males for allowing "white men to outrage all decency and law by stripping one of our women and hanging her merely on suspicion." The Woods case was peculiar in that the lynching mob included numerous black men. This part of the story influenced Wells's immediate reaction, but the protection issue was always paramount for her anyway. White mobs were going to keep lynching blacks on mere suspicion if nobody tried to stop them. What most needed to be said, Wells insisted, was that black men everywhere needed to "rise in their manhood and resent such outrages, as white men do." White men did not allow anyone to insult their women. They raged and stormed and retaliated immediately. They lynched black people and white men with no hesitation. Wells implored her Afro-American male readers to summon a similar self-respect: "God expects us to defend ourselves. When we fail to do so we have only ourselves to blame."[108]

She published this blistering call to self-defense on March 2, 1889. Later that month Wells attended a conference of the National Colored Press Association at the Metropolitan AME Church in Washington, DC, where militant black journalist John R. Mitchell Jr., editor of the *Richmond Planet,* read aloud the names of more than two hundred lynching victims, all from the past two years. Mitchell had a routine: First the recitation, then appeal to the crowd: "Don't cringe and cower. Stand up for your rights with manly dignity." As Mitchell spoke, Wells fought back tears, thinking of the many lynching victims that "had no requiem, save the night wind, no memorial service to bemoan their sad and horrible fate." Later at the conference, Wells was elected secretary of the association, a professional breakthrough.[109]

Later that year Beale Street Church pastor Taylor Nightingale asked Wells to edit his newspaper, *Memphis Free Speech,* which he founded in the church basement in 1888. Wells joined Nightingale and business manager J. L. Fleming as an equal partner of the renamed paper, the *Free Speech and Headlight,* becoming the first African American woman to run or partly own a city newspaper. Nightingale was a blustery type who bullied his congregation, a far cry from Wells's ideal of the pious, holy, reflective minister. The paper, however, was a golden opportunity for her, a turning point. Wells filled it with articles about churches, unworthy ministers, politics, schools, and black community life, welcoming Booker Washington as an ally on her unworthy-ministers trope. In August 1890 Washington blasted black ministers in the *Christian Union,* claiming that most had no business being ministers. Wells had two conflicting reactions. One, Washington was wrong to say such things in a white Protestant house organ. Why humiliate black ministers in Lyman Abbott's magazine? But, two, everything that Washington said desperately needed saying. She wrote to Washington personally, thanking him for his "manly criticism of our corrupt and ignorant ministry." No one was more "fitted" than he to "clean up" the black church in Martin Luther's reforming spirit, Wells declared. Washington wrote a friendly reply, the last exchange between them that could be called friendly.[110]

Wells took a flinty moralistic attitude toward her fellow teachers too. In the early 1890s she became convinced that some of her African American female colleagues were seriously lacking in aptitude and morality. Wells wrote unsigned editorials blasting the Memphis school system for hiring bad teachers; then she upped the ante by charging that they were immoral too. She had a theory about why the school system overflowed with adulterous Afro-American female teachers: White board members hired them for easy sex. Wells asked Nightingale to sign her editorial on this theme, reasoning that it would make a greater impact if a minister wrote it; plus she didn't want to lose her job in the school system. Nightingale turned her down, so the editorial was published unsigned. It set off a storm of accusation, denials, and a suicide, as the teacher that Wells held foremost in mind—Hattie Britton, the sister of noted singer Julia Hooks—blew her brains out with a pistol. Wells was fired from her teaching job, convinced of her righteousness. Decades later she was still convinced, explaining that her targets lacked the requisite "mental and moral character" to be teachers; their only qualification was their willingness to carry on "clandestine love affairs" and other "illicit relationships" with influential white men. Afro-American studies scholar Paula J. Giddings explains that Wells had "steely moralistic tendencies" that she did not question. According to Wells, the worst part of the episode was that parents did not thank her for exposing the bad teachers: "I thought it was right to strike a blow against a glaring evil and I did not regret it. Up to that time I had felt that any fight made in the interest of the race would have its support. I learned that I could not count on that."[111]

Again she had taken the path of righteous resistance, while ruing that she had hardly any friends. Both episodes of lonely defiance strengthened Wells for the trials to come. Shortly after Wells lost her teaching position, Nightingale fled to Oklahoma, chased by a messy conflict with his wife that became public and legally threatening to him. Now Wells and Fleming had the paper to themselves. At the time, Wells probably had no more than two good friends: Thomas Moss, a postal carrier and Sunday school teacher at Avery Chapel, who co-owned a cooperative grocery store, the People's Grocery; and his wife, Betty Moss. Then Tommy Moss was lynched in the aftermath of a dispute over a game of marbles.

Tommy Moss epitomized the ethic of clean-living, civic-minded Christian virtue that Wells prized, and the People's Grocery was located in a mostly black district of Memphis called the "Curve," so named because the streetcar line curved sharply in that area. W. H. Barrett, a white grocer, had long monopolized the grocery trade (and boozy gambling) in this area until Moss and Calvin McDowell opened a grocery cooperative across the street. Barrett was openly hostile toward Moss and McDowell, which was all it took to spark a local tragedy and exodus that changed Wells's life.

It started with a fight between groups of black and white boys over a game of marbles. Parents on both sides were drawn into the fight, as were the owners of both nearby grocery stores, and nominal fines were issued in court. Coming out of court, Barrett and his friends vowed that revenge would be swift. That night both grocery stores had armed men standing nearby to provide protection. Six armed white men, deputized for the occasion and carrying warrants instigated by Barrett, descended on the People's Grocery. Three stormed the back entrance and were promptly fired upon. According to the local white press, the deputies had come to make an arrest and were gunned down. According to five local black ministers, including Wells's pastor, Benjamin Imes, everyone knew that the deputies had come for revenge, beginning with the destruction of the grocery store. Two of the deputies were seriously wounded, and the white press described the incident as a murderous ambush against officers of the law by black hooligans.

The press identified McDowell and Nat Trigg, a postal worker, as the shooters, but police arrested forty African Americans. A lynch mob of seventy-five stormed the county jail, heading straight for the ringleaders of the People's Grocery—McDowell, Moss, and Will Stewart. Getting rid of the store was more important to Barrett's mob than sorting out legal guilt in the shooting. The three store managers were dragged to the local railroad grounds, tortured, and executed. Newspapers ran harrowing eyewitness accounts, describing the four large holes shot into McDowell's face, Stewart's stoicism while being shot repeatedly, and Moss's reportedly weepy, begging last minutes. Journalists inadvertently set off a backlash, however, by reporting Moss's last words: "Tell my people to go West, there is no justice for them here."[112]

Wells was in Mississippi when her friend was lynched. She hurried back to Memphis, later recalling, "The shock to the colored people who knew and loved both Moss and McDowell was beyond description. Groups of them went to the grocery and elsewhere and vented their feelings in talking among themselves, but they offered no violence." A white mob destroyed the People's Grocery, defying black grievers. Barrett got the remains of the store while blacks stewed over Moss's last words, feeling trapped. Wells crystallized the issue for them: "The City of Memphis has demonstrated that neither character nor standing avails the Negro if he dares to protect himself against the white man or becomes his rival. There is nothing we can do about the lynching now, as we are outnumbered and without arms. The white mob could help itself to ammunition without pay, but the order was rigidly enforced against the selling of guns to Negroes. There is therefore only one thing left that we can do; save our money and leave a town which will neither protect our lives and property, nor give us a fair trial in the courts, but takes us out and murders us in cold blood when accused by white persons."[113]

The only thing left for African Americans to do in hateful Memphis was to get away from Memphis. This was like Moses in Egypt or the black "Exodusters" that fled the South after Reconstruction ended. Wells's blunt assessment had a huge impact. Black congregations gathered and prayed about it, mulling their options. Some considered Liberia, but Liberia was far away and hard to imagine. The federal government had formally opened Oklahoma Territory to settlement in 1889. Entire congregations debated whether to move to Oklahoma, and two of them did. Thousands of black Memphians made the move singly or in groups, draining Memphis of service workers and consumers. The first large contingent of exiles contained 649 men, women, and children, in thirty wagons, sent off by a gathering of 3,000 well-wishers. Prominent black businessman Robert Church helped them leave. Church had made a fortune buying up Memphis real estate after the yellow fever epidemic. He had become the South's first black millionaire by betting on a Memphis recovery. Now he donated ten thousand dollars to the Central Oklahoma Emigration Society, which helped 4,000 Memphis blacks move to Oklahoma. Overall, approximately 6,000 blacks made the move in the first year, 20 percent of the city's black population.

Nationally, the black press erupted in unprecedented fashion over the Memphis lynching and the exodus. The Kansas *American Citizen* implored white Memphis to punish the fiendish lynchers, which would prove that "God is not dead; that religion is not a mockery, and that all of your churches should not be burned to the ground." Ferdinand Barnett, in the Chicago *Conservator*, declared furiously, "The American flag is not a protection to citizens at home, but a dirty, dishonored rag." Memphis railway officials asked Wells to urge readers to start using the streetcars again. She replied that she would do no such thing; the rail company deserved to be boycotted. The officials pleaded that northern capitalists owned the company. She replied that southern lynchers ran it. They asked why she didn't expend her energy finding the lynchers instead of telling blacks to leave Memphis and/or shut it down. She replied that Afro-Americans had run out of options in Memphis. The circuit court judge himself was probably in the lynch mob, so the court system was out of play for blacks, and the reporters would never betray their white brethren. Decades later she recalled, "Every time word came of people leaving Memphis, we who were left behind rejoiced."[114]

Having set off the exodus, Wells paid a solidarity visit to Oklahoma City, Langston City, and other Oklahoma locales. She seriously considered moving there, but Fleming preferred New York or Philadelphia, places where her renown had escalated. Wells lauded those that fled to Oklahoma and West Africa, disputing Fortune's contention that the "intelligent class" of blacks would never move to Liberia. Turner was right, she argued. There was no reason why American blacks should not return to their ancestral land; the Puritans faced daunting obstacles, too. The nationalist strain in her thought was deepening.[115]

In May 1892 Edward Ward Carmack, editor of the *Memphis Commercial*, published a vile editorial claiming that black males had degenerated since Reconstruction into beastly rapists. The most horrible thing on earth—the rape of a white woman by a black man—had reached epidemic proportions, according to Carmack. It had become impossible for a white man to leave his family at night without dreading "that some roving Negro ruffian is watching and waiting for this opportunity." Wells had little time to reply before heading for the AME General Conference in Philadelphia, but she had to say something. She noted that eight African Americans had been lynched in the past two weeks, and five were lynched on "the same old racket—the new alarm about raping white women." Wells dashed off a one-sentence preview of an article she meant to write soon about lynching, rape, and the sexual relationships between black men and white women: "If Southern men are not careful, they will overreach themselves and public sentiment will have a reaction; a conclusion will then be reached which will be very damaging to the moral reputation of their women."[116]

Rushing off to Philadelphia, Wells met Payne at the General Conference, "who fulfilled my every ideal of what I thought a Negro bishop ought to be." Otherwise she did not care for the convention, musing that the delegates would have done better to contribute their railroad fare to people in need. Giddings explains, "Few meetings are filled with more verbiage than ecclesiastical ones, and Ida was not impressed." Then Wells traveled to Jersey City, across the river from New York City, to meet Fortune, who told her that having finally made it to New York, she would have to stay. What did that mean? Fortune handed Wells a copy of the New York *Sun*, which reported that a white mob had destroyed her office, chased Fleming out of town, and left a note saying that anyone who tried to publish another issue of the paper would be killed. The *Memphis Commercial* had goaded the mob with an editorial condemning the *Free Speech*'s "loathsome and repulsive calumnies." The *Memphis Evening Scimitar*, assuming that Fleming had written the editorial, went further, declaring that the author of the *Free Speech*'s calumnies about white women should be tied to a stake in the center of town, branded in the forehead "with a hot iron," and subjected to "a surgical operation with a pair of tailor's shears." Wells was finished in Memphis.[117]

Years later she recalled, "Having lost my paper, had a price put on my life, and been made an exile from home for hinting at the truth, I felt that I owed it to myself and to my race to tell the whole truth now that I was where I could do so freely." She began with a sensational article, "The Truth about Lynching," in Fortune's paper, now called the *New York Age*. Contrary to popular opinion, Wells noted, most lynchings had nothing to do with rape. Citing a *Chicago Tribune* study, she explained that of the 728 mob killings reported from 1882 to 1891 (a low estimate), no rape was even alleged in almost two-thirds of the cases. The majority of people lynched during this period were black men, and of that group, most were lynched for challenging whites in business or politics or for refusing to be intimidated. Tommy Moss was a more typical lynching victim than any accused rapist. Moreover, Wells argued, something had changed between white women and black men since the end of slavery, but it wasn't that black men became rapists. Nobody claimed that rape was a problem during the Civil War, when white southern women were vulnerable at home. What changed was that many white women in the South established consensual relationships with black men, exposing the latter to the rage of white males. The truth was simple and almost never publicly acknowledged, she wrote: "There are many white women in the South who would marry colored men if such an act would not place them at once beyond the pale of society and within the clutches of the law."[118]

Wells provided examples and names, telling of Sarah Clark of Memphis, who swore in court that she was not white, in order to avoid prosecution for miscegenation; and Edward Coy, who was burned alive in Texarkana after his white lover sold him out; and a black coachman in Natchez, Mississippi, who fled for his life after a high society lady named Mrs. Marshall gave birth to an "unmistakably dark" baby; and Ebenzer Fowler, the wealthiest Afro-American in Issaquena County, Mississippi, who was riddled with bullets by a white mob that discovered his affair with a white woman. Wells observed that there was "hardly a town in the South" that did not have stories of this kind that everyone knew. Everyone in the South knew that the upsurge of lynching was about something other than rape. But the lynching mania fed on itself, sprawling far beyond its ostensible rationale. There was no epidemic of rape, Wells noted, but African Americans were advancing in American society and black men were engaging in a greater number of interracial relationships, which set off an explosion of lynching. Mob violence had reached the level of mass contagion, feeding a "growing disregard of human life" that spread to the North.[119]

Wells stressed that the "best men" of the South were prominent in the lynching mobs. The group that burned Coy, for example, was long on socially respectable types posing as chivalrous protectors of white women, never mind that several were fathers of mixed-race children. For that matter, Wells argued, her own experience of persecution was mostly at the hands of "leading citizens." The leading white citizens of Memphis stoked and supported the lynching of Moss, McDowell, and Stewart. Then they targeted her for complaining about it. Wells advised that only one thing had worked thus far in combating lynching, besides the obvious option of taking flight. Every black American home needed to have a Winchester rifle, she urged. The rifle should have "a place of honor" in the home for providing protection that the law did not provide.[120]

On her sexual thesis, Wells was simultaneously emphatic, ambivalent, and repulsed. The leading citizens that burned Coy and shot Fowler were "notorious" for preferring black women as sexual partners, Wells contended. They mythologized southern belles as pure-minded Christian ladies lacking sexual desire, and they vengefully punished the black men who dared to treat white women as sexual beings. They prated about defending the honor of white women while betraying them as partners, preferring black women for sex, as they had during slavery. White men were the barbarians in this picture; white women were more sexual than their husbands dared to imagine; black women were victimized by the predatory sexuality of white men; and black men caught hell for all of it, especially if they were not careful.[121]

Wells cautioned that she did not expose the sexual entanglements between black men and white women out of any desire to provide "a shield for the despoiler of virtue." She had mixed feelings about the "poor blind Afro-American Samsons who suffer themselves to be betrayed by white Delilahs." Yes, she defended the black men who got in trouble with white men by allowing themselves to be seduced by white women. The truth was not as bad as the plague of rape-accusation and lynching. Wells was searching for the truth, which yielded only a half defense of certain Afro-American men. She hated having to dip her hands "in the corruption here exposed." But the difference between the truth and the lie was enormously important, she argued: "Somebody must show that the Afro-American race is more sinned against than sinning, and it seems to have fallen upon me to do so. The awful death-toll that Judge Lynch is calling every week is appalling, not only because of the lives it takes, the rank cruelty and outrage to the victims, but because of the prejudice it fosters and the stain it places against the good name of a weak race. The Afro-American is not a bestial race."[122]

Church-lady Victorianism ran very deep in Ida Wells, but to expose the lies that fueled the lynching mania, she had to rip the bark off late-Victorian decorum. Everything about her argument was incendiary, or revelatory, depending on the reader. Fortune aimed for as many as possible, publishing a special edition of ten thousand copies, which quickly sold out, leading to a pamphlet version. The article lifted Wells to the top rank of nationally recognized Afro-Americans; the pamphlet, published under the title "Southern Horrors: Lynch Law in All Its Phases," had a long life as a staple of the anti-lynching movement. In October 1892 Wells got a thunderous reception at the Afro-American Press Association Conference in Philadelphia, where she implored that winning applause was not the point. She asked the group to launch an anti-lynching campaign based on investigative journalism and professional detective work, which it promptly agreed to do, electing her as treasurer.

That month her celebrity status was sealed by a glittering event in her honor at Lyric Hall in Manhattan, a block from Madison Square Park. Wells had moved to Brooklyn, still a separate city in 1892, where she felt homesick. She was thirty years old and starting over, having traded her *Free Speech* subscription list for a one-fourth interest in the *Age*. At the time the African American communities of New York City and Brooklyn mirrored the larger rivalry of the two cities. Brooklynites viewed their city as a cultured refuge from the crime, noise, and high rents of New York, while New Yorkers looked down on obviously inferior Brooklyn. Both cities had distinguished black literary societies that had a history of snubbing each other. In 1892 the women of these rival societies pulled together for something they could agree upon—the breakthrough importance of Ida Wells.

Wells had never given a formal speech, and she tended to feel uneasy in the company of wealthy and/or distinguished people. Lyric Hall on October 5 was loaded with them, notably Philadelphia journalists Gertrude Mossell and Frances Ellen Harper, New York physician Susan McKinney, Henry Highland Garnet's widow, Sarah Garnet, and the grande dame of high society black America, woman suffrage activist Josephine St. Pierre Ruffin, of Boston. Wells's old suitor Charles S. Morris was there, accompanied by his wife, Annie Sprague, the granddaughter of Frederick Douglass. Surveying the crowd, Wells was terrified: "A panic seized me. I was afraid that I was going to make a scene and spoil all those dear good women had done for me." She began to read her speech on the evils of lynching and was appalled to feel tears streaming down her face. This was her nightmare, to break down like a little girl in front of this crowd. Wells was mortified by her "exhibition of weakness." She had gotten through the lynching of her best friend and the destruction of her career in Memphis without yielding to "personal feelings," only to crumble at a testimonial in her honor.[123]

But the crowd loved her, giving her a huge ovation. Morris told Wells that her tears broke through the ingrained cynicism and selfishness of New Yorkers.

Decades later, still mortified at her tears, Wells consoled herself that the Lyric Hall event launched the black women's club movement. The first club, the Women's Loyal Union of Brooklyn and New York, was organized in December 1892. Similar clubs were soon launched in Pittsburgh, New Orleans, and Chicago. For women who had no hope of becoming pastors, professors, or political leaders, the club movement was a godsend, a vehicle for fellowship and activism. Wells's second consolation was that the Lyric Hall event launched her career as a public speaker.

From the beginning she fastened fiercely on one subject—the evil of lynching. Every speech called for a movement to abolish mob terrorism. Ruffin coordinated a New England speaking tour for Wells, who spoke to a white audience for the first time. Douglass, responding to "The Truth About Lynching," lauded Wells for breaking through: "Brave woman! You have done your people and mine a service which can neither be weighed nor measured. If American conscience were only half alive, if the American church and clergy were only half Christianized, if American moral sensibility were not hardened by persistent infliction of outrage and crime against colored people, a scream of horror, shame and indignation would rise to Heaven wherever your pamphlet shall be read." Douglass declared that nothing written about lynching compared to Wells's article "in convincing power." Wells asked Douglass for permission to print his letter as a preface to the pamphlet version of her article, which he granted. She hit the lecture trail, buoyed by the praise of America's greatest black leader, with whom she became friends.[124]

Douglass had recently resigned from his last public office, minister resident and consul general to the Republic of Haiti and chargé d'affaires for the Dominican Republic. He had retired to his twenty-four acre Maryland estate, Cedar Hill, where he walked the grounds, played the violin, received visitors, and revised his 1881 autobiography, *Life and Times of Frederick Douglass*. The emergence of Wells cheered Douglass like nothing else in his last years, and his friendship thrilled her long after he let her down. The second edition of Douglass's *Life and Times*, published in 1893, did not enliven the first edition, which did not compare to his riveting previous autobiographies, *Narrative of the Life of Frederick Douglass* (1845) and *My Bondage and My Freedom* (1855). The second edition of *Life and Times*, besides being a hundred pages longer than the first edition, was still flat, lacking immediacy. Remarkably, it said nothing about lynching. In the summer of 1892, however, the *North American Review* asked Douglass what he had to say about lynching, just as Wells exploded on this subject. Without mentioning Wells, Douglass supported three of her signature claims: The upsurge of lynching reflected white alarm that blacks were advancing in American society, the "best white men" had a lot of lynching blood on their hands, and the struggle against lynching was morally equivalent to the abolitionist struggle against slavery. Douglass stressed point one: "It is only when he rises in wealth, intelligence, and manly character that he brings upon himself the heavy hand of persecution. The men lynched in Memphis were murdered because they were prosperous."[125]

Wells was thrilled to have Douglass's support on these controversial arguments. Douglass offered no plan of action, but she had no strategy either, except to build a protest network. Douglass said nothing about sexual relationships between black men and white women, but Wells appreciated that he must have felt disqualified from addressing this issue, because Douglass was married to a white woman, Helen Pitts. Years later Wells addressed the issue bluntly. Douglass dearly loved Pitts, his second wife, Wells recalled. Many friends judged him harshly for marrying a white woman, which wounded him deeply. Wells too wished that Douglass had chosen "one of the beautiful, charming colored women of my race for his second wife." But Wells grieved that people treated Douglass and Pitts badly for it. Douglass told Wells he knew only two black women who treated Pitts decently: Francis Grimké's wife and her. Wells, for all her militant moralism, could not imagine "such a breach of good manners," partly because it thrilled her to be friends with "the greatest man our race has produced."[126]

Back in Memphis, Carmack resented that Wells got to be famous by making Memphis look bad. Carmack retaliated in the *Memphis Commercial*, calling Wells a "wench," the "mistress of a scoundrel" (allegedly Fleming), and a "black harlot" who railed against lynching to swell her bank account and was known to want a white husband. John Mitchell and Josephine Ruffin publicly defended Wells, who contacted Albion Tourgée. Could she sue Carmack for slander? Tourgée said yes but warned that everything she had ever said or done would be fodder in a trial. Since he was broke, he suggested that she ask Ferdinand Barnett to be her lawyer. Barnett started to build a case for Wells, telling her that he looked forward to giving Carmack the thrashing he deserved. In the end they decided not to go forward with the case, judging that the potential gains were not worth the risks. But Wells had found someone who met her requirements.[127]

In 1893 Douglass delivered on a promise to Wells by packing Metropolitan Church in Washington, DC for her first speech in the nation's capital. Mary Church (Molly) Terrell introduced Wells with a speech of her own. Molly Terrell was Robert Church's daughter, an 1884 graduate of Oberlin College, a former acquaintance of Wells's in Memphis, and soon to be a luminary in the club movement. She had taught languages at Wilberforce from 1885 to 1887 and earned a master's degree at Oberlin in 1888. She toured Europe for two years, enjoying her wealth and independence, before marrying Robert H. Terrell in 1891, a lawyer who became the first Afro-American municipal court judge in Washington, DC. In a frosty aside reflecting their longtime rivalry, Wells later recalled that although Terrell had been asked to introduce her, "she seemed to be making a maiden speech." Anna Julia Cooper, principal of the elite M Street High School and author of the recently published *A Voice from the South*, was also there. Cooper argued in her book that the educational and spiritual progress of black women would lift the black American community as a whole. Terrell and Cooper were elegant, classically educated exemplars of the "elevation" tradition of Afro-American thought, with which Wells had a conflicted relationship, and Wells subsequently clashed with Terrell. Decades after her night at Metropolitan Church, however, Wells still felt its glow, remembering the evening as a "blaze of glory" in which "most of the brilliant women of Washington" took part.[128]

The next morning Wells read about a horrifying lynching in Paris, Texas. An Afro-American accused of murdering a five-year-old girl had been tortured for hours with burning irons before being set afire. Afterward the lynch mob fought over his bones and teeth for souvenirs. Wells despaired that white newspapers and churches seemed indifferent to the barbarism of their society. To this point, her meteoric celebrity seemed to mean nothing to most white Americans. Wells was stewing over this issue when she received an unlikely invitation to speak in Great Britain.

Catherine Impey, an English Quaker activist and editor of a journal, *Anti-Caste*, devoted to liberationist struggles of peoples of color, and Isabella Mayo, a wealthy Scottish author and social activist, organized a thirty-five lecture tour for Wells. This invitation, Wells later recalled, "seemed like an open door in a stone wall." She drew enormous crowds and publicity that rippled back to the United States. Leading clergy in England signed a petition urging their American clerical counterparts to pay heed to Wells's searing indictment of lynching, which yielded speaking invitations from northern white American churches. Impey and Mayo had a falling out, forcing Wells to reluctantly forego Mayo and her money, but the publicity generated by the tour changed Wells's life. She became a fixture on the northern white social gospel circuit and at meetings sponsored by Fortune's Afro-American League. Always she began by lambasting the prevailing silence about lynching. Always she described the Memphis lynching, the Coy and Woods lynchings, and the 1891 lynching of eleven Italians by a mob in New Orleans. Always she ended with an appeal to the abolitionist spirit of William Lloyd Garrison, Nat Turner, John Brown,

Frederick Douglass, Charles Sumner, and Wendell Phillips, sometimes quoting all of them. America needed a new abolition movement as "strong, deep and mighty" as the old one, Wells implored.[129]

For Wells, speaking in the South was out of the question, and her attempts to speak in border states did not go well. But her dogged speaking across the North spurred liberals to deal with the issue. In 1892 the toll of mob killings reached 161. For the next three years Wells took every speaking engagement she could make, updating her stump speech constantly as new lynchings occurred. In 1893 Wells moved to Chicago and took a job working for Barnett at the Chicago *Conservator*, the city's oldest African American newspaper. Her kindling romance with Barnett was a factor, as was her desire to start a women's club in Chicago, which was promptly named the Ida B. Wells Club. Wells joined Douglass, Barnett, and black press historian I. Garland Penn in protesting the decision of the World's Columbian Exposition in Chicago to offer merely token representations of African American life. Meanwhile she worked hard at learning all that she could about lynching, twelve years before James E. Cutler wrote the first scholarly text on this subject.

Cutler eventually traced the term to Virginia judge Charles Lynch, who established extralegal citizen juries during the Revolutionary War. Official courts were few and hard to reach under British occupation. Those punished under lynch law were usually horse thieves or Tories, and usually punished with thirty-nine lashes. Cutler showed that in the 1830s, though most lynch victims were still white, lynch law morphed into something primarily about preserving the slave order in the South. Anyone who threatened the existence of the slave system could be whipped or hung without bothering with courts. The third phase of lynch law began after the Civil War, when lynching became an instrument of racial terror, fueled by Klan terrorism and the struggles for power under Reconstruction. In the 1880s it became ritualized, with ceremonies usually involving torture and mutilation and more explicitly racialized. Cutler and Wells both treated 1882 as a benchmark year for racial lynching, although 1886 was the first year in which more blacks than whites were lynched.[130]

Wells pressed her lecture and reading audiences to confront the escalating rampage of racial lynching in their country. One was a heartbreaking case in Bardwell, Kentucky, where a mob insisted on killing C. J. Miller even after testimonial evidence and a search animal pointed elsewhere. As a concession to its lack of evidence, the mob settled for torturing, dragging, and hanging Miller instead of burning him as it wanted. Wells put it concisely in the Chicago *Inter Ocean*: "An innocent man has been barbarously and shockingly put to death in the glare of the nineteenth-century civilization, by those who profess to believe in Christianity, law and order." The *Inter Ocean* ran a heart-stopping illustration next to Wells's article, picturing Miller hanging from a telephone pole, with a log chain around his neck, stripped to a loincloth, and eerily resembling Christ crucified, as a passive crowd looked on.[131]

In Quincy, Mississippi, a lynch mob of two hundred suspected Benjamin Jackson of poisoning a well. The mob realized, however, that it didn't know what really happened. So after lynching Jackson it came back for his wife, his mother-in-law, and two of his friends, lynching them too, hoping to find the culprit in there somewhere. Wells noted that this case of moral degradation "did not excite any interest in the public at large. American Christianity heard of this awful affair and read of its details and neither press nor pulpit gave the matter more than a passing comment." In Memphis, a black man named Lee Walker accosted two white women driving a wagon. He later claimed that he was starving and demanded something to eat; they claimed that he tried to rob them; whatever happened, they screamed and he ran off. The women reported the incident and a ten-day manhunt ensued. The assailant was repeatedly described in the white press as a rapist, never mind that no sexual assault occurred or was charged. Walker was tracked down and briefly jailed, until a lynch mob dragged him to a telephone poll, tortured him, hung him, mutilated his corpse, and tossed it into a bonfire. Ten hours before this lynching occurred, Wells got a telegram inviting her to it, but she declined to return to Memphis. Later she observed ruefully that the difficulty of her work made it hard to believe that white America had any moral feeling. Wells failed to uncover *any* information about five lynchings that were known to occur in 1893. The lynching of black Americans had become so commonplace "that neither the civil authorities nor press agencies consider the matter worth investigating."[132]

Wells worked hard at becoming harder to ignore. The Indianapolis *Freeman* and the *Memphis Appeal-Avalanche* offered characteristically contrasting reactions to her. The *Freeman* compared her to Joan of Arc; the *Avalanche* called her a "negro adventuress" set upon a "career of triumphant mendacity." Wells increasingly took in stride her compliments from the black press and black audiences, admonishing both that she did not own this subject. All of them had to become more vocal about lynching, which did not mean they had to buy her sexuality arguments, as many found them dirty and offensive. C. H. J. Taylor, the federal recorder of deeds, accused the *Conservator* of trashing its "clean" legacy by hiring Wells. Wells carefully monitored her growing reputation in white America, lamenting that it was pretty much confined to social gospel circles, unlike the crowds she had attracted in England. She became adept at handling hecklers, denying that all lynching victims were innocent. What was at issue was the right to a trial that determined guilt or innocence. Wells told friends that she craved to break beyond her white liberal audience, and she measured her effectiveness by the amount of abuse she attracted. She invited some abuse by picking a fight with the celebrated leader of the Women's Christian Temperance Union (WCTU), Frances Willard.[133]

Wells harbored a special resentment of moderate white Christian, morally high-minded, highly regarded types that were no friend to Afro-Americans. It galled her that there were so many of them. So many Christian leaders of her time were admired for their social virtue despite demonstrating little or none in the area of racial justice. Three people topped her personal list: evangelist Dwight Moody, Southern Methodist bishop Atticus G. Haygood, and Willard. Moody, the late nineteenth century's leading evangelist, preached warmhearted evangelical sermons to vast throngs in the United States and Britain, epitomizing for many how the gospel should be preached. Wells heard Moody speak twice in Memphis in 1886 and praised his sincerity and simplicity. She wanted to like Moody, because his irenic sermons struck deep chords in her. McMurray remarks that Wells was like many others in being "mesmerized" by Moody's preaching. At first Wells found it merely puzzling and disappointing that Moody did not preach against racism. Later she learned that Moody never did, and he preached to segregated audiences wherever local custom demanded segregated audiences. That gave Wells second thoughts about Moody's Christian sincerity. Moody was a bitter disappointment.[134]

Haygood became a very different example of the same thing. Far from avoiding the race issue, Haygood talked about it constantly, with greater sympathy than any southern Christian leader. During the Civil War he served as a Confederate chaplain, doing hard service in the battlefields and hospitals, especially in Atlanta. In the 1870s he assumed the presidency of his alma mater, Emory College, brilliantly saving the school from financial ruin. In the early 1880s he became the South's foremost white clerical proponent of treating black Americans decently. Haygood's book *Our Brother in Black* (1881) made its most important argument in the title. There is one human race, Haygood said, and white Christians were morally obligated to treat blacks as their lowly, hurting, undeveloped brothers and sisters. Haygood had many anecdotes illustrating his thesis that black Americans were childlike, vulnerable, morally undisciplined human beings. He praised the northern churches for building schools and churches for blacks in the South and urged that the time had come for southern Christians to take up this work. This plea found a welcome reader in ex-president Hayes, who asked Haygood to run the newly founded Slater

Fund, dispensing forty thousand dollars annually for black education. Booker Washington became a prime beneficiary of the Slater money.[135]

Wells was tolerant of patronizing ministerial rhetoric concerning her race. Haygood's paternalism did not offend her, as Wells dispensed similar moralistic judgments on a regular basis, and she was willing to swallow sanctimony from whites if they supported the rights of black Americans. A fierce defender of the northern missionaries that founded black colleges, Wells appreciated Haygood's contributions to black education, and his Christian moral leadership. *Our Brother in Black* was mostly a defense of white southern Christianity, trying to represent it at its best; Wells believed that Haygood had an important role to play in changing a terrible situation.

But Haygood's Episcopal duties in Atlanta drew him increasingly into apologetics that crossed the line into rationalizing the indefensible. In July 1893, responding to the upsurge of lynching and to Illinois governor John Peter Altgeld's release of three anarchists implicated in the Haymarket Square Riot, Haygood condemned Altgeld for endangering American society. Anarchy was the greatest enemy of any society, Haygood argued. Anarchists were a menace to society, and so was lynching. Haygood called for the creation of "Law and Order Leagues" to support a just legal system, wipe out the plague of radical anarchists, and curb the plague of lynching: "A country given over to Lynch law is damned. A government that is indifferent to Lynch law is foolish and criminal. A government that can put Lynch law down and will not try to do it is itself a traitor to government. A government that cannot, is weak and contemptible."[136]

Two months later Haygood called for northern and southern Christians to unite against lynching. Mob executions were crimes against society and God, he urged. If a government was so weak or bad that it could not enforce the law, revolution was the appropriate remedy, not lynching. But Haygood cautioned that there was a serious mitigating factor at issue in the American case; it was not enough to reiterate basic principles of just government. The recent upsurge of lynching, he contended, did not arise from any cruelty, superstition, or ignorance peculiar to the South or the United States. It arose from something honorable, the determination to protect the honor of women. According to Haygood, the rape of white women by black men had increased dramatically in recent years, so lynching had exploded in response: "No race, not the most savage, tolerates the rape of woman, but it may be said without reflection upon any other people that the Southern people are now and always have been most sensitive concerning the honor of their women—their mothers, wives, sisters, and daughters." Haygood admonished black leaders and their white northern liberal allies that the rape crisis had to stop before the lynching crisis would abate.[137]

Lynching was about rape, not race hatred. In one paragraph Haygood had destroyed his life's work in Wells's eyes, pouring gasoline on the very lie that fueled the lynching mania. Only a third of lynching victims were even *accused* of rape, so what was he talking about? Wells knew very well what motivated Haygood: Most white Americans were not remotely prepared to admit that the explosion of lynching was about race hatred. Wells replied that white southern women deserved better defenders than Haygood: "It is their misfortune that the chivalrous white men of that section, in order to escape the deserved execration of the civilized world, should shield themselves by their cowardly and infamously false excuse, and call into question that very honor about which their distinguished priestly apologist claims they are most sensitive. To justify their own barbarism they assume a chivalry which they do not possess."[138]

Haygood went to the top of the bad list, surpassed only by Willard, who denied indignantly that she belonged there. Willard was an indefatigable temperance reformer and woman suffragist. She grew up in Janesville, Wisconsin, taught at Evanston College for Ladies, and was the first dean of women at Northwestern University. In 1874 she cofounded the Women's Christian Temperance Union, which she built into a national powerhouse, serving as its president from 1879 to 1898. Willard urged women to "do everything" on behalf of temperance and woman suffrage: lobby, petition, preach, publish, and educate. She called her two-sided platform "Home Protection," contending that women deserved to vote and to be protected from the social and domestic ravages of alcohol. She also supported the union movement and federal funding for education and was quiet about her lesbian sexuality. She was immensely popular in England, where she roomed in lengthy stays with her lover, Lady Henry Somerset, president of the British Woman's Temperance Association. There she converted in the 1890s to Fabian Socialism.[139]

The general dispute between Wells and Willard centered on the question of whether Willard's brand of temperance feminism used racism as a political weapon. More specifically their feud went back to an interview that Willard gave in 1890 to a New York City temperance newspaper, the *Voice*. Willard said that "alien illiterates" ruled American cities: "The saloon is their palace, and the toddy stick their sceptre. It is not fair that they should vote, nor is it fair that a plantation Negro, who can neither read nor write, whose ideas are bounded by the fence of his own field and the price of his own mule, should be entrusted with the ballot." Willard disparaged African American voters as "great dark-faced mobs whose rallying cry is better whiskey, and more of it. The colored race multiplies like the locusts of Egypt. The grog-shop is their center of power. The safety of women, of childhood, of the home is menaced in a thousand localities at this moment, so that men dare not go beyond the sight of their own roof-tree."[140]

Twenty-one years had passed since Elizabeth Cady Stanton blasted her abolitionist comrades at the American Equal Rights Association convention in New York City for enfranchising "Sambo and Hans and Yung Tung" ahead of educated white women. Cady Stanton railed that under the Fifteenth Amendment, white women would be "subjected to the government of outside barbarians" and forced to live under "the legislation of the ignorant African." Wells, reading the Willard interview, flushed with anger that Willard amplified a familiar line of abuse. Every racist trope that Wells battled against had a place in Willard's account of what plagued American society: Black Americans were not real Americans; they were stupid and didn't deserve the vote; their growth was a catastrophe for America; they were prone to crime and drunken destruction; and they raped white women with terrifying frequency. Talking about it would not have helped Wells and Willard reach an understanding. Willard resented black opposition to the Prohibition amendment, and she blamed black voters for its defeat in Tennessee. It galled Wells that Willard claimed to be a friend of Afro-Americans, always boasting that the WCTU had black members and that her parents' home had been a stop on the Underground Railroad. Allowing black members in the WCTU was not terribly impressive when you compared them to the locusts of Egypt.[141]

Wells said so in her speeches in England. Many of Willard's English admirers refused to believe she had maligned African Americans, as Willard did not talk that way in England, which made Wells all the more determined to set them straight about the phony Progressivism of Frances Willard. But Wells had not brought a copy of the *Voice* interview to England, so she could not prove her accusation. As soon as she returned to the United States, she tried to find the article. Wells made several trips to the WCTU headquarters in Chicago in search of it, scouring back issues of the organization's official organ, the *Union Signal*, to no avail. Neither did she find a different article in which Willard said similarly offensive things. On one occasion Wells asked WCTU secretary Anna Gordon where the offensive interview had been published; Gordon professed not to know. Eventually Wells found the interview, in time to brandish it on her second trip to England, in 1894, where she blasted Willard and Haygood for slandering black men as sexual predators. English listeners asked if it was true that she criticized Moody too. Wells affirmed that Moody was like Willard: "They have given the weight of their influence to the southern white man's prejudices."[142]

Wells was starting to become famous for saying harsh things about people who were renowned for their liberality and goodwill. Her press coverage increasingly featured questions or accusations about her moral character. On her second trip to England, Wells realized that this had become a serious issue. Twice she asked Douglass to write a public letter commending her moral character. Both times Douglass replied with weak, stiff, carefully vague letters that praised her devotion to an important cause without commending her. Wells was deeply hurt by both letters. She and Douglass were mindful of the parallels between their careers. England had given refuge to Douglass in 1845, shortly after he published his first autobiography, when he was a runaway slave. He had become famous in England, staying there for almost two years, before he returned to renown in his country. Douglass had his own reputation to maintain in Britain, and he was sufficiently unsure of Wells to withhold the endorsement she craved. Wells soldiered on without him, discovering that she could overcome bad press on her own. She attracted huge audiences that yielded numerous anti-lynching resolutions. She overcame Somerset's attempts to silence her and won a battle of nerves with Willard, who was forced to defend her own reputation.[143]

Lady Somerset, seated beneath "the trees of my garden at Reigate," published an interview with Willard in the *Westminster Gazette*. Willard stuck to her line that she was nothing like a racist, but she said it dismissively, flicking off Wells as a wild exaggerator. Willard assured that she was a good liberal. She defended the rights of blacks, her parents were abolitionists, she had learned to read by reading *The Slave's Friend*, she was known for caring about Afro-Americans, and she had even been nice to Wells. Now she worried that Wells was damaging her own effectiveness by acting badly. Somerset asked about Wells's claim that white American Christians did not care about lynching; Willard replied that America's biggest Protestant denomination (the Northern Methodists) had passed a strong anti-lynching resolution. Somerset asked about the Willard interview that Wells flogged to her audiences. Willard replied that it had nothing to do with lynching or racism, things she opposed. She was against allowing uneducated people to vote, a perfectly reasonable position. Wells had erupted over nothing, imagining things that weren't there. Did Willard worry that Wells had sullied Willard's progressive image? Not at all, she claimed: "British justice may be trusted to guard my reputation in that particular issue as in all others."[144]

Wells caught the tone of airy dismissal and ridicule. She realized that this posture might work better than righteous indignation for Willard. Wells struck back immediately, protesting that the picture of two privileged white ladies bantering lightheartedly about her limitations did not comport very well with the terrible seriousness of her subject. The two ladies did not ask, in their superiority, how they could help "the Negro who is being hanged, shot, and burned," Wells observed. Their only question was how to guard Willard's reputation. Wells put it sharply: "With me, it is not myself nor my reputation, but the life of my people which is at stake." She noted that Willard had never said a word in public against lynching, until now. Wells left the implication hanging: Willard never would have said anything, had she not been shamed into it by Wells. Wells added that it was perverse to blame blacks for the defeat of prohibition in the South when hardly any blacks could vote there: "The fact is, Miss Willard is no better or worse than the great bulk of white Americans on the Negro question. They are all afraid to speak out, and it is only British public opinion which will move them, as I am thankful to see it has already begun to move Miss Willard."[145]

This reading of the situation carried the day in Britain, as Willard signed an anti-lynching petition inspired by Wells. Wells gave 102 lectures in four months on her second British tour, garnering praise and support from Archbishop of Canterbury Edward White Benson, Christian Socialist leader Charles F. Aked (pastor of London's largest Nonconformist congregation, Pembroke Chapel), *Manchester Guardian* editor William E. A. Axom, feminist journalist Florence Belgarnie, and above all, *Liverpool Daily Post* editor Sir Edward Russell, whose fervent support opened doors for Wells across the nation. Upon returning home she clutched a raft of anti-lynching resolutions and laudatory press coverage. The *Christian Recorder* gushed that an archway of roses "should greet this Joan of Arc on her return from fields of conquest."[146]

Wells, however, though pleased with her success in Britain, was in a furious mood. She was angry with black men in general and at nearly every black man that she knew in particular. Douglass, J. L. Fleming, and Taylor Nightingale headed the latter list. Wells's critics routinely accused her of salacious slander, and sometimes they recycled Memphis rumors that she had committed adultery with Fleming and/or Nightingale. Fleming and Nightingale backed away from defending Wells publicly, as did others in a position to help her. In her telling, only two Afro-American men defended her: Turner and Fortune. All others melted into cowardly silence, including Douglass, although Wells never criticized Douglass publicly.

On returning home, Wells poured out her frustration in the Indianapolis *Freeman:* "I am feeling so sorry for myself that the bitter tears have been coursing down my cheeks. I am wondering what a fool am I to sacrifice so much and suffer so much and work so hard for a race which will not defend me or protect me in defending it. Not for myself alone do I weep. My heart aches for those of my race who are being immolated every day on the altar of the white man's prejudice—hanged, shot, flayed alive and burned; over the widows and orphans made desolate; over the great bulk of the race which reads these things and whose hearts are not stirred to action of some kind on behalf of the victims; over the spirit of envy and jealousy which actuates those who can help to opposition instead of support; lastly and most of all, I weep because the manhood of the race knows itself slandered, its women and children slaughtered, its mothers, wives, sisters and daughters insulted and despoiled and traduced and still fails to assert its strength or extend its protection to those who have the right to claim it. Is mine a race of cowards?"[147]

Turner welcomed the rise of a like-minded AME radical with a crusading spirit who asked the right question. He believed that most African Americans quietly cheered for Wells while making sure not to be heard. On returning home Wells resolved that she needed a vehicle to promote the anti-lynching cause and protect her. She wanted to be a full-time movement leader, like Willard, holding the authority that came with movement leadership. That would require an anti-lynching organization modeled on the WCTU, which paid Willard eighteen hundred dollars per year plus an allowance for clerical help and a salary for her secretary. If Wells could build such an organization, anti-lynching would become the abolitionist cause of her generation and she would attain the support structure she needed to pursue it. Fortune and the *Cleveland Gazette* endorsed this idea, forming an executive council to raise money. Wells appealed to activists and church groups for support. They told her the lynching issue was too narrow and episodic to support a WCTU-like organization; plus, American audiences were unlikely to pay for lectures about lynching. Many ministers added that she had to stop talking about interracial sex, because this topic was impossibly salacious, offensive, and a loser for the anti-lynching cause.

Wells doubled down on the lecture circuit to prove them wrong. The anti-lynching cause, she insisted, would never be lifted to the status it deserved if African Americans shied away from focusing on it. Moreover, the issue of interracial sex had to be addressed because the lynching mania was fueled and rationalized by the charge that black men were raping white women. Wells would have preferred to say nothing about the sexual desires of white women. As it was, she had to raise the issue, because silence about it was deadly for black Americans. Speaking to New York *Sun* editor Charles Dana on this topic, Wells remarked that anyone who read Sir Richard Burton's *Arabian Nights* knew there was nothing new about white women falling for black men. That set off a torrent of outrage. The *New York Times* called Wells a "slanderous and dirty-minded mulatress." Black Democrat H. C. C. Astwood, a former U.S. consul to

Santo Domingo, told the *New York Times* that Wells was a "fraud" and that no
"respectable negro" had ever been lynched. Many newspapers recycled the
New York Times story, while the *Brooklyn Daily Eagle* offered to pay Memphis
to take back Wells and shut her up. Many of Wells's friends begged her to lay off
the sexual argument, pleading that there were no hard numbers to cite and the
sexual issue poisoned any attempt to talk about lynching. In Philadelphia Wells
addressed AME ministers that disliked her lynching fixation with or without the
sexual argument. Wells, incredulous at hearing AME ministers debate whether
they wanted to endorse her, told them she was accustomed to better treatment:
"I cannot see why I need your endorsement. Under God I have done work
without any assistance from my own people. And when I think that I have been
able to do the work with his assistance that you could not do, if you would, and
you would not do if you could, I think I have a right to a feeling of strong indignation. I feel very deeply the insult you have offered and I have the honor to
wish you a very good morning."[148]

Turner was the outstanding exception for Wells among AME clergy, lauding
her for standing up for the race in lonely bravery. Ransom soon became another
exception. Wells spoke across the country in 1894, addressing northern and
border state audiences in Pittsburgh, Cleveland, Chicago, St. Louis, Denver,
Topeka, the West Coast, and elsewhere. In Chicago she launched a strong anti-
lynching organization led by Barnett, black dentist Charles E. Bentley, and
white Socialist clubwoman J. C. Plummer. Elsewhere she launched weaker
organizations that were short on money and leaders. The crowds that Wells
addressed were small and often negative compared to the treatment she had
received in two British tours, to her disappointment. Then Willard surprised
her by going on the offensive.

Willard pretended there had never been any question about her opposition
to lynching. This was a Wells fabrication. As for the sexual issue, Willard had
something new to say: The alarm about black rapists was legitimate, not something cooked up by white racists. To be sure, Willard acknowledged, the
problem of predatory male sexuality cut both ways between the races. During
slavery, white men were guilty of gross immorality with black women, which
was a source of "intolerable race prejudice and hatred" in American society.
But Willard pressed for a key distinction in this area. White men and black
women had "relations" during slavery that did not amount to rape; after slavery
ended, rape became very much an issue between black men and white women.
Willard said it as plainly as possible. Black women of the past had "relations"
and white women of the present were raped. As for black women of the present,
Willard reasoned that they carried emotional scars from a slave experience that

no longer existed. Willard aimed this breathtakingly condescending contention straight at Wells: "The zeal for her race of Miss Ida B. Wells, a bright young colored woman has, it seems to me, clouded her perception as to who were her friends and well-wishers in all high-minded legitimate efforts to banish the abomination of lynching and torture. It is my firm belief that in the statements made by Miss Wells concerning white women having taken an initiative in nameless acts between the races, she has put an imputation upon half the white race in this country that is unjust, and save in the rarest exceptional instances, wholly without foundation." Every expert on this issue agreed with her, Willard claimed. Wells was not rational and she lacked any authority on her hobbyhorse subject.[149]

Wells was stunned by this attack and thrown off-balance by it. She protested that Willard distorted the facts to shore up her southern support, but Wells left it there at mere assertion, failing to make a case. It wounded her that two Afro-American WCTU members from Michigan ceremoniously presented Willard with a bouquet of flowers at the convention, a scene played up by the press coverage. Ransom, perceiving that Wells was hurting, invited her to his congregation, St. John Church in Cleveland, where he bucked her up with a fiery speech and she urged a large audience to form an anti-lynching committee. Ransom had recently tried to persuade Cleveland's city council to enact an anti-lynching resolution. He concurred with the *Cleveland Gazette* that the picture of two African American women showering Willard with flowers played a role in defeating his efforts. Addressing his home church members and many guests, Ransom urged them to side with Wells, justice, and their own dignity. Years later he recalled that Wells met "cold, or indifferent support in most of the Negro Churches of America" as she campaigned against lynching: "She had small response to awaken and organize our people."[150]

For Ransom, Wells was the pioneer of the new abolitionist Christianity that was needed. He got his bearings in social justice politics by throwing himself into the anti-lynching movement. Wells appreciated Ransom's support, but he was a young pastor just beginning to make a mark. Her mainstays of support were Fortune, Turner, Tourgée, Barnett, Ruffin, and Douglass. Tourgée and Douglass were especially important to Wells because they had large audiences that respected them immensely—the very audiences she sought to reach. In November 1894 Wells saw Douglass for the last time. Douglass had gone back to treating her in a fatherly way, and Wells was grateful for it, although not without an edge. Speaking together at a meeting in Providence, Rhode Island, Douglass gently asked Wells if she got nervous before addressing such a large crowd. He admitted that he still got nervous after fifty years of doing it. She replied: "That is because you are an orator, Mr. Douglass, and naturally you are concerned as to the presentation of your address. With me it is different. I am only a mouth-piece through which to tell the story of lynching and I have told it so often that I know it by heart. I do not have to embellish; it makes its own way."[151]

Two months later Douglass died of a heart attack and was buried in Rochester, New York. Wells was in Kansas City, where the news about Douglass crushed her. Many asked her for a tribute or memoir. Wells picked up her pen several times, tried to write something, and could not do it, overwhelmed by her feel-ings. Later she told the Indianapolis *Freeman* that hearing of Douglass's death was the saddest thing she had heard since being told she was an orphan. Wells soldiered on for several months, ending up in San Francisco, where a throng of ministers fought over what they should do about lynching. Charles O. Brown, a Congregational social gospel minister, saved the day by pushing through an anti-lynching resolution. By then Wells was physically and emotionally depleted, plus bankrupt. She told herself she had done "all that one human being could do" to stop the lynching mania: "It seemed to me that I had done my duty." In that state of mind she made a decision. Barnett had proposed to her just before her second trip to England, and Wells had put off several wedding dates. Now she returned to Chicago "to accept the offer of a home of my own."[152]

Barnett was ten years older than Wells, a widower, and a graduate of Chicago College of Law (later Northwestern University). He did not belong to Chicago's Blue Book social register, but had wealthy friends who did, notably Daniel Hale Williams, founder of the upscale Prudence Crandall Club, and S. Laing Williams, Barnett's law partner. Barnett's previous wife, Mary H. Graham, with whom he had two children, was cultivated, kindly, and socially graceful. For many years Wells had to put up with rueful comments by Chicago insiders that Wells was nothing like Mary Graham—a wounding exaggeration, since, as Giddings notes, both were highly intelligent. Barnett was attracted to highly capable women, and he was sufficiently romantic to make sure that Wells got a letter from him at every stop on her U.S. tour. Yet she was a dour bride in June 1895, the same year that Booker Washington soared to preeminence. Wells was frustrated, uneasy, and dejected. She yearned to lead a national civil rights orga-nization and felt no yearning to be a mother, yet here she was, heading down the aisle at Bethel Church. Years later she reflected that her early entrance into public agitation probably "had something to do with smothering the mother instinct." As it was, heading down the aisle, she had no intention of pulling back from her public career: "Having always been busy at some work of my own, I decided to continue work as a journalist, for this was my first, and might be said, my only love."[153]

For a while she took over the *Conservator*, served as president of the Ida B. Wells Club, and returned to the lecture circuit, taking her baby and a nurse on the road. Her first child, Charles Aked Barnett, was born exactly nine months after her wedding; Wells-Barnett boasted that she was surely the first woman to travel across the United States making political speeches accompanied by a nursing baby. In 1896 she played a role in founding the National Association of Colored Women, but it was not the organization that Wells-Barnett wanted, and she was slow to absorb that the group's president, Molly Terrell, was determined to marginalize her.

THE NATIONAL ASSOCIATION OF COLORED WOMEN AND THE AFRO-AMERICAN COUNCIL

By the mid-1890s there were many black women's organizations. Jefferson City, Missouri, had a Harper's Woman's Club, organized in 1893; Pittsburgh had a Belle Phoebe League, organized in 1894; New Orleans had a Phillis Wheatley Club, organized in 1894; Knoxville, Tennessee, had a Woman's Mutual Improvement Club, organized in 1894. All were modeled on the Loyal Union of Brooklyn and New York. Ruffin headed the Woman's Era Club of Boston, which in 1894 called for a convention to unify the local clubs into a national organization. James W. Jacks, president of the Missouri Press Association, inadvertently galvanized the local clubs by trying to deflate Wells-Barnett's reputation in England. In a public letter to London feminist and racial justice activist Florence Balgarnie, Jacks tried to "educate" Balgarnie about black Americans, explaining that he lived near lots of them: "The Negroes of this country are wholly devoid of morality, the women are prostitutes and are natural thieves and liars." Jacks had an estimate about how many black American women had no morality: "Out of 200 in this vicinity it is doubtful there are a dozen virtuous women of that number who are not daily thieving from the white people."[154]

Reading Jacks's letter, Ruffin and other African American women organized protest meetings; then Ruffin capitalized on the furor by convening a national conference in July 1895. Approximately one hundred delegates representing twenty clubs from ten states came to Boston to found the National Federation of Afro-American Women. Ruffin told the delegates that white southern women routinely excluded Afro-Americans from women's organizations because of the supposed "immorality of our women." Black women were overdue to form a national organization that confuted this misrepresentation, she urged. Ruffin overlooked, however, that a club organization not represented at the Boston meeting— Molly Terrell's Colored Woman's League of Washington, DC—already claimed to be a national organization. Terrell's group, founded in 1892, offered night-school courses on literature and languages and established a kindergarten for the children of working parents. Hard things were said about presumption and exclusion, until the two organizations agreed to merge as the National Association of Colored Women. Terrell was elected president of the NACW at its founding convention in 1896 in Washington, DC. Ruffin, Margaret Murray Washington (Booker T.'s spouse), Lucy Thurman, and Victoria Matthews were elected to leadership positions. All were genteel reformers predisposed to Bookerism. Wells-Barnett represented the Ida B. Wells Club at the founding convention. From the beginning she had a strained relationship with the new organization, although it was worse than she realized.[155]

Negatively, the group's immediate objective was to confute an ugly stereotype. Positively, it was to model black female dignity and advance the cause of civil rights, on decidedly middle-class terms. The NACW's founding convention resounded with the language of Victorian true womanhood and cultivated elevation, adopting the motto "Lifting as we climb." Women's education topped the agenda, followed by industrial training, temperance, race literature, suffrage, and domestic hygiene. Wells-Barnett supported these things but inveighed against political moderation and polite society decorum, pleading for a militant national club movement. To her it was not even debatable what the movement's top priority should be: agitation against lynching. That was a minority view, however, in the NACW.

In 1897 the NACW held its convention in Nashville, which Wells-Barnett skipped, already choosing domestic projects over national meetings. Terrell declared that the organization's purpose was to "proclaim to the world that the women of our race have become partners in the firm of progress and reform." The NACW believed that skin color should not matter, but black women were assigned a "peculiar status" in American society, so they had to band together to say that race should not matter. Terrell declared that African Americans needed what other Americans needed: purified homes and free kindergartens. If a child lacked a pure home and a good kindergarten, by the time it reached the age of six "evil habits are formed that no amount of civilizing and christianizing can ever completely break." Terrell called the delegates to their homes "to implant feelings of self-respect and pride in our children" and to enhance the progress of the human race: "Let us purify the atmosphere of our homes till it becomes so sweet that those who dwell in them carry on a great work of reform. . . . Let us purify the atmosphere of our homes till it becomes so sweet that those who dwell in them will have a heritage more precious than great, more to be desired than silver or gold."[156]

Terrell was pregnant at the time, hoping for a healthy baby, having lost two already. But her third baby died too and she adopted the NACW as her child, saying so explicitly. Her stately eloquence and refined bearing defined the group's public identity. Terrell presided over national conventions in Nashville, Chicago (1899), and Buffalo (1901). The NACW's constitution forbade an officer from serving more than two consecutive terms, but the delegates at Chicago voted to give her an additional term, after which she was voted honorary president for life at Buffalo. The Chicago convention was the NACW's big, splashy high-water mark, widely covered by an admiring press. According to Terrell, she bowed reluctantly to an overwhelming demand that she serve a third term. In truth, her operatives fought for a third term and excluded Wells-Barnett from the proceedings. Wells-Barnett asked Terrell how the organization could possibly exclude the founder of the Ida B. Wells Club. Terrell replied that many members were unwilling to participate if Wells-Barnett played an active role in the convention. The women of Chicago were especially insistent on this point. Wells-Barnett realized belatedly that Terrell had undercut her from the beginning. When Terrell subsequently told the story of the club women's movement, she managed not to mention Wells-Barnett's name.[157]

Terrell did not exaggerate, however, Wells-Barnett's difficulties working with others, especially professional-class women, and Terrell and the NACW went on to play important roles in civil rights activism. Wells-Barnett got along better with supportive males who respected her, such as Trotter and John Milholland, than she did with female peers. Her militant politics and loner-hero style did not wear well in the club movement, even as she stuck with the NACW and offered herself as a candidate for leadership positions. As a loner-hero, she could be admired; as a member of NACW, she had a reputation for taking her marbles and going home, which caused others not to vote for her, even as Terrell and the NACW became increasingly political, adopting the civil rights agendas of the National Afro-American Council and the NAACP.[158]

Wells-Barnett had a similar experience with the National Afro-American Council, though at least she held leadership positions in it before resigning in protest. This group had a backstory in the abolitionist conventions of the 1830s and Fortune's call for a national civil rights organization in 1884. The convention movement began in Philadelphia in 1830; it declaimed against slavery through the Civil War; and it still existed in the 1880s, offering speeches and proclamations concerning civil rights. In 1884 Fortune proposed that a new model was needed—a permanent organization based on local and state branches that met annually in a national convention. Speeches and proclamations were not enough, he contended. America needed an activist-oriented

"Afro-American National League" that Fortune modeled on the Irish National League. He urged: "Let us agitate! *agitate!* AGITATE! until the protest shall wake the nation from its indifference." Elsewhere he admonished: "You must fight your own battles. You must come together."[159]

Ida Wells, in her *Free Speech* period, lauded this idea as "the grandest ever originated by colored men." Mitchell organized the first local branch in 1887 (in Richmond, Virginia), and in January 1890 Fortune founded the first national black organization specifically created to challenge racial segregation, the National Afro-American League. Fortune was a race man, putting race above party or anything else. He conceived the league as a transparty successor to the abolitionist movement, an all-black organization devoted to black self-protection, at least in the North. The league did not directly challenge southern de jure segregation; instead it aimed for winnable victories against de facto discrimination in the North. The organization's high point occurred in New York State Supreme Court, where Fortune prevailed against a New York City bar (the Trainer Hotel) for refusing to serve him. For the rest of the organization's brief and depressing run, Fortune begged for financial support that never materialized. "Talk is cheap and law is expensive," he admonished. "We the race, do a great deal of unnecessary and profitless talk. The League is out to succeed. It requires the brains and the energies of the entire race."[160]

But the league did not succeed. It held a second national meeting in Knoxville, Tennessee, in 1891, and no more. In 1893 Fortune announced the group's death, leaving local chapters to fend for themselves. He had second thoughts after Wells became a sensation, briefly reviving the league, but he shut it down for good in 1894. Prominent black Republicans such as Douglass, Bruce, and John Mercer Langston never joined the league, mainly because it was not explicitly Republican and they had no interest in playing second fiddle to Fortune. The black professionals that joined did not respond to Fortune's pleas for money. Above all, Fortune's attempts to attract the masses through his newspaper failed utterly. All of this weighed heavily upon Fortune when Alexander Walters asked him in 1898 to revive the league.

The spark was the murder of a black postmaster, Frazier Baker. A white mob in Lake City, South Carolina, outraged at Baker's appointment as postmaster, responded by setting fire to his house and shooting at members of his family as they exited the house. Frazier and his infant son were killed. Walters, outraged at the Lake City lynching, told Fortune they had to try again, resurrecting the Afro-American League. Fortune replied that nothing had changed since they failed previously; a resurrected league would fail for the same reasons. Walters persisted. Fortune refused to write a call until Walters rounded up 100 supporters;

Walters came up with 115, and Fortune called for a gathering in Rochester, New York, to dedicate a statue of Douglass and resuscitate the league. Instead the group founded a new organization with almost the same name, the National Afro-American Council.[161]

For a moment Wells-Barnett hoped to have a renewed partnership with Fortune in building a national civil rights organization devoted to agitation on lynching, segregation, and disenfranchisement. She was outraged by *Plessy v. Ferguson*, which cited her lost appeal in Tennessee as a precedent for its decision to scuttle the equal protection clause of the Fourteenth Amendment. "Separate but equal" segregation, imposed by state power, was now officially what the Constitution sanctioned. Wells-Barnett wrote a "thanks for trying" letter to Tourgée for arguing the *Plessy* case, and vowed to build up the Afro-American Council. It appalled her that the *Plessy* decision stirred little immediate reaction in black communities, North and South, and that the cause of abolishing lynching had no organization—until, she hoped, now.

But Fortune had begun to unravel personally. He despaired at the state of black America, insisting that the new group would be no better than the old one. He behaved erratically at the founding meeting of the Afro-American Council, prompting Wells-Barnett to call for his removal as president, in favor of Walters. Fortune was spiraling into depression; later he self-medicated with alcohol. He agreed to chair the group's executive committee, while Walters took over as president. Walters tried gamely to build a strong civil rights organization that kept its pro-Booker and anti-Booker factions on board. He spoke as a forceful critic of lynching and segregation but ran the council with an ecumenical hand, encouraging Washington's operatives and Washington himself to play active roles in the organization. Walters supported Wells-Barnett, who became director of the council's Anti-Lynching Bureau, and he worked hard to establish an antidiscriminatory legal operation, though it won zero victories in the organization's first five years of existence. Walters reasoned that there should be room in a national civil rights organization for straightforward northern civil rights types and for the wily, accommodating strategy that Washington practiced in the South. In the early going, it helped that Washington was always willing to operate behind the curtain, sometimes in ways that conflicted with his public image.

The Afro-American Council, however, was founded just before anti-Washington sentiment began to heat up in the northern black press. From the beginning the group had bruising internal debates over Bookerism that soon flared into public view with the rise of Du Bois. A year before Du Bois published *The Souls of Black Folk*, Washington crossed a fateful line, partly as a consequence of having made a very public alliance with President Theodore Roosevelt. It was no longer enough to merely dominate black opinion; now Washington had to control it. He started with black newspapers and the Afro-American Council, in the former case buying influence, in the latter case using proxies with his customary cunning and secrecy. Having forged a close friendship and alliance with Fortune, Washington co-opted the council in 1902 by getting his followers to replace Walters with Fortune as the group's president. It was not really clear that Fortune had changed his politics or that he would be a mere proxy for Washington. Neither was it clear, in 1902, that Washington had enough leverage in the council to dominate Walters, William Pledger, Frederick McGhee, Nelson Crews, and other council heavyweights. To Wells-Barnett, however, it was terribly obvious that Washington and Fortune conspired to ruin the organization. She angrily resigned from the council, giving up the organizational vehicle that had put her back on the anti-lynching lecture circuit. Her successors as director of the council's Anti-Lynching Bureau were Mitchell and Terrell.[162]

Both of the organizations in which Wells-Barnett had vested her hope lapsed into outlets of a triumphant Bookerism. This was a grim picture. It was hard to justify exhausting yourself with a child in tow when hardly anyone was in a fighting mood. Wells-Barnett naturally had trouble accepting the rise of Terrell, who was skilled at organizational politics. Terrell considered herself a pragmatist and social-welfare progressive, emphasizing the power of human will to reform society. To Wells-Barnett, these terms were highfalutin covers for "Booker opportunism." She fretted about letting down the militants that expected her to keep alive the flame of resistance. In September 1897, when Wells-Barnett skipped the NACW convention in Nashville, she did so to pursue a cause that she shared with Terrell and the NACW: kindergarten. At the time, Wells-Barnett was seven months pregnant with her second child. Chicago did not have an all-black kindergarten, and Bethel Church did not want to establish one. Bethel Church, however, had a new pastor—Ransom, who teamed with Wells-Barnett to create one. Shortly after Chicago's first black kindergarten opened in November, Wells-Barnett gave birth to her second child, Herman. Dramatically, she announced that she was withdrawing from public life, content to stay at home with her children and a newfound mothering impulse. She was finished with writing, speaking, organizing, and agitating.[163]

That is not what happened, as Wells-Barnett gave four years to the Afro-American Council, she remained loyal to the club movement, and there were always new outrages to write about. There was also the disappointment of friends to negotiate. A new friend, feminist icon Susan B. Anthony, was exacting on this subject, just as Anthony had been with Elizabeth Cady-Stanton twenty-five years earlier. Anthony admonished Wells-Barnett that lots of women could be mothers but hardly any women had her chance to change the world. She pressed the point personally: "I too might have married but it would have meant dropping the work to which I had set my hand. I know of no one in all this country better fitted to do the work you had in hand than yourself. Since you have gotten married, agitation seems practically to have ceased." Wells-Barnett took this "well-merited rebuke" to heart. She respected Anthony and partly agreed with her. She did not say, in Anthony's presence, how their situations differed, for fear of offending Anthony. Anthony was a white woman who found financial and institutional support for her work. Wells-Barnett was a lonely black woman forced to carry on by herself, which exhausted and derailed her.[164]

She did what she could in the years that followed, lending her name to worthy efforts that came along, writing about new outrages, working with Trotter and Marcus Garvey, and supporting A. Philip Randolph's Brotherhood of Sleeping Car Porters and Maids, while raising four children. Always she yearned for the civil rights organization that would fight tenaciously and effectively against lynching, segregation, and disenfranchisement. When it finally came along, Wells-Barnett briefly tried to belong to it. But she did not like Du Bois, who epitomized intellectual arrogance and elitism to her. She did not like NAACP ringleader Mary White Ovington, who looked out for Du Bois. Above all, Wells-Barnett burned at the memory that nearly every black male she knew had abandoned her when her moment came. Otherwise she might have played the historic role that was offered to Du Bois.

As it was, the movement that she helped to inspire played down her contribution, such that she was forgotten before she was gone in 1931. Du Bois, Washington, Terrell, Willard, Carter Woodson, Jane Addams, and other luminaries wrote accounts of the time that never mentioned her. Even books about lynching, such as Walter White's *Rope and Faggot*, did not mention her. Wells-Barnett, noticing the trend at the end of her life, wrote an autobiography to fill the void—which went unpublished for forty years. But her fourth child, Alfreda M. Duster, did not let that injustice endure. Thanks to Duster, Angela Davis, and the feminist and Black Power movements of the 1960s, *Crusade for Justice: The Autobiography of Ida B. Wells* was belatedly published in 1970, rescuing Wells-Barnett for memory and the canon. Paula Giddings, in her landmark book *When and Where I Enter* (1984), lifted Wells-Barnett into the canon, eliciting incredulity from later generations that she had ever been forgotten.[165]

3

THE CRUCIBLE: DU BOIS
VERSUS WASHINGTON

A black tradition of the social gospel would have emerged had W. E. B. Du Bois never existed. It was already coming when he burst onto the scene and changed the conversation. Had Du Bois not come along, the anti–Booker Washington party would have found another leading light, the Afro-American Council would have fought over Bookerism, the Great Migration would have raised the same issues for black churches, and Reverdy Ransom, Ida Wells-Barnett, Alexander Walters, Adam Clayton Powell Sr., Nannie H. Burroughs, and Richard R. Wright Jr. would have had something like the careers they had. Even the Socialist option that Du Bois eventually took would have had black social gospel advocates without him, notably Ransom, George Washington Woodbey, and Robert Bagnall.

But Du Bois versus Washington defined the politics of the color line for the generation that launched the NAACP. It framed the debate over the future of black Americans, even for ministers who refused to choose between Du Bois and Washington. And it produced the breakthrough genius of the civil rights movement.

Long after Du Bois routed Washington in this debate and Washington passed on, Washington remained highly respected across racial lines and notably in black churches. It was not until the 1960s that it became hard to remember why Washington had been revered. In his heyday Washington's nickname, the "Wizard of Tuskegee," conveyed irony to much of the nation only because it described a black man. It acquired further irony as he began to totter. His accomplishments were colossal, and he achieved them in the face of a viciously oppressive society that erupted over any violation of Jim Crow. But Washington believed that he had no legitimate opposition, which contributed much to his downfall—nearly as much as the fact that his humiliating strategy did not work.

BECOMING BOOKER T. WASHINGTON

He was born a slave in 1856 on a two-hundred-acre tobacco farm near the village of Hale's Ford in Franklin County, Virginia. In 1901, near the zenith of his power, Washington reflected that he knew "almost nothing" of his ancestry: he did not know his birthday, and he knew nothing of his father except for a rumor that he was a white man from a nearby plantation. Washington had light brown skin, luminous gray eyes that evoked compliments throughout his life, and red-brown hair. At the age of five he was valued at four hundred dollars by his owner, James Burroughs, whose inventory for that year listed ten slaves. Washington's mother, Jane, a plantation cook, told him that he and his older brother, John, had different fathers; later there was a sister, Amanda. Washington's father probably belonged to the Ferguson farm family nearby, which had several biracial children by slave women; other possibilities were that he belonged to the Burroughs and Hatcher families. Washington later recalled that his family never ate a meal together and that he acquired his first pair of shoes at the age of eight. His single garment was a coarse flax shirt, which his brother generously wore for him long enough to break down the harsh fibers. During slavery Washington got his meals "very much as dumb animals get theirs," devouring scraps of meat and bread that fell his way from the kitchen fire, the Burroughs family leftovers, or the livestock.[1]

Since Washington grew up on a small, close-knit farming enterprise in which master and slave worked side by side, and since he grew up playing with the Burroughs children, it is probably true, as he claimed, that his owner was less harsh than many others. His brother, John, whose memories of their slave years were stronger and more detailed, confirmed Washington's account in this area, noting that a nearby master, Josiah Ferguson, whipped his slaves repeatedly. On the other hand, Washington routinely played down how bad things were or had ever been, and on the lecture circuit he had a tendency to attribute his older brother's experiences to himself. When Washington told his story in *Up from Slavery*, he mentioned no beatings and stressed that most slaves were personally devoted to their masters. When he told his story to a black audience in *The Story of My Life and Work*, he disclosed a bit more, observing that Burroughs "cruelly whipped" his slaves in only "a few cases." On one occasion Washington saw his uncle Monroe Burroughs tied to a tree, stripped naked, and beaten with a leather whip. With each blow his uncle cried out, "Pray, master!

Pray, master!" Washington, as usual, said nothing about his feelings, except that this incident made an impression on his heart "that I shall carry with me to my grave.[2]

Franklin County was Unionist but not antislavery, generally voting for the Whigs. In the Virginia slavery debate of 1832 it opposed abolishing slavery. At the Virginia secession convention in 1861 it voted to stay in the Union. When war came, the Franklin County hill farmers were less committed to it than were farmers in the Confederate lowland areas where the war was fought. Hale's Ford was rural and centered socially at the local post office. Burroughs got his mail by sending a slave to the post office several miles away. His slaves got their news about the war from the mail carrier, who discreetly listened to whites read their letters and newspapers to each other. Washington got additional news by over-hearing his masters during mealtimes at the Big House, where he fanned flies from the table. In his telling, he never knew a slave that did not yearn to be free, and he knew hardly any that held any bitterness toward whites. The slaves, owing to their "kindly and generous nature," poured out "tenderness and sympathy" for their masters, nursing them in illness, tending to their feelings, doting on their children, and wishing them well in all things. After they were liberated, the emancipated slaves felt sympathy for their former owners, who were left with no skills or slaves. At least America's enslaved population knew how to grow things and build things, Washington explained: "Notwithstanding the cruel wrongs inflicted upon us, the black man got nearly as much out of slavery as the white man did."[3]

Up from Slavery, despite its title, was not really a slave narrative. It was a look-on-the-bright-side story about living into U.S. American freedom, where even slavery folded into a progress narrative about black and white Americans flourishing together. American blacks, Washington insisted, came out of slavery stronger and with more opportunities than any group of black people anywhere in the world. Therefore it was pointless for African Americans to dwell on the horrors of slavery. There was a huge upside to be counted and what mattered was to move up.

Washington said it emphatically and reassuringly throughout his career: Most U.S. American slaves empathized with their owners during and after slavery; many were spared from cruel mistreatment; most were not bitter toward white America; nearly all wanted to help build a stronger America; and slavery opened the door of opportunity for latter-day African Americans. Washington indulged the moral pride of white southerners, mindful of "Lost Cause" mythology, especially its insistence that racial hostility became an issue only after the war: "Deep down in their hearts there was a strange and peculiar attachment to 'old Marster' and 'old Missus,' and to their children, which they found it hard to think of breaking off." In his telling, he found his way to a similarly magnanimous place. For a time, Washington suggested, he resented southern slaveholders, but he let go of resentment after realizing that bad systems made people do bad things and that people of noble spirit did not bear grudges. Even his father, a planter in Virginia Piedmont, was not to be faulted: "He was simply another unfortunate victim of the institution which the Nation unhappily had engrafted upon it at that time." As an institution, Washington assured, slavery was abhorrent; it was established "for selfish and financial reasons, and not from a missionary motive." There was no denying that he grew up "in the midst of the most miserable, desolate and discouraging surroundings." But divine Providence used human beings and institutions to accomplish God's saving purpose. So it was even with slavery.[4]

Washington Ferguson, a freedman, was the father of Washington's younger sister, Amanda. He followed the Union Army during the war and eventually settled in Malden, West Virginia, to work in the salt mines. In 1865, after the war ended, Washington's mother took her family to Malden and married Ferguson. Nine-year-old Booker pleaded that he wanted to go to school. Ferguson did not care what Jane's middle child wanted; to Ferguson, school was pointless and Booker needed to earn his keep. He sent John and Booker to work in the salt furnaces and coal mines, where the darkness and danger terrified Washington and the hard labor wore him down. Workdays began at 4:00 A.M. and continued until dark. Ferguson pocketed the pay for the two brothers, who resented their stepfather. Yet Washington clawed his way to an education through sheer determination not to be denied one. The number 8, marked on Ferguson's barrels, was the first thing he learned to read. His mother came up with a spelling book, through which Washington taught himself the alphabet. Later he seized an opportunity to attend night school, despite Ferguson's opposition; Jane eventually persuaded her husband to let Booker attend school between two daily shifts in the mines. At school, when asked for his surname, Booker named himself Washington; later, upon discovering that his mother considered "Taliaferro" to be his surname, he added it as a middle name. One day he overheard two men talking about a new school to educate freedmen, the Hampton Normal and Agricultural Institute in Hampton, Virginia. Washington later recalled, "Not even Heaven presented more attractions for me at that time." He resolved to somehow get himself to Hampton Institute.[5]

Meanwhile he caught a break and witnessed a fateful assault, both involving the family of Louis and Viola Ruffner. Louis Ruffner's family was of German-Swiss origin and had moved into the Shenandoah Valley in the eighteenth century. He owned the local salt furnaces and had taken a complicated path to the Republican Party, having belonged to the American Colonization Society and, as late as 1860, having owned twenty-six slaves. Ruffner opposed Virginia secession, however; he helped to found the new state of West Virginia, where he joined the Republican Party, and he served in the Union Army as a major general. A widower with a large family by his first wife, Ruffner married the governess of his younger children, Viola Knapp, over the protests of his older children, who never accepted wife number two. Viola Ruffner was introverted, intellectual, and cultivated, of New England Puritan bearing, twenty years younger than her husband. She fired a succession of houseboys who failed to meet her exacting demands, until she hired Washington. Between this lonely woman, who had taught English in Vermont, and her new servant, a friendship developed. Viola drilled Booker on grammar, speech, and housecleaning, and grew fond of him. She stressed that education was the key to achieving self-reliance and that he should work hard. Washington knew about working hard and he knew plenty of ex-slaves who were desperate to become literate. From Viola Ruffner he learned that disciplined hard work was virtuous, it enabled one to be independent, cleanliness was godly, and this combination won the approval of certain high-status white people.[6]

In 1869 a payday fight between two miners in Malden escalated into a racial conflagration. Malden was a border community that touted its biracial identity, but it had over two hundred local night riders calling themselves Gideon's Band or the Ku Klux Klan. A fight broke out between a group of African Americans and the Gideons, with gunfire on both sides. General Ruffner, the town's leading Republican, intervened to hold off the Gideons and was struck in the head with a brick. Washington stood nearby as Ruffner fell unconscious to the ground. Ruffner lay for days in critical condition and never completely recovered. Meanwhile, no attacker was charged or paid any consequence, and the Klan tried to terrorize all African Americans into leaving Malden. One Klan member put the group's agenda succinctly: "To clean out and finish up the niggers." Washington learned a chilling lesson: Anyone who stood up for blacks, even a prominent white employer, could be struck down with no consequence. For a while he despaired that it was hopeless for blacks in America; white southerners would never let them succeed at anything. But Washington took refuge in the African Zion Baptist Church, affiliated with the Providence Baptist Association of Ohio. He got involved in Republican politics, following the lead of his schoolteacher William Davis, his pastor Lewis Rice, and Ruffner. Above all, he held the dream of Hampton in his head, an antidote to despair. By the time that he got there, Washington was predisposed to Hampton founder

Samuel Chapman Armstrong's message of deliverance: Work hard, follow Jesus, get an education, learn a trade, keep your head down, and avoid politics.[7]

During the Civil War, runaway slaves had congregated in Hampton, Virginia, seeking the protection of the occupying Union Army at Fortress Monroe. Armstrong, a young Union Army general, had commanded black troops in Virginia. In 1866 he took charge of ten thousand former slaves at the Hampton site. Later, Armstrong directed the Freedmen's Bureau in eastern Virginia, through which he assigned the Hampton group to himself. It helped that Armstrong had a merchant friend in New York, Robert Curtis Ogden, who had connections with wealthy philanthropists, and that Armstrong knew about the American Missionary Association, as his father had been a Presbyterian missionary in Hawaii. Enlisting help from these sources, Armstrong founded the Hampton Institute in 1868 as an AMA teacher-training school. By then he believed that Reconstruction mistakenly lifted politics above education and assimilation; Hampton Institute was his response to the postwar story of his time.

The AMA, committed to educating and "civilizing" formerly enslaved people, created eight schools in the South for this purpose. Under Armstrong's direction, Hampton became a model AMA institution, combining military discipline, pious nurture, academics, and training in agriculture, carpentry, sewing, printing, and shoemaking, plus a strong emphasis on personal hygiene and grooming. Armstrong spurned Latin and ancient civilizations, judging that much of the classical curriculum was useless. Academically, Hampton concentrated on English, mathematics, history, and biology. It emphasized grammar and rhetoric, teaching that mastery of language was the mark of an educated person. It placed equal emphasis on American, English, and world history, teaching modern history as a progress narrative about the advance of Anglo-Saxon civilization. According to Armstrong, abolitionism and anti-imperialism went hand in hand with the progress of liberal, enlightened, Anglo-Saxon Christianity, although he played down the Civil War and his role in it. Crowing about the Confederacy would not be constructive. He told students that slavery had taught them to be wasteful, dependent, unreliable, and dissembling, but he would teach them to be productive, independent, self-reliant, and morally virtuous, moving into a better future. Armstrong was fond of pithy admonitions, such as, "Be thrifty and industrious," "Make the best of your difficulties," "Live down prejudice," "Cultivate peaceful relations with all," and "Vote as you think, not as you are told."[8]

Washington got there in 1872, after five hundred miles of walking and begging rides. The school's three-story brick building seemed like a palace to him, "the largest and most beautiful building I had ever seen." It sat on 159 acres of campus, ample for marching and expanding. Washington, soiled and bedraggled from travel, won over a skeptical principal, Mary Mackie, by thoroughly cleaning a recitation room. Like Viola Ruffner, Mackie was a devotee of starched, Protestant, New England work-ethic righteousness. Washington recognized the social type and exulted at passing his admissions test, joining the school's 243 students; 89 were female. The school was sufficiently overcrowded that Washington volunteered to sleep in a tent with other hardy types, braving the cold in winter. While most Hampton students worked at the institute's farm, he worked as a janitor in the academic building—a variation on the Big House during slavery—where he cultivated relationships with white teachers and administrators, especially Armstrong.[9]

For the rest of his life Washington revered Armstrong as the most generous, selfless, admirable, perfect human being he ever met. For Washington, idolizing Armstrong went hand in hand with embracing Hampton's regime of piety, learning, and vocational training; later it helped him befriend Armstrong's network of benefactors. Washington thrived and excelled at Hampton, training for a career as a teacher. He loved his teachers, especially Nathalie Lord, a Vassar graduate from Maine, who taught English composition and public speaking. Every weekday at noontime she joined Washington and two classmates in Bible study. Sometimes he took her rowing on Hampton Creek.

Washington marveled at the goodwill of his teachers. Years later he had no truck with white southern ridicule of the northern schoolmarms that came to teach former slaves. At Hampton he was enthralled to learn about Frederick Douglass and Blanche Bruce. As far as Washington knew, and was told, African Americans had no history until the African American abolitionists came along. On first impression, Washington judged that Armstrong was the best of the Yankee do-gooders—"that Christlike body of men and women who went into the Negro schools at the close of the war by the hundreds to assist in lifting up my race." Later he realized that Armstrong loved all downtrodden people, not just former slaves. Still later, upon realizing that Armstrong cherished his friendships with white southerners and felt no bitterness toward the South, Washington decided that his hero was simply a saint, one to be emulated. For the rest of his life, whenever Washington expounded on what a noble spirit looked like, which was often, he held Armstrong in mind. Always he described Armstrong as the epitome of goodness, never suggesting that Armstrong's blatant paternalism might be some kind of racism.[10]

Academically, Hampton was a high school, though Washington insisted for the rest of his life that Hampton gave him a better education than he could have attained at Harvard or Yale. Graduating in 1875, Washington took part in a commencement debate, contending that the United States should not annex Cuba even if Cuba broke free of Spain. The United States was already awash with ignorance and the ravages of a war, he urged; flooding the country with ignorant Catholics would make everything worse. After commencement he dutifully went home to Malden to teach black children, even though Malden was not really home to him anymore, as his mother had died the previous summer. Washington resisted the lure of a career in law or politics, reasoning that Armstrong was right: Education was the greatest need.

He worked hard and quietly, operating in a Klan stronghold, teaching ninety students per day and ninety more per evening, and sending his best students, plus his brother John and adopted brother James, to Hampton. He had mixed feelings about the passing of Reconstruction, judging that it should have imposed on both races the literacy and/or property requirements for wielding the vote. After teaching for two years, Washington felt some attraction to the ministry, despite believing that most black ministers were vain and shallow. The ministry attracted people for whom ministry looked easy, he judged. Washington studied briefly at Wayland (Baptist) Seminary in Washington, DC, but he chafed at the irrelevance of seminary education. At Hampton, students learned about things that mattered, plus how to make things, plus how to behave. At Wayland, in his telling, they learned a smattering of Greek and were not very disciplined or morally serious. The seminary's location in the nation's capital didn't help, as Washington judged that city life in general was corrupting, and Washington, DC, was especially so. Leaving seminary, Washington returned to Malden in 1879, just before Armstrong invited him to join the staff at Hampton.[11]

Armstrong decided that Hampton needed some African American teachers. Washington was thrilled to be asked, taking charge of a night school for black students who were too poor to attend the day school. Armstrong, however, had already expanded Hampton's mission by enrolling Native Americans. In its first ten years, Hampton's student body had been entirely Afro-American, except for one white student who entered in 1876. In April 1878 Hampton admitted its first Native American students—seventeen young Kiowa and Cheyenne warriors captured as federal prisoners of war. Armstrong felt compelled to assimilate them into white American society in the same way that Hampton assimilated former slaves. He built a three-story dormitory, inevitably named "the Wigwam," admitting forty-nine additional Native Americans in the fall of 1878, this time from western reservations, including nine girls. In 1880 Armstrong asked Washington to run the program; he balked inwardly. Washington later recalled that his assignment was to supervise "over one hundred wild and for the most part perfectly ignorant Indians." The pertinent variables, he surmised, were that Native Americans took for granted their superiority over white Americans, they had their own history of taking slaves, they considered themselves far superior to black Americans, and they denigrated blacks for submitting to slavery. But saying no to his idol was out of the question, and Washington surprised himself by managing reasonably well. He taught English, science, and geography, telling his students they belonged to one of humankind's five races, the red one, which set off murmurs of disbelief. He let them spend Saturdays outdoors, camping on a beach, which they appreciated. He sympathized, to some degree, with the culture shock of his students, noting that they were accustomed "to the open air, the chase, the war dance, athletic sports and a free and easy life." Hampton could not cut them off too abruptly "without serious injury to their health."[12]

When Washington warmed to this subject he was capable of rueful asides about assimilation. In *Up from Slavery* he recalled that Hampton's Native Americans did not like having to give up smoking, wearing blankets, and wearing long hair. Washington winked at readers: "No white American ever thinks than any other race is wholly civilized until he wears the white man's clothes, eats the white man's food, speaks the white man's language, and professes the white man's religion." In 1881, however, writing about his experiences at the Wigwam, Washington kept his guard up, celebrating that Hampton turned "savages" into civilized Christians. Bears Heart, a Hampton graduate of 1881, was an army prisoner three years removed from the Indian Territory when he enrolled at Hampton in 1878. Washington lauded Hampton for turning Bears Heart into a model citizen: "His long hair and mocassins [*sic*] he has long since forgotten, and instead of the weak, dirty, ignorant piece of humanity that he was, with no correct ideas of this life or the next—his only ambition being to fight the white man—he goes back a strong, decent, Christian *man*, with the rudiments of an English education, and hands trained to earn himself a living at the carpenter's bench or on the farm." Washington enthused that Bears Heart might represent "the beginning of the solution of the Indian question."[13]

Then Washington's life turned a corner. In 1880 Colonel Wilbur F. Foster, a Confederate veteran and lawyer, and Arthur L. Brooks, a Democratic candidate for the Alabama State Senate, asked a black Tuskegee tinsmith, Lewis Adams, what his price would be for swaying Tuskegee's black vote to their side. Tuskegee was a low foothill town of two thousand people at the end of the Appalachian Mountains chain; Adams was the town's leading Afro-American citizen, having built a substantial business in roofing, kitchen utensils, hardware, and leather-working. He replied that he wanted the state legislature to finance a normal school (teachers college) for African Americans in Tuskegee. The following year three state commissioners led by George W. Campbell asked Armstrong if he knew of any white man who might found and run a school, as Alabama had pledged an appropriation for one. In fact, the state had pledged two thousand dollars per year for a teacher's salary only; there was no building and no promise of any other support; and the state prohibited any tuition charges. Armstrong replied that he knew a "very competent capable mulatto . . . a thorough teacher and superior man . . . the best man we ever had here." Washington arrived in Tuskegee in June 1881. He was twenty-five years old, and his relationships with supportive whites had been entirely with northerners, but Armstrong assured him that such people existed in the South, at least potentially. Washington arrived in Tuskegee confident that he would find them—an unimaginable expectation to most southern blacks.[14]

Tuskegee was a Klan stronghold before the Klan existed, having spawned a vigilante organization called the Knights of the White Carnation a few months after the Civil War ended. Its leader, Cullen Andrews Battle, a former Confederate general, led terror campaigns against blacks while serving Tuskegee in the U.S. House of Representatives. When Radical Reconstruction and the U.S. Army arrived in 1867, the Klan exploded in much of the South, terrorizing African Americans and their few white allies, torching black churches and schools, and proclaiming a white nationalist myth of victimization, racial defiance, and white supremacy. This myth was strong in Tuskegee when Washington arrived. In 1882 a popular black Republican and former slave, Jack Turner, was lynched on phony charges; his real crime was that he threatened white Democratic control of Choctaw County. Later that year an Afro-American, Leonard Coker, was lynched by a mob just north of Tuskegee for allegedly murdering a white woman. His guilt was never proved, but the *Tuskegee News* declared that lynch law existed for the likes of Coker, "a fiend in human shape."[15]

Washington realized that he had no margin for error, and he learned belatedly of his no-building, no-support, no-tuition restrictions. In addition, the state mandated that no school could be founded or sustained with less than twenty-five students, and one of the projected school's three commissioners died before Washington arrived in town. Washington began by persuading Hampton's kindly treasurer, General J. F. B. Marshall, to be his treasurer, too. Marshall launched the school with a personal check, and Washington cultivated friendships with his three commissioners: Lewis Adams, George W. Campbell (who had doubts about Washington and educating black Americans), and M. B. Swanson (a local merchant). Eventually Campbell took over the school's finances. By 1881 the economy had been mired in a recession for eight years, which convinced some white neighbors that a bit of progress by African Americans might be good for the economy. These factors were just enough to make Tuskegee Institute not completely impossible, even as newspapers and an angry white nationalist undercurrent insisted that trying to educate blacks was a waste of time and money.

Washington campaigned throughout the Alabama Black Belt, recruiting students, raising money, and nurturing relationships. He taught the school's first classes in a log cabin AME church; when it rained, a student held an umbrella over his head while he taught. He made a godsend hire in Olivia Davidson, a delicate, gifted, light-colored former slave who had fled to Ohio during the Civil War. Davidson had been a classmate of Washington's at Hampton. She studied for two years at a Massachusetts teacher college and taught at a freedmen's school in Hernando, Mississippi, where the Klan lynched her brother and sister. Boston abolitionists and Mrs. Rutherford B. Hayes sponsored her education, plus her employment at Tuskegee. To Washington she was invaluable as a principal, teacher, fund-raiser, and later, much more. In 1882 Washington married former Hampton classmate Fanny Norton Smith, with whom he had a daughter, but Fanny died in 1884. Two years later he married Davidson, with whom he had two children. In the early years, Washington delegated fund-raising in New England to Davidson, but her frail health did not permit weeks of travel, so he traveled to New England while she ran the school. By 1882 the school had its first building, named after a Brooklyn banker, Alfred Porter. By 1889 there were seven buildings and the school employed twenty-five teachers, all from Hampton Institute.[16]

From the beginning Washington proclaimed that Tuskegee stood for piety, self-reliance, and industry, and that students would build the buildings. To him it was worth putting up with an occasional leaky roof if students learned they could build a dormitory or classroom. Other black schools of higher education were built and run by whites, and some excluded women; Tuskegee was different on both counts. The building program, besides saving money, enhanced student self-esteem and fostered community. It was also a winner on the lecture circuit, as Washington enthralled his audiences by describing student-workers lovingly building their own campus. In the early years Washington relied on Armstrong's abolitionist network in New England for money, especially Congregationalists and Unitarians; two Boston sisters, Ellen and Ida Mason, contributed several thousand dollars each year for over thirty years. He also tapped into the Slater Fund, newly established by textile industrialist Samuel Slater, and nearly went bankrupt learning how to make bricks, but turned brickmaking into a profitable business.

Tuskegee Institute produced graduates that established primary schools of their own. Almost every Tuskegee graduate of the 1880s went on to organize a school in a rural area or village, usually within fifty miles of Tuskegee. From the beginning the school served as an unofficial board of education for the schools it helped to create, placing teachers and helping with finances. In the late 1880s Washington superintended Congregational schools at Society Hill, Cotton Valley, and East Tallassee, Alabama, and spawned industrial schools in Kowaliga and Snow Hill, Alabama. From the beginning, too, Washington realized that these efforts were a drop in the bucket, as African Americans desperately needed publicly supported schools. He pushed hard for public education, organizing the first statewide professional group for black teachers, and tried to win black land-grant agricultural college status for Tuskegee under the Morrill Act of 1890, although Washington lost the latter bid to a black rival, William Hooper Council (of Alabama Agricultural and Mechanical College), who shamelessly spouted white nationalist ideology. By then Tuskegee had four hundred students, nearly twice as many as the University of Alabama.[17]

Meanwhile, Washington aimed higher in fund-raising while scrambling to pay for Tuskegee's expanding campus. His first wife, Fanny, like Olivia Davidson, was frail, light-skinned, beautiful, goal-oriented, and fervently dedicated to him and his cause. Washington grieved at her death, but hustled to New England for an exhausting fund-raising tour, as Tuskegee depended on his constant fund-raising. In 1886 Washington married Davidson, who had recently recovered, it seemed, from a long-standing respiratory illness. But she died in 1889, probably from tuberculosis. Tuskegee was so dependent on Washington's fund-raising that it nearly folded during Davidson's illness and death. Grief-stricken, Washington wrote to Armstrong, although actually expressing his grief was not a possibility for him. Washington was relentless in repressing his feelings. Over the course of his career he wrote tens of thousands of letters. Not one was a love letter, and none expressed a moment of joy. Even with Armstrong, his closest friend, Washington could only refer to the possibility of describing his feelings: "Few will ever know just what she was to Tuskegee and me. But I cannot trust myself to write more now." A few months later he wrote again, now desperate. Olivia's illness and death had blown a hole in his fund-raising; the school was nearly bankrupt. Armstrong sent enough money to get Tuskegee through the fall.[18]

Olivia's death took away Washington's beloved wife, the mother to his children, the virtual cofounder of Tuskegee Institute, and his best teacher and administrator. He was crushed. Nothing could fill the void that she left in his life. Olivia was his ideal, more polished than him, and brave, with integrity; she had made her life a work of art. Washington was too practical not to replace her as soon as possible, functionally. But he lost much of his optimism upon losing her, and he never let anyone get close to him again. A month after Olivia's death, Washington met Margaret Murray at her graduation from Fisk University. Murray was the daughter of a black washerwoman and an Irish railroad worker in Mississippi. She was raised mostly by Quaker teachers; she had a strong personality; and she boldly asked Washington for a teaching job, which he granted. The following year he appointed Murray as lady principal, and in 1892 he married her. Murray lacked Olivia Davidson's literary sophistication. Her evangelical faith contrasted with Washington's cool religiosity. Before they married she confessed to him that she disliked children in general and really disliked ten-year-old Portia Washington. Murray clashed with Washington's relatives, and the marriage was lukewarm emotionally. But she was a strong partner to Washington through his glory years, taking care of him, managing his household, and helping to manage Tuskegee as he spent half of each year on the road fund-raising.[19]

In the 1880s and early 1890s Washington lectured extensively to southern black audiences about the opportunities at Tuskegee and to northern white audiences about giving money to Tuskegee. He was a brilliant speaker, using a conversational style, deadpan humor, and an arsenal of anecdotes delivered without notes. In the South he gave earnest homilies about working hard, developing good habits, mastering one's self, acquiring intellectual compe-tence, and learning a trade—variations on his Sunday evening chapel talks at Tuskegee. In the North he went door-to-door during the day, soliciting indi-vidual contributions of ten and twenty dollars. At night he gave winsome, informal speeches that worked hard at developing intimacy with his audiences. Washington was not white enough for woman suffrage leader Alice Stone Blackwell, who panned that he "had too much of the Negro defects remaining," but vast crowds of white northerners found him a superb speaker. To southern blacks he projected a fatherly image and to white audiences he projected solic-itous humility, spurning the showy bombast of nineteenth-century oratory. In both contexts Washington frequently used dialect humor, especially to warm up audiences, which was doubly effective in the North because he sounded white to most listeners. According to Washington, upon founding Tuskegee he asked a handyman to clean out a henhouse to serve as the school's first class-room. The worker replied, "What you mean, boss? You sholy ain't gwine clean out de hen-house in de *day*-time?" That repeatedly brought down the house. In 1888, speaking to the Boston Unitarian Club, Washington spoofed a Tuskegee church boasting two hundred members and eighteen preachers. This led to a story about a farmworker who stopped chopping cotton, looked heavenward, and declared: "O Lawd, de cotton am so grassy, de work am so hard, and de sun am so hot dat I b'lieve dis darky am called to preach!"[20]

Northern blacks sometimes decried Washington's racial pandering, which he brushed off as humorless drudgery. Until the 1890s Washington had little contact with northern black intellectuals or communities. The great exception was Timothy Fortune, with whom Washington became friends in the mid-1880s. Fortune was Washington's first black advisor. This was a case of opposites attracting, as Fortune was high-strung, erratic, pushy, a womanizer, politically radical, and eventually an alcoholic. When Fortune began to push for the Afro-American League in 1887, Washington surprised many players by supporting it. Friendship played a role; plus Washington wanted access to northern blacks. But he kept an icy distance from northern protest movements and lamented that northern black intellectuals lacked a common touch.

He was equally tough on ministers, lampooning preachers on the lecture circuit. Washington believed that the black church overflowed with lazy, illiterate, combustible, morally undeveloped preachers. However, he wrapped his gibes in dialect humor, so he seemed only half-serious, until 1890, when he stood before a commencement crowd at Fisk and said it angrily. Black ministers were an embarrassment to the race, Washington declared; for example, Alabama had four hundred black Baptist churches and fifteen intelligent pastors. In August he published an article version of the Fisk speech in Lyman Abbott's *Christian Union*. According to Washington, three-fourths of the black Baptist ministers and two-thirds of the black Methodist ministers were "unfit, either mentally or morally, or both, to preach the Gospel to anyone or to attempt to lead anyone." Most Afro-American preaching had nothing to do with cultivating Christian virtues, he claimed. It settled for setting off groaning, screeching, and jumping. Washington lauded social ethical religion in the same phrases as his friend Washington Gladden, commending the social gospel. But very few black preachers had been trained at the leading Protestant seminaries, he lamented. Thus he called for a non-denominational Protestant seminary to train them.[21]

This article unleashed a flood of protests from African American ministers calling Washington conceited, rude, slanderous, and the like. Some charged that his attack was obviously a ruse to raise funds for his next enterprise, a seminary. Washington replied in the *Christian Union* that every bishop and presiding elder knew he was right; the stupid and immoral ministers vastly outnumbered the intelligent and upright ones. Then he went silent, realizing that this controversy was not going well for him. Washington had never previously struck an intemperate tone in public. His attack seemed out of character; moreover, defending himself on the pecuniary accusation became pointless, as mining heirs Caroline and Olivia Phelps Stokes donated ten thousand dollars for a new Tuskegee enterprise, Phelps Hall Bible School, shortly after Washington published the article. To his relief, Washington won the public endorsement of Bishop Payne, and some black notables congratulated him privately, notably Francis Grimké. But he got hammered by a barrage of angry resolutions, later recalling: "Every association and every conference or religious body of any kind, of my race, that met, did not fail before adjourning to pass a resolution condemning me, or calling upon me to retract or modify what I had said."[22]

Meanwhile, the Phelps School helped to burnish his religious credentials. Washington had a social ethical religion that adapted to the theology of wherever he happened to be, and for years he had to live down rumors that Tuskegee was secretly a Unitarian school. Tuskegee had significant support from Unitarians, and Washington's treasured friend Marshall was an officer of the American Unitarian Association. More important, Washington was obviously comfortable in the liberal, rational, socially minded milieu of the New England Unitarians among whom he fund-raised. Religion, for Washington, was a key component of a healthy, productive, disciplined personal life, with immense social benefits. That was not enough religion for some that otherwise adored Tuskegee. The Phelps School buttressed Washington's assurances that he was a Baptist and that Tuskegee was broadly Protestant. The school did not grow into a full-fledged seminary; it merely offered Bible courses for students and brief seminars for ministers. Washington continued to say that he was right about the crisis in black ministry, but he said it less sharply, taking responsibility for the effect of his tone and his criticism in a hostile society. In 1895, after Frederick Douglass died and Washington soared to Number One, Washington realized that African American ministers had enough trouble without being ridiculed by the supposed successor to Douglass.

STRUGGLE AND ACCOMMODATION

Washington had black detractors in the North as soon as he skyrocketed to national fame, though usually they confined their criticism to the living room. Often they said that Washington represented a steep fall from the roaring protest leadership of Douglass. This claim tended to fixate on the early Douglass and the memory of his last decade, when he swung back to protest politics. But Douglass and Washington had important things in common: an inspiring up-from-slavery story, ample numbers of white friends and admirers, and virtually the same stump speech, which they gave year after year. Both expounded on the hallmark of the age—progress through economic self-development.

Both urged that African Americans would never win self-respect, white respect, or their rights until they became economically powerful. Douglass had a formal, didactic stem-winder on this theme titled "Self-Made Men."

It was not merely a post-Reconstruction fallback. Douglass first offered his gospel of work and self-culture in 1859, reprised it through Reconstruction, and was still giving it in the 1880s, always appealing to Thomas Jefferson, Abraham Lincoln, and other self-made American heroes. America was rightly said to be "preeminently the home and patron of self-made men," Douglass proclaimed. "Allowing only ordinary ability and opportunity, we may explain success mainly by one word and that word is WORK! WORK!! WORK!!! WORK!!!! Not transient and fitful effort, but patient, enduring, honest, unremitting and indefatigable work into which the whole heart is put." No people, Douglass urged, were ever respected until they respected themselves, "and we will never respect ourselves till we have the means to live respectably." Afro-Americans had no chance of flourishing in America until they developed a large class of self-made citizens who achieved success and self-determination through the "self-acting, beneficent, and perfect" law of labor.[23]

Memory hung this theme on Washington because he took it further than Douglass and he did so in conscious distinction from Douglass. After he became famous, Washington reflected that Douglass was "the great defender of the race," but Douglass's life was consumed by a bitter political struggle that left him unprepared "to take up the equally difficult task of fitting the Negro for the opportunities and responsibilities of freedom." He added, "The same was true to a large extent of other Negro leaders." Bookerism was the view that Afro-Americans needed "a policy not of hostility or surrender, but of friendship and advance." Ideologically it rested on the promise that black economic progress would eventually dissolve the social friction between whites and blacks. This promise helped Washington break into the top echelon of philanthropy just before he became wildly famous and built the Tuskegee Machine. In the early 1890s he won financial support from railroad magnate Collis Huntington and the Phelps Stokes sisters, which fueled an expansion boom, doubling Tuskegee's budget, doubling its student body to eight hundred, and more than doubling its campus to eighteen hundred acres. Washington had to fend off criticism from white neighbors that he was building an empire in the name of black independence, both of which they resented. Teachers at Tuskegee dreaded Washington's returns from the fund-raising circuit because he ran his plantation with hyperactive authoritarian zeal. He railed at the slightest faults, smudges, and mishaps of his underlings, just like the planters and business barons that he lionized in his speeches.[24]

For all his success, however, Washington yearned to make an impact on the power centers of the South. To change America, he had to reach the white southern elite. He assured repeatedly that the two races got along peaceably in most of the South; at the same time, knowing better, he was anxious to break through. In his most desperately rationalizing mode, Washington told audiences that even lynching belied some indication that blacks were making progress in America; otherwise blacks would still be ignored as they were in the past. Washington opposed the Alabama Apportionment Act of 1891, which allowed white-controlled school boards to spend far more tax money on whites than blacks. The same year, and the year after that, twenty-four African Americans were lynched in Alabama. Washington could feel the noose tightening throughout the South, and he had no illusions about reaching ordinary white southerners. The one thing that might make a huge difference, he thought, was to win the attention of the white southern commercial establishment, making the case for white and black America rising together.[25]

In 1893 he made a breakthrough, seizing an opportunity to address the annual Conference of Christian Workers convention in Atlanta. Already committed to speaking engagements in Boston, Washington took a train to Atlanta that arrived ninety minutes before his return trip to Boston—all to give a five-minute speech to an audience of two thousand southern and northern whites, his first to white southern civic leaders. That opened the door, the following year, to an appearance before a committee hearing of the U.S. House of Representatives, at which Washington supported a request to fund the 1895 Cotton States and International Exposition in Atlanta.

African Americans were excluded from the 1893 Columbian Exposition in Chicago, and the organizers of the Atlanta Exposition—former Georgia governor Rufus Bullock, *Atlanta Constitution* editor Clark Howell, and exposition president Charles A. Collier—wanted to prevent a similar embarrassment in Atlanta. Bullock had been Georgia's first Republican governor and the most hated man in the state during Reconstruction. As governor he pleaded with President Grant to enforce the Reconstruction Amendments in the South. In 1871 the Klan drove him out of office and the state. In 1876 he returned to Georgia to face charges that he was a carpetbagger who looted the state. Two Atlanta juries found Bullock innocent of all charges, and he stayed to become a prominent businessman. By 1895 he was president of the Atlanta Chamber of Commerce and eager to show that the New South was real. For Bullock, the Atlanta Exposition and Booker Washington were important for similar reasons. At the House hearing, Washington asked Congress to support the exposition's plan to showcase African American history. Then he played a role in constructing the exposition's Negro building, and he agreed to speak at the opening ceremony of the Atlanta Exposition.[26]

This was the chance of a lifetime — a national audience in a southern venue. Washington did not need to be told what was at stake, but he heard it constantly anyway. The Chicago *Inter Ocean* editorialized: "The late General Armstrong predicted that this man would some day be recognized as the Washington of the negro race because he would lead it out of the bondage of ignorance and sloth which were the products of slavery." A white farmer in Tuskegee told him more jocularly that it was one thing for Washington to win over white audiences in the North, or blacks in the South, but this was another deal altogether: "I am afraid that you have got yourself into a tight place." His journey to the exposition felt like walking to the gallows: "This was the first time in the entire history of the Negro that a member of my race had been asked to speak from the same platform with white Southern men and women on any important National occasion." African Americans flocked to him, saying they were counting on him. Washington trembled at needing to represent black Americans and impress white northerners without offending white southerners. To seize the moment, he had to confute the demonization of African Americans that pervaded American society, but on Jim Crow terms; otherwise he would make everything worse. He traveled to Atlanta with his new mentor and white confidant William H. Baldwin Jr., who got so anxious that he could not bring himself to enter the exposition. Thus Baldwin did not witness the icy reception that Washington received upon entering, and the observers demanding to know, "What's that nigger doing on the stage?"[27]

Hateful depictions of African Americans escalated in the 1890s in tandem with stricter forms of segregation. Respected national publications such as *Harper's Weekly* and *Atlantic Monthly* routinely described American blacks as beastly, lazy, stupid, and degenerate. Racist imagery and prescription pervaded American advertising, journalism, literature, and entertainment. Readers were told that whites were superior to blacks in intelligence, morality, civilized behavior, and everything else that mattered. Treating blacks as equals, besides being ridiculous, would lead to interracial sexual unions, producing a mongrel race that destroyed America. In the 1830s, Jim Crow was a dim-witted, superstitious stereotype portrayed in blackface minstrel shows; by the 1890s he had turned into a vengeful type that was out to hurt white people. Other minstrel figures, such as Jim Dandy and Zip Coon, underwent similar transformations, dramatizing the necessity of the Jim Crow caste system. Every blackface minstrel show featured a "coon song" replete with racist lyrics; in the 1890s, the best-selling Tin Pan Alley song was titled "All Coons Look Alike to Me."[28]

To reduce the risk of being lynched, every Afro-American in the South had to know and follow the Jim Crow rules, also called black codes: Never offer to shake hands with a white male, which implied social equality, or with a white female, which smacked of rapist intentions. Never eat with a white person, unless it was unavoidable, in which case never be served before a white person or eat without a partition. Never speak to a white person before being spoken to, and always use courtesy titles, humbly, after being spoken to, as in "Mr. Johnson, sir." Never show affection toward another black person in public, because that offended whites. Always yield the sidewalk, and always ride in the back. Never suggest that a white person lied about anything or had dishonorable intentions. Never lay claim to greater knowledge or intelligence than a white person. Never curse a white person or laugh derisively at a white person or comment on the appearance of a white female.[29]

Washington was long practiced at appeasing white hostility when he stepped forward in Atlanta to confute the demonization of Afro-Americans and make a pitch for building America together. He opened with a blunt factual statement: "One-third of the population of the South is of the Negro race." The South could not succeed as an economic, social, or moral enterprise if it repressed one-third of its population. Washington thanked the "magnificent Exposition" for representing the "value and manhood of the American Negro," which promised to awaken a new era of industrial progress for the South. Reconstruction, he explained, tried to place emancipated slaves at the top of the social order, teaching them to prize a seat in Congress over learning how to make something or run a business. That foolishness was over, and he did not pine for it. The New South was about building up wealth from below, and Washington wanted African Americans to be part of it.[30]

He told a homely story that ended with a maxim: "Cast down your bucket where you are." Many blacks were moving to cities, some had moved to the North, and a trickle had moved to Liberia. Washington told Afro-Americans to stay where they were—on the farms, in the South—where they could become prosperous without ruining their moral character. The gospel of wealth would lift black Americans to a productive life in the New South. Washington did not exclude the professions from the places where African Americans might cast down their buckets: "Cast it down in agriculture, mechanics, in commerce, in domestic service, and in the professions." But higher education and the professions were marginal to his message that common labor was essential to a civilization; there was great dignity in it, no thriving race obsessed over its grievances, and every ascending race started at the bottom, "not at the top."[31]

Washington shook his head at white employers who lured foreign-speaking foreigners to America. What sense did that make, when there existed eight million English-speaking black Americans to work for them? Afro-Americans had no history of strikes or labor wars, he admonished. They had a history of tilling America's fields, clearing America's forests, building America's railroads and cities, and digging coal from dangerous mines. They had a history of caring for white masters, nursing their children, and crying at the graves of both. If white Americans were to cast down their buckets among black Americans, America would flourish as a civilization: "While doing this, you can be sure in the future, as in the past, that you and your families will be surrounded by the most patient, faithful, law-abiding, and unresentful people that the world has seen." America could become great by working together in industry, commerce, civil society, and religion, Washington urged, reaching for his most famous metaphor: "In all things that are purely social we can be as separate as the fingers, yet one as the hand in all things essential to mutual progress."[32]

This was the deal he had come to make. He had used the fingers/hand analogy for years, but never on a stage like this. Everything in the Atlanta Compromise speech was organized around this sentence. Washington had already won the crowd when he got to this statement, and he held his hand high above his head upon making it. He took for granted that for most whites, social equality was about the abolition of segregation, whereas for most blacks, it was about something much less significant, intimate relationships across racial lines. To the white South, social equality was something abhorrent; in the North it was layered and patchy; Washington noted that some (northern) blacks condemned every section of the nation that did not at least aspire to it. He assured that he was nothing like them: "The wisest among my race under-stand that the agitation of questions of social equality is the extremest folly, and that progress in the enjoyment of all the privileges that will come to us must be the result of severe and constant struggle rather than of artificial forcing." African Americans would get their social and political due after they made significant economic progress, Washington asserted. Every race ascended through economic advancement, and no race failed to ascend that succeeded economically. For America to be a just society, Afro-Americans had to get their rights, but first they had to make themselves worthy to exercise their rights. The deal on the table was that if white America allowed blacks to succeed econom-ically, blacks would be willing to wait for their rights.[33]

Washington figured, rightly, that southern blacks, northern whites, and southern white elites would hear the speech differently, but each in a way that came out favorably for him. His black defenders would not feel sold out, because things like racial intermarriage were not worth fighting over, and he was careful to say that his strategy aimed to regain political rights. Northern whites, he knew from his years of fund-raising tours, would appreciate his boot-strap message and his political realism. The white southern elites, he hoped, would welcome his pledge not to make a fuss about voting and other rights, because they believed their own rhetoric about a wealth-breeding New South. Washington knew that most working-class southern whites would resent his every word and being, and that he would have trouble with the blacks he accused of extreme folly. But even the Wizard of Tuskegee did not see coming the gusher of adulation that lifted him to messianic status.

Bullock rushed across the platform to congratulate Washington, setting off a roar of approval. Howell declared from the podium that Washington's speech was "the beginning of a moral revolution in America," setting off another roar. White southern women plucked flowers off their dress and threw them joyfully on stage. The keynote speaker, Judge Emory Speer, tried to follow Washington, contending that, actually, there was no race issue in the South. All that mattered was for blacks and Yankees to accept "white control of the local affairs of these States." If that happened, good southern gentlemen like him would make sure that blacks were treated fairly. The press, however, made Speer a footnote to an electrifying national story. Newspapers throughout the country published Washington's speech in full. Northern editorialists described it as exceedingly wise, redemptive, and perfect, a gift of deliverance. The *Independent* conferred the blessing of the Radical Republican tradition, declaring that Washington was "fit to be the prophet and leader of his race." Southern editorialists bit their tongues and said nothing. To them, no black American deserved such a plat-form, and Washington's success smacked of uppity race-climbing, subverting the natural order of things. It was galling that northern whites and a handful of enablers like Howell indulged Washington's attempts to lift black people to the level of whites. But Washington stymied southern critics by saying nothing smacking of bitterness or accusation, and others lifted him to Number One. Howell wrote, "The address was a revelation. The whole speech is a platform upon which blacks and whites can stand with full justice to each other." The *Boston Evening Transcript* concurred: "The speech of Booker T. Washington at the Atlanta Exposition, this week, seems to have dwarfed all the other proceed-ings and the Exposition itself. The sensation that it has caused in the press has never been equaled."[34]

Washington added to the journalistic outpouring, writing in the New York *World* that as he spoke to the crowd and absorbed its thunderous approval, "I seemed to have been carried away in a vision, and it was hard for me to realize as I spoke that it was not all a beautiful dream, but an actual scene, right here in the heart of the South." Mary E. Stearns, one of Olivia's Boston abolitionist friends, had the same feeling, gushing to Washington: "Your address is glorious! Beyond all words glorious! Olivia was with you yesterday!" Many blacks thanked him heartily for his example of moral dignity. White racism was so oppressive that commanding a national stage in Atlanta, speaking with dignified bearing, and saying a good word about the humanity of Afro-Americans was revolutionary. That came through to many prominent blacks that praised Washington, notably Fortune, J. W. E. Bowen, Edward E. Cooper, AME bishop Abram Grant, and T. McCants Stewart. Bowen commended Washington for stressing that freedmen had to be taught to "love work." Young W. E. B. Du Bois, teaching at Wilberforce College, took a similar view. Du Bois wrote to Washington: "Let me heartily congratulate you upon your phenomenal success at Atlanta—it was a word fitly spoken." In Fortune's *New York Age,* Du Bois lauded Washington for offering "the basis of a real settlement between whites and blacks in the South." Du Bois never retracted that view. For the rest of his life he said that the Atlanta speech, in its context, was a "statesmanlike effort to reach understanding with the white South." Had the white South responded with "equal generosity," the cause of racial justice would have moved forward. Instead, the South persecuted black Americans and Washington became an obstacle to racial justice.[35]

There were only a few public negative responses from African Americans. W. Calvin Chase was blistering, dismissing Washington as a "trimmer, pure and simple" who cared mostly about raising money for Tuskegee, even if he had to play down lynching and segregation to do it: "He said something that was death to the Afro-American and elevating to the white people. What fool wouldn't applaud the downfall of his aspiring competitor?" The Bethel Literary and Historical Society of Washington, DC, sharply debated the Atlanta Compromise, dividing equally between defenders and opponents. Some Bethel critics accused Washington of recently refusing to help a black Tuskegee lawyer, Thomas Harris, as he sought refuge from a mob. Actually, Washington got Harris to safety in a way that preserved deniability and defused the situation, but the story tarnished Washington's image. George N. Smith and the Atlanta *Advocate* decried the rise of Booker-style accommodation. Smith, writing in Turner's *Voice of Missions,* protested that comparing Washington to Douglass was like comparing "a pigmy to a giant" or a mountain brook to Niagara Falls. The exposition, Smith charged, was merely a moneymaking scheme for white elites, and Washington was merely their instrument to make money. The Atlanta *Advocate* opined that Washington was a throwback to "the most servile type of the old Negro" and that his name, "B. T.," stood for "Bad Taste." Turner was more conflicted. Washington was "a great man" doing "a great work" in promoting economic self-help, Turner believed. But Washington's statement about social equality was a disaster for blacks, because social equality was bundled up with every kind of equality: "He will have to live a long time to undo the harm he has done to our race." Turner feared that white Americans would use the Atlanta speech to bury the hope of racial equality.[36]

That was exactly what happened, but in 1895 a tidal wave of pro-Washington press lifted Washington from remarkable success to something much bigger. As the praise mounted and crowds surged to Washington wherever he went, he grasped that his life had changed. He became a confidant of the high and mighty and started to build the Tuskegee Machine. He hit the lecture circuit harder than ever, speaking to overflow houses in city after city, giving variations on the Atlanta address to cheering audiences. Somberly and willingly he accepted the leadership of black America. If there had to be a Number One, it might as well be him. Washington was careful to say that he had not expected the mantle of Douglass to fall on him, but he also said that he was distinctly suited to help African Americans take up the challenges of a coming new century.

Since Washington believed that his life was a success story, he did not ask why the Atlanta address had such an enormous impact. The exposition was an episode in his success story. President Grover Cleveland offered congratulations and invited Washington to be his advisor. Power broking became a way of life, as black politicians asked Washington to intercede with white political leaders, and white politicians asked him to influence black voters. The *Outlook* lauded Washington so effusively that the *Independent* cautioned against "the worship of Booker T. Washington." William Hayes Ward, writing in the *Independent* in 1898, assured that he "gave all honor" to Washington for his virtues, accomplishments, and political realism. Still, Washington was merely a "sensible, prudent man" who had to operate within the limits set down by the Alabama legislature. Ward admonished New England liberals that Washington lived in the wrong part of the country to provide the answer to America's racial crisis. Baldwin, however, told his upper-class friends that Washington *was* the answer. Armstrong had died in 1892, and Baldwin was the new Armstrong figure in Washington's life. A Southern Railway executive with Boston abolitionist family roots, Baldwin joined Tuskegee's board of trustees in the mid-1890s. By 1898 he was soliciting large gifts from J. P. Morgan, John D. Rockefeller, John Wanamaker, Henry H. Rogers, and other top-ranking American capitalists; George Eastman and Andrew Carnegie subsequently signed on. Meanwhile, Washington told Francis Grimké that Ward was "all right," but he suffered from hanging out too much with American Missionary Association types holding unrealistic political ideas.[37]

The business titans were empire builders who admired Washington's success at building a large enterprise from nothing. They appreciated his admiration of them, his embrace of Gilded Age capitalism, and his aversion to trade unions. They opened their summer homes to him as they vacationed in Bar Harbor, Maine; Saratoga Springs, New York; and other playgrounds of the upper class. They took pride in their racial enlightenment and admired Washington's work for racial reconciliation. Above all, they needed a workforce that was trained to work in their shops and mills, and no one preached the gospel of industrial education more effectively than Washington. The Atlanta speech offered the capitalist class a cheap and docile labor force that promised not to get uppity about its rights. For northern business titans this was obviously a terrific deal; for their counterparts in the New South, Washington wagered, the deal was hopefully good enough to overcome . . . everything else.

Industrial education was not conceived specifically for the education of African Americans. It was an educational reform movement with roots in the pedagogy of Swiss romantic Johann H. Pestalozzi, who espoused "learning by head, hand and heart." It had American roots at Oberlin College, Berea College, and other abolitionist institutions, and it was the cutting edge of educational reform when Tuskegee and the Slater Fund arose together. Always it touted the relevance of practical education over classical, elitist, Latin-centered education. The Slater Fund was devoted to trade education, and Tuskegee relied on the Slater Fund for fifteen hundred dollars each year during its first decade. After Washington became famous and acquired wealthy friends, Tuskegee became even more identified with vocational education, because most of its oil and railroad backers took little interest in the school's main work—training rural schoolteachers. Washington conceived Tuskegee as a teaching school *and* a trade school, requiring all students to take at least half their courses in academic subjects, which required him to mollify high-rolling friends who accused him of raising money for industrial programs that only half existed. For Washington, industrial education, teacher education, the progress of the race, the good life, and Christianity fit together. He had a favorite saying about why Christianity mattered; in effect it was Washington's theology: "Nothing pays as well in producing efficient labor as Christianity."[38]

Tuskegee's bifurcated identity created perpetual tensions, which paled in comparison to struggling for black progress on Jim Crow terms. Two public incidents exemplified the latter burden. The first occurred in 1896 at Tuskegee's commencement. Alabama governor William C. Oates and Wilmington, North

Carolina, customs collector John C. Dancy addressed the graduates. Dancy, a black conservative known for going along, lauded the New England philanthropists for supporting Tuskegee, which may have been what set off Oates. Otherwise it was hard to figure what set off Oates. Following Dancy to the platform, Oates waved his prepared speech at the audience and refused to deliver it, declaring: "I want to give you niggers a few words of plain talk and advice. No such address as you have just listened to is going to do you any good; it's going to spoil you. You had better not listen to such speeches. You might as well understand that this is a white man's country, as far as the South is concerned, and we are going to make you keep your place. I have nothing more to say to you." The crowd sat stunned and muttering. Washington bounced up in good humor, declared that Tuskegee would be delighted to hear Oates again "when we are not so fagged out," and told the crowd to rise for the doxology. Washington needed to stay on good terms with Oates, which he did. Even Tuskegee's most true-believing Bookerites, however, had to notice that Washington's strategy and eminence were not working for them.[39]

The second incident occurred at the National Peace Jubilee in October 1898 in Chicago, where a crowd of sixteen thousand celebrated America's victory in the Spanish-American War. The gathering included President McKinley and a bevy of dignitaries. Giving tribute to the four black regiments that served in Cuba, Washington figured, mistakenly, that America's soaring sense of national honor gave him a bit of slack from his usual straightjacket. He called the roll of African Americans that fought for the American nation, featuring Crispus Attucks at the Boston Massacre, the Fifty-fourth Massachusetts Regiment that charged Fort Wagner, and the black troops that joined the charge at San Juan Hill. Whenever black Americans were called to defend their nation, Washington observed, they did so with bravery and patriotic feeling: "We find the Negro forgetting his own wrongs, forgetting the laws and customs that discriminate against him in his own country, and again we find our black citizen choosing the better part." In his telling, America had won all its battles except one, "the blotting out of racial prejudices." Washington urged Americans to celebrate their victory by uniting "in our business and civil relations," building on the trench that black and white soldiers dug together to surround Santiago. Then he dramatically violated Jim Crow: "I make no empty statement when I say that we shall have, especially in the Southern part of our country, a cancer gnawing at the heart of the Republic, that shall one day prove as dangerous as an attack from an army without or within."[40]

Washington ended with a riff on the no-exceptions loyalty of Afro-Americans to the Stars and Stripes, which got a thunderous ovation in Chicago, suggesting that perhaps he had made a winning gambit. For three years he had occasionally ventured a critical word about racial prejudice or disenfranchisement in less prominent venues. But this venue was national, and he directly censured white racism, an unforgivable affront to Jim Crow. A crush of southern editorialists said so, very angrily. Even Clark Howell turned against him, charging that Washington sounded like an agitator for social equality, a far cry from the sober racial healer that addressed the Atlanta Exposition. Howell advised Washington to reimmerse himself in the real world of Tuskegee and stop playing to the grandstand. A Birmingham editor demanded to know if Washington had reneged on the Atlanta Compromise. Washington pleaded no: He always avoided the social equality issue, he seldom referred to racial prejudice, and in Chicago he singled out the South only because that was where most African Americans lived. Admittedly, in Chicago he criticized racial prejudice, but he had business and civil relations in mind, not social relations. Then he took a vow of silence and waited for the drubbing to pass.[41]

The National Peace Jubilee confirmed that Jim Crow still applied to everything Washington said in public, coincident with a rising tide of state disenfranchisement movements, segregation, and lynching. Disenfranchisement movements in Mississippi and South Carolina had already succeeded. North Carolina and Louisiana excluded nearly all black voters in 1898; in 1899 a disenfranchisement bill was debated in Georgia; and Virginia and Oklahoma disenfranchised its black voters in 1902 and 1910. In every case literacy and property tests, plus a poll tax, formed the foundation, then poor whites were cut into the deal with clauses pertaining to special understandings, good character, or one's grandfather. White primaries were equally effective and more widely adopted, excluding blacks from statewide primaries in South Carolina, Arkansas, Georgia, Florida, Tennessee, Alabama, Mississippi, Kentucky, Texas, Louisiana, Oklahoma, Virginia, and North Carolina.[42]

For white nationalist leaders like James K. Vardaman and "Pitchfork" Ben Tillman, state disenfranchisement was a mere beginning; black education and the Fifteenth Amendment had to be abolished, too. Vardaman, on his way to the governorship of Mississippi, contended that educating African Americans was destructive to the nation, not merely wasteful and stupid. He told campaign crowds that the Negro was "a lazy, lying, lustful animal which no conceivable amount of training can transform into a tolerable citizen." Tillman, who had moved from the governorship of South Carolina in 1894 to the U.S. Senate the following year, put it equally graphically at the University of Michigan. Pointing to a black student in the audience, Tillman declared: "You scratch one of these colored graduates under the skin and you will find the savage. His education is only like a coat of paint. Booker T. Washington simply equips the negro for more deadly competition with the white man; a hundred more colleges like his would only arouse more race antagonism."[43]

Washington realized that white nationalists would not stop at disenfranchisement and that disenfranchisement victories therefore put everything at risk for African Americans, not merely their political rights. He intervened directly in Georgia, helping to organize opposition to the Hardwick Bill, where a coalition of blacks and white anti-Populist Democrats defeated disenfranchisement. One of Washington's allies in Georgia was Du Bois, now teaching at Atlanta University. (Georgia, however, enacted a disenfranchisement bill in 1908.) In Louisiana Washington worked secretly to stop disenfranchisement, helping to organize and finance a civil rights opposition that fought the issue in court for years. At every turn, faced with a hateful opposition thriving on political victories, Washington found himself scrounging for allies on almost any terms. Edgar Gardner Murphy advocated black education, paternalistic segregation, and repealing the Fifteenth Amendment. He reasoned that if white Americans were relieved of fearing black political power, lynching would fade and America would move forward in race relations. In the summer of 1899 alone, thirty-eight blacks were lynched in the South, twelve in Georgia, while Washington organized opposition to the Hardwick Bill. Washington was so desperate for white southern allies that he struggled to stay on good terms with Murphy and other segregationists of his ilk. He even indulged figures in Murphy's orbit that disparaged black education; anyone who stopped short of demonizing African Americans qualified as a friend.[44]

By that criterion, things were not so bad in the South, despite the surge of lynchings and disenfranchisement. This was the spirit in which Washington wrote the signature statement of his philosophy, *The Future of the American Negro*, in 1899. Washington allowed that blacks in the North enjoyed certain privileges that blacks in the South lacked; still, the South was the best place to live, because economic competition was fierce in the North, and so was trade unionism. African Americans had a better chance of gaining citizenship rights in the South than of being admitted into northern trade unions; plus unions were bad anyway. Washington declared that black Americans should not have to relinquish any of their constitutional rights, contrary to suggestions that he believed otherwise. Moreover, he did not believe that blacks should be confined to farming, mechanics, or a similar trade. There was already a need for black teachers, ministers, doctors, lawyers, statesmen, and the like. But black America needed to build a strong material foundation to support the black professional class and the rise of the race as a whole.[45]

Toward that end, Washington worried about six things. Activist blacks in the North, lacking any understanding of conditions in the South, were harming southern blacks by inflaming white southern opinion. Tempered discussion of the rights issue was commendable, but anything smacking of accusation or anger was bound to hurt African Americans where most of them lived. Second, the entire white South increasingly allowed itself to be represented by the whims of lawless mobs, damaging the reputation of the South. It was hard to say this without seeming angry or accusatory, but Washington said it as innocuously as possible. Third, Afro-Americans were entering the twentieth century more discouraged than ever. They were beaten down by disenfranchisement and segregation movements, all on top of being told that their race had no chance of surviving Darwinian weeding out. Fighting against demoralization was Washington's highest calling, because despair was the ultimate enemy. Fourth, closely related to the first and second, many northerners knew nothing about the South except what they read about lynching and disenfranchisement. Some articles were exaggerated, Washington averred; more important, in most of the South the two races got along peaceably most of the time. Fifth, crime was increasingly a problem in the very places where blacks were denied the right to an education. Washington warned that there was a causal relationship between crime and the denial of educational opportunity. Sixth, clarifying his position about disenfranchisement, Washington supported literacy and property tests of citizenship. It was not unjust for a state to uphold a high standard in its election laws, he argued. It was unjust to enact a law that applied only to blacks, as Mississippi and South Carolina had done.[46]

Washington stressed that nothing else mattered if African Americans despaired and gave up. It was getting harder to remember that black Americans made tremendous gains in the half century just passed: "If, fifty years ago, anyone had predicted that the Negro would have received the recognition and honor which individuals have already received, he would have been laughed at as an idle dreamer. Time, patience, and constant achievement are great factors in the rise of a race." Washington risked the guffaw that he was one of the few individuals to have achieved recognition and honor. His story was his best argument: "So long as the Negro is permitted to get education, acquire property, and secure employment, and is treated with respect in the business or commercial world—as is now true in the greater part of the South—I shall have the greatest faith in his working out his own destiny in our Southern States."[47]

Instead the disenfranchisement mania surged next into Alabama, where African Americans were 45 percent of the population and where the Constitutional Convention of 1901 to disenfranchise blacks admitted no black members. Alabama's superintendent of education ridiculed the idea that blacks should have voting rights: "What a fearful mistake! What a stupendous error! What a crime against civilization!" The Fifteenth Amendment took a dreadful pounding; speakers wailed that it abused the rights of superior white people and was responsible for every slight and assault suffered by white women. Washington wrote a petition to the convention, pleading with customary flattery and indirection that Alabama had no reason to fear its loyal, hardworking, law-abiding black population. The convention had to debate whether this petition deserved to be read, eventually opting to endure its hearing. The usual schemes for admitting whites and excluding blacks were adopted, including Louisiana's grandfather clause, which admitted any citizen whose grandfather had fought in a war; at the time Washington was secretly directing a lawsuit against the Louisiana clause. J. Thomas Heflin, a rising star in Alabama politics, added that educating African Americans was as bad as letting them vote, because it encouraged them to compete with whites. Washington realized that losing the vote in his home state would damage his standing and strategy, but the outcome was obvious, so he stayed out of the ratification campaign. In the end, Alabama cut its black voter roll from 180,000 to 3,000.[48]

That was the state of things political during the period that Washington skyrocketed to fame by accommodating Jim Crow. McKinley consulted with Washington and complimented him publicly but did nothing to protect blacks from an upsurge of white terrorism. Meanwhile, a rash of best-selling books made white nationalism intellectually respectable. Charles Carroll kicked off the new century with a vile resurrection of the theory that blacks belonged to a different biological species; his book, *The Negro a Beast*, won respectful reviews, a best-selling audience, and a host of imitators. Two years later William Calhoun's similar diagnosis also conveyed its argument in the title: *The Caucasian and the Negro in the United States. They Must Separate. If Not, Then Extermination. A Proposed Solution: Colonization.* That year Thomas Dixon Jr. soared past all other white nationalists, but just before Dixon swept the field, William Hannibal Thomas showed that the field was open to black writers of a sufficiently jaundiced mentality.[49]

Thomas was a mixed-race son of free people of color in Ohio. He was denied entrance to the Union Army because of his race, but later fought with the Fifth U.S. Colored Infantry and lost an arm in battle. He taught school in South Carolina; served as a Republican lawyer, legislator, and trial judge during Reconstruction; and later worked as a Methodist minister, seminary professor, and journalist. In the late 1880s he took an ugly turn and started writing about it, sneering that African Americans were obviously an inferior race intellectually and morally. This conviction landed a prestigious publisher, Macmillan, for a book titled *The American Negro: What He Was, What He Is, and What He May Become* (1901).[50]

Basically, Thomas recycled the white nationalist lexicon of savagery with occasional appeals to his personal authority. He argued that blacks were "savage animals" when they came to America and were partly civilized by slavery. But after slavery ended and the idiocy of Reconstruction was imposed, blacks fell back into beastliness: "The negro is in every respect wholly unlike other races of men. The negro is immoral; he must be endowed with morality. He is lazy, and therefore needs to be made industrious. He is a coward; he must acquire courage. His conscience is dead, his intellect dense; one must be resurrected, and the other set aflame by the light of heaven." Thomas struggled to convey the "inconceivable mendacity" and "folly" of African Americans. In their speech, they were "silly and vaunting; in their homes, untidy and negligent; in their associations, coarse and vulgar. Their demeanor toward inferiors is pompous and arrogant, while their conduct toward superiors is always servile and craven." Worst of all, "so bestial are negro men that we have known them to lead wives, mothers, sisters, and daughters to the sensuous embraces of white men." Thomas alleged that 90 percent of black women lacked sexual virtue. In that case, presuming that slavery was off the table, what was America to do? Thomas said that a degenerate people could be saved only by "an infusion of virile blood." The best blacks were the ones, like him, that had three or four generations of white ancestors. The answer was to rid America of blackness.[51]

Reverdy Ransom later recalled that *The American Negro* "dropped like a bomb in the camp of the more intelligent colored people of the country. Everyone felt humiliated by it." The book was so "nauseating," Ransom said, so "vile and lurid" that Thomas's wife wept as she typed the manuscript. Other black social gospel reviewers denounced the book as a travesty. Alexander Walters called it "a wholesale and unwarranted slander of the negro race." Richard R. Wright Jr. condemned Thomas's "distorted and immoral imagination." Charles T. Walker enrolled Thomas in the traitors' hall of fame alongside Judas Iscariot, Benedict Arnold, and Aaron Burr. White social gospel reviewers similarly blasted the book. Jenkin Lloyd Jones called it "slovenly and unscrupulous." The *Independent* protested that Thomas "shamelessly, scandalously" libeled black Americans, doing his best to hold them "in helpless inferiority and to justify the brutes who use just his language to defend his oppression and lynchings." Edgar Gardner Murphy grieved that the *New York Times* gave the book a favorable review; the publication of this vengeful book was a "calamity," Murphy observed, and widespread acceptance of it would be "little short of a catastrophe."[52]

By that standard, the book was a catastrophe, as it won favorable reviews in the *New York Evening Post, Boston Evening Transcript, Washington Post, Chicago Tribune,* and other leading newspapers. All said that Thomas had a special authority in writing about this subject and he did it very well. A few social gospel reviewers took a similar line. John R. Commons praised Thomas for his "candid" and "entertaining" assessment of "the moral and intellectual qualities of his fellows." Abbott's *Outlook* editorialized that Thomas offered a strong account of the "mental and moral shortcomings of his own race." White nationalists were ecstatic that the book won a large audience and favorable northern reviews. Bill Arp, a widely read white nationalist, contended that the reaction to Thomas's book proved that northern sympathy for blacks had significantly diminished.[53]

The American Negro marked a new low by winning praise and respect. The Wizard of Tuskegee, alarmed at the book's reception, took a two-track approach to bringing Thomas down. For the *Outlook,* Washington wrote a polite, anonymous, mildly exhortatory review, noting that Thomas claimed special authority for his viewpoint on the basis of a racial identity that he otherwise denigrated. Thomas had an extreme case of the blues, Washington concluded, but the remedy for that was to commit one's self to the "earnest work" of uplift, not to stand apart from others and criticize them. On track two, the Wizard hired private investigators to dig up dirt about Thomas. It turned out that Thomas had a history of abusing women and stealing money from his employers. Journalist John Bruce and novelist Charles Chestnutt ran hard with the story, and Thomas was discredited, although Macmillan refused to withdraw the book, which remained a strong seller for years.[54]

UP FROM SLAVERY

Up from Slavery, not coincidentally, was published amid this mania of disenfranchisement, lynching, ramped-up segregation, and popular screeds justifying all of it, although the worst was still to come with the entry of Thomas Dixon. *Up from Slavery* was a trump card, a resort to Washington's strongest suit. He knew the power of his story, having used it for years on the fund-raising circuit. In 1896 Walter Hines Page, then of Houghton, Mifflin and Company, suggested to Washington that it was time for a book version. Two years later Washington hired a black journalist, Edgar Webber, to ghostwrite his story for a subscription house specializing in door-to-door sales. Webber produced a sloppy hodgepodge of anecdotes and documents that embarrassed Washington, so he fired Webber, took *The Story of My Life and Work* in hand, and produced a better second edition. This book sold well in the subscription trade, mostly in the black community, but it was still a hodgepodge of memoir, testimonials, letters, and news articles, and Washington yearned for a smoother telling. This time he hired Max Bennett Thrasher, a white journalist from New England, who was already doing public relations for Tuskegee. Thrasher traveled with Washington on one of his speaking tours, reworked parts of the first memoir, traded drafts with Washington, and produced *Up from Slavery*.

Up from Slavery was serialized in *Outlook* before it was published as a book. Abbott implored Washington to use more personal anecdotes, and Washington tried to comply. The book was pitched to a white audience; it dropped Washington's account of the beating of his uncle, and it barely mentioned Reconstruction. More important, it dropped the previous book's haunting section on "this terrible evil of lynching." In 1899, Fortune had changed his mind about whether Washington should say something about lynching; Washington, while vacationing in Europe to regain his health, wrote an open letter "to the Southern people." Washington explained that he kept silent because he loved the South and he grieved whenever it was criticized. Moreover, the South had no monopoly on lynching, and whites were sometimes lynched, too. But it had to be said, Washington wrote, that "the habit of lynching" had taken hold of the South, most victims were black, and lynching was "hurting" the South morally and materially: "We cannot disregard the teachings of the civilized world for eighteen hundred years, that the only way to punish crime is by law. When we leave this dictum chaos begins." Washington pleaded "for the Negro," but not only for Negroes. He told of a nine-year-old blue-eyed white boy who witnessed a lynching, returned to his mother, and said, "I have seen a man hanged; now I wish I could see one burned." Washington remarked that it would be unbearable for him to hear his son say such a thing: "I would prefer seeing him laid in his grave." Lynching was destroying the souls of the lynch mobs and their children, he implored. *The Story of My Life and Work* reprinted the letter in full, adding that white America's duty to the Negro had not ended with "those who fought for the freedom of the slaves."[55]

That had to be cut from *Up from Slavery*, which aimed for a big white audience and stuck with an uplift message. Stylistically the book was plodding, dull, literal, earnest, and unreflective, denuded of color and drama. It eschewed evocative description and cut back on Washington's "darky" jokes and other minstrel stereotypes, though it was sprinkled with a few. Washington claimed, incredibly, that the Klan no longer existed and was barely remembered in the South. Many reviewers described the book as a black version of the Horatio Alger story of a poor young man's rise to respectability. Some preferred the parallel to a real person, Andrew Carnegie, who rose from poverty in Scotland to become a steel baron in Pittsburgh; Carnegie himself endorsed this analogy with enthusiasm. Reviewer Sidonie Smith later described the book as a "businessman's autobiography." Hampton's monthly *Southern Workman*, combining paternalism and Washington reverence, emoted that Washington's respect for manual labor and "belief in the white race" made him eminently suited "to do the work that God has called him to do." The *Independent* eschewed paternalism and Washington-reverence, but cheered that *Up from Slavery* was "one of the most cheerful, hopeful books that we have had the privilege to read." Many years later reviewer James M. Cox, describing the book's style, exhausted the connotations of "inert." *Up from Slavery* treated language as matter, not as energy.[56]

But the book's inertia did not matter, because its slavery-to-eminence story was enthralling, and Washington's overcoming affinities with Carnegie, Alger, Douglass, Lincoln, and Benjamin Franklin helped him reach a huge audience. *Up from Slavery* was famous before it existed as a book, as Abbott doled it out in seventeen installments to his one hundred thousand subscribers. George Eastman, inventor of the Kodak camera, found a new favorite for his philanthropy upon reading the book. So did Carnegie, who told his assistant to "give the man a library," a neoclassical gem that became the first of Carnegie's many gifts to Tuskegee. *Up from Slavery* raked in money for Tuskegee for the rest of Washington's life and beyond it, sealing his monopoly over white philanthropy for racial progress.[57]

Many reviewers lauded the book's simple, "manly," unadorned style, and most reviewers said the book's merits were secondary to Washington himself—a paragon of virtue meriting unstinting praise who served as America's antidote to an embarrassing plague of radical white racism and lynching. The *Nation* contrasted Washington and Thomas, explaining that Thomas lifted himself above ordinary African Americans, while Washington nobly identified himself with his people. William Dean Howells, a prominent literary critic, lauded Washington's "singularly pleasing personality" and his "constant common sense." According to Howells, Washington correctly divined from his mentor, Armstrong, that the secret of happiness is to be constantly active for the good of others. Washington had music in him, Howells judged, but his heart and soul belonged to Tuskegee and the good of African Americans, and thus the dominant register of his memoir was *business*: "He has lived heroic poetry, and he can, therefore, afford to talk simple prose."[58]

The only dissenting note on *Up from Slavery* and its author, in reviews outside the orbit of white nationalism, came from Du Bois, who had recently had a falling out with Washington. They had known each other since 1894, when Washington offered Du Bois what would have been his first teaching job. Instead Du Bois chose Wilberforce. They had corresponded periodically before and after Du Bois earned a doctorate at Harvard in 1895, moved to the University of Pennsylvania in 1896, and moved to Atlanta University in 1899. They had worked together to defeat the Hardwick Bill in 1899; later that summer, when leaders of the Afro-American Council attacked Washington for playing down segregation and lynching, Du Bois defended him. A few weeks later Washington offered Du Bois another job at Tuskegee, conducting research on African American life. That tempted Du Bois, but he did not want to operate under Washington's shadow at Tuskegee, and he preferred to live in Washington, DC, where the greatest school system in the world that blacks controlled needed an assistant superintendent.[59]

Du Bois asked Washington to support him for the school position, which Washington did, writing a nice letter. But Washington's friends in the District of Columbia objected that they wanted a Booker stalwart, Robert Terrell, for the position; plus they didn't trust Du Bois. Washington made quick work of his dilemma, telling Du Bois that he still supported him but he had learned that an outsider was sure to be appointed, so would Du Bois please not use the letter that Washington had written for him? Du Bois seethed that Washington betrayed him, although Terrell was an inside candidate and he did not get the job. To Du Bois, the meaning of the episode was obvious: The Tuskegee Machine had pushed him aside. He was finished with defending Washington from critics with whom he agreed anyway. *Up from Slavery* gave Du Bois his first opportunity to say it, only a few months before Theodore Roosevelt became president and set off a spectacular controversy by having a White House dinner with America's favorite black man.[60]

Du Bois wrote that Washington got to be Number One because white Americans had tired of Negroes and they wanted to concentrate on making money. Washington accepted that making money was more important than redressing injustices; in fact, he proposed that grubbing for money should be "a veritable Way of Life" for African Americans too. The key to *Up from Slavery* was its crassness, Du Bois believed. The book perfectly mimicked the "triumphant commercialism and the ideals of material prosperity" that defined the age. Most white Americans sneered at a black boy that studied French grammar, and so did Washington. Du Bois doubted that Washington truly supported Fisk, Howard, and other black colleges, regardless of what he felt compelled to say in public venues. He also insisted that Washington was "far from a popular leader" among African Americans. There were three types of Afro-American leadership, Du Bois explained: rebellion, accommodation, and "a determined attempt at self-development, self-realization." Bookerism, despite its language of self-development, was really about commercialism and selling out. Du Bois credited Washington for his shrewdness, tact, and "very evident sincerity of purpose." Moreover, Du Bois did not cite or identify with black writers that denounced Washington: Chase, Ransom, Wells-Barnett, and Trotter. Instead, Du Bois called out five figures that sometimes lauded Washington and sometimes criticized him: Kelly Miller, poet Paul Dunbar, painter Henry Tanner, writer Charles Chesnutt, and lawyer Archibald Grimké. These were the people to watch, Du Bois claimed, if a real alternative to Bookerism was to be mounted.[61]

Du Bois had misgivings about the reflexively polemical opposition that existed, and he worried that it was terribly small, anyway. So he struck a blow for a bigger and more sophisticated opposition just before Washington leaped to another level of fame and power as a confidant of the new American president.

BECOMING W. E. B. DU BOIS

William Edward Burghardt Du Bois would have stood even taller in history had he not lived so long. He defined the problem of the twentieth century, blasted accommodation as self-defeating despair, and led the civil rights and Pan-African movements, before aligning with Communist revolution, all despite spurning, "sometimes ostentatiously," essential duties of movement leadership: "I never was, nor ever will be, personally popular." Du Bois made his greatest impact from 1903 to 1930, especially 1910 to 1920, before concluding that he would not live to see anything remotely resembling racial equality. The later Du Bois judged that the white world was too determined by the unconscious and social structural reflexes of racism to want equality. He moved from radical democratic Socialism to pro-Communism, and in later life pleaded with scholars not to overlook his later career. But Du Bois knew that he made his chief place in history during his early career, and he harbored a whiff of nostalgia for his glory years. In 1940 he put it with typically shimmering boldness: "I think I may say without boasting that in the period from 1910 to 1930 I was a main factor in revolutionizing the attitude of the American Negro toward caste. My stinging hammer blows made Negroes aware of themselves, confident of their possibilities and determined in self-assertion. So much so that today common slogans among the Negro people are taken bodily from the words of my mouth. But of course, no idea is perfect and forever valid. Always to be living and apposite and timely, it must be modified and adapted to changing facts."[62]

He was born in Great Barrington, Massachusetts, in 1868, the year that Andrew Johnson was impeached and the freedmen of the South were enfranchised. Du Bois periodically wrote his story to illustrate his unfolding ideas about race and exemplary individuality, always in the lyrical language of saga. One of his autobiographies, *Dusk of Dawn*, began by asserting that his life had deep significance only "because it was part of a Problem." Always he stressed that he came late to realizing there was a "Problem," because he had a happy childhood. He was born "by a golden river and in the shadow of two great hills," although Du Bois usually clarified that the Housatonic River running through the Berkshire Mountains was golden from industrial waste. His mother, Mary Silvina Burghardt Du Bois, was a "dark shining bronze" woman with a "heavy, kind face" who gave the impression "of infinite patience" and belonged to what he sometimes called a "mighty clan" of farmers spread out between Great Barrington and Sheffield, Massachusetts. Mary Burghardt's grandfather, Tom Burghardt, was born in West Africa, enslaved by Dutch colonist Conraed Burghardt, and served briefly in the Continental Army, which may have been how he attained his freedom. The Burghardts had forsaken farming for domestic service by the time that Willie (as they called him) was born. Mary Silvina Burghardt had an older son, Adelbert, whose father was Mary's first cousin; Du Bois always passed quickly over this half brother, explaining that he did not know what to say about his mother's first romance. Long after he was famous, Du Bois declared that he loved his mother for pouring herself out for him, yet he also seethed that she and her family pushed his father out of their life.[63]

His paternal great-grandfather, James Du Bois of Poughkeepsie, New York, was a wealthy physician of French Huguenot origins, who fathered several children with slave mistresses, including a son named Alexander, who fathered a son named Alfred with a mistress in Haiti. Alexander Du Bois tried unsuccessfully to reclaim a rich plantation patrimony in Haiti, and Alfred Du Bois was Du Bois's father. Du Bois eventually met his stern, mannered, austere grandfather Alexander, but he had no memory of his own father, who left when he was an infant. In *Darkwater* (1920), the most passionate and evasive of Du Bois's memoirs, he introduced his father with Homeric imagery: "Alfred, my father, must have seemed a splendid vision in that little valley under the shelter of those mighty hills. He was small and beautiful of face and feature, just tinted with the sun, his curly hair chiefly revealing his kinship to Africa." In this telling, Alfred Du Bois was romantic, kindly, dashing, and a dreamer, albeit unreliable: "He yielded and flared back, asked forgiveness and forgot why, became the harshly-held favorite, who ran away and rioted and roamed and loved and married my brown mother."[64]

However dashing Alfred Du Bois may have been, he was a philandering husband who almost certainly committed bigamy when he married Mary Silvina Burghardt, and he never contacted his son after he took off, despite living in New England into the late 1880s. Du Bois obscured his father's lack of interest in him by misstating his age, whereabouts, and longevity. In *Darkwater* he claimed to remember "urgent letters" from his father telling them to join him in New Milford, Connecticut, "but mother no longer trusted his dreams, and he soon faded out of our lives into silence." In *Dusk of Dawn* (1940) he remembered differently that his father, "a light mulatto, died in my infancy, so that I do not remember him." In *The Autobiography of W. E. B. Du Bois* (1968) he said that his father lived with him for "a few years" before moving to Connecticut "to build a life and home for mother and me." *Dusk of Dawn* candidly explained that Alfred was "naturally a playboy" who "never actually did much of anything" except roam and play, "always irresponsible and charming." In later life Du Bois absolved his father of any blame, claiming that his mother's clannish, rustic family got rid of Alfred because he had cultured manners and was not black enough. Du Bois told an interviewer in 1960: "The black Burghardts didn't like it because he was too white and he had a lot of extra manners which they weren't used to. . . . At any rate, they practically drove him away. . . . They made it just as uncomfortable for Alfred as they could. . . . I don't suppose it was simply a matter of color. It was a matter of culture." In his last memoir, *The Autobiography of W. E. B. Du Bois*, he put it concisely: "The black Burghardts did not like him. He was too good-looking, too white." And he had no job. From the beginning there was an "open feud" between the Burghardts and Alfred, which eventually drove Alfred away.[65]

So Mary Du Bois had a son from her love affair with her first cousin and a son from her brief marriage to a light-colored playboy with a French surname; her family apparently intervened to curtail both relationships; and she eked out an impoverished living as a domestic worker. She lived with her father until he died, when Du Bois was five years old; then the family moved to an employer's estate in town until Mary's mother died; then Mary rented a dilapidated house near the railroad tracks, two blocks from a stretch of saloons and prostitution, which she shared with a similarly destitute white family. She struggled with depression and rarely said a word. Shortly after moving next to the railroad station, she had a stroke that left her with a lame leg and a withered hand, disabling her from fulltime work. Yet Du Bois idealized his childhood. In the first place, he was grateful for it. Moreover, this telling of his story accentuated his motif about discovering there was a problem to be solved: "Having finally gotten myself born, with a flood of Negro blood, a strain of French, a bit of

Dutch, but, thank God! no 'Anglo-Saxon,' I came to the days of my childhood. They were very happy."[66]

He and his mother were companions; people commended him for being nice to her, while aunts, cousins, neighbors, and the housemates helped out. Mary admonished Willie to avoid the saloons—"the open door to hell." Otherwise she treated him as though he were already perfect. Great Barrington, a New England town of five thousand, was firmly Republican and Anglo-Saxon Protestant, with about fifty African Americans. Du Bois received good schooling and had plenty of friends, black and white. In the world of adults, he noticed, whites and blacks kept more or less to themselves, whites had the good jobs, and blacks were pretty much restricted to day labor, farming, and house service. Moreover, Great Barrington definitely had something against the incoming Irish and South Germans that labored in the mills. But Du Bois experienced almost no racial discrimination in his youth. He despised the Irish and South Germans just like his white friends, annexing "the rich and well-to-do as my natural companions. Of such is the kingdom of snobs!"[67]

In Du Bois's telling, the Berkshire Mountains, fields, and orchards in which he played were "a boy's paradise," all of which seemed to be "property of the children of the town." He lacked any sense of being a racial other until the age of ten, when a girl visiting the town refused to exchange visiting cards with him: "Then it dawned upon me with a certain suddenness that I was different from the others; or like, mayhap, in heart and life, and longing, but shut out from their world by a vast veil." Du Bois may have lost his innocence that suddenly, on the edge of puberty, like many others. But years later he seemed to place this incident during high school, recalling that in high school he "began to feel the pressure of the 'veil of color.'" Whenever the card incident may have occurred, Du Bois caught the great break of his life in high school.[68]

Frank Hosmer, Du Bois's high school principal, came from the milieu of New England, Congregationalist, abolitionist families that ran the American Missionary Association and the Freedmen's Bureau. After graduating from Amherst he had moved to Great Barrington to teach; in the late 1870s he took over as principal at Great Barrington High School; in later life he served as president of a missionary college in Hawaii, returned to Massachusetts to serve in the state legislature, and died in 1918 from overwork in the Red Cross. Du Bois was thirteen years old when he began high school, four years after Reconstruction ended. Hosmer recognized Du Bois's ability, urging him to take the college preparatory curriculum of algebra, geometry, Latin, and Greek. Only two of Du Bois's thirteen classmates took the college track, and there were no other black students in the school, except for one who attended briefly, "but

I was very much ashamed of him because he did not excel the whites as I was quite used to doing." Hosmer got the local millowner's wife to purchase Du Bois's textbooks, who repaid the favor by helping her son with his lessons. Had Hosmer been a different kind of person, Du Bois later recalled, he would have studied for an agricultural trade and thought nothing of it: "I did not then realize that Hosmer was quietly opening college doors to me, for in those days they were barred with ancient tongues." As it was, he excelled in high school and considered himself "very much" part of the town's privileged class: "In this way I was thrown with the upper rather than the lower social classes and protected in many ways."[69]

In his youth Du Bois was Episcopalian, like the Burghardts, but he followed his mother to the Congregational Church in the late 1870s and also attended the AME Zion Church, impressing both Sunday schools with his Greek. The church was an important social outlet for Du Bois; plus he loved the prose of the King James Bible. New England Puritanism pressed deep into his mind, persuading Du Bois that truth is a moral absolute transcending mere data. Though Du Bois shucked off New England theism after he got to college, he never relinquished its belief that liberty is the conformity of one's will to moral duty. At his high school graduation he gave an address on Wendell Phillips, "my first sweet taste of the world's applause." He was sixteen years old and, in his telling, "thoroughly New England" in outlook and expressive reticence, a "habit of repression" that plagued him after he became a movement leader and was expected to inspire and befriend people. Mary Du Bois died of an apoplectic stroke shortly after her son graduated, which liberated him from the prospect of having to care for her: "Now it was the choking gladness and solemn feel of wings!" Du Bois was brainy, self-absorbed, and eager to fly, though not without a "half-guilty feeling"; only years later did he feel what he had lost. Having heard that Harvard was the best college, he set his heart on Harvard, "a mighty conjure-word in that hill town." Hosmer, Congregational minister C. C. Painter, and J. Carlisle Dennis, the black steward of a rich local widow, went to work on a realistic option, and Painter rounded up money from four Congregational churches that he had served to send Du Bois to Fisk University in Nashville, Tennessee. Du Bois took for granted that he would get to Harvard eventually, "but here and immediately was adventure." He was happy to go to Fisk because he was overdue to experience the land of "slavery, rebellion and black folk."[70]

Scholars have lingered over Du Bois's penchant for autobiographical expression and doubling metaphors. Thomas Holt notes that Du Bois conceived his life as the point of departure for everything he wanted to say about race, culture, and the "political uses of alienation." Arnold Rampersad notes that Du Bois was exemplary in this respect, as autobiography is the leading genre of African American literary expression. Lawrie Balfour notes that Du Bois used autobiography to exploit the fissure between his own subjection and stardom, and his own passage from believing that ignorance was the key to racism to believing that racism was too layered, unconscious, structural, and unwieldy to have a key. These observations help to fill out why Du Bois persistently idealized his youth—to reinforce his self-understanding as an outsider who understood the dominant society from within and without. Du Bois embodied the double-consciousness that he later described as the defining condition of African Americans behind the veil of color. He had barely a glimmer of it when he went to Fisk, because he had not experienced what most blacks experienced in the United States.[71]

Fisk Free Colored School had opened in 1866 on the site of a Union Army hospital, where three officers of the American Missionary Association pledged to build a school. On its first day two hundred former slaves enrolled; within a month there were six hundred; by the end of the year it had a thousand students. General Clinton Bowen Fisk, a former colonel of a regiment of black American troops, ran the school, directing teachers from the AMA and the Freedmen's Bureau. In 1867 the school's principal, John Ogden, renamed it Fisk University, though it was actually a high school, a college to train teachers, and a school of theology to train ministers. In the early 1870s Fisk launched a spectacularly successful choir, the Jubilee Singers, which enthralled audiences across America and Europe with songs from slavery times; the enormous popularity of the Negro spirituals financed the school's takeoff. When Du Bois got there in 1885 the faculty had one black professor and fourteen white, northern, deeply religious, abolitionist professors. One was Latin instructor Helen Morgan, the nation's first female full professor in a coeducational institution, and Fisk's mostly highly regarded teacher. Fisk University was thoroughly New England in some ways, producing Afro-Saxons, or Black Puritans, but most of Du Bois's classmates were otherwise very different from any Afro-Americans he had known in New England.[72]

Some were wealthy sons or daughters of white planters; few came directly from farming backgrounds; most were children of preachers, barbers, undertakers, physicians, or privileged domestic servants. Some had faced mobs and witnessed lynchings, and nearly all were steeped in the South's lexicon of racial insult and exclusion. Du Bois later recalled that Fisk contained "sons, daughters, and clients of every class of white Southerner." He was placed in the sophomore class, in recognition of his advanced preparation, but socially he was

blown away by Fisk: "I willed and lo! My people came dancing about me—
riotous in color, gay in laughter, full of sympathy, need, and pleading; darkly
delicious girls—'colored' girls—sat beside me and actually talked to me while
I gazed in tongue-tied silence or babbled in boastful dreams." One of the
girls was Margaret Murray, subsequently Washington's third wife, who chided
Du Bois about forgetting his lines in rhetoric class. Du Bois studied eagerly
"under teachers who bent in subtle sympathy, feeling themselves some shadow
of the Veil and lifting it gently that we darker souls might peer through to
other worlds."[73]

Du Bois began to feel and conceptualize what it meant for blacks lacking his
unusual background to be black in America. Outside the Fisk campus, the
slightest contact with a white person could bring danger. For the rest of his life
he said that Fisk was his true alma mater, because Fisk replaced his youthful
egocentrism with "a world centering and whirling about my race in America."
Fisk drew him into a black world, to a point. The emotional spontaneity of
southern black worship, for one thing, frightened him: "A sort of suppressed
terror hung in the air and seemed to seize them—a pythian madness, a demo-
niac possession, that lent terrible reality to song and word." Absorbing the "wail
and groan and outcry," Du Bois realized that he would never be black in that
way; New England reticence and intellectualism were too deep in him. For a
while he stuck with placid orthodoxy, until Fisk imposed apologetics on him,
which backfired. George Frederick Wright's *The Logic of Christian Evidences*
(1880) claimed to reconcile natural science and Christian orthodoxy, which
struck Du Bois as special pleading—as ridiculous in its way as Fisk's antidancing
moralism. Du Bois later claimed that he was repelled at Fisk by the Presbyterian
heresy trials of Union Theological Seminary biblical scholar Charles Briggs.
The Briggs trials, however, occurred after Du Bois graduated from Fisk in 1888.
At commencement, graduating in a class of three women and two men, Du
Bois gave an earnest address praising Bismarck for forging a nation out of bickering peoples. This was what African Americans needed to do, "marching forth
with strength and determination under trained leadership." Then Du Bois
entered the Harvard class of 1890 with third-year status, having learned of a
scholarship fund—Price Greenleaf Aid—to diversify Harvard's ingrown white
New England constituency.[74]

He had expected to go to Harvard and his mettle prevailed: "I willed and lo!
I was walking beneath the elms of Harvard—the name of allurement, the
college of my youngest, wildest visions!" He needed money, and "scholarships
and prizes fell into my lap." Du Bois kept to himself, feeling vulnerable and
easily ignored. Had he gone straight from Great Barrington to Harvard, he

might have tried to have a social life at Harvard, which probably would have failed. As it was, three years in Nashville taught Du Bois about color caste in America, which made it easier to thrive in Cambridge's version of social segregation. A few white students broke through his protective shell, insisting on knowing him, which he mostly appreciated. His roommate, William Monroe Trotter, was socially gregarious, so Du Bois didn't see much of him either.[75]

Du Bois told himself he was at Harvard to study, which he did, studying under neo-Hegelian idealists George Herbert Palmer and Josiah Royce, pragmatists William James and George Santayana, Unitarian social ethicist Francis Greenwood Peabody, and historian Albert Bushnell Hart. He especially liked James, who took him to his home and the Philosophical Club, and Peabody, who taught a famous course under a succession of titles: "Ethical Theories and Moral Reform," "Philosophy 5," "The Ethics of the Social Question," and other variations. After twenty years of name changes, Peabody accepted James's suggestion to call the course "Social Ethics," which became the name of his field. In Peabody's conception, social ethics had three steps: Generate data, assemble and analyze the data, and discern the underlying moral unity in nature. Somewhere between the second and third steps, he taught, science passed into (idealistic) philosophy. All social issues and events were interrelated, and social ethics sought to grasp the underlying unity of the whole, including its ethical character and principles. The ideal was to use inductive method to develop general moral principles, not to isolate practical problems or to assume moral principles on a priori grounds. Du Bois, having come to Harvard as a political innocent, religiously unmoored, and a transfer student, took to the kindly and religiously practical Peabody, and to James, both of whom encouraged Du Bois to pursue his interests in sociology and history.[76]

In his senior year Du Bois took his first course with Hart and found his academic calling. By then his religion was sophisticated idealism, believing in will, ideals, and the power of spirit backed by Spirit divine. Especially he believed in the power of ethical will, an idea variously conceived but similarly emphasized by James, Peabody, and Palmer. Hart was an ethical idealist, too, and a product of New England neo-Puritanism, but academically he was a recent doctoral graduate of Freiburg and a fervent believer in German data-driven historiography. Du Bois's first course with Hart surveyed U.S. constitutional and political history from 1783 to 1861, devoting several class sessions to American slavery. Hart drilled his students in objective methodology and its German invention, telling them that good history was not the mishmash of religion, patriotism, speculation, and personality cult propaganda favored by English Victorians. Lord Thomas Macaulay's five-volume *History of England* epitomized Victorian history; Du Bois loved it, thrilled by its sweeping, aggressive style and its emphasis on heroes. Hart countered that good history was factual, austere, and rigorous, not flashy, opinionated, and obsessed with heroes. Though Hart wrote passionate articles expounding his anti-imperialist and anti-expansionist views, he told students that these writings were moral propaganda, not history. Only objective history belonged in a history course or a serious history book. Du Bois, accepting this stricture, worked hard under Hart's tutelage, and won his support for graduate study. At commencement Du Bois gave a speech on Jefferson Davis to a throng of dignitaries. Still a political innocent, impressed chiefly by the exertion of forceful will, Du Bois praised Davis for combining individualism and might-makes-right: "I told them certain astonishing truths, waving my arms and breathing fast!" He got a huge ovation, perhaps too big, "but then! I walked home on pink clouds of glory!"[77]

Increasingly disturbed by the world, but very pleased with himself, Du Bois asked for a fellowship to support his studies for a Ph.D. in social science. Harvard gave him the Henry Bromsfield Rogers Fellowship for two years of study under Hart, economist Frank William Taussig, and sociologist Edward Cummings. Taussig treated the self-correcting market laws of neoclassical theory as objective truth, which was fine with Du Bois; he wrote papers for Taussig lauding the gold standard and condemning trade-union strikers. Hart told Du Bois that to become a great scholar he had to study in Germany, specifically Berlin. Harvard had no more fellowships for him, but a friend told him the Slater Fund supported black men worth educating. "No thought of modest hesitation occurred to me," Du Bois later recalled. He applied to the chair of the Slater Fund, Rutherford B. Hayes, who politely replied that the program to which Du Bois referred had been terminated.[78]

Du Bois refused to accept that as an answer: "I went at them hammer and tongs! I plied them with testimonials and mid-year and final marks." He chastised Hayes for suggesting that the program had been terminated because no worthy applicants had emerged. If the program was an experiment, Du Bois wrote, "you ought to have had at least one case before withdrawing it; if you have given aid before (and I mean here toward liberal education—not toward training plowmen) then your statement at Johns Hopkins was partial. From the above facts I think you owe an apology to the Negro people." This injury to African Americans was "almost irreparable," Du Bois admonished, adding that he had no trouble finding benefactors to study theology or plowing, "but I never found a man willing to help me get a Harvard Ph.D." Du Bois did not expect to get the Slater money; he sought merely to get the attention of someone—anyone—on the board that might help him get to Europe. But the former president of the United States, Du Bois later recalled wryly, relented: "I wonder now that he did not brush me aside, too, as a conceited meddler, but instead he smiled and surrendered."⁷⁹

In Europe Du Bois enjoyed the two most liberating and peaceful years of his life. He felt that he experienced the unity and elegance of life: "I dreamed and loved and wandered and sang." Europeans did not look down on him, and European anti-Americanism helped him relax, as he didn't like white America either: "I was just a man of the somewhat privileged student rank, with whom they were glad to meet and talk over the world." At the University of Berlin he studied under two welfare state Socialists, Adolf Wagner and Gustav von Schmoller, who ripped laissez-faire doctrine as the rule of ignorant capitalists. The economy had to be managed by a strong guardian state. Du Bois felt over-whelmed when Wagner and Schmoller expounded on varieties of Socialism; he vowed to learn about Socialism. He also studied under political historian Heinrich von Treitschke, who wanted Germany to seize foreign lands and become a mighty empire. Du Bois, still attracted to romantic authoritarians, brushed off Treitschke's offhand slur against "mulattoes" and nodded approv-ingly when Treitschke rattled on about great men overcoming the pitiful masses to do great things. Young Max Weber lectured at Berlin, grappling with the relationships between social scientific description and universal truth. For Du Bois, however, dreaming, loving, and wandering trumped the professorial lectures. He loved German Romanticism, especially Goethe and Beethoven, and he felt free in Germany. The veil of race seemed thin to him there, though he noticed that Germans denigrated Jews and Poles. In Germany Du Bois caught a glimpse of life's beauty and acquired a respect for manners. He strolled alone through parks, dined alone at cafés, and aimed for a doctorate. He made numerous visits to a prostitute in Potsdam, had an intense affair with a Berlin shop girl named Amalie, and dreamed of his future, describing all of it in his notebooks: "These are my plans: to make a name in science, to make a name in literature and thus to raise my race. Or perhaps to raise a visible empire in Africa thro' England, France or Germany."⁸⁰

Was that grandiose? Du Bois did not think so, though he puzzled at what to call it: "I rejoice as a strong man to run a race, and I am strong—is it egotism—is it assurance—or is it the silent call of the world spirit that makes me feel that I am royal and that beneath my scepter a world of kings shall bow." An ocean removed from his anti-imperialist teachers Hart and James, Du Bois gave free reign to his romantic authoritarian impulse. Near the end of his time in Germany he also took the roll of women he had loved and left. There were five so far, counting Amalie, whom Du Bois had strung along. He felt bad for her, regretting the "life-ruin of Amalie which is cruel," but he treasured the sexual ecstasy he had experienced with her, and he left Germany lamenting only that he missed his chance to earn a doctorate at Berlin. Du Bois needed one more semester to win the prize he really wanted, but the Slater money had run out, and the Slater board let on that delving into Goethe and Hegel in Berlin was not what John Slater had in mind when he established a fund for black education. No more Slater money went to high-flying doctoral types like Du Bois; all of it subsequently paid for school buildings and primary school teachers. Du Bois had to settle for Harvard, where he became the first African American to earn a doctorate. After two blissful years wandering through Europe and studying in Germany, he went to Paris for a last look, spent his last dollar, took passage to the United States in steerage, and found himself "suddenly back into 'nigger'-hating America!"[81]

The age of miracles, as Du Bois later described his student days, had begun at Fisk and ended in Europe. Now he plunged into a career of scholarship and teaching at Wilberforce University, the University of Pennsylvania, and Atlanta University. Payne had died in 1893, the year before Du Bois got to Wilberforce. Du Bois arrived in Wilberforce, Ohio, with affectations of his German experience—cane and gloves, plus a Wilhelmine mustache and goatee. He was eager to teach Latin and Greek, as assigned, and eager to change the world immediately, which did not work out.[82]

"I had all the wild intolerance of youth, and no experience in human tangles." Later he admitted that he must have been hard to take: "I was cocky and self-satisfied. I doubtless strutted and I certainly knew what I wanted." Wilberforce, however, had problems that would have provoked a humbler Du Bois. Founded by the Methodist Episcopal Church in 1852 and refounded as an AME institution by Payne in 1863, the school was engulfed in a leadership crisis when Du Bois got there, as Bishop Benjamin Arnett, overreaching his authority as trustee chair, had fired Wilberforce's most distinguished professor, classicist William Scarborough. Du Bois was there to replace a legendary teacher. He respected the moral seriousness of his colleagues and he welcomed "my first introduction to a Negro world," apparently disqualifying Fisk for its enclosure in Nashville. But Du Bois was a bad fit for Wilberforce, an intensely religious school where revival meetings periodically wiped out classes for days at a time. Du Bois refused to lead at extemporaneous prayer; he felt stifled intellectually; he wanted to teach sociology; and he tired of dogma, revival enthusiasm, financial constraints, disciplinary duty, the machinations of Arnett and university president S. T. Mitchell, and teaching languages: "For the first time in my life I realized there were limits to my will to do." Instead of allowing Du Bois to teach sociology, Arnett and Mitchell added German, English, and history to his portfolio. Du Bois seethed, completed his doctoral dissertation, and assured himself that something better would come along; years later he likened Mitchell to the devil.[83]

Three good things happened at Wilberforce: Du Bois finished his dissertation on the suppression of the slave trade to the United States, he met Alexander Crummell, and he found a companion. The dissertation aimed at American myths about the U.S. role in the Atlantic slave trade. Building his case on government statutes, census tabulations, court decisions, naval reports, and newspaper accounts, Du Bois contended that the United States routinely violated its 1808 federal ban on slave trading stipulated by Article 1, Section 9 of the U.S. Constitution. This practice was so prevalent that by 1850 virtually all slave-trading ships heading anywhere in the Americas flew the U.S. flag for protection. In 1619, twenty slaves arrived in Jamestown, Virginia; in 1790 the United States had seven hundred thousand slaves; by 1830 there were two million; by 1860 there were nearly four million.

Du Bois argued that these extraordinary increases could not have occurred had the United States abided by its own law. Had it abolished slavery in 1789, it would have become a better country. As it was, the U.S. Constitution kept the monster breathing, Southern states demanded more slaves than they could produce, and the northern states were variously indifferent and corrupted. Decades later, following Philip Curtin's monumental work, historians sharply reduced the estimate of the Atlantic slave trade (15,000,000–50,000,000) to 9,566,000. Du Bois estimated that 250,000 slaves were illegally imported to the United States after 1808; Curtin's figure was 54,000. Du Bois underestimated the American South's success at growing its own slave force, and he missed the fact that the sugar economies of Cuba and Brazil had higher mortality rates, thus making them more dependent on importation. But Du Bois pointed to something more important than precise importation figures—the moral corruption of the nation in its hallowed constitutional beginning. And he began his career as a scholar that conceived the color line in international terms.[84]

Hart certified Du Bois's dissertation on June 1, 1895, and secured its publication as the inaugural volume of the Harvard Historical Series. That month Du Bois met Crummell at the Wilberforce commencement ceremony. Du Bois had never met a black man that he considered to be worth emulating, a point he made sharply in his speeches to black audiences in the Boston area. A few years later, in *The Souls of Black Folk*, Du Bois recalled his first impression of Crummell: "Tall, frail, and black he stood, with simple dignity and an unmistakable air of good breeding." Until that moment, the best model that Du Bois had was a half-imagined image of his cultured grandfather Alexander Du Bois. Crummell, he judged, radiated a rare blend of integrity and hope: "Instinctively I bowed before this man, as one bows before the prophets of the world. Some seer he seemed, that came not from the crimson Past or the gray To-come, but from the pulsing Now." Crummell validated Du Bois's elitism, idealism, and Pan-African internationalism; more important, he provided a model of strong and dignified black intellectualism and religious leadership.[85]

ALEXANDER CRUMMELL AND THE BLACK NATION

Alexander Crummell was an Episcopal priest, an intellectual, an Anglophile, and a former missionary and Liberian nationalist. Like many black nationalists, he was an authoritarian collectivist and racial separatist, in his case with a social gospel theology, a puritanical/Victorian moral code, an American Federalist political philosophy, a romantic idealistic racialism, and a deep admiration for Plato. He experienced the tyranny of the majority as a youth and abhorred it throughout his life, having witnessed the anti-abolitionist riots of 1834 in New York City. Like most nineteenth-century social thinkers, though with special emphasis in his case, Crummell believed that "civilized" societies got to be advanced by submitting to universal physical, moral, and economic laws. He loved West Africa and was fiercely devoted to the rise of blacks as a nation, all the while holding that almost everything about Africa's cultural legacy was backward. And he knew from experience that only a few trustworthy and noble souls existed among the whites—a moral and spiritual elite. This elite helped him overcome the bigotry and repression of other whites, lifting him into a black elite, where he preached a gospel of racial nationalism. Crummell made his early reputation as an abolitionist and his midlife reputation as a black colonialist, but he had long left behind the dream of a Pan-African Christian homeland in West Africa when Du Bois met him.

He was born in New York in 1819. Crummell's father, Bostin Crummell, was probably descended, as he claimed, from the Temne chiefs of what became Sierra Leone, although Boston *Guardian* editor George Forbes claimed to know that Bostin Crummell was a Vey educated by missionaries. In either case, he was captured and enslaved at the age of thirteen and brought to New York, where he served Peter Schermerhorn for ten years before refusing to be a slave any longer. Alexander Crummell treasured his connection to the Temne tribe, stressing that they were a noble people of "indomitable" and "unconquerable" spirit, never subdued by the British, while the "yellow" Veys were unimpressive in physicality and vigor. Still, he noted, the Veys were smart and their women were beautiful. Bostin Crummell became an oyster vendor in New York after shucking off slavery; he married an Episcopalian "Free African" from Long Island, Charity, whose family had a Quaker connection; and the Crummells lived in the Five Points district of lower Manhattan, on Leonard Street, next door to the family of Henry Highland Garnet. Conditions were harsh and morally perilous in Five Points, a memory that fueled the moralistic preaching of Crummell and Garnet throughout their careers. They grew up as friends and classmates at the African Free School Number Two, on Mulberry Street, and later the Canal Street High School, founded by New York abolitionists Lewis and Arthur Tappan. In 1834, shortly after William Lloyd Garrison completed a speaking tour in England, race rioters destroyed Lewis Tappan's home and much of the Five Points district, including St. Philip's Episcopal Church, where the Crummells were members. Crummell was stunned by the vengeance of the anti-abolitionist mob. Then he was affronted, and motivated, by U.S. vice president John C. Calhoun's declaration that he would not believe that Negros were human beings until he met one that knew Greek syntax. Crummell vowed to learn Greek.[86]

In 1835 abolitionists established the Noyes Academy in Canaan, New Hampshire. Crummell, Garnet, and classmate Thomas S. Sidney made the arduous journey together, as Crummell later recalled, "in gentlemanly garb," providing "a most unusual sight" and evoking "universal sneers and ridicule" along the way. Garnet, who was chronically ill, barely survived the trip. Soon after the trio arrived they gave abolitionist speeches at a parish meetinghouse in Plymouth and the locals erupted against the Noyes Academy: "Fourteen black boys with books in their hands set the entire Granite State crazy!" Crummell, Garnet, and Sidney averted a mob and fled the state. For the rest of his life Crummell loathed the masses, urging that the educated elite of any civilized society had to restrain the majority's stupidity and violence. The trio enrolled at Oneida Institute in Whitesboro, New York, founded by Presbyterian abolitionist minister Beriah Green, who taught biblical Greek and Hebrew to Crummell and encouraged him to aim for the Episcopal ministry. Crummell knew of three black Episcopal rectors: Absolom Jones of Pennsylvania, William Levington of Maryland, and his own rector at St. Philip's Church, Peter Williams Jr. He was fond of Williams, grateful for his moral guidance and support, and appreciated that Williams was a clerical pioneer. But Crummell chafed at his rector's timidity and diplomatic deference; Williams was no role model for him. Crummell reasoned that if he earned a degree at General Theological Seminary in New York, the white clergy would be compelled to treat him more respectfully than they treated Williams. General Seminary, however, refused to admit Crummell, ostensibly to avoid offending donors from South Carolina, and the bishop of New York—B. T. Onderdonk—treated Crummell badly, all of which set off a chain reaction of Episcopalian outrage from what became Crummell's first group of white benefactors. The key benefactors were New Jersey bishop George W. Doane and John Jay, grandson of America's first chief justice. Crummell ministered to Episcopal congregations in New Haven, Connecticut; Boston; and Providence, Rhode Island, as a lay reader and deacon, and in 1844 he was ordained to the priesthood in Philadelphia, unhappily, as most clergy shunned him.[87]

Crummell relied on his white liberal benefactors, as most white clergy resented his intrusion into their white supremacist club, and many black Episcopalians did not warm to him. Every congregation that Crummell ever served, while acknowledging that he was strong and eloquent, complained that he was contentious, accusatory, unfriendly, and disdained pastoral care. In 1840 Crummell lost his closest friend, Sidney, to illness, which cut him deeply. Soon afterward he married an eighteen-year-old woman, Sarah, with whom he had seven children, three of whom died early. The marriage was cold and mutually bitter. Nearly all of Crummell's written references to his wife were disparaging, especially concerning her chronic illnesses, and he never mentioned her by name. His harshness eventually alienated him from his entire family. In 1845 Crummell took over the Church of the Messiah, New York's second black Episcopal church. Three years later he hauled his family to England, officially to raise money for his congregation. Crummell, however, pined to be an educator, preferably as the founder of a black college. He recoiled at the anti-intellectualism of U.S. American society, and he knew that Douglass had recently found refuge and celebrity in England. In London, Liverpool, Birmingham, and other cities, antislavery clergy welcomed Crummell to their pulpits, where he preached against racism and told his story. Again he quickly acquired influential friends, especially through Henry Venn, secretary of the British and Foreign Anti-Slavery Society. Crummell thrived in England and found his calling.

From the beginning he delivered the standard Douglass-style speech against American slavery, but Crummell had never been a slave and he stressed that most slaves were heathens stripped of family, dignity, and culture. His new benefactors built up a fund for Crummell's congregation and a second fund to support Crummell. Eminent physiologist Benjamin Brodie, working with activists in Venn's circle, helped get Crummell into Queen's College, Cambridge. Crummell entered Cambridge in 1849, studying Greek and Latin classics, plus mathematics. He later recalled that at first he was "the last man in everything";

plus he suffered from poor health, as did his wife and three surviving young children. But Crummell persevered scholastically, absorbing Joseph Butler's early-Enlightenment *Analogy of Religion* and earning respectable marks on exams, all despite a dismal family situation and complaints of neglect from his home congregation. He loved England, enthusing that only there had he experienced what it felt like to be treated with respect. He thrilled at meeting leading academics, clergy, writers, and antislavery activists. One evening he heard a three-hour performance by Macaulay, a "brilliant avalanche" of history, biography, poetry, and criticism that enthralled Crummell and boosted his romantic idealism. Crummell made lifelong friends, judging that the English had distinct gifts for liberty and curiosity. Recalibrating his heroic ambitions, he conceived the idea of a West African ministry uniting blacks from the Americas, West Indies, and Africa—converting West Africans to Christianity and civilization.[88]

Crummell had shared the usual abolitionist scorn for the American Colonization Society. Now he turned aside the protests of his English and American friends that colonialism had nothing to do with abolitionist social justice. Crummell and Garnet made this turn for similar reasons, determined to apply the principles of self-help and nationalist self-determination to emancipation. Crummell undoubtedly cringed at living off the charity of white English abolitionists for five years, although he never said so. He probably exaggerated how wonderfully he was treated in England, although he never admitted that either. He could have remained in England after graduating from Cambridge in 1853, and Sarah Crummell desperately wanted to stay there instead of returning to the United States or chasing his West African dream. Instead Crummell told friends he could not remain in England, despite their entreaties to stay, and he thought it best not to return to his congregation in New York, because he was devoted to the cause of a black Christian empire in West Africa. Crummell moved to Liberia shortly after graduating from Cambridge.

He worked diligently, founding congregations and a college, preaching that Christianity was the true religion and that English Christian civilization was superior to all others by virtue of having submitted to the universal laws of nature, morality, and civilized order. For Crummell, "civilization" and English-speaking "culture" were equivalent; thus he used them as interchangeable terms. Civilization was essential to achieving black liberty, and the rule of educated black elites was essential to black progress. Many Liberians found him arrogant, as Crummell openly disdained "backward" blacks and everyone else who disagreed with him. Like Garnet, Martin Delany, and other leading nationalists, he denigrated black humanity routinely, decrying the "degraded" condition of black people. When Crummell arrived in Monrovia in 1853, Liberia had 225,000 natives, some of whom were Americanized, and 10,000 American-Liberians. Crummell grieved at the "poor benighted heathen" in the former category and focused his efforts, at first, on the colonists, whom he called "with rare and individual exceptions, ignorant, benighted, besotted, and filthy, both in the inner and the outer man." Later he worked equally with both groups, with some success, although they wearied of his accusatory sermons. Crummell's best biographer, Wilson Jeremiah Moses, described his temperament as "brooding," "vituperative," and "combative," adding that Crummell "needlessly made enemies with his sarcastic tongue." Even his friends described him as "a perfect Tsar." In 1862, when Crummell's lecture tour in the United States converted Turner to emigration activism, Crummell warned his audiences that Africa was desperately backward: "Darkness covers the land, and gross darkness the people. Great evils universally prevail. Confidence and security are destroyed. Licentiousness abounds everywhere. Moloch rules and reigns throughout the whole continent, and by the ordeal of Sassywood, Fetiches, human sacrifices, and devil-worship, is devouring men, women, and little children."[89]

The early black nationalists wanted to create a black nationality on cosmopolitan terms, which they borrowed from European and American racialism. In the name of rejecting assimilation and promoting black nationality they championed a severe form of Euro-American cultural assimilation. Their parents had been victimized by the slave wars of West Africa; thus the early nationalists were the wrong generation to celebrate anything in African culture. Neither did the slave culture of America hold anything redemptive, except, for some, the figure of Jesus. Crummell epitomized the early black nationalist predicament and solution, urging black Christians that they had a moral duty to Christianize West Africa and help unite the black race. Returning to Africa as colonists would be good for their souls and saving for West Africans. Liberia would be saved by the transplantation of Christian culture in the same way that England was saved from backwardness by the importation of Roman discipline and Christian morality. Crummell gave his best years to this calling, though Douglass knowingly accused him of exaggerating his accomplishments in Liberia. Crummell misrepresented his health too, claiming that he enjoyed robust health in the tropical heat, which was not true for him or his family.

The end came quickly for his Liberian mission. Crummell's friend Edward James Roye, leader of the True Whig Party, was inaugurated in January 1870 as Liberia's fifth president, but the following year Roye was overthrown and killed in a coup led by the nation's American-Liberian aristocracy. Crummell characterized the coup as a revolt of the ignorant against "newspapers, Colleges, improvement, civilization." The new three-person junta, he despaired, knew nothing of liberty, culture, or virtue, which put his life in danger. Crummell had seen it coming, warning with alarm in 1870 that Liberia's political class had "ignored the *national* obligation to train, educate, civilize and regulate the heathen tribes around us!" They also failed to build a viable economy and governing structure: "All historic fact shows that force, that is authority, must be used in the exercise of guardianship over heathen tribes. Mere theories of democracy are trivial in this case, and can never nullify this necessity."[90]

Crummell returned to the United States, taking over tiny St. Mary's Chapel in Washington, DC—a black stepchild of wealthy St. John's Episcopal Church. He founded a new congregation and building—St. Luke's Church—out of St. Mary's, building a solid congregation of six hundred communicants during his twenty years of ministry there. Washington, DC, was the cultural capital of black America; St. Luke's attracted notable visitors, including President Chester A. Arthur and U.S. senator Georg F. Hoar, and Crummell, despite sparking many controversies with harsh remarks, sustained a growing congregation. He gave commanding, erudite sermons and lectures, showering audiences with references to Plato, Chaucer, Shakespeare, and his favorite English idealists, especially Wordsworth. After returning to the United States he made the transition to domestic nationalism, still exalting the values and culture of English civilization and still in the name of a conservative black Christian nation, though sometimes in the language of social integrationism. Black nationalism had faded in the 1860s with the Civil War and the Reconstruction Amendments. It rebounded in the 1870s with Turner's vigorous advocacy, Crummell's return to the United States, and the fallout from Reconstruction, but it became different things to Turner and Crummell.

Crummell contended that the social principle binding all blacks to each other was as powerfully real in America as in West Africa. Fixating on West Africa was unnecessary and unhelpful. The "social principle" was the disposition that led specific groups to self-identify and work together. It consisted essentially of the conjoined experiences of mutuality and dependence, and it was the driving force behind the forging of a nation: "Men must associate and combine energies in order to produce large results." The greatest nations on earth, Crummell asserted, were Great Britain, France, the United States, Holland, and Belgium. They got to be great by submitting to the civilizing principles of growth and mastery—especially the principle of association—that obtained for all nations and races on earth: "We children of Africa in this land are no way different from any other people in these respects." It took ten centuries for the English to grow from "wild and bloody" savagery into the world's greatest nation; Crummell counseled that post-slavery black America would need a century to become great. Black Americans would not make it if they tried to forget they were black and/or failed to build race-defined organizations. There were two barriers, in his view, to blacks becoming a great people in America. The first was white racism, and the second was that many blacks were "ignorant, unkempt, dirty, animal-like, repulsive, and half-heathen—brutal and degraded." Crummell admonished that nothing could be done about the first problem, except to address the second problem. Blacks were the only people in America lacking power, and they would remain powerless as long as they had a vast underperforming underclass.[91]

White Americans would not respect the rights or dignity of blacks until blacks lifted themselves to the social standards of whites. Crummell expounded constantly on this theme without seeming to notice that most white Americans lived in rural poverty or urban tenements lacking any experience of "cultural uplift." After President Hayes dismantled Reconstruction and Douglass became marshal of the District of Columbia, Crummell got sharper about his differences with Douglass. Douglass told black audiences to remember slavery, agitate for their rights as individuals, let go of race consciousness, and spurn separatist organizations. Crummell disagreed on every count. The slave experience held nothing worth remembering, aside from giving ballast to Douglass's celebrity. Agitation was pointless and counterproductive without cultural development, notwithstanding Douglass's cheerleading for agitation. And race pride was essential to the salvation of blacks as a people, despite the urgings of too many light-colored blacks to forget about race.

Crummell had deeply ambivalent feelings about "mulattoes," distinguishing pointedly between black "negroes" and biracial "coloreds." He appreciated that the "colored" population had many highly educated individuals, "a merciful providence by which some gleams of light and knowledge came." Still, Crummell stressed that there were five hundred thousand colored Americans in 1860 chiefly because slavery destroyed the black family and slave masters mercilessly violated black women. Crummell insisted that the black American woman, upon being freed from slavery, was "a prostrate and degraded being." Nearly thirty years after the Civil War ended, he claimed that she was "still the crude, rude, ignorant mother." Crummell folded this baleful reading of black female humanity into his case for a male leadership elite, even as he claimed to be a feminist. In his telling, blacks were temperamentally conservative, receptive, religious, and law-abiding. They were not genetically or culturally prone to violence, like the Irish and Germans. Crummell condemned the "perfectly astounding" anticapitalism of white trade unionists and the loose sexual mores of modern society, imploring that the real threats to American society were class war and sexual anarchy. Black Americans, if left in peace, would change this picture through their inherent moral decency, "ready to uphold the prerogatives of enterprise, the rights of property, and the sway of Law."[92]

To become a great people, blacks needed only to be left alone, to restore the father-headed family ideal, and to build up a Christian, culturally accomplished elite. In 1885 Crummell said it plainly at Storer College in West Virginia, where he and Douglass gave dueling commencement addresses. Crummell argued that cultural uplift and accomplishment were more important than protest activism. The race problem was partly a problem of black deficiency, not merely white racism. Douglass countered that nothing was more important than protest activism to achieve equality; Crummell had it exactly backward. Crummell was undaunted, insisting that blacks had to take responsibility for their own condition, they had to do so by building strong father-led families, and that Douglass-style, integrationist protest activism distracted middle-class blacks from taking responsibility for their situation.[93]

Black America needed an accomplished Christian elite that built up black America's moral and cultural stature. Crummell said it wherever he went. He said it at Thanksgiving in 1877, enlarging on "The Destined Superiority of the Negro," where Crummell contrasted the fates of black Americans and Native Americans. Blacks were on their way to becoming a great people because they were virtuous, Christian, receptive, and adaptable. Native Americans, by contrast, stuck to their "depravity" and "gross paganism," which led straight to their "national suicide." Crummell claimed that Native Americans were feeble, uncivilized, unhealthy, and thus already decaying when the Europeans arrived. Then they perished, because "depravity prepares some races of men for destruction. Every element of good has gone out of them." Crummell admired and lamented the wasted efforts of missionaries who translated the Bible into Native American languages that soon vanished. Black Americans, by contrast, did not waste their opportunities, despite having to endure slavery: "Although great cruelty and widespread death have been large features in the history of the Negro, nevertheless they have been overshadowed by the merciful facts of great natural increase, much intellectual progress, the gravitation of an unexampled and worldwide philanthropy to the race, singular religious susceptibility and progress, and generous, wholesale emancipations, inclusive of millions of men, women, and children."[94]

The good must be cultivated, Crummell implored. He said it at Wilberforce in 1895, calling for an enlightened moral elite that lifted the black race to national greatness. Two years later Crummell founded the American Negro Academy, declaring that the organization's purpose was to undertake "the civilization of the

Negro race in the United States, by the scientific processes of literature, art, and philosophy." Crummell was an idealist, spurning the grubby materialism of British empiricism and, without saying it, Booker Washington. Materialists and empiricists were "blind" to what is saving, Crummell contended: "For they fail to see that neither property, nor money, nor station, nor office nor lineage, are fixed factors, in so large a thing as the destiny of man; that they are not vitalizing qualities in the changeless hopes of humanity. The greatness of peoples springs from their ability to grasp the grand conceptions of being. It is the absorption of a people, of a nation, of a race, in large majestic and abiding things which lifts them up to the skies."[95]

That was exactly what Du Bois already believed; hearing it from Crummell thrilled him. Crummell expounded often on the incarnation of the divine ideal in Christ and the greatness of Jesus's teaching. The cardinal principle of Christ, Crummell explained, was that of Christ's own sovereignty and rule, the kingdom of God. Jesus described a divine government already set up in the existing world, founded upon righteousness and sustained by God's love and rule. This divine kingdom had three dimensions. First, it transcended all worldly kingdoms and will prevail against the very gates of hell. Second, through the work of the Holy Spirit it produced regenerated human beings that followed the way of Christ—throwing off selfishness and domination, repudiating the spirit of revenge, abolishing war and national enmity, and recognizing that all human beings are children of God. Third, the divine kingdom held the promise of eternal well-being in an otherworldly spiritual realm in the presence and glory of God.[96]

Crummell taught that these grand ideas of Jesus's held the key to the progress and hope of the entire world. The Egyptians, Babylonians, Greeks, and Romans built mighty civilizations, but all were saturated with brutality and lust, reveling in their moral debasement. They produced some worthy art but more that was disgusting, unbearable for people cultivated by Christianity: "The paintings and the sculpture are too often vile and infamous. The condition of woman among them was degrading. Their family-life was barbarous, and not seldom shameless. Their social state presented the varied aspect of great luxury, dazzling splendor, allied to gross license and unrestrained indulgence." Crummell proclaimed that Christ changed "the moral complexion of human civilization," making the world see what is true, beautiful, good, and eternal. The Word of the gospel, wherever it spread, turned peoples against greed, domination, slavery, and war.[97]

To be sure, Crummell allowed, Christ had not yet abolished war, but "He *has been abolishing war* through all the centuries through, by the humanization which He has introduced into the policy of nations." Under the influence of Christ, the world grasped that it is a "brutish, heathen" thing to love war. Similarly, Crummell saw the redemptive, humanizing influence of Christ "in the suppression of the slave trade, in the destruction of piracy, in the abolition of slavery, in the reformation of prisons, in the progress of the temperance cause, in the improvement of tenement houses, in the increase of hospitals and infirmaries; in the care of the blind, the deaf, and the dumb; in the godly efforts to prevent the ravages of licentiousness; and in the merciful endeavors to save the victims of prostitution!" Though Christ took on flesh only briefly, suffering insult and crucifixion for his blessedness, "yet His divine face, the odor of His sanctity, the glories of His nature, and the mystical power of His resurrection come streaming down the centuries."[98]

This rendering of gospel religion had profound resonance for Du Bois, and for Reverdy Ransom, especially because Crummell, like Jesus, suffered for those he came to save. Du Bois, a fatherless intellectual, autodidactic and largely self-created, bowed for the first and only time to a role model, although Crummell disappeared from his later memoirs. Crummell, Du Bois perceived, had to battle against hate, despair, and doubt, and the greatest enemy was doubt. Crummell was a Jesus figure that accepted his anointed calling and suffered abuse and derision to save his people. Moreover, Crummell had a social gospel theology that fit his modernizing religious agenda, one focused on the progressive influence of Christ upon history. He had begun his career as a black nationalist in the narrow sense of the category and moved to a broad-sense version that rang true to Du Bois, even describing nationalist ambitions in the language of social integration. Above all, Crummell stood strong, subjecting himself to criticism and opposition but refusing to be shamed. When told that many found him to be difficult and, in particular, rigid, Crummell replied: "I am proud of this criticism. It is in evidence that I tolerated no iniquity, and that I rebuked depravity." The fact that Crummell dehumanized Native Americans did not count against his Christ-figure status for Du Bois, who also did not mention Crummell's truculence. For years to come, when Du Bois blistered black and white ministers for misrepresenting the religion of Jesus in shabby, mediocre, corrupted, and hypocritical ways, he held Crummell in mind as a Christian witness who was none of these things.[99]

BLACKS IN A NORTHERN CITY AND URBAN SOCIOLOGY

At Wilberforce, however, Du Bois judged that he was surrounded by pious mediocrity, and he became increasingly morose about it. He was in a desultory state of mind when Washington electrified America with the Atlanta address. Du Bois felt the immensity of the moment, congratulating Washington for his "phenomenal success at Atlanta." Meanwhile, he was stuck in a pathetic battle with Arnett, who tried to impose one of his low-functioning sons on the faculty. Du Bois rallied the faculty and students to strike, forcing Arnett to back down, but Du Bois did not kid himself that this small victory meant anything. Arnett was a power broker, McKinley's leading advisor on African American affairs. Du Bois had no future at Wilberforce and did not want one. In the spring he cheered himself up a bit by marrying one of his students, Nina Gormer, the daughter of a hotel chef from Cedar Rapids, Iowa. Du Bois prized Nina's cultivated manners, later describing her as "a slip of a girl, beautifully dark-eyed and thorough and good as a German housewife." Three weeks after his wedding he won deliverance from Wilberforce in a telegram from the University of Pennsylvania.[100]

Penn turned out to be a stopover of one year, long enough to rankle Du Bois for the rest of his life. He was marginally employed there, and his name did not make it into the catalog. But it was a productive turning point, as he was hired by the sociology department at Penn's Wharton School, and indirectly by the settlement movement, to write a pioneering work of black urban sociology, *The Philadelphia Negro.*

Philadelphia in the 1890s only faintly resembled its fabled past as a city of goodwilled Quakers, hardworking Germans, and a sizable black bourgeoisie. Early-nineteenth-century economic expansion drew large numbers of unskilled Irish, Scots, and other whites to the city to work in the mills and foundries. They built a Democratic machine that, in 1838, disenfranchised black voters across Pennsylvania, sparking a succession of race riots up to the Civil War. After the war the machine in Philly was Republican and blacks got patronage jobs through it, but the Gilded Age capitalists cared even less about the common good than their predecessors, while Philly became an industrial dynamo turning out steel, ships, and railroad cars.

Philadelphia had the typical northern machine government, which catered to the capitalist class and distributed patronage, which gave rise to a local Progressive/social gospel movement to clean up government and build neighborhood settlements. In Philly, Quaker activist Susan P. Wharton was a leader and founding member of the College Settlement Association. Wharton had the idea that a social scientific study of her predominantly black neighborhood, the Seventh Ward, would be socially useful. Of Philadelphia's forty thousand African Americans, nearly ten thousand lived in the Seventh Ward. Wharton pitched the idea to her neighbor Charles C. Harrison, a retired sugar tycoon currently serving as acting provost at Penn.

The settlement movement had right-leaning assimilationists that patronized African Americans and shuddered at them, left-leaning assimilationists that tried to keep their paternalism on a leash, and neo-abolitionists that conceived antiracism and cultural diversity as elementary to a just society. Jane Addams was a neo-abolitionist with a patronizing streak that she mostly stifled. The Philly CSA group had a few feminists of that sort, including Du Bois's research assistant, Isabel Eaton. For the rest of his life, however, when Du Bois mentioned the motivations of Wharton, Harrison, project director Samuel McCune Lindsay, and the CSA feminists, he professed not to care. He took for granted that paternalistic racism had the upper hand and he was hired to do a dirty job—depicting the social pathology of black Philadelphia. Officially, Penn hired Du Bois to describe how Philadelphia blacks lived and worked, which occupations they were excluded from, how many of their children went to school, and what it all meant. Du Bois, however, knew that his sponsors were mostly concerned about the spread of black poverty and black criminality, two fearful things that went together. Their theory, he later recalled, "was that this great, rich, and famous municipality was going to the dogs because of the crime and venality of its Negro citizens." David Levering Lewis puts it sharply: "The conservative CSA gentry thought of poverty in epidemiological terms, as a virus to be quarantined." Du Bois was supposed to help them contain the virus.[101]

The book that he wrote, *The Philadelphia Negro*, was obliging and not. Du Bois interviewed twenty-five hundred households, wrote grim descriptions of the Seventh Ward's poverty, vice, and crime, and sprinkled the book with patronizing admonitions that sounded like Washington or Abbott. But he also challenged racist interpretations of the situation he described. Many of his subjects balked at being interviewed; Du Bois later recalled, "They had a natural dislike to being studied like a strange species." Sociology was in its infancy, and few works on any social subject were based on empirical research. *The Philadelphia Negro* was a pioneering work in urban sociology, combining urban ethnography, social history, and descriptive statistics. The book carefully discussed Seventh Ward families, individuals, homes, street activity, and community organizations, basing its structure and method on Charles Booth's influential work *Life and Labour of the People in London* (1889). It also consulted city surveys published by the CSA and Addams's book *Hull House Maps and Papers* (1895). Du Bois did not claim that his research refuted common prejudices; in fact he affirmed that his picture of black urban existence conformed "to a large extent, with general public opinion." Life was grinding, harsh, and often deadly in the Seventh Ward. Du Bois's chapter on crime featured thirty diagrams and tables, contended that criminality was "rampant" in the Seventh

Ward, and argued that ex-slaves and their descendants were especially prone to theft, burglary, and other crimes involving violations of private property rights. Later he added that crime was also terrible in poor communities that suffered from less racial hostility than blacks experienced. The Irish and Italians were felt to be worth educating "because they were men and brothers," but white America declared of its black population: "Let them stagger downward."[102]

Du Bois showed that 80 percent of black males worked at unskilled jobs, they were excluded from the craft and industrial unions, they were excluded from most teaching and clerical positions, and they were driven out of jobs in which Philadelphia blacks had once thrived—catering and barbering. In the midst of so much harshness and exclusion, how could it be surprising that the Seventh Ward contained so much rage, hopelessness, crime, and drug use? Du Bois had a chapter in which white Philadelphians casually explained why they would never hire an African American for anything that mattered, or anything at all. A druggist stated, "I wouldn't have a darky to clean out my store, much less to stand behind the counter." An applicant for a clerk position was told: "What do you suppose we'd want of a nigger?" An applicant at a bakery was told: "We don't work no niggers here." An applicant at a candy manufacturer was told that the white workers would quit if a Negro were hired. Du Bois acknowledged that overt racial hostility had diminished greatly in Philadelphia in recent decades: "A colored man today can walk the streets of Philadelphia without personal insult; he can go to theatres, parks, and some places of amuse- ment without meeting more than stares and discourtesy; he can be accommo- dated at most hotels and restaurants." This was important, he said, "a vast advance." But the employer quotes painted a devastating picture of what blacks were up against in northern cities when they applied for any job above menial labor. White America, Du Bois argued, paid a staggering price in black crime and indolence to spare the feelings of white people that could not bear to asso- ciate with dark-skinned people.[103]

The Philadelphia Negro did not say that racial prejudice was the sole cause of black America's grim condition. Du Bois contended that race, class, economics, and feeble group morality interacted badly in the Seventh Ward and the class factor was the main driver of problems on the moral and cultural level. Most white Americans knew little or nothing about the class structure of black America. There were good Negroes and bad ones, and the good ones usually had some white blood. Du Bois countered that social class was a powerful factor in black America, where four distinct classes existed. At the top was the aristocracy, an elite of 277 families in Philadelphia (approximately 3,000 persons) that Du Bois described as prosperous "families of undoubted respectability" far removed from menial labor. The second group was the "respectable working class," which worked hard in "steady remunerative work" and was upwardly mobile. The third class consisted of the "working poor," which made a real effort but with very modest success, sometimes because its work ethic faltered. At the bottom was the "lowest class," where sloth, immorality, and crime abounded; Du Bois called it "the submerged tenth." The lower classes, he urged, had no hope of climbing out of poverty without embracing exactly the bootstrap work ethic preached by Washington: "The social environment of excuse, listless despair, careless indulgence and lack of inspiration to work is the growing force that turns black boys and girls into gamblers, prostitutes, and rascals." At the same time, unlike Washington, Du Bois stressed that the social system was stacked against African Americans: "How long can a city teach its black children that the road to success is to have a white face?"[104]

The Philadelphia Negro seesawed on this twofold theme, issuing moralistic bromides that outpatronized Washington while making it clear that white oppression prevented most African Americans from having a real chance. On the one hand, "The Negro is, as a rule, willing, honest and good-natured, but he is also, as a rule, careless, unreliable and unsteady." Put differently, Negroes "must cease to be, as they often are, breeders of idleness and extravagance and complaint. Work, continuous and intensive; work, although it be menial and poorly rewarded; work, though done in travail of soul and sweat of brow, must be so impressed upon Negro children as the road to salvation, that a child would feel it a greater disgrace to be idle than to do the humblest labor." On the other hand, white America excluded Afro-Americans from any opportunity to earn a decent living: "Such discrimination is morally wrong, politically dangerous, industrially wasteful, and socially silly. It is the duty of the whites to stop it, and to do so primarily for their own sakes." If white Americans stopped it, Du Bois noted, most people would remain where they were: "The mass would remain as they are; but it would make one vast difference: it would inspire the young to try harder." He did not comment on what that meant for the many: They could exhaust themselves in hard work and get nowhere, exactly as most black Americans already did.[105]

Du Bois was almost a Social Darwinist concerning government, and he was a flat-out elitist concerning how black America might advance. He argued that black Americans had a right to freedom for self-development and no right to any special provisions. In his colorful phrase, African Americans had no right "to ask that the civilization and morality of the land be seriously menaced for their benefit." Du Bois supported aid that furthered self-development—schools, reformatories, relief agencies, and preventive agencies. He advised white Americans to stop fantasizing about blacks withering into extinction; Afro-Americans were going to survive Darwinian weeding out. But he argued that any special provisions for blacks would disable their chance of overcoming indolence and backwardness, and he accepted that Darwinian weeding out was very much at issue. White Americans had a right to expect blacks to "make themselves fit members of the community within a reasonable length of time." Thirty or a hundred years would not be enough to "complete civilization," but African Americans had to make "every effort and sacrifice . . . [to] become a source of strength and help instead of a national burden." As for elitism, Du Bois contended that it was mere decency "to judge a people by its best classes, rather than by its worst classes or middle ranks," because the elite shows the possibilities of a group. Black America deserved, like other groups, to be judged by its elite. White America needed to recognize that a black American elite existed, and this elite needed to accept its leadership responsibilities for the race, which, so far, it was not doing. Du Bois did not yet call it the "Talented Tenth," and he did not distinguish between aristocratic and meritocratic elites. But he already had a Talented Tenth strategy based on meritocratic achievement, it was very American, and it was very much a male construction yearning for accomplished male race leaders. The black elite had to stop segregating itself from working-class and working-poor blacks, he urged. Otherwise nothing would get better and white America would continue to judge black America by its lowest class.[106]

The Philadelphia Negro got generally positive reviews that commended Du Bois's thorough research and paternalistic bromides and that ignored his emphasis on white oppression and equal opportunity. The *Nation* lauded the book as a "very exhaustive study" that wisely taught a lesson of "patience and sympathy toward the South, whose difficulties have been far greater than those of the North." The *Literary Digest* said the same thing, adding that Du Bois showed that Booker T. was right. The *Outlook* congratulated Du Bois for not bending the facts "so as to plead for his race." Reviewers did not say that the book labored too much under the sway of male moralism, a fading neo-Lamarckian Social Darwinism, or American capitalism. Twenty years later, Du Bois took pride at having authored a pioneering work of American sociology: "Nobody ever reads that fat volume on 'The Philadelphia Negro,' but they treat it with respect, and that consoles me."[107]

That was a premature judgment, as the book had many offspring in academic works on urban sociology and Afro-American life. E. Franklin Frazier graduated from the University of Chicago in 1932, went on to a distinguished career in sociology at Howard University, and based his career on studies of the black family, the black church, and the black elite. In 1957 he published a book on the African American bourgeois class that set off a firestorm of controversy. In Frazier's telling, black America had an influential bourgeoisie but no real business class, no genuine cultural identity, and a problematic matriarchal family structure. Frazier got the controversy that he expected over the second, third, and fourth arguments, but many readers were shocked at the idea that Afro-Americans had a bourgeoisie of any kind. Du Bois had a similar experience when he introduced this idea nearly sixty years earlier, which reinforced his elitism. He later reflected that at Wilberforce he held back, critically detached from the struggles of his students and colleagues, spurning their reliance on church piety. At Penn he turned that detachment to a scholarly book about urban blacks, but he still didn't know them or really identify with them. In Atlanta he became W. E. B. Du Bois, "hot and indignant."[108]

That, at least, is how he told his story. Du Bois had a powerful romantic impulse and a gift for poetic expression, and in Atlanta he encountered, far more brutally, the evils assaulting African Americans. In his telling, his immersion in Georgia racism unleashed him from the scientific straightjacket that he donned in *The Philadelphia Negro*. In *Darkwater* he put it vividly: "I saw the race-hatred of the whites as I had never dreamed of it before—naked and unashamed! The faint discrimination of my hopes and intangible dislikes paled into nothing before this great, red monster of cruel oppression. I held back with more difficulty each day my mounting indignation against injustice and misrepresentation."[109]

More or less, that *is* what happened. However, this story of a sharp transition to a different kind of writing and activism somewhat belies that Du Bois had already published the electrifying opening chapter of (what became) *The Souls of Black Folk* before he moved to Atlanta, and he kept writing academic sociology long after he became a movement leader. He did not have to encounter the searing racism of Atlanta or be horrified by the lynching and burning of Sam Hose or be traumatized by the death of his two-year-old son to write the stunning, lyrical, existential, double-minded meditation by which he exploded onto the national scene. In August 1897 Du Bois published an article, "Strivings of the Negro People," in *Atlantic Monthly*. It was his introduction to a national audience. It was also, for the magazine's audience, an introduction to a new, bracing, unimagined black intellectualism.

DOUBLE-CONSCIOUSNESS, THE RACES OF THE WORLD, AND POLITICAL ACTIVISM

G. W. F. Hegel famously reasoned that self-consciousness exists only in being acknowledged. When self-consciousness encounters another self-consciousness, it comes out of itself, finding itself in an *other* being, and it supersedes the other in doing so. The "I" of immediate self-consciousness exists for itself; its dissolution leads to a consciousness that exists for another; in the beginning these two shapes of consciousness coexist in an unequal union of opposition and dependency. One is the master (*Herr*), whose essential nature is to be for itself; the other is the slave or vassal (*Knecht*), whose essential nature is to live for another. Hegel illustrated his theory with a story about a master defeating a slave in battle. The master prevails because he does not fear death as much as the slave does. There are no laws; each experiences the other as making brute demands in a predatory struggle for survival. The master's dominance makes him the author of the law, but the law does not work for him, because the master's self-consciousness depends on the things he consumes, which he owes to the slave's labor. The master's autonomy depends on the mediation of the slave; he is not a master if the slave does not recognize his authority. But the master has no reason to believe that the slave has any authority to confer authority on him. The slave, by contrast, by obeying the master's rule, internalizes the idea of a moral right. Through his labor the slave becomes a reflective agent, learning that there is such a thing as subjecting oneself to an external law. Instead of simply fearing for his life, he masters himself, relying on his self-chosen obedience to the law, and he begins to notice that the world is created by his labor. The slave achieves self-consciousness, rising above the possession-oriented consciousness of the master, by seeing himself reflected in the products that he makes, no longer alienated from his labor.[110]

This profound insight about the sociality of consciousness and power plays a role in all modern and postmodern philosophies influenced by Hegelian or Marxist theory, and Du Bois probably had it in mind when he expounded on Afro-American double-consciousness, although he never said so. There are traces of the double-consciousness idea in other thinkers who influenced Du Bois, especially Ralph Waldo Emerson, Johann Gottfried von Herder, and William James, although Du Bois did not mention them either, and James had not yet published his two-selves idea when Du Bois wrote "Strivings of the Negro People." Whatever the mix of influences may have been, Du Bois entered the national picture with an arresting double-minded question of his own: What does it feel like to be treated as a problem? He told *Atlantic Monthly* readers that he heard this unasked question every day. It lay behind the awkward self-justifying remarks of white strangers, such as, "I know an excellent colored man in my town," or, "I fought at Mechanicsville," or "Do not these Southern outrages make your blood boil?" *The Philadelphia Negro* had a similar remark about whites who told him, immediately upon meeting, that their father was connected with the Underground Railroad. Du Bois observed in the "Strivings" article that the real question was seldom asked or answered. What was it like, for a black American like him, to be "born with a veil, and gifted with second-sight in this American world—a world which yields him no true self-consciousness, but only lets him see himself through the revelation of the other world"? The veil shut the Negro out from the world of the others.[111]

Emerson's concept of double-consciousness underwrote Emersonian spirituality. Every self possesses a doorway to the sacred realm through its own spiritual nature. Double-consciousness is the dichotomy between a grubby, calculating, sensate lower self and the higher self of a reflective soul. For Emerson, the idea of double-consciousness was transhistorical, generically human, and potentially redemptive. For Du Bois, the double-consciousness of the black American was gritty, social, historical, and problematic. It was the experience of being compelled to look at one's self "through the eyes of others, of measuring one's soul by the tape of a world that looks on in amused contempt and pity." Du Bois had never felt otherwise, "save perhaps in babyhood and in Europe." In America he felt his duality as an American and a Negro—"two souls, two thoughts, two unreconciled strivings; two warring ideals in one dark body, whose dogged strength alone keeps it from being torn asunder." This struggle to forge his double self into a better, truer, self-consciously integral self was the key to African American existence, he proposed: "The history of the American Negro is the history of this strife." It raged through every version of the hopeless debate between nationalism and integration, in which black Americans argued about which of their selves to give up. The answer was not to Africanize America, "for America has too much to teach the world and Africa." Neither did he believe in bleaching his black soul "in a flood of white Americanism," for he was certain that "Negro blood has a message for the world." The answer was to be allowed to be fully a Negro and an American, and thus "a co-worker in the kingdom of culture."[112]

Du Bois struck gold by projecting his struggle with marginality and duality onto all African Americans. Emerson worried that Americans, lacking a culture of their own, lived parasitically off European culture. Americans needed to unleash their inward spiritual capacities to create a beautiful culture based on genuine self-knowledge—something that their outward American freedom enabled them to do. Du Bois shared this idea of culture as a commonwealth of value and aspiration, and its American ideal of self-creation and individuality. The very end of human striving was to be a coworker in "the kingdom of culture." But white America was deeply problematic for blacks, a "race" that Du Bois described repeatedly as backward and undeveloped. *Atlantic Monthly* was not the place to linger over the meaning of "Negro blood" or how many races existed. Du Bois settled for a half sentence describing the Negro as a "seventh son" of the world preceded by "the Egyptian and Indian, the Greek and Roman, the Teuton and Mongolian." He boasted that slaves wrote the only true American music and that no group surpassed black Americans in espousing the Declaration of Independence. Black Americans needed practical education more than ever, Du Bois acknowledged, but above all they needed "the broader, deeper, higher culture of gifted minds and pure hearts." Black Americans needed to share in the commonwealth of (elite) culture, which began by aspiring to it. To secure the vote was a matter of "sheer self-defense," but beyond that, Afro-Americans needed work, culture, and liberty flowing together, "each growing and aiding each, and all striving toward that vaster ideal that swims before the Negro people, the ideal of human brotherhood, gained through the unifying ideal of Race." This ideal of race did not bring blacks into opposition with whites, he asserted. It operated "in large conformity to the greater ideals of the American Republic, in order that some day on American soil two world-races may give each to each those characteristics both so sadly lack."[113]

Later that year, in a speech to the newly founded American Negro Academy, "The Conservation of Races," Du Bois lingered over Negro blood and races—entangling race with nationality and offering a table of the ostensible races. Black Americans, he acknowledged, were inclined to "minimize race distinctions," since race was used against them every day. Du Bois sympathized with the minimizing but implored against it, declaring that race was terribly important. In fact, reaching back to Hegel and a succession of lesser German nationalists, Du Bois contended that race was the most important thing of all: "The history of the word is the history, not of individuals, but of groups, not of nations, but of races, and he who ignores or seeks to override the race idea in human history ignores or overrides the central thought of history." So, what was a race? Du Bois started with a mushy sociohistorical answer that answered nothing: "It is a vast family of human beings, generally of common blood and language, always of common history, traditions, and impulses, who are both voluntarily and involuntarily striving together for the accomplishment of certain more or less vividly conceived ideals of life."[114]

It was hard to say what that meant, so Du Bois offered a twofold table of the races, appealing to Darwinian biologist Thomas H. Huxley and German ethnographer Friedrich Ratzel for at least the first category. There were at least two primary races, and possibly three—"the whites and Negroes, and possibly the yellow race." And there were eight historic races—"The Slavs of eastern Europe, the Teutons of middle Europe, the English of Great Britain and

America, the Romance nations of Southern and Western Europe, the Negroes of Africa and America, the Semitic people of Western Asia and Northern Africa, the Hindoos of Central Asia, and the Mongolians of Eastern Asia." Du Bois had to know what was wrong here. Biological science was belatedly dubious about the first category, and the second category was a hopeless mess of groups lacking parallelism with the first category. If there were eight historic races, why did Native Americans not count as a race? If the English counted as a race, how could the Spanish be left out? All that Du Bois could say was that historians would judge which groups mattered enough to be deemed a historic race and which ones belonged to "minor race groups." Racial distinction surely began with physical differences, he reasoned, but there were spiritual and psychical differences that cut deeper than physical characteristics. In that case, race and nationality could not be disentangled. The Teutonic nations, for example, were united first by racial identity and common blood, but the emergent commonalities of history, law, religion, habits of thought, and a conscious striving together for certain ideals were more important.[115]

However that sorted out, African Americans were despised and brutalized in America. Even if no one could say what, exactly, a race was, white Americans had no trouble picking out one for the worst abuse. Thus Du Bois told the American Negro Academy at its founding convention that it was desperately needed: "We need race organizations: Negro colleges, Negro newspapers, Negro business organizations, a Negro school of literature and art, and an intellectual clearing house for all these products of the Negro mind." Reprising his double-consciousness thesis, he urged that black Americans were Americans by virtue of their birth, citizenship, political ideals, language, religion, and nothing else: "Farther than that, our Americanism does not go." African Americans were Negroes in everything else that mattered. They gave their country its only original music and fairy tales and its only pathos and humor amid America's "mad money-getting plutocracy." America's eight million blacks were "the advance guard of the Negro people," Du Bois declared. If they took their "just place in the van of Pan-Negroism," the Negro race as a whole would advance and Afro-Americans would insure their future as a race in America.[116]

Two things needed to happen in America, he urged. First, African Americans had to overcome their own "immorality, crime, and laziness." Second, white Americans had to permit "a more impartial selection of ability in the economic and intellectual world." Building to a dramatic close, Du Bois declared that black Americans would either conquer their vices or be destroyed by them: "We are diseased, we are developing criminal tendencies, and an alarmingly large percentage of our men and women are sexually impure. The Negro Academy should stand and proclaim this over the housetops, crying with Garrison: *I will not equivocate, I will not retreat a single inch, and I will be heard.*"[117]

The American Negro Academy loudly acclaimed this appeal to racial solidarity and idealism, with two murmurs of dissent. Scarborough, who had regained his position at Wilberforce, questioned Du Bois's rejection of assimilation. William Henry Ferris, currently studying at Harvard Divinity School on his way to the Congregational ministry, objected that individuals made races great, not the other way around. Crummell, however, was president of the academy, and elderly. He had Du Bois pegged as the successor to Douglass and himself; he strongly commended Du Bois's presentation; and no further objections were heard. No one disputed Du Bois's insulting rhetoric of disease, venality, and backwardness. No one objected that the fixation with lifting up a male elite had chauvinism problems of its own. And no one protested that Du Bois's unwieldy fusion of neo-Lamarckian social theory and Hegelian idealism was scientifically challenged at both ends.[118]

Neo-Darwinian philosopher Herbert Spencer was the commanding and unavoidable thinker of the age when Du Bois began his career. One could not be a serious intellectual without mastering Spencer's fusion of Darwinian natural selection, Lamarckian development, Malthusian population theory, early thermodynamics, laissez-faire economics, and anarchist politics. Spencer coined the phrases "Social Darwinism" and "survival of the fittest." Moreover, like Charles Darwin and everyone else that he respected, Spencer ranked human groups hierarchically from the "savage" to the "civilized." His system featured Darwinian natural-selection theory while denying that natural selection was the main mechanism for generating biological diversity. Spencer and other neo-Lamarckians contended that every individual's biological development (ontogeny) recapitulates the entire evolutionary development (phylogeny) of its species. The environment acts directly on organisms, yielding new races, and the survival of a race depends on its interaction with its environment. If there is a one-to-one correspondence between phylogeny and ontogeny, such that ontogeny repeats forms of the ancestors, the characteristics of "less developed races" must exist within the more advanced races.[119]

Life is a continuous process of development from incoherent homogeneity (protozoa) to coherent heterogeneity. Races are real and hierarchically ordered, with traits that can be measured. Any political intervention that impedes this natural process is harmful. The foremost biologist of the late nineteenth century, Ernst Haeckel, also a prominent Social Darwinist, put it with unsurpassed arrogance, opining that the hierarchical ordering of the races was obvious, intelligence was obviously the key distinguishing factor, Africans were obviously at the bottom of the human order, and any government policy that helped the unfit to survive was odious. White people had an unbroken history of superiority, Haeckel assured; in fact, the Caucasian "Mediterranean man" was the only species (excepting the Mongolian) to have arisen above nature to the status of civilization: "The Caucasian, or Mediterranean man (*Homo Mediterraneus*), has from time immemorial been placed at the head of all the races of men, as the most highly developed and perfect."[120]

The third volume of Spencer's *Principles of Sociology* was published in the same year that Du Bois addressed the American Negro Academy, 1897. Du Bois later recalled that the tenth volume of Spencer's *Synthetic Philosophy* was published in 1896 and he felt the power of Spencer's system. Many social scientists sought to discover social laws that correlated with Spencer's physical laws. Albion Small, the founding chair of sociology at the University of Chicago and founder of the *American Journal of Sociology*, countered that sociology needed to operate inductively and historically. Du Bois was mindful of the lag between neo-Lamarckian theory and what he later called "actual scientific accomplishment," although in 1897 he could not know how this story would turn out. That year he scrounged for as much consolation as he could find in the regnant theory, telling the American Negro Academy that the "same natural laws" governed the development of all races. If that meant that biology and social science vested behavioral stereotypes about "racial temperaments" and the like with the force of biological law, Du Bois was prepared to swallow the stereotypes, as long as he got to interpret them.[121]

Small contended that Spencerian sociology was too theory-laden and deductive, analogizing from chemistry and genetics to social processes, although Chicago sociologists stereotyped just as vigorously, now on sociohistorical grounds. Meanwhile, biologists admitted that they could not find a determinant of racial difference and basis of racial classification. Huxley and French anthropologist Paul Broca focused on skin color, but that got nowhere. Others, including Broca, pressed hard on facial angles, jaws, and skull size, to no avail, as Caucasians alone included every possible head shape. For a while Huxley, Broca, Haeckel, Friedrich Müller, and many others believed that human hair must hold the answer, but that got nowhere too. Then early-twentieth-century biology refuted the strong version (one-to-one correspondence) of recapitulation theory and social science turned away from neo-Lamarckian explanations. Had Du Bois launched his career a decade later, he surely would have eschewed neo-Lamarckian explanations of "race," which might have tempered his racial romanticism. But that is speculative and not what happened, and scholars have clashed over Du Bois's culpability in treating race as a biological category, and/or adopting a sociohistorical theory of race with a biological component, and/or legitimizing essentialist notions of racial temperament.[122]

Wilson Jeremiah Moses contends that Du Bois's early racial romanticism was sloppy, "Anglo-chauvinist," and basically impervious to science. His three-and-eight formulation was "a thoughtless concatenation of non-comparable entities"; somehow the English but not the French deserved the status of a race; and Du Bois's terminology was "disgracefully inconsistent." Moses assails Du Bois for using "race" and "nation" interchangeably, "with reckless abandon," and he confused civilization with culture, too: "The basis of Du Bois' raciological theory was not rational, but mystical; it was not grounded in reason, but in something akin to faith." In this telling, Du Bois had too much in common with the central European nationalists that he read at Fisk, Harvard, and Berlin. He imitated their superheated racialist prose and, with Crummell, but also Marcus Garvey, represented "the culmination of a tradition that conceived black nationalism in European terms."[123]

Philosopher Anthony Appiah agrees that Du Bois pushed aside the scientific approach to race, replacing biological and anthropological data with sociohistorical constructs based on theological beliefs. Du Bois believed, Appiah explains, that "socio-historical races each have a 'message' for humanity—a message which derives, in some way, from God's purpose in creating races. The Negro race has still to deliver its full message, and so it is the duty of Negroes to work together—through race organizations—so that this message can be delivered." In essence, Du Bois offered "a revaluation of the Negro race in the face of the sciences of racial inferiority." Appiah concludes that this approach, although "allegedly" sociohistorical, fell short of adhering to sociohistorical evidence, too, because Du Bois "explicitly" set his theologically based sociohistorical scheme "over against the scientific conception."[124]

Historian Joel Williamson agrees that Du Bois was predisposed not to let science get in the way of his racial romanticism, but Williamson plays up the Hegelian influence, contending that Du Bois was imbued with Hegelian idealism, not mystical faith. Hegel interpreted world history as the struggle of the spirit of freedom to realize itself through specific historical peoples, and so did Du Bois. Hegel traced the self-realization of Spirit through six great historical peoples—the Chinese, Indians, Persians (culminating with the Egyptians), Greeks, Romans, and Germans—and Du Bois added the Negro as a "seventh son" born with a veil and second-sight. In voodoo belief, Williamson notes, the seventh son is the fortunate one, born with the gift of prophecy. Hegel gave short shrift to North America because it represented the future, and he was concerned with History. Du Bois filled out the Hegelian vision of where history was going, in which the black American struggle for freedom played the leading role: "Out of slavery and out of the later striving of black folk for whiteness in an oppressive white world came a rising sense of black soul."[125]

On this reading, Hegelian idealism helped Du Bois affirm the white culture that was in him. He refused to disparage the ideal of freedom, the conceptuality of civil rights, or the intellectualism that he got from white culture. The two warring ideals within him were Hegelian antinomies, clashing toward break-through. Williamson's Hegelian Du Bois celebrated that black Americans had begun to move toward self-consciousness in struggling for their freedom. He believed and taught that when black people knew their souls, they would know God truly as the divine Spirit of freedom, and History would move forward. Upon knowing themselves, blacks would know their whiteness too and be at peace with the whiteness within them. Du Bois had a vision of black and white joining together to create a nation based on human equality and freedom. Williamson does not call it a Christian vision, as he believes that Du Bois had moved through and beyond Christianity, like Hegel. But Hegelian idealism conceptualized everything that Du Bois took from Christian theology.

Moses catches part of the problem, Appiah catches it more accurately, and Williamson aptly expounds the Hegelian cast of Du Bois's early philosophy. But each of them underestimates Du Bois's commitment to scientific truth. Moses scores against Du Bois's Germanic racialist tendencies, but he ignores that neo-Larmarckian theory reigned in biology and social science during Du Bois's early career and that Du Bois felt obligated to square his account with it. Appiah correctly describes Du Bois as a sociohistoricist, but Du Bois did not believe that this approach set him against biology and anthropology, contrary to Appiah. The lure of neo-Lamarckian theory, besides its prestige in the academy, was its behavioral theory of evolution and its insistence that the same laws of nature applied in all disciplines and to everything. Evolutionary theory promised to unite biology, physics, social theory, history, and philosophy.

The prestige of this enterprise was very high when Du Bois entered the academy, and as political theorist Adolph L. Reed Jr. aptly notes, Du Bois believed he was being scientific when he adopted the sociohistorical version of evolutionary process espoused by Chicago sociologists. Chicago sociologist William I. Thomas, describing the folk psychology method in 1896, taught that all communities contained survivals of stages of social evolution and culture through which they had passed. The next year Du Bois described the development of existing races in phrases that closely approximated Thomas's neo-Lamarckian formulation. The physical differences among races, Thomas wrote, carried little significance, but the formation of "artificial or historic races, through the influence of *milieu* and the diffusion of a common fund of beliefs, sentiments, ideas, and interests among a heterogeneous population brought by hap and chance into the same geographical zone, is taking place before our eyes at the present moment, and is a matter of history; and we are safe in assuming that in this the process of the formation of true races is repeating itself." Du Bois said the same thing, except for physical differences, adding that as the "sociological and historical races of men began to approximate the present division of races," the "spiritual and physical differences of race groups which constituted the nations became deep and divisive."[126]

Williamson renders the entire matter as a philosophical issue for Du Bois, but the same objection applies to Williamson. Du Bois realized that he did not know whether evolutionary philosophy would endure or be refuted, but he never thought he was defying science, and he adopted the best natural scientific and social scientific accounts that he knew. He updated Hegelian idealism with better science than Hegel possessed, an approach taken by every Hegelian philosopher. Moreover, Williamson's emphasis on Du Bois's Hegelianism over-looks that Du Bois stopped talking about double-consciousness after he dropped neo-Lamarckian race theory, became a Socialist, pulled back on his moralistic idealism, read Freud and Marx, and adopted a more stringently cultural conception of race.

Du Bois never explained why he dropped the double-consciousness idea after publishing *The Souls of Black Folk* in 1903. Even his subsequent discussions of the book did not mention this idea, though scholars repeatedly treat it as the key to Du Bois's thought and/or African American experience. Sociologist Gunnar Myrdal, famously depicting the "American dilemma" in 1944 as the tension between the American creed and American racism, described Du Boisian double-consciousness as an analogous "dual pull" in the "Negro world." Education scholar Carol B. Stack described Du Bois's image as the definitive expression of the "conflicting and warring identities between being a Black and an American in a white world." Among the many recent reinterpretations of this idea, Lawrie Balfour describes it as a trope marking the dialectical experience of uplift and oppression, Robert Gooding-Williams says that Du Bois used it to criticize unimaginative black political leaders, and Cornel West says that Du Boisian double-consciousness is about the cultural obstacles to black self-recognition. Literary critic Henry Louis Gates Jr., introducing the 1989 Bantam edition of *The Souls of Black Folk*, bypassed the book's political arguments while describing double-consciousness as an illuminating trope that hurtles through the decades—"Du Bois' most important gift to the black literary tradition . . . without question."[127]

Reed, sociologist Lawrence Bobo, and historian Ernest Allen Jr. counter that this focus on double-consciousness depoliticizes Du Bois and makes him too idealistic. Du Bois stopped talking about double-consciousness because it smacked of the evolutionary progressivism that he also dropped (Reed), or it wasn't a social scientific explanation of anything (Bobo), or its point was to legitimize the success of Talented Tenth achievers in the white world (Allen). Critics of the emphasis on double-consciousness usually say that Du Bois eventually replaced a faulty concept of race with a chastened social-constructionist understanding, following the trend in sociology, and/or that his early statements about race and double-consciousness should not be invested with meaning transcending the political context that Du Bois himself left behind.[128]

These critiques assume that the early Du Bois conception of race was problematic, owing to faulty science and/or romantic racialism. One prominent line of countercritique says that Du Bois's early writings about race should not be taken so literally; otherwise it is hard to explain why the later Du Bois sometimes made blatantly essentialist claims about race temperament. Political theorist Manning Marable contended that Du Bois conceived race entirely as a cultural category throughout his career. Everything that Du Bois said on behalf of racial pride was meant to defend the cultural integrity and identity of black people. Literary theorist Houston A. Baker Jr. similarly says that racialist ideology, in Du Bois's use of it, had a progressive trajectory conveying a blues-inflected black cultural authenticity, "a field of 'particular' or vernacular imagery unique to the Afro-American imagination."[129]

In the latter rendering there is such a thing as progressive essentialism, and someone, perhaps Baker, is the judge of racial authenticity. Social theorist Paul Gilroy counters that all constructive concepts of blackness and racial thinking must be rejected; race is a toxic concept that underwrites racism and reactive solidarities. In his early work, *The Black Atlantic*, Gilroy featured Du Boisian double-consciousness as a precursor of Gilroy's analysis of the politics of fulfillment and transfiguration. Subsequently Gilroy consigned double-consciousness to the nineteenth century, judging that this idea carries fading power in a postmodern age of multiple identities in which culture is diffused through virtual technologies. Gilroy suggests that Du Bois himself, had he lived into our time, would have spurned the usual, obligatory, double-minded resort that race is socially invented but must be taken seriously because of its "embeddedness in the world."[130]

Du Bois himself, recalling his struggle to decide what he believed, explained that he first confronted scientific race dogma at Harvard, he decided that he could accept evolution and survival of the fittest "provided the interval between advanced and backward races was not made too impossible," and he balked "at the usual 'thousand years.'" Then he moved to an emphasis on culture and cultural history, at Harvard and Berlin. This emphasis, he suggested, subsequently deepened in him. In Berlin Du Bois was already skeptical about arguments concerning brain weight. Upon beginning his career at Atlanta, he dropped the table of races. In his early career he resisted the high-flying generalizations of evolutionary science and philosophy, because they could mean anything and science was turning against them. Du Bois gave himself to a positivist approach to his consuming subject: "Facing the facts of my own social situation and racial world, I determined to put science into sociology through a study of the condition and problems of my own group. I was going to study the facts, any and all facts, concerning the American Negro and his plight, and by measurement and comparison and research, work up to any valid generalization which I could. I entered this primarily with the utilitarian object of reform and uplift; but nevertheless, I wanted to do the work with scientific accuracy." Passionately committed to the black race, but also mindful that "race" was cultural, complex, and changing—"a changing racial group"—Du Bois believed that sufficient enlightenment would abolish racism.[131]

He gave thirteen years to Atlanta University, another institution established by AMA missionaries after the Civil War. Du Bois thought he had some idea of what to expect from having studied at Fisk and taught at Wilberforce, but that notion was quickly eviscerated. Atlanta University was an outpost of latter-day abolitionism surrounded by an unremittingly hostile city and state. Founding president Asa Ware had come to Atlanta from Yale and established the school's motto, "I will find a way or make one." Ware died in 1885 and was succeeded by Horace Bumstead, who tried to continue Ware's legacy, building up a New England–style liberal arts college, with faculty trained mostly at Yale and retaining a classical curriculum. Bumstead added Tuskegee-style vocational training to the curriculum, but his appointment coincided with a rising chorus of opposition to higher education for blacks throughout the Deep South. Even Tuskegee was widely condemned, which left Atlanta University with no base of white support in a seething neighborhood.[132]

Faculty and students were treated as pariahs, entering dangerous territory whenever they stepped off campus. White faculty members were condemned as "nigger teachers" and vilified for eating with blacks in the dining hall. In 1887 the state government eliminated the university's annual land-grant appropriation because it had white students: "The co-education of white and colored persons in this state is in direct conflict with the fundamental law and the long established policy of the state of Georgia." Atticus Haygood spoke up for the university, risking condemnation for excusing racial integration. Haygood noted that only fourteen white students were at issue and their northern parents taught at the university, doing noble work that southerners should have done. It was indecent to punish the university for having northern white professors who had children. But Haygood was drowned out by an enraged public. Bumstead bravely held the school together, and in 1896 he decided that Atlanta needed a sociologist specializing in "conditions concerning the Negro." Some colleagues thought the position should go to a graduate of Atlanta or Fisk; Bumstead replied that he wanted the best candidate, from wherever. Some colleagues objected that Du Bois was not very religious; Bumstead replied that there were "indications of genuine religion" in Du Bois's passion for racial justice. Du Bois and Bumstead forged a lasting friendship on the basis of that recognition. Years later Bumstead reflected that Du Bois, although reticent about religion, lived by one that was deep in him, out of which he drew when he occasionally conducted evening devotions at the university. And Du Bois pointedly inserted this recollection into his last autobiography.[133]

Atlanta shocked Du Bois and changed him. The naked hostility battered him and wreaked deeper damage on Nina, who lacked the refuge of campus and scholarship. In April 1899 a farmer in nearby Palmetto, Sam Hose, shot and killed a white farmer after an argument over a debt. Hose was swiftly lynched and burned to death. A white mob of two thousand men, women, and children ripped his body to shreds, fighting over fragments of his teeth and bones for souvenirs. Hose's blackened knuckles were displayed in a grocery store window on Mitchell Street near Atlanta University. Du Bois tried to respond calmly, writing a careful statement of the facts for the *Atlanta Constitution*. He was on his way to the newspaper office, garbed with cane and gloves, when he heard about the knuckles on display nearby. He froze in place, turned, and walked back to the university. Emotionally he was thrown into a different place; later he recalled: "I began to turn aside from my work." Du Bois could not produce calm social science when African Americans were being brutalized and lynched. He continued to direct the Atlantic Conference, which produced social scientific studies on Afro-American life. For the next decade, scholars, activists, religious leaders, and public officials made their way to Atlanta to attend Du Bois's annual conferences and to meet Du Bois. Jane Addams, anthropologist Franz Boas, and reform activist Mary White Ovington were among them. But Du Bois turned aside from big-scale works on urban sociology. He reasoned there was no demand for it anyway; he could write sequels to *The Philadelphia Negro* without making any difference.[134]

In that frame of mind he suffered a personal tragedy in May 1899 when his two-year-old son Burghardt contracted an intestinal infection, nasopharyngeal diphtheria. Du Bois knew of two or three black physicians in Atlanta, whom he tried to reach, unsuccessfully. Burghardt struggled, untreated, with a mounting fever for ten days and died. His death deeply wounded Du Bois and crushed Nina. She never forgave her husband for dragging her to a hostile city that had almost no black doctors and where no white doctor would treat a desperately ill black child. Nina passed from dreading and fearing the South to loathing it. In *The Souls of Black Folk*, Du Bois enclosed an agonized elegy to Burghardt that emphasized Du Bois's pain. Nearly a half century later, in an obituary for Nina, he belatedly acknowledged that she experienced Burghardt's death differently than he did: "In a sense my wife died too. Never after that was she quite the same in her attitude toward life and the world. Down below was all this great ocean dark bitterness. It seemed all so unfair. I too, felt the blow. Something was gone from my life which would not come back. But after all Life was left and the World and I could plunge back into it as she could not. Even when our little girl came two years later, she could not altogether replace the One."[135]

His work and the sheer hostility of the world pulled Du Bois back into both, though he was not quite ready to say that he returned on different terms. In August 1899 he defended Washington at the National Afro-American Council meeting in Chicago, admonishing Ransom against radical overzealousness. Du Bois recognized that Washington walked a daily tightrope merely to survive in Alabama, and he knew that Washington was not as accommodating as his cagey speeches to white audiences. By then Du Bois had negotiated the streets of Atlanta for two years, radicalized by its naked hatred but also realizing that Murphy's constant warnings of powder-keg doom were not exaggerated. Murphy pleaded with Washington not to risk setting off a bloodbath. Du Bois, for all his rage, was chastened by the dangers. Thus he almost ended up working for Washington.[136]

Du Bois hesitated to throw himself into anti-Washington politics because he was averse to movement politics. He could not picture himself as a political leader, slapping people on the back and holding coalitions together. Plus he had misgivings about the anti-Booker leaders who had emerged. Trotter bitterly attacked Washington from the safe climes of Boston. Wells-Barnett had similar self-dramatizing tendencies after fleeing the South. Chicago attorney Edward H. Morris charged that Washington's silence about lynching made him responsible for it. Du Bois doubted that strident anti-Washington polemics would build what was needed—a national movement for civil rights and an international movement for black unity.

The first person to get something going on the latter idea was Henry Sylvester Williams—a lawyer from Trinidad, trained in Canada, and practicing law in London. In 1897 Williams founded an organization of West Indian professionals seeking friendly conversation and a spirit of unity among Africans and others of African descent, the African Association. His organization struggled to grow beyond its West Indian professional base, but in the summer of 1899 Williams met Washington, who agreeably came to a meeting. Washington had almost no interest in African solidarity. He liked Williams, however, and he was launching a program in Togoland in cooperation with the German colonial administration and a quasi-private cartel in the cotton industry. Basically the plan was to send three Tuskegee graduates to Togoland to set up vocational training centers that brought credit and publicity to Tuskegee. That gave Williams just enough to work on: Would Washington finance a conference bringing together Africans and people of African descent? A few months later, after Washington surprisingly said yes, Williams came up with a name for his idea, coining the term "Pan-African."[137]

The Pan-African Congress met for the first time in July 1900 in London, sponsored by a famous African American leader who took little interest in Africa. Thirty-three women and men representing people of African descent from Abyssinia, Antigua (British West Indies), Canada, Dominica (British West Indies), England, Gold Coast (West Africa), Haiti, Jamaica (British West Indies), Liberia, Saint Lucia (British West Indies), Scotland, Sierra Leone (West Africa), Trinidad (British West Indies), and the United States met on July 23, 24, and 25 in Westminster Town Hall. The spectators included a smattering of Quakers and representatives of the Aborigines Protection Society; Williams got Alexander Walters to preside; and the United States had the largest delegation, with ten members, notably Du Bois and Anna Julia Cooper, who was about to become principal of M Street High School. Du Bois, for the first time in his life, found himself among blacks that equaled him in brilliance and academic achievement, notably Benito Sylvain of Haiti, a former aide-de-camp to Emperor Menelik of Abyssinia (Ethiopia), Samuel Coleridge-Taylor, a musical prodigy from London, and John Alcindor, a London physician from Trinidad on whom Williams relied in building the Pan-African Congress.[138]

This was not a radical outfit. These were Victorian Afro-Saxonists, who moved about the palace and grounds, as Walters later recalled, "with an ease and elegance that was surprising; one would have thought they were 'to the manor born.'" No one in this cultured group doubted there was such a thing as good imperialism. Williams regularly petitioned the British government to live up to its highest pieties about itself. The previous week he had criticized Great

Britain, in a speech in Dublin, for failing to support the rights of black Africans in South Africa. The Pan-African Congress followed suit, petitioning Queen Victoria about the governing policies of her subjects in South Africa, especially Kimberley and Rhodesia. It asked the queen and the Colonial Office to abolish the so-called "indenture" system (the legalized bondage of native Africans to white colonists), racially segregated transportation and walkways, compulsory labor on public works projects, and restrictions on acquiring property and voting. The queen, through her envoy, replied that she was "graciously pleased" to reply: "Her Majesty's Government will not overlook the interests and welfare of the native races."[139]

There is no indication that the Colonial Office was alarmed or even mildly surprised by anything said at the congress. Years later, after Du Bois became famous, scholars assumed that he must have inspired the congress and dominated its proceedings. Du Bois contributed to this mistaken impression by never mentioning Williams in print for over forty-five years. As it was, Du Bois played a secondary role in creating and guiding the early congress. Williams died young, at forty-two, and his role in history had to be rediscovered by a later generation of scholars. He was, however, the founding organizer of the Pan-African Congress. He served as general secretary of the organization during its early years (Walters served as president and Du Bois as one of many vice presidents, representing the United States). Williams ended the conference ingeniously by asking Du Bois to address the nations of the world.[140]

Du Bois's opening sentence had the hallmarks of his soon-famous style, replete, as Lewis observed, with "grave cadence" and "momentous phrasings": "In the metropolis of the modern world, in this the closing year of the Nineteenth Century, there has been assembled a Congress of men and women of African blood, to deliberate solemnly upon the present situation and outlook of the darker races of mankind." Then came a sentence with momentous phrasing of a higher order: "The problem of the Twentieth Century is the problem of the color line, the question as to how far differences of race, which show themselves chiefly in the color of the skin and the texture of the hair, are going to be made, hereafter, the basis of denying to over half the world the right of sharing to their utmost ability the opportunities and privileges of modern civilization."[141]

Du Bois allowed that by European standards, which he did not question, "the darker races" had fallen behind in cultural achievement. But this was a relatively recent development bearing no reflection on the ability of the darker races. If the "world of culture" allowed blacks to become educated and culturally accomplished, human progress would advance. But if blacks continued to be denigrated and abused, the consequences would be deplorable, "if not fatal, not simply to them but to the high ideals of justice, freedom, and culture which a thousand years of Christian civilization have held before Europe." Du Bois assured that the modern world was progressing beyond the spirit of class, caste, and birth privilege: "Let the world take no backward step in that slow but sure progress." Specifically, the aspirations and family lives of Africans should not be sacrificed to the greed of the powerful. Christian missionaries should stop hiding behind the "ruthless economic exploitation" of the people they evangelized. The British nation, "the first modern champion of Negro freedom," should crown the abolitionist work of William Wilberforce and Bishop John W. Colenso by granting self-government rights to the black colonies of Africa and the West Indies "as soon as practicable." The U.S. American nation should revive the spirit of Garrison, Phillips, and Douglass, overturning the "unrighteous oppression" of black Americans. The German Empire and French Republic, "true to their great past," should remember "that the true worth of Colonies lies in their prosperity and progress." Du Bois enthused that Congo Free State was about to become "a great central Negro State of the world" and that Abyssinia, Liberia, and Haiti had won their independence.[142]

He did not say that the "Great Powers of the civilized world" should immediately liberate their colonies. Even Du Bois took for granted that colonialism would run for decades more, and should do so. On behalf of the Pan-African Congress, however, and trusting in the "deep sense of justice of our age," he appealed to the great powers to recognize "the righteousness of our cause."[143]

Du Bois returned home from London delighted to have started something that transcended U.S. American racial politics. As the nineteenth century ran out, he celebrated the birth of Nina Yolande Du Bois, which brought him closer to Nina Gomer Du Bois, for a while, than previously or after. He formed a deep friendship with John Hope, a classicist at Atlanta Baptist College for Men (later its president for thirty years, which was renamed Morehouse College in 1913). Hope graduated from Brown University and could easily have passed for white, or, if he chose, an honorary white man in northern academic society. Instead he chose to live in the South as a voluntary Negro. Du Bois needed a friend that he treated as an equal. Hope filled that need during Du Bois's Atlanta years, as did George Towns to a lesser degree. Towns had studied at Atlanta University and Harvard, returning to Atlanta University to teach pedagogy and English just before Du Bois arrived. Towns publicly opposed Bookerism before Du Bois came out and helped to nudge Du Bois in that direction.[144]

Du Bois believed that *Up from Slavery* was not the book that African Americans needed to survive the upsurge of lynching and repression, and he shuddered at Washington's growing eminence. The latter factor was decisive. It was terrible enough that blacks were terrorized and oppressed. Even worse was that violent white repression was becoming taken for granted, so normalized that white politicians and clergy did not feel compelled to apologize for it. Du Bois saw it happening in Atlanta. He despaired that colleagues treated Washington as the final word on racial politics. The tyranny of Bookerism was degrading and suffocating; Du Bois later recalled, "Things came to such a pass that when any Negro complained or advocated a course of action, he was silenced with the remark that Mr. Washington did not agree with this." So Du Bois wrote *The Souls of Black Folk*.[145]

Actually he assembled most of it, cutting and polishing nine essays from *Atlantic Monthly, Dial, World's Work, New World*, and *Annals of the American Academy of Political and Social Science*. His publisher, McClurg and Company, also owned the *Dial*, an ambitious Chicago magazine for which Du Bois had recently reviewed *Up from Slavery* and *The American Negro*; in the latter review he pleaded for no more books that defamed an entire people. Years later Du Bois recalled that he had been wary of assembling a book, since essay collections nearly always fell flat, and he suggested inaccurately that his chapter "Of Mr. Booker T. Washington and Others" was the book's only new piece. But his mistaken recollection highlighted what mattered—that the Washington chapter was the key to the book. He would not have authored *The Souls of Black Folk* had he not felt compelled to say that Washington was wrong to play down the right to vote, wrong to disdain black colleges and black intellectual aspiration, and wrong to blame the victims of racism for racial oppression. Above all, Du Bois later recalled, "I resented the Tuskegee Machine." But he proceeded cautiously, developing a nuanced argument and avoiding an accusatory tone. His target, after all, was the most admired man in America, then at the peak of his influence, riding a sympathetic backlash against an absurd controversy. Simplistic polemics would not create a viable alternative to the Wizard of Tuskegee.[146]

"THE MOST DAMNABLE OUTRAGE"

In September 1901 an anarchist assassinated William McKinley, putting Theodore Roosevelt into the presidency. Within hours of taking office, Roosevelt summoned Washington to the White House for advice about federal appointments in the South. The two men were already on friendly terms, as Roosevelt had sought Washington's advice during the 1900 election, Washington had been TR's guest at his home at Oyster Bay on Long Island, and TR had been finalizing plans to visit Tuskegee when McKinley was assassinated.

Washington was crucial to Roosevelt's plan to break Mark Hanna's control of patronage in the South. On October 16, Washington arrived in Washington, DC, to meet with Roosevelt and received a note inviting him to dinner that evening at the White House. Roosevelt had not thought about how the dinner scene would play in the South. He told Tourgée that he paused momentarily at setting a precedent, felt a rush of embarrassment at pausing, and issued the invitation. Washington, receiving the invitation at the home of his friend Whitefield McKinlay, hesitated before accepting. This was sure to go down badly in the South, but what else could he do? That evening Washington dined with Theodore and Edith Roosevelt, their three sons, and their seventeen-year-old daughter Alice Lee, plus TR's hunting partner Philip Stewart.[147]

The first day response was encouraging, as African Americans and white liberals celebrated a historic breakthrough. On the second day newspapers throughout the South exploded in rage and disbelief, which carried on for months. The *Richmond Dispatch* headlined, "Roosevelt Dines a Darkey." Other headlines described TR as "A Rank Negrophilist" and "Our Coon-Flavored President." The *Atlanta Constitution* was more wordily didactic: "Both Politically and Socially, President Roosevelt Proposes to Coddle Descendants of Ham." A subhead declared: "President's influence with southern white men gone." Newspapers that had banished the n-word brought it out of retirement, following the lead of the *Memphis Scimitar*: "The most damnable outrage which has ever been perpetrated by any citizen of the United States was committed yesterday by the President, when he invited a nigger to dine with him at the White House. . . . By inviting a nigger to his table he pays his [Southern] mother small duty. . . . He has not inflamed the anger of the Southern people; he has excited their disgust."[148]

The press coverage was long on disgust. Roosevelt was condemned for an obscene violation of Jim Crow decency and for promoting the mongrelization of the Anglo-Saxon race. Washington was condemned for violating his Atlanta Compromise, stinking up the White House, and disrespecting white women. The Raleigh *Post* was moved to verse anchored by "vigor" and the n-word. The *Richmond Times* howled that TR's invitation signaled "that white women may receive attentions from Negro men; it means that there is no racial reason in his opinion why whites and blacks may not marry and intermarry, why the Anglo-Saxon may not mix Negro blood with his blood." The New Orleans *Times-Democrat* taunted its readers: "White men of the South, how do you like it? White women of the South, how do you like it? Everyone knows that when Mr. Roosevelt sits down to dinner in the White House with a negro, he that moment declares to all the world that, in the judgment of the President of the United States, the negro is the social equal of the white man." White nationalists had unbearable imaginings of Washington lusting after Alice and touching her thigh under the table. They recycled the Jim Crow convention, which they had used against Washington for years, that any white man who dined with a Negro was also inviting him to have sex with his sister or daughter. The *Geneva Reaper,* a Populist weekly in Alabama, took the next step, declaring that Roosevelt "might now just as well sleep with Booker Washington, for the scent of that coon will follow him to the grave, as far as the South is concerned."[149]

Some white southern editorialists were harsher than others, and some fixed greater blame on Roosevelt than Washington, but virtually all blasted the dinner as a terrible mistake. The *Montgomery Advertiser,* which was normally sympathetic to Washington and proud of its temperate respectability, asked readers to mostly blame Roosevelt for this fiasco. The *Birmingham Age-Herald,* equally pro-Washington and temperate, felt obliged to fall in line, declaring that Washington damaged Tuskegee and the hard work of a lifetime in one evening. The *Richmond News* similarly wailed against the massive destruction of one evening, though it blamed Roosevelt. With so much condemnation coursing through moderate white southern newspapers, it was hard for white nationalist leaders to outflank the coverage rhetorically. But they managed to do so. James K. Vardaman, in a protest that helped him win the Mississippi governor's seat in the next election, declared: "President Roosevelt takes this nigger bastard into his home, introduces him to his family and entertains him on terms of absolute social equality. . . . The White House is so saturated with the odor of the nigger that the rats have taken refuge in the stable." Ben Tillman, now a U.S. senator, announced that Washington's dinner would require remedial genocide: "The action of President Roosevelt in entertaining that nigger will necessitate our killing a thousand niggers in the South before they will learn their place again."[150]

The new president was shocked and bewildered by this outpouring. At first he blamed "the idiot or vicious Bourbon element of the South," vowing that he would invite Washington to dine "just as often as I please." He told Tourgée that if a mere dinner caused such a fuss, it was probably overdue, and he had no regrets. Then he learned that even his white allies in the South were condemning him, and TR changed his tune, assuring that he had not meant to make a big statement about racial equality or anything like that. The dinner was merely a spontaneous gesture of hospitality. Washington got no more dinner invitations to the White House, which was fine with him. The incident damaged his reputation in the white South for the rest of his life. Editorialists could not mention race relations or black participation in politics without reblasting Washington's insolent dinner in the White House. Arkansas governor Jeff Davis, campaigning in 1904, replayed the dinner constantly: "Can you think of anything dirtier, nastier than that?—eating with a nigger." Davis told campaign crowds that every honorable southern male, faced with a black man who tried to walk his white daughter home from church, would shoot him dead. But poor Alice Roosevelt was given no choice by her disgusting father: "Let me tell you, we are not going to have any nigger equality down here as long as we can pull a trigger and there are shotguns and pistols lying around loose."[151]

Many politicians and writers capitalized on that feeling and refueled it. One author outstripped all others in promoting, defending, and dramatizing white rage: Thomas Dixon Jr. The son of a Baptist preacher and slave owner in Shelby, North Carolina, Dixon was born in 1864 and grew up amid the controversies over Reconstruction. He graduated from Wake Forest College and studied briefly at Johns Hopkins University under Richard T. Ely, which exposed him to social gospel liberalism. Dixon tried to be an actor in New York but failed. He took up the law in North Carolina, but was bored by it. He was a sensational speaker, with a taste for drama, which helped him find his first calling—Baptist preaching. In several pastorates Dixon drew overflow crowds, eventually returning to New York, where he had to move from a large church on Twenty-third Street, to an auditorium, to a music hall to accommodate the crowds. Often he preached on social and political topics, especially Tammany Hall corruption. He also gave social gospel sermons about the unity of the human race under the fatherhood of God. But Dixon seethed inwardly over racial resentments; he was high-strung and vindictive, plus guilt-ridden over his mother's difficult life; he strained paternalistically to treat blacks as fellow human beings; and in the 1890s his resentments consumed him.[152]

In 1899 Dixon quit the ministry, moved to an estate in Virginia, and took up full-time lecturing. Often he lectured on the Spanish-American War, which he viewed excitedly as a victory for Protestant Anglo-Saxon expansion. His racist feelings were further excited by North Carolina's gubernatorial campaign of 1900, in which Charles B. Aycock swept to victory. The Democratic Party had a favorite slogan dating back to the 1868 presidential campaign: "This is a white man's country. Let white men rule." That was exactly what Aycock believed. Like other southern victors in 1900, he campaigned on a platform of white supremacy and racial segregation. Two years later Dixon erupted into a literary career after attending a dramatization of Harriet Beecher Stowe's *Uncle Tom's Cabin.* For years he had seethed over the unbearable smugness and stupidity of northern white liberals. On his lecture tours Dixon compiled notes for a race novel that refuted his models for this genre—Stowe and Tourgée. Watching *Uncle Tom's Cabin* propelled Dixon into action. In two months he poured out a stunning, vicious, lyrical, perversely romantic, best-selling book, *The Leopard's Spots: A Romance of the White Man's Burden* (1902). Dixon's editor, Walter Hines Page of Doubleday, Page & Company, was so enthralled by the manuscript that he kept reading it while walking to his office on Fifth Avenue and was injured by a passing taxicab.[153]

The Leopard's Spots was a revenge-fantasy sequel to *Uncle Tom's Cabin* and a rebuke to Tourgée's claims that African Americans were accomplished and deserved to be equal citizens. It also rebuked Washington's plea that white Americans should care about black Americans lifting themselves up. Stowe's Simon Legree returned as a Scalawag Reconstruction leader. Stowe's educated, biracial George Harris returned to romance the daughter of a northern politician, who discovered how wrong he had been about race and Reconstruction. Dixon's protagonist, Charles Gaston, modeled on Aycock, had a pastor and substitute father, John Durham, who preached about delivering his state from "the black death." Durham taught that slavery partly civilized a savage race, but blacks returned to beastliness after slavery ended, lusting uncontrollably after white women. Durham warned, "The beginning of Negro equality as a vital fact is the beginning of the end of this nation's life." Gaston grew up to overthrow a black Republican government and restore white control. As governor he disenfranchised African American voters, but he had a soft spot for black industrial education. Durham, all-knowing on racial matters, countered that educating blacks for anything was a terrible mistake. The only solution was to drive blacks out of America. Gaston, finally seeing the light, thundered climactically: "If we attempt to move forward we are literally chained to the body of a festering Black Death! This is a white man's government, conceived by white men, and maintained by white men through every year of its history—and by the God of our Fathers it shall be ruled by white men until the Archangel shall call the end of time!"[154]

Dixon overflowed with tender feelings about the Lost Cause of southern civilization. He served up wooden plots, melodramatic dialogue, stereotyped characters, and a zoological lexicon, describing blacks as apes, baboons, beasts, brutes, gorillas, monkeys, mules, and snakes. Five times, in italics, Durham declared that the future American would be either Anglo-Saxon or "mulatto." One drop of Negro blood was enough to ruin anybody. *The Leopard's Spots* sold over a million copies, making Dixon famous; then he published *The Clansman: An Historical Romance of the Ku Klux Klan* (1905). This book, a story about the biracial mistress of a clansman and her biracial lover, heightened Dixon's sexual trope, exhausting his society's stereotypes about the sexual degeneracy of blacks. *The Clansman* sold over a million copies, too, providing the basis for a play of the same name and Hollywood's first blockbuster, D. W. Griffith's *The Birth of a Nation* (1914), which glorified the Klan for its noble, brave, redemptive, patriotic defense of white America from unbearable blacks.[155]

In Dixon's telling, Afro-Americans were beastly, stupid, immoral, and a drag on American society, and black Africans of unmixed racial lineage were worse. Few blacks remained who knew their place and behaved decently, Dixon complained. Their number declined drastically after the disaster of Reconstruction, in which "African barbarism" and the rule of "black apes" was imposed on the ruins of a noble southern civilization. According to Dixon, there were two kinds of racial prejudice, depending on whether the race in question acted from a position of inferiority or superiority. The "mean" kind of racism hated a superior race; Dixon reflected that inferior groups sometimes victimized Jews in this way. But there was nothing wrong with despising an inferior race. That was racial self-preservation. Dixon explained to a New York audience, "You can't swallow a single nigger without changing your complexion." Dixon shuddered at the many white Americans who claimed to admire Washington. They were dangerously misguided, he warned, for Washington was a wolf in sheep's clothing. He pandered to white Americans in assuring tones but conspired to lift his race above white Americans. If the cult of Washington continued to grow, it would surely lead to a race war.[156]

Washington keenly understood that white nationalist rage had surged out of control. He had to calculate the chance of a violent episode every time that he spoke in the Deep South away from Tuskegee, and for months after the White House dinner he stayed in the North. Editorialists ripped him for sending his daughter Portia to Wellesley College in Massachusetts; then they ridiculed her when she washed out. A popular coon song immortalized the dinner. Vardaman based his next campaign on name-calling, describing Roosevelt as "the coon-flavored miscegenationist in the White House." Washington, trying to stay positive, told Roosevelt that "something good" would eventually come from the horrendous pounding they were taking.[157]

Something good did accrue to Washington. Though he lost control of his image in the white South, he soared higher than ever in the nation's regard, reaping a huge sympathy backlash and raking in money on the fund-raising circuit. Many northern whites grasped for the first time what Washington was up against in the South. His relationship with Roosevelt made him a political power player of the first order, selecting federal judges, federal marshals, postmasters, census takers, and other federal appointees. Washington's ability to make patronage appointments offered a precious counterweight to the plague of disenfranchisement that drove African Americans out of the political system. Thus he took the risks to his reputation and work of being a political boss, without putting it that way, since putting it that way would not have played to his favor. Taking on all that was no easy task for the bookish and conflicted sociology professor from Atlanta University.

"OF MR. BOOKER T. WASHINGTON AND OTHERS"

The Souls of Black Folk was an electrifying manifesto and a poetic work of spiritual prophecy. Du Bois announced that the new century of seemingly over-whelming and impregnable white European supremacy would actually be about something else—the relation of the world's darker races to the white privileged ones: "The problem of the Twentieth Century is the problem of the color line." He employed the language of prophecy boldly, using the word "seer" five times and the words "prophet" and "prophecy" twice each. Du Bois artfully fashioned the book, heading each chapter with a double epigraph pairing Negro spirituals with verses by Byron, Schiller, Whittier, Elizabeth Barrett Browning, Swinburne, Tennyson, and others. The chapter titles began with the preposition "Of," in the manner of the Church of England's Thirty-nine Articles of Religion, as in "Of Our Spiritual Strivings." He began with black/American double-consciousness and moved to a backstory chapter on the overlooked achievements of the Freedmen's Bureau before coming to his keystone chapter, "Of Mr. Booker T. Washington and Others," where Du Bois acknowledged that African Americans of his time lived in the age of Booker T. Washington.[158]

Reconstruction had come and gone, memories and ideals of the Civil War had faded, an age of tremendous commercial expansion had begun, and Washington distinctly offered a strategy for black Americans. Du Bois recalled that it surprised white southerners to hear a Negro make such a proposal, but many were sufficiently relieved to applaud. Northern whites admired Washington for building on the work of northern white missionaries. African Americans murmured a weak word of protest and fell into silence, too confused and beaten down to know what else to say. Du Bois judged that Washington's greatest achievement was to win a significant amount of sympathy and coopera-tion from certain white southerners. This had seemed "well-nigh impossible," but Washington did it, building Tuskegee into a thriving enterprise. Then he cut a deal with the white South in the Atlanta Compromise, which won so much approval that Washington became "the most distinguished Southerner since Jefferson Davis, and the one with the largest personal following."[159]

His second greatest accomplishment was to win favor and then power in the North, which he pulled off by adopting "the speech and thought of triumphant commercialism." Du Bois had a grudging word of half endorsement on this theme, but it took him a while to get there, because this point grated on him. He hated that Washington's philistine shtick on the lecture circuit routinely skewered poor blacks holding intellectual aspirations. Du Bois pictured a lone black boy "poring over a French grammar amid the weeds and dirt of a neglected home." It was a picture drawn from Washington's stump speech and recycled in *Up from Slavery*. To Washington, Du Bois claimed, this picture was the height of absurdity. Washington played it for laughs to white and black audiences, but he was serious about it, and offensive. He got to be great by being narrow and insensitive. That, Du Bois said, was how people usually became great in a commercial society. Du Bois lined up with Socrates against Washington, while acknowledging that Washington overflowed with tact and complexity in pursuing his narrow aim; otherwise he could not have steered between "so many diverse interests and opinions," winning the respect of millions.[160]

Du Bois noted that Washington was the second black American to make an impression on white Americans and the first to be selected as a leader by white Americans. All black leaders before Washington had become leaders "by the silent suffrage of their fellows," none besides Douglass had impressed white America, and all had sought to lead only people of their own race: "But Booker T. Washington arose as essentially the leader not of one race but of two—a compromiser between the South, the North, and the Negro." In truth, Du Bois cautioned, Washington's claims on the South and the Negro were weak. The key to the Atlanta Compromise and Washington's power was his standing in the rich and dominant North, which had grown weary of the race problem and had huge investments at stake in southern enterprises. The North was eager to cooperate with the South so commerce could proceed. Washington offered Bookerism as a solution, and the North crowned Booker T. the leader of black America. Washington was so successful that even most blacks accepted his leadership, despite the price.[161]

Bookerism, Du Bois contended, was the old slave strategy of survival through submission, updated to the age of commercial expansion and commercial ideology. Specifically, it asked black Americans to concede political power, civil rights, and higher education, at least for the present. This policy now had a fifteen-year track record, including ten years of undisputed domination. And what was the return? Disenfranchisement, the creation of a distinct status of civil inferiority, and reductions in aid to higher education for blacks. Du Bois did not mean that Washington advocated any of these things, "but his propaganda has, without a shadow of doubt, helped their speedier accomplishment."

Bookerism promised that if blacks let go of political rights, accepted their status as a servile caste, and aimed for nothing higher than vocational training, they would become economically prosperous. But that deal was plainly not working out. American blacks could not own property or manage their own businesses if they had no right of suffrage to defend their right to property. They could not be thrifty and self-respecting if they were condemned to civic inferiority. And even Tuskegee could not operate without teachers trained in black colleges.[162]

There were two schools of black dissent from Bookerism, Du Bois asserted; at least, two were needed. One was a throwback to Nat Turner's slave rebellion, preaching hatred of the white South and opposition to most of the white race. This school righteously blasted the outrages of white racism, and it harbored no hope for blacks in America. It wanted African Americans to build a nation somewhere else, preferably West Africa. But this program was more hopeless than ever, now that America ruled over "weaker and darker peoples" in the West Indies, Hawaii, and the Philippines: "Where in the world may we go and be safe from lying and brute force?" The other school still did not exist, Du Bois argued, recycling his appeal in the *Up from Slavery* review. This school would battle for the right to vote, civic equality, and the education of youth according to ability. This time he cited four people, calling out Kelly Miller and Archibald Grimké again, plus Francis Grimké and J. W. E. Bowen. It was difficult to imagine how such men could "much longer be silent," Du Bois declared, trying to rally the opposition that he wanted.[163]

The "thinking classes of American Negroes" had a heavy moral responsibility to discharge, Du Bois urged. It was to state "plainly and unequivocally" the just demands of black Americans, "even at the cost of opposing an honored leader." Du Bois did not want an opposition that refused to recognize its potential allies in the white South. The South was not "solid," he observed. Ignorant white southerners simply hated Negroes, working-class white southerners lived in fear of competing economically with Negroes, capitalist white southerners cared only about using Negroes as laborers, and some educated white southerners believed that an ascending black race would be a menace to human development. But some white southerners were allies of the Negro; usually they were "sons of the masters." Growing that group was imperative. Moreover, speaking of fairness, Du Bois acknowledged that Washington was not always accommodating, having opposed disenfranchisement bills and spoken against lynching. But Washington encouraged millions of Americans to believe that southern discrimination was justified because African Americans were degraded; he pedaled a self-serving falsehood about black education, and he rose higher and higher as blacks were put down. Du Bois was for Washington and against him. He was for striving with Booker T. when he preached "Thrift, Patience, and Industrial Training for the masses," and he was for "unceasingly and firmly" saying no when Booker T. apologized for injustice and demoralized black Americans.[164]

The Souls of Black Folk had further chapters about the South, higher education, the Talented Tenth, the Negro church, Crummell, and the spirituals. Du Bois regretted that the Freedmen's Bureau did not get a longer run, claiming that even Reconstruction might have been unnecessary had the South not responded to defeat with vengeance and Black Codes. He anticipated C. Vann Woodward's discontinuity rendering of southern history by a half century, with similar problems, lamenting the overthrow of the old planter class by a new class of ruthless capitalists. The old, quasi-feudal South, Du Bois explained, was at least restrained by hierarchy, paternalism, and noblesse oblige, and the capitalism of late-nineteenth-century England and the northern United States was at least restrained by unions and factory laws. But the postwar South unleashed capitalism in its full savagery, shredding the "best elements of the South." Du Bois could be florid on this subject, lamenting that the rod of empire passed in the South to "the sons of poor whites fired with a new thirst for wealth and power, thrifty and avaricious Yankees, shrewd and unscrupulous Jews." In this telling, Jews were odious — "the Jew is the heir of the slave-baron" — and democracy was not (yet) a force for progress in the South. Moreover, like the Woodward school of a later time, Du Bois overlooked that many white nationalist leaders had slave masters in their family tree.[165]

The Souls of Black Folk used the phrase the "Talented Tenth" only once, but almost every chapter had a gloss on it. It was there in the Washington chapter's sections on black higher education. It was named in a chapter titled "Of the Training of Black Men," where Du Bois showed that the number of black graduates from northern colleges and black graduates from southern Negro colleges had quadrupled since 1875: "Here, then, is the plain thirst for training; by refusing to give this Talented Tenth the key to knowledge, can any sane man imagine that they will lightly lay aside their yearning and contentedly become hewers of wood and drawers of water?" The Talented Tenth was featured in a chapter titled "Of the Wings of Atalanta," where Du Bois blasted Bookerism for turning the black world upside down. In the past, he wrote, the preacher and teacher embodied the ideals of black America — "the strife for another and a juster world, the vague dream of righteousness, the mystery of knowing." In the age of Booker-style religious materialism, however, "the danger is that these ideals, with their simple beauty and weird inspiration will suddenly sink to a question of cash and a lust for gold."[166]

Du Bois inveighed against being wooed from the struggle for righteousness and the love of knowing to regarding "dollars as the be-all and end-all of life." Later that year, in a speech titled "The Talented Tenth," he put it aggressively: "The Negro race, like all races, is going to be saved by its exceptional men. The problem of education, then, among Negroes must first of all deal with the Talented Tenth; it is the problem of developing the Best of this race that they may guide the Mass away from the contamination and death of the Worst, in their own and other races. . . . Was there ever a nation on God's fair earth civilized from the bottom upward? Never; it is, ever was, and ever will be from the top downward that culture filters."[167]

Du Bois knew well that most of the black intelligentsia lived in the North—several hundred families in a national Afro-American population of more than nine million. In the South there were not more than fifty such families, and most felt intimidated by the Tuskegee Machine. More than anything else, this was what drove Du Bois to defy Washington. He knew plenty of prosperous northern blacks that sneered at Washington in their living rooms and never felt "led" by him in any way. A handful of others blasted Washington publicly, but not very effectively. Moreover, Du Bois had colleagues in the South who qualified for the Talented Tenth but who trembled before Washington's power to make or break their careers. The very people that Du Bois wanted most were too afraid of Washington, so far, to be called out. No rhetoric of democracy or "building from below" meant anything to Du Bois in a context where Washington exemplified building from below and trade unionism was violently racist. Bookerism lifted the race on degraded terms, refusing to lift the veil, which actually denigrated black people, even as Du Bois granted that Washington deserved to be commended and supported for his training of teachers.

The purpose of life was to ennoble humanity, and the purpose of the elite was to be of service to the mass of humanity. Black America needed an elite that roared for the humanity and dignity of black people. Du Bois dialed up a stunning rhetorical flourish to seal the point, evincing what mattered most to him: "I sit with Shakespeare and he winces not. Across the color-line I move arm in arm with Balzac and Dumas, where smiling men and welcoming women glide in gilded halls. From out the caves of evening that swing between the strong-limbed earth and the tracery of the stars, I summon Aristotle and Aurelius and what soul I will, and they come all graciously with no scorn nor condescension. So, wed with Truth, I dwell above the Veil."[168]

The early responses to *The Souls of Black Folk* were telling, determinative, and variegated. The book was ignored with a few exceptions in white southern newspapers and studiously ignored in the entire black press that Washington controlled. It was widely reviewed in the secular white northern press, praised by some very influential white political outlets, lauded by the few Afro-American publications not controlled by the Tuskegee Machine, and sharply debated by white social gospel leaders. All of these responses played a role in lifting Du Bois to a movement leadership role that he only half-wanted and could not refuse.

Deep South reviews were uniformly vengeful, and border-state reviews were generally less so, as editorialists debated whether Du Bois or Washington better reflected the feelings of black Americans. But most white southern reviewers said the book was unintelligible on its own terms, ignorant of what really mattered, and, usually, harmful to America. Often they rehearsed Lost Cause mythology. There was no race problem during slavery. The slave masters treated their slaves like family. The race problem began after the Civil War, as Reconstruction stoked Negro resentment and infuriated the defeated white South. And northern liberals of both races failed to grasp any of these things.

The influential Louisville *Courier-Journal* described *The Souls of Black Folk* as "a crudely written book characterized by incoherent statements and disconnected arguments." According to the *Courier-Journal*, Du Bois better represented black Americans than did the "steady-minded Booker Washington," because Du Bois reflected "their actual and illogical grasp at power and their exaggerated estimate of any mental attainment among themselves." The *Nashville American* judged that the vast majority of African Americans agreed with Washington's approach, but it warned: "This book is indeed dangerous for the negro to read, for it will only excite discontent and race hatred and fill his imagination with things that do not exist, or things that should not bear upon his mind." The *Christian Advocate*, published in Nashville, reported that it was impossible to say what the point of the book was, since Du Bois wrote in a "highly colored" and "somewhat incoherent" fashion that was "characteristic of his race." However, to the extent that Du Bois had any intelligible thoughts, "one suspects that the author is basing his hopes on social equality." The *Christian Advocate* admonished Du Bois to stop feeling sorry for himself and start taking responsibility for his problems. The *New York Times* dispatched the book to an anonymous white southerner, who allowed that Du Bois was talented and the book was generally interesting. However, Du Bois understood almost nothing about the South, including black southerners, and for all his portentous exertions, his real agenda was simply to "smoke a cigar and drink a cup of tea with the white man in the South."[169]

Reviewers from the Deep South had no doubt that *The Souls of Black Folk* was pernicious. The *Keystone* of Charleston, South Carolina, denounced

Du Bois for being "restless and dissatisfied with the irrevocable fate of an infe-
rior race." It warned that the book would cause much harm. The *Houston
Chronicle* said the same thing while proposing to do more about it. The
Chronicle urged prosecutors to indict Du Bois for inciting rape; more ambi-
tiously, it wanted federal and state officials to deport all African Americans to a
U.S. colony. In the meantime it admonished black Americans to follow
Washington: "The hatred Du Bois preaches to the negro leads to crime, race
riots and endless trouble. The book cannot fail to do much harm."[170]

In two notable white southern reviews Du Bois was not ignored or denounced.
One was a border state newspaper, the *Louisville Post*, which fair-mindedly
summarized the book's arguments, made no complaints about unintelligibility
or evil will, and praised Du Bois's "remarkable piece of work" and his "poetic
and effective style." The *Post* was no exception to standard-fare paternalism. It
repeated the stock trope that black Americans had slavery to thank for being
civilized, opined that Washington's realism was wiser than Du Bois's "utopia-
nism," and recycled Washington's plea for patience. In the life of a race, the
Post admonished, "two hundred years is but a day." Du Bois needed to absorb
the wisdom of patience. But the *Post* recognized that *The Souls of Black Folk*
was an important work: "We should know what intelligent negroes think of the
negro-problem."[171]

The other exception was a review in the *South Atlantic Quarterly*, by John
Spencer Bassett, a leading historian at Trinity College (later renamed Duke
University). Bassett was a Booker man, with an edge. He founded the *South
Atlantic Quarterly* in 1901 to provoke southern discussion of the race issue, and
two years later he made himself a pariah by opining that Washington was the
second greatest southerner of the past hundred years, surpassed only by Robert
E. Lee. Bassett added that blacks in the South were being bludgeoned out of
their cowardice and that a great struggle over racial equality was coming. These
statements set off a furor. The Raleigh *News & Observer* campaigned against
Bassett, angry whites across the state demanded his firing for comparing
Washington to Lee, and Bassett eventually decamped to Smith College in
Massachusetts, although Trinity defended his academic freedom. Bassett's
review of Du Bois was an augur of his fate. On the one hand, Bassett commended
Washington's cry for peaceful cooperation; on the other hand, he agreed with
Du Bois that this appeal was not working: "Professor Du Bois' protest is not a
violent one. It is the cry of a man who suffers, rather than the reproach of a man
who hates. It is a plea for soul opportunity, and it bears the evidence that its
author while he was writing realized the hopelessness of it all." Bassett felt the
hopelessness upon reading a current best seller, *The Negro a Beast*: "A more

stupid book it is impossible to conceive." But the same terrible age that produced *The Negro a Beast* produced *The Souls of Black Folk*, so perhaps there was some basis for hope.[172]

The Souls of Black Folk got few reviews in black publications because the Tuskegee Machine controlled the black press; repressing dissenting voices worked better for Washington than arguing with them. But the few Afro-American reviews that Du Bois got helped him break through, even as they usually avoided saying that Du Bois rejected the Tuskegee approach. Wendell Phillips Dabney, a friend of Du Bois's, led the way in the Ohio *Enterprise*: "SHOULD BE READ AND STUDIED BY EVERY PERSON, WHITE AND BLACK. We cannot find language to express our appreciation of this production, which, from every point of view, can well be termed 'a masterpiece.'" The AME *Christian Recorder* commended the book's "penetration of thought and a glow of eloquence that is almost unexampled in the literature on the Negro question." The reviewer (probably Richard R. Wright Jr.) observed that Du Bois could have used his academic achievements to separate himself from his persecuted people; instead he applied his extraordinary attainments "to the cause of race improvement." William Monroe Trotter's Boston *Guardian* praised the book's "vigor, spontaneity and spirituality," offering no objections. The *Dallas Express* was equally succinct and a bit more effusive: "His style is terse, his logic unrefutable, his argument unanswerable. The reader of this book is simply charmed and chained."[173]

A few reviewers stepped out a bit further in preferring Du Bois to a usually unmentioned you-know-who. The *Detroit Informer* declared: "So far ahead of anything written on this subject is this excellent work, that we claim a place for it among the archives of English classics." There was no cant or bombast in Du Bois, the *Informer* continued, "no pettifogging or cringing, no irritation or smoothing things over." The *Progressive American*, a New York newspaper, put it acidly: "It is one of the best books ever written in defense of the Negro's position on the policy of submission and surrender, which is now a popular fad among worshippers of Mammon in black skins." John Daniels, writing in the Boston periodical *Alexander's Magazine*, published a review for the ages, with a keen sense of the book's likely historic significance. Upon reading *The Souls of Black Folk*, Daniels observed, "one feels the mystery and the awe of what people call 'the Negro Problem.' One is filled with sympathy for the Negro, and a sense of the brotherhood of man. One sees vividly the despair, the bitter misery of the Negro in his social degradation. One is exalted by the dominating spirituality of the book. And withal, one feels all the time the fine, sensitive embittered nature of the author." Daniels did not find the book to be hopeless, pessimistic, cynical, unrelenting, or vengeful: "It is simply and finally a voicing of the bitterness in the Negro's soul, the sorrow that things are as they are, which is not inconsistent with the hope of better things." *The Souls of Black Folk* was not an argument, not even an anti-Washington argument, Daniels contended; it was a poem, an appeal to the heart: "Give the book its highest place; not that of a polemic, a transient thing, but that of a poem, a thing permanent."[174]

The Souls of Black Folk got vast attention in the white northern press, mostly positive. Nearly always it featured the Du Bois versus Washington angle, sometimes by reviewers that were surprised to learn that the Wizard had significant black opposition. Two very big outlets, *Literary Digest* and *Collier's Weekly*, gave the book a major lift even as the former scoffed and the latter sneered. *Literary Digest* puzzled that Washington and Moses apparently had opposite problems with their following. The Hebrews in the wilderness yearned for the fleshpots of Egypt and practical things, but Washington's opponents accused him of fixating on practical things and ignoring their higher selves. *Collier's* warmed up its huge audience in August 1903 with a piece of racist tripe titled "The Black Man's Soul." Black people were "gently and happily barbaric," the editors claimed. "The pathos of the negro is a Northern invention." As long as blacks had enough food and warmth, they were happy, although black women were notoriously promiscuous, which unfortunately delivered their untethered sons into criminal lifestyles. *Collier's* suggested that castration was probably an appropriate punishment "for bad black men." With that baseline in place, the magazine reviewed *The Souls of Black Folk* the following month, charging that educated blacks like Du Bois were obsessed with their rights instead of their obligations. Du Bois was a "poetical, melancholy, wistful, attractive" dreamer. Washington was a sensible leader. "Let the negroes follow Mr. Washington."[175]

The *Chicago Tribune* introduced a question that intrigued several reviewers: Since Du Bois was at least half white, which parts of the book were white? *Tribune* reviewer Elia W. Peattie praised Du Bois's passion, eloquence, and insight, which compelled "profound respect." But she worried that Du Bois littered his book with riddles about double-consciousness and the like that did not sound black, which led her to question whether it was "the white man in Du Bois which so tortures itself with questions which may not be answered." Perhaps "mulattoes" had special problems that were better left unasked?[176]

The *New York Evening Post* fueled similar speculation in the name of heading it off. More important, this review, which was reprinted in the *Nation* and undoubtedly authored by Oswald Garrison Villard, won a large audience for the book. Villard was the grandson of William Lloyd Garrison, heir to his father Henry Villard's railroad fortune, and owner of the *New York Evening Post* and the *Nation*. He was a Booker man, but *The Souls of Black Folk* impressed him: "Mr. Du Bois has written a profoundly interesting and affecting book, remarkable as a piece of literature apart from its inner significance. The negro-phobist will remind us that Mr. Du Bois is not as black as he has painted himself, and will credit to the white blood in his veins the power and beauty of his book." Villard countered that Du Bois's soul was blacker than his face, as evidenced by the book's exquisite tenderness, emotionality, and imagination. To be sure, Du Bois on the lecture stump was "coldly intellectual." To know him from that context was to be unprepared "for the emotion and the passion throbbing here in every chapter, almost every page. It is almost intolerably sad." In addition, Du Bois was brilliant and learned, and he demolished "the cheap nonsense, of which we hear so much" about the choice between full and restricted suffrage. The real choice was between full suffrage "and a new form of slavery." Villard suggested that Washington deserved a fairer accounting than Du Bois provided, but he concluded that Du Bois deserved to be taken seriously, an outcome that this review did much to obtain.[177]

The three most influential journals of white liberal opinion were the *Nation*, the *Independent*, and the *Congregationalist*. All three lauded Du Bois, which alarmed the Tuskegee Machine. William Hayes Ward, like Villard, still consid-ered himself a Booker man, because he greatly admired Washington. But he had never believed that Bookerism was the solution to America's racial crisis, and he had said so in the *Independent*. Now he said that *The Souls of Black Folk*, though unfair to Washington, was a breakthrough: "As an index to the negro's inner life and feeling and as a revelation of the negro's appreciation of his unique situation in American social life, *The Souls of Black Folk* will be of incal-culable service. It is the best and most logical expression of the clear facts of race hatred yet made by any student of the negro question." The *Congregationalist* enthused that *The Souls of Black Folk* soared above everything in the field, and it commended Du Bois for justly, accurately, and eloquently exposing the limi-tations of Bookerism: "If it is the duty of white America to understand the souls of the black citizens before they pass final judgment, then it will be the duty of leaders of opinion to read this book with an open and sympathetic mind." Other white social gospel liberals similarly commended the book. Chicago Unitarian minister Jenkin Lloyd Jones had local friends on both sides of Du Bois versus Washington: Wells-Barnett, Barnett, and Charles Bentley versus Monroe Work, S. Laing, and Fannie Barrier Williams. Jones said that Du Bois was mostly right, but he needed to be fairer to Washington, so the two groups could work together.[178]

Lyman Abbott was in no mood for pulling together with, let alone praising Du Bois. He resented the coming of Du Bois. In Abbott's telling, Du Bois was "ashamed of his race," but Washington was "proud" of his race. Du Bois made the white man the standard, but Washington looked for a standard in the ideals of his own race. Du Bois sought to "push the negro into a higher place," he demanded the right "to ride in the white man's car," and he demanded the ballot "for ignorant black men because ignorant white men have the ballot." Washington was wiser on every count. Washington sought to make black men "larger," he worked to "make the black man's car clean and respectable," and he sought to "make the black man competent for the duties of citizenship, and wishes no man to vote who is not competent." Du Bois wanted to base black education on the university model, while Washington wisely based it on "the common school and the industrial school." Du Bois wanted to teach Negroes "to read the Ten Commandments in Hebrew," but Washington wanted Negroes "to obey them in English." Du Bois regarded labor as "barely more honorable than idleness," but Washington regarded industry as "the basic virtue." Abbott implored that choosing Du Bois over Washington would be a catastrophe. Black Americans should not push themselves forward or think about themselves or fuss over their problems. They needed to concentrate on getting ahead, attaining property, and making themselves worthy of the rights and privileges of citizenship.[179]

Abbott and Washington Gladden had been friends for many years, and Gladden had only recently met Du Bois, upon speaking at Atlanta University's baccalaureate. But Gladden was deeply impressed by Du Bois. He read *The Souls of Black Folk* on the train home from Atlanta. He was offended by Abbott's review. The following Sunday he said so from the pulpit, telling his congregation that Du Bois's book marked a turning point: "I want you all to read it. It will give you, I think, a deeper insight into the real human elements of the race problem than anything that has yet been written."[180]

A Gladden sermon had to end with assurances about progress and hope, even on this subject. In Atlanta, during the same week that he met De Bois, Gladden preached at Henry Hugh Proctor's congregation, First Congregational Church. Proctor asked him where America's race problem was headed. Gladden told him "it was going to be liberty and opportunity and manhood for the Negro." The South would change, Gladden assured; it was changing already: "It is impossible that these millions of white Christians should shut out of their minds the great ideas of human brotherhood which are accumulating in human thought, which envelop them like an atmosphere, and which are changing, everywhere, the spiritual climate. It is impossible that they should resist the altruistic understanding of this faith."[181]

It could not be that racism would prevail in America. It simply could not be, if America was becoming more Christianized, that white American Christians would continue to denigrate the humanity of Afro-Americans. Actually believing that helped Gladden learn from Du Bois, which helped Du Bois acquire a following among social gospel leaders. At a crucial moment, Gladden's endorsement was a breakthrough. Afterward Gladden heralded the book to his lecture audiences, even as he assured that the AMA stood "for no unnatural fusion of races, for no impracticable notions of social intercourse." Though Gladden practiced social equality, he judged that fighting for it was misguided when the right to political equality was under siege. Social equality was slippery and relative, but justice was neither. Christian morality and the demands of justice required nothing less than "perfect equality for the Negro before the law, and behind the law." Gladden's advocacy on this issue triggered a barrage of hate mail. He later admitted that the "bitter and violent" letters he received gave him a new realization of what African Americans were up against in his beloved country.[182]

The Souls of Black Folk thrilled Reverdy Ransom, who welcomed Du Bois to the racial justice party, and Richard Wright Jr., for whom higher education was very personal as a justice issue. The book's inspiring power was crucial to its historic significance. In 1913 William Ferris recalled that the book changed his life and the lives of many fellow African Americans that he knew. *The Souls of Black Folk* "proclaimed in thunder tones and in words of magic beauty the worth and sacredness of human personality even when clothed in a black skin." The book helped Ferris believe that the divine light shone in his soul. In barely a few years, Ferris claimed, *The Souls of Black Folk* became "the political bible of the Negro race" and Du Bois became "the long-looked-for political Messiah, the Moses that will lead them out of the Egypt of peonage, across the Red Sea of Jim Crow legislation, through the wilderness of disfranchisement and restricted opportunity and equality of rights."[183]

The book had an equally significant impact on figures who went on to say that Du Bois–style radicalism and Washington-style conservatism were both indispensable to the civil rights movement that was needed. Adam Clayton Powell Sr. and Henry Hugh Proctor were prominent in this school, as was Gladden, who declared: "I fear that Mr. Washington is putting too much weight on economic efficiency as the solvent of race prejudice. All that Booker Washington is doing we may heartily rejoice in, but there are other things that ought not be left undone." In 1909, shortly before black and white neoabolitionists finally launched a vehicle for racial justice that got somewhere, Gladden reflected that although most southerners did not believe in racial justice, "it is the opinion that must prevail, because this is a moral universe."[184]

Certainly it was Gladden's experience that he lived in a moral universe. Du Bois had a profoundly different and conflicted experience. He never let go of believing that life is a challenge to live up to one's moral duty, and he soon gave himself entirely to heroic moral leadership in a liberationist cause. But being black in America shredded Du Bois's belief that he lived in a moral universe, and he said that his life had significance only "because it was part of a Problem." If not for the "Problem," he would not have spent his life in social justice movements. Du Bois would have taken his brilliant mind to Harvard, embarked on a glittering career, and enjoyed the world as it was: "Had it not been for the race problem early thrust upon me and enveloping me, I should have probably been an unquestioning worshipper at the shrine of the established social order and of the economic development into which I was born."[185]

Instead he was thrown into the outrageous, howling, demeaning, oppressive problem of race, which became unavoidable, which led him to "other things" that he hated about the world too. Every black social gospeler had a humbler version of the experience of being thrown into a terrible problem that became unavoidable.

4

IN THE SPIRIT OF NIAGARA

When Du Bois told the story of his life in 1920, he described a succession of triumphs from Great Barrington to New York. Every chapter of his life ended with a success that led to the next stage of his battle to confute the white world's denigration of black humanity and ability. He had dreamed of Harvard, becoming an editor, studying in Germany, earning a doctorate, joining a racial justice organization, and speaking "to my people and of them, interpreting between two worlds."[1]

Now he was a famous intellectual and movement leader who had cut Booker Washington down to size and launched the civil rights movement through the National Association for the Advancement of Colored People (NAACP) and its journal, *The Crisis*. Du Bois told this story of fabulous success so breathlessly that it was easy to miss the major counterfactual to it—that in 1909 he had hit a dead end. His situation at Atlanta University had become untenable and he had staked everything on the Niagara Movement, which crashed after a brief, rhetorically sparkling, organizationally dysfunctional run. Had Du Bois not cut a deal with white liberals to form the NAACP, the civil rights movement would have remained a smattering of grouplets and individuals despairing over what to do about America's worsening plague of racial oppression.

In the same month—April 1903—that McClurg and Company published *The Souls of Black Folk*, Booker Washington held a gala conference at Madison Square Garden to celebrate Tuskegee. This event was the apogee of William Baldwin's high-end networking for Tuskegee. Former president Grover Cleveland kicked off the gala with a racist riff on the "grievous amount of ignorance" and "sad amount of viciousness" and "tremendous amount of laziness and thriftlessness" of black America. Cleveland lauded the white South for treating its mostly unbearable black population with remarkable kindness and patience, concluding that white southerners should support the only Negro who provided a solution to "the vexatious negro problem of the South." Lyman Abbott piled on in the same vein, contending that African Americans were far from deserving the rights of citizenship and that only Booker T. had an answer. Edgar Gardner Murphy said the same thing more viciously, describing black Americans as "a rotting body . . . polluting the atmosphere we breathe." Washington must have winced as the invective piled up, but he stayed in char-acter—ceremonious, cagey, opaque, deferential. Two days later Andrew Carnegie gave him $600,000 in U.S. Steel bonds—$450,000 for Tuskegee's endowment and the rest for Washington.[2]

That was a mixed blessing, too, as Washington's white southern and black northern critics exploded over the Carnegie gift. Southern editorialists condemned it as northern interference in southern race relations that strength-ened Washington's base of power independent of white control. William Monroe Trotter, who ripped Washington every week, had no trouble fitting the Carnegie gift into Trotter's usual story about a power-mongering opportunist who had sold out his people. The only upside that Trotter could see was that perhaps New England would be spared Washington's fund-raising tours now that Carnegie had more than doubled Tuskegee's endowment and put the Wizard himself on Easy Street.[3]

Trotter had cofounded the *Boston Guardian* in 1901, six years after he gradu-ated from Harvard. His father was a prominent black Democrat who served as recorder of deeds in the Cleveland administration. Having inherited a small fortune of approximately twenty thousand dollars, Trotter plowed it into civil rights journalism, leading a band of Boston radicals that included journalist George Forbes and lawyers Archibald Grimké, Clement G. Morgan, and Butler Wilson. Grimké was a respected Boston attorney and diplomat, born into slavery and a storied biracial family in Charleston, South Carolina. His slave-owning father, Henry W. Grimké, had a white family with his wife, who died young, and a second family with his enslaved concubine, Nancy Weston, the mother of Archibald and Francis Grimké. Henry Grimké also had two younger sisters, Angelina and Sarah Grimké, who became famous abolitionists after leaving the South. In 1868, sixteen years after their brother's death, the Grimké sisters discovered that they had black nephews studying at Lincoln University. They befriended the Grimké brothers, subsequently paying for Archibald and Francis to study law at Harvard and Howard, respectively. Francis went on to Princeton Theological Seminary and a longtime ministry at Fifteenth Street Presbyterian Church in Washington, DC; Archibald served as consul to Santo

Domingo (the Dominican Republic) before returning to Massachusetts and helping Trotter found the *Guardian*. In 1903 Archibald Grimké became president of the American Negro Academy, a position he held until 1919. Having him in their corner conferred gravitas on the Boston radicals as they rallied opposition to the reign of Bookerism.[4]

Trotter pleaded for a new generation of black heroes who dared to "throw off the shackles of fear, of obligation, of policy and denounce a traitor though he be a friend." Booker Washington, he charged, was the worst kind of enemy because he betrayed blacks and robbed them of their moral agency. The Wizard of Tuskegee, speaking in March 1903, declared that a single respectable home or farm was worth more than all abolitionist speeches combined. Trotter, incredulous, asked Afro-Americans how they could listen to such "claptrap." The abolitionists were Trotter's heroes. He organized Boston's memorial celebrations of abolitionists and idolized Garrison especially. Trotter had a bust of Garrison on his desk and a personality much like Garrison's: intense, vivid, self-righteous, ascetic, alternately abrasive and charming, and fired by an independent ethical religion. The abolitionist tradition, to Trotter, mattered far more than homes or farms. He challenged readers to summon their dignity and repudiate their nonleader. In June 1903 Trotter reported, sadly, that apparently there would be no upside to the Carnegie gift, as Washington did not intend to lessen his attacks on the rights of Afro-Americans: "Tuskegee has proved the most deadly enemy of Negro liberty, more deadly than the south itself, because it comes in the guise of a friend."[5]

In that case, anything that brought him down could be justified. The *Guardian* mercilessly, brilliantly, and at times outrageously skewered the Wizard. Nothing was too personal or vindictive if it struck a blow. Trotter had a slew of epithets for Washington, calling him "the Great Traitor," "the Great Divider," "Pope Washington," "the miserable toady," "the Benedict Arnold of the Negro race," "the Exploiter of all Exploiters," and "the Heartless and snobbish purveyor of Pharisaical moral clap-trap." He caricatured Washington's manner, speaking style, family, and physical appearance, sometimes describing a monster that had nothing to do with Booker T. According to the *Guardian*, Washington's forehead "shot up to a great cone," his "vast mastiff-like rows of teeth" meshed together like a vice, his eyes were "dull and absolutely characterless," and anyone who met up with him should call the police before going to bed. On July 30, 1903, the Boston chapter of the Bookerite National Business League held a public meeting at the Columbus Avenue AME Zion Church, where Fortune and Washington spoke. Trotter's group was amply present. Catcalls began at the first mention of Washington's name, and it got worse after

Washington stepped forward to speak. Trotter had nine protest questions that he wanted to ask, but fights broke out across the sanctuary, the police were called, somebody stabbed a police officer with a hatpin, more police arrived, and Trotter was hauled to jail. Finally Washington gave his speech, shouting over an uproar. The following day, and for weeks afterward, Washington played down the incident to journalists and President Roosevelt. He was embarrassed, fearing that the "Boston Riot," as the press called it, would hurt him. White New Englanders told him they were shocked to discover that he had such enemies. That shock, plus Washington's belief that he had no legitimate opponents, caused him to mobilize the Tuskegee Machine against his tiny band of critics.[6]

The master of accommodating diplomacy to white America could not tolerate insubordination from black Americans anywhere, so he tried to crush his critics before they cut him down to size. Washington was not open to being one black leader among others. Trotter shrewdly told Du Bois that this was the Wizard's fatal weakness: "The real issue as to Washington is his lust for power, his desire to be a political leader, to be a czar, his clandestine methods of attempting to crush out all who will not bow to him." Du Bois had tried, until the so-called riot, to stay on good terms with Washington. In early 1903 he seriously considered a job offer from Washington. He taught at Tuskegee in the summer of 1903 and dined with Washington in early July, although when he told this story subsequently, Du Bois placed the riot in July 1905, on the eve of the Niagara Conference. That misconstrued the turning point of his career. Washington tried to control Du Bois, who chafed at being manipulated and smoldered over the school superintendent episode. Then Du Bois judged that his disagreements with Trotter were mostly about style and that Trotter's assessment of Washington rang true.[7]

By August 1903 the two sides were arming for battle and Du Bois felt compelled to choose between them, realizing that both sides were watching him. Kelly Miller, allergic to taking sides, displayed his inner conflict in an article comparing Douglass and Washington. Douglass was "like a lion, bold and fearless," Miller wrote, while Washington was "lamblike, meek and submissive." Douglass escaped from personal bondage, "which his soul abhorred," but Miller could imagine Washington rising into the favor of his master had not President Lincoln intervened. Douglass roared for the rights of blacks, criticized white racism, and acted on principle, while Washington emphasized the shortcomings of his race and acted prudentially. On the other hand, Miller respected Washington's genius and the demands of a commercial age. Douglass lived in a time of moral giants like Lincoln and Garrison, but Washington lived in a time of merchant princes. Had Washington lived in Douglass's time, he would have been "hooted off the stage," but had Douglass lived into the twentieth century, he "could hardly receive a hearing." Miller ended with an explosive point that he put as blandly as possible: Black Americans did not choose Washington to be their leader and they did not find him to be a "magnetic personality." It was a select portion of white America that "set up Booker Washington as the divinely appointed and anointed leader of his race." Miller concluded that it would be a good thing for America, and even for Washington, if pro-Booker white Americans stopped assuming that all criticism of Washington was a "sacrilege."[8]

In September Washington went to France to clear his head and recharge. He read Miller's article in Paris, plus a fresh batch of *Guardian* attacks, with alarm. Clearly, Miller still wanted to have it both ways, but if he had to be this insulting to keep his standing with northern intellectuals, things were worse than Washington had thought. When Washington returned from Europe he told Robert Ogden it was time to go after Du Bois, the real force "behind the mean and underhanded attacks that have been made upon me during the last six months." He claimed to have proof that Du Bois had plotted against him. In fact, he had no proof, because Du Bois had not orchestrated anything against him. But Washington was right that Du Bois was his biggest problem; Trotter's influence was already fading in the aftermath of the Boston fracus.[9]

In October Washington asked Du Bois to help convene a group to address "the weighty matters that now confront us as a race." They bargained briefly over the invitation list, until Du Bois gave up. Washington pressed hard for the conference that he wanted. He was willing to put up with a sharp critic like Chicago lawyer Edward Morris or Chicago physician Charles Bentley, but not both. He wanted Fortune and J. W. E. Bowen to be there, as both were influential and favorable to him. He was willing to indulge a sermon from Francis Grimké, but doubted it would be worth hearing. Du Bois was no match for the Wizard in this area. It didn't help that Carnegie financed the conference, although Washington had to override Baldwin and Ogden to proceed, as they feared that any dialogue with northern liberals would play badly in the white South. To Washington, that risk was worth taking, as long as the proceedings were not recorded. He had to regain control in the North, and he was a skilled conference performer. In November he told a national conference of sociologists that at Tuskegee they didn't just study racial injustices: "We eat them for our breakfast, for our dinner, for our supper. We live on them day in and day out." Washington had something similar in mind for his dialogue with the anti-Washington camp, barring Trotter, who was deemed beyond the pale.[10]

The conference took place at Carnegie Hall in January 1904. There were twenty-eight African American participants: five were decidedly critical of

Washington (Du Bois, Morris, Archibald Grimké, Minnesota attorney Frederick L. McGhee, and Clement Morgan), four or five belonged to the Miller camp of straddlers, and the rest were pro-Washington. Approximately twenty white players, all pro-Washington, came to the opening plenary, where Carnegie, Abbott, Ogden, Baldwin, Villard, and others lauded the Wizard's wisdom and greatness. By all accounts Washington dominated the proceedings after the white benefactors departed. He affirmed that he supported civil, political, and public equality, and higher education for the elite. He was gracious, charming, and personal, outperforming the dry and inwardly seething Du Bois. Washington won over the straddlers with his apparent sincerity and reasonableness. Even Archibald Grimké was swayed by Washington's moving account of racist affronts he had suffered, especially over the White House dinner. By the end Du Bois had only three supporters in his corner, as Grimké publicly praised Washington's performance. Washington took advantage by calling for a Committee of Twelve, stacked with his supporters, to coordinate future activities, on which Du Bois, Bookerite Hugh Browne, and he would serve as conveners. Writing to Baldwin afterward, Washington reported that his opponents were "either silenced or won over to see the error of their way."[11]

Charles Anderson urged Washington not to rest content with this victory. Anderson was a light-colored, tough-talking, self-made businessman, a New York Republican politician and chief accountant for the New York State Racing Commission. By January 1904 he had become one of Washington's chief advisors on political matters. A few months after the Carnegie Hall conference, Washington got Roosevelt to appoint Anderson as collector of internal revenue for the Second District in New York City, where Anderson supplanted Fortune as Washington's chief advisor. Three weeks after the conference, Anderson gave Washington some welcome advice about dealing with the Du Bois group: "He is whipped oftenest who is whipped easiest." Washington's opponents, Anderson urged, were college types who never accomplished anything except graduating from a snotty college: "A good thrashing would convince these young upstarts, with their painful assumption of superior intellectuality, that they had better spend their time in some less dangerous occupation."[12]

That was exactly what Washington already believed. Du Bois had always felt uneasy in Washington's company because he never expressed himself frankly. The Wizard was wary, secretive, slippery, and manipulative, whereas Du Bois was fast-talking and voluble, concealing nothing. Du Bois felt Washington's disdain when they were together, and he perceived that the Committee of Twelve was heading to a consolidation of Washington's power. It enraged Du Bois that Miller and Grimké capitulated to Washington's ostensible leadership. He was done with that. In April Du Bois said it publicly in a farewell titled "The Parting of the Ways."

"THE PARTING OF THE WAYS"

Black Americans, Du Bois declared, were seriously divided over the scope of education, the necessity of the right to vote, the importance of civil rights, conciliating the white South, and their own future. One side of this debate carried on the tradition of Payne, Crummell, and Douglass. Its proponents argued that the "broadest field of education" should be open to blacks; one could not be a free citizen of a republic if one lacked the ballot; self-respect and equal civil rights went together; social peace could not come at the price of one group surrendering "the essential rights of manhood"; and Afro-Americans should not settle for anything less than full political and civil rights.[13]

The accommodating tradition, on the other hand, reflected the shallow commercial spirit of its age. "The gospel of money has risen triumphant in church and state and university," Du Bois lamented. Americans no longer aspired to ideals or even talked about human rights. Instead they prized the vulgar question of what somebody or something was worth, and they cheered as their nation swaggered about the world in battleships, "looking for helpless peoples whom it can force to buy its goods at high prices." Du Bois assumed that America's infatuation with materialism would not last: "It will pass and leave us all ashamed." But while it lasted, "it strangely maddens and blinds us."[14]

The age proclaimed that the greatness of the nation was its money; thus, religion, politics, and education became devoted to moneymaking. Things of higher learning could wait until one became rich. Politics did not pay and it caused trouble. Earning a living was more important than personal dignity and freedom. Humiliation, for some, was the price of earning a living. Du Bois acknowledged that nobody said these things "quite so flatly and bluntly." The accommodating tradition merely emphasized industrial education, played down the rights to vote and freely associate, told blacks they had to earn their right to their rights, emphasized the shortcomings of Afro-Americans, and played down the hostility of white Americans. Du Bois judged that there was just enough truth in this prescription to make many blacks overlook what was terribly wrong in it. Certainly, the "shiftless and poor" had to acquire discipline and skill, ignorance could not vote intelligently, rights and duties went together, and social peace was essential. Nobody denied any of these things. But Du Bois did deny "that Negro colleges are not needed, that the right of suffrage is not essential for black men, that equality of civil rights is not the first of rights and that no self-respecting man can agree with the person who insists that he is a dog."[15]

Du Bois pressed hard on self-respect and human dignity. Without naming Washington, "The Parting of the Ways" railed against unnamed champions of industrial education that listened "complacently" to insults directed against black Americans and silently allowed "a new slavery to rise and clutch the South and paralyze the moral sense of a great nation." Most African Americans did not agree with Washington on the key points at issue, Du Bois contended: "I speak advisedly when I say that the overwhelming majority of them declare that the tendencies today are wrong and that the propaganda that encouraged them was wrong." Most of the black press said otherwise because the party of accommodation controlled it. Du Bois countered that accommodation was wrong and a failure: "We refuse to kiss the hands that smite us." His party, the majority of American blacks, insisted on gaining "every right and privilege open to a free American citizen." As for the third party, the back-to-Africa nationalists that held no hope for America, Du Bois respectfully disagreed: "I believe that black men will become free American citizens if they have the courage and persistence to demand the rights and treatment of men, and cease to toady and apologize and belittle themselves. The rights of humanity are worth fighting for. Those that deserve them in the long run get them."[16]

Miller, distraught over "The Parting of the Ways" and Washington's heavy hand, wrote plaintively to Du Bois: "Is it war to the knife, and knife to the hilt?" The answer was yes. Washington whipped the Committee of Twelve into line, restoring his patented equivocations and priorities, and Du Bois resigned from the committee. Archibald Grimké resigned, too, as a protest against Washington's domineering treatment, then rescinded his resignation, struggling with Miller to prevent a factional war. Du Bois admonished Grimké and Miller to stir up their courage. It was a "clear misfortune to the Negro race" that they submitted themselves to dictation from Washington and provided cover for him: "I am sorry, very sorry to see it. Yet it will not alter my determination one jot or tittle. I refuse to wear Mr. Washington's livery or put on his collar."[17]

On his way to launching the Niagara Movement, Du Bois composed a statement of faith. "Credo" was modeled on the second-century Apostles' Creed, but Du Bois's creed featured social ethical and spiritual convictions. It began with God and race: "I believe in God, who made of one blood all nations that on earth do dwell. I believe that all men, black and brown and white, are brothers, varying through time and opportunity, in form and gift and feature, but differing in no essential particular, and alike in soul and the possibility of infinite development. Especially do I believe in the Negro Race: in the beauty of its genius, the sweetness of its soul, and its strength in that meekness which shall yet inherit this turbulent earth." Du Bois believed in "Pride of race and lineage and self," enough to denigrate no person's father, and in service, "from the blackening of boots to the whitening of souls." He believed that the Devil worked to repress struggling human beings, "especially if they be black." He believed in "the Prince of Peace" and that armies are the "tinsel and bragga-docio of oppression and wrong." He believed that the death of powerful white nations was foreshadowed by their "wicked conquest of weaker and darker nations." He believed in "Liberty for all men" to live, vote, and associate "as they will in a kingdom of beauty and love." He believed in the training of chil-dren for life and righteousness, and he believed in patience—"patience with the weakness of the Weak and the strength of the Strong, the prejudice of the Ignorant and the ignorance of the Blind; patience with the tardy triumph of Joy and the mad chastening of Sorrow."[18]

"Of one blood" was a gloss on Acts 17:26, a passage frequently cited by ante-bellum abolitionists, which linked Du Bois's creed to abolitionism and the Bible. William Ward published the nine-paragraph "Credo" in the October 1904 *Independent*, burnishing Du Bois's spiritual credentials. Du Bois was not a godless intellectual removed from the biblical cadences and imagery of the black church. He embraced the prophetic ethical religion of Jesus. He defied a white oppressor that did not see the beauty and genius of the Negro race. He believed that people of color had no stake in white America's wars of empire. And he wanted black Americans to believe that their liberation from oppression and exclusion was coming. Francis Grimké rejoiced to Du Bois: "God has gifted you, in a remarkable degree, with vision and power of statement." His credo was exactly what black Americans needed "more than anything else—the assertion of the truth, clearly, forcibly, never mind who it offends, who is pleased or who is not." Grimké wanted the credo to receive "the widest circulation. It ought to be hung in all of our homes, and in all of our school houses." For sixteen years it was Du Bois's second best-known publication, and it hung on many living room walls. Then Du Bois reprinted it as the opening page of *Darkwater* and the credo was mounted on many more walls—a counter-Word for the generations that dreamed of deliverance from America's racial caste system.[19]

In 1904 John Wesley Edward Bowen and journalist Jesse Max Barber launched *Voice of the Negro*, a national magazine. Bowen was born into slavery in New Orleans in 1855; three years later his father purchased his freedom; he fought in the Union Army and later became a Methodist Episcopal minister; and in 1887 he became the first African American to earn a doctorate at Boston

University. Teaching at Gammon Theological Seminary in Atlanta, he espoused
the personal idealism of his mentor at Boston University, Borden Parker Bowne.
Politically Bowen was conservative in the Booker line, but he partnered with
a young managing editor from Virginia and Illinois, Barber, who favored Du
Bois. Under Barber's influence *Voice of the Negro*, published in Atlanta, played
a significant role in the parting of the ways.[20]

At the time the main vehicles of opposition to Bookerism were the *Boston
Guardian*, *Washington Bee*, Chicago *Conservator*, Chicago *Broad Ax*, and
Cleveland Gazette. These were the very places—except for Washington, DC,
where the *Colored American* competed with the *Bee*—where Washington had
a shaky following and no successful press outlet, despite trying to create both. In
Boston the pro-Washington *Colored American Magazine* teetered on bank-
ruptcy until Washington got his National Negro Business League ally Fred
Moore to purchase the magazine and move it to New York. In every case
Washington kept his involvement secret. Though it was widely believed that
Washington kept the pro-Booker press in line with subsidies, his operatives
protected his secrets and denied that he purchased influence. In December
1904 Barber offended Washington with a sarcastic anti-Booker editorial, "What
Is a Good Negro?" The following month Du Bois charged in *Voice of the Negro*
that Washington had recently paid three thousand dollars to influence black
newspapers in five unnamed cities.[21]

This figure was in the ballpark, but Du Bois had only anecdotal backing for
it. Publicly, Washington denied that he paid money to influence any editorial
line. Privately, he vowed to crush *Voice of the Negro* and Barber. Washington
believed that only indirection, ambiguity, and secrecy would work for him. If he
straightforwardly launched his own magazine he would lose his capacity to
fudge his position. He could only control the discourse by getting proxies to
speak for him. He could not say what he truly believed, whatever that was, and
he had to be deceptive about what he did, even though it was obvious that he
bought editorial influence.[22]

Du Bois did not have these problems, although he ate some crow for lacking
proof. Black newspapers accused him of smearing a great black leader. Ward
asked Du Bois if he had anything further to say about the controversy. Du Bois
replied that he was getting hammered by the very papers that had "sold out to
the Syndicate"—the *New York Age*, Chicago *Conservator*, Boston *Citizen*,
Washington *Colored American*, *Colored American Magazine*, and Indianapolis
Freeman. Oswald Garrison Villard, pressing harder, admonished Du Bois that
it would be a very serious matter to make such an accusation lacking "positive
proof." Du Bois, panic-stricken at the prospect of offending Villard, pleaded

with Trotter to send him "every scrap of evidence you have. . . . Give me *facts* & hurry them to me." But Trotter had only more anecdotes and circumstantial evidence, which Du Bois relayed in a long letter to Villard, who replied that Du Bois had not proved anything. Villard added that he did not believe there were "any essential differences" between the viewpoints of Du Bois and Washington, since Washington supported higher education for blacks. Du Bois replied that he did not need smoking-gun evidence to know what was going on and he did not have to believe that Washington was a rascal to conclude that the "general tendency of his policies is dangerous." Then he waited for the furor to pass; proof had to wait for historian August Meier, a half century later. Du Bois later recalled that he resented the way that Washington built, employed, and lied about the Tuskegee Machine: "All this is a common method of procedure today, but in 1904 it seemed to me monstrous and dishonest, and I resented it."[23]

In 1904 Du Bois began to drop Socialist-leaning statements into his speeches. Speaking to the American Missionary Association convention in October, he declared that America's worsening race problem was a sign of America's worsening class war. Socialist economist Isaac Max Rubinow reached out to him. Rubinow had worked for the federal government and the city of New York, developing the nation's earliest health and social security insurance plans. He told Du Bois that in his view, "the actual foundation of the race prejudice is the desire of the stronger to exploit the weaker, though of course historical causes have contributed to the survival of these prejudices." Racial abuse was rooted in the "same desire of exploitation" that fueled the class war. As for Bookerism, Rubinow wrote, it was simply naive to claim that all blacks, or all whites, should be capitalists; Bookerism was a remedy "for the *few*, while what is necessary is relief for the *many*." Rubinow asked Du Bois if he agreed. Du Bois replied that he was still far from Rubinow's Socialism, but he sympathized with the Socialist movement and he had "many socialistic beliefs."[24]

The year 1905 would have been terrible for Washington even if Du Bois had not founded the Niagara Movement. *Letters from Tuskegee*, a book purportedly written by a music teacher at the white Alabama Female College in Tuskegee, but more likely by a white nationalist ghostwriter, incited a large readership with salacious tales about rampant sexual immorality among Tuskegee students and faculty. Washington was reduced to denying that Tuskegee had an ethos of promiscuity. Georgia politician Tom Watson restored his racist credentials by accusing Washington of believing in black superiority. In 1904, as a Populist candidate for the American presidency, Watson criticized southern Democratic leaders for exploiting racial prejudice: "What a blessed thing it is for Democratic leaders that they always have 'the nigger' to fall back on! For thirty years they have been doing business on 'the nigger,' and today he is their only stock in trade." The following year Watson smoothed his return to the Democratic Party by bashing Washington: "What does Civilization owe to the negro? Nothing! *Nothing!! NOTHING!!!*" Washington was reduced to denying that he had ever claimed that blacks were superior to whites.[25]

Meanwhile Thomas Dixon's *The Clansman* became a runaway best seller, entertaining a million readers with its melodrama about happy blacks during slavery, beastly rapist blacks during Reconstruction, and the glorious work of the Ku Klux Klan. A stage version of *The Clansman* played to overflow audiences throughout the South in the fall of 1905, complete with live horses, a burning cross, and a climactic lynching. In August Dixon ramped up book and ticket sales by skewering Washington in the *Saturday Evening Post*. According to Dixon, Tuskegee was a subterfuge for racial equality and mongrelization, and Washington was building up an independent black nation. An explosion would occur when southern blacks began to compete with southern whites for jobs. Dixon assured that the white southerner would not stand for competing with blacks: "He will do exactly what his white neighbor in the North does when the Negro threatens his bread—kill him!"[26]

That month Washington set off another firestorm over social equality by eating dinner with department-store magnate John Wanamaker at the United States Hotel in Saratoga Springs, New York. The story got extra juice when the New York *Evening Journal* falsely reported that Washington had escorted Wanamaker's daughter to the table. The Wanamaker story enraged the same people that erupted over the White House dinner, and more, as the *Montgomery Advertiser* and other previous defenders despaired of Washington's incorrigibility. Many harsh things were said about his arrogance, insolence, power-hungry presumption, and sending his children to white schools; Washington gently replied that it was impossible for him to raise money in the North without consorting with white people socially.[27]

By then Washington's image across the white South was badly damaged. From opposite standpoints, white southern critics and black northern critics increasingly used the phrase "Wizard of Tuskegee" with a sneer. The Wizard paid a huge price for becoming a political boss, and he made some bad decisions; his worst decision was still to come. But his main problem was that he tried to do the impossible. He became preeminent by promising a cheap and docile labor force to New South capitalists, but most white southerners were opposed to blacks succeeding at anything, which fueled a backlash. In February 1905 Du Bois convened a secret meeting at the Buffalo home of anti-lynching activist Mary B. Talbert to imagine the Niagara Movement. Trotter, John Hope,

Charles E. Bentley, and twenty-nine others were there. The group drew up a list of fifty-nine black male educators, lawyers, ministers, physicians, publishers, and businessmen—the invitation call for a founding conference in July.

NIAGARITES

The Niagara Conference was supposed to take place in Buffalo, but the racial prejudice of a Buffalo hotel manager compelled a last-minute switch to the Erie Beach Hotel in Ontario, on the Canadian side of Niagara Falls. The switch inadvertently threw off Washington's spy, Boston attorney Clifford Plummer, who saw nothing in Buffalo for three days and reported that the conference never happened. Twenty-nine members of the Talented Tenth came to Ontario and thereafter called themselves Niagarites. Women were excluded because Trotter and others didn't want them. In the early going, Du Bois bowed to antifeminist sentiment. The founders included Howard University medical professor Henry Lewis Bailey; Jesse Max Barber; Charles Bentley; Beverly, Massachusetts, lawyer Robert H. Bonner; Kansas attorney and judge I. F. Bradley; Harrisburg, Pennsylvania, lawyer William Justin Carter; Baptist pastor and (from 1908 to 1911) seminary president James R. L. Diggs; Newport, Rhode Island, Congregational pastor Byron Gunner; Howard University law professors William H. H. Hart and William H. Richards; AME Sunday School Union Publishing House trustee Richard Hill; John Hope; Washington, DC, attorney Lafayette M. Hershaw; Cincinnati, Ohio, lawyer George Henry Jackson; Boston lawyer Edwin B. Jourdain; Chicago bookkeeper James S. Madden; Frederick McGhee; George Frazier Miller; Clement Morgan; Virginia businessman Freeman Henry M. Murray; Boston Baptist pastor William Henry Scott; Kansas City, Missouri, lawyer B. S. Smith; *Cleveland Gazette* editor Harry C. Smith; Columbus, Ohio, businessman Harvey A. Thompson; and Baltimore Baptist missionary Garnett Russell Waller. Several social gospelers who could not make it to Niagara identified with the group from the beginning and thus considered themselves founders, notably Ransom, Wright, Francis Grimké, William H. Ferris, and Monroe Work. Miller and Archibald Grimké were not at Niagara because Du Bois didn't invite them.[28]

The Niagarites met agreeably for three days; it helped that Du Bois and Trotter were on good terms at the time. The group formed an organization with ten committees, elected Du Bois as general secretary, and commissioned a "Declaration of Principles," authored by Du Bois and Trotter. There were nineteen principles, beginning with progress, suffrage, and civil liberties, and ending with agitation, help, and duties. Du Bois and Trotter touted black progress over the past decade, especially the "increase of intelligence, the buying of property, the checking of crime, the uplift in home life, and [the] advance in literature and art." Their case for "manhood suffrage" rested on the claim that "no man" deserved to be entrusted wholly with the welfare of his neighbor. They defended the right of all American citizens to equal treatment in public venues and sharply criticized economic exclusion, noting that in the rural South the denial of equal opportunities amounted to "peonage and virtual slavery." The Niagara Declaration called for universal public education and a color-blind court system. It pleaded for the right not to be subjected to unhealthy living conditions. It noted "with alarm" the escalating hatred of white Americans for black Americans, declaring: "We pray God that this nation will not degenerate into a mob of boasters and oppressors, but rather will return to the faith of the fathers, that all men were created free and equal, with certain unalienable rights."[29]

Du Bois and Trotter blasted American employers for exploiting Afro-Americans as scab laborers, and unions for excluding blacks as members. They declared that any form of discrimination based simply on race or color was "barbarous," a relic of "that unreasoning human savagery of which the world is and ought to be thoroughly ashamed." For example, the Jim Crow car was an assault on the humanity of blacks, forcing them to pay "first-class fare for third-class accommodations." One year before Theodore Roosevelt dramatically abused 167 black soldiers, the Niagara Declaration protested that America routinely mistreated black soldiers, refused to promote them, and excluded them from military academies. Under the category, "War Amendments," Du Bois and Trotter urged the federal government to enforce the Reconstruction Amendments. They repudiated "the monstrous doctrine that the oppressor should be the sole authority as to the rights of the oppressed." Since Trotter lacked word-painting talent, it was obvious who wrote certain sentences: "The Negro race in America, stolen, ravished and degraded, struggling up through difficulties and oppression, needs sympathy and receives criticism; needs help and is given hindrance, needs protection and is given mob-violence, needs justice and is given charity, needs leadership and is given cowardice and apology, needs bread and is given a stone. This nation will never stand justified before God until these things are changed."[30]

That could have been a climactic ending, but there were still things to say about the church, agitation, help, and duties. Du Bois and Trotter professed to be "surprised and astonished" at the capitulation of white American churches to an upsurge of white American racism. They had not expected this from ministers who preached about "human brotherhood." They replied, simply, "This is wrong, unchristian and disgraceful to the twentieth century civilization." On agitation, they roared for freedom and justice: "We do not hesitate to complain, and to complain loudly and insistently. To ignore, overlook, or apologize for these wrongs is to prove ourselves unworthy of freedom. Persistent manly agitation is the way to liberty, and toward this goal the Niagara Movement has started and asks the cooperation of all men of all races." The movement was exclusively black, but it wanted help from white neo-abolitionists. It affirmed that rights were linked with duties—the duties to vote, work, obey the laws, respect the right of others, be clean and orderly, educate their children, and "respect ourselves, even as we respect others."[31]

The Niagara Declaration was a manifesto, a protest, and a prayer. Its language of equal rights was an echo of the 1848 "Declaration of Sentiments," when Elizabeth Cady Stanton, Lucretia Mott, Frederick Douglass, and others founded American feminism at Seneca Falls, New York, but the Niagara Declaration steered clear of feminism and any explicit recognition of parallels or precedents. Its condemnation of employer/union economic injustice was rare for black literature of the time and taken straight from Du Bois's speech to the American Missionary Association. The businessmen and Howard professors must have choked at Du Bois's broadside against American capitalism. Du Bois's personal authority also carried the day for some participants who had mixed feelings about Trotter. By Du Bois's calculation, his group at Niagara constituted .02 percent of the black population and a tiny fraction of the Talented Tenth. But he was delighted to start something; in a group photo, Du Bois looked away from the camera with a hint of playfulness. The conference got almost no press notice, as Clifford Plummer thwarted coverage of the conference he missed. For press notice, Du Bois had to rely on in-house Niagara organs: the *Bee, Voice of the Negro, Boston Guardian, Gazette,* plus a breakthrough story in the *Boston Evening Transcript,* which announced the existence of an alternative to the Afro-American Council.[32]

The Niagara Movement was incorporated in January 1906. Washington derided it as a handful of intellectuals from three cities—Boston, Chicago, and Washington, DC. He dominated New York and Philadelphia, and he dominated all the places that Niagarites not from Boston, Chicago, and Washington, DC, came from. But Washington did not feel secure in his dominance. He worked zealously to crush the Niagara group, which falsified his insistence that Du Bois did not matter. *Voice of the Negro,* under Barber's stewardship, had a brief run as Niagara's unofficial organ. Barber knowingly accused Washington of meddling in other people's business; at the time Barber had to cope with Emmett Scott, Washington's chief operative, as a staff colleague. Barber admonished that great figures moved history forward by writing great works and inspiring people to fulfill their ideals; Washington, however, obsessed over small things that should have been beneath his dignity. That ended Barber's career as soon as the Wizard had a pretext for making a move. When the pretext arrived—the Atlanta riot— Washington gave an object lesson in small-minded punishment by driving Barber out of Atlanta and thwarting his journalistic career.[33]

Du Bois believed that the Niagara Movement needed a galvanizing magazine of its own. His first attempt to provide one, the *Moon Illustrated Weekly*, lasted thirty-four issues—long enough to publicize the group's moment of glory from August 15 to 18, 1906, at a place of ineffable historical resonance, Harper's Ferry, West Virginia. There the Niagarites celebrated the one hundredth anniversary of John Brown's birth, at Storer College, another school launched by AMA abolitionists. Du Bois, at the time, was writing a large, powerful, lyrical, complex biography of Brown, so the locale overflowed with resonances for him. At Harper's Ferry Du Bois offended Trotter by organizing a Women's Auxiliary, although women were still barred from meetings, and Ransom stole the show with an electrifying address.

Du Bois wanted as much religious support as he could get. In *The Philadelphia Negro* he argued that the black church played an incomparable role in black American life by promoting general intelligence and setting moral standards. The church distinctly provided a language and space for social discourse, maintaining a continuous membership. It antedated the family in black American experience, preserving some functions of African tribal organization. It sought to improve social conditions, and above all, it provided an indispensable source of transcendent meaning. In *The Souls of Black Folk* Du Bois added that the slave "spoke to the world" through the sorrow songs, which were rarely secular. The spirituals were nearly always about strife and exile, groping toward "some unseen power" and sighing for eternal rest. For Du Bois, leaving religion aside was not in play. Rallying the black church to social justice activism was essential, which required movement leaders that spoke the language of gospel faith and were themselves church leaders.[34]

Ransom gave a stem-winder on John Brown and the meaning of it all, getting a tumultuous reception. His speech had perfect pitch for the aggrieved, determined, defiant, but somehow still optimistic spirit of Niagara. Du Bois responded with a cadenced, hastily written, tightly composed "Address to the Country." He asked Hershaw to deliver it, on the last night of the conference, avoiding any performance comparisons with Ransom. The work of the "Negro hater" flourished in America, Du Bois began. The situation had become so desperate that some "weaker brethren" were reduced to whispering for mere decencies, ruling justice out of play. The Niagara Movement, by contrast, roared for the United

States' founding ideals, lest America become "the land of the thief and the home of the Slave." Du Bois stressed that America was the worst of the civilized nations in its treatment of racial minorities. No other nation proposed to adopt "so cowardly a creed" as the one enshrined in Jim Crow and *Plessy v. Ferguson*. Du Bois lingered there in disbelief: "And this is the land that professes to follow Jesus Christ."[35]

The Niagara Movement demanded full manhood suffrage, "and we want it now, henceforth and forever." It demanded the abolition of discrimination in public accommodation, the right to social freedom, and the rule of law applied equally to rich and poor, capitalists and laborers, and whites and blacks. Contrary to prevailing white opinion, "We are not more lawless than the white race, we are more often arrested, convicted, and mobbed." Lastly, the Niagara Movement demanded a real education for all black children, "the development of power and ideal." It was repugnant to educate blacks merely to be servants: "They have a right to know, to think, to aspire."[36]

On Friday morning Du Bois led the Niagarites in a silent, barefoot procession down a steep road, cupping candles against the morning breeze, to the old arsenal at Harper's Ferry, paying homage to Brown's memory. On Sunday evening Du Bois ended the conference with a final word about Brown and righteous rebellion: "We do not believe in violence, neither in the despised violence of the raid nor the lauded violence of the soldier, nor the barbarous violence of the mob, but we do believe in John Brown, in that incarnate spirit of justice, that hatred of a lie, that willingness to sacrifice money, reputation, and life itself on the altar of right. And here on the scene of John Brown's martyrdom we reconsecrate ourselves, our honor, our property to the final emancipation of the race which John Brown died to make free." Du Bois insisted that justice and humanity had to prevail. He refused to surrender "the leadership of this race to cowards and trucklers." He rang the roll of abolitionist heroes: Garrison and Douglass, Sumner and Phillips, and Nat Turner and Robert Gould Shaw. He thanked God for the abolitionists of the past, and those of the present day, "few though their voices be, who have not forgotten the divine brotherhood of all men white and black, rich and poor, fortunate and unfortunate."[37]

This time the press coverage was stronger, led by Villard's *Evening Post*, but Washington's domination of black politics was about to end in any case, destroyed by two explosive events. The first was unfolding as the Niagarites made their votive procession to Brown's fort.

On August 13, 1906, a ten-minute shooting spree in Brownsville, Texas, killed a bartender and wounded a police officer. The incident occurred in a dance hall area outside Fort Brown, where the Twenty-fifth U.S. Infantry Regiment was housed. The soldiers at Fort Brown, from the day of their arrival three weeks earlier, had been subjected to racial taunting and abuse, as 167 of the 170 soldiers were black. Townspeople jeered and threatened the soldiers, refused them entry to bars, pushed them off sidewalks, beat up several of them, and inevitably accused them of assaulting a white woman. When the shooting spree broke out, soldiers believed that a white mob was attacking and townspeople believed that the soldiers were retaliating for recent assaults. An armed mob demanded that the troops be punished, but every soldier signed an affidavit denying any prior knowledge about the shooting or participating in it.

The army investigated but got nowhere. The mayor of Brownsville produced a soldier's cap and some army rifle shell casings—weak evidence, circumstantial, and probably planted. The fort's white commanders reported that every black soldier had been in the barracks at the time of the shooting, answering a roll call under a curfew. Moreover, the Twenty-fifth was a crack regiment, having fought in Cuba, the Philippines, and the Great Plains against the Sioux. The U.S. inspector general assigned to the case, however, a white South Carolinian, concluded that this was a case about uppity blacks and group insubordination. He recommended a blanket dishonorable discharge, explaining that Negroes had a reputation for covering up for each other and recently they had become "much more aggressive" about their rights. Roosevelt read this report as the Niagara Conference concluded.[38]

At the time Roosevelt was the most popular American president among blacks since Lincoln, notwithstanding that he spent most of his presidency trying to regain white southern support and he sometimes slurred blacks as an inferior group prone to break the law. Black Americans appreciated TR for dining with Washington, for wanting their support, and for breaking with Republican lily-white appointment policy in the South. Washington had recommended an African American, William Crum, as collector of the Port of Charleston, South Carolina, and TR stuck with Crum after white southerners erupted against the appointment. In 1904, black support for Roosevelt helped him fend off a nomination challenge engineered by Mark Hanna at the GOP national convention. Black Americans wanted to believe they had a friend in the White House. By 1906, to sustain that belief, they had indulged a slew of racial slurs, Roosevelt's downplaying of the dinner, and, when campaigning in the South, his appeals for white racial purity. Black Americans trusted, as the November midterm election approached, that Roosevelt would handle the Brownsville situation justly.

Roosevelt, however, carefully bided his time. He bought the inspector general's verdict: The real issue was black insubordination, a conspiracy of silence. If the innocent were determined to protect the guilty, to hell with them. It didn't matter that the soldiers were treated badly; they were soldiers and had a duty to take it. Soldiers were a firewall against anarchy—always TR's raw nerve. Just before the election Roosevelt told Washington that he planned to fire all 167 black soldiers without trial. Washington was appalled. He pleaded with Roosevelt not to do it. Later he asked Roosevelt to let him investigate what had happened; learning the truth would surely be better than arbitrarily sacking everyone. Roosevelt said an inquiry would pointlessly prolong the issue. He was done with the Brownsville case. Secretary of War William Howard Taft, making the same objection, got the same reply. On the day after the midterm election, in which Republicans retained control of the House and gained four seats in the Senate with overwhelming Afro-American support, Taft announced that all 167 of the black soldiers were dishonorably discharged and barred forever from reenlisting. Six were Medal of Honor winners and some had served more than twenty-five years.[39]

Black communities across the nation exploded with disbelief and outrage, as did many white newspapers. African American support for Roosevelt evaporated overnight and never returned. Protesters flooded the White House with telegrams. Ransom and Trotter organized a protest meeting that packed Faneuil Hall in Boston. Fortune pressed the analogy to lynching, blasting Roosevelt for "carrying into the Federal Government the demand of the Southern white devils" to hand over innocent black men to mob vengeance. That set the tone and terms for many editorialists and ministers. Many protested that Roosevelt did more to legitimize the lynching mentality than the white nationalists sitting in congressional seats and gubernatorial chairs. A North Carolina Baptist convention protested that no president would have done such a thing to white soldiers. The New York *World* stressed that Roosevelt had no idea how many soldiers might have been involved; no amount of ignorance made any difference to America's president. The Unitarian *Christian Register* was incredulous at Roosevelt's verdict that up to 160 soldiers were willing to ruin their lives over an ostensible secret. The *New York Times*, sympathetic as usual to the white South, opined that Roosevelt needed to stop black impudence before it got out of hand. Still, even the *Times* blanched that the government's case contained "not a particle of evidence" proving the guilt of any soldier. Ohio Republican U.S. senator Joseph B. Foraker rallied opposition in Congress, blasting Roosevelt for betraying his oath to uphold the Constitution.[40]

Roosevelt was astonished by this outpouring, and defiant. The more that blacks and northern white critics condemned the wholesale firing, the madder he got at blacks and northern white critics. "I have been amazed and indignant at the attitude of the negroes and of shortsighted white sentimentalists as to my action," he told a friend. "It has been shown conclusively that some of these troops made a midnight murderous and entirely unprovoked assault upon the citizens of Brownsville." In fact, historians subsequently upheld the gut reaction of black communities that the government lacked any credible evidence against anyone and that Roosevelt's action was indefensible. Roosevelt insisted that black churches got the racial angle exactly wrong. Had the troops been white, white Americans would not have defended them, but "the colored people have made a fetich [*sic*] of the innocence of the troops." As the furor rolled on and the condemnations piled higher, Roosevelt opined that the lynching analogy was apt, favoring him. He found himself sympathizing with white defenders of lynching, and not only because they praised him for punishing the Brownsville 167. Lynching apologists always said that whites had to step outside the law to exact justice because blacks banded together to shelter criminals from the rule of law. The president of the United States found himself reconsidering his previous disagreement with this argument, and thus, with lynching: "I had never really believed there was much justification for the claim of the Southern whites that the decent Negroes should actively or passively shield their own wrongdoers; or at least I had never realized the extent to which this statement was true; but this Brownsville business has given me the most serious concern on this very point." In December Roosevelt's annual address to Congress stooped to that level, fulminating against "the negro criminal," especially "the negro criminal who commits the dreadful crime of rape," and above all, Afro-Americans that upheld each other in criminal behavior.[41]

Booker Washington, had he signed off at this point, might have salvaged a better closing decade and legacy. All he had to do was divulge that he strenuously opposed Roosevelt's action. He may have believed—probably wrongly—that a few of the soldiers were guilty, but that was never the point. Du Bois openly doubted that the entire group was innocent. The point was that wholesale punishment was atrocious, something on which Du Bois and Washington agreed. But Washington treasured his political power and he sincerely believed that things would get worse for blacks if he lost his role as a patronage broker. He told Anderson that being disloyal to "our friend" in the White House was not an option for him. He would take whatever criticism came from sticking with Roosevelt, even after Fortune pleaded with him to break away, and even as Afro-Americans across the nation reeled from two stupendous assaults—Brownsville and the Atlanta riot.[42]

On September 22, a marauding mob of ten thousand mostly young whites in Atlanta savagely beat every black person it could find in the streets. The mob pulled black passengers off trolleys, hunted down black employees in shops, and chased down blacks trying to escape, also pillaging the train station, post office, and white-owned businesses. The spark was the usual canard about protecting white women from black rapists. The rioting carried on for five days, killing more than twenty people and injuring hundreds. Washington traveled to Atlanta as soon as order was restored, aiding in the work of reconstruction. Du Bois, returning home by train to his terrified family, composed a prayerful cry, "A Litany of Atlanta." Some passages were immortalized in church bulletins, and some were too raw for church bulletins:

> Is this Thy justice, O Father, that guilt be easier than innocence, and the innocent crucified for the guilt of the untouched guilty? . . . Wherefore do we pray? Is not the God of the fathers dead? . . . Behold this maimed and broken thing; dear God it was a humble black man who toiled and sweat to save a bit from the pittance paid him. . . . Doth not this justice of hell stink in Thy nostrils, O God? How long shall the mounting flood of innocent blood roar in Thine ears and pound in our hearts for vengeance? . . . Bewildered we are, and passion-tost, mad with the madness of a mobbed and mocked and murdered people. . . . Surely Thou too are not white, O Lord, a pale, bloodless, heartless thing? . . . Forgive the thought! Forgive these wild, blasphemous words. Thou art still the God of our black fathers, and in Thy soul's soul sit some soft darkenings of the evening, some shadowings of the velvet night.[43]

The *Independent* published Du Bois's passionate litany shortly after he rushed home to sit on the steps of South Hall with a shotgun, protecting Nina and Yolande. Washington tried to bring together white and black civic leaders in Atlanta, issuing an appeal in *Outlook* for racial reconciliation. He tried hard, claiming to believe that the riot provided a new opportunity for black and white cooperation. The bitter ironies, however, were widely noted. The city in which Washington supposedly cut a deal with white America had turned monstrously hostile to blacks. The parties on the white side of the deal were fewer and less motivated than in 1895, as the New South had rushed on for a decade of commercial boom in tandem with unleashed racial rage.

In the aftermath of Atlanta and Brownsville, Fortune urged Washington to cut his ties to Roosevelt and speak for racial justice. But Washington had never upbraided a white authority figure in his life; this was not a likely time to start. Instead he replied with a Machine move, secretly buying the *New York Age* and softening its editorial line. Fortune, angered and despairing, already losing his battle with alcoholism, cut his ties to the *Age* and Washington. He drifted closer to Du Bois's position, but for Du Bois it was sad to witness Fortune in decline. Adam Clayton Powell Sr. was among the first to say that Washington had something worse than a loyalty problem. Powell told the *New York Times* that some Afro-Americans in his circle believed that Washington was responsible for Roosevelt's mounting hostility to blacks: "The awful march of events since the famous Roosevelt-Washington [dinner] makes a thoughtful man ask: Has the colored race been sold for a mess of pottage?" In the pulpit of Abyssinian Church, Powell put it more sharply, declaring that Washington's friend in the White House had gone from being "enshrined in our hearts as Moses" to being "enshrouded in our scorn as Judas."[44]

Washington went down with Roosevelt, clinging to power but dismally lamenting to friends that he could not say what he really thought. Alexander Walters went over to the Niagara camp after Brownsville and Atlanta, declaring to the Afro-American Council in October 1906: "The object of our enemies is to make us serfs. It is nonsense to cry peace when there is no peace. We are determined to rise or die in the attempt to obtain our rights." The following July, the Afro-American Council, chaired by Walters and no longer a support group for the Wizard, voted to censure Roosevelt.[45]

Du Bois was the opposite of Washington—flush with energy and moral authority, feeling the momentum swing his way and saying what he thought, but lacking money, infrastructure, employee security, and political power. He launched a new monthly, *The Horizon: A Journal of the Color Line*, giving himself wholly to propaganda journalism, with help from two loyalists, Hershaw and Murray. The *Horizon* reported on global struggles against white imperialism and specialized in zingers against the Booker/Abbott/Murphy school of racial paternalism. Du Bois lamented that the cause of civil rights lost its most brilliant advocate, Fortune, when it needed him most, a victim of his own vices and the "Arch-Tempter," Washington, who came "smooth-tongued and cynical, with gold." Now it was too late for the debt-ridden and deteriorating Fortune to lead the movement.[46]

The *Horizon* teemed with advice about books, magazines, and newspapers, striving to expand and shape the black reading public. Du Bois implored readers to buy books instead of borrow them and to avoid the Sunday newspaper, which was always a "hodge-podge of lie, gossip, twaddle and caricature." Every self-respecting black American needed to read a daily paper, a race paper, a weekly "digester," a monthly picture magazine, and an "Encourager." In January 1907 Du Bois opined that the best race papers were the *Guardian* and the *Voice of the Negro*, and every Afro-American needed a weekly digest from the *Independent*, "the bravest and fairest in its stand on the Negro problem." The other prominent Congregational weekly paper, the *Outlook,* stood for "militant hypocrisy in ethics and literature." The following January Du Bois told *Horizon* readers to make their own decisions about daily and race papers. The digester, however, had to be the *Independent;* Ray Stannard Baker's "wobbly, but trying hard" *American Magazine* was the best picture monthly; and *Horizon* was clearly the best Encourager, please send donations. In the early going, *Horizon* blasted Roosevelt repeatedly, declaring that the president did not like black people, never had one as a friend, never did much to earn his outsized black support, and now slammed the door of opportunity "most emphatically in the black man's face."[47]

Since most readers of *Horizon* had never voted anything but Republican and regarded Socialism as something foreign and anti-American, Du Bois had to address rumors about his politics. In the second issue he confirmed that he had become some kind of socialist, "a socialist of the path." He did not advocate socializing everything, but he believed that railroads, coal mines, and many large factories "can and ought to be run by the public and for the public." His new friend Mary White Ovington was a strong influence in this area. Ovington had grown up in a cultured, Brooklyn, abolitionist, feminist, Unitarian family. She was deeply involved in reform movements and had recently cofounded a settlement in San Juan Hill, an African American neighborhood just north of Hell's Kitchen in Manhattan. In 1904 Du Bois invited her to his annual Atlanta Conference of Negro Problems. Ovington had friends across the spectrum of left-wing movements, and her friendship with Du Bois became central to her many-sided activism. In 1905 she joined the Socialist Party, telling Du Bois that racial injustice and capitalism worked together. She got him to read Socialist writers, especially books by her friend John Spargo. She worked on Ray Stannard Baker too, who became the first prominent American journalist to feature the color line as a justice issue; Baker cofounded the *American Magazine* in 1906 and wrote a best-selling book, *Following the Color Line* (1908), which helped to coalesce the activist community that founded the NAACP. Du Bois, increasingly certain that civil rights work and black anti-imperialism needed a Socialist underpinning, told *Horizon* readers that in Socialism lay "the one great hope of the Negro American."[48]

For a militant and financially strapped enterprise, the Niagara Movement grew impressively; by any other standard, it was a small enterprise. It boasted 170 members at the Harper's Ferry conference. By 1907 it had 380, and it peaked in 1908 with 450. The questionable state of black Republicanism loomed large in 1908. Roosevelt pandered to white supremacy in the South, increasing his national popularity, which would have carried him to a third term had he not declared in 1904 that running for reelection in 1908 would be unseemly. Roosevelt wanted to take it back, but Democrats hung the pledge around his neck and the Republican Party reluctantly nominated Taft, who hated politics. Taft wanted to be chief justice of the Supreme Court. Since Taft was a lily-white Republican in the mold of Hanna and McKinley, Du Bois urged blacks to show their contempt for the Republican Party's unabashed contempt of them. In early 1908 Du Bois despaired that there was nothing to choose between Taft and Democratic front-runner William Jennings Bryan: "'tis the Devil and the Deep Sea." The Socialists were the only party that treated black Americans as human beings, he contended. But Du Bois had already wasted his vote in 1904, and the stakes were too high in 1908 to do it again. By March he was ready to hold his nose and vote for Bryan, who at least had a populist conscience, and who did not boast—like Taft—about driving blacks out of politics in the South. Du Bois warned *Horizon* readers that if Taft's reactionary wing of the Republican Party prevailed in the election, "we are sentenced for a century to Jim Crow cars, peonage and disfranchisement." He pleaded with them to stop fretting about deserting the Republican Party, for the party had already deserted them.[49]

From the beginning the Niagara Movement had debilitating factions and a desperate lack of money, which killed it. Du Bois had three treasurers in three years; J. Milton Waldron was the middle one. Du Bois's correspondence with all three was unremittingly depressing. Du Bois feuded with Trotter, who could not play Number Two to anyone, and Trotter feuded with Clement Morgan, splitting the Boston stronghold. The organization was nearly broke by the time it met in Boston in 1907, and the Boston conference was a letdown from Harper's Ferry, except for twenty female delegates wearing spectacular hats and full-length dresses. Du Bois ended the Boston conference in Faneuil Hall with another stirring speech titled "Address to the Country." The following year, at Oberlin, he could not muster stirring oratory for a small and dispirited gathering. Ovington was admitted as the group's first white member, a foretaste of the NAACP, but she had to miss Oberlin because of her father's declining health. Du Bois tried to merge Niagara with the Afro-American Council, Negro Academy, and Negro American Political League, convincing Walters, Archibald Grimké, and Waldron to help make it happen at the Oberlin gathering. But the shriveled turnout deflated visions of synergy. Du Bois had labored for the past five years on a biography of Brown that proved to be too lumbering, uneven, and unsettling to attract readers or favorable reviews, despite its sparkling passages. Though Washington's star had fallen, his Machine still monopolized racial philanthropy and stifled press attention to the existence of Niagara.[50]

Most important, the Du Bois–Trotter relationship ended shortly after the Boston conference. Morgan fought with Trotter to retain control of the Massachusetts chapter, and Du Bois sided with Morgan against Trotter, who teamed with Waldron to found a rival organization in April 1908, the Negro American Political League, out of the old National Equal Rights League. Losing the Trotter faction killed the Niagara Movement. Trotter was a magnet for militants that found Du Bois to be too intellectual and coolly self-certain. For Du Bois, excluding women from the movement was indefensible, and excluding whites meant that the movement would always be poor and marginalized. He and Trotter fought over both things, plus the politics of militancy and Trotter's rivalry with Morgan, until it became pointless to keep fighting. In theory, Trotter wanted white allies, but in actuality, he had trouble finding any he could stand; civil rights activist John Milholland was a rare exception. Moreover, Trotter distrusted any organization he could not control, and he lost one of his closest allies, Ferris, during the schism with Du Bois. Each made a strong case against the other. Ferris said that Trotter was impossible to work with, and Trotter said that Ferris mooched off him for years. The Negro American Political League morphed a succession of incarnations called the National Independent Political League, the National Independent Political Rights League, the National Independent Equal Rights League, and finally the National Equal Rights League. All stressed that they were organizations "of the colored people and for the colored people and led by the colored people." The Niagara Movement had a last conference hurrah in 1909 in Sea Isle City, New Jersey, and a last year of political journalism in 1910.[51]

To the end, the *Horizon* was sparkling, biting, and scathingly humorous. It paved the way to the success of *Crisis* and the NAACP by building an audience for Du Bois's brand of propaganda journalism. A Chicago reader asked Du Bois to "talk more about the bumptious negroes up in the North" who harmed race relations by showing off, talking loudly, dressing even louder, and generally acting "very impertinent, chesty and fresh." Would Du Bois please use his influence to make the bumptious types less obnoxious? Du Bois could sympathize: "Bumptious people are trying. The loud-mouthed and flashily dressed do much to spoil an otherwise bearable world. America has invented the striking words 'chesty' and 'fresh' because they express something peculiarly American but not on that account the less obnoxious or harmful." Still, had the correspondent ever noted that young people as a whole tended to be off-balance and somewhat full of themselves? Or that Europeans found Americans as a whole to be obnoxious? Did the correspondent admonish youthful white people when they carried on obnoxiously? To be sure, "What is more trying than that boy of eighteen or twenty who knows it all? Who sets the fashions, kicks the cat, and contradicts the Lord!" But we should not suppress the boy, Du Bois advised, or even admonish him to be less obnoxious: "Wait! Look! Listen! Let him grow; he may be Martin Luther bursting his chrysalis, or Alexander Dumas trying his wings; he may foreshadow a mighty people in travail."[52]

Du Bois tired of hustling for money to organize conferences, publish *Horizon*, and travel to meetings. For most of his career in Atlanta he lacked even a workable office. His bosses at Atlanta University, Horace Bumstead and Edmund Ware, were supportive and admiring, but Du Bois knew that his battle with Washington cost the university financial support every year. Du Bois was so strapped for money that he nearly missed the December 1909 meeting of the American Historical Association in New York, where he presented a paper on "Reconstruction and Its Benefits"—the core of his subsequently massive, revisionist lifework on Reconstruction.

At the AHA Du Bois was reunited with his teacher, Hart, who paid his travel fare. Hart was still an admirer, although Du Bois had not made it easy for him. Hart was a trustee at Howard University, and he wanted all people that cared about African Americans to pull together. Washington had a strategy and Du Bois had a strategy; what was the problem? In 1905 he wrote proudly to Du Bois: "I hear of you everywhere." But he also heard that Du Bois said harsh things about Washington. Was that really necessary? Hart wrote: "So far as I understand, there is no innate lack of harmony between your purpose in life and his. You take a certain thing which must be done, viz. the higher education of those who can profit by it; he takes another end of the same problem; naturally each of you thinks that his interest is the more important; if you did not, you would exchange activities. But I do not see how either excludes the other." Hart shuddered at Trotter's ridicule of Washington, and he could not imagine that Du Bois and Trotter were allies, even though people told him it was so. Du Bois told his teacher to get over it; the informers were correct. He had nothing against Washington personally, "but his platform has done the race infinite harm & I'm working against it with all my might. Mr. W. is today chief instrument in the hands of a N.Y. clique who are seeking to syndicate the Negro & settle the problem on the trust basis. They have bought & bribed newspapers & men."[53]

At the AHA Du Bois stared down the dean of "Negro misrule" orthodoxy, Columbia University historian William Archibald Dunning. There was an upside to Reconstruction that historians overlooked, Du Bois contended. Negro rule inaugurated democratic government, free public schools, and progressive social legislation in the South. Unfortunately, the federal government failed to get behind the Freedmen's Bureau, which was weak to begin with, poorly financed, and quickly abandoned, allowing the South to institute new forms of slavery. The historians applauded; Hart told Du Bois that Dunning himself gave high praise to his presentation. But Du Bois was ignored in the field for the next twenty-five years, as were others (including Hart and black Republican politician John Lynch) making similar arguments, while a succession of historians and journalists continued to say there was no upside to Reconstruction. Historians did not seriously reconsider what happened under Reconstruction until Du Bois published *Black Reconstruction in America* in 1935.[54]

Du Bois still wanted to believe that rigorous, enlightened scholarship would break the tyranny of ignorance and bigotry that rationalized the abusive treatment of his race. Every page of *The Philadelphia Negro* was suffused with this hope, and Du Bois was clinging to it as he lectured to the AHA; standing there was important to him. But Du Bois probably would not have given himself to movement propaganda activism had he actually believed it. Afro-Americans were being terrorized and he doubted that his original rationale for an academic career was true. Scholarship, at least in the short run, was no better than Bookerism at breaking the tyranny of white ignorance and bigotry. This doubt was confirmed, for Du Bois, when he submitted his lecture on Reconstruction to the *American Historical Review.*

One breakthrough conviction that Du Bois and Washington shared was that the word "Negro" should be capitalized. Both prevailed with skittish publishers to break convention in this area. *The Suppression of the African Slave Trade* and *The Philadelphia Negro* were among the first books to have the noun placed in capitals, and *Up from Slavery* introduced a vast audience to the idea that employing the upper case was an elementary decency. Du Bois, upon reading the proofs for his article in the *American Historical Review,* had one request of managing editor J. Franklin Jameson: "I always ask editors, as a matter of courtesy to allow me to capitalize the word Negro. They usually do so and I trust you will do the same."[55]

Jameson was a major player in the field; he taught for many years at Johns Hopkins, Brown, and the University of Chicago, directed the historical research department at Carnegie Institution, and headed the Library of Congress Manuscript Division. He replied that the journal had good reason not to capitalize the word for anyone else and not to make an exception for Du Bois. "Negro," after all, was not a proper name. Du Bois pushed back. The journal's uniformity of practice, he replied, was not a "sufficient excuse" for inflicting a "personal insult" on him, a Negro scholar with feelings on the subject. Jameson was incredulous. It "astonished" him that he, the "grandson of an old Abolitionist, brought up to know no difference between black and white" could be accused of insulting a colleague of any race. He was a race-blind liberal; he had no prejudice; nobody questioned that. The word *"negro"* was Spanish for black, Jameson noted. It had nothing to do with nationality—"negro" was not like American, German, or Hindu. It belonged in the same category with white man, brown man, and red man—a mere characterization of physical traits: "The question was simply one of typography."[56]

Du Bois backed down on the article, but not the argument. He told Jameson he had not meant to imply that the "personal insult" was from him. It was merely the usage to which Jameson subscribed that was insulting. "You are mistaken about the authority of that usage," Du Bois contended. On the Continent and in England, the word was almost always capitalized. Even in the United States it was commonly capitalized "until about 1840 when 'negroes' became definitely cattle for all time." If the *Outlook* could find its way to capitalizing the word, Du Bois was sad that the *American Historical Review* could not: "I am therefore exceedingly sorry to see you range yourself with the least authoritative & more insulting usage."[57]

CREATING THE NAACP

On August 14, 1908, Springfield, Illinois, erupted in a devastating race riot. Racial tension had built up in Springfield over competition for jobs in mining and rail transportation between black and white newcomers from the South. A white woman charged that a young black man raped her; another white woman egged on a mob that gathered at the jail; and hundreds of marauding white rioters killed seven black Americans by gunfire and two by lynching. Thousands of white citizens calmly looked on for two days while the mob chased down every black person it could find.

The Springfield riot shocked northern white liberals into action. Chicago social gospeler Graham Taylor found it a "sorry comment upon American civilization" to have produced a "new race of white barbarians" who believed they had no means of protecting themselves "except the blood and fire of extermination." Taylor allowed that there were "barbarians" on both sides of the racial divide in Springfield and America; still, the root cause of America's continuing racial pathology was the insistence of white Americans on isolating and holding down blacks. The Springfield rioters had to be punished, but more important, the United States had to build a civilization that eliminated white racism and civilized "our barbarians, both white and black." That year Taylor's network of social gospel progressives played a leading role in founding the Federal Council of Churches.[58]

Meanwhile, white liberals in New York plus a handful of Afro-Americans created the NAACP. William English Walling called it into existence with a searing article in the *Independent* titled "The Race War in the North." Walling was a Socialist author and New York settlement worker who had grown up in a wealthy Kentucky former slaveholding family. He was nearly as outraged by the public reaction to the Springfield riot as by the marauders. He and his wife traveled to Springfield as the riot took place, expecting to meet horrified onlookers. They found that most civic and political leaders responded commendably, but the "masses of the people" in the shops and streets were another story: "We at once discovered, to our amazement, that Springfield had no shame. She stood for the action of the mob. She hoped the rest of the negroes might flee. She threatened that the movement to drive them out would continue." Then the press coverage mused about "mitigating circumstances" that made such a thing possible in the home of Lincoln. Walling replied that Springfield exploded because of race hatred, not mitigating circumstances. The whole country was becoming like the worst parts of the South, and America was overdue to become alarmed about it: "Either the spirit of the abolitionists, of Lincoln and of Lovejoy, must be revived and we must come to treat the negro on a plane of absolute political and social equality, or Vardaman and Tillman will soon have transferred the race war to the North." On the basis of that either/or, Walling ended with a two-question question: "Who realizes the seriousness of the situation, and what large and powerful body of citizens is ready to come to their aid?"[59]

Mary White Ovington, reading Walling's article, vowed to build a large and powerful national organization to fight racism. She prodded Walling to get something started. The two of them plus social worker Henry Moskowitz drafted a call for a meeting on Lincoln's one hundredth birthday, February 12, 1909, sending it to Ovington's contacts in reform circles. Muckraking journalist Charles Edward Russell was the fourth member of the original group, which knowingly added a fifth member, Villard, before the meetings began in earnest. Villard had been talking about launching a "Committee for the Advancement of the Negro Race" since 1906. *The Souls of Black Folk* had made an impact on him. Then he investigated the peonage system and was appalled, charging that it reinstated slavery in the South. Villard's pro-Booker friends in the South begged him to pull back from lashing the South, and he replied that the time had come for outside criticism. Then Atlanta exploded and Villard told Ovington and other reformers that they needed to create a new civil rights organization. He took this message to the Afro-American Council in 1906, calling for an organization with a research and publicity bureau, a legal division to fight court cases against racial discrimination, a special committee to investigate lynching and peonage, a lobbying operation at the federal and state levels, a committee to organize mass protest meetings, and a monthly magazine. It was a blueprint for what became the NAACP. The reformers already regarded this organization as Villard's idea when they began to meet; plus he was rich, smart, aggressive, connected, and far more influential than any of them.[60]

From the beginning Ovington was the key to the group's unusual bridging of racial, gender, and class lines. The early meetings convened at Walling's apartment on West Thirty-ninth Street in Manhattan, adding Ray Stannard Baker, social worker Lillian Wald, Rabbi Stephen Wise, Unitarian minister John Haynes Holmes, and two Afro-American members—Bishop Walters and Ovington's friend William Henry Brooks, pastor of St. Mark's Methodist Episcopal Church in New York. Soon the group became too large for Walling's living room and it moved to the Liberal Club on East Nineteenth Street, where William Bulkley, a New York City public school principal, became its third black member. The next dozen members included William Ward, social worker Florence Kelley, and Du Bois's former collaborator Isabel Eaton. Villard, though brusque and egotistical, was the ringleader, and grateful to be asked. A supporter of Ovington's San Juan Hill settlement, he later recalled that "no greater compliment has ever been paid to me" than to be asked to cofound the NACCP. He also greatly admired Ovington, lauding her for "an unselfishness, a patience, a sweetness of spirit, and a kindliness hard to describe adequately." Villard rewrote the call, declaring: "This government cannot exist half slave and half free any better today than it could in 1861, hence we call upon all the believers in democracy to join in a national conference for the discussion of present evils, the voicing of protests, and the renewal of the struggle for civil and political liberty." Sixty people signed the call, released to the public on Lincoln's birthday, launching the National Negro Conference. Eight were African Americans: Du Bois, Walters, Brooks, Bulkley, Waldron, Wells-Barnett, Francis Grimké, and Mary Church Terrell. Many of the sixty signers did not know each other, but they all knew Ovington.[61]

The daytime meetings of the founding conference took place on May 31 and June 1, at New York's Charity Organization Hall, and the evening mass meetings were held at Cooper Union. Villard invited Washington, who dispatched his spies instead, admonishing Villard that he did not believe in agitation. Three hundred delegates attended and approximately eleven hundred spectators. Nearly one-third of the delegates were women, an echo of the abolitionist past before abolitionism and woman suffrage split over the Fifteenth Amendment. Jane Addams, Mary McDowell, Lillian Wald, and Florence

Kelley headed a formidable group of social workers. Other white female delegates included labor lawyer Inez Milholland (John Milholland's daughter), suffrage activist Fanny Garrison Villard (Oswald's mother), and Unitarian minister Celia Parker Woolley, a founder of Chicago's Frederick Douglass Center. The white male intellectuals included philosopher John Dewey, literary critic William Dean Howells, and comparative-literature scholar Joel Spingarn. Overall, the white progressives divided politically into three main groups—Socialists in the orbit of Ovington, Walling, and Russell; old-style Republican Protestants like Villard, Ward, and John Milholland; and liberal reformers less defined by ideology or religion. According to the *New York Times*, the gathering was roughly half black and half white. According to Du Bois, African Americans were overwhelmingly outnumbered. Du Bois noted that spectators seemed most interested in the "darker and less known" faces sprinkled among the prominent white people. The black contingent included Walters, Brooks, Bulkley, Du Bois, Wells-Barnett, Ransom, Miller, Scarborough, Terrell, Trotter, Waldron, Barber, and Archibald Grimké. By Du Bois's reckoning, the conference consisted of four groups: "Scientists who knew the race problem; philanthropists willing to help worthy causes; social workers ready to take up a new task of Abolition; and Negroes ready to join a new crusade for their emancipation."[62]

Ward gave the opening keynote, a ringing call to build a movement for equal rights. White academics spoke for the rest of the morning, on an assigned subject: Scientific evidence of human equality. They obligingly corrected two centuries of scientific racism concerning "racial inferiority," brain size, and research cited by insurance companies to justify denying coverage to blacks. Columbia University anthropologist Livingston Farrand acknowledged that his topic—race differentiation—was hard to discuss intelligently because nobody knew what a "race" was. Cornell University neurologist Burt Wilder, brandishing charts and photographs, said there were no significant differences of mental capacity between whites and blacks. Though whites had heavier brains than blacks and tended to have fewer prefrontal deficiencies affecting reason and judgment, blacks were not significantly different from whites in manifesting lateral or ventral depressions of the prefrontal lobe. This information was received appreciatively. Columbia University philosopher John Dewey said that racism deprived society of social capital, there was no such thing as an inferior race, and the current trend in biological science emphasized environmental factors. Columbia University political economist Edwin Seligman challenged the audience to be social-scientific for a moment—if they were white southerners, they would have the same views about social equality and politics that most white southerners held. Social evolution proceeds very slowly, Seligman cautioned.[63]

The conference participants got through a biracial lunch at Union Square Hotel, where the locals registered no irate reactions, to Ovington's relief. A few years earlier southern newspapers had excoriated Ovington and Villard for hosting a biracial gathering of the Cosmopolitan Club at a New York restaurant; Ovington dreaded a second round of "unspeakable" mail. The afternoon speakers were Woolley, Du Bois, Bulkley, and Walling. Woolley argued that a racial justice organization should treat racial, gender, and economic injustice as interlocking variables. Du Bois argued that blacks needed political power to abolish the new slavery of disenfranchisement, Jim Crow, and poverty. Bulkley argued that southern racism stupidly did not recognize the value of developing an intelligent laboring class, and it drove skilled workers into the ranks of unskilled labor. Walling argued that a movement opposing racial injustice should target the antilabor alliances of northern and southern economic elites.[64]

These calls for an emphasis on economic justice displayed a serious yearning for a labor movement not overwhelmingly segregated and hostile to black workers. Meanwhile, the organization being birthed needed to find some wealthy white backers, who were unlikely to prize trade unions. The success of this enterprise depended on Villard, who was still friendly with Washington. That provoked much anxiety about whether the organization would turn into another Booker T. production. According to Washington spy Charles Anderson, Du Bois convened a secret dinner meeting with Wells-Barnett, Barber, Walters, Waldron, Nathan Mossell, and John Milholland to keep Bookerism at bay. Later that night the conference reconvened to discuss the day. Somebody questioned whether agitation was a good thing. Russell said that too much agitation could not have occurred, since he had learned more about racism that day than in his entire life. Barber said the crisis of racial injustice was fundamentally political, not economic. Trotter said the crisis was fundamentally political and that Taft had become the biggest problem of all. Wells-Barnett, weary of boastful speeches, admonished that she had "launched" the agitation in the United States and England and they had not supported her. Was it going to be different this time?[65]

The following day there were more speeches, and the National Negro Conference debated what kind of group it should be and which forty people should lead it. Resolutions were offered and ripped apart, jeremiads were delivered, appeals to trust and goodwill were voiced, and feelings were hurt. Ransom warned against creeping Bookerism. Wells-Barnett gave her stock speech that lynching was "color-line murder" requiring a national remedy—a federal antilynching law. Discussion from the previous day was rehashed and critiqued.

Trotter, Waldron, and Wells-Barnett pressed hard for militant resolutions and minimal white leadership. Ovington later recalled that Trotter and Wells-Barnett were at the "height of their power" and held "little belief in our sincerity." At one point someone suggested that Washington should have a role in the organization; according to Du Bois, a woman jumped to her feet and cried out angrily, "They are betraying us again—these white friends of ours."[66]

In this group, that protester could only have been Wells-Barnett. Political contention and points of order rolled on through the day and evening, past midnight. Trotter did not suppress his low regard for Villard and others present, and Villard found the speeches, suspicion, and acrimony hard to take. He told his uncle Francis Garrison: "After the Resolutions were introduced we had a very hard time and the colored men wrangled for an hour over them, the Rev. J. M. Waldron and Trotter behaving very badly, speaking incessantly, and making the most trivial changes in the language, always with a nasty spirit. Trotter was really unbearable and I took great pleasure in telling him so at the end of the evening." Villard added that many Afro-American participants apologized to him personally for the "ill-concealed hostility" of Waldron and Trotter, and he acknowledged that African Americans, having been "tricked so often by white men," had a right to be suspicious. Still, it was a "trying" experience to launch this enterprise. As the evening wore on, Villard was tempted to announce that he and Walling would do it by themselves; the rest were welcome to leave.[67]

Instead the National Negro Conference came out of Cooper Union with resolutions much like the Niagara Movement and Milholland's Constitution League, a biracial organization founded to defend the Fourteenth and Fifteenth Amendments. The platform of the new organization demanded full manhood suffrage, the same education for blacks and whites, and enforcement of the Reconstruction Amendments. It also condemned lynching, disenfranchisement, wage slavery, and the manipulation of workers by appeal to racism. Female suffrage was not addressed, as this group was determined not to relive the storied schism of May 9, 1869—the American Equal Rights Association convention at nearby Steinway Hall. Du Bois described the final product gratefully as "a visible bursting into action of long gathering thought and brooding." Ovington judged that some of the fierce arguing was valuable, as a counterweight to going "namby-pamby at the last," and some was not, as every activist group had a few "cranks." She was grateful for Russell's courtesy in chairing the evening-long debate; otherwise the group might have blown up. Ovington had another insight that cut deeper and more revealingly, telling Villard that sometimes she forgot that "the Negroes aren't poor people for whom I must kindly do something." Instead they were "men with most forceful opinions of their own."[68]

Du Bois enthused that the conference was a great success. The National Negro Conference, he declared, was something new in bridging the differences of color, class, and types of activism: "So the conference adjourned. Its net result was the vision of future cooperation, not simply as in the past, between giver and beggar—the older ideal of charity—but a new alliance between experienced social workers and reformers in touch on the one hand with scientific philanthropy and on the other with the great struggling mass of laborers of all kinds, whose condition and needs know no color line."[69]

That turned out to be true, but the group stewed in turmoil as Du Bois wrote these hopeful words, because the founding conference did not determine what kind of organization this was going to be and it ended with a debacle over the governing body. Du Bois served as chair of the nominating committee that named the Committee of Forty that would govern the new organization. He was the only African American on the nominating committee, which included Walling, Russell, Ovington, Milholland, and Villard. At the end of the conference, Du Bois announced the governing body. Most were relieved that the governing group did not include Washington; on the other hand, it did not include anyone in the Trotter/Waldron/Wells-Barnett faction, even though someone in the know had assured Wells-Barnett that she was on the list. The conference took a quick voice vote and headed for the exits. Wells-Barnett, in her telling, tried to take it philosophically, reasoning that her plate was full anyway. But Milholland stopped her as she left Cooper Union, saying it was "unthinkable" to exclude her—"you, who have fought the battle against lynching for nearly twenty years single-handed and alone when the rest of us were following our own selfish pursuits." Milholland told Wells-Barnett that the nominating committee had named her to the governing body; she headed the list that they agreed upon. For some reason, Du Bois had eliminated her name.[70]

Wells-Barnett claimed to take the insult calmly. Then Ovington swept past her on the sidewalk, looking very pleased, "with an air of triumph." Wells-Barnett took it that Ovington was preening about her removal from the governing committee. Ovington told a different story: She was desperate for some time-alone decompression. Her father had died a few days earlier, and she was too wrung out from managing the conference to celebrate its completion: "I was exhausted physically, mentally, emotionally." Whatever happened, the sidewalk encounter was a fateful moment. Wells-Barnett was summoned inside, where Du Bois, Milholland, Walling, and Russell stood waiting for her. Du Bois offered a lame explanation of what happened. He had taken the liberty of replacing her with Bentley, for two reasons. One, Du Bois thought of Wells-Barnett and Ferdinand Barnett as representatives of the Douglass Center in Chicago, but

Celia Woolley would represent the Douglass Center, which she founded. (For that matter, Bentley was a member of the Douglass Center, too.) Two, Bentley would represent the Niagara Movement.[71]

The first reason was too ridiculous to merit a response, as Ida Wells-Barnett vastly transcended the Douglass Center. As for Bentley, Wells-Barnett noted that he had not bothered to attend the conference, so he must not have thought very highly "of your movement." Wells-Barnett was already describing this enterprise as a vehicle to lift up Du Bois. Du Bois retreated, offering to add Wells-Barnett to the Committee of Forty. She turned him down, an angry decision that she later regretted: "Those white men had done all they could to rectify the deliberate intention of Dr. Du Bois to ignore me and my work. I was too furiously indignant at him to recognize my obligation to try to hold up their hands." The next day, Milholland tracked down Villard, urging him to rectify Du Bois's mistake. Villard replied that the conference had voted on this and he had no authority to alter the list—which did not stop Villard from dropping and adding names for weeks to come. Milholland told Villard that he would step down to make room for Wells-Barnett; Woolley too told Villard she would step down to make room for Wells-Barnett. Villard took no interest, at first, in these remedies, as he was the dominant player in this group, he loathed the contentious manners of Trotter, Waldron, and Wells-Barnett, he didn't want their politics on the governing committee either, and he had probably arranged with Du Bois and Ovington to get rid of Wells-Barnett.[72]

Ovington and Du Bois had their own reasons for keeping Wells-Barnett at bay. Ovington was informally in charge of who was in and who was out, she had a close and admiring relationship with Du Bois, and it was already her job, having recruited Villard, to keep him satisfied. On one occasion Ovington wrote that Wells-Barnett and Trotter were "fitted for courageous work, but perhaps not fitted to accept the restraint of organization." Elsewhere she put it more pointedly about Wells-Barnett, acknowledging that Wells-Barnett was "a great fighter, but we knew that she had to play a lone hand. And if you have too many players of lone hands in your organization, you soon have no game." Ovington already had a favorite lone-handed player, Du Bois, with whom she sided for the next twenty years when he conflicted with friends or foes. Du Bois was fine with being the only African American on the nominating committee, as he hoped that this venture would turn into exactly what Wells-Barnett suspected—a vehicle for him to shine. Du Bois had no peer relationships with strong black women like Wells-Barnett or Terrell, he had no interest in being bossed or admonished by a black heroine who did not look up to him, and he enjoyed being admired by white feminists like Ovington, Eaton, and

Woolley. Du Bois and Ovington were good for each other's careers. Both of them benefitted from Wells-Barnett's embattled relationship with what became the NAACP.[73]

The Committee of Forty was charged with calibrating the organization's ideological posture, selecting its board of directors, and hiring its staff. Villard decreed that service on the committee would not be compensated financially, thus skewing the group's work toward well-healed white males for whom this was no problem. After he took over from Walling as committee chair, Villard decreed that all personnel decisions would be the exclusive province of the committee chair. Eventually he succeeded Walling as chair of the board, too; in the meantime, Villard tried to whittle down the number of black members, fighting with Walling, even as Walling prevailed on expanding the governance committee to fifty members. The core African American members were Du Bois, Wells-Barnett (who changed her mind, for a while, about serving), Bentley, Scarborough, Terrell, Walters, Hershaw, educator Leslie Pinckney Hill, and Richard R. Wright Jr. Walling and Ovington pressed for more black members, adding Brooks, Waldron, Archibald Grimké, and Philadelphia physician William A. Sinclair. Walling tried to get Kelly Miller and Philadelphia minister E. W. Moore on the committee, too, but that never happened; he did not try to add Ransom, since Ransom was too radical for Villard.[74]

For a year the evolving NAACP had no office, program, or settled name, while insiders debated two rival visions of the organization. Some members thought the group should be primarily a white organization that changed the discourse about race in American society. Villard and his circle of genteel reformers held out for this idea, which relied on membership rallies, fund-raising, and articles in the *Nation*. The second group held out for an interracial activist organization focused on civil and social rights. Walling pressed hard for this idea, as did Ovington, Russell, Milholland, and most African Americans on the governing board. The second group, led by Walling, argued that the National Negro Conference by whatever name needed to provide a platform for Du Bois.

Since the group was centered in New York, Du Bois was a secondary player in the deliberations that determined its future. Villard viewed Du Bois as icy, arrogant, difficult, gifted, and too radical. Du Bois was distinctly valuable to the cause, but he had to be controlled. Villard had no intention of setting up Du Bois with a salary and movement vehicle. He would have been happy for Du Bois to stay in Atlanta and come to New York for executive committee meetings. As usual, Du Bois got what he wanted, and as usual, he got it by fiercely sticking to a principle about what he wanted and by inspiring loyalty to him on that basis, not by cutting a Booker-like deal. On the other hand, to the Trotter faction, Du Bois's success with white liberals showed that he was a shrewd player, in his own way, of the racial diplomacy game.

The latter point was in question during the months preceding the group's turning point conference of May 1910. In November 1909 Villard and Du Bois had a frosty exchange over Villard's review of Du Bois's book on John Brown. The backstory was complicated, as Du Bois had planned to write a biography of Douglass, and in 1909 Villard was completing his own voluminous book on Brown. In 1903 historian Ellis Paxson Oberholtzer asked Du Bois to write a biography of Douglass for Philadelphia publisher George W. Jacobs & Company. Du Bois said yes, but two months later Oberholtzer wrote back sheepishly, reporting that Washington had belatedly decided that he wanted to write the Douglass book. Would Du Bois be willing to switch to someone else? Du Bois was gracious, suggesting a book on Nat Turner; eventually they settled on Brown, which Du Bois needed five years to write.[75]

John Brown wrestled strenuously with its subject, stressing Brown's moral hatred of slavery, his friendship with Douglass and other abolitionists, and Brown versus Douglass concerning the raid on Harper's Ferry. The book was a vindication of Brown and an echo of Douglass's demurral. Du Bois presented Brown as a hero and religious visionary, notwithstanding that he murdered five proslavery ruffians in Kansas and set off a failed insurrection at Harper's Ferry. In Du Bois's telling, Brown had a simple, moral perspective about what had to be done, and Douglass had a complex perspective that took politics into account, plus the fact that blacks would have hell to pay for a failed insurrection. Douglass kept his balance and Brown did not, but both were right about what was needed, even while disagreeing. Du Bois said it emphatically: Nothing compared to the effect of Brown's utterances from prison before he was executed. Brown shook the foundations of American slavery more than anyone, a fact that Douglass later appreciated. Most Americans preferred not to grapple with the challenge that Brown presented to his own time, or with the fact that he remained a challenge to succeeding generations of Americans. Du Bois spoke for Brown at the end of the book, admonishing American readers not to write him off: "You may dispose of me very easily—I am nearly disposed of now; but this question is still to be settled—this Negro question, I mean. The end of that is not yet."[76]

Du Bois relied on long quotations to make his points, which proved tiresome to reviewers; he made some factual slips, and he did not make use of important source material that Villard (also trained by Hart) used in his forthcoming book on Brown. But Du Bois powerfully brought to life Brown and his time, and his book had an ample scholarly basis. He would have accepted a review in the *Nation* that noted the book's strengths and weaknesses. However, the unsigned review he got was carping and brittle, exposing small errors that only Villard would have recognized, and in Villard's commanding style. Things that mattered, on which Du Bois and Villard mostly agreed, were swept aside in favor of scholarly minutiae that belittled Du Bois. Du Bois submitted a letter pointing out that several of his supposed errors were judgment calls; moreover, regarding sources, he favored writers that were eyewitnesses of what they wrote. Villard's assistant, P. E. Moore, sent a bureaucratic reply, sticking to the *Nation's* carping points, admonishing that Du Bois apparently did not grasp the concept of a source, and reporting that Du Bois's letter would not be published. Du Bois protested that this response failed the test of minimal courtesy. He realized that his book had shortcomings, "but savagely to emphasize these so as to give an impression of total falsity is a contemptible thing to do." Even worse, the *Nation* gave him no opportunity to defend himself.[77]

There was another back and forth between Du Bois and Moore; then Villard intervened. He was shocked and amazed that Du Bois would suggest that Villard had been unfair to him, perhaps out of book rivalry. After all that he had done for Du Bois! Villard's usual patrician self-righteousness went into over-drive. He had praised *The Souls of Black Folk*, brought attention to the book, invited Du Bois to his uncle's memorial service, and made him a major player in the new civil rights organization. Nothing would have made Villard happier than to write a glowing review of Du Bois's new book, if only the book deserved it. As it was, Villard could only hope that Du Bois, once he recovered his senses, would recognize "the injustice that you have done." Du Bois, steering away from righteousness issues, told Villard that the dispute between them was not about getting too much or too little praise, blame, appreciation, or condemnation. The issue in dispute was simply a question of justice. He did not write these letters to complain about the review: "I complain of your fear to publish a courteous answer to its ridiculous misstatements."[78]

Villard would never be a friend, but Du Bois had everything riding on their ability to work together. The following month, while pondering whether his life was about to change, Du Bois had a poignant exchange with his dearest friend, John Hope, over a similarly slippery question of friendship/righteousness/politics. In January 1910, relaxing with Du Bois, Towns, and a small group of Niagarites, Hope revealed that Washington had recently helped him secure a ten-thousand-dollar gift from Carnegie. Du Bois chided his friend for selling out, perhaps not mentioning that he had begged Carnegie for money, too. Hope was deeply wounded, enough to write a nineteen-page letter filled with contrition, self-justification, and tender feeling. He told Du Bois that he had never felt compelled to justify himself to anyone, until now: "Why Du Bois? Because I have followed him; I believed in him; tried even, where he was not understood, to interpret him and show that he is right; because I have been loyal to him and his propaganda—not blatantly so, but, I think, really loyal; and because, in spite of appearances, I am just as truly as ever a disciple of the teachings of Du Bois regarding Negro freedom." Hope loved, admired, and followed Du Bois. At the same time, he had Atlanta Baptist College in his hands, which compelled him to nurture a friendship with Washington. Was this not possible? Hope stressed that he and Du Bois had been friends for nearly ten years; at least, he thought they were friends: "I write to ask, no matter whether you doubt the wisdom of or resent my action, are we friends?"[79]

Hope reminded Du Bois that he had always stood for his views, never lacking courage, and had always been loyal to Du Bois, never lacking faithfulness: "But, Du Bois, may there not be a *tyranny* of views? Have we not required such severe alignments that it has been sometimes as much a lack of courage as a mark of courage to stand either with Du Bois or Washington to the absolute exclusion of one or the other in any sort of intercourse?" It hurt him, Hope confessed, to be accused of apostasy, especially since he was "not truly apostate." But he tried to do the right thing, which was often less clear to him than it was to Du Bois, who did not ask himself what other people thought: "That is genius. I am a plodder. My even petty thinking calls for great travail of mind and spirit; and, in the process, I carry along most hospitably all opposing views with which I am acquainted. I am plodding, canny—you go on the wings, and are daring." Did that mean that they could not follow the truth and be loyal to each other? Had things come to a point that Hope had to repudiate Washington to be Du Bois's friend? "I write to ask you whether you have me in your heart—not on your calling list or your mailing list but in your heart—on your list of friends. I am asking this question fearlessly as a strong man would ask his chieftain. I will receive the answer just as fearlessly. And however it may be, I shall be loyal to my chieftain still."[80]

Du Bois returned the favor of speaking directly. He treasured Hope's friendship and had never doubted Hope's loyalty to him. He did not believe that Hope had surrendered the principles they shared, and he would not "easily" surrender their friendship even if Hope did so. He shuddered at seeing his friend caught in Washington's net, but he accepted that Hope had no real choice in the matter, since Washington monopolized aid to black institutions. Du Bois implored Hope to hold fast to one fact as he struggled to keep his college alive: "Washington stands for Negro submission and slavery.

Representing that, with unlimited funds, he can afford to be broad and generous and most of us must accept the generosity or starve." To take the money was to allow oneself to be bound and gagged, Du Bois cautioned. He understood that Hope and others like him had to do it. Even for himself, Du Bois could only hope that he would not have to beg for the Wizard's favor: "I may have to place myself in that position yet, but, by God, I'll fight hard before I do it."[81]

The NAACP was the chance of a lifetime for Du Bois and an alternative to pleading for the Wizard's favor. It nearly expired in the year that elapsed between the founding conference and the second conference. Villard tried and failed to raise money for the group, Walling had to resign as chair for personal reasons, and everything fell on Villard and Ovington to keep the organization alive. Villard and his mother covered the expenses, hiring an executive secretary, settlement activist Frances Blascoer. As the day approached for the second meeting of the National Negro Conference, on May 12, 1910, at the Charity Organization Society, Walling urged Villard to provide a vehicle and salary for Du Bois. Walling believed that Du Bois transcended the group's ideological factions and that Villard had to get over his misgivings about Du Bois. By then Villard did not like Walling either, but he respected Ovington and Milholland, who pressed him to support Du Bois, activism, and a strong role for Afro-American board members. Du Bois and Villard were cordial to each other at the conference, shaking hands "across the chasm," as Ovington put it. After the conference Villard still voted against hiring Du Bois, but Ovington, Walling, and Milholland prevailed, settling the issue about the kind of organization this was going to be. Ovington wrote: "From that time on no one doubted where we stood."[82]

The second conference chose Walling as chairperson, Milholland as treasurer, Villard as assistant treasurer, and venerable Boston attorney Moorfield Storey as president. Storey came from blue-blood stock, Harvard Law School, and a clerkship with Charles Sumner during Reconstruction. He had a distinguished law practice and was renowned for his defense of civil liberties, property rights, the gold standard, and anti-imperialism. In the 1880s he was a leader in the Mugwump movement; in the 1890s he became a leader in the anti-imperialist movement, chairing the national Anti-Imperialist League from 1905 until its dissolution in 1921. Storey's establishment credentials and commitment to civil rights made him ideally suited to head the NAACP. He did not attend meetings but represented the organization—which had a thirty-person executive committee limited to fifteen New Yorkers—and waged its early court battles. Shortly after the second conference ended, the committee chose a cumbersome name of eight words that no one really liked, but which stuck, surprisingly to everyone.

Villard wanted "Advancement" to be in the name, and Du Bois preferred "Colored" over the alternatives, to reflect his conception of the organization as a liberationist vehicle for all people on the nonwhite side of the color line. For years afterward insiders debated other names, such as the Emancipation League, the Garrison Association for the Advancement of Colored People, the Lincoln Association for the Advancement of Colored People, the Association for the Advancement of Colored People, the Garrison-Douglass Association, and the League for the Advancement of Colored People. Some said the group should adopt the name that best described what it was, the New Abolition Movement. Joel Spingarn said so repeatedly. But others always replied that this name would scare off white southerners, thwarting any chance of establishing southern chapters; thus it was never put to a vote. The second conference paved the way to the name that prevailed and to the NAACP becoming an organization that featured Du Bois's movement journalism.[83]

Nearly a month after the conference ended, Walling wrote to Du Bois, apologizing for the delay. Wealthy Bostonians and New Yorkers had departed for their summer vacations in Cape Cod and Europe, so fund-raising was difficult. Walling tried to shake down the governing board for a salary fund, with little success. He assured Du Bois they would raise enough money for a decent salary—twenty-five hundred dollars plus expenses. He did not want to lose Du Bois, not realizing that Du Bois was ready to accept any invitation. In a closing word, Walling regretted that he and Du Bois were not "old and intimate" friends, because he had a bad conscience about urging Du Bois to take a risk. As it was, recognizing the sacrifice that Du Bois would be making, Walling could only say, "The moment is a critical one for your work and public activities." Du Bois replied that he agreed about the moment and he wanted to take the risk. On July fifth he announced his resignation from Atlanta University, explaining that he had accepted the position of director of publicity and research for the NAACP. There was no time for a ceremonial farewell, as Du Bois hurriedly moved to New York, already imagining the sensational monthly magazine he would create.[84]

CRISIS AND AUDACITY

On the first morning of his new job, Du Bois learned that the NAACP still lacked a source of funding for his job. Villard told him, "I don't know who is going to pay your salary; I have no money." Du Bois chose not to worry about that. Villard had provided two offices at the *Evening Post*'s building in downtown New York at 20 Vesey Street. Du Bois figured that one office would be his editorial desk and the other would house the rest of the NAACP operations. If he had an office and some provisional support, he could launch a magazine; surely the white liberals would come up with a salary fund. The white liberals were aghast at the magazine idea. They had nobody in place at Vesey Street except Ovington, who worked without salary, and a secretary who felt threatened by Du Bois, and who eventually resigned. They were further chastened by Du Bois's track record with magazines—the *Moon* lasted a few months, and the *Horizon* expired just as Du Bois moved to New York. In both cases he had alienated friends who had financed his dream of magazine glory. The new abolitionists had not launched the NAACP to start a magazine, and they did not want to make the new organization depend on the success of a magazine. Du Bois was undaunted, urging that his next magazine would be a game changer that would propel the NAACP into national prominence. Villard, surprisingly, got behind this idea, believing that his influence would expand if the magazine succeeded. The others, less surprisingly, recognized that Du Bois was the one with star power.[85]

Ovington, Walling, and Du Bois had a planning meeting in early August, at which either Ovington or Walling proposed *The Crisis* as the magazine's name, christened after James Russell Lowell's abolitionist poem of 1844, "The Present Crisis." The first issue of *The Crisis: A Record of the Darker Races* was published in November 1910. It listed Villard, Russell, Barber, Kelly Miller, poetry editor William Stanley Braithwaite, and managing editor Mary Dunlop Maclean as contributing editors—two white males, three black males, and one white woman. That was mostly for show, however, as Maclean ran the magazine, moonlighting without pay from her day job at the *New York Times*, and Du Bois wrote most of the copy. Maclean was indispensable to Du Bois during the launch years. A young Englishwoman who had grown up in the Bahamas, she joined the *Times* as a full-time staff writer and attended the first National Negro Conference, where she asked Russell how she could help. Her skill and tireless buoyancy helped to make *Crisis* an immediate sensation. In an early issue Maclean wrote a stunning Afrocentric essay on the black sources of Egyptian civilization, but she died young, in 1912, leaving a grieving staff and a hugely successful magazine.[86]

From the beginning the magazine featured a section on politics and society titled "Along the Color Line," a canvass of press coverage and correspondence titled "Opinion," an editorial section, a section on recent atrocities against Afro-Americans titled "The Burden," and a section describing not-to-miss recent articles and books. It had a special section titled "The Ghetto" that tracked the spread of residential segregation, especially in border states and the

North. Soon it added a section on women's issues. The inaugural issue of November 1910 had sixteen 5 x 8 pages, plus a cover page with a woodcut of a black child. It described in detail the founding of the NAACP, explaining that *Crisis* was the organization's official organ. It implored against the trend in northern cities of establishing separate public schools for black children. Du Bois protested: "Separate them by color and they grow up without learning the tremendous truth that it is impossible to judge the mind of a man by the color of his face."[87]

In the early going, Du Bois reported on his travels to speaking engagements and conferences, reflecting that "the race problem" differed in time and place; it was not just one thing. In Ohio alone it was several different things. Toledo, rushing to become an expanding commercial center, pushed aside its "half forgotten" black community. Cleveland, very different, had racial gains to defend against an upsurge of segregation and disenfranchisement coming from the South. At Oberlin College Du Bois met black and white students privileged to walk "on sacred ground, on ground long since consecrated to racial equality and hatred of caste and slavery." In most of the white South he heard constantly that black Americans were lazy and stupid; that was the crux of the race problem. Du Bois replied that in Georgia, Virginia, and North Carolina, blacks owned forty million dollars' worth of taxable property in 1900, despite being oppressed by mob violence, wage discrimination, hostile municipal policies, and lack of facilities for saving. By 1908, he added, blacks owned seventy-four million dollars' worth of taxable property in these three states, a "simply astounding" increase of 87 percent.[88]

The race problem was different things in different places, but everywhere it was about the ravages of white racism. Du Bois explained, "In the time of slavery we had the subterfuge of colonization to tempt the conscientious mind; in the time of Reconstruction we had the subterfuge of threatened Negro domination to blind those who ought to have seen; in the days since Reconstruction we have had the subterfuge of industrial inefficiency to make people forget race prejudice." In all three phases, the teaching of Jesus was simply tossed aside, along with ordinary decency: "It is the object of the National Association for the Advancement of Colored People to impress the fact upon the American people that the foundation difficulty of the race problem is this despicable race prejudice, and that unless we attack this central difficulty we never shall settle this problem."[89]

Du Bois's faith in himself was vindicated immediately. In a "fit of wild adventure" he ordered 1,000 copies of the inaugural issue, which quickly sold out. The December run of 2,500 sold out, too, and the magazine climbed to 9,000 net paid copies per month the following year, earning a move to larger headquarters at another *Evening Post* address, 26 Vesey Street. After that, the magazine climbed by over 1,000 copies per month for years to come, soaring to 75,000 in 1918 and peaking at 104,000 the following year. A little over a year into this spectacular run, Du Bois groped for some measure of how well he was doing, asking Barber how big the *Voice of the Negro* had been in its heyday. Barber replied that the peak was 17,000. That was a bitter memory for Barber in 1912, as he had resorted to dentistry. Du Bois later recalled, "*The Crisis* came at the psychological moment and its success was phenomenal." Its early success far outstripped the NAACP's, which had eleven hundred members by the end of 1912, organized into eleven branches. Du Bois reflected that the magazine was perfect for the psychological moment because it was filled with relevant news that black Americans could not get elsewhere, it ran lots of "blazing editorials" that stoked controversy, and it risked something truly novel—displaying pictures of ordinary black Americans.[90]

The *Crisis* outstripped all sources of information about Afro-Americans, and it said so stridently. Du Bois blistered much of the black press for anti-intellectualism, superficial reporting, and bad grammar. Calvin Chase accused Du Bois of high-minded arrogance and of writing in "Harvardized English." Du Bois replied that the *Bee*, to do something useful for the race, should report on something besides weddings and murders. More than once he suggested that too many (unnamed) editors perpetuated semiliterate ignorance. Some who felt accused pushed back that arrogance and Harvard were very much at issue. The *Age* editorialized that Du Bois damaged his cause by denigrating the very people he wanted to recruit. That caused heart palpitations for the white liberals who had just entered this discussion. Storey fretted that Du Bois's experience of taking abuse from people lacking his brilliance had turned him into a vengeful type unsuited for his job. The NAACP passed a resolution praising the black press for doing a great job. Du Bois published the resolution without comment.[91]

The *Crisis* was strong and unbridled about the black church, black women, white women, the politics of gender, and electoral politics. Du Bois, putting it aptly years later, recalled that when he wrote an editorial, he "talked turkey." In May 1912, anticipating national conventions of the black Methodist and Baptist denominations, Du Bois courted singular anguish by taking on the black church. He bowed with deep respect, he assured, before the institution that saved the race during slavery. The black church "instilled and conserved morals, it has helped family life, it has taught and developed ability and given the colored man his best business training." Thanks to the black church, blacks had somewhere to go and somewhere to be somebody wherever they went in the United States.[92]

But the black church was far from what it should be, Du Bois admonished. It had a handful of accomplished and morally impressive leaders and a vast horde of lousy ones: "The paths and the higher places are choked with pretentious, ill-trained men and in far too many cases with men dishonest and otherwise immoral." With so many unworthy leaders, it was hard for anyone who was not a cunning opportunist to get ahead in the church. There were lots of "hustling businessmen, eloquent talkers, [and] suave companions" in the clergy, but precious few "burning spiritual guides of a troubled, panting people" that modeled unselfishness and righteous idealism. Du Bois wanted a better church to play a stronger role in American society. As it was, the trends were in the wrong direction: "Today the church is still inveighing against dancing and theatergoing, still blaming educated people for objecting to silly and empty sermons, boasting and noise, still building churches when people need homes and schools, and persisting in crucifying critics rather than realizing the handwriting on the wall." To change this picture, the churches had to groom distinguished leaders, weed out the "noisy and unclean leaders of the thoughtless mob," and initiate "positive programs of education and social uplift."[93]

This was milder than Washington's famous reproach of 1890 and the first such reproach in a national publication since 1890—for reasons that quickly rained down on the NAACP. Du Bois offended some of the same people that blasted Washington for harming the black church. Du Bois, however, was not in the reconciling business; he was trying to light a fire. Two years later he scorched his former employer, Wilberforce University, for falling behind. The old Wilberforce was sadly lacking in many ways, Du Bois declared, but the new Wilberforce was worse. The new Wilberforce had debilitating battles between the university (the College of Liberal Arts, which the church ran) and the Normal Department (which the state ran). Du Bois did not let friendship stand in the way of ripping Wilberforce's mediocrity and its current president, Scarborough, who had lauded and supported Du Bois. Du Bois wounded and embarrassed Scarborough, with no apology.[94]

Repeatedly, *Crisis* editorialized about women and feminism, refusing to be locked into a sorry either/or that pitted abolitionism against woman suffrage. Du Bois believed that the best measure of any society's civilization was the status of women within it. The ultimate measure of a society's enlightenment was its willingness to emancipate women—especially black women. His novel *The Quest of the Silver Fleece* (1912) pressed on this theme, suggesting that even the race question ultimately reduced to the ownership of women. White men wanted to own and control all women, having their way with them sexually whenever they felt like it. They resented any infringement on this desire, such

as the existence of black men. Du Bois believed that this explained the explosion of white male rage in the South during and after Reconstruction. White
men had to do something with the rage and lust that consumed them after they
lost their ready access to black women's bodies. They had already sentimental-
ized white women as delicate types lacking sexual desire, so they had a problem
with their own sexuality after they could not control or rape black women with
impunity. *Silver Fleece* conjured a black heroine antithesis of rapist white
culture—the luminous Zora, a dark-skinned, self-cultured embodiment of intu-
ition and humanity who read Plato, Tennyson, and Spencer, symbolizing the
hope of human redemption.[95]

Zora was nothing like the symbol of obsequious, sexless, uneducated,
matronly black humanity that the white South proposed to immortalize. In 1911
the *Athens Banner* of Athens, Georgia, kicked off an outbreak of nostalgia for a
Lost Cause invention—the old, doting, happy black mammies of the South.
This movement was still building steam in 1923 when the United Daughters of
the Confederacy pushed for a statue in the nation's capital to commemorate
how the bucolic plantation families of old loved their mammies. Du Bois took
an early shot, in 1912, at burgeoning mammy nostalgia, noting that the black
mammy of the proposed statues was always "of the foster mammy, not of the
mother in her home, attending to her own babies." After slavery, when the black
mammy retreated to her home, white mothers condemned her for selfishly,
lazily caring for her own children. Then they condemned her when she trained
to be a teacher instead of nursing white children. Du Bois celebrated black
motherhood as an act of rebellion against white racism: "Let the present-day
mammies suckle their own children. Let them walk in the sunshine with their
own toddling boys and girls and put their own sleepy little brothers and sisters
to bed. As their girls grow to womanhood, let them see to it that, if possible, they
do not enter domestic service in those homes where they are unprotected, and
where their womanhood is not treated with respect. In the midst of immense
difficulties, surrounded by caste, and hemmed in by restricted economic opportunity, let the colored mother of today build her own statue, and let it be the
four walls of her own unsullied home."[96]

In April 1913 more than one hundred people were trampled when cavalry
troops from Fort Myer clashed with a woman suffrage march on Pennsylvania
Avenue in Washington, DC. White spectators hurled epithets at the suffrage
marchers, while black spectators maintained a sympathetic quiet. Du Bois
found the contrast instructive, unleashing his sarcasm: "White men are on the
firing line, and if they don't want white women for wives they will at least keep
them as prostitutes. Beat them back, keep them down; flatter them, call them

'visions of loveliness' and tell them that the place for woman is in the home, even if she hasn't got a home. If she is homely or poor or made the mistake of being born with brains, and begins to protest at the doll's house or the bawdy house, kick her and beat her and insult her until in terror she slinks back to her kennel or walks the midnight streets." Du Bois stressed that the white men berating their sisters and mothers in the streets did not lack rational coherence: "Don't give in; don't give her power; don't give her a vote whatever you do. Keep the price of women down; make them weak and cheap."[97]

Kelly Miller, in 1915, wrote an article for *Crisis* opposing woman suffrage. According to Miller, women were weaker than men, and women's child-care responsibilities precluded taking responsibility for public matters. Moreover, women were already protected under male suffrage; allowing women to vote or hold office would be dangerous. Du Bois kept a straight face for a paragraph, then gave up: "The statement that woman is weaker than man is sheer rot. It is the same sort of thing that we hear about 'darker races' and 'lower classes.' Difference, either physical or spiritual, does not argue weakness or inferiority." As for men protecting women with their votes, Du Bois pointed to the millions of women who were unmarried, widowed, deserted, and "those who have married failures." As for risk, Du Bois offered a variation on his signature statement: "The meaning of the twentieth century is the freeing of the individual soul; the soul longest in slavery and still in the most disgusting and indefensible slavery is the soul of womanhood."[98]

When he warmed to this theme Du Bois wrote his most searing prose. White feminists felt the depth of his conviction, appreciating that it extended to them. Some tried to overlook what they knew of his promiscuous personal life and his bad treatment of Nina. Du Bois indulged himself sexually on the lecture circuit, where he spoke up to fifty times per year, and he had mistresses at every stage of his career. Louie Davis Shivery, an English teacher married to a dentist, was his main paramour during his Atlanta years. Mildred Bryant, a piano teacher in Chicago, was one of his mistresses for over thirty years. Jessie Dunlop Fausset, midwife of the Harlem Renaissance, was another sexual partner. Du Bois did not acknowledge the humiliation that he doled out to Nina by bullying her, ignoring her, and carrying on with other women, though he was a dutiful father to Yolande.[99]

However Du Bois may have rationalized his behavior, and despite his frosty treatment of strong black women in general, he expressed vividly in his writing that nothing cut him deeper than everything he knew about the vile mistreatment of black women during and after slavery. He expected, on Judgment Day, to forgive the white South for many things. He expected to forgive slavery, "for slavery is a world-old habit." He expected to forgive the South for defending the Confederacy, remembering its rebellion "with tender tears," and wailing and strutting about its Lost Cause and its pride of race: "But one thing I shall never forgive, neither in this world nor the world to come: its wanton and continued and persistent insulting of the black womanhood which it sought and seeks to prostitute to its lust." Du Bois thought about it whenever somebody invoked Taft's statement about allowing the gentlemen of the South to take control of America's race problem: "I cannot forget that it is such Southern gentlemen into whose hands smug Northern hypocrites of today are seeking to place our women's eternal destiny—men who insist upon withholding from my mother and wife and daughter those signs and appellations of courtesy and respect which elsewhere he withholds only from bawds and courtesans."[100]

The presidential election of 1912 was novel for featuring four major candidates, all of whom made a pitch for the votes of progressives and one of whom ran as a party-label Progressive. Taft won the Republican nomination partly by erasing what remained of the party's interest in civil rights. Teddy Roosevelt created the Progressive Party after failing to win the Republican nomination. Eugene Debs attracted enormous crowds as the Socialist candidate. Woodrow Wilson, upon winning the Democratic nomination on the forty-sixth ballot, campaigned as a different kind of Democrat—one that might respect the humanity and dignity of black Americans.

Du Bois would have supported Debs had the Socialists held any chance of winning or had Debs dropped his party's evasiveness about race. Du Bois voted for Debs in 1904, and he was a member of the Socialist Party when the 1912 campaign began. There were many things that Du Bois admired about Debs— his passion for economic justice, his nondogmatic approach to Socialism, his command of the written and spoken word, his inspiring oratory on the campaign trail, his French Protestant background, and his personal antiracism. Debs was a race-blind progressive who condemned racism as abhorrent and refused to address segregated audiences. But the Socialist Party had a Negro-phobic right wing led by Wisconsin politician Victor Berger; it had a core of trade unionists who took pride in keeping blacks out of unions; and Debs dealt with his party's race problem by trying not to talk about race. He told audiences that he offered nothing to blacks except Socialism, which would abolish racism.[101]

Du Bois bristled at the sophistry of that answer. Instead of facing the fallout from making an issue of racial justice, Debs hid behind the Marxist slogan that there was no race problem apart from the general labor problem. Sometimes Du Bois said that Debs was not worth supporting as long as he dodged the race issue. Sometimes he put it more generously, acknowledging that Debs took a "manly stand for human rights irrespective of color," which was brave in America. In either case, Du Bois argued, Debs was not going to win, so blacks needed to choose among the other three parties. Socialists replied that Du Bois was not much of a Socialist if he could not muster a vote for Debs. Du Bois, respecting that sentiment, resigned from the party, later observing that the average American Socialist could "scarcely grasp" the hatred that blacks experienced in the South. The Socialists did not see the Socialist imperative of explicitly becoming "a party of the Negro." Du Bois admonished them to face up to reality, instead of betraying Socialism: "The Negro Problem is the great test of the American Socialist."[102]

That left a choice between the sitting enemy in the White House, a known enemy burnishing his progressive credentials, and the candidate of the historic Democratic enemy. Du Bois described it as a choice between a Republican Party that had "promised and failed," a Progressive Party that had "failed and promised," and a Democratic Party that "merely promises." He liked Roosevelt's Bull Moose agenda on workplace issues and social insurance, especially an eight-hour workday, retirement security, and unemployment insurance, plus female suffrage. Du Bois was willing to overlook TR's presidency if the Progressive Party convention in Chicago passed a strong plank on civil rights—specifically, a plank that he proposed via Jane Addams, Henry Moskowitz, and Joel Spingarn. Spingarn was a wealthy liberal Republican and literature scholar who loathed the growing corporate culture of university life. This loathing had caused him recently to resign from Columbia University, protesting Nicholas Murray Butler's dictatorial presidency. Spingarn joined the NAACP shortly after its founding and had cachet with the liberal Republicans who convened at Chicago. But Roosevelt had not changed on the politics of race. TR hustled for lily-white southern delegates, his operatives excluded most of the black delegates that showed up to vote for him in Chicago, and the Du Bois plank died in a platform committee meeting. The so-called Progressive Party could not muster a vote on a decent plank against racial discrimination, despite boasting a who's who of social workers and social scientists among the delegates. TR piled on by warning Spingarn that Du Bois was a dangerous character. Thus Du Bois found himself hoping that Wilson might be better than he seemed.[103]

The bitter Progressive Party outcome and TR's parting shot about Du Bois left Du Bois wanting to be persuaded to support Wilson. Walters sold him on Wilson by citing his personal dealings with the candidate; it helped that Villard knew Wilson and said the same things. Du Bois knew the risks. Wilson was studiously vague about the rights of blacks, Princeton had been closed to African Americans during Wilson's presidency there, and the South was still solidly caste-ridden. There had not been a southern president since Zachary Taylor, or a Democratic president since Grover Cleveland. But Du Bois told *Crisis* readers it was worth finding out if the Democratic Party could be democratic at the national level, as it was already in the North. The best real-world option was to bet on Wilson: "He will not advance the cause of oligarchy in the South, he will not seek further means of 'Jim Crow' insult, he will not dismiss black men wholesale from office, and he will remember that the Negro in the United States has a right to be heard and considered."[104]

Upon assuming the presidency Wilson promptly falsified every one of these predictions, filling Du Bois with revulsion and alarm. Wilson officials purged a dozen African Americans from the federal government, segregated clerks in the Treasury and Postal Departments, and bragged about it to southern Democrats. Six months into Wilson's first term, Du Bois pleaded with him to change course. He noted that white nationalists were thrilled with the administration, crowing that they had a friend in the White House: "They and others are assuming this because not a single act and not a single word of yours since election has given anyone reason to infer that you have the slightest interest in the colored people or desire to alleviate their intolerable position." Du Bois protested that Wilson officials doled out "personal insult and humiliation" to black workers, herding them "as though they were not human beings." In places where herding was impossible, the government installed cages around black employees to separate them from longtime white colleagues. Du Bois appealed: "Here is a plain, flat, disgraceful spitting in the face of people whose darkened countenances are already dark with the slime of insult. Do you consent to this, President Wilson? Do you believe in it? Have you been able to persuade yourself that national insult is best for a people struggling into self-respect?"[105]

Du Bois desperately wanted to believe in September 1913 that Wilson had a different future in mind. The *Crisis* had not supported Wilson so he could launch "an indefensible attack on a people who have in the past been shamefully humiliated." Some people, Du Bois observed, believed there was no limit to the abuse that white America should be able to inflict on black Americans. At the moment, Congress was flooded with bills to expand Jim Crow. Democrats had not controlled the presidency *and* Congress since before the Civil War, and southern Democrats were seizing the moment, proposing bills to ban interracial marriage, extend residential and transportation segregation, ban African Americans from the army and navy, and bar people of African descent from immigrating to the United States. Du Bois appealed to Wilson as a human being, a statesman, a person who touted his sense of fairness, and a cosmopolitan sophisticate: Please stop abusing us. Moreover, if politics negated all that, there was one thing more: Please remember that "we black men of the North have a growing nest egg of 500,000 ballots." If Wilson wanted any black votes next time, he had to change course immediately. Du Bois ended on a personal note. He had not yet apologized to readers of *Crisis* for supporting Wilson: "But at the present rate it looks as though some apology or explanation is going to be in order very soon."[106]

By then *Crisis* was a major player in black politics, notwithstanding its subsequent apologies for endorsing Wilson. Du Bois knew it was happening when the Republican, Democratic, and Progressive Parties took out full-page ads in the magazine to reach black voters. The *Crisis* soared because it offered matchless coverage of the issues, it pulsated with Du Bois's fearless and opinionated spirit, it crusaded for civil rights, and it shredded the journalistic convention that nobody wanted to look at pictures of African Americans. At the time most white newspapers refused to publish pictures of blacks, except criminal suspects. Even black newspapers spurned pictures of ordinary black Americans, offering pictures of celebrities, who sometimes paid for the coverage. Du Bois recalled, "In general, the Negro race was just a little afraid to see itself in plain ink." The *Crisis* conveyed and displayed Du Bois's contrary conviction that black embodiment was beautiful.[107]

All of that was just the beginning, which fueled the ascension of the NAACP. The *Crisis* was unabashedly political, taking positions on political issues and supporting the NAACP in courtroom battles that won stepping-stone victories on civil rights. In 1911 the NAACP worked out a cooperative relationship with the Urban League to map out boundaries. The Urban League focused on housing and economic issues, and the NAACP focused on civil rights. By 1913 the NAACP had branch offices in Boston, Baltimore, Kansas City, Washington, DC, Detroit, and St. Louis. That year Du Bois and Villard clashed at a board meeting and the entire operation froze for a perilous moment. Villard was routinely imperious, Du Bois was sensitive to slights real and imagined, and Du Bois's radicalism was hard for Villard and other board members to swallow. Villard charged that balance and fairness meant nothing to Du Bois; every issue was a rant against white people, which misrepresented the NAACP. If *Crisis* had any interest in being an honest broker, it should publish a monthly list of crimes committed by black Americans. Du Bois, from that point onward, could not regard Villard as an ally, but he had to stay on decent terms with him, as the NAACP existed in his shop. Faced with an ultimatum from Villard, the board chose Du Bois over Villard, who resigned as board chair and as a contributing editor of the magazine, while remaining active in the organization, plotting his next move.[108]

Spingarn succeeded Villard as board chair, and the NAACP moved to spacious quarters at 70 Fifth Avenue, where Du Bois built an eight-person staff wholly answerable to him. Spingarn basically sided with Du Bois, believing that Du Bois was right to focus on building up the NAACP's black constituency and that he should be free to say what he believed without being censured by board members. Throughout 1914 and 1915 the NAACP fought internally over the tensions between its two halves. The organization had begun with a thirty-member board, a board chair (Villard), a president (Storey), two vice presidents (Milholland and Walters), a volcanic publicity director, and a salaried secretary (Blascoer, who resigned in 1911 after clashing with Du Bois, giving way to a tougher personality, May Childs Nerney). Now the organization was being defined in the public eye by a radical magazine that conceived the civil rights struggle in the United States as the driving wedge of a global movement to empower blacks. Every board meeting had an argument about that. Walling implored board directors that Du Bois was their star. They had to walk the extra mile not to offend him; otherwise it would appear that white liberals and black plodders could not abide being led by a black intellectual with star power. Du Bois made essentially the same argument, pointing to the success of the magazine, which had thirty-three thousand subscribers by early 1914.

But more than half of the NAACP's annual budget of eleven thousand dollars came from eighteen white donors. Some were conservative white liberals who subscribed to Villard's sense of fair play in talking about race. They focused on the Reconstruction Amendments and they wanted Du Bois to stop talking about social equality, since that reduced to interracial sex, a losing issue for the NAACP. They cringed at his claim that the only morally decent arguments against racial intermarriage were pragmatic. Florence Kelley was voluble on the latter subject, protesting that Du Bois did not speak for her on social equality. A more liberal group of white liberals realized that social equality was unavoidable; the NAACP could not confine itself to the Fourteenth and Fifteenth Amendments. But even some of the liberal liberals wanted Du Bois to cool down the race talk. Race should not matter, they argued; the job of the NAACP was to delegitimize race talk and racial favoritism. Jane Addams and John Haynes Holmes lined up with that wing of the NAACP. This was not merely an argument between Du Bois and privileged whites, as many black NAACP insiders criticized Du Bois on similar grounds, especially Archibald Grimké, Butler Wilson, William A. Sinclair, and William Pickens. Du Bois, in their telling, was too radical about social equality and global racialism, he treated them rudely, he spent too much money, and he bypassed opportunities to promote the NAACP. Grimké moved to Washington, DC, in 1913 to head up the NAACP chapter and to be near his brother. The star-power argument did not work with him, as he did not look up to Du Bois.[109]

Du Bois did not want to be the leader of the NAACP, but for a while it appeared that he would have to take over or leave. Villard made a power play in the spring of 1914, getting himself appointed treasurer, through which he tried to wrest control of the organization. Du Bois told Ovington that Villard had said it to him plainly: He was determined to gain control of the NAACP and *Crisis*, breaking Du Bois's power and ending the separate-but-equal nonsense. For the first time Du Bois pictured the opposite—himself as a movement organization leader. If he had to take over the NAACP to keep *Crisis* going strong, he was willing to do it. He told Ovington: "I am sorry that the impression is widespread that I do not receive or desire any advice. It is not true." He claimed to believe that he and Villard had no political disagreements; politically, he felt closer to Villard than to anyone else in the NAACP. The problem was that Villard was accustomed to giving orders to African Americans "and he simply cannot bring himself to work with one as an equal." Du Bois observed that "every conceivable effort" had been made over the past three and a half years to force him into a subordinate position to "some other official," usually Villard. More recently the board had tried to raise money from the same "reactionary sources" that bankrolled Washington: "We have at last fully developed the art of compromise and retreat." Du Bois insisted that he was not the one who threatened to betray the principles on which the NAACP was founded. He lifted the NAACP to renown by fighting for its principles.[110]

Ovington was Du Bois's rock at the NAACP, politically and as a friend. She defended him against all critics even as she worked to hold the organization together. She tried repeatedly to help Villard see the world as Du Bois did, from the perspective of an oppressed people that struggled not to be shackled, denigrated, and otherwise ignored. Spingarn accused her of idolizing Du Bois and of overprotecting him; she allowed that perhaps he was right. However, Ovington explained, "To me, the rest of us on the Board are able journeymen doing one day's work to be forgotten tomorrow. But Du Bois is the master builder, whose work will speak to men as long as there is an oppressed race on earth."[111]

That was dead-on, although Du Bois eventually got through the NAACP's organizational crisis by bonding with Spingarn, exactly as Ovington sought. Replying to Du Bois in April 1914, Ovington asked him to imagine that the editor of *Crisis* was a white abolitionist with all the right views. This imaginary editor would sometimes offend Afro-American readers without being conscious of it. He would patronize more than he realized, dictate too much, and rub readers the wrong way, all as he felt that he did nothing but speak the truth. If he said anything other than what he did say, he would feel that he had compromised his conscience and principles: "He would be absolutely honorable and yet he would offend."[112]

Ovington judged that the same thing was happening to Du Bois, inevitably. No black man could espouse the NAACP's principles without setting off white readers in various ways without realizing it. The trick was to become more sensitive to how and why it happened. The NAACP, Ovington argued, had to care about the problem because it was a biracial organization that spoke to black and white audiences. Villard offended black allies by giving them orders, and Du Bois offended white allies "by calling them hogs, by saying that they are reactionary heathen." Ovington asked Du Bois to think about the difference between a biracial civil rights organization and a Socialist organization. Du Bois wanted to preach race consciousness in the same way that Socialists preached class consciousness, but the NAACP liberals had not signed up for that. He was wrong to say that he stood for NAACP principles while his critics stood for selling out. Even the part about the NAACP retrogressing was untrue, she said. In the early going, they had to fight to keep Washington off the governing committee. Now they were building a national movement to abolish lynching and segregation. To be sure, Ovington allowed, things got said at board meetings that smacked of paternalism and selling out: "But the *work* of the organization, which is what I can judge by, has been aggressive as it should be."[113]

The NAACP, for all its internal tensions, had in fact stepped up under Spingarn's leadership. The organization threw itself against the flood of Jim Crow legislation pending in Congress, playing a key role in defeating most of it. Grimké was invaluable in this work, showing up at hearings on pending legislation, sometimes on a moment's notice. He grilled lawmakers to explain why they needed to expand the reach and punishments of racial caste. In addition, the NAACP launched a thirty-year crusade against lynching, calling for a federal law to prosecute lynch mobs, and it rallied opposition to D. W. Griffith's motion-picture travesty, *The Birth of a Nation*—Hollywood's biggest success until *Gone with the Wind* (1939).

Birth of a Nation dramatized to millions the Dixon fantasy of beastly blacks, evil carpetbaggers, and noble Klansmen. President Wilson, treated to a private showing at the White House, was quoted as enthusing that the film was "like writing history with lightning" and "all so terribly true." Supreme Court Chief Justice Edward White, a former Klansman, heaped similar praise on the film. Dixon, thrilled at the film's enormous commercial success, declared: "Every man who comes out of one of our theatres is a Southern partisan for life—except the members of Villard's Inter-Marriage Society who go there to knock." The NAACP and Trotter's NIPL responded by ramping up their campaigns against lynching. Nearly one hundred blacks and a score of whites were lynched in 1915, the highest in a decade. One of the lynch mobs—in Waco, Texas—captured a mentally impaired field hand from a courthouse, dragged him from a car, cut off his ears, doused him with kerosene, chopped off more body parts, and burned him on a tree on the courthouse lawn, all in a celebrative atmosphere. Du Bois described it graphically, featuring a cover picture of the brutalized victim, Jesse Washington, suspended from a lynching tree. In a rare occurrence, Du Bois lauded Trotter for standing up to Wilson at a controversial meeting at the White House, but *Crisis* minimized Trotter's role in the fight against lynching. Trotter had quit the NAACP out of rivalry with Du Bois and his own misgivings about biracial liberalism, and the resentments were deep on both sides.[114]

Meanwhile, the NAACP fought court battles against segregation and disenfranchisement, especially grandfather clauses. Storey's brief against Oklahoma's Voter Registration Act of 1910 was accepted as a friend-of-the-court argument in *Guinn v. United States* (1915), which ruled that Oklahoma's grandfather clause was unconstitutional. That was a huge breakthrough. In April 1917 Storey argued before the Supreme Court that Louisville's residential segregation by city ordinance violated the due process clause of the Fourteenth Amendment (*Buchanan v. Warley*, 1917). That November the Court ruled in Storey's favor. By mid-1917 the NAACP had nine thousand members. Two years later it had ninety thousand members and more than three hundred local branches—a windfall from the group's court victories, its appointment of James Weldon Johnson as field secretary, and a decision by Spingarn and Johnson to capitalize on the court publicity by recruiting black members in the South.[115]

Spingarn's aggressive strategy set off a surge of self-confidence and good feeling within the organization. From early on he had a strong relationship with Du Bois. As a Jew, Spingarn knew about prejudice; moreover, he was elegant, cultured, and intellectually accomplished, things that Du Bois prized. Du Bois knew there were board members who vented to Spingarn instead of Walling or Ovington about him. He knew there were constant complaints that *Crisis* soaked up too much money, space, and attention, and it misrepresented the NAACP. Still, he was stunned when Spingarn criticized him in October 1914 for sowing "an atmosphere of antagonism" in the organization. Spingarn cautioned that it went far beyond Villard, Nerney, and disgruntled white board members. Most black board members complained about Du Bois, and "even some of your most intimate friends feel toward you a mingled affection and resentment." Spingarn appreciated why Du Bois was sensitive about being slighted; he could even overlook Du Bois's unwillingness to admit that he was ever wrong about anything. But Du Bois seemed not even to try to work with others or to care what they thought. He elevated every slight personal difference into a question of principle. Everyone said this, Spingarn wrote. Moreover, they were right: "Whenever I have come to talk over such matters with you, and to effect some form of cooperation by which all of us could fight for the truth together, I found that I could not act toward you as I would toward other co-operators in a great cause. You had to be approached with care and diplomacy, and made to do things by wheedling and questioning, as children are induced to do them."[116]

It was time to say this bluntly, Spingarn reported, because Du Bois's critics were marshaling the votes to fire him. Du Bois had to mend his ways before it was too late: "The time has come to put an end to this tragic trifling. . . . We cannot go on unless your talents are subordinated to the general welfare of the whole organization, and the rift between the various departments of the Association is closed once and for all. There can be no Crisis and no non-Crisis; that way of dividing our work has failed; both must be one."[117]

Du Bois was known for terse one-sentence replies. He replied to Spingarn with the longest letter he ever wrote, a plea to think big. He had no doubt "that my temperament is a difficult one to endure." Disputing that would be ridiculous. Du Bois also knew that whenever he had a free hand, he accomplished great things. That was all he asked, "a reasonable chance to finish the big thing which is now scarcely begun." The *Crisis* was on its way to becoming "one of the great journals of the world." If only the NAACP would leave him alone, *Crisis* would become a center of enterprise and cooperation exceeding the dreams of all black Americans: "But for heaven's sakes let me do the work. Do not hamper and bind and criticize in little matters." Du Bois urged that the purpose of *Crisis* was "to make the NAACP *possible.*" The NAACP had to refuse to be content with accomplishing a few small things: "The great blow— the freeing of ten millions—and of other millions whom they pull down—that means power and organization on a tremendous scale."[118]

To be accused of "tragic trifling" was absurd, and Du Bois resented it. Moreover, he did not bruise as easily as those who cried about their hurt feelings. Du Bois thought the NAACP got along remarkably well, all things considered. It was a "heaven of peace and concord" compared to the Anti-Slavery Society. When did white liberals become so sensitive? Yes, he might have been less harsh when Villard proposed to publish an ongoing list of black crimes, but Villard had been sticking it to him for two years and he exploded. Du Bois cautioned Spingarn that "no organization like ours ever succeeded in America." The antislavery societies were organizations of white philanthropists that wanted to "help" the Negro. The black-only groups froze out "their white co-workers by insolence and distrust." Historically, and currently, everything tended to break along the color line. Spingarn did not see the color line everywhere, Du Bois judged, "because there is no shadow of the thing in your soul." Ovington saw it because she lived intimately with African Americans. Villard and Nerney were oblivious to the color line; consciously they had no color prejudice, but unconsciously they took white supremacy for granted with every waking breath. Thus Nerney, a secretary, never accepted Du Bois's authority.[119]

Authority was the keystone issue for the NAACP, Du Bois concluded. "Since there must be some center of authority that center must be white or colored. If the head is colored, the whites gradually leave. I have seen the experiment made a dozen times. If the head is white, the colored people gradually drop out of the inner circle of authority and initiative and become clerks—mere helpers of white philanthropists working 'for your people.'" This was why Du Bois resisted the verdict that "separate but equal" had failed in the NAACP. Was *Crisis* failing? Was the NAACP failing? Very few NAACP insiders saw the real issue, Du Bois said. He saw it, and Ovington saw it. He hoped there were others. Since the color line was terribly real, the NAACP needed to have two mutually supportive but independent authorities.[120]

Du Bois ignored the irony of saying that "separate but equal" had to be the ruling principle of the NAACP. Spingarn pushed back, declaring that expenses for *Crisis* had soared out of control and the magazine had to be a responsible steward of the organization's resources. Du Bois replied that in that case, he would take complete control of *Crisis* and relinquish his NAACP salary. The next board meeting overwhelmingly rejected that proposal, but Du Bois engineered a compromise that was better than winning: The magazine was incorporated, a special fund controlled by him was created for *Crisis*, and the magazine got its own committee, controlled by Du Bois and Ovington. There were more rounds of sparring after Du Bois loudly proclaimed victory, but the structure that got the NAACP through its takeoff phase, on the way to becoming a powerhouse, was finally settled upon.

THE END OF BOOKER T.

The year 1915 would have been a turning point for Du Bois and the NAACP if only for the anti-lynching campaign, *Guinn v. United States*, and the resolution of the organization's structure. But it was also the year that Booker T.

Washington died. Du Bois later put it surprisingly blandly, noting that Washington's death "coincided with a change in Negro attitudes." This coincidence was overdetermined. Washington had lost much of his political influence with the defeats of Roosevelt and Taft. He had tried to derail the NAACP by deploying spies and running negative stories about the organization in the black press, which repelled straddlers. His health had deteriorated since the early 1900s, as Washington's overwork, stress, arteriosclerosis, and high blood pressure ganged up on him, plus his high-fat diet. He probably had diabetes, too, and in later life his vacations did not break the downward spiral.[121]

Then he had endured a humiliating barrage of publicity over a bizarre scrape in Manhattan. On March 19, 1911, Washington took the subway from his room at the Manhattan Hotel in midtown—his usual New York residence—to an address on West Sixty-third Street near the southern end of Central Park. In his telling, he came there to meet with a Tuskegee accountant visiting New York, having been directed to this address by a letter from Emmett Scott, which Washington destroyed because it contained confidential information. He rang the buzzer several times, paced back and forth, departed from the building and returned, and was assaulted by a resident, Henry Ulrich, who accused him of attempted burglary. Washington tried to get away, but Ulrich chased him, beating him with a walking stick that a passerby donated, inflicting deep gashes on Washington's face and head, until he fell into the arms of a police officer. At the police station Ulrich started with the burglary charge, added that Washington was drunk, and claimed that Washington got the gashes by falling onto a fire hydrant and a curb. Washington, perfectly sober and cordial, countered that he was Booker T. Washington. The officers arrested Ulrich for assault and sent Washington to a hospital. Meanwhile, Ulrich's wife arrived at the police station to charge that Washington had accosted her with an offensive greeting: "Hello, Sweetheart."[122]

The following morning New York newspapers ran sensational stories featuring, in order, the sweetheart allegation, the beating, the drunkenness charge, and the burglary charge. Washington replied that he had never said anything like that to a woman in his life, much less a white woman he did not know. He had also never been drunk, and he clearly lacked a motive to burglarize a low-rent apartment. The story exploded into a national psychodrama. Newspapers stoked a frenzy of speculation about Washington's apparent sexual proclivities on the road, never mind that his reputation for sexual rectitude had been impeccable up to that moment. The neighborhood was seedy, it was not far from the Tenderloin prostitution district, and Washington had no proof of why he was there. He tried to cut a deal with Ulrich that would clear him of moral taint, but it didn't work out. The story was so huge that Washington had to be vindicated; otherwise it would be an unbearable blot on his name.[123]

Villard wrote a strong resolution expressing moral support for Washington and a weak one expressing regret at what happened. The NAACP rejected the former resolution vehemently and endorsed the latter one on a divided vote. It didn't help that Washington was waging an ugly vendetta against Walling in the *New York Age*, all the while still denying that he owned the *Age*. Villard tried to turn Washington's crisis into the occasion of a truce between Tuskegee and the NAACP, but that got only a few weeks of lip service on both sides, which Du Bois shredded: "If we continually dodge and cloud the issue, and say the half truth because the whole stings and shames; if we do this, we invite catastrophe. Let us then in all charity but unflinching firmness set our faces against all statesmanship that looks in such directions."[124]

In the early going of Washington's nine-month nightmare, there was a great deal of editorial support for him that countered a good deal of speculation on whether he had a thing for white prostitutes. Even Trotter and Harry C. Smith tried to be generous at first; Trotter declared that he took no interest in kicking Washington while he was down. But the story dragged on too long to keep saying that, and by August, Trotter and Smith were blasting Washington for loitering in a seedy district and bringing disgrace on the entire race.[125]

Washington's confidence that the trial would go well for him was predicated on his sterling reputation and the fact that his two accusers had credibility issues. Mrs. Ulrich, it turned out, was somebody else, a housewife in New Jersey lacking any idea of her husband's whereabouts until he suddenly became tabloid fodder. The woman that claimed to be Mrs. Ulrich, Laura Page Alvarez, was separated from her actual husband, a man of Spanish surname by whom she had a daughter. She claimed to be Mrs. Ulrich moments before she claimed that Washington called her "sweetheart"; meanwhile, nearly everything that Ulrich claimed was unbelievable. Ulrich, however, was acquitted on the grounds that some doubt remained about his motive for attacking Washington. Washington never provided a convincing account of how he ended up in a dubious place or why he did not call ahead to an accountant that had no connection to this address. If he covered up for a lover, he paid a huge price, but exposure would have gone worse.

For Washington the episode was a cruel ending. To most of the public this was how he went out, though he conducted speaking tours in Florida in 1912 and Louisiana in 1915. Aside from the testimony of a brute lacking any credibility, the scandal rested entirely on the claim of a low-credibility white woman that a black man had called her "sweetheart." Washington's friends noticed that he never mentioned any other aspect of the episode. He told the Grimké brothers: "The hardest part of the whole outrage was the conspiracy to make it appear that I addressed indecent words to a woman, something I never did in my life." It must have cut Washington deeply that he, of all people, was victimized by this particular lie. Yet it took almost nothing to bring down even him.[126]

After Washington died, Du Bois declared that his death marked an epoch in the history of America: "He was the greatest Negro leader since Frederick Douglass, and the most distinguished man, white or black, who has come out of the South since the Civil War." Du Bois did not doubt that Washington achieved an enormous amount of good, and he did not want to be remembered as having said otherwise: "He directed the attention of the Negro race in America to the pressing necessity of economic development; he emphasized technical education, and he did much to pave the way for an understanding between the white and darker races." On the other hand, Washington did not understand the growing bond between politics and industry that made corporate capitalism a different kind of beast, he did not understand the deeper foundations of human development and flourishing either, and his strategy for racial reconciliation was based on caste. Du Bois was grateful that Washington accumulated land and property, empowered thousands to become productive citizens, and tried to prevent African Americans from getting killed or run over: "On the other hand, in stern justice, we must lay on the soul of this man a heavy responsibility for the consummation of Negro disfranchisement, the decline of the Negro college and public school, and the firmer establishment of color caste in this land."[127]

Du Bois could feel the tide turning in his direction, even as African Americans reeled from an upsurge of lynchings and Jim Crow enhancement bills. In 1916 the NAACP planned to hold its annual meeting on Lincoln's birthday, February 12. Then it learned that Scott and the Bookerites were planning to hold their memorial service for Washington on that day. Spingarn saw an opportunity—a unifying conference at his home in Dutchess County, New York, south of the Berkshire Mountains. The guest list ran the gamut of black and white civil rights activists, from Trotter to the NAACP to Scott. The implicit agenda was to reflect on what the NAACP should do in the epoch of the NAACP.

Putting it that self-consciously was thrilling to Du Bois, although he did not say publicly that was the agenda. Du Bois organized the conference, placing straddlers Robert Terrell and James Weldon Johnson in moderating roles, plus John Hope and educator Lucy Laney. All were trusted by the Booker faction but also friendly with NAACP leaders. Laney shared a tent with Mary Church Terrell, NACW president Mary B. Talbert, and Nannie Burroughs. At the last minute Trotter and Washington's successor at Tuskegee, Robert Russa Moton, declined to attend, an inadvertently helpful decision. The Amenia Conference marked a turning point. Instead of deliberating in secret, as Du Bois had planned, the group developed a spirit of camaraderie over three days and announced its conclusions. Du Bois later recalled, "We all believed in thrift, we all wanted the Negro to vote, we all wanted the laws enforced, we all wanted to abolish lynching, we all wanted assertion of our essential manhood." They differed on how to get these things, but Amenia marked the beginning of a new era in civil rights work. It certified that the torch had passed to NAACP-style activism, literally in Johnson's case, as Amenia brought Johnson into the NAACP.[128]

But the NAACP was changing, too. Johnson joined the staff as field secretary on the eve of America's entry into World War I. He was the NAACP's first officer from the South, let alone its first to come from the Tuskegee network. Born in Jacksonville, Florida, Johnson had joined the Florida bar, composed "Lift Every Voice and Sing," served as U.S. consul to Venezuela under Roosevelt and Taft, and authored *The Autobiography of an Ex-Colored Man* before he was forty. Now he resolved to help the NAACP expand its black membership—in the South. Johnson was an ideal candidate for the job—magnanimous, talented, energetic, and quietly charismatic. He urged southern blacks to join the organization, and they did. He tried to push the NAACP into the South without stirring a white backlash, which proved to be impossible. Then black soldiers returned from World War I in no mood to resume their former subjugation. In 1919, organizing the NAACP's national conference in Cleveland, Ovington realized that the group had turned a corner. The NAACP was founded on the white liberal model of philanthropic activism, but at Cleveland the white delegates found themselves in a solidarity organization focused on the status of blacks as citizens and "constantly learning from them." The years of white direction ended just as NAACP leaders fell out with each other over their nation's plunge into World War I.[129]

THE WAR AND THE COLOR LINE OF EMPIRE

President Wilson and Republican contender Charles Hughes sent greetings of support to the Amenia Conference, but Du Bois angrily told readers in October 1916 that both were odious. Some NAACP liberals took heart that Hughes sometimes sounded like a pre-McKinley Republican; others said he was just a slicker lily-white from New York. Du Bois emphatically took the latter view, adding that Wilson got only one thing right—placing a decent, principled, able justice on the Supreme Court, Louis Brandeis. Otherwise, Wilson was a nightmare for black Americans, plus an imperialist who had toppled Mexican president Victoriano Huerta in 1914, invaded Haiti in 1915, and sustained U.S. occupations of Nicaragua and the Dominican Republic. Du Bois railed against the invasion of Haiti, declaring that Haiti deserved to work out its own destiny and that it was already more civilized than Texas: "SHAME ON AMERICA!"[130]

The imperial angle was distinctly illuminating to Du Bois, helping him to synthesize his belief in the solidarity of peoples of color with his belief that racial injustice and capitalist exploitation were powerfully linked. The NAACP had plenty of black members, epitomized by Miller, who equated black progress with free market capitalism, and plenty of white members, epitomized by Storey, who similarly believed that "capitalism" was a name for the freedom principle and its benefits in the economic sphere. Du Bois offended both groups every time he editorialized about the ravages of capitalism. Until the Great War, however, Du Bois merely recycled conventional Socialist criticism of capitalist inequality and commercialism, and he fended off objections that Socialist ideology stripped ordinary people of their economic freedom. Europe had barely plunged into war in 1914 when Du Bois began to reflect on the role of Africa in causing the European empires to stumble into carnage and destruction.

In May 1915 Du Bois published an essay on the imperialist causes of World War I that preceded V. I. Lenin's similar theory by two years. Du Bois took a quick pass at the long view, noting that agriculture and trade flourished in Africa long before Europe ceased to be a wilderness. The pertinent history, however, was tellingly recent. Du Bois observed that it began when Welsh-born American journalist Henry Stanley took an epic journey down the length of the Congo River in the late 1870s. Britain was skittish about plunging into Central Africa, but King Leopold II of Belgium invested in Stanley's plan to tap the Congo's riches, and the "scramble for Africa" was on. That led to the Berlin Conference of November 1884, where the European powers sorted out their imperial claims in Africa with ineffable hubris. Even Du Bois lacked the words for it, settling for "contemptible and dishonest beyond expression." England, having pushed earliest and hardest, got four million square miles of African territory; France got approximately the same amount; Portugal got three-quarters of a million square miles; and Spain and Italy got substantial chunks. Stanley's exploits paved the way to the creation of the Congo Free State, which Leopold owned privately and which fell into "murder, mutilation, downright robbery," like the others. Germany, a late player in this enterprise, was granted an area half the size of the entire German Empire in Europe—a sizable payoff for joining the pillage of Africans lacking any say in the matter.[131]

The equation of color with inferiority was the crucial point in this story, Du Bois argued. Here the European powers took an important lesson from the British and American slave trades. The pillage and rape of Africa could be called something else if black people were less than human. Du Bois explained, "Thus the world began to invest in color prejudice. The 'Color Line' began to pay dividends." England was already deeply invested in Africa, "cleaning away the debris of the slave trade and half consciously groping toward the new Imperialism." France was keen to build a northern African empire stretching from the Atlantic Ocean to the Red Sea. Germany, shut out from Central and South America by the Monroe Doctrine, sought colonies in Africa and Asia. Portugal renewed and expanded its historic claims to African territory. Du Bois noted that in 1875 the European powers controlled one-tenth of the African continent. By 1900 they controlled virtually the entire continent. This was what drove Europe to war—the scramble for economic riches by rival capitalist nations creating mutually exclusive economic bases of power.[132]

The very emergence of modern capitalism drove the capitalist powers into "undeveloped" markets, beginning with England. English economist John Hobson, in his classic text *Imperialism* (1902), contended that England established "imperialism as a political policy" in the early 1870s. As long as England held a virtual monopoly of world markets for important manufactured goods, it did not need modern imperialism; the old kind worked just fine. In the early 1870s competition from Germany, the United States, and Belgium impaired England's capacity to sell its manufactured goods at a profit. Hobson observed, "The encroachments made by these nations upon our old markets, even in our own possessions, made it most urgent that we should take energetic means to secure new markets. These new markets had to lie in hitherto undeveloped countries, chiefly in the tropics, where vast populations lived capable of growing economic needs which our manufacturers and merchants could supply." England tried hard to stay ahead of the competition, but its rivals seized and annexed territories for the same purpose. Hobson concluded: "Every improvement of methods of production, every concentration of ownership and control, seems to accentuate the tendency. As one nation after another enters the machine economy and adopts advanced industrial methods, it becomes more difficult for its manufacturers, merchants, and financiers to dispose profitably of their economic resources, and they are tempted more and more to use their Governments in order to secure for their particular use some distant undeveloped country by annexation and protection."[133]

Hobson's analysis was already growing into its career as a pillar of neo-Marxist theory when Du Bois drew upon it, although Du Bois did not mention him. Following Hobson, Du Bois did not say that capitalism always overpowered liberal democracy, trade unions, Socialist movements, or even peace movements. The great Western movements opposing exploitation and imperialism had huge achievements to their credit, he acknowledged. But progressive movements played a role in accelerating the flow of finance capital to parts of the world lacking Socialist and anti-imperialist movements. Du Bois applied this Hobson thesis to his own social and generational context. Democracy was supposed to be the answer to the terrible problems of inequality, exploitation, and oppression, he observed. The ship of state was supposedly launched on the "broad, irresistible tide of democracy." Yet as democracy spread, so did the rule of might. The modern state was founded on a paradoxical combination of democracy and imperialism, as in the increasingly democratic and imperialist United States. Du Bois noted that even the rankest American imperialists gave speeches praising democracy: "It is this paradox which allows in America the most rapid advance of democracy to go hand in hand in its very centers with increased autocracy and hatred toward darker races, and which excuses and defends an inhumanity that does not shrink from the public burning of human beings."[134]

Du Bois did not want to sneer at the democratic faith of his liberal and Socialist allies, which he shared. He was a progressive who believed in radical democracy. But the seemingly paradoxical wedding of democracy and imperialism was not really puzzling, he argued. "The paradox is easily explained: the white workingman has been asked to share the spoil of exploiting 'chinks and niggers.' It is no longer simply the merchant prince, or the aristocratic monopoly, or even the employing class, that is exploiting the world: it is the nation, a new democratic nation composed of united capital and labor." The union movements still had a long way to go in attaining a just share of the wealth they generated, and they did not reach the poor and excluded classes beneath them, "but the laborer's equity is recognized, and his just share is a matter of time, intelligence and skillful negotiation." Du Bois had a rosy view of the middle-class future of the American and European union movements. The capitalist class would yield to the unions as long as it found new markets to exploit. The national bond in a modern capitalist nation was not based on something as flimsy or sentimental as patriotism, loyalty, or ancestor worship, he argued. It was based on the wealth that created a middle class and that flowed down to the working class: "Never before was the average citizen of England, France, or Germany so rich, with such splendid prospects of greater riches."[135]

Most of this new wealth, however, came primarily "from the darker nations of the world," and its accumulation depended on the exploitation of Asians, Africans, South and Central Americans, West Indians, and South Sea Islanders. Du Bois acknowledged that the "older exploitation" still existed in parts of white America, Russia, and Europe. It was fading, however, and it was not the reason why the Germans and British were slaughtering each other. The nations at war took for granted their right to rule and exploit the darker nations of the world. The war was about which group of white nations would do so. Every available resource of modern science and religion had been marshaled to this end, buttressing the modern idea of racial superiority: "Thus arises the astonishing doctrine of the natural inferiority of most men to the few, and the interpretation of 'Christian brotherhood' as meaning anything that one of the 'brothers' may at any time want it to mean."[136]

Du Bois acknowledged that Japan was a problem for this scheme, as the Japanese had thus far escaped the color bar with no indication of wanting to ally with white nations against brown, black, and the rest of the yellow peoples. The Japanese nation demanded white treatment, which did not bode well for white hegemony. China, in addition, was increasingly independent, complicating the Western domination of China. But Africa was not complicated, Du Bois observed. Aside from a flicker of self-consciousness in Abyssinia, and civil rights stirrings in the United States and the West Indies that elicited "ruthless repression," the peoples in and from Africa were docile, repressed, and dominated. In short, "Africa is prostrate"; notwithstanding that, but also because South Africa had gold and diamonds, Angola and Nigeria had cocoa, the Congo had rubber and ivory, and the West Coast had palm oil. This was the "real secret" of the European war, Du Bois contended: "We speak of the Balkans as the storm-center of Europe and the cause of war, but this is mere habit. The Balkans are convenient for occasions, but the ownership of materials and men in the darker world is the real prize that is setting the nations of Europe at each other's throats today."[137]

This was a grim picture, even with Du Bois's confidence that unionism had a bright future in the rich nations. If Progressive movements accelerated the imperial logic of modern capitalism, what were they to do? Du Bois answered that they needed to "remove the real causes of war" by universalizing democracy. If the liberal, union, anti-imperialist, and Socialist movements wanted to create "real peace and lasting culture" in the world, they had to struggle for democracy everywhere, not just at home: "We must go further. We must extend the democratic ideal to the yellow, brown, and black peoples." Democracy is distinctly powerful and transformative, he urged, "a method of doing the impossible." To abolish the causes of war, the defenseless needed to attain "democratic weapons of self-defense." That meant three things: One, Africans needed to own their own lands. Two, "we must train native races in modern civilization," principally through education. Three, colonialism had to be abolished everywhere. Except for the English, Du Bois observed, nobody cared about Africa in the early nineteenth century, and for the English it was just a matter of salvaging something from the scraps of the slave trade. Now white Europe was at war over things it wanted in Africa, and Du Bois warned that the darker races would not endure their subjection forever: "They are going to fight and the War of the Color Line will outdo in savage inhumanity any war this world has yet seen."[138]

Du Bois stressed that he was a peaceable type who hated war. He was for "peace and the civilization of all men." But he was deadly serious about universal democracy and "civilizing" all people, which predisposed him to Wilson's rhetoric about saving the world for democracy. In August 1916 Du Bois cheered the Irish Republican uprising against the British, telling *Crisis* readers that "no human group has ever achieved freedom without being compelled to murder thousands of members of other groups who were determined that they should be slaves." Black Americans would do well to imitate the "foolishness" of the Irish, he admonished. The following month he mused that the war would be good for racial justice, destroying the modern order that imposed white racist ideas of beauty and accomplishment. Du Bois looked forward to a postwar order that prized "brown and black men and women with glowing dark eyes and crinkling hair." In January 1917 he predicted that Poland would gain self-determination from the war, offering another example of a repressed race attaining "a chance for self-development after a high noon of despair."[139]

The following month Spingarn began to campaign for a training camp for African American officers; he lobbied government officials and spoke at college campuses. Spingarn told Du Bois he would respect whatever position Du Bois took about intervention and black officers. As for himself, he was determined to abolish race discrimination in the armed forces, even if he had to start with a segregated training camp. Du Bois thought about it for three weeks before linking arms with Spingarn and military integration. It helped that Du Bois's friendship with Spingarn was the closest he ever held with a white male. He also had friendships with Walling and Russell, who supported intervention. As soon as Wilson took America into the war, Du Bois cheered heartily, lining up with Spingarn against the pacifist wing of the NAACP (led by Ovington and Addams) and the neutralist wing (led by Villard).[140]

Du Bois took up his new cause with customary bravado, lashing at critics who said that America should not intervene, or that the NAACP should not fight for military integration, or at least, that fighting for a segregated training camp was absurd. He reasoned that black Americans put up with segregated schools and Jim Crow cars "because it would be suicide to go uneducated [or] stay at home." This was like that, a "damnable dilemma" created by black America's white enemies: "We must make the choice else we play into their very claws. It is a case of camp or no officers." Trotter issued a blistering reply, describing Du Bois as "a rank quitter of the fight for our rights." At the very moment that Afro-Americans finally held a bit of leverage, Du Bois "betrayed the cause of his race." The *Afro-American* and the *Chicago Defender* rallied similar opposition to Du Bois, who had nearly finished his June editorial when the army announced that one thousand black officers would be trained at a segregated camp in Des Moines, Iowa. "We have won!" Du Bois exulted. Years later he was more rueful: "The War Department squirmed. We had to fight even to be segregated. We fell out among ourselves."[141]

The army had a distinguished candidate to run the camp, Charles Young, a black lieutenant colonel recently returned from Wilson's adventure in Mexico. The army hastily retired Young on bogus grounds, ostensibly concerned about his blood pressure, to avoid the spectacle of an African American training black captains and lieutenants. There were more damnable dilemmas to come, inevitably. The draft called up eighty-three thousand blacks, and the law decreed that they were to be trained separately from whites and trained as laborers, not soldiers. Black draftees were harassed mercilessly, enduring epithets and mistreatment. The *Crisis* railed against all of it.

Spingarn got a waiver from the age regulation for officers, at the age of forty-three, to get himself appointed as an infantry major. He got Ovington to be his temporary replacement at the NAACP, which pleased Du Bois, but Spingarn's position at the NAACP and his published remarks that white America gave black Americans little to fight for got him in trouble with the army's Military Intelligence branch. Spingarn seethed at hearing his patriotism questioned. He got revenge by getting himself placed in Military Intelligence, then doubled down by asking Du Bois to accept a captaincy in it. Besides revenge, Spingarn had a deeper motive—protecting the NAACP and Du Bois from violating the new Sedition Act, which contained harsh penalties for anything spoken or written that was deemed to be hostile to America. Du Bois was fifty years old, the commission would have allowed him to keep his job at *Crisis*, and he had no interest in going to jail. He gave barely a moment's thought to the perils and trade-offs before saying yes. Belatedly asking the NAACP for approval, Du Bois explained that he would address "pressing grievances of colored folk which hinder the prosecution of the war."[142]

He had never believed that ordinary limitations applied to him. The captaincy was like getting into Harvard or inventing *Crisis*: a challenge to achieve something stupendous through his outsized intelligence and will. Du Bois did not think about how the army intelligence bureau might be less accommodating than Harvard or the NAACP. He told astonished friends that he saw no inconsistency between doing military intelligence and carrying on his radical activism. Years later, having thought about it, Du Bois allowed that in 1918 he was touched by war psychology and some recent victories. The government had commissioned over seven hundred black officers; blacks had been granted representation in the Departments of War and Labor; most of the recent segregation ordinances had been defeated; the Red Cross, for a while, employed black nurses; and Wilson belatedly spoke against lynching. Du Bois did not admit, even many years later, that the military commission turned his head. He and Spingarn were overimpressed with the prospect of wielding military power.[143]

In July 1918 Du Bois published an editorial titled "Close Ranks." It was not what he usually said, though he pretended not to notice. He really wanted the military commission. Years later, claiming a hazy memory, Du Bois did not explain that he received the captaincy offer on June 4, he wrote the editorial on June 6, the printer's deadline was June 10, and his physical exam for the army would be on June 15. "This is the crisis of the world," he announced in the editorial. "For all the long years to come men will point to the year 1918 as the great Day of Decision." Du Bois urged that blacks held "no ordinary interest" in the outcome of the war, for German militarism posed a life-or-death threat to the aspirations of the darker races for equality, freedom, and democracy: "Let us not hesitate. Let us, while this war lasts, forget our special grievances and close our ranks shoulder to shoulder with our own white fellow citizens and the allied nations that are fighting for democracy. We make no ordinary sacrifice, but we make it gladly and willingly with our eyes lifted to the hills."[144]

Black editorialists and activists were incredulous at being told to forget their special grievances for the rest of the war, much less to hear it from Du Bois. He took a thrashing in the black press. Trotter was stunned into near-silence. The *Pittsburgh Courier* wrote, "Dr. Du Bois has seldom packed more error into a single sentence." The New York *News* condemned Du Bois's "crass moral cowardice." Archibald Grimké told NAACP board members that if they supported Du Bois's commission and Du Bois remained at the magazine, he would take his Washington, DC, branch out of the NAACP. Grimké's friend Neval Thomas, also addressing the board, declared that Du Bois had "reversed his whole life, and is no more good to us." Niagarite Byron Gunner, resisting the latter conclusion, wrote to Du Bois: "I simply find myself unable to conceive that said advice comes from you. It seems to me that the impossible has happened and I'm amazed beyond expression." Did somebody write the July editorial under Du Bois's name? Du Bois told Gunner that he wrote the editorial, it conveyed his "exact thought," and it was "entirely consistent with my well-known attitude."[45]

The *Crisis* stuck to that line for two more issues, even as Du Bois took more upbraiding from the black press and as the NAACP board refused to approve his request. "Our country is at war," Du Bois implored. "The war is critical, dangerous and world-wide. If this is our country, then this is our war. We must fight it with every ounce of blood and treasure." At the time, and years later, Du Bois rationalized that his opponents on the NAACP board were pacifists (although Ovington supported him). In fact, a majority of the NAACP board supported America's intervention, but Du Bois got only five votes for his proposal to be an army captain and the *Crisis* editor simultaneously. In the only pass that he ever took at explaining what happened, Du Bois wrote blandly, "Fortunately the matter never came to an issue." He never had to decide whether to destroy his career by sticking with an impulsive and bizarre decision, because army Negrophobes saved him from it. He did not try to say, years later, what he might have decided had the army not canceled the special bureau plan. Spingarn and Du Bois came under attack from white southern officers in the intelligence branch, the bureau proposal was terminated, and the army sent Spingarn to the front in France with the Sixth Army Corps. Twenty-two years later Du Bois could not say that he still believed what he wrote in 1918, nor could he say that he ever did. He doubted that things would have gone worse had Germany won the war. He tried to remember what he really thought in 1918, but it wasn't clear to him: "Perhaps, despite words, I was thinking narrowly of the interest of my group and was willing to let the world go to hell, if the black men went free." Perhaps if black Americans had boycotted the war, the world might have been saved for blacks and whites. But that was never going to happen, and his proposal to do so might have "slaughtered the American Negro body and soul. I do not know. I am puzzled."[46]

That was in 1940, however, after another world war had erupted and Du Bois had given up on idealism and civil rights liberalism. In December 1918 Du Bois brimmed with idealistic visions of a transformed world order. Wilson, heading to the Paris Peace Conference aboard the *George Washington*, expounded his Fourteen Points and League of Nations proposals to officials. Du Bois, meanwhile, regaled reporters on the press ship *Orizaba* with his proposals for

Pan-African unity and a vast state in central Africa. Du Bois tried to meet with Wilson to pitch his idea of reviving the Pan-African Congress. Then he hooked a ride on the *Orizaba* after learning that Wilson was sending Moton to Paris to represent black America at the conference and to pacify black American soldiers in France.[147]

Du Bois had the official backing of the NAACP to organize a pan-African conference at the peace conference. He based his vision of a postcolonial Africa on Wilson's point V—an "absolutely impartial adjustment of all colonial claims." Du Bois did not believe that Africa would plunge into chaos if the colonizers went home. He burned with resentment at white Europeans and Americans who said that it would. In the heady aftermath of the war, while Wilson gave bravura speeches in European capitals, Du Bois believed that Wilson's new world order might be a springboard for Pan-Africanism. He reasoned that Pan-Africanism was like Zionism; moreover, in the patronizing tradition of Crummell, Du Bois stressed that African Americans should play a leading role in "civilizing" Africa: "The African movement means to us what the Zionist movement means to the Jews, the centralization of the race effort and the recognition of a racial fount." It was imperative for African Americans to "help bear the burden of Africa" without diminishing their efforts to liberate themselves in America: "Amelioration of the lot of Africa tends to ameliorate the condition of colored peoples throughout the world."[148]

The Wilson administration, however, took no interest in adding Pan-African activism to its liberal internationalist agenda. Wilson told Du Bois in November 1917 that he was too busy to meet with him. Wilson's chief aide, Colonel Edward M. House, listened politely to Du Bois's proposal for a Pan-African Congress, but promised nothing. In Paris, Wilson officials brushed off Du Bois's requests for a conference or a meeting. Moton got respectful treatment in France and Du Bois got U.S. Army intelligence agents wherever he went, who made no secret of their hostility to Du Bois. That did not stop Du Bois from reliving his ecstatic German student experience of losing the veil, at least among Europeans. He told *Crisis* readers that in Paris he laughed and bantered with Europeans without feeling "the *Thing*—the hateful, murderous, dirty *Thing* which in America we call 'Nigger-hatred.'" Du Bois reexperienced what it felt like to while away an evening in interracial company without feeling defined by his race. Still, for three weeks he failed to get anywhere with his own government, the French government of Georges Clemenceau, or the British government of David Lloyd George—until he approached Blaise Diagne.[149]

Diagne was the *commissaire général* for French West Africa and represented Senegal in the French Parliament. Born in Senegal in 1872, he had risen from poverty to become a French colonial customs officer. In 1914 he won election to the French Chamber of Deputies, overcoming objections that no native African belonged in the French Parliament. Three years later Clemenceau, faced with German troops closing in on Paris, named Diagne as high commissioner for the republic with special authority for French West Africa. Diagne raised an army of 680,000 West African soldiers to defend France, plus a force of 238,000 laborers. Clemenceau, overflowing with gratitude, offered Diagne the French Legion of Honor; Diagne declined, pleading that he had only done his duty, which was reward enough. By 1919 Diagne was one of Clemenceau's closest friends, and he outranked all of France's colonial white officials. He was a Pan-African by his lights but a French colonial above all. To many African anticolonialists he was anathema, but Du Bois could respect Diagne's wager that fighting for the empire might yield a better life for his people. Du Bois had made that wager, too; plus he was desperate for a sponsor, so he approached Diagne. Diagne agreed to try, taking the Pan-African conference proposal to Clemenceau, who replied: "Don't advertise it, but go ahead."[150]

Clemenceau had no intention of endorsing independence for Africans or Asians. He had spent the past month ridiculing Wilson's idealism, snorting that even God had only ten points. The French premier was reason number one why Du Bois's fondest hopes for a generous peace and a new world order were going nowhere. But Clemenceau undoubtedly enjoyed tweaking Wilson's self-righteousness by giving a stage to a black American who reminded the world of how America treated blacks. Moreover, Clemenceau owed Diagne, and he probably trusted Diagne's guarantee that the conference would say nice things about French colonialism. Diagne made good on the latter promise for years to come as president of the Pan-African Congress.

The refounded Pan-African Congress met on February 19, 1919, at the Grant Hotel in Paris. The Wilson administration took it badly, declaring that the conference was a mistake and no passports would be issued for American delegates wishing to attend. Wilson officials worried that Du Bois would go on about lynching, segregation, and/or the army's treatment of black soldiers; they were slow to grasp that Africa really mattered to Du Bois and the delegates. Eminent journalist Walter Lippmann, editor of the *New Republic* and a key advisor to Wilson, was an exception. Very few prominent white Americans not connected to the NAACP interacted with Du Bois or took any interest in his work. Lippmann, however, respected Du Bois, encouraged his work, and reached out to him in Paris, congratulating him on organizing the conference.[151]

Fifty-seven delegates representing fifteen nations participated, including twenty-one West Indians, sixteen U.S. Americans, and twelve delegates from nine African states including the Belgian Congo, Ethiopia, Liberia, and Egypt. Several European nations were represented, Walling and Russell took part, and the congress got strong press coverage that often mistakenly described it as the first assembly of its kind. It helped that Du Bois had bantered with white journalists on the *Orizaba*, a rare occurrence for him. From the beginning he sparred with Diagne, who said that French imperialism was good and the other kinds, especially British, were bad. Du Bois drafted the report of the congress and was selected to continue as its secretary. The refounded Pan-African Congress, like its predecessor, was far from radical. It made no mention of an autonomous state in Central Africa. It did not call for immediate self-determination for any colony. In a moderate tone it asserted that land and other resources "should be held in trust for the natives" while natives acquired the capacity to effectively own "as much land as they can profitably develop." The congress declared that capital should be regulated to prevent the exploitation of native peoples and natural wealth. And it stated that Africans should be allowed to participate in the government "as fast as their development permits." These statements were foundational for subsequent Pan-African conferences, but in Paris the conference was a sideshow. Pan-African leader Kwame Nkrumah, the first president and the first prime minister of Ghana, later recalled that for European leaders "the very idea of Pan-Africanism was so strange that it seemed unreal and yet at the same time perhaps potentially dangerous."[152]

Refounding the Pan-African Congress was half of Du Bois's agenda in France; the other half was to gather information on how the American military treated its black soldiers. The electrifying May 1919 issue of *Crisis* contained his findings. Only one black division (the Ninety-second) had received its full complement of personnel and support, and white officers grossly exaggerated disciplinary problems in it, inflating five rape convictions to thirty. Racist treatment was the norm, the worst white officers were assigned to black units, and the high command denigrated black soldiers that were sent into fights lacking maps, grenade launchers, or signal flares. Arbitrary transfers and arbitrary courts-martial were rampant. By the time Du Bois got to France, there were hardly any African American officers left from New York's three National Guard units, as all were sent home as quickly as possible. Du Bois summarized: "First, was the effort to get rid of Negro officers; second, the effort to discredit Negro soldiers; third, the effort to spread race prejudice in France; and fourth, the effort to keep Negroes out of the Regular Army." Moton, Du Bois noted, was supposed to be on the case, but Moton looked the other way, enjoying the afterglow of Washington's prestige. Emmett Scott was supposed to be on the case, too, writing an official report commissioned by the government. Scott's report was cautious, methodical, and generally positive. Du Bois charged that Scott whitewashed things that he must have discovered: "If Mr. Scott did not know, why did he not find out? If he did know, what did he do about it?"[153]

The *Crisis* zoomed to over one hundred thousand subscribers during this period, setting off an impassioned controversy in the black press over Du Bois's attack on Scott. Some NAACP stalwarts sided with Scott, fearing that Du Bois put the NAACP in jeopardy by blasting the military so aggressively. Du Bois took no interest in protecting his right flank. His "Close Ranks" cheerleading for the war had battered his image, emboldening a new generation of critics to condemn him as a sellout. Du Bois returned from France in a fighting spirit, still defending the logic of "Close Ranks," but vowing to move forward as a radical double-minded American and Pan-African:

> This is the fatherland for which we fought! But it is *our* fatherland. It was right for us to fight again. The faults of *our* country are *our* faults. Under similar circumstances, we would fight again. But by the God of heaven, we are cowards and jackasses if now that the war is over, we do not marshal every ounce of our brain and brawn to fight a sterner, longer, more unending battle against the forces of hell in our own land.
> We return.
> We return from fighting.
> We return fighting.
> Make way for Democracy! We saved it in France, and by the Great Jehovah, we will save it in the United States of America, or know the reason why.[154]

A hellish racial backlash was about to explode when Du Bois returned to New York in April 1919. Northern cities seethed from failing to accommodate the Great Migration and America's recent foreign immigrants. Southern newspapers warned returning black soldiers that expectations of decent treatment would be handled swiftly. Labor strikes across the country shut down shipyards, coal mines, and steel factories. A national panic over American Bolshevism ensued. The U.S. government waged a vicious crackdown on leftists. The "Red Summer" of 1919 racked up a frightening toll. Race riots broke out in over twenty cities, fourteen black Americans were burned in public, and over sixty were lynched. Du Bois declared that blacks needed to defend themselves against racist violence: "When the armed lynchers gather, we too must gather armed." South Carolina congressman James F. Byrnes, a Tillman protégé on his way to eminence as a U.S. senator, U.S. Supreme Court justice, U.S. secretary of state, and South Carolina governor, was one of several southern congressional representatives to demand that Du Bois be prosecuted under the espionage act. Byrnes charged that Du Bois appealed to the prejudices of Afro-Americans, "which can have no other result than to incite them to deeds of violence." Du Bois replied that Byrnes was in Congress illegally because people like him had taken away the right of blacks to vote in South Carolina.[155]

There was never a time during Du Bois's twenty-five-year association with the NAACP that he did not scare or rankle key board members, white and black. The conflict between operating a free-spirited literary magazine and being the voice of a civil rights organization was never resolved. As a board member and a paid employee, Du Bois personified the conflict uniquely. Du Bois had a more global idea of racial advocacy than most members of the NAACP and most readers of *Crisis*. He had just enough allies on this issue and others to get his way in the magazine, but the NAACP board did not sign up for Socialism or Pan-African ideology, and Du Bois's fiery editorials often condemned the very people that the NAACP tried to recruit as allies.

Du Bois got his way in the magazine because his success had lifted the NAACP in the first place and he had four staunch white allies when he needed them—Ovington, Russell, Walling, and Spingarn. He told himself that the board was inevitably conservative, representing capital and investment, while his job was to run an independent magazine that led a liberal organization to radical reform. That rationale gave him ten years of freedom as *Crisis* climbed to a hundred thousand subscribers and paid his salary. Then the magazine got a second decade of glory by launching the Harlem Renaissance, as Du Bois worked under Johnson and fostered a group of artists that compelled recognition, though subscriptions fell off sharply.

Four developments, all of them budding as American troops came home from the war, determined how Du Bois spent the 1920s. One was the reactionary backlash in American politics. Another was the emergence of a black Socialist tradition that attacked Du Bois from the left and helped to pull him in its direction. The third development was the Garvey phenomenon—a massive explosion of populist black consciousness centered on a charismatic Jamaican that morphed into a back-to-Africa movement. Fourth was the Harlem Renaissance of the "New Negro," a cultural flowering willed into being by the Talented Tenth. All were concerns or movements that diminished the black church as a source of resistance and hope, though Reverdy Ransom and Mordecai Johnson said that the New Negro movement was a cultural version of the black social gospel.

The theologians of the black social gospel had to make a case that the church was still relevant to the struggle for civil rights and social justice, even as this struggle increasingly employed ideological, political, and cultural modes of discourse that marginalized Christianity. They worried that the poor migrant newcomers were becoming a permanent underclass that had no faith in God or America. They worried that black intellectuals were losing faith in God. They implored churchgoers not to rest content with otherworldly or anti-intellectual religion. The struggle for justice would go nowhere if it spurned the faith of ordinary churchgoers in the religion of Jesus. Du Bois's religiosity was ambiguous, the black social gospelers acknowledged, but he spoke the language of spiritual prophecy and he emphatically embraced the religion of Christ, describing Jesus as "a man who despised the prejudices of his time; who associated with and loved people to whom his fellow countrymen would disdain even to speak: who discovered among the lowest and meekest the loftiest and sweetest souls and who laid it down as a guiding rule of life to 'Do unto others even as you would that others would do unto you.'"[156]

That was exactly what the black social gospelers preached as the touchstone of good religion. They were gospel-centered theological progressives committed to the inward and outward flourishing of God's kingdom. Du Bois did not side with them merely for political reasons, a posture he accused Carter Woodson of taking. Woodson's pioneering *History of the Negro Church* (1921) contrasted the social gospel wing of the black church to its conservative majority that opposed protest activism. Du Bois ripped Woodson for missing the religious point of black religion: "Everything is there except the church; except the inner spirit and motive of that marvelous faith and unreason which made a million black folk on the shores of exile dance and scream and shout the Sorrow Song; which raised from smoking entrails the witch-figure of that old black preacher, whose trembling hands built a spiritual State within a State, guarded and groomed it and made it spawn a new freedom for a world-old race, made it build and guide, shelter and teach, lead and train a people." Du Bois urged that black progressive religion lacking much religion would be no more saving than the conservative black churches Woodson criticized. It would be a disaster to strip prophetic religion merely to its politics: "The Negro church is the mighty central fact of American Negro History. It is independent, unique, and Negro through and through, despite all imitation. It is a great astonishing, a contradictory social triumph with its feet in the African jungle and its head in Heaven."[157]

Du Bois stopped defending the black church a few years after he stopped working for the NAACP. But his early and middle career writings about the black church helped three generations of church leaders imagine a liberating and transformative church. Moreover, he never stopped speaking the language of spiritual prophecy—invoking and mobilizing the virtues of holiness, prophetic opposition to injustice, and sacrifice. In his early career he put it idealistically and in his later career he put it in the hard-edged language of radical Socialism. But he always said that good religion had work to do in the world, it inspired and mobilized the spirit of love, and this spirit enabled genuinely religious people to sacrifice their well-being for the sake of others: "The true joy of living dwells in that Higher Life, that sitting above both sunshine and shadows, that values them at their worth and strives to wind them to his will. In that higher life, my friends, there are three things: Work, and Love and Sacrifice—these three—but the greatest of these is Sacrifice." Du Bois rightly viewed his work as a religious calling in the sense that mattered. And he inspired ministers and lay activists who heard the gospel of social justice through him.[158]

5

New Abolition Bishops

The new abolitionists launched a national civil rights organization that did not sputter and fail like the previous ones. They identified the new abolition with the struggle against lynching and the rights of the battered Fourteenth and Fifteenth Amendments. They supported women's suffrage while disagreeing about the priority they should give to fixing the Fifteenth Amendment's failure to enfranchise women. Some of them conceived the new abolition as a global struggle for the liberation of all people of color. All of them sought to build up the small middle-class activist groups that composed the civil rights community.

But small groups of middle-class activists were not going to transform U.S. American society by themselves. To be serious about abolishing racial caste, the new abolitionists had to reach deep into religious communities through which millions of Americans made moral and spiritual sense of their lives. Two Methodist trailblazers, Reverdy Ransom and Alexander Walters, stood out in this cause, legitimizing the social gospel in the AME and AME Zion churches. It helped that both became bishops, but they took strikingly different paths to the episcopacy and toward legitimizing social justice religion.

Ransom was the Du Bois figure in black social Christianity, clearing a path for something new and expounding it brilliantly. But his AME ministerial colleagues kicked him out of Chicago and Boston for doing so, thwarting his efforts in the two cities that seemed best suited for black social gospel ministry. Ransom had to create his own constituency to legitimize the social gospel and himself in his denomination. Walters, by contrast, was the blessed child of his denomination, picked for stardom, nurtured unfailingly along the way, and rewarded early, all of which he repaid by devoting himself to the church.

Politically, Ransom and Walters helped to break the Republican monopoly on black church loyalties, though with customary differences. Ransom pushed for democratic Socialism and militant abolition politics, and no one ever called him a smooth operator. Walters helped to redefine the black Christian political mainstream by playing leadership roles in the Afro-American Council, World Society of Christian Endeavor, Negro American Political League, National Colored Democratic League, and NAACP. Ransom, characteristically, had to fight to be heard in the Afro-American Council and NAACP, while Walters led the Afro-American Council and was a founding vice president of the NAACP. Both, however, were strong, self-confident, eloquent types, brimming with race pride and dignity, and gifted at holding a crowd. Together and differently they challenged the black church to ramp up its commitment to making society a subject of redemption.

BECOMING REVERDY RANSOM

Reverdy Cassius Ransom was deeply aware that he was not a self-made success; thus he titled his autobiography *The Pilgrimage of Harriet Ransom's Son* (1949). He was born in January 1861 in Flushing, Ohio, the only child of a powerful, loving woman who assured him that he was "let down from the skies." Ransom never mentioned his father, although according to family tradition he knew that his father was black, and Reverdy resented that people assumed otherwise from his red hair. A local member of Congress, John A. Bingham, paid Ransom's mother, Harriet Johnson, five dollars in gold for the right to name her son after two politicians, Reverdy Johnson of Maryland (a prominent lawyer and subsequent Senate defender of President Andrew Johnson) and Cassius Marcellus Clay of Kentucky (an antislavery Whig and later Republican who served in the 1860s as minister to Russia). Ransom got his surname from the man who eventually married Harriet, George Warner Ransom, although Reverdy Ransom may have acquired the name before his mother married. During the Civil War he lived with his mother and maternal grandmother, Lucinda Williams, in the latter's two-room log house and occasionally saw Union soldiers crossing through Ohio.[1]

In 1865 Harriet left her mother's house to work as a domestic servant in Washington, Ohio, placing Reverdy with George Ransom's parents, who owned a farm nearby. For Reverdy Ransom it was a difficult transition. Harriet paid the Ransoms to care for him; there were numerous Ransom children in the house, who did not welcome him; he was constantly hungry and plagued with scary voices in his head; and George Ransom's sister treated him badly, calling him "that little red-headed devil." At night Reverdy joined his mother in the unheated attic of a Washington merchant, one of the homes in which she worked. He dreaded the cold attic and the Ransom household; at the same time, he was deeply influenced by the Ransoms, his mother's religion, and his mother's white employers. Harriet and the Ransom family were active members of the AME Church, which was organized in Ohio in the 1820s and surged with the migration of blacks to Ohio after the Civil War. In later life Reverdy expressed gratitude for the model of hard work and faithful belief that the Ransom family had given him, though his stepfather was unconverted during Ransom's childhood. Harriet's employers were prosperous, educated, proslavery northern Democrats who took for granted that their children would go to college. In the early 1860s only five states permitted working-class black males to vote, and all were in New England, where only 4 percent of the nation's free blacks lived. Ohio, part of the Old Northwest territory, was hostile terrain for Afro-Americans, especially the newcomers. Yet Ohio was a magnet for black migration, mostly for geographical and economic reasons. From her employers Harriet got her ideas about how her son should speak and carry himself, and she vowed that he would go to college.[2]

Even with a determined mother, Ransom was a long shot to make it to college. In 1869 Harriet moved to nearby Cambridge, a town of twenty-five hundred with approximately three hundred African Americans. Some were former slaves or children of former slaves; others were descendants of rural Ohio blacks of the antebellum period. Nearly all scraped out a subsistence living. Ransom attended a segregated school in the local AME church, where a white man taught all classes and made little attempt to keep order. Ransom was fascinated by history and geography, but heard the same lessons year after year. When Ransom was thirteen Harriet demanded that he be allowed to attend the public school. "I can still see the finger of Professor McBurney pointing and waving while he told my mother: 'You must take your child right down there to the colored school where he belongs, we cannot admit him here." Thus Ransom returned for more of the same, while yearning for a Latin textbook. Harriet performed laundry services in exchange for private tutorial lessons for Ransom, and he worked as a janitor in exchange for algebra lessons. He later recalled, "There was almost no high aspiration among the colored youth of our community and nothing to inspire it. Few books and papers were available. The Church was the social centre of our life."[3]

Ransom's friends derided him for aspiring to college. Often he attended the local Court of Common Pleas, where he watched lawyers interrogate witnesses and make legal arguments. Ransom studied the lawyers intently and read voraciously: "I was almost daily in the homes of our most cultured and wealthy white people, for whom my mother worked. I took note of their customs, manners, and conversation even to the form of their words and the modulation of their voices. I was ever trying to explain and reconcile their world to the one in which I lived among my own people." Why was there such a chasm between the black and white Americas? Why was he prohibited from attending public schools? Why were black people poor? Harriet replied that ignorance was almost always the answer; the solution was to be educated. Her dream for him centered on Wilberforce University. Ransom took a summer course to qualify and was admitted to Wilberforce in 1881. But in the spring of 1881 Harriet Ransom had to overcome two crises to get her son to college.[4]

Her savings turned out to be less than needed; Harriet Ransom responded by selling the family cow and mortgaging her house. The bigger crisis was that Reverdy impulsively married Leanna Watkins in February and she became pregnant. Many years later he shuddered at the memory: "It is a strange caprice of fate that most people, usually in youth, or at the threshold of their career, have an experience, or tragedy, that puts a mark upon the heart, mind, or spirit, that one carries through life. In all such lives there is a sealed room, the privacy of which no one is permitted to tarry long upon the threshold of its poignant memories." His friends had sex without getting married. He had religious scruples against doing that, so he got married: "We lived in a community of free morals. We were both in our teens. She was one of the finest and the best among us. She was comely to look upon, added to this, the correctness of her life and conduct caused her to stand apart from most all of the other girls in her group." Undaunted, Harriet Ransom declared that even teenaged fatherhood would not stand between her son and a college education. For eight years she took charge of the next George Ransom, named after her husband, while Reverdy headed for Wilberforce University.[5]

Ransom enrolled at Wilberforce the year after Turner was elected bishop; thus he got there just as the AME Church in the South embarked on its binge of school launchings and Payne railed against all of it. In 1852 the Cincinnati Conference of the Methodist Episcopal Church had founded the university and village of Wilberforce in honor of British abolitionist William Wilberforce. The village's original name was Tawawa Springs, as Native Americans appreciated its health-giving waters. Early nineteenth-century planters liked the springs, too. They summered in Tawawa Springs, accompanied by their concubines and children, at a 350-room resort hotel. A bit later, after the Panic of 1837 and Ohio abolitionism killed off the hotel, the planter class used it as a university for its biracial children. Fugitive slaves, free blacks, and the racially mixed families of slave owners settled the community in the 1830s and 1840s; the Northern

Methodists incorporated the university in 1856; and the school closed in 1862 as a casualty of the Civil War. The following year Bishop Payne, who had served on Wilberforce's board of trustees, bought the university for ten thousand dollars. Payne refounded the school as an African Methodist Episcopal Church institution; in 1891 it spawned a seminary, Payne Theological Seminary.[6]

Bishop Payne, though newly embattled in the denomination, dominated the AME Church in the North and shaped Wilberforce firmly in his image. Wilberforce was a "praying school" that stressed learning, service to one's race and nation, and above all, Godly living. It was thoroughly middle-class and Afro-Saxonist, holding compulsory chapel services twice per day. Two AME bishops—Payne and J. A. Shorter—lived at Wilberforce, reinforcing the school's earnest piety. Benjamin Arnett lived there, too, before his elevation to the episcopacy in 1888. Payne inveighed against emotionalism, which he called "an incurable religious disease" for "the most stupid and headstrong." He loathed the camp-meeting ring shout, which he called "most ridiculous and heathenish," and the spirituals, which he called "cornfield ditties." He insisted that holy living was unfailingly rational, sober, and devout; he censured all perceived affronts to his Episcopal authority; he was deeply committed to sustaining Wilberforce's status as the intellectual center of the AME Church; and he took pride in Wilberforce's commitment to racial integration. Wilberforce practiced what it preached, boasting that its predominantly black male faculty included three white female professors and an interracial marriage of two beloved professors, William S. Scarborough and S. C. Scarborough. Academically, however, Wilberforce disappointed Ransom; he shook his head at the same mediocrity that later distressed Du Bois. The largest of the school's six departments was the department for remedial education. Richard R. Wright Jr. later noted that Wilberforce was "little more than a high school" in the late nineteenth century. But Ransom appreciated that it preached racial equality: "Racial self-confidence, self-respect, dignity, honor, the ambition to achieve in every line of endeavor, were taught and encouraged."[7]

In this environment he belatedly joined the church. As a youth Ransom had enjoyed watching others come forward to be saved, especially when mourners wailed and rolled on the floor, and he felt the call to follow Jesus. But the "mourner's bench" was not for him; if he had to become the object of a frenzied spectacle to join the church, he could wait. Wilberforce provided the quiet, orderly religion he needed to convert. As a freshman Ransom joined the church; as a sophomore he transferred to Oberlin College after winning a scholarship there. Scarborough told Ransom that Oberlin was an outstanding school that had treated him well during his student days in the late 1860s. That was enough to convince Ransom, who wanted a rigorous education with a "broader and more liberal" curriculum. However, Oberlin's social climate did not live up to its abolitionist reputation. Black students were excluded from the college's social life, and a new regulation segregating African American females was instituted in the women's dining hall. Ransom helped to organize a protest against the latter policy, gave a speech against it, and promptly lost his scholarship by faculty action. That sent him back to Wilberforce, cutting him deeply; a few years later he wrote an upbeat memoir of his college days that made no mention of his year at Oberlin.[8]

In a chastened and appreciative mood, Ransom made the best of being at Wilberforce. On his first try he had worried that "a Faculty composed of colored men" did not compare to the better white schools. Now he was grateful that Wilberforce practiced racial equality and wanted him. On his first try he had chafed at the school's regimented social relations. Males and females were not permitted to speak to each other on campus or walk together; games and dancing were forbidden; meetings between males and females were permitted once per month, in chaperoned "socials" lasting two hours; and Ransom felt estranged from his uneducated bride. None of that improved for him on his second try. He chafed for two more years at Wilberforce, yet made a home there. At Oberlin Ransom felt called to ministry; at Wilberforce he decided to complete his college and theological education at the same time. Always short of money, Ransom vowed not to stay in school any longer than necessary.[9]

He had two delicate problems, however, in training for the ministry. One was his troubled marriage. Ransom downplayed that he was married, and he divorced Watkins shortly after graduating from Wilberforce. The other problem was his theological liberalism, the origin of which he never explained. Ransom may have heard about liberal theology at Oberlin, but Oberlin was militantly orthodox in the 1880s, having acquired the old Andover Seminary journal *Bibliotheca Sacra* as a forum for fighting off liberal theology. Perhaps a Wilberforce or Oberlin teacher piqued Ransom's curiosity by criticizing liberal theologians. Perhaps he read Horace Bushnell or a Unitarian theologian on his own. In any case, as Ransom later recounted, he spent much of his time at Wilberforce concealing his beliefs from theologian T. H. Jackson, whose conservatism was rigid and emphatic. Jackson condemned everything smacking of heresy or doctrinal temporizing. For Ransom, that created intellectual, moral, and vocational problems. He rejected Trinitarian doctrine, accepted evolutionary theory, and reasoned that all doctrines were "man-made," not divine. Ransom had a conflicted conscience about concealing his liberal views, and thus he doubted whether he belonged in the ministry.[10]

In his junior year he was licensed to preach, which gave Ransom the opportunity to hone his speaking skills. In his senior year he served a church in nearby Selma, Ohio, where he courted his second wife, Emma Connor; by then Ransom was determined to see if a theological liberal could make it in the AME ministry. Poetically he wrote to himself that he would not "sneak" deceitfully into God's temple for the sake of winning fame or acclaim: "I'd rather dwell in poverty obscure / and all the pangs of poverty endure / than for the honors which the Church can give / through life a timorous hypocrite to live." His 1886 graduating class numbered eight men and one woman. Ransom lamented for years afterward that most Wilberforce students did not make it to graduation. His stepfather, not yet a Christian, was appalled that Ransom wasted his education on the ministry; George Ransom railed that educated black men had no business begging their living off poor blacks. Harriet Ransom, on the other hand, made a memorable scene at her son's graduation. Every member of the graduating class delivered an oration or essay. Ransom gave an oration on "Divine and Civil Law," contending that Afro-Americans, having fought to save the Union from disintegration, deserved equal treatment under the law, not the current regime of discrimination. His speech was wildly applauded. Harriet Ransom, sobbing with joy, forced her way onto the stage to embrace her son. A reporter wrote that the scene evoked tears throughout the crowd. For the rest of his life Ransom remarked that he and his mother graduated together: "She saw the fruit of her sacrifices, the fulfillment of her hopes, and with characteristic impulsiveness gave expression to the happiness that thrilled her."[11]

Ransom struggled for years with a troubled conscience about pretending to be theologically conservative; nonetheless, he entered the ministry as a disciple of Payne. In 1886, when Ransom took his first pastorate, Payne had been a bishop for thirty-four years. For Payne, the cause of keeping African Methodism ascetic and impeccably orthodox was a consuming passion. Ransom's education and early ministry coincided with Payne's years of embattlement with Turner and Cain, the rise of southern power in the denomination, the explosion of southern AME schools, and the rise of liberal theology as a movement in American churches. Payne thought that impious southern rebellion was his biggest problem in the denomination. He did not see liberal theology coming through one of his own protégés.[12]

Bishop J. P. Campbell assigned Ransom to a tiny congregation of thirteen members, most of them elderly, in Altoona, Pennsylvania, and another congregation of seven women, five of them widows, in Hollidaysburg. Ransom's next assignment was a mission parish in Allegheny City, Pennsylvania, that had five members. He protested to Payne, who chastised him: "Begone! Leave my

presence! There are people there!" Ransom found hundreds of people there,
"living in wretched tenements in the alleys, and in shanty boats along the river
front." Newly married, he and Emma visited the tenements and boats daily,
building up his church. He bought a house in a white neighborhood, which the
neighbors promptly stoned, nearly hitting his infant son Reverdy Junior. The
AME Church routinely assigned young pastors to impossible posts like
Allegheny City; Ransom bitterly objected that it was wasteful and degrading to
send the church's most promising ministers to places that crushed their spirit.
Sixty years later he was still complaining: "There can be no virtue in being
hungry, or in being deprived of the ordinary comforts of life."[13]

Ransom used his connections to Payne and Wilberforce to get on a better
career track. In April 1890 he published a sharp attack on C. S. Smith, director
of the AME Sunday School Union, for using a revised version of the Apostles'
Creed. Smith eliminated the phrase about Christ's descent into hell; Ransom
acidly replied that it was a very serious thing for a church functionary to break
the "golden chain of faith" just because he did not believe some part of the
church's creed. Invoking Princeton theologian A. A. Hodge, Ransom charged
that Smith's revision was a "dreadful violation" of Christian solidarity that led to
mysticism and pantheism. He also took Payne's side in the controversy over
AME colleges, contending that the AME had too many, which diminished
Wilberforce, and he wrote a glowing memoir of his Wilberforce days, describing
the school as the pride and intellectual showcase of the denomination. In
September 1890 Payne rewarded him with an attractive parish in Springfield,
Ohio. Payne told Ransom that North Street Church had "carpets on the floor,
cushioned pews, stained glass windows, and a marble pulpit." On the other
hand, the bishop dolefully cautioned, Ransom's eventual successor would
undoubtedly "mar or destroy all you have been able to build up."[14]

Ransom's gratitude to Wilberforce was genuine, although it masked misgivings that he freely expressed in later years, and he later stressed that his private
theological views were liberal from the start. He gave three years to Springfield,
acquired a reputation as an outstanding preacher, and attended the World's
Parliament of Religion in Chicago, which was held in connection with the
Columbian Exposition of 1893. The parliament and exposition both impressed
him as momentous signs of modern progress. Taking pride that Arnett spoke at
the parliament, Ransom enthused that it was a good thing for the world's religions to grow in mutual respect and understanding. He also attended lectures by
Josiah Strong and Washington Gladden and was introduced to Ida Wells. Later
that year, after Ransom had been promoted to St. John Church in Cleveland, he
enthused that African Americans shared in the progress of American civilization.

"In these closing years of the nineteenth century, 'progress' is a word upon every tongue," he observed. "Men of every rank and calling conjure with this word." American science, invention, manufacture, statecraft, art, literature, and religion were flourishing. But Ransom cautioned that the true mark of progress was spiritual renewal, not growth in machines or products. It was Martin Luther defying the Catholic hierarchy, Richard Allen taking a "manly stand for manhood Christianity," and Abraham Lincoln issuing the Emancipation Proclamation. Black Americans, Ransom observed, profoundly appreciated the church, school, and home—the pillars of high civilization. Wherever blacks moved, they promptly built churches. Despite being deprived of education, they made greater efforts to become literate than any people in history. Despite having their families ripped apart by slavery, they built new families as circles of virtue. All of this counted in the tally of American progress, but the year 1893 also witnessed "no abatement of the barbarities" that African Americans suffered at the hands of white Americans. The United States was still a nation in which innocent blacks were lynched by racist mobs. Ransom allowed that not all Afro-Americans were innocent; true criminals of every race had to be punished: "But for these lynchings and burnings there can be no excuse, for the law is on the side of the lynchers; the courts, juries, militia are in their hands."[15]

He warned that America could not be truly civilized and savagely terrorize blacks at the same time: "This epidemic of mob violence, of outrage, and crime is making deep inroads upon the nation's constitutional authority and moral strength." It was shameful that "the southern lyncher, backed by public senti-ment, has no need to seek cover for his crimes." Northern newspapers reported lynchings with rarely a word of condemnation. Southern authors rationalized racist murder by depicting blacks as too dangerous and inhuman to be dealt with by mere law; thus the lynchers were praised as saviors of civilization. Ransom observed that many Afro-Americans, being marked for denigration and abuse, had lost all hope: "The field of opportunity is largely closed against us." Others fantasized about returning to Africa. America was not that hopeless, he urged. African Americans were Americans, and they needed to be courageous: "The man or the race who falters and retreats because the door of opportunity and endeavor is slammed in his face is unworthy of the goal he seeks. . . . Let the Negro continue to act the brave, the manly part."[16]

Very few ministers talked like that in the 1890s, or supported Wells when she did so. Ransom also had a pastoral voice, preaching the gospel of clean, ethical, productive living and admonishing black youths to spurn the indulgences of white youths: "The white boys and girls of this country have standing at their backs centuries of glorious achievements, and if they stop to play a little by the way, or if they stray from the way and give themselves to vices and follies, they have a foothold in the earth that you don't possess." White youths, he explained, could afford to be frivolous, because they had power. Their fathers owned the banks and manufacturing companies. They stood to inherit the mansions on Cleveland's Euclid Avenue and Prospect Street, where John D. Rockefeller, Henry Payne, and other Standard Oil millionaires lived.[17]

Ministering to the city's largest black congregation, Ransom despaired of fathers who gambled and mothers who drank. He noted that some mothers dispatched their children to buy alcohol: "No matter what excuse you frame for a woman that sends her child to a saloon, I say there is something the matter with the mother-heart in that woman." That came from a deep wellspring of feeling and memory. Ransom adored his mother and was grateful to her, but every woman in his family drank whiskey and dispatched children to obtain it: "Every two or three days, they would give us children ten or fifteen cents and a little tin bucket and send us for whiskey. Every morning before prayers and breakfast, they each drank a toddy and gave some to all the children." Though Ransom preached blistering sermons against vice, he was tender with individuals who struggled with sexual moral lapses or alcoholism. The memory of his own first marriage embarrassed him, and he struggled with alcoholism. Near the end of his life he confessed with typical honesty that his alcoholism had been "a serious handicap to my reputation, my usefulness, and my spiritual power."[18]

With echoes of Crummell, Ransom preached Du Bois–like romantic racialism before Du Bois burst into view. Race, Ransom asserted, whatever it was in itself, spilled into nationality and endowed given groups with particular traits or characteristics. In 1894 he preached on "Race Soil," urging the youth of St. John Church to take advantage of their disadvantages. Ransom argued that Jews, Greeks, Romans, and other "races" had made their distinct contributions to the world and were now either gone or exhausted. Black people, however, were just beginning to make their mark. The natural gifts of the black race were beginning to flourish in an explosion of racial development and productivity: "We believe that with his natural music talent, the Negro will cause sweeter harmonies and prettier melodies to waft in the air than ever enraptured the human soul. Eloquent of speech, he will plead the cause of God and the welfare of mankind with such tones of power that neither rostrum nor the forum ever heard. His deep emotional nature will be the foe of tyranny and oppression and as a religious vehicle will carry the triumph of the King of Kings into the seats of pride and power, and over the dark and barren regions of the globe." Two years later, after he had moved to Chicago, Ransom put it in global terms, urging that the black race in Africa, the West Indies, and North America shared a common history of denigration and abuse and a common destiny of lifting the world to a higher spiritual plane.[19]

Ransom thus believed in Pan-African racialism before Du Bois wrote about it, and he became a Socialist long before Du Bois did, converting during his ministry in Cleveland, where the city's class divisions drove him to think about political economy and the relation of economic forces to racial privilege. In this area Ransom took a distinctive path, one influenced by his attraction to national politics and to George Herron's Christian Socialism. Herron's popular books of the 1890s called Americans to replace capitalist greed and inequality with Socialist equality. Ransom absorbed Herron's writings and imagined a different kind of political ministry than the black church model of his mentor, Arnett.[20]

Payne avoided politics and racial justice activism, concentrating entirely on building up the AME Church. Arnett, however, was deeply involved in Republican Party politics. He served one term in the Ohio legislature (1885–1887), playing a key role in abolishing the state's Black Codes. The Ohio Civil Rights Act of 1886 abolished school segregation and boosted Arnett's political influence two years before his elevation to the AME episcopacy. Arnett cultivated close ties with Ohio Republican senator Mark Hanna and his protégé, Ohio governor William McKinley. For Arnett, political activism was mainly about patronage. Hanna was good for black patronage in the North and a bulwark of lily-white reaction in the South, which Arnett tolerated, which yielded for him a plum assignment as chaplain of the Republican National Convention of 1896 in St. Louis.

Though Ransom was schooled in the Payne critique of political religion, it impressed him that Arnett got a free pass to practice a political ministry. Arnett took a fatherly interest in Ransom, the two became friends, and Arnett's ministry legitimized Ransom's political interests, providing cover for him. Ransom, however, took little interest in machine politics or patronage. For him, political ministry centered on the social justice interests of African Americans, especially in electoral politics, and the best politics combined Socialism and civil rights. Winning favors from establishment politicians was pedestrian by comparison. In Cleveland Ransom formed a local chapter of the Anti-Lynching League, serving as its president. In 1896 Arnett placed him in the best city for that kind of ministry, Chicago, giving Ransom a choice between a relatively affluent parish on Wabash Avenue, Quinn Chapel, and a large parish west of State Street, Bethel Church. Ransom chose Bethel, where Ida Wells-Barnett, newly married to Ferdinand Lee Barnett Jr., was a member.[21]

THE SOCIAL GOSPEL IN QUESTION

When Ransom got to Bethel Church in 1896 he drew crowds that overflowed the sanctuary's seating capacity of nine hundred. At first he credited his scintillating preaching, but then noticed that other black churches were overflowing, too. The migration surge from the South had begun, although the starting point for when it became "great" is usually assigned to a year between 1910 and 1915. To Ransom, the surge of migrants seemed immense already by the late 1890s. Black ministers in the South cited Booker Washington on this supposedly baleful development, warning that migrants would be overwhelmed by the North's competitive harshness and corrupting urbanity. Many northern ministers openly agreed and others muttered about it. From the beginning Ransom countered that blacks were compelled to flee white southern hostility and that they had greater opportunities in the North. At the same time, he recognized that the flood of migrants created new social challenges for the churches and cities, necessitating a social ethical response. The churches had to create social welfare programs and acquire the skills to run them. He later recalled: "The number of these people increased so rapidly that the colored clergymen of the city were bewildered. They were unprepared by training, experience and vision, to cope with the moral, social and economic conditions so suddenly thrust upon them."[22]

Ransom's first Thanksgiving sermon in Chicago was a stem-winder titled "The Industrial and Social Conditions of the Negro." His text was Isaiah 9:3: "Thou hast multiplied the nation, and not increased the joy." This text applied directly to black Americans, who lost ground as the nation expanded stupendously. Ransom observed that Afro-Americans played important roles in building the American nation, during and after slavery. It was only recently, with the scourge of lynching and Jim Crow, that African Americans lost their foothold in the economy. Until recently, blacks dominated the barbershop business, but now they were "reduced to blacking boots." They dominated the laundry business but failed to organize, so immigrant whites took over the laundry business. They used to control the catering business but lost that too, and now they were losing their working-class jobs in the hotels and factories. Even in the railroad companies, Ransom observed, "the only job they can get now is as porters."[23]

It was extremely difficult, Ransom acknowledged, to keep knocking on doors after white America slammed the door in one's face "a good many times." All he could do was encourage his congregants to be brave, to strive for excellence, and to persevere, in the manner of Ida Wells-Barnett. "During all these years, only one voice has been raised until two continents were compelled to hear," he said. Wells-Barnett doubled her trouble by banging defiantly on closed doors. She made numerous black enemies by doing so, which made her all the more exemplary: "When a voice stands out and pleads, some, because it is not their voice, some because they are not getting the glory, a fat political job, and don't want to hurt the feelings of the powers that be, will sink the interest of the race for their own personal gain and personal safety." Ransom exhorted his congregants not to give up on America, despite being oppressed by white Americans and sold out by unworthy black American leaders, because America was still their best chance, "the grandest field for action."[24]

At Bethel Church Ransom organized a Men's Sunday Club and took on the trip-wire issue of interracial relationships. The Sunday Club met weekly to discuss moral and social issues, swelling to over 500 members; it became the prototype for AME Sunday Forums across the nation. Ransom opened the church to the Manassa Society of Chicago, an organization of biracial married couples, which grew to include over 350 couples. During his eight years in Chicago, the first four of which he spent at Bethel Church, Ransom wedded 104 black men to white women and 3 white men to black women. The plantation cast a long shadow over these weddings; sometimes Ransom acknowledged it. The union of black women to white men evoked deeper traumatic memories than the union of black men to white women. On the other hand, even the suggestion of black men uniting with white women sent much of America into paroxysms of loathing and hysteria.

Ransom had this ministry pretty much to himself among Chicago's churches. The only other Chicago congregations that welcomed interracial couples were Roman Catholic. Ransom stressed that in his experience, the white women who married black men were not immoral types, contrary to popular opinion. They were "good hard-working women" who worked as maids, waitresses, clerks, and secretaries at places of employment where they formed relationships with black coworkers. Most of these couples, Ransom noted, bought their own homes and were upstanding citizens. Since they were "thrown back upon themselves," they were strongly predisposed to save their money and provide for their children. Many had children who went to college and became professionals, although some tried to pass for white, sadly. Ransom took particular pride in this aspect of his ministry, delighting at the success of the interracial couples he helped. His romantic idealism usually triumphed when he counseled engaged interracial couples about what they would be up against.[25]

When Ransom moved to Chicago, the lack of a national civil rights organization frustrated and appalled him. How could it be that the Afro-American

League fizzled out for lack of a following at the very moment that racial hysteria exploded in America? Why were black Americans rolling over for a black leader they did not select? A bit later, after McKinley was elected president and Walters founded the Afro-American Council, what were blacks to say about a Republican president who did nothing for them? What could be done to ensure that the newly founded Afro-American Council did not lapse into Bookerism?

Ransom pressed for militant answers. Having supported McKinley as governor of Ohio and benefited from Arnett's favor, Ransom cheered when McKinley was elected president in 1896. He soon gave up believing, however, that African Americans had a friend in the White House. In August 1899, Washington told the National Association of Colored Women convention in Chicago that the "Negro problem" could be solved only in the South, and by education. The day after the NACW convention ended, the Afro-American Council convened at Bethel Church. Fifty-three delegates from thirty-seven states attended. Washington did not attend, as Fortune advised him to avoid any entanglement in embarrassing things that might be said. Instead Washington dispatched Emmett Scott to protect his interests at the convention, he agreed to have Margaret Washington make a speech, and he summoned Walters to a meeting in his hotel room, where he admonished Walters to restrain the group's militant wing.[26]

Ransom was the leader of the militant wing. He probably learned directly from Walters what Washington had said to him, although Ransom's subsequent account of this incident mistakenly conflated events from two different conventions. Whether or not he heard it straight from Walters, Ransom was offended that Washington tried to control the convention without bothering to attend it. Insult was added to injury when the Washington camp canceled Margaret Washington's speech at the last minute. Ransom, freshly appointed as a council vice president, unleashed a tirade, urging the group to cancel Washington's membership: "I know of no man who has received more advertising from his connection with the Negro race than has Booker T. Washington. He has posed as the leader of the colored people and the Moses who was to lead his people out of the wilderness. Yet he has hung around the outskirts of this council casting aspersions and contempt on its proceedings. He has refused to come inside. He sat in his room at the Palmer House and sent for our president to wait upon him. No such man ought to claim to be our leader. We want the country to know he is nothing to us. We hold him in contempt."[27]

That was nowhere near the mainstream view of this group. Editorial condemnation rained down on Ransom for denigrating the Moses of black America. Walters defended Washington's absence, reasoning that Washington was an intermediary between the races, not the leader of an activist organization. Du Bois admonished Ransom for misrepresenting the group's diverse views with "ill-timed and foolish" words. Washington was "one of the greatest men of our race," Du Bois declared. Ransom backed down, declaring that he respected Washington and should not have spoken so harshly. He apologized to Washington, praising his "most fruitful and remarkable" career and pledging to support Washington in "any line of work" that Washington pursued. The pledge overcompensated for rashness, making a promise that Ransom soon regretted. For Du Bois, Ransom's outburst was an early marker of how not to oppose Washington. Radical belligerence was self-marginalizing. In this case, it also rallied backlash support for Washington during his glory phase.[28]

But Ransom had served notice that the cause of racial justice militancy had a new voice in a surprising place, the AME ministry. In Chicago he flourished; years later he called it the site of his golden years. Richard R. Wright Jr., having served as Ransom's assistant for a year, later agreed that Chicago was Ransom's heyday, although Wright mistakenly claimed that Ransom "fell under the influence of the 'Social Gospel'" during his Chicago ministry. Ransom was already a social gospeler when he got to Chicago. There he formed friendships with white civic leaders Jane Addams, Graham Taylor, Mary MacDowell, Frank W. Gunsaulus, and Clarence Darrow, as well as black civic leaders Edward H. Morris, Theodore Jones, Edward H. Wright, and S. Laing Williams. Gunsaulus, a prominent social gospel activist, combined ministry at Plymouth Congregational Church with serving as president of Armour Institute of Technology. Darrow, a superstar lawyer, was deeply involved in racial justice causes, often providing legal counsel for Afro-American organizations and individuals. Morris and Williams were prominent lawyers, though Morris shared Ransom's antipathy to Washington, while Williams was a Booker operative. Gunsaulus and Darrow encouraged Ransom to launch a settlement-house ministry. Years later, when tempted to despair that all whites were racist, Ransom would think of Gunsaulus and Darrow to pull back from despair.[29]

On political economy Ransom urged that a strong commitment to social justice should lead to democratic Socialism. Fundamentally, he argued, Socialism was about democracy as a means and end. The Socialist alternative opposed anarchic government and overcentralized government, seeking to make ordinary people the owners of their economic fate. It centered on the rights and needs of human beings, which were universal: "Socialism and industrial reform is not a question of race; it is not confined to the boundaries of any nation or continent; it is the question of man." Ransom conceived Socialism as the sign and goal of the coming solidarity of the human race. It had little following among

Afro-Americans, but that would change as they increasingly took account of the big picture. Until recently, Ransom reasoned, blacks struggled merely to survive poverty, ignorance, homelessness, denigration, and violence. They had little occasion to reflect on "the deep questions that concern the destiny of nations or the welfare of mankind." Moreover, most labor organizations had the word "white" in their constitutions, and they despised blacks for taking jobs as strike-breakers. For Ransom, the answer to this sorry picture was to include blacks in the universal struggle for economic justice and Socialism: "We shall see the steeples of a new civilization rising. A civilization which shall neither be Anglo-American, Asiatic, nor African; but one which, recognizing the unity of the race and the brotherhood of man, will accord to each individual the full reward which the free exercise of his powers has won, and the right to stand upon an equal plane and share all of the blessings of our common heritage."[30]

Believing in Socialism was compatible with believing in America, Ransom insisted. In 1897 he told the Ida B. Wells Club at Bethel Church that he took pride in being an American Christian because American Christianity produced the "highest type of man" in the world. Confucianism, Buddhism, and Islam produced impressive human beings, he allowed, but none compared to the American Christian, who had the largest heart and brain, the most productive economy, and the strongest civilization in the world. America's worst fault was that it degraded the manhood and womanhood of Afro-Americans, and women got it worse than men: "Our womanhood was degraded by the slave hut. No woman under heaven could develop and grow into large proportions under those conditions. The miserable hovel or hut which she was compelled to call her home and the conditions under which she was compelled to live meant stamping out the higher and nobler instincts in her nature and the degradation of womanhood. The springs of maternal affection were almost sapped by the abominable and damnable system. Wifely devotion was made almost impossible." Ransom stressed that this was "recent history," still playing out. It was painful but necessary to recall the history, just as it was difficult but necessary to believe that something better lay ahead: "We find that we are not cultured yet, that social life among us is very crude; we have only the rudiments of it." But it was happening, undeniably: "There is coming a time—the day is almost at hand—when the better elements among us are beginning to class themselves together, and they are saying to those who are not fit for respectable association, 'If you want to stand on this plane, you must qualify yourself by virtue, by intelligence and culture so to stand.'"[31]

In 1898 Ransom joined the patriotic stampede for the Spanish-American War. A few white social gospelers held out against patriotic gore and militarism, but Ransom wanted to be counted as a good American and for black Americans to be included in American democracy. His connection to McKinley was also a factor, and Ransom believed that manifest destiny went with freedom, democracy, and Christian civilization. The Illinois State Militia had only one black unit, a battalion headquartered in Chicago. Ransom campaigned for a black regiment led by black officers, won the Illinois governor's support, and recruited the full quota of the regiment at his own expense, using Bethel Church as sleeping quarters for volunteers. After the war he spoke for the city of Chicago at a huge celebration. Ransom shook his head at anti-imperial critics. The republic was not ending, he chided: "However loudly they may shout their notes of warning, the great mass of the nation is borne forward by the current of events. The step, once taken, cannot be retraced. In a new sense we have become a world power." Ransom stood squarely with the social gospel faction that wanted to Christianize imperialism. America at its best invaded only to liberate, he assured: "While other nations subjugate alien peoples, we must liberate them. While others exploit the material resources of foreign lands, we must develop them." It was a good thing to have a missionary spirit, if the goal was human solidarity and liberation. Christianity and Socialism were inherently missionary faiths: "The necessity for cooperation among men, their mutual interests, and the common good are bounded by no race or clime. The destiny of our race is bound up with the destiny of humanity, even as the destiny of our nation is bound up with the destiny of the world."[32]

By 1899 Chicago was the hub of the settlement movement. Ransom asked Addams and Taylor what it would take to launch a settlement; Addams said it would take a lot of money. She made the first contribution and helped Ransom get financial backing from Mrs. George Pullman (widow of the Pullman railroad founder) and Robert L. Lincoln (Pullman company president and son of President Abraham Lincoln). Arnett supported Ransom's decision to leave Bethel Church, and in December Ransom announced that he had secured enough money and a building to launch a combined settlement house and church. The Institutional Church and Social Settlement opened in July 1900 in a renovated railroad mission on Dearborn Street. It had a gymnasium, dining area, kitchen, eight large rooms, and an auditorium seating twelve hundred. The building was kept open twenty-four hours per day to meet the needs of the neighborhood. The program, modeled on Taylor's program at Chicago Commons, included boys and girls clubs, a nursery, a kindergarten, sewing and cooking classes, concerts, discussion groups, and lectures. In its first three years the center serviced eight thousand children and offered instruction in voice, piano, and organ. A women's club of thirty members offered assistance to the poor and ill, sewed for the nursery children, distributed clothing, and conducted literary discussion groups. The center also conducted regular Sunday worship services and a Sunday school. Ransom praised the church for serving vital community needs that most churches did not address.[33]

From the beginning his colleagues bitterly disagreed, especially AME pastors. They charged that Ransom replaced gospel evangelism with social work, copied white social gospelers, and took unfair advantage of his large following at Bethel Church. Sometimes they claimed that his work undermined their programs. Ransom replied that he preached and practiced the gospel, Bethel's support was a good thing, and the parallel church programs were fictional. He later recalled: "It was entirely beyond their conception of what a church should be. Their only appeal was preaching, praying, singing, shouting, baptizing and Holy Communion, but going out into the street and highways, bearing a message of social, moral, economic and civic salvation they did not believe to be a function of the church." Ransom insisted that the abolitionist spirit of the AME Church made it perfectly suited for the social gospel idea of struggling for society-wide social justice. He got in trouble for pressing the point to colleagues who thought he had lost his mind.[34]

First they tried to eliminate him as a Sunday morning competitor. Shortly after Abram Grant replaced Arnett as presiding bishop of Illinois, Ransom's fellow ministers went to work on Grant, persuading him that Ransom should not be allowed to preach on Sunday mornings. Archibald J. Carey and A. L. Murray were the ringleaders of the anti-Ransom campaign. Grant told Ransom he would have to make do with Sunday evening and weekday sermons, which Ransom did for several weeks. Turner was appalled by this turn of events, telling Ransom: "I am the Senior Bishop of the church and regardless of what Bishop Grant says, I order you to preach." The following Sunday morning Ransom held a service, standing beside Turner, who announced that he would not preach that morning because he had come to hear Ransom. Ransom preached an improvised barn burner, and Turner announced: "Great God! Just think of anybody trying to silence a voice like that on Sunday morning. My God! How that man can preach." That ended the Sunday morning prohibition, and the ministers resorted to a stopgap, telling congregants they were forbidden from taking communion at the Institutional Church or from supporting, in any way, Ransom's not-a-real church.[35]

In August 1901 Ransom took his first trip abroad as a delegate to the Third Ecumenical Methodist Conference, held at City Road Chapel in London. Eight bishops traveled with him, including Arnett, who pushed for Ransom's selection as a delegate. The group took a tour through Lucerne, Milan,

Florence, Pisa, Rome, Naples, Genoa, and Paris. For most of the trip, the group saw the usual things and had the usual tourist experiences. In Paris, however, Ransom had a revelation—the Du Bois experience of feeling liberated from the veil: "For the first time in my life I was enveloped in an atmosphere that seemed absolutely free of any prejudice whatever on account of color. I felt a sense of freedom I had never known before." It stunned him that such a thing was possible. Ransom felt exhilarated, until it struck him, harder than ever, that his homeland was exceptionally racist and he would soon be returning to it. Upon returning he was doubly chastened, as AME ministers refused to shake hands with him in the street or ask him about his trip. Ransom realized what that meant. His colleagues were plotting to get rid of him.[36]

Ransom courted more dangerous trouble by campaigning against the gambling racket on Chicago's South Side. There were over fifteen hundred branches of the numbers racket in Chicago. In 1902 a grand jury indicted 110 racketeers, but they were never brought to trial, which strengthened the syndicate. Ransom had the requisite courage for standing up to bullies and predators. The racketeers infuriated him, especially for preying on school children. He implored local police to crack down, which didn't happen; sometimes officers told him they could not find the perpetrators. He persuaded a journalist to take photographs of the numbers offices, but the reporter was assaulted and his camera smashed.

Finally Ransom preached a series of sermons against the gambling trade. The racket struck back, dynamiting Institutional Church. The blast blew out windows and opened huge cracks in the walls and foundation stones. Ransom was defiant, telling the *Chicago Evening Post* that racketeers would have to kill him to shut him up: "They may burn this place, but if they don't burn me with it the police and firemen may cool the embers, and I will stand on the ashes and keep pegging away. If this church stands I will make my next talk against the evil from its pulpit next Sunday. Be sure I will protect my life." The following Sunday he preached against the racketeers, holding a loaded revolver underneath his Bible, taunting from the pulpit, "Dynamite and violence are a poor answer to an argument." Ransom's crusade against the gambling racket got national publicity and results, leading to the arrest of 128 members of the syndicate, though he acknowledged that he merely slowed down an odious business that ensnared some of his parishioners. The *Chicago Tribune* editorialized, after the dynamite attack: "The colored clergyman against whom this attack was directed is doing a noble work and one much needed, for many of his own people are victims, but neither he nor all the clergymen in the city, acting alone, can break up this nefarious business."[37]

By the end of his Chicago ministry in 1904 Ransom had a national reputation for his preaching eloquence, the settlement ministry, taking on the numbers
racket, mediating a stockyard strike, and his ongoing opposition to Washington.
In 1903, on the Sunday after the "Boston riot," Ransom declared from his pulpit
that Washington was not a true leader or representative of black Americans. It
was perverse to call Washington a black leader when he surrendered the rights
of black Americans: "A colored man should have the right to vote, to own his
own home, to transact his business, have a fair trial if he commits a crime, just
as a white man does." That was what black Americans really believed, Ransom
said. It looked otherwise from the black press only because Washington
controlled the black press.[38]

That went down very badly with Ransom's ministerial colleagues, who
resented his growing fame anyway. For some, scheming to get rid of Ransom
had become an obsession. In 1904 they convinced the AME Church's new
presiding bishop of the Chicago area, C. T. Shaffer, to dispatch Ransom to the
Indiana conference as a presiding elder. Bishop Grant, a close ally of Washington,
played a key role in hatching the plan. Upon hearing of his imminent departure
Ransom confronted Shaffer, pleading that he did not want to be a presiding
elder, much less in Indiana. If he had to leave the Institutional Church, he
wanted to move to Evanston, which would keep him in the middle of things
in Chicago.

Shaffer coolly denied that any plan existed, admonishing Ransom that he
made appointments only at the AME annual conference, as everyone knew.
Ransom replied, "You are a liar." He knew that Shaffer had already cut a deal
involving David Cook, A. J. Carey, and him, with him being dumped in
Indiana. Ransom felt abused by his small-minded colleagues and by Shaffer's
capitulation to pressure. Shaffer's lying about it drove him over the edge;
infuriated, Ransom declared that he would not accept any appointment from
Shaffer "to any church whatsoever." Had he lacked a protector, Ransom might
have sabotaged his career right there, or might have swallowed his pride. As it
was, Arnett had become presiding bishop of the New England conference, so
Ransom ended up in New Bedford, Massachusetts. Wright later recalled that
AME pastors did not care for the social gospel or Ransom; Ransom's successor,
J. W. Townsend, did their bidding, vowing to make Ransom's settlement "a
regular AME church, to cut out the social foolishness and bring religion back."[39]

New Bedford was a shock for Ransom. He was used to large crowds, noise,
and strenuous activities, but in New Bedford all was small and tranquil: "Here
I found the atmosphere and people so quaint, so subdued, so unlike the general
forms of community life I have ever known, I sometimes thought I was like a

disembodied spirit trying to get acquainted with the modes of life in the spirit world." He had met plenty of bland, colorless white people in his time, but in New Bedford even the black people were that way. Their worship was cold and formal, they had no spontaneity, and they spurned the spirituals. Many were also kindly. Ransom made some friends in New Bedford but was relieved, after nine months, when Arnett found a better fit for him, at the Charles Street AME Church in Boston.[40]

THE SPIRIT OF NIAGARA

That put Ransom in Boston in the year that Du Bois and Trotter founded the Niagara Movement. Boston was proud of its abolitionist heritage, which it memorialized with statues and anniversary celebrations. The roll began with Crispus Attucks, the first to give his life for freedom in the Revolutionary War. It included Phillis Wheatley, a slave who was brought from Senegal to Boston in the mid-1750s and became a distinguished poet. Boston was the birthplace of black freedom in America. Massachusetts abolished slavery in 1780 through the Declaration of Rights, authored by John Adams, and the state finalized full manhood suffrage without regard to race in 1790. Boston was the home of David Walker, whose fiery abolitionist "An Appeal in Four Articles" terrified slaveholders in 1829, and of William Lloyd Garrison, who founded the abolitionist movement in 1831 by founding a newspaper, the *Liberator*. Bostonian Wendell Phillips, the "Golden Trumpet" of abolition, joined the movement after witnessing an aborted lynching of Garrison. Frederick Douglass headed a long list of Boston black abolitionists that included author William Wells Brown, orator Charles Lennox Remond, and Underground Railroad organizer Peter Howard.[41]

Ransom soaked up Boston's abolitionist lore upon moving there, sprinkling his sermons and lectures with it. He worked hard at building up Charles Street Church, a historic congregation located at the foot of Beacon Hill, on the corner of Charles and Mt. Vernon Streets, where few African Americans lived anymore. In the eighteenth century blacks had settled near the wharfs in the North End. In the early nineteenth century they had clustered near Beacon Hill, in the city's West End. At Charles Street Church black members were confined to the gallery, which motivated them to buy the building in 1876. By the end of the nineteenth century most black Bostonians had moved to the South End or Roxbury. Ransom worried that he could not live on the church's meager salary of twelve hundred dollars, but the trustees and stewards told him the church's diminished membership could not afford a better salary. Ransom cut a deal with them, over their objection, keeping the entire collection raised on the first and third Sundays of every month. Within four months Ransom no longer needed the third week's collection for himself, as his powerful preaching swelled the congregation's membership.[42]

He made an early splash by addressing the National Reform Convention, at Park Street Congregational Church on Boston Common, on the topic "How Should the Christian State Deal with the Race Problem?" Ransom moved straight to his thesis: "There should be no Race Problem in the Christian State." Jesus treated everyone the same, Ransom observed. Jews, Samaritans, Syrophoenicians, Greeks, and Romans had bitter conflicts along racial, religious, ethnic, and class lines, but Jesus broke down barriers, treating all human beings alike as human beings, dispensing with "all the Old Testament laws and ordinances that prevented Jew and Gentile from approaching God on an equal plain." Ransom stressed that America did not bring blacks to America to be human beings. Then God spoke to America through the Civil War, freeing blacks to scrounge a meager, persecuted existence on "the fringes of the industrial world." The gospel of the "New South" was about confining Afro-Americans to the status of a "peasant class," Ransom observed. This project was a crime against "the very life of human spirit." It did not deserve to be associated in any way with Christianity. If American Christianity stayed on this path, "Christianity will un-Christ itself."[43]

Emma Ransom made a similar mark shortly after the Ransoms moved to Boston. Invited to introduce herself to the community in August 1905, Emma spoke on "The Home-Made Girl" before the convention of the Northeastern Federation of Women's Clubs. The homemade woman was not a product of superficial social trends or fashions, she argued. Her moral character was molded in the home; it was morally serious without apology; and it conceptualized human existence as an "opportunity for usefulness." Emma Ransom, like her husband, was fond of Victorian pieties about the "charm," "graces," "refinement," and "manners" of the true woman. Like him, however, she was also frank in turning the table on white racism. White male predators had raped black women for centuries, yet what did white America prattle on about hysterically? That black men raped white women. There was no evidence, Emma admonished, that black males were distinctive in this area, which did not stop white Americans from pretending otherwise. She urged the clubwomen to keep up their guard and their dignity, keeping white men "and all other men in their proper places." Black women had new opportunities in the age of the club movement: "The colored woman of today has before her an empire, unconquered, unsubjugated and untraversed; she has it in her power to make her beauty, the dream of art and the inspiration of poetry; her virtue and culture win her the devoted admiration of men and become the charm of society; her industry and frugality lay the foundation of material prosperity."[44]

That year marked the centennial celebration of Garrison's birth, a two-day affair in Boston, at Faneuil Hall. Ransom gave the closing address. Black Americans vastly outnumbered whites in attendance, but numerous state officials showed up, as did Julia Ward Howe, the poet, reformer, and composer of the "Battle Hymn of the Republic." Ransom observed that very few great figures had the carrying power to extend into another century and that Garrison became one of them by refusing to compromise with the enemies of human freedom. Garrison based his crusade on the Bible and the Declaration of Independence, Ransom noted; his legacy consisted of the Thirteenth, Fourteenth, and Fifteenth Amendments. In 1905, however, the Fourteenth and Fifteenth Amendments were more bitterly opposed than in 1870. Now it was seriously in question whether Afro-Americans were condemned to be aliens in their own country and deprived of civil and political rights. Ransom implored the audience not to let it happen: "I feel inspired tonight. The spirits of the champions of freedom hover near. High above the stars, Lincoln and Garrison, Sumner and Phillips, Douglass and Lovejoy, look down to behold their prayers answered, their labors rewarded, and the prophecies fulfilled." He refused to despair that America was incapable of becoming a racially integrated union: "This nation will evolve a people who shall be one in purpose, one in spirit, one in destiny, a composite American by the commingling of blood."[45]

For two days of Garrison speeches, a parade of noted white speakers tried to stir the crowded audience. The *Boston Evening Transcript* reported that no speaker came close to Ransom: "They cheered, they shouted, they threw their handkerchiefs and hats into the air. They were for a few minutes in a tumult of enthusiasm and fervor, and Rev. W. H. Scott, who was presiding, had to call on the band to aid him in restoring order." The *Boston Herald* concurred: "The applause was simply tremendous, frequently compelling the speaker to pause for several minutes. At its close the scene was indescribable. Women wept, men embraced each other. Guests on the platform rushed upon the orator with congratulations, the program was forgotten and only the playing of the band restored order and made it possible to proceed." Howe caressed Ransom's hands and stared at him adoringly, which got a lot of newspaper play.[46]

The following year Ransom electrified the second Niagara conference, at Harper's Ferry. In a booming voice, brimming with self-confidence and a sense of theater, Ransom declared that a person like John Brown appeared only once or twice in a thousand years. Brown towered above all others, like Mont Blanc, the king of the mountains, or like Melchizedek (Genesis 14), who had no predecessors or successors. He was a singular man of action who belonged to no party or school. The abolitionists had spellbinding speakers like Henry Ward Beecher and Wendell Phillips, but Brown felt called by God to *do* something: "God sent him to Harper's Ferry to become a traitor to the government in order that he might be true to the slave." Brown tried to spark the slaves to rise up and strike for their freedom. Spurning the slow trickle of the Underground Railroad, he set fire to the slave system in its homeland. That was still the point, Ransom urged: "The Negro will never enjoy the fruits of freedom in this country until he first demonstrates his manhood and maintains his rights here *in the South,* where they are the most violently protested and most completely denied."[47]

He stressed that 1906 was not much different from 1859. Before the Civil War, the northern states and federal government allowed the South to treat blacks pretty much however it wanted, and that was still the case. Theodore Roosevelt was "absolutely silent" about enforcing the Fifteenth Amendment, and his secretary of war, William Howard Taft, insultingly dismissed blacks as political children. Ransom allowed that Taft was right about one thing; American blacks had a "childlike faith" in the Republican Party. But finally, "the scales are falling from the Negro's eyes. He is being disillusioned by the acts of a *Republican Congress,* the speeches of members of a *Republican cabinet,* and the silence of a *Republican president.*" Politically awakened blacks realized that Republicans were nearly as bad as Democrats on racial justice, Ransom observed. Despite contrary appearances, Afro-Americans were not divided about what they wanted; all ten million wanted an equal opportunity to "every avenue of American life." They were divided only about how to get there. One group took the very slow road, counseling patient submission to humiliation and degradation; the other group refused to be "remanded to an inferior place." The second group recognized the importance of property and economic development but refused to barter "its manhood for the sake of gain." It believed in hard work but did not believe "in artisans being treated as industrial serfs."[48]

Ransom declared that the soul of John Brown marched on in the courageous resistance of the second group: "The Negroes who are aggressively fighting for their rights have the press against them and the weight of public opinion. They are branded as disturbers of the harmony between the races, but they have the same spirit that animated the founders of this nation." Ransom drew the link to the founders. The Niagara Movement was not simply a fight for the rights of Afro-Americans, he argued. It defended the American nation by calling the United States to its own best meaning, fighting on the ground of "our common manhood and equality." If the Declaration of Independence was not a lie, and a righteous God still ruled in heaven, it had to be that black Americans were on their way to taking their place in America's household as equal to all others.[49]

He got a tumultuous reception. The applause went on and on, intense and refusing to let go, overshadowing the applause for other speakers. Antislavery veterans exulted that they had heard nothing like it since the abolitionist stem-winders of the 1850s. Besides being cathartic, the speech had perfect pitch for the spirit of Niagara. Max Barber called it the most eloquent address he had ever heard. Du Bois later recalled: "That speech more than any single other event stirred the great meeting. It led through its inspiration and eloquence to the eventual founding of the National Association for the Advancement of Colored People."[50]

Ransom's two years in Boston heightened his profile in the church and racial justice movements. His bravura speeches at Faneuil Hall, Harper's Ferry, and other venues made him by far the AME Church's dominant personality in New England. But that created the same problems for him in New England that he had in Chicago. His clerical colleagues did not appreciate his press clippings, radical friends, social gospel theology, or self-dramatizing tendencies. They basked in no reflected glory from Julia Ward Howe's admiration. Moreover, in between Ransom's riveting successes at Faneuil Hall and Harper's Ferry, he took a humiliating beating in the press, which his colleagues cared about very much.

In the spring of 1906 William H. Councill invited Ransom to give the commencement address at Agricultural and Mechanical College of Huntsville, Alabama. Ransom's wife and mother, many church members, and most of his friends urged him not to go. Why would Councill, the epitome of opportunistic black subservience to white nationalism, want Ransom to speak at his school? How could this possibly go well? Ransom brushed them off, deciding that this was an unusual opportunity. He bought a ticket at the Southern Railroad office in Boston, where he was assured there would be no problem taking a sleeping car from Boston to Huntsville. On the train he settled into his seat and began to study his speech. As far as Ransom could tell, there were no problems from Boston to Tennessee, although he gave a pamphlet containing his Garrison centennial speech to a porter, as was his custom while traveling. At some point as the train neared Newport, Tennessee, Ransom became aware that a woman seated across from him was staring at him and his travel bag, which was covered with foreign stamps. She asked if he were foreign; Ransom replied that he traveled a lot. She asked if he spoke English; he tried to avoid further conversation by replying in French. Ransom went back to his speech, with no hint of trouble.[51]

A bit later two white men who had boarded in Newport pulled Ransom from his seat and kicked him, demanding to know his nationality: "Ain't you a nigger?" Both accusers were delegates to the state convention being held in Nashville; one was a lawyer, William McSween. Ransom replied to McSween: "I beg your pardon, sir, I am an American." This reply set off a tirade of indignation. McSween and Edward Mills accused Ransom of harassing a white woman, passing himself off as a French count, and distributing subversive literature to a railroad employee. Ransom protested that he had not interfered with anybody nor misrepresented himself, but the men dragged him two coaches forward into the Jim Crow car. A sympathetic porter told Ransom the two men would be getting off at Knoxville, which relieved Ransom, as his belongings were still in the sleeper. After the train left Knoxville, Ransom returned to his seat, only to find that McSween and Mills had not departed. They treated him roughly, cuffing his hands, kicking and grabbing him, dragging him back to the Jim Crow car, and slamming him with his leather bag. No one else on the train said a word during the entire episode; Ransom noted ruefully that no African American spoke to him or came near him during the rest of the trip to Huntsville.[52]

The train arrived at 2:00 A.M. in Huntsville, where no one welcomed Ransom. He found his way to a hotel serving blacks but could not bring himself to crawl into the bed. Ransom later recalled, "I was sick, sore, and exhausted; the odor of the place was so bad, and the bed looked so dirty, I could not, tired as I was, lie upon it." He sat on the bed, leaning on his elbow, to get through the night. The next morning Ransom learned that his train incident was a front-page story in local newspapers and his speech had been canceled. Ransom spoke briefly to a black journalist with the Associated Press, Charles Stewart, and waited for a visit from Councill and/or someone on his staff, which never occurred. He had not eaten or slept since leaving Boston. He had to find his way back to the train station, shunned by passersby black and white, who gave him "such looks as shall be fastened in my memory as long as I shall live."[53]

As Ransom headed back to Boston, the story went national, usually blaming Ransom. In the dominant version he claimed to be French or German, he offended the train lady in the first place by eating next to her in the dining car, he was arrogant and flippant, he showed up drunk at Councill's home, and he drunkenly flopped into bed with his boots on, forcing Councill to cancel the speech and remove him from the school grounds. The dining car was a fabrication, as Ransom knew very well to avoid the dining car. Even the French aspect was mostly an attempt to avoid an unpromising conversation. The fact that Ransom had a drinking problem gave legs to the story after Fortune and

Washington got hold of it, but he insisted that he did not drink on the train, and in any case, he never saw Councill.

For Fortune, still in his Booker phase, and for Washington, the story was a godsend. Fortune blasted Ransom in the *New York Age*, reporting that he offered two students a nip of whiskey on the train and that he was notorious for needing a drink. Washington urged Fortune to keep it up: "The scoundrels in Boston are trying to make Ransom out a saint and I see no reason for our lying down while the enemy is constantly at work." Washington supplied fresh rumors, and Fortune published them, telling readers that drunken arrogance was an old story with Ransom, which had chased him out of Cleveland, Chicago, and New Bedford. Fortune taunted and ridiculed Ransom: "Everyone knows Ransom knows that an investigation is just what he does not want. An investigation might investigate Ransom in Cleveland, or Ransom in Chicago." Ransom needed his "little nips" to get through a normal day, and he turned out to be a coward when it mattered: "Why in the world did not Ransom fight and have his dead body in the car, as he has been advising Afro-Americans in the South to do? It seems to be one thing to give advice in Faneuil Hall and quite another to put in practice in the South."[54]

Ransom's friends stood up for him. The *Boston Post* reported that Ransom's mistreatment "aroused widespread indignation and severe denunciation among the colored citizens of Boston and Cambridge." George W. Forbes said that Councill invited Ransom to discredit him and that Councill, a shameless opponent of black American rights, was not exactly a reliable source of information concerning Ransom. The New England AME Conference, though hardly a cheering section for Ransom, recognized a smear campaign after it got rolling. Ransom had lost his protector in the meantime, as Arnett was in failing health; he died in October 1906. Turner replaced Arnett, calling the conference to an ecclesiastical trial in Providence, Rhode Island, in July 1906. Turner took the drinking accusation very seriously, as he explained with customary roughness: "As everybody knows, we hate liquor as we do the devil, and regard everybody a fool who drinks it. And as for a preacher using it as a beverage, we would walk ten miles to hear a jackass bray, before we would walk fifty yards to hear him preach. Indeed we would not hear a liquor-drinking preacher babble in the pulpit at all. Especially a colored preacher, for he has no brains to waste."[55]

One of Ransom's ministerial colleagues, D. A. Graham, forcefully reproved Ransom for embarrassing the church with his immoral behavior. In executive session another cleric, C. P. Cole, made a passionate case against Ransom, mostly recycling the newspaper rumors. Ransom arose to defend himself, perhaps admitting that he struggled with alcohol but denying that he drank on the night in question. It helped that Councill did not claim to have seen Ransom drunk, and Turner described the rest of the journalistic bashing as "garrulous prattle." Turner recounted: "Men listened and wept like children, and the writer himself had to use his handkerchief more than once, and after about two hours the doctor was unanimously acquitted and his character passed, Dr. Cole voting for his acquittal, and hand clasps and hand shaking was the order of the day. Thus ended one of the biggest excitements in any part of our connection for years."[56]

The episode was not really over, however, as Ransom's colleagues did not like having to defend him. More important, they hated being outshone by him. In 1907 Turner told Ransom that he could not ignore the outpouring of complaints against him. The ministers resented Ransom's high profile activism and they were not going to shut up about it. Turner confided that he might have to remove Ransom from Boston, much as he hated the idea: "This is not saying that I am going to do it, but I fear I may want to do it, from the contingency of present apprehension." Ransom was incredulous; his ministry in Boston was a smashing success. He later recalled that Charles Street Church was growing and thriving: "No minister belonging to my group was so much in demand for the various activities in the city of Boston, as I was." But that was the problem. Two months later Turner moved Ransom to Bethel Church in New York City, which at least was large and prestigious, located on West 25th Street. Ransom was too big to be shuffled off to Indiana, and Turner respected him. He took the transfer with a heavy heart and gave five years to Bethel Church.[57]

That put Ransom on the southern boundary of the Afro-American section of Manhattan, an area roughly bounded by 25th and 59th Streets, between 6th and 8th Avenues. In the 1880s most black New Yorkers lived in Greenwich Village. Then they moved uptown to the Tenderloin and San Juan Districts, making way for the Italian immigrants that moved into the Village. In the 1920s black New Yorkers poured into Harlem, a move that Ransom's church anticipated by planting its parsonage on 129th Street in Harlem. But for the five years that Ransom served Bethel Church, most black New Yorkers and their churches were located in two districts. Abyssinian Baptist Church was then located at West 40th Street and led by Adam Clayton Powell Sr. Another prominent, mostly black congregation, St. Philip's Protestant Episcopal Church on West 25th Street, attracted congregants mostly from the upper social strata. Mother AME Zion Church on West 89th Street reflected the migration of Afro-Americans from one section of the city to another. It started on Church Street in 1800, moved to the corner of Bleecker and West 10th Streets in 1864, moved to West 89th Street in 1904, moved to 136th Street in 1914, and settled on 137th Street in 1925.[58]

Ransom plunged into the life and politics of his new city with customary vigor. He prowled the streets for prostitutes, inviting them to join the church, which some did. He welcomed actors and musicians, which confirmed for many pastors that he catered perversely to immoral types. Ransom countered that his style of ministry resembled that of Jesus. He added that he thought for himself, serving as the lackey of no church or party. Above all, he roared for equal rights, vowing to "vigorously oppose the enemies and betrayers of the race." Upon learning that New York had no Afro-American police officers, Ransom organized a coalition of ministers, business owners, and professionals, contending that black crime in Boston, Pittsburgh, and Newport had declined because these cities employed black police officers. This argument got nowhere with Republican officials, so Ransom helped Tammany Hall win the mayoral race, which kept its promise by appointing blacks to the police department. Ransom was a major player in breaking the Republican monopoly in New York, as blacks joined the Democratic Party over the police issue.[59]

In 1908 Ransom ran for the editorship of the *Christian Recorder*, already signaling how he intended to influence a denomination that was nowhere near as outspoken about racism and social justice as he believed it should be. The memory of Huntsville was too fresh for him to win the annual conference election, but Ransom addressed it directly, admitting that he had an alcohol problem in the past. Ransom claimed he was long finished with alcohol, analogizing that he and drinking were as far from each other as the throne of God was from the gates of hell. At the time he was in one of his periodic strong-willed sobriety phases. Later that year Ransom supported William Jennings Bryan, imploring African American audiences that their leftover sentimentality about the Republican Party was ludicrous in the wake of the Brownsville episode. He organized a rally at Bethel Church, at which *New York Age* editor Fred Moore, a Booker operative, was nearly mobbed for exhorting blacks not to abandon Taft. The year after that Ransom followed Du Bois from the Niagara Movement to the NAACP, believing that Du Bois had a keen sense of how radical to go without going too far.[60]

When Washington blundered into his nearby Tenderloin scrape in 1911, Ransom was unsure what to think or say. Everything about the episode was strange or absurd, including the fact that Washington showed up afterward at Ransom's doorstep, plastered with bandages, instead of calling on Charles Anderson or Fred Moore. Later that week Anderson asked Ransom for permission to hold a pro-Booker rally at Bethel Church. Ransom consented and the Bookerites spoke, plus a few others including Adam Clayton Powell Sr. and John Haynes Holmes. Theodore Roosevelt and Alexander Walters were unable to come but supported the gathering. Oswald Villard pointedly declined to come. Holmes was one of the few NAACP liberals who were willing to defend Washington's character. Ransom merely looked on; years later he was halfheartedly sympathetic: "Whether Mr. Washington was innocent or guilty, I think the overwhelming majority of Americans believe that Mr. Washington was too great a man and rendered too large a service, not only to members of his own race, but to his country, to be further humiliated and challenged."[61]

In November 1911 he was less charitable. Speaking at a centennial memorial for Wendell Phillips at Plymouth Church in Brooklyn, Ransom blistered Washington as a traitor who routinely betrayed black Americans and thus deserved no standing as a black leader. The first speaker, NAACP cofounder Charles Edward Russell, put the audience to sleep with an hour-long recitation. Plymouth pastor Newell Dwight Hillis asked Ransom if he would prefer to give his speech on a later occasion; Ransom assured Hillis he would bring the crowd to life. In a scorching address Ransom declared: "The traitors within the ranks of our race are known. They have neither our confidence nor our hearts." Ransom charged that the Booker machine was still taken seriously only because it was bankrolled by white wealth and used by politicians for partisan advantage. It was lionized by a newspaper establishment "whose approving voice is the mouthpiece of a decadent public opinion which would let the Negro question 'work itself out' under the baleful influence of the many degrading forms of Jim Crowism."[62]

Accommodation and abuse were linked inseparably in Ransom's mind. The lesson of his bruising trip to Huntsville, he said, was that accommodating racist abuse did nothing to reduce it. Hampton Institute poured out accommodating Afro-Americans every year, which did not stop the South from ramping up Jim Crow. Atlanta had a black college on "every hill," yet blacks were murdered in Georgia "with more impunity than any man would dare to take the life of a good dog."[63]

Ransom's years in New York coincided with the establishment of the Federal Council of Churches, in which he served for many years. He represented the AME Church on the Federal Council, worked on the council's executive committee, and chaired its Race Relations Commission. He admired the council unabashedly on everything besides racial justice, stating that it was the best and most effective institution in American Protestantism. On racial justice he appreciated that the council occasionally issued fine words—Ransom usually wrote them. It galled him that nothing changed in the member churches. One statement got a typically distressing reaction. The council observed: "There is also among the Negroes an increasing distrust of the white race, and a growing contempt for its religion and its sense of justice—feelings which are breeding a new spirit of antagonism and aggression. And through all this tangle of suspicion and hatred, in this professedly Christian land, mob violence strikes unimpeded, deepening the Negro's distrust, and inflaming the worst passions of lawless Whites." At the council's next meeting, a white minister from Texas denounced the statement, contending that lynching was a legitimate method of protecting white women. The Federal Council, asked to repudiate its statement in the interest of "peace and harmony," responded by toning it down, declaring that lynching aggravated the crime problem, weakened the force of law, and threatened to destroy civilization. Ransom resigned himself to the milder statement: "It did not satisfy radicals like myself and others, but we realized that we were living in the United States and not in the millennium."[64]

Ransom had a vision of American blacks and whites going forth "hand in hand" to teach the world how to build a democratic, interracial, Christian society. It was not an incidental theme for him, or something he trotted out merely at wartime, on ceremonial occasions, or at Federal Council meetings. It was fundamental to his social gospel vision of a redeemed creation. He stressed that if black Americans got their rights in the United States, they would be in a position to play a uniquely redemptive role in the world by virtue of being Americans: "The Negro himself can perhaps do more than any other to silence confusion by proving for himself and for the blacks throughout the world that he is capable of attaining to the very highest and best within this civilization. For the Negro here is the only Negro on the face of the earth in vital daily contact with the white man within the same government on terms of equality. If he fails through ignorance, incapacity, laziness, shiftlessness, courage, in a sense the black race throughout the world has failed." Ransom exhorted black and white Americans to show the world that color was superficial. What mattered was the "common humanity and manhood" of all human beings: "From the shores of this country the Negro and the white man should go forth, hand in hand, to teach Russia, Japan, England, India, Europe, and Africa how men of different races may live together upon terms of equality, of fraternity, and of peace."[65]

This vision of global transformation flew on the wings of the progressive belief in progress and the social gospel expectation of Christianizing and democratizing the world. Yet Ransom watched the racial pathology of his country grow more insidious and hopeless. In 1911, at the height of white social gospel optimism, he observed that America's racial oppression had become so terrible that white progressives cowered even from mentioning it: "We have actually arrived at the place where it requires courage and may entail sacrifice—political, moral, or financial—for a man, black or white, to plead for justice for the Negro." Ransom saw it happen at religious and political gatherings. The range of permissible speech about racial justice narrowed as America got meaner. Any white minister or activist who spoke up for the rights of blacks was immediately denigrated as "a fanatic who would foist upon the white people social equality with the blacks, while making them in some sections politically dominant." President Taft, bowing to white hostility, announced that he would appoint no blacks to office in any community where whites objected. Ransom noted acidly that Taft belonged to the party that blacks routinely supported.[66]

Near the end of his New York ministry in 1912, after he had already accepted his next post, Ransom revealed that his passion for racial justice had belatedly tempered his enthusiasm for American manifest destiny. On June 5 the Taft administration invaded Cuba to protect American interests. Two weeks later, on the eve of the Republican National Convention, Ransom expanded on his stock theme that Afro-Americans had lingered too long in a pathetic reliance on the Republican Party while their rights were annulled. The United States was not the only place where blacks suffered under vicious racism, he observed. Wherever the white man roamed, he proclaimed his lordship over darker-skinned people. Now the U.S. Marines were proclaiming it in Cuba. Ransom declared: "We are against any American government in Cuba whose object is to set up a white man's government on that island. If this government by its might crushes the present revolt of the blacks of Cuba against injustice, it may by its intervention proclaim peace, but it will be the peace of despotism and everlasting disgrace to a nation whose chief claim to greatness rests upon the fact that it stands for free self-government without distinction of blood, religion, or race." He was finished with enlisting black Americans to subdue people of color in foreign lands. Instead of putting down brown insurgents in the Philippines or black ones in Cuba, Ransom declared he would prefer to see every black American soldier discharged, court-martialed, or imprisoned for desertion.[67]

BUILDING A SOCIAL GOSPEL CONSTITUENCY

By then he had made a career move that rescued him from the whims and politicking of bishops. In 1912 Ransom ran for editor of the *A.M.E. Church Review.* He campaigned with a dramatic flair, imploring that the church's quarterly journal be politically nonpartisan, committed to principles and ideals instead of parties, fiercely committed to justice, and sufficiently ambitious to take on "the great international and world questions of peace and war, arbitration, colonization and the exploitation and government of the backward people of the earth." Ransom took no interest in "supine" or "colorless" journalism. He stood for journalism "that has backbone, conviction, principle, on all the great questions of government which so vitally affect the moral, intellectual, social, and industrial welfare of the people." He upped the drama: "The audience is assembled, the stage is set; we now await the rising curtain to reveal in the foreground the black Garrisonian journalist who will make good this solemn declaration: 'I am in earnest. I will not equivocate. I will not excuse. I will not retreat a single inch— *And I will be heard.'*"[68]

The *A.M.E. Church Review* was the brainchild of Benjamin Tanner, who founded it in 1884. At the time Tanner was editor of the *Christian Recorder.* He was frustrated that few African American authors got published in white journals, and he enlisted Turner's support for an AME journal; Turner pushed it through. L. C. Coppin succeeded Tanner as editor of the journal after Tanner became a bishop in 1888. H. T. Kealing, a Texas layperson, succeeded Coppin in 1896 but died in office. C. V. Roman, a medical college professor, was appointed by the publication board to finish Kealing's term. Roman taught at Meharry Medical College in Nashville and had been educated in Canada. He came to the 1912 General Conference expecting to be elected in his own right as the incumbent editor. He was genteel and high-minded, with a tendency to look down on preachers, causing him to underestimate Ransom's ability and appeal. Though Ransom had been driven out of Chicago and Boston, he had a following that prized him as the Du Bois of black Methodism. Ransom won the election handily. Shortly afterward he received one of Du Bois's typically terse and puckish letters, flashing delight:

> My dear Dr. Ransom:
> Let me congratulate you upon your election to the Editorship of the Review. It is about time you had a new picture taken, and I should like a copy of [it for] the *Crisis.*
>> Very sincerely yours,
>> W. E. B. Du Bois[69]

The journal gave Ransom an independent base as a general officer of the denomination, responsible only to the General Conference. It also gave him a vehicle to convert AME clergy to his viewpoint and legitimize himself. Tanner had conceived the *Review* as a literary journal with denominational backing, not a sectarian bulletin board, although it also covered denominational news. From the beginning it featured prominent Afro-American writers such as Frederick Douglass and Frances Ellen Harper. More important, it provided an outlet for less known authors. Tanner housed the *Review* in Philadelphia, where it remained until Kealing moved it to Nashville. Ransom moved it back to Philadelphia, adding George E. Haynes and George W. Forbes to the masthead. Haynes, the first African American to earn a Ph.D. at Columbia University, taught social science at Fisk University and served as associate editor of the *Review*. Forbes, a Boston militant, served as literary reviewer.[70]

Under Ransom's direction the *A.M.E. Church Review* featured black scholarship, educated the church and its ministry, and reported on major developments in theology, ethics, culture, science, and the arts. Above all, it advocated racial justice. Ransom aimed directly at the Talented Tenth, citing Du Bois. Politically, Ransom outflanked most of his writers to the left, but he featured writers that shared his belief in the power of Christianity to bring about social change: Haynes, Wright, Walters, Miller, and Scarborough. Other frequent contributors included Fortune, Forbes, Villard, Alice Dunbar, novelist Charles S. Chestnutt, and diplomat Richard T. Greener. Ransom paid close attention to Du Bois and cooperated with him. The *Crisis* regularly featured church news, and Ransom featured items about *Crisis*. Ransom and Du Bois worked together on lynching, segregation, disenfranchisement, electoral politics, and economic justice, and they advertised and sold the two publications as a package deal.[71]

The 1912 election was an exception. In the early going, Ransom leaned toward Roosevelt, hoping that TR's candidacy offered a breakthrough for progressive politics. Ransom implored that voting for Taft was unthinkable. Taft prattled that black Americans needed to be held "in tutelage to the white people" and they did not deserve the same education as whites. Surely, Ransom argued, Taft had killed off what remained of black sentimentality about the Republican Party. As for Roosevelt, though his presidency ended badly, Ransom reminded readers that black Americans had liked him up to Brownsville, and afterward TR went back to standing up "for justice and a square deal to the Negro." For a while Ransom was ready to give Roosevelt a second chance, because he could win and he had returned as a progressive who railed against economic injustice.[72]

That ended abruptly, shortly after the Progressive Party convened and Roosevelt refused to seat the black southern delegates. Ransom disavowed his previous leanings, blasting TR as "monstrous, unpatriotic, unjust and politically immoral." He seemed to be set up for the recourse that Walters and Du Bois took. The *Review* cautiously informed its readers that "some" black leaders had opted for Wilson, at first not mentioning that the notable figures in question were Walters and Du Bois. Later the journal sponsored a freewheeling debate in which Ransom played a careful hand. He was new to the job and eager to establish himself in it. He opened the journal to defenders of each candidate and commented editorially on the pros and cons. Ransom had doubts about Wilson, even as a lesser evil, and he knew for sure that "the Democratic Party is today as of old, controlled by southern sentiment." He cautioned that the mainstream of the Democratic Party still wanted to repeal the Fifteenth Amendment. Moreover, in much of the country the Fifteenth Amendment was already nullified, thanks to the hostility of Democrats and the arrogant opportunism of Republicans. In the end Ransom chose not to say how he came out. He probably voted for Debs, but did not make a case for doing so. Du Bois soon wished he had played it that way.[73]

Ransom's January 1913 edition of the *Review* celebrated the fiftieth anniversary of the Emancipation Proclamation. Turner wrote the lead article, a reminiscence of the proclamation and its time. Walters wrote about the legacy of the proclamation, Villard described the NAACP's agenda, and Washington offered his customary defense of industrial education. Ransom could not resist tweaking Washington:

> For more than a score of years there has been at work an insidious influence, under the guise of philanthropy, to fix the Negro in a place of permanent inferiority. He is to be educated along the lines which will make him a better servant; he is to be free to buy land and own homes (provided his 'white neighbors' do not object to his presence in that vicinity) and work independently upon the soil; he may apply himself to trades and work at a minimum wage in the South and in the North work not at all, if the Labor Union objects; he may have a bank account, but it will not buy him comfort or convenience in travel, or entrance to places of entertainment, or that make for the culture of intellect or the higher elevation of the spirit; he may own land, but his broad acres give him no voice in the laws under which he is taxed or in the choice of the men who are to administer them, neither do they give him equal standing in the courts, nor protection from the violence and fury of the mob.[74]

Ransom implored that any strategy not opposed to all that was not worth considering.

After a year of editing the journal, Ransom and Emma decided that running a journal was not enough for them in a world of suffering and need. In September 1913 they launched a mission church in the Tenderloin district and moved to an apartment there, ministering to the homeless and broken. Ransom rented a store on West Thirty-seventh Street between Eighth and Ninth Avenues, a few doors from a gambling hall, calling his mission the Church of

Simon of Cyrene, after the figure that helped Jesus carry the cross to Calvary. There the Ransoms ministered to what he called "the bad Negroes . . . the Negroes of the slums." Ransom put it plainly to his readers: "The editor of the *Review* has lifted up the cross of Christ down in what is known as 'New York's Black Tenderloin.' It is hell, but we have plunged into it, and never have we known such joy in the service of our blessed Lord as we find in offering the lifeline to the poor human derelicts who have suffered moral shipwreck and have been dragged by the treacherous undertow of degeneracy and vice." Churches rarely ventured into such areas, where "many old hulks of human wrecks lie stranded." Ransom admonished that mainstream denominations like the AME Church were just as middle-class and cut off from the urban poor as the established white denominations.[75]

The Ransoms shared the life of the urban poor, touring the saloons and gambling joints, declining to say anything about religion. They preached only at church, visited the sick and lonely, and kept moral criticism to a minimum. Their neighbors, treated with unaccustomed respect, grew to love and trust both Ransoms. Ransom stocked the mission with food after learning that prostitutes tended to be flush one day and broke the next. He became friends with the local police captain, frequently coming to the police station to assume responsibility for a bailed or paroled prisoner. In the early going, the local AME clergy fiercely opposed the mission, charging that Ransom was on another ego trip, one power base was not enough for him, he was sure to steal members from them, and his ministry implied some kind of criticism of them. The loudest complainer was Benjamin W. Arnett Jr., Ransom's successor at Bethel Church, who made Ransom promise not to poach members from him.[76]

But the Ransoms endured at the mission church, giving eleven years to it. Ransom understood why churches avoided the seamy parts of cities; part of him even agreed that they should, as every congregation had to protect its children. But the churches gave themselves too much leeway in this area, he judged: "The Negroes of character, intelligence and means have withdrawn themselves too far from the ignorant, the depraved and struggling mass. These cannot rise without their aid, but the more neglected will tend to drag the upper stratum of the race down to the depth wherein they lie." Somehow, he urged, "these two extremes" had to be brought together, "until each stands uplifted under the inspiration of a quickening touch, girded with new power and strength and animated with unity of purpose." In the final analysis, the churches could not claim to be Christian if they spurned this basic gospel principle: "Shall we sit smug and comfortable in our large churches, or go forth with Jesus Christ into the highways and seek for the sheep that are lost until we find them?" Eventually that argument prevailed in the AME Church, at least regarding Ransom. In June 1915 the New York annual conference accepted Ransom's mission church as part of the conference and appointed a full-time pastor to it.[77]

By then Ransom was embroiled in an aftermath controversy over Trotter's quarrel with Wilson in the White House in November 1914. Ransom was ecumenical in his militant politics, belonging to Trotter's National Independent Political League (NIPL, an arm of Trotter's National Equal Rights League) as well as the NAACP. In 1913 Trotter and Wells-Barnett had led an NIPL delegation that held a surprisingly encouraging meeting with Wilson. The militants called for an end to racial segregation, and Wilson welcomed their concern. A year later the militants returned to the White House, determined to press harder.

Wilson was in a bad way. His wife, Ellen, had died in August, and Wilson relied on female companionship. Wilson's confidant Edward House later recalled that Wilson was "not fit to be President" at the time because he was too grief stricken to think clearly. But this meeting would have gone badly in any case. Trotter stated bluntly that the group had returned because segregation was worse than ever in the federal bureaucracy. Wilson replied that measures had been taken to protect blacks from white antipathy: "Segregation is not humiliating but a benefit, and ought to be so regarded by you gentlemen." If only people like Trotter would stop telling blacks that segregation was humiliating, they would recognize its benefits. Trotter interrupted, protesting that Wilson made things worse for African Americans by "drastically" imposing segregation in the federal government. Wilson snapped, "Your manner offends me." The president was unaccustomed to being interrupted, much less admonished in a passionate manner, much less by an Afro-American. Trotter replied respectfully that he was being earnest, not passionate. Both men got louder and interrupted each other. Wilson flushed with anger. Trotter told Wilson that he, Du Bois, and Waldron were catching hell for having endorsed him for president. Wilson replied that being president was far worse; his burdens were intolerable; they had no idea. Then he expelled the delegation from his office. Trotter promptly held a news conference at the White House, providing verbatim quotes, which was as shocking in 1914 as the confrontation itself.[78]

The white press condemned Trotter for unbelievable rudeness and presumption, while much of the black press gasped and looked away. Du Bois backed Trotter to the hilt, declaring that Trotter expressed "the feelings of nine-tenths of the thinking Negroes of this country," whether or not they said so. Du Bois had ignored Trotter's earlier trip to the White House out of personal rivalry, and he soon returned to not giving Trotter his due, by playing down Trotter's role in stirring a national reaction against *The Birth of a Nation*. For a moment, however, something was too important to let personal rivalries get in the way. Du Bois praised Trotter for standing strong; Wilson, on the other hand, was by birth and education "unfitted for largeness of view or depth of feeling" on the matter of racial justice.[79]

For Ransom there were no conflicts to untangle. He was close to Du Bois and he greatly respected Trotter. In December 1914 Ransom organized an NIPL rally at Bethel Church to defend Trotter and the NIPL delegation against a firestorm of press criticism. Ransom, Adam Clayton Powell Sr., and NIPL national president Byron Gunner spoke at the rally. The following month Ransom reprised himself on the meaning of Wilson versus Trotter: "Shades of Jefferson Davis, defend us! When in the memory of Presidents, Confederate or otherwise, did ever the 'grinning,' 'good-natured,' 'patient,' 'non-resistant creature,' so address a Chief Executive?" Ransom stressed that Trotter said nothing that was actually offensive. Wilson got offended simply because Trotter did not approach him "with shuffling gait, cringing, hat in hand; but standing erect like a man."[80]

From the pulpit and podium, in the streets, and in the *A.M.E. Church Review*, Ransom expounded on the moral and psychological meaning of being proud of one's blackness. Pride motivates human beings to adventure, risk, endure, and triumph, he urged: "Find a man who has no pride and you have one whose past is inglorious and whose future is without hope." Ransom liked to say there was a "pride of race" that lifted the "gifted spirits" of a group to greatness, winning "a crown of fadeless immortality." There was also a pride of race that bred intolerance and contempt; whenever it prevailed in a dominant class, it produced shrunken souls, "like a withered leaf." The ideal, for Ransom, was pride of personality that transcended race. Grounded in the recognition of the divine light within each soul, "this pride becomes the highest form of meekness which inherits the earth and the heaven, too." It had peers, but no superiors "in a world which slowly, more and more, revolves from darkness into light."[81]

On January 11, 1915, the U.S. House of Representatives voted 228 to 60 to prohibit intermarriage between whites and blacks in the District of Columbia. The penalties maxed out at one year in prison and five thousand dollars in fines. Mixed couples entering the city were subject to prosecution, and all mixed marriages were legally voided. The House averted the complexities of the "one drop" rule by asserting that a Negro was anyone possessing one-eighth or more of Negro blood. Ransom opted for sarcasm: "We count ourselves happy in this move of the U.S. Congress to disentangle and legally define our veri-colored racial identity." Still, he cautioned, African sunshine was a "powerful resolvent," which had a "sly way of revealing, even to the thirtieth degree, the rich pigment it has held in solution." The new law, he added, would not correct what needed correcting—white men denying the humanity of black women by day and using them for sex at night. Ransom tried not to offend readers that did not share his position about interracial marriage. He allowed that there was room for a range of views about whether the state should discourage intimate inter-racial relationships. But one aspect of the House statute, he implored, was not debatable. To nullify the existing marriage of a mixed couple and subject them to prosecution was an "abomination."[82]

With the passing of Turner and Washington in 1915, Ransom could feel the turning of an age. There would never be another Turner, nor should there be, Ransom wrote. Turner was a force of nature with enormous virtues and faults. He built up the AME Church in the aftermath of slavery; he fought against lynching and Jim Crow with unsurpassed heroic moral defiance; and he inspired Afro-Americans to be self-confident, even as he blistered them for their shortcomings. Ransom judged that the AME Church had done very well in making Turner a bishop, for Turner provided the kind of leadership that the church needed in his time. Now that Turner was gone, the church had to rethink what it needed from its leaders. Ransom hoped the next bishops, besides being pious, would be figures of "broad culture and refinement, of liberal education and breadth of vision." As for Washington, Ransom vowed to speak with "great consideration and restraint." Washington was obviously great, "the mightiest hand that has laid hold of both races in the last thirty years." Like Turner, he was very much a product of his times. Unfortunately, Washington's era was the age of the capitalist blowout, when Andrew Carnegie could be considered an important thinker. Thus Washington became "the high priest of the subordination of his race to the spirit of a materialistic age." The "new age" that Washington prophesied, Ransom declared, had now passed with the passing of Washington. Ransom tried to be hopeful that his age would be known for overturning Washington's wrongheaded subordination of equal rights and social justice to economic self-interest.[83]

On one level there was a surge of activism that seemed to bear out this hope. Ransom praised the NAACP and played up his participation in it, urging *Review* readers to support the NAACP's anti-lynching fund. At the political level he struggled not to despair. Wilson versus Hughes in 1916 pitted a known enemy against a mere opportunist. Ransom judged that Hughes sounded better than Taft because the Republicans realized they had to win back the votes of blacks and white progressives. The party had become too identified with big business to win national elections, so it resorted to the "Old Black Mule," the black vote. Ransom told readers to play hard to get: "Let him kick, refusing to be saddled, bridled and mounted politically until approached in the proper spirit, and until there is open and avowed assurance of just and liberal treatment." Ransom hoped that Hughes would win and be surprisingly progressive. Instead, Wilson edged Hughes in a close election (277 to 254), and Ransom despaired that Republicans would probably abandon black Americans again.[84]

"He kept us out of war" worked for Wilson in 1916. The following year, after Wilson took the United States into World War I, Ransom stuck close to Du Bois, making the same arguments about defending America and accepting the segregated training school for black officers. More important, he made the same argument about laying aside special grievances. Some Afro-Americans were reluctant to fight for America, Ransom observed. This was a terrible mistake, for it was under the American flag that black Americans were "made free men and citizens, clothed with a constitutional liberty beyond that enjoyed by the people of any other country." Ransom urged black Americans to prove their loyalty to America by easing off on the unrealized promise of America. He played his part, preaching Wilsonian sermons about the hope and ideal of global democracy. Ransom mustered enthusiasm for the infusion of black officers, even if they had to be trained separately. He lauded Wilson's belated (July 1918) condemnation of mob violence in America, although Wilson did not mention black Americans. Ransom caught some backlash for his patriotic splurge, although nothing like the one that lashed Du Bois; one of his articles was actually titled "Close Ranks."[85]

Ransom did not begrudge Wilson when his stature briefly soared to dizzying heights at the end of the war. He appreciated that Wilson was somehow sincere and idealistic about the self-determination of nations, despite his racism. But the postwar politics were bruising, and Ransom judged that Wilson overplayed his hand. In 1919, after Wilson refused to negotiate over his League of Nations proposal and the U.S. Senate rejected it, the AME Church's Committee on the State of the Country endorsed the Senate's position, contending that Wilson's plan would have placed the United States at the mercy of unfriendly foreign powers. Ransom made sense of this outcome by invoking a strained analogy between the American government and the AME Church. The Monroe Doctrine, he observed, though lacking a place in the U.S. Constitution, was nonetheless "the most zealously guarded and sacredly cherished" statement of the principles by which the United States related to other nations. The AME Church had its own Monroe Doctrine, the principles of AME founder Richard Allen. In this doctrine, discrimination in the church of Christ on the basis of nationality or race was forbidden. Ransom contended that just as the United States stayed true to its anti-imperial identity by staying out of the League of Nations, the AME Church steered clear of all alliances and programs "that would invade or compromise the Negro's religious liberty, equality, and manhood."[86]

By this reasoning, the rank imperialism of the Monroe Doctrine was an anti-imperial warrant for refusing to build structural alternatives to war, empire, and the domination of the weak by the powerful. Years later Ransom took it back, asserting that the best vision of a decent world order came from "Woodrow Wilson's fertile brain" during a compressed and turbulent period near the end of World War I. Wilson, Ransom judged, was not as great as Franklin Roosevelt, who would "loom larger in history" because of his greater magnetism and "broader humanitarian spirit." Wilson's shriveled personality would surely militate against revisionist history favoring him. But Ransom gave Wilson his due: "Wilson's place is safe because it embodies most of the ideals we are now trying to achieve."[87]

In 1918 Ransom flirted with a career switch to politics. The United Civic League, an independent organization founded in 1913 by John M. Royall, sought greater representation for black Americans in electoral politics. In 1918 the group asked the Republican Party in New York to run Ransom as its candidate for the Twenty-first Congressional District, which included Harlem, where upward of 120,000 blacks had moved. The party said no, so Ransom ran for Congress as an independent backed by the Civic League. Republican officials went to work on Ransom. Party leader Johnny Lyons, campaign manager for Republican candidate John A. Bolles, offered Ransom a state office in return for dropping out of the congressional race. Ransom told Lyons that the Civic League had some really good lawyers who would be great for a state office. Lyons countered that the party would be willing to put Ransom in the state senate; Ransom still wasn't interested. Lyons offered Ransom five thousand dollars to withdraw from the race. Ransom told Lyons he could not be "bluffed, bribed, or bought." In that case, Lyons asked, what did he want? Ransom, in his telling, replied, " 'You go to hell! Get out of here!' "[88]

Ransom ran against Bolles and Democrat Jerome Donovan. The 1918 New York elections had special significance because women were entitled to vote for the first time. When the race began, approximately 50,000 voters were enrolled in the Twenty-first District. In theory that number had the potential to double, although party operatives did not expect more than 1,500 women to register. That put a premium on the existing 6,500 registered black votes. Republican operatives, feeling entitled to the entire black vote, scoured Ransom's petitions and got him thrown off the ballot. Ransom ran as a write-in candidate, but most of his votes were thrown out, too, as election officials claimed that voters misspelled his name. In the end he won 465 votes and resolved that running for office was not for him.[89]

That raised the question of whether Ransom was ready to be a bishop. By 1918 he knew that he was on track to become one, even though AME southerners voted for southerners and thus won most of the bishops' chairs. Ransom had a growing following on social gospel theology, the NAACP, black Methodist union, the Garvey movement, economic justice, the politics of racial justice, and the importance of Ransom. In 1920 the AME Church elected five bishops at the General Conference in St. Louis. Ransom did not want to be a bishop, as he did not want to be a church administrator. Secretary of missions would have suited him better. But friends pleaded that the church needed a militant northern bishop, so Ransom agreed to be placed on the ballot.

He detested the campaigning for bishops' chairs that consumed general conferences. Ransom and Wright believed that southern campaigning had seriously corrupted the denomination. They used their editorial perches at the *A.M.E. Church Review* and the *Christian Recorder* to implore against it, and Ransom refused to campaign. On the first ballot William D. Johnson (a Georgia minister) and Archibald J. Carey (still in Chicago, but a Georgia native) were elected. On the second ballot Maryland native William Sampson Brooks was elected fresh off pastorates in St. Louis and Baltimore at which he had retired large parish debts. On the third ballot Morris Brown College president William A. Fountain, Tennessee minister William Tecumseh Vernon, and Ransom headed the field. Ransom found Vernon unbearable, a showboat that specialized in "grotesque" demagoguery and bragged about being darker-skinned than other church leaders, rubbing his cheeks. Vernon had no theological training and very little ministerial experience. At the convention, however, he won a bishop's chair with a spectacle performance, spreading his legs wide apart as though standing astride America and Africa, rocking himself from side to side, and crying out, "Turner, shake two Continents! Turner, shake two Continents!" Ransom bristled at losing to Vernon. Still, that left the fifth bishopric to be decided, still on the third ballot. Ransom ran ahead of Fountain by two to one in the early going, until the reader of the tallies oddly stopped calling Ransom's name. His southern votes were not counted, and Fountain was read into a bishop's chair. Ransom felt conflicted about the outcome, as the election seated four new southern bishops and a northern bishop from the South, and gave Ransom four extra years of freedom.[90]

That year the three black Methodist denominations almost merged, as proposals for an organic union passed in all three churches. Ransom was a

longtime advocate of uniting black Methodism, having called for it as soon as
he took over the *Review*. Once the union movement made headway, however,
he found himself cautioning merger enthusiasts to slow down and think it
through. Ransom pressed one question: Did the three black Methodist denominations have the same spirit? The AME Church had an abolitionist spirit from
its birth, he stressed. It was deeply involved in politics, it remained true to its
abolitionist origins, and it did not apologize for being abolitionist and political.
The AME Church defended the right to be voted for, not merely the right to
vote. The church may have wavered here or there, Ransom allowed, but it
never had the spirit of "compromise or subserviency." He was not willing to
merge with the Colored Methodist Episcopal Church if doing so put the AME
Church's abolitionist legacy at risk. It was hard enough to deal with backsliders
and accommodationists at AME conventions. By Ransom's reckoning, the
AME Zion Church was close enough to the spirit and tradition of the AME
Church that a union between these denominations made sense. But the merger
process underway merged all three denominations, which made him anxious.
Ransom protested that the CME Church did not have an abolitionist spirit and
it remained in "tutelage" to the ME Church South. He supported an organic
union, but not at any price. If union was worth having, it could take place in
stages. Rushing to a full-fledged union would be a terrible mistake.[91]

As it was, the black Methodist churches failed to merge anyway, and a decade
later Ransom tried to revive the merger initiative, without success. Aspirants for
the episcopacy did not like their chances for election in a united church, and
by then there was too much history to overcome. Many held it against Ransom
that he objected when the chance had come to unify black Methodists. He
always replied that hanging separately was better than pulling off a premature
union, though he was against hanging separately.

THE GARVEY EXPLOSION AND THE
HARLEM RENAISSANCE

Ransom's solidarity with Du Bois was personal, ideological, and strategic. He
delighted when people likened him to Du Bois. He admired Du Bois for putting
the equal rights agenda back in play after the disaster of Bookerism. He shared
Du Bois's determination to walk the narrow path of sensible radicalism. Like
Du Bois, he urged that civil rights militancy was better than revolutionary rejec-
tionism and back-to-Africa defeatism. When Trotter, Wells-Barnett, and Marcus
Garvey blasted Du Bois for urging black Americans to put aside their grievances
and fight for America, Ransom supported Du Bois and the war effort. When the

Garvey movement soared after World War I, Ransom preferred to say what was good about it, and even Du Bois later claimed that he felt a twinge of sympathy at first. But Ransom quietly supported Du Bois after Du Bois felt compelled to say what was wrong and disastrous about it.

Marcus Garvey set off the first popular explosion from below—a mass movement of downtrodden black Americans and West Indian immigrants. He was born in St. Ann's Bay, Jamaica, in 1887. His father, a voracious reader, was a stonemason and small landowner, and his mother was a domestic worker. Garvey's cantankerous father impoverished the family with court battles over petty grudges, and only one of Garvey's ten siblings survived into adulthood. In 1900 Garvey was apprenticed to his uncle, a printer and avid reader with a large library, which Garvey devoured. Garvey had a Du Bois–like story about losing his racial innocence; in his case it happened at the age of fourteen when a white playmate's parents forbade her from playing with Garvey. In 1906 he moved to Kingston to work as a compositor in a printing firm. There Garvey met a follower of Pan-African founder Henry Sylvester Williams, Jamaican physician Robert Love, whose newspaper *Jamaica Advocate* heightened Garvey's racial consciousness.[92]

Garvey joined the printers' union, which got him blacklisted in the private sector. In 1910 he left Jamaica to explore Central America, where he witnessed the exploitation of Jamaican laborers in the banana and coffee cartels of Panama. In 1912 he moved to London for schooling and to see what life was like for blacks in Europe. Garvey took courses in law and philosophy at Birkbeck College and worked for the *African Times and Orient Review*, where he absorbed the Islamic Pan-Africanism of publisher Dusé Mohamed Ali. On occasion he held forth at the Hyde Park Speakers' Corner, where he cited Dusé Ali, Martin Delany, Booker Washington, and Henry McNeal Turner on behalf of black unity. In 1914 Garvey returned to Kingston to found the Universal Negro Improvement Association and African Communities (Imperial) League; the following year he briefly met Du Bois at a garden party.

Garvey's organizing in Jamaica got nowhere. In his telling, he failed because the island's biracial population identified with the white colonizers. Assimilation in Jamaica worked for the mixed-race population, which was treated as near-white, locking out the pure-black majority. Garvey decided that building a back-to-Africa movement in Jamaica was impossible; the best place to try was the United States. Reaching out to Washington, Garvey moved to the United States in 1916, visited Washington at Tuskegee, and moved to New York, where he spoke nightly on Harlem street corners. His breakthrough came on June 12, 1917, when Hubert Henry Harrison invited Garvey to address Harrison's Liberty

League of Colored Americans to a packed house of two thousand Harlemites at Bethel AME Church. Garvey got a tumultuous response and quickly overtook Harrison as a race leader in Harlem.[93]

Liberty League rallies turned into United Negro Improvement Association (UNIA) rallies, drawing enormous crowds. Many of Garvey's early followers were recent West Indian immigrants, as thirty thousand West Indians poured into Harlem between 1915 and 1924. West Indians in Harlem had to deal with being black in the racist United States and with not being welcome in their African American neighborhoods. Garvey took little interest in African American history and culture, a point that Du Bois eventually pressed against him. But Garvey was gifted at expressing racial grievance, connecting with audiences Du Bois did not reach. Garvey told his audiences that their gut feeling about NAACP liberals was right—people like Du Bois were elitists who just wanted a place at the white man's table. When Du Bois called black Americans to close ranks, Garvey's newspaper, the *Negro World*, gave a scathing response: "They enslave their children's children who compromise with sin."[94]

Acquiring the *Negro World* was a breakthrough for Garvey, which enabled him to publicize his rallies and expound his vision of returning to Africa. Garvey had a vision of ocean liners steaming to Africa to create a new base of black wealth and build an African Zion, a superstate headed by him. This vision thrilled a huge audience that read Garvey's newspaper and packed into his rallies at Liberty Hall. Donations poured in for his Black Star Line ships, which he accepted as donations until a district attorney told Garvey that he had to incorporate. The line was capitalized at ten million dollars, and two million dollars' worth of stock was offered for sale. Garvey launched additional enterprises, bought Liberty Hall, and in July 1918 fully incorporated the UNIA. But as the stock began to sell, the UNIA liquidated debts it had acquired prior to incorporation, which was illegal. In 1919 Garvey was wounded by gunfire and staggered into a Black Star Line meeting, bandaged and limping, which gave him martyr status.

From the beginning Du Bois held a low view of Garvey's enterprise, but he kept it mostly to himself. In August 1920 Du Bois gave a snotty interview to journalist Charles Mowbray White, telling White that Garvey's followers were "the lowest type of Negroes, mostly from the West Indies." The following month, however, Du Bois finally mentioned the Garvey movement in the *Crisis*, without mentioning Garvey by name. Du Bois treaded cautiously, telling readers that the "rise of the West Indian" represented a "new ally in the fight for black democracy."[95]

Implicitly, this was a story about the vast outpouring of West Indians into the United States; thus Garvey himself was incidental. Du Bois explained that foreign-born blacks in the United States had doubled in the first decade of the twentieth century, and doubled again in the next decade, averaging five thousand per year. North Americans, Du Bois observed, being "naturally provincial," tended to forget that the twelve million blacks in the United States constituted less than half the black population of the New World. There were six million blacks in the West Indies and nine million in Central and South America. Du Bois reasoned that the situation in South America was much like in the United States. In South America, the black population was in the minority, and it needed to assimilate with the dominant society, which was happening. Thus very few South American blacks migrated to the United States. In the West Indies, however, people of color held strong majorities, where biracial blacks held leadership positions and black peasants were locked out. In Haiti, biracial blacks teamed with the black underclass to drive out the white colonizers. Elsewhere biracial blacks moved into power, supported by the British. In both cases, Du Bois said, resentment among the "great mass of Negro peasantry" fueled a racial consciousness that wanted nothing to do with amalgamation. This mass of black peasants, having fled to the United States, was now marching in great parades and overflowing auditoriums throughout Harlem. Du Bois offered a sympathetic word: "The movement is yet inchoate and indefinite, but it is tremendously human, piteously sincere and built in the souls of a hardworking, thrifty, independent people, who while long deprived of higher training have nevertheless very few illiterates or criminals. It is not beyond possibilities that this new Ethiopia of the Isles may yet stretch out hands of helpfulness to the twelve million black men of America."[96]

Shortly afterward, and for many years thereafter, whenever Du Bois was challenged to prove that he had not opposed Garvey from the beginning, he pointed to this statement. In 1920 he told White that he would not raise a hand to stop Garvey. Du Bois might have stuck longer to that pledge had Garvey remained vaguely Socialist with a whiff of Leninism. But Garvey took a right turn in the fall of 1919, chastened by the postwar crackdown on leftists. He purged the UNIA of Socialists and condemned all radical movements targeted by the federal government. Garvey stressed that he was committed to black capitalism, opposed to trade unions, and comfortable with white conservatives. He studded his speeches with Booker Washington references, lauding capitalist achievers in Booker fashion. Often he laced his call for an African Zion with a Social Darwinist warning: "The weaker and unprepared group is bound to go under." If blacks did not build an empire of their own in West Africa, they would shrivel and die in the Americas. If repudiating radical allies helped Garvey steer clear of the Red Scare and the Palmer raids, he was willing to do it. He told his followers they had no time to waste "over the white man's politics." The UNIA was devoted to lifting the black race, creating black wealth, raising an army for Africa, establishing an African Zion, and nothing else.[97]

The Garvey movement electrified people who were nobody in U.S. American society by day but who marched in colorful uniforms at night under black, red, and green banners calling for black children of Africa to rise up. They packed the largest venues they could find, overflowing the old Madison Square Garden. In August 1920, twenty-five thousand marched through Harlem, replete with Knight Commanders of the Distinguished Order of Ethiopia, Knight Commanders of the Sublime Order of the Nile, Black Cross Nurses, African Legions, and high school bands. Garvey rode in a convertible, resplendent in a regal plumed helmet. He claimed that the UNIA had four million members; Du Bois, already tracking Garvey's labyrinth of enterprises and shady finances, judged that three hundred thousand was closer to reality.

Even that low estimate far outstripped other attempts to build a mass movement. In August the UNIA sponsored an International Convention of the Negroes of the World, issuing a manifesto titled "Declaration of the Rights of the Negro People of the World." There were fifty-four declarations, headed by the right of all black men, women, and children to live freely as citizens of Africa, "the Motherland of all Negroes," and the principle of "the supreme authority of our race in all things racial." It affirmed "the inherent right of the Negro to possess himself of Africa," condemned "the atrocious crime of whipping, flogging and overworking" black people anywhere, and declared that no black had a right to "battle for an alien race without first obtaining the consent of the Black peoples of the world, except in a matter of national self-defense." Reaching further, the manifesto demanded "that the governments of the world recognize our leader, and his representatives chosen by the race to look after the welfare of our people under such governments."[98]

Ransom welcomed this statement as "an encouraging awakening," the most militant declaration ever issued by "the rank and file of Negroes." Some would take it as a joke and others would dismiss it as "harmless oratory," Ransom predicted. He thought British colonizers would take it more seriously, as the chief point of the declaration was "to arouse and inspire black people throughout the world to preserve their national and territorial inheritance in Africa." Ransom had two cheers for Garvey, setting aside Garvey's racism and his back-to-Africa fixation, which smacked of reactionary smallness. To inspire racial pride in millions of lowly blacks was a tremendous achievement, Ransom acknowledged. Moreover, though Garvey railed nonsensically against light-colored blacks and black intellectuals, he deserved to be recognized as an exponent of the Pan-African faith that Du Bois pioneered.[99]

Du Bois wanted Garvey to fail, but not spectacularly, as that would be humiliating for Afro-Americans and calamitous for the masses of people who lost their money—a throwback to the crash of the Freedmen's Bank in 1874. Du Bois's early attempts to deflate Garvey focused on two things: Garvey's obsession with racial purity had no place in the United States, and his dubious financial dealings reeked of calamity. Before Du Bois could press the former argument, however, he had to clear the air about what he believed about racial intermarriage. For a decade he had laid off this subject except for an occasional aside that always evoked a backlash, which was chastening. In November 1920 he announced that in the interest of "justice and clear thinking," the *Crisis* was due to take a public stand.[100]

Du Bois believed "most emphatically" that romantic relationships across racial lines were a bad idea. Racial intermarriage "involves too great a strain to evolve a compatible, agreeable family life and to train up proper children," he argued. But the legal question was whether racial intermarriage should be against the law. Du Bois urged that this issue was not debatable in a decent society: "Either white people and black people want to mingle sexually or they do not. If they do, no law will stop them and attempted laws are cruel, inhuman and immoral. If they do not, no laws are necessary." The American South, Du Bois observed, offered "an awful and abiding example" of what came of denying such a fundamental right. There were powerful and convincing social reasons why people of different races should not marry, Du Bois concluded. But there were no legitimate moral, physical, or mental reasons, contrary to racist propaganda.[101]

That set off the usual backlash hysteria about miscegenation, which Du Bois took in stride. It also cleared the way for him to attack Garvey, which he had delayed longer than he could stand. As Du Bois expected, Garvey accused him of racial treason. In December 1920 Du Bois tried to take the high road, offering pro and con on Garvey while laying off the sensitive issue of racial purity. Garvey was hard to characterize, Du Bois wrote. He was obviously an eloquent and inspiring racial leader who "has become to thousands of people a sort of religion." Unlike many people, Du Bois said, he was not ready to say that Garvey was unscrupulous. On the other hand, it was clear that Garvey had "very serious defects" of temperament and training: "He is dictatorial, domineering, inordinately vain and very suspicious. He cannot get on with his fellow workers. His entourage has continually changed. He has had endless lawsuits and some cases of fisticuffs with his subordinates and has even divorced the young wife whom he married with great fanfare of trumpets about a year ago. All these things militate against him and his reputation."[102]

The following month Du Bois had more things that militated against Garvey. The UNIA offered no serious account of its assets and expenses, there was ample evidence of financial mismanagement, and Garvey's hostility toward light-colored blacks had no place in the United States. Du Bois explained, "There is no doubt but what Garvey has sought to import to America and capitalize the antagonism between blacks and mulattoes in the West Indies." Pigmentocracy was alien to the African American experience, Du Bois admonished. It was also stupid, "absolutely repudiated by every thinking Negro." Garvey stressed that privileged people of color in the United States were always light-colored, as in Jamaica. Du Bois replied that if Garvey did not drop his attacks on biracial people, he would be dismissed as a demagogic bigot: "American Negroes recognize no color line in or out of the race, and they will in the end punish the man who attempts to establish it." Garvey aspired to unite all blacks, but sneered at light-colored blacks. He had big plans for Liberia, but did not bother to consult the Liberian government. Above all, Du Bois concluded, if Garvey did not clean up his finances, disaster was inevitable: "He can have all the power and money that he can efficiently and honestly use, and if in addition he wants to prance down Broadway in a green shirt, let him—but do not let him overwhelm with bankruptcy and disaster one of the most interesting spiritual movements of the modern Negro world."[103]

By then Du Bois was used to being heckled at speeches outside NAACP circles and anywhere in Harlem. It got worse after Garvey was indicted for fraud in 1922 and fought to stay out of jail, unsuccessfully. Garvey responded by lurching to the far right—pandering to the Klan, linking arms with Mississippi archracist senator Theodore Bilbo, courting favor with John Powell's Anglo-Saxon League of America, and stooping to anti-Semitism. He declared that he vastly preferred the Klan to the NAACP. The NAACP, in Garvey's telling, merged the worst kind of blacks and the worst kind of whites, producing a hypocritical integrationism that shook down feckless white liberals to bankroll Du Bois and a self-serving anti-lynching campaign. Du Bois replied with two kinds of polemics. One was scathingly factual, detailing Garvey's fantastical bookkeeping and his penchant for doubling down on bad business decisions. UNIA delegates wanted to know where their money had gone. Garvey's rise to popularity rested on one thing, Du Bois argued—his revival of "a pretty thoroughly discredited dream," a vision of exiled blacks overtaking Africa. But Garvey squandered the money of unknowing people in record time.[104]

Garvey's trial for fraud in 1923 revealed that the Black Star Line had done remarkably little with stunning sums of money. The *Yarmouth* made three disastrously expensive trips to the West Indies in three years; the *Maceo* made half a trip, aborting in Santiago; and the *Shadyside* went up and down the Hudson River a few times. Garvey was denied bail, jailed briefly in the Tombs Prison, and convicted. All the while he played the racial martyr. In prison he wrote a memoir, "The Negro's Greatest Enemy," which blamed his problems on "light colored Negroes in America and the West Indies." The martyr business and Garvey's ramped-up campaign against racial integration unleashed Du Bois and others in his circle. NAACP branches director Robert Bagnall was scathing and vicious:

> A Jamaican Negro of unmixed stock, squat, stocky, fat and sleek, with protruding jaws, and heavy jowls, small bright pig-like eyes and rather bull-dog-like face. Boastful, egotistic, tyrannical, intolerant, cunning, shifty, smooth and suave, avaricious; as adroit as a fencer in changing front, as adept as a cuttle-fish in beclouding an issue he cannot meet, prolix to the 'nth degree in devising new schemes to gain the money of poor ignorant Negroes; gifted at self-advertisement, without shame in self-laudation, promising ever, but never fulfilling, without regard for veracity, a lover of pomp and tawdry finery and garish display, a bully with his own folk but servile in the presence of the Klan, a sheer opportunist and a demagogic charlatan.

Whether or not Garvey was insane, Bagnall concluded, he was certainly a demagogic charlatan, and probably insane: "Certainly the movement is insane, whether Garvey is or not."[105]

Du Bois must have pondered whether he needed to top that. He opted for trying, unleashing a blistering polemic against Garvey's "unbelievable depths of debasement" while insisting that he had "almost leaned backward" to avoid any injustice to Garvey: "Marcus Garvey is, without doubt, the most dangerous enemy of the Negro race in America and in the world. He is either a lunatic or a traitor." Du Bois explained that Garvey had launched a scurrilous campaign to derail racial integration. Garvey forged alliances with every powerful white racist he could reach, declaring that no black American would ever become an American citizen, returning to Africa was the only solution for blacks, and a race war would be unavoidable if the NAACP succeeded in its aims. Du Bois remarked, "We would have refused to believe that any man of Negro descent could have fathered such a propaganda if the evidence did not lie before us in black and white signed by this man." The only difference between Garvey's propaganda and the usual white nationalist tripe was that Garvey's was worse:

"Not even Tom Dixon or Ben Tillman or the hatefulest enemies of the Negro have ever stooped to a more vicious campaign than Marcus Garvey, sane or insane, is carrying on. He is not attacking white prejudice, he is groveling before it and applauding it; his only attack is on men of his own race who are striving for freedom; his only contempt is for Negroes; his only threats are for black blood." Du Bois dismissed Garvey's complaint that he was temporarily denied bail for being black, noting that the UNIA had to be warned repeatedly against intimidating witnesses and that Garvey "openly threatened to 'get' the District Attorney."[106]

Du Bois revealed that he had ample personal experience with UNIA threats: "After my first and favorable article on Garvey, I was not only threatened with death by men declaring themselves his followers, but received letters of such unbelievable filth that they were absolutely unprintable." On one occasion his friends hired secret police protection for him out of fear that Garvey's agents intended to kill him: "Friends have even begged me not to publish this editorial lest I be assassinated. To such depths have we dropped in free black America! I have been exposing white traitors for a quarter century. If the day has come when I cannot tell the truth about black traitors it is high time that I died." Du Bois did not want this issue to be about him, however. What mattered was to end Garvey's public career. Black Americans had "endured this wretch" for too long, bending over backward not to offend his followers. Du Bois declared: "The end has come. Every man who apologizes for or defends Marcus Garvey from this day forth writes himself down as unworthy of the countenance of decent Americans. As for Garvey himself, this open ally of the Ku Klux Klan should be locked up or sent home."[107]

That was a painful verdict for some who had not withstood the dangers and vituperation that Du Bois experienced. Most NAACP insiders readily accepted Du Bois's version of what happened and what it meant, usually saying so with a bit more reserve than Du Bois and Bagnall used. Some, like Ransom, grieved that the first mass movement of black liberation ended badly, having deserved a better leader and outcome. George Forbes, writing in *A.M.E. Church Review*, spoke for Ransom and himself in summarizing the Garvey debacle: "His great talent, restless energy and marvelous magnetism deserved a better fate. We never saw in his scheme anything other than arrant charlatanism, but his ability to draw the masses together and build up in them a confidence in a leader of their own was at least something."[108]

Some *Crisis* readers judged Du Bois more harshly. Ira May Reynolds, a Harlem resident, was one of them. Reynolds told Du Bois that she and "quite a large number of the readers of your magazine" believed that things would have

gone differently had Du Bois tried to cultivate a relationship between the
NAACP and the UNIA. Instead, he devoted himself to "sending Mr. Garvey to
jail and trying to wreck the Universal Negro Improvement Association."
Reynolds sharply reprimanded Du Bois: "This has been considered by a great
many who have looked into the case as unmanly and cowardly." Garvey was not
the issue, she admonished; she and her friends took no interest in defending
Garvey. What mattered was the movement that Garvey inspired into being,
something that Du Bois had failed to accomplish: "You must know that while
you may destroy the individual you cannot destroy an organization or a principle which has been so deeply embedded in the minds of the people as the
work of Mr. Garvey."[109]

Du Bois never admitted that things might have gone better had he not
personally loathed Garvey from the beginning. Garvey had insecurity issues
and a volatile ego, which made him hypersensitive to perceived sleights. He
had to know from early on that Du Bois looked down on him—the very experience of denigration that fueled Garvey's rage against light-colored officials and
intellectuals. In the 1920s, every time Du Bois gave a speech in a locale that
Garvey had reached, he knew he was in for a rough time. There was bitter irony
in this outcome, as Du Bois's anger got hotter and more Garvey-like during the
very period that he condemned Garvey. Not coincidentally, this was the same
period in which the Dyer anti-lynching bill was filibustered to death in the
Senate (1923) and Congress passed one Anglo-Saxonist immigration bill after
another (1917, 1920, and 1921). Some black leaders applauded the new immigration restrictions as a boon to black labor. Du Bois countered that the collusion
of nativists, Nordic elitists, and trade unionists to keep poor foreigners out of
America was reprehensible, a pillar of the new white supremacy.[110]

Darkwater seethed at the postwar refashioning of white supremacy in which
Nordic whiteness was the ideal, non–Anglo-Saxon whites struggled to assimilate, America adopted the southern "one-drop" rule for blacks, and "mulatto"
was dropped from the U.S. census (as occurred in 1920). U.S. American society
as a whole opted for binary racial ordering, with people of color representing
the defining opposite of the national ideal. Du Bois observed that by this reckoning, the darker people belonged to "mudsill" populations underneath a rising
tide of melted ethnic immigrants: "We push below this mudsill the derelicts
and half-men, whom we hate and despise, and seek to build above it—
Democracy!" American democracy was founded on exclusion, "a feeling that
the world progresses by a process of excluding from the benefits of culture the
majority of men, so that a gifted minority may blossom." Du Bois dreamed of a
deeper and wider democracy extending to people of color, poor whites, and

women, "a world of service without servants." But it *was* a dream, and he was getting angrier.[111]

Du Bois's scathing articles of the 1920s gave the impression that for him it was all going downward. But this was also the period that Du Bois, Alain Locke, James Weldon Johnson, Charles S. Johnson, and Jessie Redmon Fausset fostered the Harlem Renaissance and the "New Negro." Du Bois had spent his entire career calling for the Harlem Renaissance; thus it was somewhat force-fed. David Levering Lewis described it as "a cultural nationalism of the parlor, institutionally encouraged and directed by leaders of the national civil rights establishment for the paramount purpose of improving race relations." In other words, the *Crisis* and Charles S. Johnson's *Opportunity* magazine, the organ of the National Urban League, willed the Harlem Renaissance into being in the 1920s, and two successive secretaries of the NAACP spent much of their time nurturing and promoting it. The name obscured that much of the "Harlem" Renaissance took place in Washington, DC, and that the term "New Negro" had been used since the 1890s.[112]

Du Bois versus Washington always cut to contrary opinions about what it would take for blacks to be respected and self-respected in American society. Later, Du Bois had similar arguments with NAACP professionals who focused solely on civil rights legislation and legal cases. Always he contended that African Americans would not win their rights until they produced a body of art compelling recognition. The *Crisis* built up slowly to its breakthrough in this area, publishing essays and poems by Charles W. Chesnutt, Fenton Johnson, Benjamin Brawley, Jessie Fausset, and James Weldon Johnson. This period—1910 to 1920—was a low point for black writers, producing few literary works of note. Du Bois's novel *The Quest of the Silver Fleece* was published in 1911; Johnson published his acclaimed *Autobiography of an Ex-Colored* Man in 1912; and Du Bois published *Darkwater* in 1920. That was it for significant books during the decade in which the civil rights movement took off.[113]

After World War I, however, a stream of gifted black writers moved to Harlem, notably Arna Bontemps, Claude McKay, Wallace Thurman, Zora Neale Hurston, Nella Larson, and Langston Hughes. Harlem had long been the Mecca of black artistic and intellectual existence, but publication was out of reach for black writers in racist America, and Harlem itself only became the favored location for New York blacks in the 1920s. The new artistic arrivals came into a different situation mainly because the *Crisis* and a decade of civil rights activism opened doors for them.

In 1919 Du Bois hired Fausset as the magazine's literary editor. The daughter of a New Jersey AME minister, Fausset had graduated from Cornell University in 1905 with a degree in classical languages. By 1919 she was a prolific poet, essayist, and short story writer; later she authored four novels. Fausset had barely moved into her office when she began to attract talented writers to the magazine. Her gallery soon included Langston Hughes, Countee Cullen, Claude McKay, Georgia Douglas Johnson, Jean Toomer, and Gwendolyn Bennett. Hughes wrote his first publications for Fausset. Later he called her the midwife of the Harlem Renaissance, though more accurately, there were three midwives: Hughes, Fausset, and Charles S. Johnson. Charles S. Johnson, an enterprising editor, turned *Opportunity* into a must-read magazine and tabbed Locke to edit the movement's signature anthology, *The New Negro.* James Weldon Johnson forecast in 1922 what the renaissance would mean for black America: "The final measure of the greatness of all peoples is the amount and standard of the literature and art they have produced. The world does not know that a people is great until that people produces great literature and art. No people that has produced great literature and art has ever been looked upon by the world as distinctly inferior."[114]

This Du Boisian conviction enlivened the *Crisis* during the years that Johnson and Walter White served as leaders of the NAACP, though never as much as they wanted, as Du Bois's writing stuck mostly to the politics of a wretched time. Johnson and White were enormously successful in mentoring new writers, attracting attention to them, and building up the NAACP. Du Bois might have played a larger role in the literary boom he fostered had he not been consumed by the wretched politics. In his contribution to *The New Negro,* Du Bois contended that the problem of the twentieth century was still the color line, globally: "Modern imperialism and modern industrialism are one and the same system; root and branch of the same tree." The labor problem that supposedly transcended everything else in the modern world was actually one side of the race problem, "and the black man's burden is the white man's burden." Du Bois observed that every great empire has a "dark colonial shadow" and empire is always "the heavy hand of capital abroad." The problems of the color line and economic exploitation went together, especially in the periphery of the "world-embracing industrial machine," where "unseen and inarticulate, the determining factors are at work."[115]

That was a different key and mode from the literary fare that Locke featured in *The New Negro.* Du Bois's other major contribution to the renaissance, *The Gift of Black Folk* (1924), similarly stressed global politics, though with lyrical touches. Edward McSweeney, chair of the Knights of Columbus Historical Commission and a former immigration officer at Ellis Island, commissioned *The Gift of Black Folk* as an antidote to the triumphant Anglo-Saxon racism of the recent immigration bills. McSweeney observed that American Catholics, Jews, blacks, and Germans had similar problems in the aftermath of World War I; thus he also commissioned books on Jews and Germans in the making of the United States. The idea that cultural pluralism was essential to U.S. American democracy, and one of its best aspects, was of recent vintage. Josiah Royce, Horace Kallen, Waldo Frank, and Randolph Bourne were its early-twentieth-century champions. Du Bois enriched this intellectual tradition by arguing that African Americans played a key role in creating a pluralistic United States and in compelling Americans to accept their nation's cultural pluralism—at least to the extent that they did so. The democracy of the American founders, Du Bois argued, was an Athenian type resting on slavery, male hegemony, and class hierarchy. U.S. American democracy became more democratic by expanding the franchise, abolishing slavery, and building a pluralistic republic, crucially by leveraging the gift of black folk—the gift of soul.[116]

"The Negro is primarily an artist," Du Bois declared. This thesis cut both ways, he realized, because racists loved to go on about the "sensuous" nature of black people, and Du Bois had his own history of neo-Lamarckian and Hegelian racialism to overcome. *The Gift of Black Folk* suspended Du Bois's anxieties about racial essentialism, however, contending that only one race ever held at bay "the life destroying forces of the tropics," and that by doing so, it acquired "in some slight compensation a sense of beauty, particularly for sound and color, which characterizes the race." Blacks conveyed a "spirit of gayety" and "exotic charm" wherever they lived, Du Bois argued. Thus, American slaves created the first great American music. Du Bois loved to tell the story of George White, a white treasurer at Fisk University, who fell in love with the sweet, powerful, sublime melodies of the slave songs and thus launched the Jubilee Singers. Music was "always back of this gay Negro spirit," Du Bois observed. Music suffused the poetry of Phillis Wheatley and Jupiter Hammon, the abolitionist polemics of David Walker, the preaching of Henry Highland Garnet, and the historiography of R. B. Lewis. In the 1860s, slave narratives multiplied; in the 1870s black writers turned to politics and Sojourner Truth added her story to the slave narratives.[117]

Du Bois noted that the recent outpouring of black literature was "large and creditable," though little of it qualified as great: "The time has not yet come for the great development of American Negro literature." Black Americans were too oppressed by economic stress and racial persecution to produce great literature, he judged. Tellingly, the same thing was true of the white American South, in reverse. Citing H. L. Mencken, Du Bois observed that the white South had forty million people in a territory six times bigger than Germany or

France, yet it lacked a single poet, novelist, composer, or critic of distinction. Blacks were not the only victims of their persecution; the white South was stunted and consumed by its obsession with putting down black people. A great black literature was surely coming, Du Bois believed, because blacks had a "peculiar spiritual quality" that had long illumined black religion. He called it "a certain spiritual joyousness; a sensuous, tropical love of life, in vivid contrast to the cool and cautious New England reason; a slow and dreamful conception of the universe; a drawling and slurring of speech; an intense sensitiveness to spiritual values."[118]

Twenty years before anthropologist Melville Herskovits and sociologist E. Franklin Frazier set off a storied debate over African cultural retentions in African American culture, Du Bois drew a straight line from Africa to the United States on one thing, religion. Plantation slavery destroyed everything from Africa except the power of the priest, he argued. The preacher interpreted the supernatural and comforted the sorrowing, expressing "rudely but picturesquely, the longing and disappointment and resentment of a stolen people." Gradually, over two centuries, the black church became Christian. In 1924 it remained by far the central social institution in Afro-American life. Du Bois believed that in religion as in democracy, black Americans posed the crucial test of whether white Americans believed what they said. If white Americans had any sincerity about following Jesus, they needed to show it in how they treated blacks.[119]

As far as Du Bois could see, the only Americans who practiced way-of-Christ humility and nonviolence were black Americans. White Americans asserted themselves and took possession, Du Bois observed. This was understandable as a rebound from European oppression; moreover, he appreciated that white Americans built up a vital, bustling, prosperous nation. On the other hand, white American self-assertion was "in many of its aspects a dangerous and awful thing. It hardens and hurts our souls, it contradicts our philanthropy and religion." Black Americans had a gift to offer in this area. It was the gift that black folk had long offered to the New World: "Thus, in singular and fine sense, the slave became master, the bond servant became free, and the meek not only inherited the earth, but made that heritage a thing of questing for eternal youth, of fruitful labor, of joy and music, of the free spirit, and of the ministering hand of wide and poignant sympathy with men in their struggle to live and love, which is, after all, the end of being."[120]

Ransom agreed on every count, drawing on Du Bois's distinct tropes, and preaching that black people had unique gifts of soul to contribute to the building of radical, pluralistic, American democracy. Ransom gloried in the Harlem Renaissance, prizing especially Chesnutt, Cullen, Hughes, and McKay. He loved the idea of a New Negro, expounding on this theme before Locke made it famous in 1925. Moreover, Ransom topped Du Bois on the spiritual freedom of blacks, declaring: "In the highest and best sense, the black people are the only free people in the United States today."[121]

Ransom explained that white Americans were chained to their prejudices and traditions. Even when white Americans resolved to live by the gospel, and thus tried to act in the spirit of justice and charity, they found themselves "restrained because of their chains," unable to break free of their bigoted beliefs about the inferiority of darker people. Black Americans did not have these problems: "Black Americans cherish no animosity, bear no contempt, or scorn, for their white fellow citizen." When white Americans claimed that blacks contributed little or nothing to America, blacks generally took the insult graciously, waiting for whites to see that they were partners with black Americans in the building of American civilization: "For three hundred years they have spoken the same language, worshipped God in identical articles of religious faith, and without a single betrayal upon the black man's part, they have sustained their country with a common loyalty and patriotism." Ransom put it poignantly, pleading for the recognition that "these dark Americans cherish the high ideals of their fellow countrymen." Black Americans read the same books, cared about the same things, and wanted the same things for their children as white Americans: "They drink from the same fountains of aspiration and inspiration that are both the hope and the glory of a great free people."[122]

He shuddered to think that white Americans might take seriously Garvey's back-to-Africa spiel. Though Ransom knew many destitute African Americans, he knew hardly any that planned to move to Africa. He exaggerated to make the point, claiming that the only trace of Africa in the lives of African Americans was "the ever fading color of their skins." Black Americans were Americans "in aspiration and hope, in faith and destiny," he stressed. Their distinct contributions to American civilization were immense, despite being denigrated. Black Americans compelled white America to live up to the justice ethic of American democracy. Culturally and morally, America would be a meaner, more selfish, less interesting, and less soulful place without its African American population: "These dark Americans have stood as the crucial test of the spirit of freedom and liberty that lies back of all our legal enactments, moral standards, and spiritual attainment. By their influence the heart of America has been softened with more kindness, a sweeter spirit has filled its life and a stronger wave of emotion has swept the whole range of its philanthropy and religion."[123]

Black American scholarship obviously lagged far behind that of white America, Ransom said. But the influence of black soul reverberated everywhere in American society, and Afro-Americans were beginning to make a mark in literature and scholarship. Here the peaceable gifts of black soulfulness were sure to have a rich bounty. Ransom had long believed that God brought blacks to the United States to become its spiritual conscience. In the mid-1920s, deeply impressed by Mohandas Gandhi's nonviolent resistance to British rule in India, Ransom urged that blacks were called to bring white racists to repentance through Christian love, nonviolent protest, and scholarship. In 1925 he put it plainly: "The intelligentsia of this race must bear no weapons of violence to combat the Ku Klux Klan, the lynchers and the mobs. They will not evade the menace which these bear to the peace and stability of our nation, but they will transfer the struggle to a higher plane, where intelligence and character may meet it in a decisive battle of brains." Ransom had always conceived moral and spiritual idealism as intrinsic to the gospel. Under Gandhi's influence he preached that violence delayed the day of reconciliation, even violence waged in the name of justice. Beyond whatever politics the word of the gospel may call Christians to support, the gospel is radical and transforming because it is spiritual: "The brute and beast within us must yield the final palm of victory to the supremacy of mind."[124]

In that mood and mode Ransom sang of "the New Negro" through whose "birth of freedom" God made all things new. Europe and Asia were receding, Ransom believed, while "America's unfinished arch of freedom waits." The New Negro came "with laden arms, bearing rich gifts to science, religion, poetry and song." Through him labor and capital would come together, finding "the equal heritage of common brotherhood," and statesmanship would be ruled by the "stewardship of justice." Ransom had an eschatological vision of racial reconciliation:

> With ever-fading color on these shores,
> The Oriental sunshine in his blood
> Shall give the warming touch of brotherhood
> And love, to all the fused races in our land,
> He is the last reserve of God on earth,
> Who, in the goodly fellowship of love,
> Will rule the world with peace.[125]

This vision of a coming commonwealth of freedom was religious for Ransom. It was his understanding of what it meant to pray, "Thy kingdom come." The situation for blacks in the United States was terrible and desperate, yet it was also distinctly promising, filled with redemptive possibilities that reverberated to the ends of the earth. On the one hand, white America routinely slandered

Afro-Americans as stupid, immoral, and inferior; it happened even in highly respectable forums.[126]

On the other hand, it was redemptive for America when blacks gained power and moral agency, as long as they did so on Christian terms. The gospel, Ransom urged, is about being saved from the slavery of egotism, selfishness, and will-to-power. Black Christianity modeled what it looked like to take the teaching of Christ to heart. Moreover, the black American story was not merely a narrative of oppression, for black Americans had precious advantages over all other blacks in the world. Ransom enthused, "He is the best housed, the best fed, the most intelligent, the best educated, and enjoys more freedom in the United States of America than any other group of Negroes on the face of the earth."[127]

More than any other group, the black American "placed his faith in God and the brotherhood of man set forth in the principles of American democracy." Ransom argued that the dialectic of oppression and freedom distinctly worked toward social salvation in the African American quest for social justice. America had what the world needed, but America's redemptive power was diminished by white America's mistreatment of its black population, which stood for Americanism at its best. The more power and well-being black Americans gained, the more the United States became the best version of itself: "We have it in our power to be foremost in the rank of the men and women who are the salt of the earth and the light of the world for all men everywhere who strive for peace on earth and goodwill among men."[128]

Ransom's tireless preaching of this message won a large following in the AME Church, which carried him to a bishop's chair. He still did not want to be a bishop, but twelve years as a general officer of the church gave him a national base in the denomination, and he had spent his career trying to become as influential as possible. Thus he found it impossible to resist the "weight, authority, influence, and . . . power" that came with the position. In 1924, at the age of sixty-three, he visited Harriet Ransom in Cambridge, Ohio, shortly before heading to the AME General Conference in Louisville, Kentucky. His mother had been ill for two years; he asked if she were praying for his election. She replied, "No, I have already prayed for you, and God has answered my prayer. He let His glory shine round about. When you are elected, let me know." In Louisville he was elected as the forty-eighth bishop of the AME Church and assigned to the Fourteenth Episcopal District of Kentucky and Tennessee.[129]

Ransom lost none of his edge or fire during his twenty-eight years as a bishop. Yet the job did turn him, as he feared, into an administrative functionary. His best speeches and writings were the early ones. Afterward, Ransom's life was consumed with committee work, financial planning, Episcopal supervision, and personnel decisions. He became a bishop partly to reform the episcopacy, at which he succeeded. He tried to merge the black Methodist churches, at which he failed. Mostly he devoted himself to survival work, while preaching that the church must not be satisfied with mere survival.[130]

Ransom had campaigned for church reform for years before he became a bishop. He wrote that he wanted "a church where ignorance cannot breed, nor superstition hide; a church where innocent credulity cannot be bent to selfish ends; where narrowness and selfishness cannot command a hearing; a church where greed, bigotry, and power shrink from the light of heaven-born, high instructed men who walk with Jesus in redemptive paths." The church needed "enlightened men" who followed Jesus in the real world, Ransom urged. He had barely become a bishop when he went after the church's Episcopal oligarchy, protesting that many AME bishops presided over the same district year after year, often in the same section of the country in which they had grown up. The Episcopal Committee was stacked to allow bishops to build permanent power bases for themselves. Ransom charged that this cushy setup bred complacency and provincialism, leading almost inevitably to corruption and other abuses of power. Bishops became dictators over their little principalities; they knew only their own part of the world; and they rewarded sycophants, who played the game so they could become bishops. Ransom posed an either/or: "Shall We Have Eighteen Ecclesiastical Principalities or a Connected Church?"[131]

That question set off a firestorm in the AME Church, where Ransom battled many southern bishops who detested him, led by Joseph Flipper and South Carolina bishop John Hurst, and his old rival A. J. Carey. Ransom also vied with his friend Wright, still editor of the *Christian Recorder,* and several others who had his back on other issues. All vehemently opposed Ransom's proposal to rotate all bishops on a regular basis. Wright protested that the Bible said nothing about rotating bishops and neither did the church's discipline, so who was Ransom to overthrow the system? Wright's northern allies agreed that at least under the current system they had some protection from southern domination. Ransom replied by escalating to an explosive issue, corruption. Everyone knew, he said, that certain bishops had become rich through serving as bishops, and thus disgraced their calling. In February 1928 Ransom implored a Bishops Council meeting in Birmingham, Alabama, that the moral integrity of the denomination was at stake. The following May the General Conference convened in Chicago, where Ransom's coalition of reformers, led by presiding bishop John Albert Johnson, proposed to rotate all bishops who had served in one district for two or more quadrennium conferences. Flipper angrily protested that delegating the assignment of bishops to the Episcopal Committee was a mere convenience and the General Conference had no authority to change how the Episcopal Committee operated. If the General Conference approved the reform proposal, the bishops would ignore the conference and assign themselves as they saw fit.[132]

That display of Episcopal arrogance helped to set off a landslide. The reformers were going to win anyway, but shortly after Flipper made his threat, Johnson called for a vote and the reform proposal passed by 641 to 203. Ransom and Johnson had two days to savor their victory; meanwhile, the old guard of defeated bishops took over the Episcopal Committee. Carey tried to cut a back-room deal with Ransom, promising that Ransom could have New York if he used his influence to keep Carey in Chicago. Ransom replied that Johnson deserved to return home to New York at the end of his career. Carey persisted, replacing New York with Philadelphia. Ransom replied, "I will have nothing to do with your combination or with your methods. You have a millstone about your neck that will drag you down until you sink." The following day Ransom and Johnson got their comeuppance from the Episcopal Committee. Johnson was exiled to Kentucky and Tennessee, where he died later that year; Ransom later recalled that the assignment "wounded his pride and broke his spirit." Ransom was banished to the Thirteenth District of Louisiana, which had only three annual conferences and a tiny mission conference. His followers took it hard; the church was still putting down Ransom even after he made bishop. Ransom took it in good humor, reasoning that New Orleans should be interesting. His two years in Louisiana were among the most enjoyable of his life.[133]

If Ransom had gotten his way, the black Methodist churches would have merged at some point during his years as a bishop. He kept trying to facilitate a three-way union but failed. He worked on a two-way merger with the AME Zion Church, but that failed, too, despite a moment of hope at the 1928 General Conference in Chicago. Opponents taunted Ransom with his own warnings of 1922, which frustrated him. He had never meant to give ballast to provincial types or to derail the merger process. He wanted a merger that proceeded cautiously, preserved the abolitionist traditions of the AME and AME Zion churches, and strengthened black Methodism. Upon failing to get it he founded the Fraternal Council of Negro Churches, an association of twelve black denominations, in 1934. The group met until 1939, lapsed for two years, and tried again in 1942, but it never coalesced. The council lacked funding and leaders who had time for it. Near the end of his life Ransom bitterly summarized why the three black Methodist churches never managed to unite despite holding the same polity and the same articles of faith. The leading causes, in his view, were "bigotry, narrowness of mind and spirit, selfish personal ambition on the part of church leaders, and lust for personal prestige, honor and power."[134]

Had Alexander Walters matched Ransom's longevity, the two leading black social gospel bishops might have pulled off one of Ransom's ecumenical dreams. As it was, Ransom was elderly before anyone viewed him as a mainstream churchman, and Walters was gone by the time it happened.

ALEXANDER WALTERS AND MAINSTREAM SOCIAL CHRISTIANITY

We have met Walters enough times already for him to be familiar. Ransom spent most of his career trying to get the AME Church to stand up for racial justice, a national social justice agenda, and progressive theology. For much of that time he had to battle merely for his right to advocate such things in the church. Walters, leading a less explicitly activist denomination, had an easier time legitimizing the social gospel within it, mainly because he influenced the mainstream from within it.

Walters was born into slavery in 1858 in the kitchen of the Donohue Hotel in Bardstown, Kentucky. His father, Henry Walters, was the son and slave of his father, Michael Donohue. Alexander's mother, Harriet Mathers Walters, had two owners in Missouri and Larue County, Kentucky, before she became Donohue's property. On his father's side Walters was distantly related to Abraham Lincoln; from his light-colored mother he inherited his tall, commanding, robust physicality and his independent spirit. On one occasion Harriet Walters witnessed a fight between Donohue and one of his sons in which the son tried to stab Donohue. She seized the fully grown younger man by the seat of his pants and nape of his neck, carried him across the kitchen, and threw him into the grape arbor, greatly impressing her own son. Harriet Walters, besides being fiery and determined, could be obstreperous. On one occasion she hurled a rolling pin at Donohue after he reprimanded her for serving a late breakfast. Donohue tried to sell her for attacking him, but his wife intervened, pleading that Harriet was precious to her. Walters was relieved not to lose his mother; years later, while saying nothing about his father, he recalled, "My mother was as brave as a lion."[135]

Harriet Walters was a fervent AME Zion churchgoer. She had eight children: four died in infancy; Alexander was number six; and she died when he was twelve years old. Walters was very short on personal stories about slavery; for him life began after the Civil War, when he studied under a succession of three private school teachers. As an adolescent he walked five miles each day to school, where he received private instruction from an educator and race leader from Lexington, Rowan Wickliffe. Wickliffe asked the local AME Zion and Baptist churches to select a likely candidate for ministry, whom he would teach without charge. Walters's church selected him. For Walters that settled, at the age of twelve, the question of what he would do with his life. He later recalled, "I was very studious, caring little for sports and the usual boys' pursuits. I was very serious minded, ever looking forward to the vocation which I believed was predestined for me." Elsewhere he recalled, "I was born to preach the gospel."[136]

Walters studied under Wickliffe for four years, finding a role model. He waited tables in Louisville and worked on steamboats on the Mississippi and Ohio Rivers, living briefly with his older brother Henry in Louisville, where he took private instruction in physics and rhetoric from two teachers at the local high school. At the age of eighteen he was licensed to preach at the AME Zion Church in Indianapolis. The following year he joined the Kentucky Conference of the AME Zion Church and married a young woman from Louisville and Indianapolis, Katie Knox. Walters's first ministerial assignment was a Methodist circuit lacking a congregation, a trying beginning. He also served churches in Cloverport and Louisville. In 1883 Bishop J. W. Hood assigned Walters to Stockton Street Church in San Francisco, where he spent the three happiest years of his life. He later recalled, in the phrases of Wesleyan sanctification theology: "I can truthfully say that I lived a sanctified life; I did not possess adamic nor angelic perfection, but perfect love."[137]

Julia Foote, a noted revival preacher, lived with the Walters family in San Francisco, filling the home with her spiritual serenity. Foote was born to former slaves in Schenectady, New York, in 1823. In 1844 she was expelled from her home congregation in Boston for contending that her pastor and her husband held incorrect views on sanctification. For decades she traveled across the country as an evangelist, sometimes preaching to thousands of people at holiness revivals. In 1894 Foote became the first woman in the AME Zion Church to be ordained a deacon, and in 1900 she became the second woman to be ordained an elder. Walters treasured her friendship and spiritual beauty. On September 9, 1884, he had a powerful experience of illumination, awaking with "a wonderful weight of glory; it seemed to me that heaven had entered anew into my soul, and all the day long it was 'Glory, Glory, Glory.'" This experience inspired Walters to preach every night for three months, reviving his congregation. In San Francisco Walters became the first black member of the Men's Bible Club sponsored by the Young Women's Christian Association, and he denounced the Supreme Court's 1883 decision abrogating the civil rights of

Afro-Americans, appealing to President Arthur. He attended the Republican National Convention in Chicago in 1884, sadly concluding that Republican delegates no longer cared about the rights of black Americans or even pretended to do so. Near the end of his ministry in San Francisco Walters had a vision in which a spiritual being told him that he would become a bishop. He trembled at the thought but was told to trust in the guidance of the Holy Spirit. For the next eight years he took for granted that he was destined to be a bishop; in San Francisco he built the AME Zion Church's showcase house of worship.[138]

In 1886 Hood moved Walters to Thompkins Chapel in Chattanooga, Tennessee, where he conducted a successful revival and expected to settle in. The city was soon flooded, however, and Walters lost his health under the physical and emotional strain of cleaning up. His illness necessitated a transfer to Knoxville, where Walters regained his health and spent two years healing factional splits at Loguen Temple Church. At every stop he emphasized personal holiness, spiritual discipline, social engagement, and race pride. William J. Simmons, catching Walters on the way up in 1887, described him as an exemplary pastor and race leader, "honored and loved by all who know him," and an excellent orator: "He is affable, kind and gentlemanly, winning by his elegant manner all those who come in contact with him. His habits of life are plain, his methods of work practical, and his success is always of the highest order." Walters was twenty-nine years old at the time. The following year he was appointed to Mother Zion Church in New York.[139]

Mother Zion was at a low point, still housed in a commodious brick edifice on Bleecker Street in Greenwich Village with room for two thousand in the sanctuary. This time Walters had to preach every night for nine months to revive the congregation. For six months he preached about law and ethics, until Katie told him to preach some gospel love. As usual Walters called upon Foote to help preach the revival, plus a battery of clerical and lay friends, including several women. In an earlier generation Walters would have preached heaven, personal religion, abolition, race pride, and not much else. As a social gospeler he preached personal religion on Sunday morning and social religion on Sunday night. Walters was a pioneer of social justice activism in the AME Zion Church, but he had no dramatic story to tell about taking lumps for it. The way was comparatively smooth for Walters. In 1892 he was elected bishop at the AME Zion General Conference in Pittsburgh, when he was thirty-three years old. Walters made a promise to God: "I promise to love Thee fervently, and to serve Thee diligently all the days of my life. And to do all in my power to bring the ministry, over which I am appointed to preside, up to the highest standard of moral and Christian integrity." His first Episcopal assignment took him to the

Seventh District of Kentucky, Missouri, Arkansas, California, West Tennessee, Mississippi, and Oregon.[140]

Walters's grounding in gospel religion strengthened and legitimized his political ministry. It helped that the custom of supporting one's pastor in public was as strong in AME Zion congregations as in AME and Baptist congregations. Had Walters ministered in a remote area when the social gospel took off, the theology of making society itself a subject of redemption would have taken longer to reach him. As it was, ministering in New York, he was immersed in it. Walters joined forces with Fortune shortly after moving to New York, where he signed the call for an Afro-American League in November 1889. He played a leadership role in the league's New York City branch and chaired the executive committee of the league's state organization. The league's first big rally, a protest against Jim Crow railroad cars, took place at Mother Zion. There former politician John Mercer Langston contended that the cause of equal rights needed lawyers more than preachers; Walters appealed for more of both. His election as bishop the following year was a godsend for the struggling civil rights movement.[141]

Walters projected robust self-confidence and deep conviction. He had a commanding presence and sounded white to white audiences, especially because he was light-colored, all of which played to his advantage in racially mixed settings. In his early years as a bishop to a far-flung district he devoted himself to building up the AME Zion Church and making its ministry more effective. Walters had a global consciousness, however, traveling to England with the mostly white Sunday School Union in 1889 and returning the following year to address the World's Christian Endeavor convention in London. The national branch of the latter organization remained the chief vehicle of his two-sided spiritual and political activism long after Walters persuaded Fortune to launch the Afro-American Council in 1898 and became the group's president.

Francis E. Clark, a Dartmouth College graduate and Congregational minister in Portland, Maine, founded the Christian Endeavor Society in Portland in 1881. From the beginning it was ecumenical and interracial, focused on involving teenagers and young adults in social ministry. This was a wellspring of the ecumenical movement's commitment to internationalism and the social gospel. The Christian Endeavor Society trained young adults for socially relevant ministries, serving as a prototype for the World Student Christian Movement launched in 1895. Clark started with a handful of youth at Williston Congregational Church in Maine. Two years later there were chapters across the United States. By the early 1890s there were chapters in England, South Africa, India, China, Bermuda, Japan, France, Turkey, Spain, Australia, Samoa,

Mexico, Chile, Brazil, Egypt, Germany, Siam, Guatemala, Italy, Bulgaria, Russia, and the Philippines. By the early twentieth century the society had nearly four million members and over seventy-seven thousand chapters. Walters's address to the world convention in 1890 made him a player in the organization.[142]

In London Walters told the society that its commitment to spiritual regeneration, Christian mission, interracial fellowship, and young people struck the right chord. He came from a country in which people like him were denigrated because of their color and formerly enslaved condition, "for neither of which we are responsible." He came to London knowing that blacks had white friends in the world, because his nation produced Abraham Lincoln, William Lloyd Garrison, Wendell Phillips, John Brown, Charles Sumner, Henry Ward Beecher, and others of the abolition generation. This list had multiplied since emancipation, Walters assured, and Clark was foremost on the post-emancipation list. Walters loved the society because it stood for Christian unity and "the deepening of the spiritual life." Too much evangelism focused on believing certain things about Christ's atonement, leaving out the part about being righteous: "They seem to have forgotten that the object of Christ's coming into the world was to save them from their sins. That the whole plan of salvation is the complete restoration of mankind to the image of God. Purity of life is one of the indispensable requisites for happiness and effectual service."[143]

Walters preached way-of-Jesus, Wesleyan, social gospel perfectionism, urging that the essential task of Christian proclamation was to show how Jesus lived, setting forth "His self-denial, His meekness, His purity, His blameless life, His spirit of prayer, His submission to divine will, His patience in suffering, His forgiveness of His enemies, His tenderness to the afflicted, the weak and the tempted, and the manner of His death." Jesus is the "perfectly pure model" of the sanctified life, and the only one, Walters held: "Piety flourishes just in proportion as the pure example of Jesus Christ is kept before a people." This was why revivals worked; people heard about Jesus every night, not just Sunday. Walters implored the young Christians to fight against alcohol, bribery, racial prejudice, and predatory business trusts. Alcohol was a "hydra-headed monster of wickedness" that destroyed individuals, families, and everything else it touched. Bribery had become a way of life in a corrupt age. Racial prejudice humiliated and oppressed many of God's children. Business combinations crushed the poor and exalted a handful of greedy capitalists. Walters urged the young Christians to "consecrate" themselves to the righting of wrongs: "You are to strike in defense of those who are oppressed. Hear the Master say today, 'To the work! To the work!'"[144]

The Christian Endeavor Society was perfect for Walters, and he for it. In 1894 he was elected to the group's board of trustees, on which he served for the rest of his life. In 1895 he gave a stem-winder at the national convention in Boston that boosted his prominence in civil rights politics. Walters started boldly with a word about what he wanted to be called. The term "Negro," he noted, had become perverted by its close association with a slur word that black Americans hated, so he did not want to be called that. "Black" and "colored" were better, but many people who were "forced into our ranks" by a racist society were more white in color than either black or colored, which made the color words uncomfortable for them. Walters observed that a few years earlier, Fortune had begun to use the term "Afro-American" as an analogue to "Anglo-Saxon." Walters preferred this term over the others. "Afro-American" made sense, he reasoned; he was an American by way of Africa. In fact, this was the only term that rightly designated people of African and American lineage, though Walters soon went back to using "Negro" and "black" interchangeably with "Afro-American." He did not like words that defined him by color alone, but he deferred to convention and used them anyway.[145]

Walters shook his head at critics like Turner who claimed there was little difference between the racism of the American South and the rest of the country. What were they talking about? His life was rich and full in the North, he went wherever he pleased, and he had white friends. Where was that possible in the South? Throughout the South, Walters stressed, Afro-Americans were routinely treated harshly and threatened with violence, many were lynched, and they were subjected to Jim Crow railroad cars and excluded from white hotels, restaurants, schools, and hospitals. Everywhere else, he observed, "we are treated fairly well." To be sure, Afro-Americans were often excluded from trade unions and public works, but there was no comparison between the South and the rest of the country. A year before *Plessy v. Ferguson* made it harder to say, Walters told the Christian Endeavor Society that the civil rights movement was primarily about compelling the white South to treat Afro-Americans more like the rest of America did.[146]

To make that happen, nice churchgoing types like them had to agitate for racial justice. Walters urged that wise agitation was indispensable, as distinguished from the other kind: "By wise agitation I mean an intelligent, reasonable, yet manly presentation of the discriminations and outrages to which we are subjected. We are not afraid to give credit to all who are friendly to our cause or who aid us in any way, shape or form, whether they be in the North or South. I would not have you think for a moment that we are unappreciative or ungrateful for past favors; neither would I have you think that we will be

contented with less than our equal rights as guaranteed to us by the Constitution."
It should not be that difficult to keep one's balance in this area, Walters believed,
though unbalanced behavior abounded. One had to call things by their right
names. Some people were oppressors and some were oppressed; this had to be
said plainly. Walters implored his young, mostly white Christian audience that
agitation was the "watchword of oppressed people for the centuries; it is a cry
which the oppressor has always endeavored to stifle."[147]

Walters had a closing word about Afro-Americans who claimed that Afro-
Americans were too religious. It was not possible to have too much good religion, he contended. People who said that Afro-Americans were too religious had
a prejudiced idea about religion, though certainly, some kinds of religion were
not helpful: "No one can have too much piety. A person can have too much
superstition, too much emotion, but not too much common-sense piety."[148]

As oppression worsened, Walters sorely regretted the lack of a civil rights
organization. He didn't know how to attract the masses to civil rights activism,
but he understood acutely the other main problem. Fortune said it constantly—
black American leaders were too quarrelsome and independent to work
together. If only more of them were like Walters! Walters stewed over this
problem until 1898, when Isaiah Loftin was lynched for accepting a Georgia
postmaster position. Walters wrote in the *New York Age* that Loftin was cut
down for no other reason than being black. There was no reason to believe the
perpetrators would be brought to justice, and the economic situation was
getting worse for Afro-Americans. Therefore "it becomes absolutely necessary
that we organize for self-protection."[149]

Walters dragged Fortune into it, rounding up members for the Afro-American
Council and agreeing to serve as president after Fortune told the founders in
Rochester, New York, that this group would not work, either. Walters gave himself
wholeheartedly to the council. He hammered out its agenda, spoke across the
country, and urged that the civil rights community had to unite its conservatives,
moderates, progressives, and radicals. Under his leadership, meeting on December
29, 1898, at the Metropolitan Baptist Church in Washington, DC, the council
adopted a tenfold agenda. It pledged to oppose lynching, challenge segregation in
court, enact state laws supporting the Fourteenth and Fifteenth Amendments,
advocate prison reform, encourage a "healthy migration from terror-ridden sectors
of our land" to law-abiding states, support industrial and higher education, promote
Afro-American businesses, educate the public about racial justice, "elevate" Afro-
American morality, and secure federal funding for equal education. This agenda
carefully blended the ideologies of the group's pro-Washington and radical wings,
as did Walters's address, a model of sensible agitation.[150]

Walters inveighed against the "everlasting shame" of America's racist founding. Afro-Americans lacked the option of being nostalgic for a mythic past, for "every possible effort was put forth to keep him down." To "so-called friends" who advised Afro-Americans to keep quiet about the abuses inflicted on them by white people, Walters had withering questions: "Shall we not speak out when innocent men and women of our race are burned at the stake, hung to the limbs of trees and shot down like dogs? Shall we look on indifferently while our women are insulted and outraged by Negro-hating white men? Shall we say nothing while thousands in the rural districts in the South are robbed of their meager earnings?"[151]

Morally, silence was not an option in the face of such persecution. Walters declared, "There can be no real peace in America until this problem is solved, and solved according to the rules of equity." He observed that white America readily spent blood and treasure to liberate Cubans and Filipinos from Spanish oppression. Where was the comparable concern for Afro-Americans? "We, your brethren in black, appeal to this powerful, enlightened Christian conscience, to this humanitarian spirit which has caused this nation to do so much for Cuba, Hawaii and the Philippine Islands." The federal government had to provide a public education for all Afro-Americans, and white America had to stop excluding Afro-Americans from decent jobs. Afro-Americans, Walters acknowledged, had moral and educational deficiencies to overcome, but the moral deficiencies were easily exaggerated, and often were: "Our enemies demand of us perfection. They are unreasonable. They require among us in twenty short years a state of moral rectitude which they themselves, with far more favorable opportunities, have not realized in one hundred times twenty."[152]

Walters got a tremendous ovation, which suggested for a moment that he had a chance of uniting the civil rights community. For a while his rhetoric got hotter, mostly in response to the lynching of Sam Hose outside Atlanta. Addressing the New Jersey Methodist Conference in Jersey City a few days after the Hose lynching, Walters charged that lynching was white terrorism, not a response to black criminality: "This cry [that] we must protect our Southern white women, is leading us on to another bloody struggle; it is the Southern white man's subterfuge to satiate his implacable hatred for the negro." Reprising his trope about white America helping Cuba and the Philippines, he added that Spain never treated Cubans and Filipinos "as barbarously" as Arkansas, Texas, North Carolina, South Carolina, and Georgia treated many Afro-Americans. Walters confided that he found it difficult to stomach America's exertions on behalf of "equitable and beneficent government" for Cubans and Filipinos, given the circumstances.[153]

Back in America, he warned, a race war was building: "The greatest problem of America today is not the currency question nor the colonial possessions, but how to avoid the racial war at home. You cannot forever keep the Negro out of his rights." Slavery turned the Afro-American into a coward, Walters said. Every Afro-American was taught to fear the white people. Thankfully, that was ending: "He is rapidly emerging from such slavish fear, and ere long will contend for his rights as bravely as any other man." Walters ended on a surprisingly militant note: "In the name of the almighty God, what are we to do but fight and die?"[154]

That startled journalist John Edward Bruce, normally a fiery black nationalist, who judged that Walters overstepped. Bruce warned that most black Americans were not up for fighting and very few whites were ready to aid blacks "in a crusade against the lawless white mobs of the south." No race on earth was more clannish or united than American whites, he cautioned. If a race war broke out, northern whites would rush to support southern whites and blacks would be slaughtered. If that seemed pessimistic to northern blacks who had a few white friends, Bruce advised them to consider the fate of America's native population. In addition, Bruce did not think, contrary to Walters, that white America's adventures in Cuba and the Philippines had an idealistic motive. Bruce generally admired Walters, believing that he had the best temperament for race leadership among current race leaders; years later he praised Walters as a "big-hearted, whole-souled, generous man." But Bruce admonished Walters to practice what he preached, keeping his balance. Any talk about a race war would go badly for black Americans.[155]

Walters soon stepped back from "fight and die" rhetoric, urging that agitation had to be sufficiently calibrated not to get people killed. He called on black Americans to observe a national day of prayer and fasting (Friday, June 2, 1899) and called on black ministers to preach about lynching and racial justice the following Sunday. Turner, Hood, Francis Grimké, and others endorsed this call, and solidarity services were held in churches across the country. In Philadelphia Walters addressed a joint meeting of the local Afro-American Council and the Methodist Preacher's Union (a white organization), imploring civic and religious leaders to oppose the escalating violence against black Americans. Philadelphia journalist Gertrude Mossell agreed with Bruce that Walters was distinctly important to the racial justice cause, though Walters had critics in the black press.

Did a minister have any business leading the Afro-American Council? Wasn't this the problem with civil rights politics, that it had too many ministers? Calvin Chase was acidic on this theme, deriding the council as a miserable joke not worth discussing, which did not stop Chase from condemning it repeatedly.

According to Chase, the council had far too many ministers, notably Walters, whom Chase ridiculed as "erratic, vacillating ... impetuous and rattle-brain[ed]." Few critics recycled Chase's personal denigration of Walters, but many critics agreed that blacks already prayed too much and overrelied on ministers. Journalist C. C. Steward urged that a single double-barreled rifle did more to stop mob terrorism than all the prayers lifted to heaven. Bruce replied that prayer and racial justice militancy went together:

> Pray for hearts pierced through with sorrow
> Burdened down with woe and grief
> Pray for sold whom the tomorrow
> Offers but a slight relief,
> Heaven hear us,
> And defend us, Help, O, help our blind belief.[156]

This was the backstory to the Afro-American Council convention of 1899 in Chicago, at which Washington admonished Walters to stifle his left flank, Ransom erupted against Washington, and Du Bois chastised Ransom for over-stepping. Though Du Bois later downplayed his role in the council, in the early years he was an active member of it. Walters held the council together at the 1899 convention by defending Washington for staying away. The following month, having reelected Walters as president, the council established its national headquarters in Washington, DC, and blasted President McKinley for refusing to defend the rights of black Americans. Walters devoted his speeches to federal legislation against lynching and organized the council around this objective. At the same time he stirred a controversy by urging Afro-Americans to develop some political independence.

Walters did not say that blacks should leave the Republican Party or become Democrats. He said that blacks should challenge the Republican and Democratic Parties to compete for their support. Alarmed critics did not hear it that way, however. According to Chase, Walters made the council more pitiful than ever by telling Afro-Americans to leave the Republican Party. Chase explained, already forgetting that he ridiculed the council from the beginning, that Fortune conceived the council as "a strong race organization." Then came the ministers, and the organization quickly became ridiculous: "The preacher has killed the Council. Whenever there are too many Methodist preachers mixed up in any institution, you can just come to the conclusion that pot-house politics must enter." Two Republican officials heeded Chase's call to quit the council, and several council leaders tried to limit the damage, explaining that Walters spoke only for himself and he did not oppose the Republican Party. Edward Cooper, editor of the *Colored American*, reasoned that the council was a coalition of administration Republicans, anti-administration Republicans, Democrats, independents, prohibitionists, female suffragists, and others committed to race advancement, not a party. Du Bois and Bruce agreed, but Bruce chastised council leaders for apologizing for Walters. The council didn't need wet nurses, Bruce admonished, especially overzealously defensive ones. The only people who disagreed with Walters were afraid of losing their jobs or their shadows.[157]

The Afro-American Council had not meant to say quite so explicitly that it was political but not partisan. Walters pushed the group to say it publicly, affirming the diversity of views within its membership. In the early going the group pushed hard for HR 6963, a bill sponsored by House Republican George H. White (North Carolina) to make lynching a federal crime. White leaned on Massachusetts legal scholar Albert E. Pillsbury's defense of the constitutionality of federal anti-lynching law, contending that the federal government was empowered to protect the lives of its citizens. White offered the bill in January 1900, but the House refused to vote on it or to allow White to read it into the *Congressional Record*.

The council responded by mobilizing its Anti-Lynching Bureau. Wells-Barnett, John Mitchell Jr., and White conducted speaking tours to drum up support for the bill. Walters and others lobbied members of Congress. White read into the *Congressional Record* racist statements by House and Senate colleagues, which yielded permission to read HR 6963 into the *Record*. That summer he and black Republican stalwart John R. Lynch, a veteran of the Reconstruction Congress, tried to get the Republican National Convention to take a stand against lynching. Lynch's resolution would have reduced representation in Congress for states that did not comply with the Fourteenth Amendment. Wells-Barnett, lecturing along the East Coast, implored that the entire nation was morally responsible for the escalation of mob terrorism and that lynching was destroying the moral fiber of the nation.[158]

For a while the Afro-American Council was the nation's leading authority and activist organization on the plague of lynching. It pressed white Americans to recognize that lynching was about race hatred, not defending white women from black rapists, and it had become a defining aspect of American culture, not an episodic spasm of the lunatic fringe. But Republicans failed to rally against lynching, and White's bill died in the House Judiciary Committee. Walters's pitch for political independence got ballast he did not want, as there was almost no difference between the Republican and Democratic National Conventions of 1900 concerning the right of black Americans not to be lynched or disenfranchised.

In the summer of 1900 New Orleans erupted in a race riot, Chase roiled the council by demanding that it get in line with the Republican Party, and Walters delicately danced with the Washington issue again. Washington wavered on whether he should attend the council convention; Walters told him: "Don't think for a moment that I believe you disloyal to our cause. There can be no conflict between the Afro-American Council and yourself. You are contending for the industrial development of the Negro, while we are contending for his civil and political rights. I am with you in your work and I believe you are with us in ours. We understand that you would take the same stand that we are taking but for your school."[159]

Walters treated Washington gingerly because Walters wanted a united front of pro-Booker, anti-Booker, and straddler activists. But Washington had no interest in legitimizing a diversity of views about Bookerism. The success of the council compelled Washington to take it over; otherwise his dominating racial leadership was in question. Washington seeded the council with his operatives, plotting a takeover that took three years to pull off. In 1900 Walters told the council's convention that its immediate business was nothing less than the struggle for "complete civil and political rights." Meanwhile the convention battled over partisan politics again before deciding not to change its nonpartisan stance, and Washington gave his customary speech on industrial education, carefully avoiding any mention of attacks on the Reconstruction Amendments or the council's agitation against the attacks. Afterward a reporter asked him if he had anything to say about recent disenfranchisement and segregation legislation; Washington replied in full Wizard mode: "I would be delighted to give you an interview on that subject if I felt it advisable to talk, but I must decline."[160]

The council had no national organizer, so the burden to make news fell on Walters. Wells-Barnett helped out in this area, publicizing her speaking tours and writing about the council's anti-lynching, legal, legislative, and business bureaus. In public she explained that the bureaus carried out the council's main work and everything else was secondary. In private she implored Council officers to hire a national organizer and they complied by hiring her. At the 1901 convention in Philadelphia, Emmett Scott replaced Du Bois as head of the business bureau, ostensibly to help the council work with Washington's newly founded National Negro Business League. In 1902, as the council entered its fourth year, Walters believed the united front was working. He was still president, Fortune and White served as vice presidents after White lost his congressional seat, Fortune guarded Washington's interests, and Wells-Barnett ran the Anti-Lynching Bureau. But the Bookerites were gaining control of the committees. That year Frederick McGhee ran a pro-Washington convention in St. Paul, Minnesota, where a nominating committee stacked with Bookerites replaced Walters with Fortune and demoted Walters to director of the executive committee. The slate was rammed through in a confusing and disorderly vote, and Fortune became president, outraging Wells-Barnett, who resigned from the council in protest.[161]

Many delegates pleaded that nothing had changed and Wells-Barnett should not leave. She replied that everything had changed and she would not work under Bookerites. McGhee soon regretted his role in paving the way for the Booker takeover. Trotter blasted the council, declaring that he no longer trusted Du Bois because Du Bois capitulated to Washington's coup. That helped to turn Du Bois, who winced at being on the wrong side. Meanwhile, Scott wrote to Washington gleefully: "It was wonderful to see how completely your personality dominated everything. . . . It is not hard for you to understand that we control the Council." The latter boast was undeniable by 1903, when the council installed Bookerite William Steward as president. The following year the Tuskegee Machine completely took over at the convention in St. Louis, reelecting Steward as president, electing the brothers John Quincy Adams and Cyrus Field Adams as vice president and secretary, electing James Guy as national organizer, and filling the bureaus with Booker operatives, too. Walters was retained as executive committee director, but the Afro-American Council no longer spoke like Walters about fighting for civil rights.[162]

Walters took his demotion graciously, tried to swing the council back to sensible agitation, and waited. He regretted losing Wells-Barnett, but tried to keep his ego out of it. He respected Fortune and sought to work agreeably with him. Walters went on giving his customary speeches, telling an audience in Richmond that God called McKinley to eternal rest because God hated what McKinley did to blacks in America: "We are contending under God for legal rights, every one of them, and we should boldly say so. The duty of the hour is to press this fight, and every Negro who has a drop of manly blood in his veins will come up to the colors." Meanwhile Booker operatives seeped into the council and Du Bois struck hard with *The Souls of Black Folk*. Fortune took a job with the Treasury Department as special immigration agent, studying conditions in Hawaii and the Philippines, which made him an absentee president. Council vice president William Pledger did most of Fortune's job while Walters sorely regretted that the council scored no legal victories in its first five years. Walters's frustration with the council's legal bureau (especially White) drove him to rationalize that perhaps the crafty Booker operatives would do better. At the council's 1903 convention in Louisville, a large portrait of Washington was placed on the stage—a galling display of hubris to the new abolitionists who had been pushed aside.[163]

Walters stayed in the picture by sticking to his position and practicing organizational diplomacy. The Tuskegee takeover did not smell as bad if Walters retained a leadership role, and some members remained in the organization only because he was still there. Walters gave them hope in 1904 by reasserting himself, emphasizing his differences with Washington. His disillusionment with Roosevelt was a key factor. Walters was a chief purveyor of the view that blacks had a friend in the White House. By 1904, however, Walters realized that TR was just another politician with no intention of risking anything for Afro-Americans. Walters began to say it stridently, which brought him into conflict with Booker Washington. Then Du Bois founded the Niagara Movement in July 1905 and Walters told friends he had to regain the council presidency. Otherwise, sensible agitators like Mitchell and Francis Grimké might gravitate to Niagara and the council would be ruined. The following month Walters won back the council presidency and McGhee told the *Washington Bee* it was too late to matter. The Bookerites had already destroyed the council, McGhee said. The situation was so bad that Fortune abandoned the council, even though he was responsible for much of what went wrong. McGhee played down that he bore considerable responsibility, too. McGhee wished that Walters had fought for the council when it was worth saving. Instead he acquiesced "for harmony's sake," cooperating with Bookerites and their "death-dealing" methods. McGhee charged that the aim of the Bookerites, all along, was to kill the council. This they had accomplished. Trying to revive it was pointless.[164]

Wells-Barnett took the same line, blasting Walters and the council in the *New York Age*, except that she spurned the Niagara Movement too, before and after it welcomed female supporters. For her this was a period of painful exits. Wells-Barnett lost the vehicle for her anti-lynching activism when she quit the council. She left Bethel Church after Ransom's successor, Abraham Lincoln Murray, got away with sexually harassing the wife of a church board member. Wells-Barnett later recalled that she could not remain at Bethel, despite its enormous importance to her, because Bethel's minister was "a man who had become so notoriously immoral." She also had a bitter falling out with the president of the Ida B. Wells Club, Agnes Moody, which further estranged Wells-Barnett from the National Association of Colored Women. Later she joined the NAACP at its founding, but that was short-lived, too.[165]

Walters was the opposite of Wells-Barnett on the matter of working with others. He refused to give up on the Bookerites, he maintained a comradely friendship with Trotter, and he moved closer to Du Bois politically. Walters was for anything and any group that tried to spark a serious civil rights movement. He shrugged off the attacks on the council and his leadership, countering that the council lobbied the McKinley and Roosevelt administrations, it testified before government committees, it launched numerous legal test cases, and it rallied the public against lynching. In July 1905 the council's legal bureau won its first victory, prevailing in circuit court over a streetcar segregation law in Florida; shortly afterward the state supreme court upheld the circuit judge's decision. *Cleveland Gazette* editor Harry Smith, though a committed Niagarite, lauded the council on its victory and praised Walters for not giving up on the council. The following year Du Bois acknowledged that the council was surprisingly renewed with activist vigor; in his telling, it happened because the Niagara Movement challenged Walters to shake things up. Du Bois assured readers that he anticipated no merger with the council and no self-effacing statements. Two years later he had to eat some crow, pleading that the Niagara Movement and the Afro-American Council stood for "essentially the same things," along with the Negro American Political League and the Negro Academy. Du Bois proposed to merge the four organizations, but by 1908 all four were depleted and exhausted.[166]

Walters was emphatically a believer in being faithful, whether or not the council succeeded, although he also touted the council's successes. In the spring and summer months preceding the Atlanta riot of 1906, Walters toured the country with a stump speech making the case for the newly renewed council. Always he began with the post-slavery story of the Afro-American people, drawing on his experience. Black Americans came out of the Civil War asking what they should do to be saved, Walters recalled. The answer they accepted was to get educated, improve their morals, acquire money, and rely on the party of Lincoln to secure their civil and political rights. They made a "wild and commendable rush for the schoolroom," surprising themselves by their academic successes. They built churches and improved their morals, bought houses and built up wealth, and rode in carriages to church—only to see the party of Lincoln sell them out in 1876 for "a mess of political pottage."[167]

Reconstruction was terminated, Afro-Americans lost their rights across the South, and they tried to organize for self-protection. Walters told the story of the Afro-American League's swift fall into "innocuous desuetude," explaining that its leaders "had reckoned without their host." According to him, the Afro-American Council did not repeat this mistake. It stayed in touch with ordinary people, campaigned across the nation, and concentrated on real-world activism. It had the same objectives in 1906 that it espoused at its founding a decade earlier—making no allusion to recent backsliding. It was the first Afro-American organization to oppose lynch law "in all of its forms," and it remained staunchly opposed to lynching. Walters noted that lynching had become less frequent in recent years, attributing the drop-off "in large part" to the council's agitation. Moreover, the council was the first organization to challenge Jim Crow in court, and it encouraged other organizations to take up this work. This was the most important thing that Afro-Americans could do in the present situation, he exhorted: "Go into the courts and fight it out." At the local level, Walter acknowledged, the movement was sure to lose many cases. The crucial thing was to keep pushing, play for the long term, and believe that justice would prevail in the higher courts: "Being persistent in our efforts, I am of the opinion that we shall win in the end."[168]

He gave high priority to prison reform. The South's convict-release system was slavery by another name, Walters charged, "a stench in the nostrils of good men and women." Making progress on this issue was difficult because everybody feared criminals and most people had no personal acquaintance with southern prisons. Walters admitted that he had to rely on what others told him about prison conditions. But they told him the prison camps were "hells on earth," perpetrating more cruelty than "any other department of the Southern government." Walters assured that some black prisoners were "very, very wicked." He put it stronger, declaring that the "greatest bane" of Afro-American life was the existence of its "criminal class," an "inflowing tide" of thieves and predators. Eliminating black criminality was a terribly serious matter of the highest priority, he stressed. But that did not justify imposing an extremely wicked system of reconstituted slavery on all black prisoners. The prison issue by itself was reason enough for black southerners to move somewhere else. As it was, Walters lamented, there were many reasons.[169]

He was equally frank about the black church, urging that it needed a stronger dose of the social gospel: "I am of the opinion that the Negro Church should place greater emphasis upon the ethical part of religion and put forth more strenuous efforts to reach the masses. My people like all others need the Christian religion to save them. The greatest saving force in the world is the regenerating force of Christianity." With Washington, Walters affirmed that Afro-Americans needed industrial education and wealth. With Du Bois, he affirmed that Afro-Americans needed higher education and an abolitionist spirit. More plainly and forcefully than Washington or Du Bois, he proclaimed that all people were helpless and hopeless without God.[170]

Walters tired of hearing that the council had not accomplished anything, countering that it deserved more credit. Defeat and self-effacement prevailed when the council was formed, he recalled. There was no organization crying for equal rights for black Americans: "It was the council which clarified this oppressive atmosphere. At the time, it was the only voice heard in the wilderness as a distinct racial organization, crying aloud for equal rights for the black man and formed to fight oppressions of all kinds." He welcomed the Niagarites to this work, assuring there was plenty to share. On that somewhat upbeat note Walters ended his stump speech, calling newcomers to the struggle. In September 1906 he published the speech in the *Colored American Magazine*.[171]

That month Atlanta exploded into five days of lynching and mayhem, and Walters dispensed with his upbeat story about things getting better. Now he said that nothing was better after years of struggle against white racism. Addressing the council's convention in New York, he declared: "The object of our enemies is to make us serfs and they are going to continue to do everything in their power to obtain their object." In that case, Walters urged, it was pointless to speak of reconciliation or making peace. The struggle for equal rights was everything; there could be no peace without equal rights. Walters went back to speaking about fighting to the point of victory or death, no longer worried how that would sound in the *New York Times*: "We may use diplomatic language and all kinds of subterfuge, but the fact remains that the enemy is trying to keep us down and that we are determined to rise or die in the attempt."[172]

The Atlanta riot and the Brownsville debacle delivered Walters from having to worry that Bookerism would make a comeback. Walters and the council teamed with Milholland's Constitution League to keep the pot boiling over Brownsville. Nearly two hundred delegates attended the council's 2007 convention in Baltimore, plus a contingent of well-wishing Niagarites. Walters told them that racial discrimination had to be "fought to the death." Booker operatives John C. Dancy and Melvin Chisien tried to restrain the convention, without success. Dancy implored the council not to repudiate Roosevelt for Brownsville. Delegates advised Dancy to make a safety move, by exiting quickly; then they formally condemned Roosevelt. They also pledged to support the Niagara Movement, lauding its fight against Jim Crow. Du Bois was appreciative, declaring in *Horizon* that the council had "unhorsed Booker T. Washington, repudiated his doctrines, and fairly spat upon him."[173]

Walters was not for spitting, but he felt sufficiently desperate to go all-in for the Democratic Party. In 1908 he supported Bryan for president with arguments that took little notice of Bryan. Afro-Americans desperately needed a political game changer, Walters implored. Allowing Republicans to take black votes for granted had yielded a Republican Party that did nothing for blacks. Walters urged that the time had come to try something else—supporting Democrats, especially at the top. It was not enough to talk about being more independent;

the only way to change the status quo was to follow through on the threat to oppose Republicans. Walters got edgy about doing so, showing up at Taft's stump speech at Cooper Union in New York. Walters demanded to know if Taft was willing to give a speech justifying Roosevelt's treatment of the Brownsville soldiers. Taft refused to answer, so Walters showed up at Taft's next speech, and the next one, and several more after that, demanding an answer. Every time that Taft brushed off the bishop he made news, alienating black voters.[174]

On the one hand, black political activism was surging; on the other hand, the organizations were reeling from financial stress and lack of members. Du Bois was so frustrated by organizational problems, especially his conflict with Trotter, that in 1907 he nearly resigned on two occasions from the Niagara Movement. The following year Trotter and Du Bois both approached Walters with proposals that did not include each other. Du Bois and Trotter were finished with each other, but each was desperate to build an organization that took advantage of the new political moment. Walters was always eager to build something better. With Trotter and Waldron he launched yet another organization in 1908, the National Negro American Political League, which sought to prevent Roosevelt *and* Taft from winning the Republican nomination. That gave new meaning to "quixotic." After the election the group changed its name to the National Independent Political League and elected Walters as its president. Meanwhile, Walters and Du Bois proposed to merge the Afro-American Council and the Niagara Movement. Walters joined the Washington, DC, branch of Niagara as a gesture of unity, but the merger idea stalled at Niagara's sparsely attended meeting in Oberlin, just as Springfield exploded into a race riot, which sparked the NAACP.[175]

It must have burned Du Bois and Walters to be called by white liberals to create a civil rights organization, after the two of them had spent years begging the same people to support the organizations that existed. Neither of them, however, said it aloud. In a sense, Walters became the NAACP's first black member, being the first Afro-American to join the group in Walling's living room where the organization was created. The year 1908 stood out for Walters, in a career filled with organizational activism. Besides entering the orbit of the Democratic Party and campaigning for Bryan, which later led him to found the National Colored Democratic League (which he ran as president), Walters cofounded the National Negro American Political League, joined the Niagara Movement, and cofounded the Federal Council of Churches, in which he served as a member of the Executive Council Committee and on several commissions. The following year, he helped found what became the NAACP, which he served as the group's first vice president and a board member, and he spoke at the National Negro Conference of 1909, calling for a biracial organization that aggressively fought for equal rights.[176]

But the NAACP was a different kind of organization than the Afro-American Council had been. The cultural politics were more secular and racially mixed. Du Bois infuriated Walters in *Crisis* by claiming that black churches were riddled with bad bishops and corrupt financial practices. Walters recoiled at the harsh personal attacks on Washington that he heard in NAACP circles, especially after Washington had his scrape near the Tenderloin district in 1911. Then Walters played a controversial role in the 1912 election and aftermath, which drove him out of the NAACP.

Walters played hardball for the Democrats in the 1910 midterm election. He and Du Bois sent out a circular telling black New Yorkers that if they wanted to see Afro-Americans in the city police and fire departments, or black soldiers in the state guard, they had better start voting Democratic. Two years later, as president of the National Colored Democratic League, Walters told black audiences that the Republican Party had been running from them for over thirty years. The only way to regain what had been lost was to win the favor and support of Democrats: "If the inimical legislation enacted against the Negro is to be repealed it must be done by the Democratic Party, which is now willing to accept the Negro vote and guarantee a fair deal." Democracy was the watchword and tendency of the age, Walters reasoned. Democratic Party leaders increasingly understood that they had to become more democratic to succeed at national politics. Walters had met white southern Democrats who wanted to leave behind the racist legacy of their party. If a sizable contingent of blacks were to vote Democratic, Walters reasoned, "the so-called black menace will be removed." White southerners would stop fearing that another round of "Negro misrule" was coming.[177]

Always it came back to that—the white southern fear of being ruled by black people. Walters told Afro-Americans they held some power to dispel this fear, merely by splitting their votes. His lecture-circuit audiences protested that Democrats would disenfranchise blacks throughout the nation if they got into power. Walters told them to get a grip. Three-fourths of the states were not going to repeal the Fifteenth Amendment. The Republican Party was good at scaring gullible black voters, and it got more political benefit than it deserved from appointing a few blacks to office. This was a form of political bondage, Walters admonished; blacks were overdue to break free. He was finished with the usual runaround, in which Afro-American leaders appealed for relief to the White House, where they were told to petition the court, where they were told to petition the Republican Congress, where they were told to go back to the court. Republican politicians had no plans to do better for their black supporters, Walters contended. The only way to get their attention was to walk away from them.

In the summer of 1912 the National Colored Democratic League had a campaign bash at Carnegie Hall to which it invited the Democratic candidate, Woodrow Wilson. He could not attend but told Walters in a letter: "It would afford me pleasure to be present, because there are certain things I want to say. I hope that it seems superfluous to those who know me, but to those who do not know me perhaps it is not unnecessary for me to assure my colored fellow-citizens of my earnest wish to see justice done them in every matter, and not mere grudging justice, but justice executed with liberality and cordial good feeling. Every guarantee of our law, every principle of our Constitution, commands this, and our sympathies should also make it easy." Wilson asserted that he had a long-standing "sympathy" for black Americans, adding: "I want to assure them through you that should I become President of the United States they may count upon me for absolute fair dealing and for everything by which I could assist in advancing the interests of their race in the United States."[178]

That was quite a mouthful—"justice" three times, plus "liberality and cordial good feeling" and "absolute fair dealing," and two references to sympathy, plus "everything" else, all vaguely lifted above grubby specific things like lynching, disenfranchisement, and segregation. Walters must have noticed the vagueness, but he spoke across the country on Wilson's behalf, persuading black audiences to vote Democratic. The same letter convinced Du Bois to play a similar role in the election, in which one hundred thousand southern Afro-Americans voted for Wilson. Brownsville mattered more than Walters and Du Bois combined, but Walters and Du Bois played a significant role, as did Villard, who helped many white liberals get behind Wilson.

Disillusionment set in swiftly. For a few months the new president played along as Villard campaigned for a National Race Commission, but Wilson backed out in August 1913, pleading lack of support in the Senate. In the meantime, Wilson ramped up segregation in the federal government, setting off enraged protests from Villard, Du Bois, and the NAACP. Wilson told Villard that he segregated black government workers for their own comfort and protection, and his administration consulted with "a number of colored men" on this issue. That was unbelievable to Villard. Who did Wilson consult? Villard pressed Wilson's secretary, Joseph Tumulty, and perhaps some cabinet members for an answer. Someone told him the issue had been discussed at a cabinet meeting on April 11, 1913, where Postmaster General Albert S. Burleson reported that he had conferred with "Bishop Walters and other prominent Negroes," some of whom approved the administration's plan. Villard angrily told Wilson that any black leader who approved the plan, if exposed, would immediately become a pariah. Then Villard publicly accused Walters of being the guilty party. Walters was deeply offended at being outed. The NAACP board compounded the humiliation by declining to defend him, and Walters resigned from the NAACP board in November 1913.[179]

Walters never explained what happened, although it was not hard to figure out. Wilson had no Afro-American advisor, believing that he didn't need one and was better off politically without one. To Walters, that attitude was grievously mistaken; plus, Walters believed that the advisor should be him. Moreover, Walters incurred suspicion in NAACP circles by defending Washington from an onslaught of personal criticism, which made it easier for NAACP allies to turn on him, which made Walters feel betrayed by the NAACP. All of that made it easy to forget Walters after the NAACP went on to glory, yielding shelves of books on this subject that barely mentioned him or the Afro-American Council. Shawn Leigh Alexander, recounting the history of the council, rightly counters that it was no less important than the Niagara Movement in paving the way to the NAACP. Moreover, although Walters rolled over during the early Wilson administration, currying favor with the new president, he did not linger there. Wilson told his cabinet that he never made any promises to black Americans "except to do them justice." Walters burned with remorse at having assured black Americans that Wilson cared about them. He admired Trotter for standing up to Wilson in the White House. He protested that Wilson's "New Freedom" only applied to white people. In 1915 Wilson tried to mollify Walters, asking him to be minister to Liberia, but that was less than Walters deserved and he was finished with providing racial cover for Wilson. Plus he wanted his friend James L. Curtis to get the job.[180]

Two years later Walters still had not completely given up on Wilson, but he was unsparing about Wilson's legacy thus far: "I regret to say that he has failed to realize any of the expectations raised by his fair promises and sweet-sounding phrases about justice and equal opportunity uttered in his pre-election days." It amazed Walters that Wilson could not bring himself to carry out the routine ceremonial aspects of his job concerning black Americans. Wilson got through his first term without visiting a single Afro-American school, church, or gathering of any kind, including Howard University's commencement. Walters knew that he diminished his reputation by supporting a politician who only pretended to respect the dignity and humanity of black Americans. All he could say was that he was sorry about Wilson, but he would not apologize for taking a chance on a Democrat: "Since I have nothing but the good of my people at heart, I have nothing to fear nor need I be disturbed by the unjust criticism so freely indulged in in some quarters."[181]

Walters might have reconciled with the NAACP leaders had Wilson been the only issue, since they went through the same dance with Wilson. Hurt feelings prevailed, however, because Walters insisted on remaining friendly with Washington, which they could not abide. Walters recoiled from the attacks on Washington's character and legacy after the tide turned against Washington. Since Walters had nothing but the good of his people at heart, and he had a long record of racial justice militancy, he believed that he deserved better treatment from NAACP insiders than he got. He had kept his balance, kept the Afro-American Council going, stood up for racial justice, and modeled Christian charity. He had thrown himself into political activism because he was committed to the flourishing of Afro-Americans, not because he loved politics. He had to care about politics because he cared passionately about the well-being of Afro-Americans; on the other hand, the sphere that he loved without qualification was the black church. Thus he devoted himself to the AME Zion Church, the Afro-American Council, the National Colored Democratic League, the Federal Council of Churches, the Ecumenical Conferences of World Methodism (which he attended in Washington, DC, London, and Toronto), and the United World Society of Christian Endeavor.

Walters coped with a weak heart throughout his career. In 1915, two years before his heart gave out, he addressed Christian Endeavor's fifth world convention, in Chicago. He reprised his usual themes, emphasizing that race has no biological meaning, the human family is a unity, and all human beings are equally the children of God. "History plays havoc with the vainglorious boasting of national and racial conceit," he declared. "Where are the Babylonians, the Assyrians, and the Egyptians, who once lorded it over the face of the earth?" Making the same point differently, Walters cited Aristotle's sneering at "barbarians" that later produced Shakespeare, Bacon, Newton, and Kant. Looking ahead, Walters expected Japan to become a great power, as the Japanese had a "keen intellect and aggressive spirit." He thought that China, India, and the nations of Africa might become powers on the world stage, though it was too soon to say. Walters did not need to know what God was doing in the world to believe that God had a plan for the world. He could respect the world's great religions while believing that Christianity was the highest revelation of God's truth.[182]

For Walters, the love ethic of Jesus was perfect, transforming, and universal. Christ was "the inspirer of all the reform movements of the world." Thus,

Christianity, rightly understood, was essentially progressive, a river of progress. In its first thousand years, the Christian river of progress was only ankle deep. In its second thousand years the water reached knee level. Walters took the long view historically. It would probably take another two thousand years for Christianity to reach its highest development and "conquer all evils," he figured: "Christ our conqueror is riding on gloriously and has the ages before Him."[183]

Walters believed in the guiding work of the Holy Spirit in the world: "We are just beginning to understand that the Holy Spirit is the executive of the Godhead; that He is the Eternal Spirit; the vital force in the world." He believed that redemption was real and always available, for Christ died on the cross to bring all people to God: "Redemption is an established fact, and men are being saved through this great truth." Lastly he believed in the "brotherhood of man," which Walters called "the acme of the teachings of Christ." Everywhere the struggle for this truth was fierce, and for some it was brutal: "But I am not discouraged. I remember it has ever been thus, but more; I remember that time, preparation and the leaven of the Gospel and an earnest struggle has brought about most happy results, and enabled the people that were once considered inferiors to take their places as equals."[184]

He had all three of the defining marks of black radicalism — critique of white domination, respect for Africa, and agitation for liberation — yet Walters was at home in the church and America. He exuded the strengths of the radical tradition while averting its pitfalls of narrowness and chauvinism, an accomplishment owing to his charitable spirit, passion for justice, and ecumenism. He died on February 2, 1917. Ransom, aptly summarizing Walters's legacy, cut straight to the church issue, noting that Walters was "a man of the Church" but too great to be a "churchman." Walters had a forceful personality, an alert mind, and a broad vision, Ransom explained. He saw the social justice core of the Bible and was too deeply immersed in the politics of racial justice to be confined "by the narrow boundaries of denominational lines." Though Ransom judged that Walters was not as astute as Arnett, lacking Arnett's capacity for subtle distinctions and complex arguments, Walters was like Arnett in "keeping his Church and race in touch with the larger national and international movements." Besides being extraordinary, Walters was an exemplar, something more important. Ransom wished that every Afro-American bishop were a social gospeler, taking "an active, unswerving, outspoken position in advocacy of the interests of his people, whether they be industrial, moral, social, or political." As it was, Ransom lamented, the three branches of black Methodism raised up few broadminded, strong, inspiring leaders, which made the churches vulnerable to being led astray by Booker Washington. Walters was a great exception, one of the very few. Walters saw that the churches had untapped ability to change society: "Bishop Walters realized this and made the most of it. The bench of bishops of our Negro churches should never be without at least one such personality."[185]

RANSOM'S LATER CAREER

Ransom was equally extraordinary, but he lived through the bitter years when the language of hope and idealism faded to near extinction. In 1930 Ransom's banishment to the tiny district of Louisiana ended abruptly, as Bishop John Hurst died and the Bishops Council added the Seventh District (South Carolina) to Ransom's duties. Ransom had criticized Hurst for appointing himself to South Carolina. Now Ransom found himself bishop of two Episcopal districts and ten annual conferences. Moving to the state capital, Columbia, South Carolina, which General Sherman had burned, Ransom was fascinated by the state's distinct history and culture. Half the state's population was Afro-American, consisting mostly of agricultural and industrial workers, many of them descendants of the last two slave ships from Africa. Ransom encountered African retentions that were new to him—language idioms variously spoken from Savannah to Charlestown, plus tribal practices of Gullahs off the coast of South Carolina and Georgia. He found that many elderly people held "strange ideas about occult influence and practice." One woman warned him to be careful what he ate, because their last three bishops had died in the past five years from eating the wrong thing.[186]

The run of deaths was real, as was the district's recent turmoil and polarization. The state's Piedmont and Charleston sections seemed to hate each other, the Ransoms learned. For two years Ransom and Emma soaked up local lore and waged a peacekeeping ministry. In Charleston a woman harshly criticized William David Chappelle, the first of three recent bishops to expire. Ransom tried to say that Chappelle had some good points, but she cut him off: "Yes, I know all of that, but he's an Up country nigger." Ransom won high praise in South Carolina for helping the district deal with its internal conflicts while the Depression took hold. It helped that South Carolinians produced enough food to feed themselves. He later reflected proudly that the church in South Carolina was the "greatest single influence making for racial self-respect, racial self-confidence, and a society of friendly cooperation and goodwill."[187]

On the lecture circuit he was more militant, delivering a fiery address at the Metropolitan Opera House in Philadelphia in March 1930. Ransom's subject at

Philadelphia was Crispus Attucks and his legacy. Attucks died for American independence in 1770, Ransom observed, confronting the enemy "on State Street in Boston." At every turning point of American history, black Americans were there, playing a key and loyal role, nearly always without recognition, in a hostile context: "The white man yields nothing, even to his own poor laboring masses, through sympathy or love. He yields not to the persuasion of logic or the sanctity of his religious creeds. He only yields or compromises in the face of aggressive, determined, uncompromising power." Since white America yielded nothing out of charity or religious feeling, black Americans needed to struggle for justice in the fighting spirit of Attucks: "We can most signally honor Crispus Attucks and the men of our race who have fought to establish and preserve this nation by emulating in the paths of peace the virtues they displayed in war. We can only gain our rights by our fights."[188]

The twenty-ninth AME General Conference met in Cleveland in May 1932, climactically for Ransom and the denomination. Ransom had railed about Episcopal corruption for years. The rotation reform helped, he believed, but not enough to change the culture of corruption. He kept the issue in play, seemingly without much effect, not realizing that a stampede was mobilizing. Years of protests about Episcopal corruption and abuse of power came to a head at Cleveland. Anger overflowed from the beginning of the convention, speakers declared that corruption had to be rooted out, and lay members demanded to be represented on the Episcopal Committee that made decisions about how many bishops were needed, where they should be assigned, and which ones should be suspended, retired, or defrocked. The committee recommended that Bishop Vernon be suspended for mishandling funds. Bishop Henry Blanton Parks lost control of a stormy convention that refused to hear Vernon's appeal or that of his defenders. Though Ransom detested Vernon, he winced at the mob atmosphere and Vernon's humiliation. Then the same thing happened to Bishop Joshua H. Jones, with Ransom in the presiding chair. Jones was declared guilty of mishandling money in the church's bellwether First District (Eastern Pennsylvania, New Jersey, Delaware, New York, and New England) and expelled from the assembly without being allowed to give his version of what happened.

Jones had grown up in South Carolina, served as president of Wilberforce University, been elected to the episcopacy in 1912, and accepted the assignment to Philadelphia in 1928. He borrowed funds on his personal security to save numerous heavily mortgaged congregations and guided the First District through the early years of the Depression. He was a clean-living moralist who blasted ministers that drank, which Ransom resented. He was also an extremely able steward of the church's business, guilty of no financial delinquency, as an extensive investigation subsequently confirmed. The latter verdict did not come in time for Jones, who died within a year of being suspended. Ransom subsequently grieved that the AME Church smeared and condemned one of its best leaders: "The General Conference was in the grip of mob psychology. It was on the loose and completely out of control." In his telling, he had tried to establish order and failed: "I called to my assistance some of the most honored and respected bishops among us. They would neither hear nor heed the voice of anybody. They yelled, howled, and shouted. . . . Thus the curtain was lowered on the official life of one of the most dynamic and forceful men that has ever presided over the administration of affairs in the AME Church."[189]

That was a true representation of Ransom's eventual feeling. The church's mistreatment of Jones, and even of Vernon, haunted Ransom for the rest of his life. Always he stressed that some of the denomination's most revered leaders stoked and led the mob. He hoped, he would say, never to witness anything like it again—failing to acknowledge that he been the leading instigator of what happened. Ransom had tried to force his rival into retirement, only to set off something bigger than he had intended. In his memoir he whitewashed his role, never mentioning that he had been Jones's leading accuser. That offended the usually unflappable Wright, who had long been a friend and ally to Ransom but was closer to Jones. Wright seethed for years that Jones, "a home-loving man of impeccable character," was brought down by a mob that drank, stole church money, and/or otherwise "led lewd lives." It mollified Wright, slightly, that Ransom subsequently described Jones as an honorable victim of a mob. But Wright resented that Ransom never acknowledged his role in the fiasco after doing more "than any one man to hurt Bishop Jones." In his authorized history, *The Bishops of the African Methodist Episcopal Church*, Wright settled the score with a blistering accusation, writing that Ransom and his followers had meant to end Jones's career, "but their plans got 'out of hand' and they killed him, and wrote the saddest page of AME history." This bitter charge did some whitewashing of its own, however, because Wright possessed the financial records that could have absolved Jones at the 1932 convention. Wright skipped the proceeding in the belief that doing so would enhance his chance of being elected to the bishopric the following day.[190]

The Cleveland conference marked a turning point for Ransom because it sent him home to Wilberforce, the Third District, where he spent the rest of his life. Though Ransom had railed against ecclesiastical fiefdoms, he settled into one for the rest of his career and beyond, in Arnett's old house, Tawawa Chimney Corner. Wilberforce was drowning in debt and otherwise floundering, and it was too precious to the AME Church to be allowed to go under. Thus, Ransom got an exemption from his own prescription of rotating bishops.

Moving to Wilberforce in May 1932, he inherited months of backlogged debt to unpaid professors and staff, unpaid bills to the university's essential service providers, and a thirteen-thousand-dollar personal debt to Bishop Jones, whose son Gilbert Jones was president of the university. Ransom, still believing he had acted justly in attacking Bishop Jones, declared that he would "have nothing to do with anybody connected with Bishop Jones." Plus, Ransom knew who he wanted for Wilberforce—Charles H. Wesley, currently dean of the Graduate School at Howard University, who aspired to be a bishop. Turning around Wilberforce would be good for Wesley's ecclesiastical ambitions. Years later, trying to clean up this part of the story, Ransom explained that he assumed that Bishop Jones was furious at him, which disqualified Ransom from being able to work with the younger Jones. So Ransom fired the younger Jones, hiring Wesley as president. Wesley lasted one month and abruptly resigned, explaining that the situation at Wilberforce was impossible—a bit worse than he expected.[191]

Wilberforce had two boards of trustees, one for the College of Liberal Arts, which belonged to the AME Church, and one for the Combined Normal and Industrial Department, which belonged to the state of Ohio. In 1887, when Arnett brokered this arrangement, the state board had three members appointed by the state and three by the church. But that eroded over time, creating a deeper division between the two parts of the institution. The AME Church regarded the school belonging to the state as a department of an AME university, but the state of Ohio gradually came to view the state school as a separate institution that happened to be located at Wilberforce. Naturally, the state school had a stronger financial base. Most of the newer buildings belonged to the Combined Normal and Industrial Department. If not for Andrew Carnegie, who donated Carnegie Library to the College of Liberal Arts, the difference would have been extremely lopsided.[192]

Du Bois warned Wesley what to expect. The president of Wilberforce, Du Bois explained, had "practically no support and no income," while the superintendent of the state school held nearly all the power. The Ohio state government was disgusted with Wilberforce and sick of pouring into it money that got wasted. But the state was caught "between the devil and the deep sea," Du Bois said. If the state abandoned Wilberforce, the school would collapse immediately and Ohio blacks would raise hell. Moreover, Ohio whites wanted Wilberforce to stay in business because they did not want black students at Ohio State University or other white colleges. So, a divorce would not work.

Du Bois told Wesley that the presidency was worth having only if it combined the two offices, holding authority over both departments. Otherwise, "you are going to be in an impossible position."[193]

Wesley took that counsel to heart, arriving at Wilberforce determined to persuade Ransom to persuade the state government to let Wesley run the entire operation. That had no chance of happening, so Wesley was gone in a month, returning to Howard. Ransom later recalled, trying to put it mildly, "This was to us a disconcerting blow and made our confusion more confused." Next he turned to Wright, who was still editing the *Christian Recorder* after running unsuccessfully for the episcopacy. Wright's candidacy for the episcopacy had been wiped out when the anti-Jones mob took down Jones. Thus, it took some chutzpah for Ransom to turn to his former parish associate, who had earned a doctorate in sociology and gone on to a distinguished clerical career. Everyone described Wright as agreeable, thoughtful, emotionally stable, analytical, and energetic. He had turned the A.M.E. Book Concern into a profitable enterprise, edited the *Christian Recorder* with consummate efficiency, made a small fortune in real estate, and had extensive experience managing community banks. Ransom counted on Wright's loyalty to Wilberforce and his ability to run an institution.[194]

Though Wright had a top-tier academic background and had taught briefly at Payne Theological Seminary, he had opted against an academic career. He no longer thought of himself as an academic type, and he felt inferior intellectually to Wesley. If Wesley could not handle this job, who was he to succeed Wesley? Ransom told Wright to get over it; Ransom and Wilberforce needed him, so he was drafted. Wright had a healthy ego, and he was determined to be a bishop. But to grow into his ego in this context he had to do the job for a while—an old story with him, as he had an overachieving father who still overshadowed him in some contexts. Introducing himself to the faculty, Wright declared that he knew less about education than any of them and he probably could not pass Wilberforce's admission test to be a student. That shocked and dismayed the professors; things were sure to get worse at Wilberforce. Instead, Wright got the school's finances under control and smoothed things over with the state government. He hired Gilbert Jones as dean of the College of Education, a risky move that strengthened the faculty and smoothed things over with the Jones family. Wright told audiences that black Americans lacked power because they lacked education; thus, he was devoted to restoring Wilberforce. During the worst of the Depression he made Wilberforce stable again; then he became a bishop in 1936. Years later, reflecting on the turnaround at Wilberforce, Ransom gave credit where it was due: "To Dr. Wright belongs the honor of placing the university on its feet to travel the road of development and progress."[195]

In Ransom's later life the nationalist strain in his thought grew stronger, by survival necessity. It amazed him, in the 1930s, that the same nation that demeaned and terrorized its own blacks could muster sympathy for persecuted Jews, Armenians, and Irish. Repeatedly Ransom protested that Afro-Americans had never been anything but loyal Americans and faithful Christians, but what did it get them? For generations they believed that if they went to church, showed good character, got an education, and learned a trade, they would be granted equal rights. "But their disillusionment is almost complete, since they find Christ has not been able to break the American color line. If Jesus wept over Jerusalem, he should have for America an ocean of tears."[196]

White Americans feared their precious culture would be Africanized, Ransom reflected. Thus they repressed blacks viciously. But why were they so fearful? That question haunted him. "We hear no fear expressed of our country being Germanized or Jewized; we hear no cry going up from North or South against Irish political ascendancy. Is there any evidence anywhere in a single page of American history where the Negro has been less patriotic and true to our institutions than any of these elements which we have named?"[197]

Ransom protested that Afro-Americans had problems of their own to overcome; it was cruel and perverse that they also had to overcome a hateful, violent, fearful white majority that believed in its own superiority. Ignorance was a huge problem in the black community "because he is denied in every possible way any encouragement to learn." There was much poverty, "because he must receive always the lowest wage when permitted work." There were many slums, "because segregation forces him there, and studied policy denies him modern sanitation and health supervision." But some things were getting better, Ransom observed: "He is recovering from a condition of promiscuous breeding and concubinage to one in which family life is being established and respected. He is learning to respect law, despite unlawful mobocracy both in certain courts and in the commonwealth. . . . He is increasing in race-consciousness, racial self-respect, racial self-reliance."[198]

Ransom stumped hard for Franklin Roosevelt in 1932, chairing the National Colored Citizens Roosevelt for President Committee. Mostly he made an economic argument, emphasizing that 95 percent of Afro-Americans belonged to the laboring class. Though both major parties were undeniably capitalist, Ransom wrote, the Democratic Party was closer to "the great body of the common people." Democrats cared more about economic fairness and were more likely to help the poor and working classes. Ransom urged that if black

Americans were to finally renounce their overlong loyalty to the Republican Party, it would "free our spirits equally as much as Mr. Lincoln's Proclamation freed our bodies." Between elections, however, Ransom was more rueful about real-world options. Afro-Americans had to get what they could out of electoral politics, but the limits of that in a racist society were grim and "bewildering."[199]

In 1933 the World Fellowship of Faiths held an anniversary commemoration of the 1893 Parliament of World Religions. Both events were held in Chicago. For Ransom, Arnett's speech at the parliament was a favorite memory, but in 1933 Ransom heard many speakers say that the major religions were essentially alike. He had too much at stake in Christianity to sing along. Ransom stood for ethical, progressive, world-conquering, Christian personalism and had no intention of standing on any other ground. The religion of Jesus is the absolute religion, he asserted. Nothing else comes close it: "Jesus taught that God is the father of all mankind; all people of every race are brothers and sisters, and are therefore equals. They should be united and governed by the Supreme Law of Love. Love God supremely; love your neighbor as you do yourself." If one is committed to this idea of good religion, Ransom insisted, one must embrace the objective of Christianity, which is "to supercede all other religious faiths and become the one universal and dominant kingdom of God from sea to sea and from river to the ends of the earth. With it there is neither accommodation nor compromise. Christ must be exalted over all and above all, God blessed forevermore." The real thing, Ransom admonished, is the absolute and progressive religion of Jesus. There is nothing weak or compromised in it: "He offers a way of salvation and life, and points to himself and his followers as witnesses to its truth. Take it or leave it. It is new wine and cannot be retained in old wine skins."[200]

As usual, Ransom moved to his immanent eschatology of a Christianized world: "If Christianity is to be established on the earth and the brotherhood of man with peace, justice, righteousness, the stage for its consummation is completely set here in the United States of America." On this point, however, in his later career, Ransom usually took it back shortly after saying it. How could he keep saying that black and white America would save the world together when white America viciously oppressed black America and thereby lost its soul? The later Ransom taught that the white nations and Asia were headed downward, while the future belonged to the children of Africa and their descendants. "Asia, Europe, and America have had their day, or are now standing at the zenith of their power," he declared. These powers did not represent any conceivable "spiritual and social future" for humanity. They stood for weapons, wealth, power, diplomacy, science, technology, logic, and philosophy, all of which had failed or were failing: "The spiritual and social pathway of humanity is strewn with the debris of their inadequacy." The white world never created a great religion, and its substitutes were barren. The hope of the world was in the last place that white America thought to look: "The African and his descendants are the last spiritual reserves of humanity."[201]

Sometimes he put it in world-historical terms. The pyramids, the Pantheon, and the Colosseum were the "tombstones" of Egypt, Greece, and Rome, Ransom observed. They marked the spots where grotesque civilizations destroyed themselves in materialistic celebrations of supremacy and power. Similarly in modern times, the ascendancy of the "black race" was served and prepared by "the colonizing, exploring, inventive, and materialistic white man." Ransom explained that the black race lacked "natural aptitudes and special endowments" for success in "the realm of things material, scientific, or commercial." The black imagination was primarily literary, artistic, and spiritual. It was not controlling or grasping but looked to the future, which was open. It brought mind and heart together, struggling to comprehend how white America could lynch five thousand black Americans in seventy years. Ransom predicted that if ever a great epic poem were written about the American experience or a great American symphony composed, the author or composer would be an African American.[202]

That was still an echo of Ransom's early buoyancy, but only an echo. The tasks of ecclesiastical administration and the sheer torment of coping with a racist society wore him down. In his later career Ransom could still give a strong speech or sermon. Wright, introducing Ransom's book *The Negro: The Hope or the Despair of Christianity* in 1935, declared that he had heard Ransom speak more than a dozen times per year for the past thirty-five years, "and he is today my favorite orator." But Ransom's days of enthralling racially mixed audiences with scintillating oratory were long past by 1935. His later audiences were church and civic groups, not surging crowds of movement activists. Ransom felt the difference. He was keenly aware that for all his later eminence as a bishop, his world got smaller. In 1936 he told the AME General Conference: "The world has little interest in us or concern about us as to what we do and what we say here. To them, we are just a group of Negroes here legislating and voting on matters that concern our church." That was not the life he had sought before he took the bishop's chair. The older he got, the more fondly he remembered Chicago.[203]

As it was, Ransom's sense of shrinking despite ecclesiastical station was a harbinger of his fate. Wilberforce became consuming again after Ohio elected a Republican governor, John Bricker, who clashed with Wright's successor, D.

Ormonde Walker, mainly because Walker was an outspoken Democrat. Ransom tried to buy some peace for Wilberforce and himself by firing Walker in 1942. Instead he bought more trouble and realized that he should have stood up for Walker, a strong president. Briefly Wright returned to Wilberforce to serve as interim president. Then Wesley returned as the first president ever elected by both boards of the institution—the deal he had wanted a decade earlier. At one time Wesley may have loved the AME school in the way that Payne, Arnett, Scarborough, Walker, and Ransom loved it. Upon taking over at Wilberforce, however, he favored the state school and demoralized the AME school, which cut Ransom deeply. Wesley let the College of Liberal Arts run down, he rarely met with faculty, and he devoted himself to the state school.[204]

The conflict between Ransom and Wesley got terribly personal the year after Emma Ransom died in 1943. Ransom took up a romantic relationship with the dean of women at Wilberforce, Georgia Myrtle Teal. He was eighty-three years old and used to being married; she was thirty-nine and eager to marry Ransom. The Ransom family split on whether it trusted her or was happy for him. Ransom's grandson, Reverdy Ransom III, who had been raised mostly by Reverdy and Emma, bitterly opposed the new union. He broke Ransom's heart by stealing and publishing Teal's love letters to Ransom, which contained critical remarks about Wesley. The Wilberforce community buzzed for weeks over the letters, humiliating Ransom and refueling the Ransom-versus-Wesley standoff. One of Teal's letters warned Ransom that his grandson had sided with Wesley against him. Ransom readily forgave his grandson for betraying him, but Teal never did. In 1947 Wilberforce lost its accreditation by the North Central Association and the board belatedly fired Wesley, who staged a piece of self-pitying theater that moved a group of students to burn Ransom in effigy. Ransom, eighty-six years old, watched from the front window as his stuffed likeness blazed and burned out. He long outlived this drama at Wilberforce, outlasting Wesley and spending his last years as the grand old sage of Wilberforce, finally giving out at the age of ninety-eight. But Wesley hurt Wilberforce by hanging on to the presidency of the College of Education and Industrial Arts, forcing a divorce between the two schools.[205]

Ransom lived to see his closest friend, Joseph Gomez, become a bishop, and his treasured friend Walker become a bishop, both in 1948, to his delight. At the same annual conference in Kansas City he was thrilled when the AME Church voted overwhelmingly to ordain women, after years of debating the issue. Ransom retired in 1952, having outlasted those who might have written about his early career. As it was, the year before, Ransom sadly ended a long-running friendship that had wounded him for years, by writing a breathtaking letter to

Wright. Ransom could not bear the hypocrisy of their friendship any longer, because Wright bantered routinely about Ransom's struggle with alcoholism, usually for laughs. Ransom observed, "When you speak of me in public as well as in private you cannot refrain reverting to what you seem to regard as my outstanding pit of damnation." Wright regaled listeners with drunk-Ransom stories, lately adding that he hoped "this wife" would get him to stop drinking. Usually he said it in a jocular way, but Ransom detected "a razor blade edge of derision bordering almost onto contempt." At the age of ninety-seven, Ransom decided to square things with Wright: "I have helped you more than anybody else to obtain every outstanding position you have held in the AME Church. I am not now and never was your personal enemy; but from now on I want no more of your smiles, or your words that carry poisoned arrows, or the shake of your hand that conceals a dagger that strikes to kill when my name comes up either in private talk or public speech."[206]

Ransom was fortunate to get a biographer, theater professor Annetta L. Gomez-Jefferson, who knew him well and loved him. Near the end of her excellent biography, *The Sage of Tawawa*, she wrote, "Alcohol was the albatross around his neck. Few knew the anguish he suffered and the depressions he experienced because of the power it had over him. Those who loved him suffered with him." Others did not realize how they wounded Ransom by snickering about his alcohol addiction, even after he experienced public humiliation for battling with it. Friends who did not act like friends wounded him especially. It took Wright fifty years to find out. Gomez-Jefferson got Ransom exactly right: "He was not a saint and would have been the first to acknowledge his own weaknesses. He was, however, a humanitarian, a visionary, a dynamic orator and preacher, a radical thinker in his day; and he knew how to be a friend. Most of all, he was a spiritual and never doubted the reality of God in his life."[207]

At Ransom's funeral Gomez-Jefferson's father, Joseph Gomez, eulogized Ransom as a survivor and "prevailer." The glory of Ransom was the "glory of survival" and the heritage he bequeathed was "that of the prevailer," Gomez declared. Jacob was the prototype, and Ransom was the "modern pattern of prevailing power." That suggested enduring influence, although Gomez had to realize that Ransom was already forgotten outside of black Methodism. Du Bois reached for a larger claim more explicitly, ranking Ransom as an orator "in the category of Demosthenes." Du Bois grandly assured: "He has erected a monument in the history of African Methodism, America, and the world which shall last throughout time and eternity."[208]

On the contrary, Ransom was almost completely forgotten. Books on the black church and black religious radicalism barely mentioned him; he was ignored in histories of the social gospel and American Christianity, and even voluminous histories of the civil rights movement never mentioned him. This legacy of forgetting persisted until Calvin Morris published a valuable book on Ransom in 1990 and Anthony Pinn published a valuable sampler of Ransom's writings and sermons in 1999, leading to Gomez-Jefferson's biography of 2002.[209]

Ransom's vision did not really diminish in his later years. He would have preferred to work in large organizations that struggled for a cooperative commonwealth. But they did not exist, and the necessity of resisting the downward slide of unrelenting racial oppression prevailed in his daily choices. Woodrow Wilson marked a turning point for Ransom, a forced recognition that progressive refinement and sneering racism could go together. Ransom called Wilson "unpatriotic, undemocratic, and fiendish." He struggled with the bitter irony that Wilson was liberal, cosmopolitan, and fervently moral, aside from being a racist. To be sure, Ransom had some racialist assumptions of his own that easily flipped into the opposite of what he intended, believing that races were genetically endowed with particular traits. Thus he assured that blacks were "naturally" gifted at music, speaking, friendliness, feeling, and spirituality, and were not suited for math, logic, or science. He overlooked that Du Bois avoided "nature" talk when singing this song and that Du Bois never said that blacks were short on mathematical and scientific ability. Ransom fell into the racialist trap of suggesting that race marked something beyond cultural identity and difference, but his purpose was to abolish racist ordering, not to perpetuate it. His statements about racial traits bore the marks of one who came of age intellectually in the 1880s, when neo-Lamarckian Social Darwinism excited and traumatized many minds.[210]

In 1935 Ransom dedicated his book *The Negro* to the memory of two champions of the true commonwealth that he missed. One was Trotter, who showed up at the Paris Peace Conference in 1919, implored the diplomats to outlaw racial discrimination, and faded from prominence in the 1920s, tagged as impossibly belligerent. In 1934 Trotter plunged to his death from the roof of his apartment building, apparently by suicide. Ransom grieved at losing Trotter, the epitome of antiracist militancy. He hailed Trotter as "the consistent and uncompromising champion of Freedom, Justice, and Equality."[211]

The other late friend to whom Ransom dedicated his book was Jane Addams, who had died in May 1935. To Ransom, Addams symbolized the path of raceblind progressivism that he might have preferred for himself had he shared her privileges or had America taken a different path. He lauded her as one "who knew neither race, class, nor creed, in her long effort to build a better humanity and to make a better world." By noting that Addams had no creed, Ransom underscored that his heroes in recent social justice activism—Du Bois, Trotter, Addams—had not made their home in the church. He wished intently that there were more people like him in the church. He would have preferred to have competition for his standing as the Du Bois figure in the AME Church. But he was more responsible than anyone for bringing the social gospel into the mainstream of the AME Church. He belonged fully to the black radical tradition. And he prefigured everything that came to be called liberation theology.[212]

SEPARATISM, INTEGRATION, SOCIALISM

The tensions built into the black social gospel were strongest among the Baptists. They debated separatism versus assimilation more contentiously than any other tradition. They had the biggest denomination, the National Baptist Convention, but waited until 1895 to assemble it. They were free of bishops but prone to fundamentalism. Since they lacked ecclesiastical governing boards, they thrashed out their internal debates in public, where sectarian language had to be translated. By the time that black Baptists formed a denomination, the party of separation had prevailed, playing up Booker Washington's bootstrap ethic and politics.

For the majority that established the National Baptist Convention, the church was a refuge from a hostile white society. Black Baptists used the philosophy of self-help to survive Jim Crow, preaching a gospel of advancement through education. The majority party, however, wanted two things that conflicted with each other: To be separate and to play an important role in American politics and society. The problems at each end were compounded by the declining fortunes of Booker Washington politics.

The leading black Baptists of the late nineteenth and early twentieth centuries were Washington, William J. Simmons, E. C. Morris, Nannie H. Burroughs, and Adam Clayton Powell Sr. All espoused a social gospel in the broad sense of the category, and Powell was a full-fledged social gospel progressive who preached liberal theology and worked hard for the NAACP. These figures achieved prominence by differently proposing how black Americans should resist racial oppression and achieve self-determination. Some Baptist leaders were separatists on ecclesiology and politics, many were separatists on ecclesiology but integrationists to variable degrees on sociopolitical issues, and some were integrationists across the board. For Morris and Burroughs, ecclesiastical separatism was a source of strength. For Simmons, Washington, and Powell, it was something to move beyond. For George Washington Woodbey, this was not the right issue. Woodbey launched a small but historically significant Baptist school of thought by taking seriously the logic of social gospel Socialism.

The first Baptists were seventeenth-century English Puritans who broke with other Puritans over baptism of believers, not infants, and baptism by immersion, not sprinkling. From the beginning the Baptist tradition was a hybrid offspring of the Anabaptist and Reformed traditions. Baptists fused the Anabaptist emphasis on spiritual freedom and believers' baptism with the Reformed emphasis on scriptural authority and the Reformed aversion to Anabaptist communalism. They fashioned a distinctly individualistic Protestantism based on the right of individuals to interpret Scripture and the necessity of individual conversion. This form of Protestantism flourished in only two places, England and the United States, but in the United States it eventually surpassed all other Protestant denominations. The Baptist emphasis on conversion yielded a theology of the church as a body of regenerated believers, which distinguished eighteenth-century American Baptists from their fellow Calvinists in the Congregational, Reformed, and Presbyterian denominations.

More important, the Baptist movement outgrew other denominations because it sprang from the working class and spoke to working people with simplicity and evangelical power. The same thing was true of the Methodist movement after it emerged in the late eighteenth century. The iconic figure of the Methodist movement was the circuit rider, an evangelist supported by Methodist order and Wesleyan theology. The iconic figure of the Baptist movement was the farmer preacher who moved with the people into an expanding frontier. Long before Methodism existed, the Baptists had a history of minority status everywhere in the United States except Rhode Island. Then they grew dramatically in the so-called First Great Awakening (1730–1760). The Baptists clashed over atonement, dividing between general Baptists (Christ died for all people) and particular Baptists (Christ died only for the elect), which heightened the separatist tendencies of the latter group. The particular Baptists were by far the larger party, especially in the Middle Colonies. The huge gains that particular Baptists made in the First Great Awakening laid the groundwork for their explosive growth in the so-called Second Great Awakening (1790–1830).[1]

No denomination came close to the Baptist and Methodist churches in attracting African American converts. In the First Awakening, Baptist missionaries welcomed slaves and free blacks; in the Second Awakening, slaves and free blacks were authorized to preach in Baptist and Methodist churches, where revival meetings were virtually identical. The first association for black Baptists was founded in 1834 in Ohio, the Providence Baptist Association. After the Civil War blacks fled the white southern churches and formed Baptist organizations at the local, regional, and national levels. Black and white missionaries from the North initiated the new organizations beyond the congregational level, yielding uneasy coalitions and charges of carpetbagging.

The Consolidated American Baptist Missionary Convention, a national denominational structure, was founded in 1866. It supported southern black Baptists as they fled white churches to form their own congregations and state conventions. The Baptist General Association of Western States and Territories was founded in 1873, and the New England Baptist Convention was founded in 1874. These regional associations eroded the national convention, leading to its demise in 1879. In 1880, missionary William W. Colley and others concerned about the dearth of black Baptist missions founded the Baptist Foreign Mission Convention. In 1886 William J. Simmons of Kentucky spearheaded a new national convention, the American National Baptist Convention, and in 1893 William Bishop Johnson of Washington, DC, founded the National Baptist Education Convention. By then most black Baptist leaders agreed there were too many conventions. They also chafed at lacking a vehicle for publications of their own, as the American Baptist Publication Society refused to publish the writings of African Americans, due to pressure from Southern Baptists. Thus the National Baptist Convention was born in 1895 in Atlanta, merging the three conventions founded in 1880, 1886, and 1893.[2]

WILLIAM SIMMONS, E. C. MORRIS, AND BLACK NATIONALISM

Youthful, brilliant William James Simmons was the catalyst of Baptist convergence. Simmons was thirty-seven years old when he almost single-handedly organized the American National Baptist Convention. At the time he was president of State University at Louisville, editor of a popular Louisville newspaper, the *American Baptist,* and president of the National Negro Press Association. Simmons was born into slavery in Charleston, South Carolina, in 1849. As a child he escaped with his mother, Esther Simmons, and two siblings on the Underground Railroad, landing in Philadelphia, where his uncle Alexander Tardieu, a shoemaker, shielded the family from slave traders. Tardieu had studied under Daniel Payne during Payne's early career in Charleston. Tardieu tutored Simmons for years, fearing that Simmons would be exposed as a runaway slave if he attended school. As a teenager Simmons was apprenticed to a white dentist in Bordentown, New Jersey, and fought for the Union Army at Petersburg, Virginia. After the war he accepted Jesus at the Baptist church of Bordentown, where pastor J. W. Custis groomed him for the ministry, and the (otherwise) all-white congregation paid for his education at Madison University (later renamed Colgate) of New York. Simmons subsequently studied at the University of Rochester, where he preached to a black Baptist church on Sundays, and at Howard University, where he delivered a graduation address on Darwinism in 1873.[3]

From early on Simmons developed a three-pronged ministry of preaching, academic administration and teaching, and political activism; later he added journalism. He caught the last part of Reconstruction in Ocala, Florida, accompanied by his wife, Josephine Simmons, with whom he had seven children. There Simmons ministered to a small congregation, served as principal of Howard Academy, served as Reconstruction deputy county clerk and county commissioner, and stumped the county in 1876 speaking for Rutherford B. Hayes. When Reconstruction ended, Simmons joined the exodus of northern blacks from the Deep South. He taught briefly at a public school in Washington, DC, accepted a pastorate in 1879 at the First Baptist Church of Lexington, Kentucky, and made his career move the following year, assuming the presidency of the Normal and Theological Institute of Kentucky.[4]

This school was owned and controlled by the General Association of Colored Baptists of Kentucky. Located in Louisville, it had twenty-five students and two teachers when it opened in 1879. Individual Baptist congregants made monthly contributions of five cents to finance the school, and congregations were taxed. The school fell to eleven students when Simmons got there in 1880, but a decade later it was thriving with over two hundred students. There were four reasons why the school (renamed in 1884 as State University and again as Simmons University in 1918) flourished. Simmons was a hardworking, charismatic leader in the Booker mode, inspiring black Baptists to care about the success of their school. He gained a national reputation through his journalism and his deep involvement in post-Reconstruction politics. He amplified his national reputation by contending forcefully for a national black Baptist denomination. And he supported the organizing efforts of black Baptist women.[5]

The Normal and Theological Institute of Kentucky was a secondary school with some theological instruction when Simmons got there. He added a college department, incorporating the liberal arts curriculum he had studied at Howard University. By 1885 Simmons had built State University into a four-sided college, normal, preparatory, and model school. In 1882 he added journalism to his portfolio, taking over as editor of the *American Baptist*. From the beginning of his academic and journalistic career, Simmons contended that industrial education and the liberal arts were both indispensable and that each had to be protected from the other. He put it with characteristic verve in a pamphlet on industrial education: "If the industrial craze be not watched, our literary institutions will be turned into workshops and our scholars into servants and journeymen. Keep the literary and industrial apart. Let the former be stamped deeply so it will not be mistaken. We need scholars."[6]

He was equally emphatic that women had leadership roles to play in the church and academy. Simmons attended northern white Baptist conferences at which women's groups developed their own service and advocacy agendas. He recognized that women, if organized, could be a source of creativity and power in the church. Thus he was predisposed to feminist activism, in 1883, when the General Association of Kentucky excluded women from its meetings. Mary V. Cook, a Latin and philosophy professor at Normal and Theological Institute, and other black Baptist women decided to form their own convention. Simmons organized the first meeting of the Baptist Women's Educational Convention of Kentucky and promptly relinquished his authority in it, leaving the women to devise their own agenda. The group grew dramatically, attracting representatives from nearly every black Baptist church in the state. It rewarded Simmons by recruiting students and raising money for State University; it also supported mission work. By 1900 the women's convention had paid off the school's debt and built a dormitory for women.[7]

Simmons played a similar role in founding the American National Baptist Convention and nurturing what became a powerful women's organization in the National Baptist Convention, although progress in the latter case was slow and painful, and Simmons did not live to see it play out. In April 1886 he issued a call in the *American Baptist* for a national convention. That August Simmons pulled off a merger of mostly southern congregations at a convention in St. Louis. The church could not carry out its evangelical mission if it lacked a denominational structure, he urged. That was the main thing; in addition, black Baptists needed to know each other, they needed vehicles for their intellectual work, and they needed a forum to discuss issues of concern to African Americans.[8]

Opponents countered that "Baptist unity" was an oxymoronic concept. Many put it personally—they were Baptists because they did not like denominational structures. Disunity was a Baptist hallmark, a predisposition fitting congregational polity and individual interpretation. Simmons refused to believe that Baptists could not work together for common purposes that mattered. Certainly, he acknowledged, Baptists were splitters, but that did not mean that

an ever-growing number of Baptist start-ups and split-offs could not be marshaled
into a national convention: "If the Baptist churches had not been the churches
of God, our enemies would have killed us long ago. It can stand apparently
more worldly mismanagement and live than all the other bodies on earth. A
Baptist split only produces another Baptist church." He had a closing argument,
something that galled him. There were more black Baptists than black anything
else, but the Baptists accomplished less than other groups due to their "want of
organization." Simmons wanted his group to wield more power in American
society. He was careful to say that spiritual strength was more important than
political power, but he insisted that these things belonged together. Black
Baptists were failing at their Christian social ethical mission precisely because
they did not work hard enough at attaining power in American society.[9]

Like Turner, Simmons belonged to the generation that tried to get as much
as it could out of Radical Reconstruction and was forced to make bitter adjustments afterward. He put it plainly in the early 1880s, advising African Americans
to stop waiting for Republicans at the federal level to grow a spine. Both parties
now espoused "the pernicious doctrine of State Rights," he explained. Thus,
black Americans needed to limit the damage at the state level and pay less
attention to national politics: "The days are slipping by and our children are
growing into manhood and womanhood—we are fast passing away. Shall we
live deluded with the hope that the general government will bring to us a
panacea for all our ills? No; we must court the favors of the people of the State.
We must be for progress wherever found. We must act wisely. Indeed the
Republican party could not, if it would, help us. They are debarred by statutes,
and sentiments stronger than statutes. Let us study State interests, its schools
and its development in every direction." Simmons urged Afro-Americans to
vote for white liberals and nonracist white Populists wherever they existed,
wherever blacks were allowed to vote. But that was less important, he contended,
than building up black organizations. In places like Kentucky, there was rarely
anybody worth voting for anyway. What mattered, above all, was for African
Americans to build up their own organizations, their own power, and their race
pride in a country that belonged equally to them.[10]

He pressed hard on the latter point, stressing that black Americans took pride
"in our beautiful country" and were therefore jealous of its good name. Afro-
Americans were "American sovereigns ourselves," Simmons declared. It was
ridiculous that "we, born Americans, finding distinctions in law, should be
driven to appeal to a portion of the same body politic for rights and equalities."
White America made the United States look bad by forcing black Americans to
"bend the supplicant knee, craving that we might be given that which appears

rightly ours without contest." Simmons added that white America made America look even worse, even if it didn't think so, by treating foreigners better than it treated Afro-Americans: "We also feel humiliated that a foreigner who has never felled a tree, built a cabin, or laid a line of railway, seems more welcome to this shore, and is accorded every facility for himself and children to make the most of themselves . . . while we, seeing them happy in a new-found asylum, and knowing you from our youth up . . . are compelled to beg your favors."[11]

Simmons was an early singer of the song about Afro-American soul and musicality that Du Bois and Ransom picked up. Usually the prologue overflowed with nineteenth-century metaphors: "The warm blood of the Negro that haunts the channels of his veins with ancient Egyptian and Ethiopian fires has been tempered in the climate of the South and reduced to that proportion which robs it of its sluggishness, subdues it of wild passion and holds it by reason, while the trials of the past have been the friction that brightens, the winds that toughen, and the frosts that ripen." The white South, he noted, had never written a great song, poem, or book: "It has been reserved for us. The only American music was born on the plantations and wrung from aching hearts as wine from the luscious grape. It has touched the heart of the learned and engaged the attention of the scientific musician. As the Indian faded in the North before the white man, so the white man of the South must yield to us, without, however, a bloody conflict. We shall gather wealth, learning and manhood, and occupy the land."[12]

He cut a large figure, inspiring admiration and emulation. Ida Wells described Simmons as "truly a big man, figuratively and physically." Simmons was the first to pay Wells for her journalism, paying her a dollar per week; for the rest of her life Wells said that she owed her greatest professional debt to Simmons, not Fortune. In 1887 Simmons published a huge book titled *Men of Mark: Eminent, Progressive and Rising.* It contained sketches of 177 black American men of note. Frederick Douglass, Richard Allen, Henry Highland Garnet, and Daniel A. Payne were among the eminent. Booker Washington, T. Thomas Fortune, Alexander Walters, and Francis Grimké were among the rising. Simmons told a story of remarkable cultural and intellectual accomplishment in the face of brutal hostility: "I wish the book to show to the world—to our oppressors and even our friends—that the Negro race is still alive, and must possess more intellectual vigor than any other section of the human family or else how could they be crushed as slaves in all these years since 1620, and yet today stand side by side with the best blood in America, in white institutions, grappling with abstruse problems in Euclid and difficult classics, and master them? Was ever such a thing seen in other people? Whence these lawyers, doctors, authors, editors, divines, lecturers, linguists, scientists, college presidents and such, in one quarter of a century?"[13]

Black Americans needed heroes and had them, Simmons declared: "I admire these men. I have faith in my people. I wish to exalt them; I want their lives snatched from obscurity to become household matter for conversation." Simmons described Henry McNeal Turner, ascending at the time to the eminent category, as "one of the most influential men in the United States" and perhaps the nation's greatest contemporary orator. His entry on Turner was otherwise uncharacteristically restrained, sticking to a recitation of facts. Probably Simmons did not want to embarrass his gruff friend, who read a draft version and probably wrote part of it. That did not stop Turner, in his introduction to the book, from reciprocating with the most admiring piece he ever wrote about anyone.[14]

Simmons was an unsurpassed educator, Turner observed: "Students admire, respect and stand in awe of him; his teachers are proud of him, trust his judgment and abide by his decisions." As a writer Simmons was equally accomplished: "His editorials are racy, versatile and logical. He contends for rights and cries down wrongs. He is extensively copied, and has the personal respect of every editor and prominent man in the country." As a speaker he was a spellbinder: "At times, in the heat of debate, the whole grandeur of his soul is transfused into his countenance; and his hearers are electrified as only true eloquence can electrify." The motto that fit him best was "God, my race and denomination." Simmons held "tenaciously" to his religious views, Turner noted, but he respected the right of others to hold different theologies. Turner admired Simmons's ability to hold a strong position without being dogmatic or belligerent: "Dr. Simmons is loyal to his convictions, sympathetic, independent, far sighted, therefore a wise counselor, methodical and liberal. . . . To friends he is faithful; to enemies he shows a steady resistance, but no aggressiveness." *Men of Mark*, Turner believed, was a work of epochal significance. He predicted that someday "the name of Dr. Simmons will be as familiar to the millions as that of Herodotus, Josephus, Pliny, Plutarch and other historians enshrined in the gratitude of the world."[15]

That was grandly off the mark, oddly not anticipating that Simmons would make his greatest contribution as the builder of a mighty denomination. *Men of Mark* sold poorly as a subscription book, disappointing Simmons, who wanted to use the profit for a companion volume on black women, which he never wrote. Some chapters were ghostwritten by the subjects. Though Turner oddly played down Simmons's work as an ecclesiastical power broker, by 1887 he was a major figure in church politics, wielding a vast patronage system. That year Simmons took over the Southern Department of the American Baptist Home Mission Society, a sizable addition to presiding over the American National Baptist Convention (ANBC), running a newspaper and a university, training and placing clergy, awarding doctor of divinity degrees, and staying involved in politics. He seeded the ANBC, as much as possible, with women's convention activists, placing Mary Cook and State University professor Lucy Wilmot Smith on the executive committee, although he and they confronted stubborn opposition to female leadership in the church. Simmons also launched the first black religious women's monthly in the United States, *Our Women and Children*, declaring: "We shall defend *Women from Wrongs and demand for her Justice*."[16]

In 1887 Simmons proposed an alliance between the ANBC and the American Baptist Publication Society (ABPS). The ABPS had never taken much interest in African American readers, officially on the ground that illiteracy rates were still very high in the black South (approximately 50 percent in 1890). But Simmons was highly regarded in the ABPS, his school trained ABPS missionaries, the ABPS employed several black ministers as agents, and the ABPS hierarchy realized it lacked a morally respectable reason for ignoring the black churches. Society officials quietly followed an indefensible policy for fear of offending the Southern Baptist Convention. The ABPS and Simmons took a first step forward, announcing that the January 1890 issue of the ABPS journal *Baptist Teacher* would contain articles by three black ministers — Simmons, Walter H. Brooks, and Emanuel K. Love. This plan was short-lived, as white Southern Baptists erupted in outrage. The ABPS had little chance of staying in business financially if it lost southern support, so it canceled the agreement. Black Baptists were equally swift in blasting the ABPS for its cowardice, and the ABPS got what it had long carefully avoided — a public fight over racism.[17]

White southern ministers condemned the ABPS for suggesting that blacks had any business writing for ABPS publications. J. W. Ford, a white minister from St. Louis, lit up an American Baptist Home Mission Society conference by warning that black ministers had to be put down before it was too late. Ministers like Simmons refused to bow down to the "moral mastery" of white people, Ford explained. If black ministers could not be relied upon to tell African Americans how to behave and where they belonged, white America would be forced to wipe out the black population: "The alternative is to elevate or exterminate, to use the Bible or bullet. There is either one or the other of these alternatives for the black man of the South. A great national peril calls for a great national movement." Numerous black and white ministers repudiated Ford's declaration, which gave it extra life.[18]

Meanwhile, the separatist wing of the American National Baptist Convention grew larger and inflamed. If separatists like Brooks and Harvey Johnson could not write for the American Baptist Publication Society, they were wasting their time trying to have fellowship with white Baptists. Black Baptists needed a big national convention with its own publishing society. The point was not so much to escape from the dominant white culture, which was impossible anyway, but to develop alternative institutions and structures. The figures making this argument called themselves separatists, sometimes using "progressive" as an interchangeable term. They had most of the major players in the ANBC — Brooks, Harvey Johnson, William Bishop Johnson, John Frank, Richard H. Boyd, Sutton Griggs, E. C. Morris, and, with caveats, Emanuel Love.

The antiseparatist party was opposed to labels, so historians had to name it. "Accommodationist" implied too much in relation to Bookerism, so Princeton historian James M. McPherson called the antiseparatists "cooperativists," although this term is problematic, too. Some historians, leaning on the connotations of "cooperative," place Simmons and Selma University president Edward M. Brawley in this camp, which is misleading. Simmons and Brawley mediated the fight between separatists and antiseparatists. The major figures on the antiseparatist side were North Carolina ministers Calvin S. Brown, Albert W. Pegues, and Samuel N. Vass; Virginia ministers John M. Armistead and Anthony Binga Jr.; and Maryland minister W. J. Howard. Most had more formal education than the separatists and were strongly inclined to say so, having graduated from Shaw University or Richmond Theological Institute. Many worked for the northern societies, and all accused the separatists of being ungrateful for the generous mission support of northern white Baptists. The defining issue between the two camps was whether black Baptists should have a comprehensive convention of their own that overthrew the subservience of blacks to whites. Simmons did more than anyone to fulfill the dream of the separatist party, even as he mediated between the two camps and cooperated with his white friends in the Home Mission Society.[19]

There were several flashpoint issues in the 1880s that brought the conflict to a climax in the early 1890s. G. M. P. King was a paternalistic white principal of Wayland Seminary, known for nurturing black students, enforcing discipline, and insisting on being appreciated. In 1882 he set off a furor by angrily pushing a student into a chair. Alumni petitioned the Home Mission Society to fire King; Home Mission secretary Henry L. Morehouse told King to apologize; and King apologized privately to black ministers. But King refused to apologize to the student unless she apologized first for cursing him, which set off another round of accusations featuring threats by Brooks and other separatists to break free of the Home Mission Society. Another controversy featured Edward M. Brawley and Charles E. Becker, a low-performing president of Benedict Institute in Columbia, South Carolina. Brawley called for more African American teachers at Benedict, protesting that Becker treated black faculty like children. Becker told the South Carolina Baptist Convention that he was appalled by the "ignorance and degradation of the colored people" and that the religious condition of black Americans was "immeasurably worse than it was in slavery." After that eruption, Brawley had only to quote Becker to win the argument, as he did across the state. Morehouse told both combatants to stop fighting in public, but implicitly he sided with Brawley by creating an interracial board of trustees at Benedict.[20]

In both cases time was running out on Home Mission Society paternalism, as separatists felt humiliated at being bossed by white presidents and at depending financially on the society. The financial realities, however, were forbidding. Brooks urged Afro-Americans in 1883 to build their own schools; Simmons replied: "Does he not know that if our brethren rise, most of them will sit down again? . . . I state from positive knowledge that the colored people are not able to support the schools now maintained in the South." If white money disappeared from the schools, Simmons warned, the schools would collapse. Very few, if any, would survive. Simmons played the game adeptly, standing for race pride and social justice while struggling not to lose financial and moral support from white northern institutions. Selma University president Charles L. Purce judged that Simmons got the balance right. African Americans controlled zero schools "that have attained to anything," Purce admonished. "It is all nonsense for any of us to say we can support them, and then will not do it."[21]

The separatists did not really disagree, although their rhetoric sounded otherwise. They counted on Simmons to leverage his influence to their advantage. Though they talked about building their own schools, the bottom line was something else. They wanted to control the Home Mission Society's schools and to control the northern money, which they continued to count upon. Simmons was crucial to both objectives, a point noted insightfully by McPherson and religious historian James M. Washington. Conferences of the American National Baptist Convention were long on political discussion, which caused white Baptists to charge that the convention was not very religious. ANBC leaders replied that they lived under a social crisis and thus operated in crisis mode. They did not come to ANBC meetings to hold spectacle worship services or discuss theology. They came to discuss what they should do about their existence under white oppression. The accommodation wing of the ANBC said the critics had a point, while Simmons played mediator, holding the convention together. He urged that if the two wings prayed together and struggled hard enough to find God's agenda for black Baptists, their ideological differences would subside.[22]

Instead Simmons's big heart shockingly gave out in October 1890, when he was forty-one years old. Simmons had battled heart stress and edema since May. The *New York Age* called his death "a calamity to the race." The ANBC, in its grief, lauded Simmons as "one of the greatest Negro leaders of the Nineteenth Century, and one of the foremost Baptists in the world." A special committee, appointed and led by Brawley, proposed to memorialize Simmons by creating a national university in his name. This proposal reignited the usual disputes about the limits of ANBC resources and the viability of separatist church politics, now in the absence of the group's charismatic leader. Brawley succeeded Simmons as president of the ANBC, but the separatists did not accept him as their leader. Brawley, like Simmons, was a staunch denominationalist, but Brawley, a light-colored Afro-American born free in 1851, fervently advocated racial integration. He preached that black Baptists "should merge race feeling in the broader spirit of an American Christianity. This is the proper aim; for it is Christlike."[23]

To separatist leaders loathing white dominance, this was not the proper aim. Brawley espoused muddling through, as did his successor as ANBC president, Michael Vann. The separatists, led by E. C. Morris, Walter Brooks, Harvey Johnson, and Emanuel Love, struck hard for a big denomination and a publishing house of their own. In 1895 North Carolina minister Albert W. Pegues proposed to incorporate the existing Education Convention, Baptist Foreign Mission Convention, and American National Baptist Convention into boards of education, foreign missions, and home missions of a new convention. That became the structure of the National Baptist Convention, founded in 1895 in Atlanta, where Henry McNeal Turner urged the delegates to embrace separatist ideology and Henry Lyman Morehouse urged them not to give up on integration. Morehouse pleaded that race should not be divisive in the church of Christ: "Don't reproach us, brethren, *because we are white*—we can't help it. We may not be altogether lovely, you may not be altogether lovely; but we are to love one another even as Christ loved us."[24]

That sentiment was routed by the excited anticipation of building something huge and powerful that white people did not control. Baltimore pastor Harvey Johnson urged the 1896 convention to sever relations totally: "I believe in an entire separation, because of existing circumstances and conditions of things. I have not always believed and felt that way, but I do now." Johnson assured that he did not advocate hatred or antagonism toward white Americans. He advocated black self-determination, a separatist position driven by the fact that "the white man's race-pride and race-prejudice so entirely and completely unfits him to accord to us in his organizations." Emanuel Love agreed, acknowledging that doing so was not possible for him until 1895, when Benjamin Griffith died. Griffith was a kindly longtime secretary of the American Baptist Publication Society. Now that Griffith was gone, Love felt free to say that black Baptists needed a convention and publishing house of their own: "I will stand or fall, live or die, with my race and denomination; where they die, 'I will die, and there will be buried.'"[25]

That was a sign that this matter had been settled, at least for the overwhelming majority that established the National Baptist Convention in 1895. By then, E. C. Morris had emerged as the leader of the separatist majority and its demand for a publishing house. Elias C. Morris was born into slavery in Murray County, Georgia, in 1855. After the Civil War he moved with his parents to Chattanooga, Tennessee, and later to Stevenson, Alabama, where he had some schooling and served a three-year apprenticeship to a shoemaker. He joined the Morning Star Baptist Church of Stevenson in 1874 and was licensed to preach the following year. He moved to Helena, Arkansas, where he scratched out a living as a shoemaker and supply preacher. In 1879 the Centennial Baptist Church of Helena called him to be its pastor. The following year Morris joined the Baptist State Convention of Arkansas.[26]

So far this was a familiar narrative to black Baptists, but Morris had leadership skills that stood out as soon as he joined the state convention. In 1882 he was elected president of the convention, which reelected him for nine successive years. He served briefly as state missionary under the American Baptist Home Mission Society. He cofounded the first black Baptist newspaper in Arkansas, *Arkansas Times*, later renamed the *Baptist Vanguard*, which he edited for four years. He was active in state and national Republican politics. In 1884 he founded Arkansas Baptist College, which he served as chair of the board of trustees during his eleven-year pastorate in Helena. During the period that Morris became the leader of a new national convention movement, he edited a popular weekly newspaper, the *People's Friend*.

Morris's breakthrough as a national Baptist leader occurred in 1892 when he opposed Brawley's effort to create a national university. The educated elite of the ANBC chastised Washington for skewering black clergy as uneducated and incompetent. They did so, however, only on morale grounds; Washington should not have embarrassed the black church in a white magazine. Otherwise Brawley and the antiseparatists believed that Washington was obviously right.

For them, as for Payne in the AME context, the remedy for ministerial igno-rance was to build a flagship Baptist university, not to squander scarce resources on a variety of local black institutions.

Morris broke through as the champion of increasingly separatist Baptists and their demand for local black control. He thwarted the move to create a national university, aided by Brooks and Love, which forced the Brawley antiseparatists to settle for a new education convention. The following year, in 1893, Morris electrified a majority of the ANBC convention with a speech titled "The Demand for a Negro Baptist Publishing House." Speaking for the twenty-person Committee on the Publication House, Morris urged that black Baptists needed to build their own schools, businesses, and institutions, and they needed a publishing house above everything else. He did not take pride "in feeding the leopard of race prejudice, by drawing and making prominent the colorline," but black Baptists were overdue to provide a legacy for their children: "We are in duty bound by virtue of what has been done for us, by the providence of God, to provide better things for our children, than our fathers were allowed to provide for us." Black Baptist ministers and academics had no place to publish their sermons, articles, and books, he noted. At the same time, youths were graduating from school with no place to apply their skills and knowledge. Morris admonished delegates that black Methodists were far ahead of them: "If we never have to conduct the business side of our religion, we shall never know how. . . . If there is any one thing in which the colored Baptists are behind their brethren of other denominations, it is in business enterprises of this kind." Establishing a publishing house immediately was "imperative," Morris urged.[27]

The convention agreed, formally adopting the resolution of the publication committee: "We shall never attain to the broad influence and elevated dignity of so vast a body of Baptists, so long as our literary productions remain unpub-lished." Morris was elected president of the new convention at its founding, a position he held for twenty-seven years. In 1896 the convention established the American Baptist Publication Society, under the leadership of Richard Boyd, fulfilling a cherished dream. The following year the convention formally sepa-rated from all white Baptist societies and braced for schisms, knowing that schisms were inevitable. The first big one occurred in 1903, the Lott Carey Separation, which cost the convention many of its most educated ministers. This schism was fought mostly over cooperation with white Baptists and the location of the foreign mission board, producing the Lott Carey Missionary Convention. A huge schism occurred in 1916, as a group calling itself the "National Baptist Convention, Unincorporated" broke off from the parent group. Here the issue was whether the original convention owned the publication society. The third schism occurred in 1961 when the convention's lack of support for Martin Luther King Jr. and the civil rights movement caused L. Venchael Booth to organize a breakaway denomination, the Progressive National Baptist Convention.[28]

Each of these schisms replayed debates over separatism and racial integration that Simmons would have recognized. But the National Baptist Convention fulfilled Simmons's dreams for it in the early going, using its numerical strength to become the most aggressive agent for racial justice and social change among all African American churches. Morris put it buoyantly in his presidential address of 1899, hailing the "wonderful record and unparalleled progress made by the Baptists since the organization of this Convention." The founders had one purpose, Morris declared, putting it negatively for a moment: "To save this wing of our great and invincible denomination from disgrace." Positively, they showed "that in the onward movement of the great army of God in the world Negro Baptists are a potent factor."[29]

Morris began with his customary assurances and admonitions. God must have wanted the black Baptists to unite; otherwise they would not have overcome the many obstacles thrown in their way. Scoffers had to stop saying that black Baptists could not unite, and holdouts needed to join the fold, because unity had already occurred and the holdouts were embarrassing themselves. The National Baptist Convention bore no animosity toward white Christians and did not favor any kind of racial prejudice: "We admit, however, that practically, and not constitutionally, the color line has been drawn by the establishment of churches and schools for the 'colored people.'" Black separatism was about building up the black community, not about despising people on the other side of the color line. The convention did not oppose cooperative efforts with white agencies, especially ecumenical coalitions at the local and state level. It insisted only that such cooperation had to be mutual and absolutely equal, something "that this country is not yet ready for."[30]

Morris gloried in the irony that African Americans possessed the only national Baptist convention. The Northern Baptist and Southern Baptist Conventions, having divorced over slavery, remained far apart, but "from Maine to California we are one." Heading such a large enterprise cost him some intellectual freedom. Morris noted gravely that America was divided over the war in the Philippine islands. The bitter argument between expansionists and anti-expansionists made "the horizon dark with commotion." This was a very serious matter, Morris observed, but he risked no opinion about it, and he did not say whether the convention should address it. All he could say was that Christians should ask God to "establish peace among the nations."[31]

On domestic order he was more definite and prescriptive. Morris was ardent about law and order, imploring the convention to stand against the escalating lawlessness of the age. Lynching was not simply a manifestation of race hatred, he argued. It was an aspect of an epidemic of anarchy and mob violence that swept far beyond race hatred or any particular section of the nation: "The people have become crazed and have lost their respect for the law and the administration of the law, and unless there is a change no man will be secure in life or property." Morris admonished there was no cowardice in obeying the law; to the contrary, the cowards were the criminals and mob-inciters: "I would counsel my people everywhere to be law-abiding, no matter how much they may suffer thereby. . . . Ministers of the Gospel and good people everywhere should lift their voices against all classes of crime which is blackening the record of our country. The man who will not lift his voice in defense of the sacredness of the home and the chastity of the women in this country, is unworthy to be called a man." Respect for the law had to be reestablished in America, Morris implored. The church had a large role to play in insisting upon it. And the National Baptist Convention would not be deterred from doing so.[32]

On foreign missions he had more admonition, reporting that the entire convention had only eleven missionaries in the field. This record was inexcusable, Morris declared—especially because the Foreign Mission Board was trying hard. To be sure, the convention had some structural problems in this area. More important, ordinary churchgoers were selfish and myopic, failing to support the mission board. Morris urged that anything less than fifty missionaries was unacceptable for a big convention that claimed to be Christian: "We can no longer hope to retain the confidence and respect of other peoples of the world, unless we do more for the redemption of the heathen, and especially those of our fatherland."[33]

Morris turned to his pride and joy, the Home Mission Board, which created the American Baptist Publication Society. The publishing house, though only three years old, was already "one of the most notable heritages the Negro Baptist ever did, or ever will have." It employed sixty-eight workers and spoke to the world "in one tremendous voice." For decades, Morris recalled, remembering how it felt, "scores of our young men and women" graduated from school "without the slightest hope or encouragement." They had no way of being heard in a society where whites did not care what any black person thought. The black church had to take responsibility for this problem, Morris observed: "The sun has forever gone down on any race of people who will not encourage and employ their literary talent. How could the Negro Baptists ever hope to be or do anything while they were committing literary suicide?"[34]

Morris expected the forthcoming census of 1900 to show that there were almost two million black Baptists in the United States. Many were "crude and undeveloped," he stressed: "They know but little of the practical side of Christianity." Morris took for granted that the movement for social Christianity marked a huge step forward in American Christianity and that black Baptists needed to practice their own version of it. He wanted black Baptists to think big thoughts about their future. They entered the nineteenth century as chattel slaves. They closed the century as "a happy, free people, having built more churches and school houses, in proportion to their numbers, than any people dwelling beneath the sun." There was already ample proof, Morris implored, that black Baptists had tremendous potential to change the world and liberate "the millions bound in heathen darkness."[35]

Had Morris not been very conservative on social issues, he might have applied his liberation argument to black Baptist women who wanted their own convention. But Morris and most of his colleagues did not have the feminist spirit of Simmons. In 1892 the Foreign Mission Convention had refused to allow women to form an auxiliary organization. Morris took a dim view of the power base that women built up at State University and the ANBC. Even if women had their own issues, that did not give them a right to their own convention, which would drain energy from the real convention run by men. He opposed the efforts of feminist leaders to form an auxiliary convention to the National Baptist Convention. Even after they created one in 1900, Morris tried to undermine it, telling S. Willie Layten that women could have a board within the convention answering to its (male) leaders. A separate convention not answering to male leaders, however, was out of play—never mind that black Baptist women had been building one for twenty years. It fell to twenty-one-year-old Nannie Helen Burroughs to explain that the logic of separatist upbuilding applied emphatically to women.[36]

NANNIE H. BURROUGHS AND BLACK BAPTIST SISTERHOOD

Nannie Burroughs came into a feminist tradition that paved the way for her and that she helped to boost at a propitious moment. She was born in 1879 in Orange, Virginia, to a cook, Jennie Burroughs, who moved to Washington, DC, in search of gainful employment. Nannie's father, John Burroughs, an itinerant preacher, never joined the family in Washington. Both of her parents were former slaves. Jennie Burroughs provided a model of personal and financial independence that made a deep impression on Nannie, who became an only child after her younger sister died in early childhood. Burroughs was schooled at M Street High School, where her teachers included Anna Julia Cooper and Mary Church Terrell. After graduating in 1896 she sought a position as a teaching assistant but was aced out by a rival candidate with lighter color and more pull. She wrote to Washington asking if she could be a typist at Tuskegee, with the same result. The former rejection cut her, yielding a vow: "I would someday have a school here in Washington that politics had nothing to do with, and that would give all sorts of girls a fair chance and help them overcome whatever handicaps they might have." Elsewhere she recalled: "It came to me like a flash of light and I knew I was to do that thing when the time came. But I couldn't do it yet, so I just put it away in the back of my head and left it there."[37]

For the rest of her life Burroughs brushed off conservative male constraints and middle-class family conventions, stressing something that made her controversial in the National Baptist Convention (feminist ideology), something that defined her career (the dignity of working-class women's labor), and something that defined her denomination (race pride). She made her first feminist connection at the age of sixteen, joining the National Association of Colored Women at its founding in 1896. Burroughs began her work life the following year in Philadelphia, working as an associate editor of the *Christian Banner*. In 1900 she moved to Louisville, where she worked as a secretary for the Foreign Mission Board of the National Baptist Convention. That put her in the middle of the Baptist women's contention for a convention of their own. Burroughs's association with the feminist community got her a speaking role at the NBC's national convention of 1900 in Richmond, Virginia, where she delivered a brassy speech titled "How the Sisters Are Hindered from Helping." She told the delegates not to kid themselves about their support of women. Baptist women had long-standing grievances about being suppressed, the new convention was no improvement, and Burroughs had come to express the "righteous discontent" of the sisters about this state of affairs. The convention responded by authorizing the largest formal organization of black women in the United States, the Woman's Convention Auxiliary to the National Baptist Convention.[38]

The Woman's Convention consisted entirely of National Baptist Convention members. From the beginning Burroughs was its leader, first as corresponding secretary until 1947 and subsequently as president until her death in 1961. The group held its annual meetings jointly with the NBC. In the early going, Burroughs established her personal authority by defying Morris and other leaders who tried to undermine the separate status of the Woman's Convention and by prevailing over WC secretary Virginia Broughton, who thought that Burroughs should defer to the older generation of feminist leaders. In both cases it mattered that the Woman's Convention was distinct from the club movement and even the Baptist women's activist tradition out of which it germinated. The preceding groups were predominantly middle class, and the club movement arose as a response to the racist denigration of black women by a white journalist. The Woman's Convention was overwhelmingly working class, and it arose as a response to the sexism of black male church leaders.

Burroughs stressed both points upon launching the organization. By her count she labored 365 days during her first year in office, traveled 22,000 miles, delivered 215 speeches, organized 12 Woman's Convention societies, wrote over 9,200 letters, and received over 4,800 letters. She and Broughton, upon settling their rivalry, worked together to build a large and vital organization. Fortunately for them the church's second most powerful figure, Home Mission Board chair Richard Boyd, defended their right to a separate organization supported by the NBC. Burroughs contended that black women undertook indispensable work in society, they deserved respect for it, and they needed their own base of power in the Baptist Church. By 1903 the Woman's Convention represented nearly 1 million women; by 1907 it had 1.5 million. Most were domestic laborers.[39]

On the lecture circuit Burroughs was blunt, personal, and often caustic, stressing personal character and correct behavior. Having joined the club movement at its founding, she shared its concern about how Afro-American women were perceived in American society. Always she spoke about the dignity of supporting one's self through labor and the necessity of developing a strong, productive, moral character. Sometimes she worked up to moral admonition, and sometimes she started with it. Burroughs shuddered at blacks that bleached their faces and straightened their hair. She assured that if "fair Negroes" were morally superior to "black Negroes," she would be the world's foremost advocate of bleach and straightening products. As it was, the "superior types of manhood and womanhood [are] found in thoroughbred Negro men and women." To Burroughs, it was pathetic to become fair through bleach "without any thought of an ounce of character to go along with it." What mattered was personal character, but anyone that bleached or straightened blared to the world that he or she had a distorted soul.[40]

The same principle held for attraction, she argued. Any black man that favored a bleached woman had something wrong with his soul, and any black woman that tried to become white had the same problem: "A true woman wouldn't give a cent for a changed appearance of this sort—a superficial nothing. What every woman who bleaches and straightens out needs, is not her appearance changed, but her mind. She has a false notion as to the value of color and hair in solving the problem of her life." Burroughs was persistent on this topic, urging that "the race would move forward" if African American women spent half as much time trying to become "better" as they spent trying to look white. It was pointless to look for exceptions, or try to become one: "Verily, verily I say unto you, that the women who spend most of their time improving their outward appearances are invariably the same women who are preparing themselves to darken their characters and make more crooked their lives."[41]

Black women, Burroughs judged, were guiltier than black men of wanting to look white, and black men were guiltier of wanting a white partner. Both desires were reprehensible to her, but Burroughs took greater offense at black men who failed to protect black women from white men seeking "social equality of the wrong sort." Burroughs stressed that having the courage to protect women was essential to being a virtuous man. In her experience, virtue was in short supply. White men defended their women fiercely, protecting even their prostitutes, while many black men failed to protect even "their best women." Burroughs elaborated: White men protected their prostitutes so zealously that blacks had to be careful not to insult them, "and yet these same white men who will die for the vilest of the vile among their own women, dare attempt to walk with impunity in our most sacred confines." To be sure, Burroughs acknowledged, African American men generally treated women of both races respectfully, unlike the contempt that white men routinely handed out to black women. Still, black men had something to learn from white men about standing up for the women of their race, even for women that did not deserve it.[42]

On the lecture stump Burroughs usually started with the defense issue, which led to the importance of women being worthy of being defended, which led to the problems of black women prostituting themselves to white men or holding romantic relationships with white men. Burroughs grieved that such women existed: "It is criminal for any woman of our race to tolerate for a moment such relations with men who have no more respect for black women than the door-keeper to Dante's Inferno has for St. Peter." Afro-American women had to train their sisters to be self-respecting, Burroughs urged. Things would be much better in the United States if there were no black women that made themselves sexually available to white men. Race relations would improve, the slanders against black women would diminish, and women would be less endangered: "It is the duty of Negro women to rise in the pride of their womanhood and vindicate themselves of the charge by teaching all men that black womanhood is as sacred as white womanhood." Though Burroughs always had a message for black men—be virtuous and productive—she spoke primarily to black women: "God help us to so live that we may raise the standard higher and higher until the name 'Negro woman' will be a synonym for uprightness of character and loftiness of purpose." If that happened, she promised, "a new day will break upon ten million people."[43]

Burroughs had barely launched the Woman's Convention when she began to talk about founding a trade school for young women. She broached the idea at the first annual conference of the Woman's Convention in 1901, forming a fund-raising committee. In the early going, most of the NBC's male leaders did not support it. Burroughs contended that improving the employability of African American women was enormously important for the advancement of the African American community and that the church needed to train women to be productive lay religious leaders, establishing community centers. In 1907 an NBC committee headed by Burroughs bought a house in the Lincoln Heights section of Washington, DC, to house the National Training School for Women and Girls. Burroughs assumed nearly complete control, a point of controversy in the NBC for forty years. The school opened officially in 1909 with Burroughs as president, situated on eight acres on a hill northeast of the Capitol. It received most of its funding from black Baptist women, none directly from the NBC and almost none from whites. Burroughs guarded her independence and control, making sure that the deed established no legal connection to the NBC or the Woman's Convention. The school started with thirty-one students and grew steadily, reaching two thousand students twenty-five years later.[44]

The National Training School attracted students from across the nation and the Caribbean, offering instruction at the high school and junior college levels in missionary work, homemaking, domestic service, clerical work, farming, and printing. Homemaking was a major category incorporating housekeeping, decorating, laundering, and home nursing. Burroughs told students they were being trained in spiritual character; everything else was secondary. Domestic work was important labor deserving professional status. All forms of honest labor should be done conscientiously and with dignity. Every form of domestic labor deserved to be decently compensated and needed to be unionized. No job was too small or too menial not to be done with professional self-respect. Congregations should address the needs of communities by developing social welfare programs run by women. To Burroughs, Christian duty, a strict moral code, productive paid labor, and racial self-help went together. She urged: "Don't be idle. Don't scorn labor nor look with contempt upon the laborer. Those who encourage Negro women to loaf, rather than work at service for a living are enemies to the race." In other words, "An idle woman is seldom a virtuous woman."[45]

Burroughs called this approach "idealizing the real," an early step toward realizing the ideal. Most Afro-American women were going to be domestic workers, she stressed. That was not going to change in the foreseeable future. What could change was how they felt about it, how they approached it, how others felt about it, and how well it was compensated. In 1909 Burroughs told the Ninth Annual Session of the Woman's Convention, "We may have the poorest, but we are going to do the best that can be done with what we have. Our table linen will be as white as that used in the Executive Mansion. If we eat out of tin plates and drink from tin cups, they will be as clean and shining as the finest china and cut glass, and we will serve with as much grace as those who have the best." In that spirit she provided the school's motto: "Work. Support thyself. To thine own powers appeal." Sometimes she said the school rested on three tools for racial advancement—the Bible, the bath, and the broom. Woman's Convention speeches and pamphlets abounded with admonitions about the importance of bathing, maintaining a clean house, and using correct manners, all in the earnest spirit of the National Training School, otherwise known as "The School of the Three B's."[46]

Every year the Woman's Convention was a feat of cooperation and planning, drawing thousands of housemaids, cooks, missionaries, and Sunday school teachers to segregated cities. Extensive housing networks in the homes of area people had to be arranged to house and feed the delegates. Women came to the convention to be inspired by each other and to draw strength for the fight against poverty and abuse. Burroughs took pride in her friendship with Washington, who began speaking to Woman's Convention gatherings in 1902. The first speech was catastrophic. Someone yelled, "fight," which was misheard as "fire," setting off a stampede that killed over one hundred people. Washington never failed to oblige Burroughs afterward, addressing every Woman's Convention until his death in 1915. Other featured speakers over the years included Wells-Barnett, George Edmund Haynes, Emmett Scott, James Weldon Johnson, Mary Talbert, and John Hope. Burroughs wore proudly the nickname she acquired, hearing it constantly in introductions: "the female Booker T. Washington."

She revered Washington, and in the early going, she and the Woman's Convention operated with Washington's charity and bootstrap model of social outreach. On the protest politics of civil rights, however, Burroughs sided with Du Bois and the NAACP. By 1910 she also stopped spurning social gospel sociology, especially its focus on transforming social structures. Evelyn Brooks Higginbotham, in her pioneering and magnificent work on Burroughs and the politics of respectability, stresses that respectability and social justice politics fit together for Burroughs: "The politics of respectability, while emphasizing self-help strategies and intra-group reform, provided the platform from which black church women came to demand full equality with white America." Burroughs roared for respectability, but the Great Migration compelled her to think about social structures too. Migrants poured into northern cities, and the settlement movement led the way in helping cities to respond creatively. From 1910 to 1920, the numbers were staggering. In Chicago the Afro-American population soared from 44,000 to 109,000. In Detroit it soared from 5,000 to 40,000. In New York the figures were 91,000 to 152,000, and in Philadelphia the figures were 84,000 to 134,000. Burroughs realized that her organizations had to take up the social gospel concerns with urbanization and industrialization. She said it explicitly at the Woman's Convention of 1912, urging delegates to read socio-logical literature on urbanization and calling for a new Social Services Committee to address urban poverty.[47]

J. Milton Waldron provided a local example of settlement ministry just as Burroughs was founding the National Training School. In 1901 Waldron had launched a social welfare program at Bethel Baptist Church in Jacksonville, Florida, featuring a kindergarten, an insurance company, a night school, and a cooking school. Waldron founded the insurance company as a church society but eventually opened it to the entire black community of Jacksonville. In 1907 he moved to Washington, DC, where he established a similar program at Shiloh Church and teamed with Monroe Trotter to form radical political orga-nizations. Henry Hugh Proctor's First Congregational Church in Atlanta and Lacey Kirk Williams's Olivet Baptist Church in Chicago created similar social welfare programs that became institutional anchors of the black social gospel.[48]

Being a black church, in the first place, was synonymous with helping African Americans survive a hostile society. Then urbanization and the Great Migration compelled black churches to develop social programs. A church would create a program to provide nursery care, job training, or recreation. It would be drawn into debates about what urbanization had wrought and whether the churches were morally obligated to welcome the migrant stranger. The question itself was unwelcome in many middle-class congregations, but the idea of the "institutional church" took hold in this context of growing urbaniza-tion combined with contention over the new migrants. The institutional church provided a new kind of organizational vehicle for racial self-help and self-determination. As urbanization and the Great Migration accelerated, church leaders had to think about what was happening to the concept of ministry. Many ministers staunchly opposed everything smacking of the social gospel, protesting that it distracted from saving souls. Some drew the line at traditional charity ministries. Some were drawn into more social work than they thought was appropriate for churches. Others consciously crossed the social gospel line into activist work for social justice.

Burroughs joined forces with social gospel proponents of social work and social justice ministry. It appalled her that this issue was controversial in the National Baptist Convention. She blasted her opponents repeatedly, always singling out ministers that confined Christianity to otherworldly singing, praying, preaching, and altar calls. Too many preachers preached "too much Heaven and too little practical Christian living," she protested. In her telling, the bad ministers were uneducated, dramatic, and low on personal morality. They were "sleek, lazy, jack leg" types that knew how to gain a following among the poor and uneducated and how to exploit them. Burroughs identified three kinds of ministers in the NBC. The first type was educated, moral, successful, socially conscious, and dedicated to community uplift; this was a small group, but growing. The second type was poorly educated and short on achievements, but conscientious and sincere. This was the largest group. The third type was the church's biggest problem and its second largest group among the minis-ters—the lowlife "grafters" that exploited poor and vulnerable congregations. The "grafters" did immense harm to the church, Burroughs charged. They drained its resources, betrayed the gospel, misled poor congregants, and made the church look bad. Everything depended on convincing ordinary church-goers not to tolerate "men who go into the ministry to dodge hard work."[49]

The same principle applied to congregations, she urged. If a congregation did nothing to improve the life of its community, it had no business being a church and no community should support it. In 1913 the Woman's Convention opened a settlement house in Washington, DC, employing a professional social worker and featuring a soup kitchen, clothing program, health clinic, voca-tional education classes, and recreational activities. Just as Burroughs argued that domestic work deserved the status of a profession and should be unionized, she supported the progressive call for professionalized social work. Social work would acquire greater social respect as it acquired a specialized literature and training, she reasoned. Moreover, there was a dire need for black female experts in this field, because white specialists nearly always misrepresented the experi-ence and social conditions of African Americans. Burroughs respected Jane Addams but emphatically did not care for most white feminist settlement workers. She gagged at the white-gloved college graduates who came to study the "interesting slum problem." She charged that privileged white women undertook settlement work "for no other reason than to show her finery and to let her less fortunate sisters see how brilliantly she shines." Burroughs implored the social reform organizations to recruit working-class African American women. If middle-class white feminists ran the settlement houses, nothing would change.[50]

The middle-class club movement, however, had a role to play in this situation. At least, Burroughs wanted her fellow club members to take it on. In 1918 she urged NACW president Mary Talbert to organize a conference on problems that postwar industrialization posed for black women. In most places the NACW had stronger ties to church work than its national conventions suggested, a two-way necessity that Burroughs appreciated. The club movement was primarily a vehicle for middle-class black women who were disqualified by gender from being ministers. But most of them were deeply tied to their church communities, and even in its formal structure the NACW had departments for church clubs, evangelism, and other religious work. For Burroughs, advocating for working-class women did not exclude forming alliances with middle-class organizations or trying to climb into them. She was a latter-day champion of Booker-style social mobility for Afro-American churchwomen.[51]

In the 1920s Burroughs followed up her own suggestion to Talbert by founding the National Association of Wage Earners, a reform group promoting greater opportunities for black women in business enterprises. Burroughs served as the group's president, and three NACW leaders headed the national board — Talbert, Mary McLeod Bethune, and Richmond banker Maggie L. Walker. Criticizing capitalism was not on the agenda for this group; Burroughs wanted to get Afro-American women into the system. But the organization's nine-point program pressed the limits of its bourgeois reformism, advocating worker training, job placement, a living wage, safety standards, grievance procedures, uniforms, reform legislation, "elevating" the "migrant classes of workers," and "enlightening" women about unions. Burroughs told African American women that the key to their success in an increasingly technological society was their willingness to work hard and efficiently. Often she suggested that women made better employees than men, and nearly always she was blunt and colorful in expressing her opinion.[52]

"The Negro race is a child race," she was fond of saying, invoking a Booker maxim. "The Negro is highly endowed with things of the spirit," notably love, forbearance, music, faith, and hope, "but he is not cultivating them." This was a variation on Burroughs's staple theme that spiritual character mattered more than anything and that Afro-Americans were gifted in this area but they squandered their gifts. According to Burroughs, African Americans sabotaged their spiritual and moral vitality "by cultivating an insatiable love for the material at the expense of higher virtues." She begged black leaders to stop boasting about material progress: "He brags about what he owns, but he goes to others for what he needs. The time spent in bragging should have been given to the development of qualities of soul." She derided black leaders for excelling at only one thing besides bragging and consuming—begging for money from philanthropists. Burroughs exhorted: "Complete absorption of thought, time, and strength to the acquisition of material things, spells moral death and spiritual death to any race. The Negro in his puerile state of mind is conjured into believing that things—houses, land, bank accounts, second-hand knowledge, and rights—will get him a place of power in this material civilization. *They will not.* He cannot catch up with the Anglo-Saxon materially, but he can catch up with him spiritually and morally."[53]

Anglo-Saxons got to be rich by using their brains to satisfy vital human needs, Burroughs reasoned. They built up a complex, bountiful, technologically sophisticated civilization, one that increasingly neglected matters of spirit for material achievement. Burroughs respected that Anglo-Saxons once had spiritual character; otherwise they would not have succeeded. She wanted Afro-Americans to do what Anglo-Saxons had already done: "The Negro must use his brains to supply some vital needs." But there were no material needs that Anglo-Saxon civilization could not satisfy, she judged. Black Americans had no chance of winning at that game; plus, the game had evolved into something that was bad for human beings anyway. Burroughs urged that African Americans were uniquely endowed to save America spiritually: "The Negro is not being taught the tremendous achieving power of his virtues. He is not being taught to glorify what he is. When he learns that he has the leaven that is needed in this American lump, he will put it in." White America gave lip service to Jesus and the Beatitudes, but black Americans were the real Christians. Burroughs anticipated black liberation theology in criticizing white Christianity and in stressing that black is beautiful: "When the Negro learns what manner of man he is spiritually, he will wake up all over. He will stop playing white, even on the stage. He will rise in the majesty of his own soul. He will glorify the beauty of his own brown skin."[54]

For Burroughs, good religion was idealistic, both rhetorically and spiritually. She implored that what matters in life is to live up to the highest ideals and spiritual purposes: "I believe it is the Negro's sacred duty to spiritualize American life and popularize his own color instead of worshipping the color (or lack of color) of another race." She yearned to see Afro-Americans let go of their fascination with white people, white things, and succeeding at a white game: "No race is richer in soul quality and color than the Negro. Some day he will realize it and glorify them. He will popularize black." God wanted African Americans to "rise and shine," Burroughs said, working out their own salvation. Ministers needed to preach about this in the right way. Burroughs urged them to preach that African Americans needed education, but with all their getting, they needed common sense more. They needed clothes, but more important, they needed to get clean. They needed houses, but more important, they needed to build homes. They needed their rights, but more important, they needed to get right: "Preachers, teachers, leaders, welfare workers ought to address themselves to the supreme task of teaching the entire race to glorify what it has—its face (its color); its place (its homes and communities); its grace (its spiritual endowment)."[55]

Burroughs never forgot when and where she entered: at the founding of the club movement, which began as a response to racist slurs on the moral dignity of black women. She crusaded against the racist white myth that black women were morally lax. Hegemonic convention was perverse in this area, for, in fact, Afro-American women were morally superior to other Americans, especially white people. Burroughs and her followers pressed this theme at Woman's Convention meetings. In 1910 the convention noted that "a certain class of whites" frequently spread across all sections of the streetcars, forcing blacks to sit near them. African Americans often reacted by demanding a seat, or by squeezing in, or by nearly sitting on the lap of a white passenger. The Woman's Convention made a plea for moral respectability: "Here is an opportunity for us to show our superiority by not squeezing in. Let us at all times and on all occasions remember that the quiet, dignified individual who is respectful to others is after all the superior individual, be he black or white."[56]

Burroughs built the Woman's Convention into a fund-raising powerhouse for the National Baptist Convention. She built the National Training School into a sprawling enterprise that, by 1929, included eight buildings spread across eight acres. The school boldly promised its students: "We specialize in the wholly impossible." Having built two nationally prominent symbols of black social Christian feminism, Burroughs spoke with confident authority about what was lacking in black life and what she had to overcome to command attention. She was often caustic on both subjects, sparing no hurt feelings. She skewered the Du Bois–Woodson revisionist line on Reconstruction, contending that black men squandered their political opportunities for petty patronage payoffs. Intellectuals did not impress her anyway, especially Du Bois; Burroughs hated the self-congratulatory talk about the Talented Tenth. When Du Bois made a stormy exit from the NAACP in 1934, Burroughs did not lament his departure. It was time for the race to "close ranks," she advised, poking at a sore memory. Ironically, Du Bois was moving at the time toward Burroughs's emphasis on black-owned institutions, but she stressed that intellectual leaders were like other black leaders in doing little for ordinary African Americans.[57]

The previous December, Burroughs had addressed an AME Church forum on the subject "What Must the Negro Do to Be Saved?" Her answer was widely reprinted and characteristically blunt: "Chloroform your 'Uncle Toms.'" Burroughs protested that self-regarding black leaders lived well off their status without helping ordinary people: "The Negro must unload the leeches and parasitic leaders who are absolutely eating the life out of the struggling, desiring mass of people." She judged that churches, schools, and political organizations overflowed with self-serving types. Without these so-called leaders, she charged, black Americans would be one hundred years ahead of where they were: "I don't care whether they are in the church as the preacher, in the school as the teacher, in the ward as politicians—the quickest way to get rid of them is the best way, and the sooner the better. They are luxurious, expensive, unworthy. They have sold us for a mess of pottage." The great emancipators, she said, were dead. The leaders of the present day were worthless and she did not believe in looking for replacement leaders: "We must arise and go over Jordan. We can take the promised land. The Negro must serve notice on the world that he is ready to die for justice. To struggle and battle and overcome and absolutely defeat every force designed against us is the only way to achieve."[58]

Burroughs grieved that the Depression drove black men to a new low of humiliation. She admonished black women that they wrongly coddled black men, failing to expect enough of them. She could see a long-term calamity coming for a generation of black men that never found a first job: "The manhood of the race is going to weeds—going to waste. Go up and down the streets in Negro ghettos and see for yourself. Social deterioration has set in. Negro men are entirely too idle and they are entirely too satisfied at being idle. They are doing too much sitting down, hanging out and hanging around. Men cannot be made under these conditions, they are unmade." When Burroughs hammered on this theme, which was often, her daily grind showed through. She spent her days teaching women domestics that worked two jobs, took care of their families, and went to school on the side. She knew their stories and sympathized, but implored mothers and wives to stop spoiling the men in their lives: "They ruin good men and make bad men worse. They run after them, support them and let them sling around as if they were rags."[59]

By her reckoning, Anglo-Saxons loved four things: liberty, home, women, and life. Burroughs respected this list, telling African Americans they erred in accepting poor substitutes: "When we make up our minds to not take substitutes for them, we'll get them." Sometimes she put it categorically, with no caveats, declaring that Afro-Americans would someday become powerful in the same way as the whites that preceded them: "The same thing that made the white race great will make the black race great." Sometimes she reduced the four things to one—the power of gospel love. Anglo-Saxons got to be great because they had the gospel, and blacks would become great by taking the gospel to heart. Sometimes Burroughs said that blacks took the gospel more seriously than Anglo-Saxons and sometimes it seemed too obvious to say. On the former occasions she explained that African Americans spurned Anglo-Saxon individualism. Anglo-Saxons always pushed forward as individuals, building an individualistic culture of materialism. Burroughs urged that blacks had to rise together "as a great race or group." She could not resist adding that black women were much closer to doing it than black men: "The Negro mother is doing it all. The women are carrying the burden. The main reason is that the men lack manhood and energy." Black men sang too much, shirked their work and family commitments, and were too easy on themselves: "The men ought to get down on their knees to Negro women. They've made possible all we have around us—church, home, school, business."[60]

Many National Baptist Convention men did not care for this refrain, which stoked an undercurrent of grumbling against Burroughs through her sixty years as a church leader. She had to defend her organizational authority, reminding NBC leaders that the Woman's Convention brought money, programs, and women into the NBC, not the other way around. She proved doubly troublesome by remaining unmarried, which did not stop her from dispensing advice about dating and marriage. She proved triply upsetting by refusing to let the NBC claim any part of her school or property, despite numerous attempts to wrest control from her. For church leaders holding one idea of what a church lady should be like, the voluble, caustic, powerful, unmarried Burroughs proved hard to take. But for her vast following of church activists, workers, colleagues, and students, she was an inspiring tower of strength and integrity, a realized impossibility. They were thrilled when she told white audiences: "We don't want your teachers, we have our teachers; we don't want your furniture, nor your clothes, we have plenty of clothes; we don't want your doctors nor your preachers; we have our doctors and our preachers; we don't want what you have earned; all we ask of you is a man's chance. What we ask is fair play and to be let alone."[61]

That was the spirit of the National Baptist Convention as she understood it, or at least as she wanted it to be. African Americans asked for nothing but elementary fairness and to be left alone. In 1942 Burroughs told the Woman's Convention: "Our real progress now depends upon two-tenths of the race that have climbed to middle ground by their own boot-straps; the clean, plain, honest, dependable, hardworking class, the back-bone of the race." The top tenth was self-indulgent and did next to nothing for the race, she judged. The lower seven-tenths, meanwhile, were mired in a "complete social economic and spiritual blackout." The economic Depression had not subsided for black Americans, and neither had the psychological Depression. A decade later, a year before Montgomery, Burroughs puzzled that the Depression had given way to a lot of strange talk about race. She waved off the "great noise about the race problem," countering that there was no such thing. There was only the fact that white Americans treated black Americans despicably. African Americans, despite their treatment, were making "wonderful progress," so there was much talk about a race problem: "They know that we are getting near them. They realize more than we, that we are coming." Burroughs begged them, on the way, to stop bleaching and straightening: "I am sorry we are colored as we are. I am sorry all of us are not black." Always she felt morally obligated to end on a note of hope: "Yes, we are living in a dark period and it is going to be worse for a while, but I believe that God will lead his people through."[62]

Burroughs shrugged off the perils of racial separatism and what was later called "essentialism," knowing that she confronted far worse problems. She shrugged off the objection that her emphasis on bathing, grooming, and middle-class manners reinforced the very stereotypes of racial denigration that she aimed to oppose. She was dogmatic about everything smacking of the sexualized life of the street. Juke joints, dancing, alcohol, gambling, jazz, immodest women's fashions—all were tools of the devil to lure impressionable youths from holy living. When pressed in this area, Burroughs was adamant about jazz and dancing; neither could possibly be forms of cultural resistance to oppression. Both were corrupting and degrading to her, like the bright-colored designer clothes that exposed women's bodies. Barbara Savage aptly notes that Burroughs railed about cleanliness and self-care not because she had class pretensions or worried about the prejudices of white racists: "She worried that the masses of black people were deeply demoralized, their spirits being so broken by racism and oppression that they no longer had the self-respect necessary to engage in the most basic acts of bodily and domestic cleanliness, pride of person, and physical modesty." Everything that Burroughs said in this area was devoted to healing demoralization and inspiring self-respect.[63]

This passionate concern helped to keep her in the Republican Party. In the 1920s Burroughs served as president of the National League of Republican Colored Women, urging black women to use the power of the ballot. In the 1930s she saw no reason to join the surge of African Americans to the New Deal and the Democrats. "I am not a political rat running from party to party," she declared. In the first place, joining a southern-dominated party that still used all-white primaries and the poll tax to exclude black voters was out of the question. Moreover, the New Deal offended her Booker-bootstrap moral sensibility. Burroughs warned that FDR's welfare programs would breed dependency and laziness among American Americans, especially men. She declared in September 1933: "So far as the Negro is concerned, America's present plan of economic recovery makes him a parasite, a degenerate, a pauper, a confirmed loafer." The Democratic Party, to her, became a perfect nightmare under Roosevelt, still dedicated to racist barriers in the South, but now committed to coddling an underclass of dependents. She said it with a barrage of accusations, decrying the new "army of enforced idlers" and the new "moral slavery." Burroughs grieved that the high unemployment of the 1930s combined with Roosevelt's social welfare policies drove African Americans to their lowest point since slavery, a new low "in our *hearts* and *minds* and *spirits*." She told the 1934 Woman's Convention that millions of black Americans were sitting down "waiting for somebody to deliver them, waiting for their second emancipator — and millions of others are happy and satisfied to live below the common level of decency."[64]

The following year Harlem exploded. Many claimed that Communists stoked and manipulated black discontent in Harlem. Some used Burroughs's rhetoric against her, pointing to a culture of idleness and failure. She countered a flood of explanation, knowing that she understood the rioters better than the journalists, officials, and academics proffering opinions. Communists did not set off the Harlem riot, Burroughs contended, and it was not a race riot. Harlem had a "human revolt" against a train of oppression: "The causes of the Harlem riot are not far to seek. They lie buried beneath mountains of injustices done the colored man in every state and in every relationship, through years of 'patient sufferance' on his part." Every day and every year, for decade after decade, blacks were robbed of their inalienable rights: "They have been goaded, hounded, driven around, herded, held down, kicked around and roasted alive. In Harlem the cornered rats fought back."[65]

Burroughs's powerful advocacy of racial uplift brought her a larger and more devoted following than any black church leader of her time before the coming of Adam Clayton Powell Jr. Culturally she was a Baptist-rooted black nationalist, and politically she was a pragmatic Republican. The church needed to be a home and refuge, a place where white racism did not intrude, although Burroughs had white allies, notably her counterpart in the Southern Baptist Convention's Woman's Missionary Union, Una Roberts Lawrence. In politics she worked hard for the Republican Party and the NAACP, spurning the futility of sectarian nationalist politics. Burroughs was a strong advocate of the NAACP becoming what it needed to be, and what it became—a predominantly black organization—and she served on its board of directors, though she objected that the organization was overly impressed with lawyers, well-heeled donors, and intellectuals. Had Burroughs cared more for Du Bois personally, she might have acknowledged that he sounded like her when he quit the NAACP. As it was, she resented that he damaged the NAACP on his way out.[66]

She respected plain speaking and had a gift for it. Burroughs possessed in abundance the gift for emotional connection that distinguished the best revival preachers and, notably, Garvey. She boldly spoke for the working poor from the perspective of the working poor. It did not faze her when she offended sensitive egos in polite society. Burroughs followed up blunt remarks with blunt explanations, not let-me-clarify walk-backs. She yearned never to see another interracial couple, sharing Garvey's feeling that the Talented Tenth was too white and deeply invested in its cultured whiteness. And she did not apologize for saying so. In 1950 an interviewer asked Burroughs how she felt about blacks that married whites. She "snorted," arose from her chair, and waved off the blacks in question: "Just something gone, but nothing missing. Let them go. . . . They should have been gone long ago."[67]

Burroughs had a millennial vision of deliverance from a hostile white world: "There is an army of them down in the bottoms that you have never seen, and never will see until you walk the streets of the New Jerusalem." God would not tarry forever, she promised. God was coming to save the lowly people and to crush "all the avarice, the secular spirit, worldly schemes, ignorance, and practical indifference."[68]

The only black Baptist leader of Burroughs's generation to approximate her renown achieved it in the other wing of the black Baptist social gospel—its upwardly mobile, middle-class, assimilated wing. Adam Clayton Powell Sr. had deep things in common with Burroughs—a defining commitment to the way and spirit of Jesus, a conviction that African Americans distinctly followed the spiritual ethic of Jesus, and a belief that blacks would flourish in the United States if they gave themselves completely to the claim of Jesus upon them. Powell greatly admired Burroughs and recognized her as a kindred spirit. He served on the board of Burroughs's school. Routinely he described her as one of America's greatest race leaders and one of the world's greatest women. He appreciated that Burroughs got to be renowned by calling people out and practicing what she preached.

But Powell's very success as a progressive Baptist minister lifted him to a life of privilege that disqualified him, to many, from calling out his ministerial colleagues. He took it very hard when ministers told him it had happened. Tellingly, it happened as a consequence of supporting a challenge from Burroughs. Though Powell lavished praise on Burroughs, and though Burroughs admired Powell's virtues and ministry, she was more guarded in returning the compliments, for Powell epitomized the privileged, honored, culturally assimilated, colored-not-black type of black leader that Burroughs regretted existed.

ADAM CLAYTON POWELL SR. AND THE ABYSSINIAN LODESTAR

Adam Clayton Powell was born at the junction of Soak and Maggotty Creeks in Franklin County, Virginia, in 1865, three weeks after the Civil War ended. Very little about his family background is certain, but his mother was Sally Dunning, a woman of African, Choctaw, and German descent, and his biological father was probably a slave owner named Llewellyn Powell, a planter of German descent who lived ten miles away at Hale's Ford. Some scholars claim that Dunning was Llewellyn Powell's slave, but census records indicate that Dunning and her mother and grandmother were free people of color, and there is no proof that Llewellyn Powell fathered Adam Clayton Powell. Powell later told his children that their grandmother was "a tall, rather fierce Negro-Indian woman." Sally Dunning was homeless at the time she gave birth to her fair, blue-eyed son Adam. A former slave, Anthony Dunn, gave her shelter during the birth; Dunn had a letter "P" branded on his back for having run away from Llewellyn Powell. In 1867 Sally married Dunn, who took in many others, eventually acquiring a family of seventeen people, all living in a one-room log cabin and eking out a bare existence as sharecroppers. In later life Powell had very little to say about his mother and stepfather, but Adam Clayton Powell Jr. met his step-grandfather once, describing him as "very shy, illiterate, a small dark-brown man" who had served as a church deacon and who showed him the "P" branded on his back.[69]

Powell Senior's early life was desperately poor, though his feats of memory contained a glimmer of his future. Until he started school at the age of seven, he had one piece of clothing, a shirt made of a bleached flour sack. His bed was a bag filled with cornhusks. In decent crop years he ate corn and wheat; at other times he had to subsist on dried apples and black-eyed peas. A charitable white teacher, Jake Bowles, had a school five miles away. Walking to school, Powell warmed his feet by thrusting them under cows lying on the ground.

On his first day of school Powell memorized the alphabet. On his second day he memorized it backward. His stepfather, duly impressed, challenged Powell to memorize the gospel of John, which he accomplished. Dunn supported Powell's reading interest, subscribing to a weekly newspaper, through which the family learned that a black man could earn a dollar per day in West Virginia. The family moved to Coldsburg to tend a farm, where Powell earned $50 per year, his mother earned $144 and his stepfather earned $360. Coldsburg was a very rough place, and Powell fell in with coarse, hard-drinking, roughneck neighbors. He later recalled: "The chief aim of the average man was to possess a pistol, a pair of brass knuckles and a jug of hard liquor. Fights were numerous and life was cheap." There were no role models, as even the preachers drank and thieved. Powell blended in, later recalling that nearly everything that happened to him in West Virginia was "a mental and moral disaster." In August 1884, guarding a melon patch for hire, Powell shot a prowler in the backside, who turned out to belong to a prominent white family. Powell fled "to keep from being lynched or murdered," moving to Rendville, Ohio, a company town run by coal mine owner W. P. Rends. But Rendville was even worse, "the most lawless and ungodly place I have ever seen." Powell, nineteen years old, added gambling to his thieving, carousing, and violent lifestyle, repeatedly drinking and gambling away his earnings as a miner, until revival came to Rendville.[70]

The local Baptist and Methodist congregations preached revival every night for two months. Powell had not attended church in years, but one Sunday morning, in a drunken stupor, he made his way to the Baptist Church, where the preacher, D. B. Houston, fell into a comalike trance, converting Powell without saying a word. Powell later recalled that the minister's emotionally over-whelmed testimony sent an arrow of conviction to his heart. Conversion enthu-siasm swept the town. Coal mines were shut down for a week, gambling tables were burned in a bonfire, and saloons went out of business. Five of the converts later became ministers. Powell, fresh from his conversion, moved to Washington, DC, hoping to attend law school at Howard University. He was not admitted, so he worked as a hotel janitor and waiter. In 1888 he applied to Wayland Seminary and College (later named Virginia Union University), where he was admitted to the normal and theological schools and where Wayland president G. M. P. King became a father figure to him.

King encouraged Powell, taught him, befriended him, and doted over him. Powell loved King in the adoring and grateful way that Washington loved General Armstrong. He later recalled, "If all the Christians in the world proved unfaithful, I would still know that Christ lived on earth during my lifetime because I met Dr. King." Powell said nothing about King's problems with black students who did not warm to his white savior paternalism. To Powell, King was a Christ figure, unambiguously a savior, plus a cherished friend: "To me he possessed the magnetism of the polestar. His life radiated beauty, goodness, courage, honesty, truth and love. These virtues cannot be taught by words. They can only be imparted by a life which possesses them in great abundance."[71]

In 1889 Powell married Mattie Fletcher Shaffer, the daughter of Col. Jacob Shaffer and his light-colored black mistress. The heir to a family brewery, Jacob Shaffer founded an academy for African Americans after the Civil War, Christiansburgh Academy, and his daughter Mattie was shy, reserved, and cultured, of regal beauty. Adam and Mattie Powell lived briefly in Philadelphia before moving to New Haven, Connecticut, in 1893 to minister at Immanuel Baptist Church, where Powell found his voice. All seven of New Haven's black churches, in his telling, were spiritually dead when he got there. The frosty intellectualism of Yale University cast a pall upon the black churches, even though they had no members from Yale.

Powell brought evangelical conviction to New Haven, preaching a revival that renewed his congregation. He wrote a small book on the history and mission of his congregation, declaring that if black Americans kept their right eye on God and their left eye on economic productivity, they were sure to succeed. Branching out intellectually, he absorbed the academic culture of New Haven and studied modern theology and philosophy. He took classes at Yale Divinity School under philosophical theologian Samuel Harris, studied Hebrew under divinity school student William H. Ferris, and studied Kant independently with his friend I. N. Porter, a physician and member of Immanuel Church. Powell invited Yale students to his home and congregation, welcoming many. He more than doubled his income by delivering two stock lectures on the pay-lecture circuit, "The Stumbling Blocks of the Race" and "My Black Cats." In 1895, upon hearing Washington deliver the Atlanta Compromise speech, Powell wrote a third lecture, "Broken, but Not Off." The chains of slavery were broken, Powell lectured, but black Americans were still handcuffed by ignorance, superstition, prejudice, intolerance, and injustice.[72]

Powell thrived in New Haven. An impressive figure at six feet, three inches, he wore Brooks Brothers suits and laced his carefully written sermons with references to his course work at Yale. His congregation grew from one hundred to thirty-six hundred, and his two children, Blanche and Adam Jr., were born in New Haven, in 1898 and 1908. Powell Junior later recalled of his father: "He was a man of great vanity, and he had something to be vain about. He was a handsome figure." Powell Senior often cited Benjamin Kidd's Darwinist *Social Evolution*, assuring that Christian teaching was compatible with Darwinian theory. He published an article on the religion of Frederick Douglass, which he folded into his pay lectures; later he gave a lecture series on abolitionism to

New Haven ministers. A progressive Republican, Powell tried, unsuccessfully, to win political patronage for blacks in the state legislature. He exuded cosmopolitan self-confidence, moving between cultures and developing friendships with white civic leaders, especially bankers Peirce Welch and Julius Twiss, Yale board secretary Anson Phelps Stokes, and probate circuit court judge Livingston Cleveland. Powell forged similar friendships with white and black ministers, frequently exchanging pulpits with them. He spoke at so many white Baptist conferences that he felt a twinge of embarrassment, realizing that the constant praise he received was spiritually perilous: "On my arrival they welcomed me as a brother beloved and during the fifteen and a half years of my stay, not a single one of them—and many were southerners—even by the faintest implication made me feel that I belonged to a backward race." In 1904 Virginia Union University proudly awarded Powell an honorary doctorate. In 1908 he set off laments across Connecticut by accepting a call to Abyssinian Baptist Church in New York.[73]

New Haven said good-bye with three large receptions at which speakers lauded Powell for his eloquence, wisdom, collegiality, and goodness. Ferris, later describing the outpouring of praise, judged that Powell had four things going for him: "A manly personality, native preaching ability, a desire to broaden his knowledge and widen his horizon and a passion for serving humanity." That was exactly how Powell wanted to be known. In his telling, there were three living options in theology: fundamentalism, modernism, and progressivism. Fundamentalists prescribed belief in unbelievable things, beginning with biblical inerrancy. Modernists replaced the living God of the Bible with a naturalistic ideology bordering on deism or atheism. Progressives worshipped the biblical God of love and embraced the social gospel of Jesus without submitting to literalistic tests of orthodoxy. Powell identified with the progressives, boasting that he was "among the first Baptist preachers to proclaim a social gospel." Later he recalled that aside from a bout with tuberculosis, his ministry in New Haven could hardly have gone better, but he was "too full of energy" to stay there: "I needed a heavy load to steady me." Powell Junior put it equally vividly, later recalling: "His wanderlust grew like a virus and it has infected me too."[74]

Abyssinian Church presented a huge challenge. At the time it was a shell of its former glory on Waverly Place in Greenwich Village. The congregation was founded in 1808 as a protest against being segregated in the balcony of First Baptist Church on Gold Street. It wandered for decades in the Thompson Street area until the congregation found a home on Waverly Place in 1856. There, Abyssinian had twenty-nine years of superchurch expansion under the leadership of William Spellman, who was succeeded by Robert D. Wynn of

Norwich, Connecticut, who implored the congregation to move to Harlem. Wynn pleaded for sixteen years and resigned in frustration, giving way to Charles S. Morris in 1902. Morris moved the congregation to Fortieth Street near Eighth Avenue, in the middle of Manhattan's red light district. Though Morris was a great orator, he had a short run at Abyssinian, having dragged the congregation to seedy midtown Manhattan by taking on debt. He further alienated many congregants by converting to tongues-speaking and other holiness practices. When Powell got to Abyssinian, the congregation had dwindled to sixteen hundred members and was carrying a one-hundred-thousand-dollar debt. He also learned that some Morris diehards opposed his call and that Powell was supposed to live with his family in a flat across the street from the church, where brothels operated upstairs and next door.[75]

This underwhelming reception was deliberate, as the faction that wanted to restore Morris as pastor took charge of Powell's accommodations. The congregation was deeply split between a majority that wanted formal and refined worship services, and a strong minority that wanted fervently emotional worship services. Bridging that divide was Powell's strong suit. He won over the congregation with an every-night revival lasting four weeks. He lived in the flat for two years, putting up with the neighborhood. He built up the congregation with eloquent preaching and a knack for generating publicity. He and Morris let on that Morris had urged Powell to accept the call to Abyssinian, which bought closure to the Morris issue. Then Powell resumed Morris's campaign against the neighborhood industry, blasting Mayor William Gaynor and a succession of others for allowing prostitution to flourish. Powell had little success with City Hall on this issue until "boy mayor" John Purroy Mitchel took office in 1914. Mitchel shut down every house of prostitution on the block, and Powell cheered him on, both withstanding intense public criticism. The last prostitute to be arrested was a vocal member of Abyssinian who enlisted her twelve-year-old daughter in the trade; two years later the daughter died of syphilis.[76]

Powell accepted that urbanization heightened the social responsibilities of churches. It was not enough for the church to rail against vice, he contended. Urbanization and the Great Migration ramped up the scale of human need in American cities, yet many churches reacted by becoming less hospitable. Powell lamented that bars, ballrooms, pool halls, and brothels offered more hospitality than the average church. This was a defining challenge for the church, he urged. If people hung out on street corners, they were arrested. If they holed up in their stuffy flats, they died of consumption. It was graceless and small-minded for churches to rail against bars and pool halls while providing no alternative places for people to recreate: "To save a man is to get him out of a bad environment and to put him into a good one with Jesus Christ as his example, ideal, and inspiration. Let the colored Christians of New York give the people churches with reading rooms, social rooms, gymnasiums, sewing rooms, and domestic science rooms that are physically clean and morally pure where people can spend their afternoons and evenings in mental and social betterment and you will see a revelation among the people of this city."[77]

After Mitchel cleaned up Fortieth Street, Powell and Ransom preached blistering sermons against "social prostitution"—parties at which middle-class women drank, smoked, flirted, and had sex. Powell was surprised to learn that such gatherings existed and that women from Abyssinian Church indulged in them. He gave "a scathing tirade against female wickedness in high places" and was stunned by the backlash. Powell received more than twenty anonymous letters denouncing him furiously; one contained a death threat. As always throughout his career, however, he got strong support from the black press, especially the *New York Age*. Editorialists praised Powell for upholding Christian morals, the letters were favorable by ten to one, and Abyssinian reaped a bounty of new members. Powell later reflected that the black press nearly always took the right side in public controversies over morality. More broadly and personally, the black press nearly always lauded Powell as a beacon of wisdom and goodness. The rift between the pro-Washington and anti-Washington press did not apply to Powell. He won public renown by winning constantly admiring treatment in black newspapers.[78]

Powell was a fount of quotable preaching, espousing a practical social Christianity fused with conservative personal morality. Often he began a revival sermon with a statement about the necessity of progressive theology. Modern people cared about deeds, not creeds, he urged: "Discovery, science, invention, education, imperialism, free speech, a more liberal and better interpretation of the Bible, have literally changed the face of the earth and revolutionized our mode of thinking and acting. Our church methods must be reconstructed if we are successfully to meet the demands of these changes." Powell's sermons abounded in maxims about getting "heaven into men," not men into heaven, and getting the "hell out of men," not keeping men out of hell: "When you get a man into heaven, he is not worth anything more to his family and the world; but when you can get heaven into him, you have done a great deal for Christ and humanity." Powell was fond of saying that Christ taught people to pray for the kingdom to come to us, not for us to go to the kingdom. God wants to save the world, but too many ministers talked only about the afterlife: "The majority of men do not care a lollipop about church doctrines, they are looking for practical application of the Spirit of Jesus in the everyday life of our members."

Excessive preaching about doctrines and the afterlife would kill Christianity, he warned: "While we have fought over useless creeds, the doors of hell have been crowded with those whom we should have saved. Acquaintance with church creeds does not save men. This is the most damaging mistake the church and clergy have made."[79]

Conservatives lost the gospel by dogmatizing it, and worldly modernists lost it by letting go of Jesus. The integrative third way was second nature to Powell. He was theologically liberal *and* evangelical, an exponent of biblical criticism *and* biblically centered, and politically pro-Washington *and* anti-Washington. Having modernized his theology was no reason to stop preaching revivals, Powell believed. At a revival in Indianapolis he offered a wager: "If you will show me a dancing, card-playing, theatre-going Christian that has won a single soul to Jesus in ten years I will walk back to New York." Powell charged that modernists drained the life and ethical urgency out of religion, which was pointless, because Christianity was nothing without gospel-centered spiritual feeling. Every person, Powell taught, had a spark of the divine ultimate reality. For many this spark remained buried underneath "the rubbish of ungodliness." When a person bowed in prayer "with a heart cleansed of carnal rubbish, the little Ultimate Reality in his soul rises like the tide to meet the great Ultimate Reality, which is God, and he becomes conscious of the fact that he is in touch with the source of power." In 1900 Powell attended the Christian Endeavor Conference in London, at which Walters spoke. There he saw the future of Christianity, a fore-taste of the fact that God did not care about creeds and denominations: "Christians of all faiths are getting together to conquer Gog and Magog in the valley of Armageddon." Sometimes he caught himself in dramatic mode, scaling back to mundane things. Speaking at a revival, Powell offered a puckish addition to the Beatitudes, a grateful comment on his experience: "Blessed is that preacher who has the unbought friendship of the newspapers."[80]

On racial justice Powell worked a similar both/and, by combining political gradualism and civil rights agitation. He epitomized the faction of the black social gospel that lauded Washington for his greatness and criticized him for being too accommodating. In 1906 Du Bois spoke at St. Luke's Episcopal Church in New Haven, and Powell endorsed him. Du Bois was a third-way mediator like himself, Powell reasoned; he showed the way between Washington-style accommodation and Trotter-style belligerence. Powell urged that there had to be a realistic form of civil rights militancy that kept its head and did not lapse into conservatism or radicalism. He was so determined not to choose sides that he denied that Du Bois had done so. Powell stuck to this both/and position long after he became a charter member of the NAACP and the National Urban

League. In the Urban League he focused on housing issues in collaboration with George E. Haynes. Like Haynes, Walters, Francis Grimké, and Henry Proctor, Powell combined forceful civil rights advocacy with deep respect for Washington, taking for granted that Washington was a legitimate civil rights leader of enormous accomplishment and importance.[81]

In his later career Powell found a succinct way of putting it, and he got more prescriptive about it. But he took the same two-ways approach throughout his career. There were two methods of approaching racial justice, he would say. One method emphasized mutual understanding and forbearance, and the other emphasized legal action and mass pressure. Both methods were "right and absolutely necessary." In later life Powell contended that black Americans had made a huge mistake by dividing between radicals and conservatives. Kelly Miller, trying to prevent the schism from occurring, had wrongly tagged one side as the conservative party, which inadvertently added fuel to the breakup. Powell pleaded that there was no such thing as black conservatism. Black Americans had no stake in preserving a system that oppressed them, so what was the point of dividing into factions?[82]

In his early years at Abyssinian Church, Powell laid off the Harlem issue. First the congregation had to trust him. Then the Great Migration ballooned, Powell moved to Harlem personally, and he urged the congregation to follow. African Americans were pouring into Harlem and Abyssinian needed to follow them there. Plus, Powell recognized that the push of business along Broadway and Seventh Avenue was going to push blacks out of midtown anyway. Wynn had resigned in 1902 after the congregation refused to leave Waverly Place. Morris got the congregation to Fortieth Street, but that was a half measure. In 1911 Powell began to preach on this issue, urging that Jesus organized the church in Jerusalem because Jerusalem had the most people. The black population of Harlem doubled in the next few years, and white Harlemites fled in panic, leaving behind many of New York's most beautiful homes, elegant brownstones designed by Stanford White. Real estate values plummeted. Powell urged Abyssinians to take advantage of the incredible bargains, following his example. He bought a gorgeous home on 136th Street, assessed at $17,500, for $6,000. A few years later he sold it for $15,000 and bought a palatial home on 134th Street, where Adam Clayton Powell Jr. had a privileged childhood, doted upon by his parents, his sister, Blanche, and a nurse.

The senior Powell shook his head that few Abyssinians took advantage of white flight from Harlem. Then the Garvey movement electrified black Americans. Powell later recalled, "The cotton picker of Alabama, bending over his basket, and the poor ignorant Negro of the Mississippi Delta, crushed beneath a load of prejudice, lifted their heads and said, 'Let's go to Harlem to see this Black Moses.'" Sharing a neighborhood with Garvey and his followers, Powell sometimes got rough treatment in the streets from Garveyites, and he prohibited his son from playing outdoors. The younger Powell grew up with little sense of his racial identity; though race was mentioned in church, it got little mention at home. Powell Senior protected his son from hurtful experiences, admired Garvey's emotional connection to oppressed blacks, and dreaded Garvey's threat to create a new black religion that left Christianity and white civilization behind. At least 80 percent of New York's black clergy shared his dread. Powell's summary judgment on Garvey was poignant and deeply felt: "He is the only man that ever made Negroes who are not black ashamed of their color."[83]

Powell told Abyssinians that boasting about degrees of color had no place in the Christian church or a decent society. The coming of the war and the surge of migrants had fueled Garvey's ascension. Black Americans took little notice of World War I in its early years, but as soon as Wilson intervened, the war became a very emotional issue. Powell was deeply conflicted, hating the prospect of intervening and feeling its unavoidability. The one thing he knew for sure was that Du Bois was wrong about the meaning of the war for civil rights. This was the moment to strike hard for equal rights, Powell urged. History proved that oppressed people usually secured their rights when their oppressors faced a crisis. Powell blasted Du Bois and "all the big Negroes" for saying that wartime was no time to make a fuss about special grievances. Going to war, he countered, was precisely "the psychological moment" for African Americans to demand their rights: "While we love our flag and country, we do not believe in fighting for protection of commerce on the high seas until the powers that be give us at least some verbal assurance that the property and lives of the members of our race are going to be protected on land from Maine to Mississippi."[84]

Powell shuddered at what he was expected to do. How could he tell Afro-Americans that they should kill and be killed for American democracy? He rallied patriotic support anyway, recruiting soldiers for the New York National Guard's all-black Fifteenth Regiment and organizing war-bond sales and programs for war relief. True patriotism, he preached, was love of one's country plus something higher—an unselfish devotion to the highest ethical and spiritual ideals. Powell warned that empires died from internal corruption and decay, not because they lost wars: "May I plead with you then for the sake of permanency and prosperity of our own people not to forget that while we are fighting a ferocious enemy abroad, we must also fight at home for those high ideals of liberty, justice, equality, and purity. Patriotism is not only a love for one's country and nation but a love for weak suffering people everywhere."[85]

He held out hope that African Americans would get better treatment after fighting for America in Europe. On July 28, 1917, Powell helped Du Bois, James Weldon Johnson, and the NAACP organize a stunning "Silent Protest Parade" in New York. Nearly ten thousand black Americans marched down Fifth Avenue without a word or gesture, accompanied only by the sound of muffled drums, protesting against mob terrorism and racial segregation. The protest got meager press coverage. The following year Powell cofounded a group called the League of Darker Peoples, which planned to attend the Versailles Peace Conference and stage demonstrations in Europe. But Powell suffered a nervous breakdown in the summer of 1918, exhausted from tension and overwork, and was forced to take a three-month emergency vacation. The Red Summer of 1919 and its twenty-five race riots wiped out what remained of his hope that the war would aid the cause of racial justice. By the early 1920s Powell believed that the war had made everything much worse for African Americans.[86]

Meanwhile he pressed hard for Harlem. In 1920 Abyssinian Church bought six lots on 138th Street between Seventh and Lenox Avenues, and Powell pitched a tent near Seventh Avenue, next door to Garvey's Black Freedom Hall. There he conducted revivals for two summers and urged his congregation to think big. The *New York Age* ran a splashy announcement that another big downtown church was moving to Harlem. Powell preached stewardship sermons twice per month, trying to raise a building fund, which the congregation resisted. They did not want to move, the projected costs were staggering, they did not want to contribute, and they disliked the idea of going deeply into debt again. He later recalled, "They were never more united or seemingly in love with me, but they were simply indifferent to my costly Harlem dream." Powell told church officers he was considering resigning; they laughed, believing he had to be joking. In December 1921 he gave up in frustration, announcing his resignation to a shocked congregation: "I am leaving your church to devote myself to evangelistic campaigns, the delivering of lectures and the publishing of sermons because you do not believe in progressive and aggressive leadership." That broke the impasse, and the congregation pledged to build in Harlem.[87]

Powell wanted to employ black builders, but he found only one carpenter and three masons. He was appalled, and repentant. From the pulpit he disavowed every negative thing he had ever said about Washington's advocacy of industrial education. He had always respected Washington, he stressed. Powell knew Washington personally and he had never doubted that Washington was an exemplary proponent of social Christianity. But Powell had blasted Washington numerous times for selling out the rights of blacks and/or moving too slowly, and he had said it in snappy ways that got press coverage. Now he took back the snappy put-downs about industrial education. Seething over his failure to find skilled black laborers, Powell apologized profusely, declaring that Washington could not have been more right about education. Higher education was fine for those who were good at higher education, but the majority of Afro-Americans needed to train for skilled labor jobs. It galled Powell that Abyssinian Church paid white laborers fourteen dollars per day to build the new Abyssinian. He raged in the pulpit, gazing at underemployed holders of college degrees. The only African American church to cost $100,000 was Union Baptist Church of Philadelphia. Abyssinian Church, Harlem, a Tudor-Gothic showcase featuring an Italian marble pulpit and seating two thousand in the sanctuary, was dedicated in 1923. It cost a breathtaking $335,000, and the congregation celebrated by sending Powell to Europe for a three-month vacation.[88]

Having dragged Abyssinian to the heart of black Harlem, Powell worked hard at being a good neighbor and at strengthening his relationships with black and white civic leaders. He was a buoyant symbol of the church's role in the Harlem Renaissance, a period of optimism and growth in Harlem. John D. Rockefeller Jr. offered to pay off the church's entire sixty-thousand-dollar debt on the condition that he would appoint one member of the board of trustees. The congregation's United Boards turned him down and paid off the debt in four years. Powell lauded the church's determined independence. He also led its community activism, especially in the anti-saloon movement. Alcohol destroyed individuals and communities, he implored; moreover, Harlem needed black-owned businesses that trafficked in something else. Powell chastised ministers that did the minimum or less for Prohibition, pleading that too much of Harlem's nightlife and economy centered on "hootch"—bootlegged alcohol—though Powell quietly drank gin in the privacy of his study. In the 1920s Abyssinian played a vital civic role by sponsoring more than fifty clubs and organizations, including a night school, a Red Cross unit, recreational facilities, and a home for the elderly. Powell remained active in the NAACP and Urban League, having served on the NAACP's finance committee since the organization's founding and having joined its board of directors in 1912. He taught at Union Theological Seminary and Colgate University, lecturing on racial justice, and he enthused from the pulpit that black Americans were entering the middle class, especially in Harlem. He persisted in holding outdoor tent revivals despite receiving threats to his life from white racists and Garveyites. Always he argued that the church had a crucial role to play in building a good society and it was not doing anywhere near enough.[89]

Powell rejected separatist arguments about integration, admonishing separatists not to spurn their white allies. He read the roll call of "healthy" black colleges and universities, stressing that none would exist if black Americans had lacked white Christian allies. In the next breath he would say that separatists were right about African Americans needing to take responsibility for their institutions. Afro-Americans financed only two "worthwhile" colleges, he judged, and both were dying. There were no good schools that were self-supporting and doing well. Powell implored that this situation had to change. It was "bad for the white man and worse for the Negro" that the best black schools depended on white charity.[90]

On all such matters he spoke with authority, claiming that he probably knew more about the desires and aspirations of Afro-Americans than anyone. In support of this boast Powell noted that he ministered to America's largest black congregation and he had a national ministry: "I am therefore speaking with authority which comes from long years of the most intimate contact, south and north, when I say that Negroes want equality; nothing else will satisfy them and nothing else will help them to help themselves out of their present low estate." He did not mean social equality, a "pernicious doctrine" that meant only one thing in America, something that almost no African American cared about. Powell put a number on it, judging that no more than one out of ten thousand African Americans cared about the right of black men to have romantic relationships with white women. Black Americans wanted equality of opportunity "in the struggle of life," he asserted. They wanted an equal chance at a decent life for themselves and their children, and nothing else and nothing less. Sometimes he put it negatively: "If the Negro fails to make good after being given equality of opportunity, let him go down in American history as a serf and a third-class citizen." Sometimes he reached for a Booker-like way of saying it: "The Negro welcomes the chance to rise or fall by the best standards of the American white man."[91]

Powell believed that black Americans had more Christian charity than any other group, but he did not believe that all racists were white: "Race prejudice is the most deadly poison in the world today, and there is just as much of it in the Negro's system as there is in the white man's. It will require years, perhaps centuries to eradicate this poison." Each race had characteristic strengths and sins, he contended: "My race needs the white man's courage, initiative, punctuality, business acumen and aggressiveness. The white man needs the Negro's meekness, love, forgiving spirit and the emotional religion as expressed in his folk songs." From the pulpit and lectern he railed against Afro-American extravagance: "We eat too much, drink too much, sleep too much, frolic too much, talk too much, show off too much and bury too much money in the graveyards." Funeral spectacles, especially, galled him; Powell despaired at presiding over "show off funerals." What idiocy to waste precious money on expensive coffins! He pleaded that cutting down on showing off would be very good for equality.[92]

For some there was a contradiction between celebrating the superior Christian charity of black Americans and supporting the militant civil rights activism of the NAACP. For Powell these things fit together as complementary sides of his social gospel idealism. He supported Johnson, Du Bois, and Walter White at the NAACP, enthusing that America finally had an effective civil rights organization. He was an active supporter of Burroughs's National Training School and served on its board. Always Powell stressed that he was idealistic because Christianity was idealistic. The gospel of John taught that the Word became flesh and dwelt among us, and human beings beheld the glory of the Father in Jesus, full of grace and truth. That was the epitome of idealism, Powell taught; you cannot get more idealistic than Christianity. In Christianity, Jesus is the ideal, "the only ideal ever seen by the human eye." Jesus taught people to love their enemies and turn the other cheek; thus, so did Powell. Jesus was serious about the meek inheriting the earth. He taught that enemy-love, nonretaliation, and forgiveness were the very heart of the gospel, and he suffered for others on the way to Calvary. If one proposed to follow Jesus, Powell urged, one had to take up the costly, fellow-suffering discipleship of the Sermon on the Mount. Young German theologian Dietrich Bonhoeffer, attending Abyssinian Church in 1930 as a student at Union Theological Seminary, was enthralled and convicted by Powell's preaching of the costly grace of the nonviolent gospel of Jesus. Hearing Powell and worshipping at Abyssinian, Bonhoeffer was shaken out of his snotty elitism, being moved by the oppression of African Americans and the failure of the white churches to promote racial justice.[93]

Powell's tendency to cast himself in the Jesus role, however, grated on fellow ministers, as in 1918, when a blowout with black Baptist ministers caused him to confine his religious activism to Abyssinian Church. That year the Colored Baptist State Convention asked Powell to identify what Harlem Baptists needed most. He made a case for an all-purpose religious, social, and educational center, reasoning that most of the new Harlemites from the South and the West Indies had little education and were too old to attend public schools. The best investment would enhance their education and socialization. Powell added that Burroughs would be the best person to run such a center. The convention applauded, and Powell met with financial backers of the (white) New York Baptist City Mission, making the same pitch. They were supportive, asking to meet with the (black) Baptist Ministers Conference to organize the center.

One hundred black Baptist ministers showed up. Powell later recalled that he expected the group to "canonize" him and the white benefactors as saints and heroes. Instead the ministers erupted as soon as Powell stopped talking, berating Powell and his white friends, calling them "czars," "usurpers," "denominational wreckers," and the like. One minister delivered a fifteen-minute tirade against the idea of a community center before asking what it was. Powell explained that it was a place where the people of a community could learn things and be together. The minister replied: "That's what I thought. We don't want nothin' like that. We want a place where folks can git religion." All but eight of the ministers agreed that they did not want the center and they did not care for Powell's attitude. Powell stalked away in disgust, vowing to waste no more time on outreach efforts with his Baptist colleagues, a pledge he kept for eleven years.[94]

Abyssinian Church set up its own food and clothing ministries and paid for two missionaries in Africa. Powell lamented that many ministers fixated on their institutions with little regard for the needs of others. He protested that such churches fed the stereotype of the church as a self-centered institution that drained the resources of the community and cared only about its own survival. In the 1920s Powell added that the fight against the liquor trade in New York rested on "two or three papers and two or three churches." This had to stop, he pleaded. The churches barely pretended to oppose the bootlegging industry, but caving in to it would not build a healthy society or economy. Later, when the Depression came and Powell's son joined the church staff, Abyssinian launched an ambitious food pantry and an unemployment relief fund. Prohibition, plus the lack of a better choice, kept the elder Powell in the Republican Party through the 1920s. In 1932 he became New York's first black elector in the Electoral College. Powell felt sorry for Herbert Hoover, believing that Americans scapegoated him for their failures, notably their moral failure to give up hootch.[95]

Powell also ramped up his sexual morality activism by preaching against "the evils of moral degeneracy and sex-perversion." In 1929 he declared that gay sexuality was more prevalent than church people believed and that many ministers were guilty of "abnormal sexual activities." It was bad enough to have gay ministers who somehow rationalized their perversion, Powell contended. Even worse was that some congregations knowingly put up with it. He admonished that only a "rotten" congregation would keep a "rotten" pastor: "I do not blame ministers with low ideals for preaching, but I do blame and condemn the church for keeping them." This sermon got widespread press coverage, most of it favorable to Powell. Kelly Miller, usually critical of the black church, lauded Powell as a prophet. Many of Powell's fellow pastors, however, gave him icy treatment, and he got some angry letters, including a death threat. Powell was appalled that some ministers upbraided him privately for targeting gays and lesbians. He believed that his outspokenness on this issue amplified his standing as a brave guardian of moral decency. There was no public controversy over his insistence on casting a spotlight on vulnerable gays and lesbians. There was only some back-and-forth over whether he exaggerated the extent of the "problem." Powell countered that "the ethical standards of the educated" had declined drastically. He was proud of playing a leading role on the issue of gay sexuality, warning, "These sins are on the increase and are threatening to eat the vitals out of America."[96]

To some degree Powell had the Ransom experience of espousing a social gospel that felt threatening to many ministerial colleagues. Like Ransom he took plenty of criticism on this subject, which he recounted for decades. Powell implored that society needed more leaders "with broad hearts and liberal minds" and no more leaders with provincial minds. Many ministers took that personally. Powell put it sharply: "The world is sick of these little, narrow, two-by-four, contracted men, interested in nothing but 'my family,' 'my church,' and 'my race.' I am appealing for men who will get in touch with world currents and world movements, men with cosmopolitan spirits, men whose purview has been so broadened that they can say, 'The world is my country and all mankind my countrymen.'" Black Americans, Powell urged, needed to care about disarmament, creating a world court, establishing just relations between labor and capital, and building a global ecumenical movement "for the salvation of mankind." From the pulpit he lauded Gandhi as "the greatest embodiment of moral force in this universe," because Gandhi fought courageously and nonviolently for "the moral betterment of humanity." The world's best Christian happened to be a Hindu. Powell urged his audiences to be like Gandhi: "If we are going to save the manhood of our own race and going to help to save the manhood of the world, we must accept the Bible as our guide and Christ as our moral and spiritual ideal."[97]

Powell became America's most famous and admired black minister by preaching a two-winged social gospel—evangelical and progressive—and by accentuating his differences with fellow ministers. Like Ransom, he hammered ministers for "feeding the people on fundamentalism and religious traditions instead of telling them how to get food and fundamental human rights." Ransom, however, took in stride that many ministers fervently disliked him. Powell never accepted that as his fate. In December 1930 Burroughs published an article challenging African American leaders to do something to help poor and vulnerable people get through the winter. She chastised prominent blacks for hibernating comfortably while others froze and starved. Powell, responding to Burroughs, announced that he had recently pledged one thousand dollars to launch Abyssinian's food pantry and that members had responded in kind by donating fifteen hundred dollars. Powell added that he was still driving a 1926 car (a Packard), even though church officers wanted to give him a new one, and he told congregants to donate to the pantry instead of making their usual "hand-shake" Christmas donations to him. He declared that if every black minister followed his example, no black American would go hungry this Christmas. Powell broke it down nationally, explaining what ministers should do. There were ten thousand well-off ministers who should donate their entire salary for January, February, and March. The second tier of ten thousand ministers should donate half their salary for these months, and the third tier of ten thousand should donate one-fourth. Anyone who failed to do this, he admonished, had no business preaching about the sheep and goats of Matthew, chapter 25.[98]

It was probably this sermon on Matthew 25, which Powell titled "A Hungry God," that made the deepest impression on Bonhoeffer, as Reggie L. Williams suggests in his perceptive book *Bonhoeffer's Black Jesus*. According to the avalanche of black ministers that responded, however, "A Hungry God" delivered the most obnoxious and self-righteous Christmas appeal ever written. The ministers found every conceivable way of saying that Powell lived in a different world from them, he was a privileged character and publicity hog, his luxurious home was magnificently furnished, their congregations did not offer them new Packards and European vacations, and he should get a clue. Sometimes they implied or stated exaggerated ideas of Powell's lifestyle, which he set straight years later. Some of them knew that Powell's relentless moralism had alienated his son for years, although father and son reconciled in 1930. The avalanche of indignation deeply wounded Powell; he called it "the longest, bitterest and the most disappointing of all the fights of my life." The New Jersey Baptist Ministers' Conference cut him deepest. Powell thought he had many friends there, but they issued a blistering letter repudiating his "scathing strictures against the Negro ministry" and praying that God would make Powell "more liberal in the gift of human kindness for your (imaginary) weak brother." Years later Powell recalled that only three ministers defended him and that the attack of the ministers upon him "constitutes the most shameful chapter in Negro church history."[99]

Powell's off-kilter sense of historic grievance had something to do with his eminence and much to do with his belief in his righteousness. He deserved to be loved and admired; moreover, any knock on him hurt the black church; above all, the backlash against him was monstrous for disregarding his pure motives. He was still reeling from this episode in 1931 when cultural critic H. L.

Mencken published a bigoted screed claiming that black Americans had no accomplished thinkers and its ministers were ignorant fundamentalists. Powell replied with immense dignity, summoning a blend of moral outrage and restraint that would have served him in his feud with the ministers. Many Afro-American ministers were modern, progressive, learned, and emphatically not fundamentalist, Powell replied. Wright, Bowen, and Bishop Matthew Wesley Clair headed the Methodist list, while Mordecai Johnson, Vernon Johns, Walter Brooks, Miles Fisher, and Powell's former associate pastor Horatio S. Hill headed the Baptist list. Powell agreed with Mencken that fundamentalism was "a negation of every intellectual decency." He and Mencken agreed about inerrancy doctrine and fundamentalist dogmatism. But intellectual decency was not the only kind that fundamentalists violated.[100]

For example, at the very time that Menken's article appeared, a mob in Maryville, Missouri, lynched a black man by fire. Powell guessed that 95 percent of the Maryville lynchers were fundamentalists, and not all were "white trash," either. Many were business executives, lawyers, and judges. These modern Americans, a large gathering of men and women, burned an innocent man, watched his naked body writhe in flames, and felt no shock to their sense of decency. Powell stressed that Mencken's magazine, the *American Mercury*, passed in silence over this indecency. He urged Mencken to think about the indecency of ridiculing African American ministers under the circumstances. Black ministers loved the white people who hated them, preaching Christian charity. Moreover, "the average Negro is also superior to the average white American in long suffering, patience, meekness, veracity and love."[101]

This contention that black Americans uniquely practiced the forgiving, enemy-loving ethic of Jesus was a staple of the theology that Powell, Ransom, and Walters bequeathed to the civil rights generation of Martin Luther King Jr. Powell lionized Gandhian nonviolent resistance to oppression before Mordecai Johnson, Howard Thurman, Benjamin Mays, and William Stuart Nelson established a Gandhian resistance tradition at Howard University. To those who urged that blacks had to become less loving and forgiving to get ahead, Powell replied that there were two methods of conquest. One was to fight for supremacy, as the Hebrews did in ancient Canaan. The other was the method of "spiritual meekness," which Jesus taught and epitomized. It was too soon to say that Jesus was wrong about the meek inheriting the earth, Powell contended. So far it had worked for Afro-Americans. Native Americans fought the white conquerors from Plymouth Rock to the Pacific Coast, and they were annihilated: "Today they are a pitiful remnant and a racial nonentity." Black Americans adopted the Jesus philosophy and survived. Powell put it sharply, contending that

Afro-Americans survived slavery and Jim Crow to become powerful in America only because their Christian meekness saved them: "Had not thousands of Negro ministers preached the meekness of Jesus to their people, they would have long ago suffered the tragic fate of the Indians."[102]

African Americans, Powell asserted, never tried to get even with their enemies. For him this was a statement of historical fact, an ethical norm, and a theology, expressing the very heart of the gospel. The spirituals expressed the gospel faith in its purest form. Black Americans retained this faith despite the train of abuses inflicted on them. Powell explained, "These spirituals are the finest revelation of the will and heart of God outside of the Bible. There is not a line of revenge or a word that breathes the spirit of vindictiveness in any of these original folk songs." He added that African Americans accepted the holy and biblical assumption that vengeance belongs to God alone. Powell made a special point of saying it at antiwar rallies. As a veteran of gatherings at which the evils of war were denounced, Christian theology was sometimes pitched aside, and the rhetoric sometimes got pretty hot, Powell was always ready with a Christian antiwar sermon. But he preferred to let the choir sing. Sometimes he took Abyssinian Church singers along to make sure it happened. "It" was the singing of a Christian spiritual way of being in the world: "I'm gonna lay down my sword and shield, down by the riverside. . . . I ain't gonna study war no more."[103]

Powell preached that hymn to the end of his pastorate, always cautioning that Christian love and nonviolence had nothing to do with relinquishing the struggle for social justice. His controversial sermon on Matthew 25 and the hunger of God eloquently proclaimed that Christians were called to amplify God's life-giving power on earth. His words were cited long after the controversy faded: "We clothe God by clothing men and women. Jesus interpreted this as meaning to clothe men and women when they are naked. When you give men and women coats, shoes and dresses you are giving clothes to God. If the Bible does not mean this it does not mean anything." Earlier that year, encouraged by recent boycotts in Chicago, Powell employed the boycott method in Harlem, organizing a Committee for More and Better Jobs. Whites held most of the jobs in Harlem, and nearly all the good jobs, he protested. New York Telephone Company, boasting zero black employees, emerged as a leading boycott target. Powell organized a boycott campaign against the phone company through the churches. It failed for lack of organizational know-how, but the idea took root, yielding boycott movements that did not fail.[104]

In 1937 Powell turned Abyssinian Church over to his son, Adam, who had overcome a sickly preadolescence, poor grades in high school, years of hell-raising rebellion against his father, poor grades at Colgate University, heartbreak at the death of his beloved sister, Blanche, and an aborted seminary experience at Union to become a dynamic pastor and community leader. He later recalled, "When my father stood in the pulpit, he was awesome in his Prince Albert coat as he thundered his holy invectives against the sins of that day. He preached so hard that his starched collar and cuffs always wilted." Abyssinian Church, on Powell Senior's twenty-nine-year watch, grew from sixteen hundred to fourteen thousand members, its budget soared from six thousand dollars to thirty-five thousand dollars, its ministerial staff expanded from one to three, and its Sunday school soared from two hundred to sixteen hundred participants. In the form of a charge to his son, Powell summarized his mission theology in one sentence: "Preach with all the power of your soul, body, and mind the old-time simple Gospel because it is a fountain for the unclean, food for the hungry, drink for the thirsty, clothing for the naked, strength for the weak, a solace for the sorrowing, medicine for the sick and eternal life for the dying."[105]

He had a plan for his retirement—write some books—but no plan to change his message. Powell had preached basically the same message for forty-four years, believing that the gospel was the power unto salvation and that African Americans embraced it like no other people. There were two methods of achieving racial justice, he would say: Washington and Du Bois symbolized the two methods, and both were absolutely necessary. Routinely Powell praised Washington as America's second greatest black leader and one of the greatest Americans ever, in the top tier with Lincoln and Douglass. Washington had played his role magnificently, but the movement needed both methods, and it was succeeding by employing them. As a pastor, Powell preached with confidence about where this story was headed. In his retirement he stopped saying it was headed in a good direction and that black Americans were distinguished as a class by their enemy-loving, Jesus-following soul.

The urban riots of the 1940s stunned Powell into deciding that he had been wrong about the direction things were going, for ample majorities in most black communities were finished with "love your enemies." In the early 1940s he warned that virtually every U.S. American city with a significant black population seethed on the edge of catastrophe or had already exploded. Powell traveled extensively in his early retirement and lingered longer than previously when he got somewhere, which fueled his dread. He passed for white whenever possible on southern railcars, which allowed him to hear racial epithets that many whites reserved for white-only company. Powell reported that some of the things he heard were more shocking to him than the lynchings that occurred in the same towns. He acknowledged that he could not work up much interest in news reports about World War II, because American cities everywhere felt like volcanoes: "The greatest danger to the civilization of the United States is not Germany, Japan, or any other foreign country but the vitriolic hate which exists between the white and the colored living within its borders. This hatred is at an all-time high and is mounting higher every day." White Americans, instead of worrying so much about the war in Europe, needed to think about American cities exploding from resentment.[106]

The American Civil Liberties Union, in a pamphlet written in 1943 by Winifred Rauschenbusch (Walter Rauschenbusch's eldest daughter), identified twenty-three cities that teetered on the edge of a racial explosion: Birmingham, Alabama; Bridgeport, Hartford, and New Haven, Connecticut; Chicago, Illinois; Indianapolis and Gary, Indiana; Alexandria, Baton Rouge, and Shreveport, Louisiana; Detroit, Michigan; Baltimore, Maryland; Newark, New Jersey; Columbus, Ohio; Philadelphia, Pittsburgh, and Chester, Pennsylvania; Providence, Rhode Island; Houston and Dallas, Texas; Memphis, Tennessee; and Washington, DC. Rauschenbusch did not list Los Angeles, California; Beaumont, Texas; Mobile, Alabama; and Harlem only because they had already erupted, although she listed Detroit, which had exploded, too. Many towns located near army bases faced similar dangers. Powell, reviewing this list, warned that if five more cities blew up, the rest would be swept away in fire, a horrible epitaph on what came of Jim Crow and the Great Migration.[107]

Beaumont erupted on June 16, 1943, on the basis of a rumor that a black man had raped a white woman. The story was pure fiction, but it set off a raging white mob that attacked every black man, woman, and child it encountered. Powell wrote, "Suppose a woman had been raped, she was not raped by all the colored men in town! Certainly no colored woman or child raped her! What unreasonable, unforgivable race hatred!" In the same mood he made a sudden, wrenching transition to the victims of white racism: "The Negro used to be the most lovable, forgivable being in America, but the white man's prejudice, hatred, and lies have changed the Negro's psychology. He is just as full of hell, hatred, and lies as the white man."[108]

Detroit erupted on June 20, 1943. In Detroit a black man cried out in Belle Isle that a white man had thrown a black woman and her baby into the river. There was nothing to this story, either, but a mob numbering in the thousands set the city on fire, killing nine whites and twenty-five blacks. Powell went to Detroit the following year to study conditions there. He judged that Detroit had become "the greatest racial battleground in the United States" because huge numbers of its black and white communities were impoverished migrants from the South at its worst: "I talked to common whites and Negroes and found enough hate on both sides to blow Detroit into hell." Housing conditions were atrocious for both groups, and blacks hated the police for tyrannizing them. Powell remarked, "This Negro minority not only hates the officers of the law but they hate anything that looks white. They would kill a white cat if one passed through their neighborhood." This situation put Powell at risk, as he was sometimes mistaken for white. In one black Detroit neighborhood he was subjected to "the most vile and threatening language" imaginable, and he could not get served at a lunch counter, either.[109]

Harlem erupted on August 1, 1943. A white police officer attempted to arrest a black woman in Harlem for disorderly conduct; a black police officer from New Jersey intervened, striking the white cop, and the white cop fired a shot at the fleeing black cop, slightly wounding him. At the street level this quickly became a story about a white cop unloading a full magazine of his revolver into a prone Afro-American army sergeant, killing him. A gang of black soldiers smashed white business establishments in West Harlem, making a symbolic statement. A second wave of rioters came through, bent on looting, with no interest in symbolism. Powell had conflicted respect for the first wave and loathed the second wave. Some people in the second group were hardened criminals and some were too frivolous to be criminals, he judged, but all wanted something for nothing: "They never work except when they are forced and that is only for a short while. The job never quite suits them." Powell mocked the looters for asking God not to find a job for them. In radical parlance, he noted, an "Uncle Tom" was any African American who did not contend for his or her rights. Powell declared that every looter was an Uncle Tom, lacking the dignity of black personhood.[110]

Some Uncle Toms did very well for themselves, Powell acknowledged. For example, "this type of Negro furnishes most of the wit and humor of the race." Many looters made comical sport of their inner emptiness, a pathetic strategy for which Powell had limited tolerance, although he admitted it was better to be lazy, destructive, and comical than to be just lazy and destructive. At least the humorous types had a spark of hope. Powell noted that Abyssinian Church had a long-standing ministry to "hoodlums." The church provided a community house with a gymnasium and recreation rooms, which the gangs defaced and destroyed, sometimes comically. This cycle of provide and destroy went on for years, until Abyssinian put the gangs in charge of the community house. By Powell's lights this was a last-resort gamble, but it worked. The gang leaders acquired dignity and moral seriousness by taking responsibility for the center. Powell stressed that he had been a hoodlum, so he knew what it felt like. The church had saved him from a short, destructive, and meaningless life. Now the church had to pour itself out for a generation of nihilistic wreckers: "Don't shoot them. Don't send them to a reform school. Don't brutalize them, but brotherize them."[111]

Powell's writings of the 1940s teased readers with glimpses of the whirlwind that had overtaken his life—his son's dramatic political ascendance. Powell Junior developed a powerful political base in Harlem by crusading for jobs and housing during the Depression. He organized mass meetings, rent strikes, and public campaigns, pressuring businesses and utilities to hire black workers. In 1941 he led a bus boycott in Harlem and won election to the New York City Council as the city's first black council representative. In 1944 he won election to the U.S. House of Representatives representing New York's Twenty-second Congressional District. His father, applauding each victory, told stories of Powell Junior leading a picket line on Seventh Avenue, hatless and flamboyant, before rushing home for a quick shower, sliding down the staircase, and zooming to Pittsburgh for a mass meeting, violating "every traffic law" as police officers looked away, "for they know he is incurably crazy." John Brown was crazy in the same way, Powell Senior observed proudly, and so was Martin Luther. Privately, father and son grieved the death of Mattie Powell in 1945, described by both as quiet, steely, loving, and Teutonic, a perfect pastor's spouse. Powell Senior soon married a blond, light-colored nurse forty years younger than him, Inez, with Powell Junior's approval, while Powell Senior admonished his son against womanizing, arrogance, and outrunning his base. The two Powells, however, genuinely loved and admired each other, and supported each other.[112]

Adam Clayton Powell Jr. was a complicated case who understood that the race issue was more complex than his subtle understanding of it. His father achieved fame and influence by claiming, sincerely, that the race issue was simple. It was simply the fact that African Americans wanted the same chance at a decent life that white Americans possessed and white Americans refused to allow it. Powell Senior preached that if only white Americans would allow blacks to have equal rights, the race problem would be solved. As it was, "until this is done, there are going to be riots, ruin, and hell." He was incredulous that white Americans, knowing the solution, preferred to see their cities burn. Powell shuddered at the still-growing nostalgia for the slave South, although he liked one thing about *Gone with the Wind*: "The one great lesson Margaret Mitchell tried to teach her beloved lazy South is that living on Negroes is gone with the wind." He admonished white Americans to stop putting down black soldiers that came home claiming their rights. It was hard enough to survive the Depression, he pleaded. Why couldn't whites and blacks work together to rebuild America?[113]

Powell liked Eleanor Roosevelt on the subject of social equality—that it was something to be shared among friends, not something to be legislated. He loved the NAACP and complained that there were too many black-only organizations working on the race problem. Black-only politics was a waste of time, Powell chided. If the racial nationalists wanted to do something worthwhile, they should learn carpentry or engineering. Powell granted a partial exception to A. Philip Randolph's March on Washington movement, because Randolph was a great man who "has always sacrificed any selfish ambition for the good of his race." That sentence resounded with double meaning in 1945, for Powell Junior had recently upstaged Randolph dramatically at a Madison Square Garden rally organized to honor Randolph. But Powell believed that even the March on Washington movement would be more effective if it included white activists.[114]

The NAACP was the gold standard in this area. Powell was an insider when Walter Francis White rebuilt the NAACP in the 1930s. He revered White for rescuing the NAACP from the devastating blows it took from the Depression. He treasured White for turning the NAACP into an aggressive national organization emphasizing court battles, lobbying, and local chapters. He cherished White for risking his life to investigate lynching and campaign against it. And he identified with the light-colored race leader who gave his life to the fight against racism when he could have passed for white. According to Powell, White was the ideal leader of the NAACP after James Weldon Johnson and White got it through the 1920s. White was a "a veritable dynamo and easily the outstanding radical among Negroes." To this high praise, Powell added a religious gloss: "That God could wrap up in such a small amount of skin as much natural ability, common sense, and moral, intellectual and physical energy as he has wrapped up in Walter White is still one of His modern miracles."[115]

Powell respected the kindly, gifted Johnson, and he routinely lauded Du Bois as the intellectual genius of the race. But White was his idol, because White turned the NAACP into a powerhouse advocate of the simple concept of antiracist activism that Powell espoused. Du Bois needed to be Du Bois, so Powell wished him well after he left the NAACP, with minimal commentary. The NAACP, however, needed to be a bureaucratic juggernaut of lawyers, accountants, field secretaries, supportive local chapters, and lobbyists—which White created.

WHITE, DU BOIS, THE NAACP, AND THE CRISIS OF CAPITALISM

Walter Francis White had blue eyes, blond hair, a supercharged personality long on charm and gregariousness, and a seemingly inexhaustible passion to abolish America's racial caste system. He was born in Atlanta in 1893 to parents of mixed race belonging to an influential church, First Congregational, where Henry Proctor was the pastor. First Congregational was founded by freedmen and the American Missionary Association after the Civil War. White graduated from Atlanta University in 1916, worked briefly for Standard Life Insurance Company, and helped to organize an NACCP chapter in Atlanta. In 1918 Johnson hired him for the NAACP's national headquarters, where White became Johnson's assistant national secretary.[116]

Johnson had pushed the NAACP into the South as its field secretary and thereby fueled its transition into a predominantly African American organization. As national secretary he managed the transition and built up the organization. When the 1920s began the NAACP was a growing, still mostly white, and still mostly volunteer organization, with 220 branches. It had a white president (Joel Spingarn), a white chair of the board (Ovington, who replaced Spingarn in 1919), and one white employee (publicity director Herbert Seligmann). The transition to becoming a different kind of organization had already begun when Johnson and White took over the NAACP, but they carried it out, turning the NAACP into a large professional enterprise run by black employees, which made the national secretary and his executive associates, not the board chair, responsible for executive decisions. By the end of the 1920s the NAACP had 325 branches in forty-four states.

Johnson led by genial example, got people to work together, and represented the organization with consummate dignity. He made a genius move in hiring White, who leveraged friendships with white literary brokers Carl Van Vechten and Alfred A. Knopf to power the Harlem Renaissance. White schmoozed with donors, professionalized the operation, and undertook dangerous assignments in the South, passing for white to investigate lynchings. Risking his life repeatedly, White investigated forty-one lynchings and eight race riots, interviewing perpetrators and the families of victims. He revealed his racial identity to blacks while gathering material, which heightened the danger and helped him make quick exits when necessary. White's reporting gave ballast to the NAACP's campaign for a federal anti-lynching law. He wrote graphic, horrifying, detailed descriptions of ritual brutality, and he stressed that fundamentalist ministers often played prominent roles in lynch mobs and local Klan organizations. In 1929 he published a book on lynching that ruled the field for decades, *Rope and Faggot: An Interview with Judge Lynch.*

The book distilled White's reporting and featured a blistering chapter on religion, contending that the lynching mania could only have occurred in a Christian society. White virtually equated racist terrorism with fundamentalism. Christianity, he stressed, was the only religion to draw the color line, and the Klan was loaded with fundamentalist ministers for whom believing in Christianity and hating blacks were identical: "It is the Christian South, boasting of its imperviousness to the heretical doctrines of modernism, that mutilates and burns Negroes, barbarities unmatched in any other part of the world." White noted that when William Joseph Simmons refounded the Klan in 1915, he and his operatives required "no especial shrewdness" to recognize "that Baptist and Methodist preachers were the very best material for Klan organizers." Though White worked hard to sustain friendly relationships with the NAACP's religious base, recognizing that the organization depended on religious leaders and institutions for its existence, he guarded its secular image. By the time that he published *Rope and Faggot*, White was the strongest force at the NAACP, outstripping Johnson, who struggled with poor health, and Du Bois, who relied on Johnson's gentle leadership style. Du Bois and Ovington remained friendly allies in the 1920s, but Ovington's adoration passed from him to Johnson, as Du Bois perceived. Ovington treasured Johnson's combination of kindly reasonableness and moral passion, appreciating that he "knew when, and when not" to exert his authority, and that Johnson was unfailingly gracious, "always the gentleman." Moreover, Du Bois detested White, which dramatically worsened Du Bois's already vulnerable position at the NAACP.[117]

When Du Bois told the story of his falling out with White and the NAACP, he acknowledged that White was brave, hardworking, and accomplished. The problem was that White was pathologically selfish and egotistical. In 1931 Johnson took an unpaid leave on account of poor health, leaving White in charge. According to Du Bois, White had worked effectively as Number Two, but White unleashed was a nightmare. As soon as White became Number One, albeit still lacking the title, "his attitude and actions were unbearable." This operation could not work if White gave free reign to his egotism and volatility. Du Bois organized a staff revolt, drafting a protest that Seligmann, field secretary William Pickens, branches director Robert Bagnall, and assistant secretary Roy Wilkins signed. Addressing the board of directors, on which he sat, Du Bois claimed that the entire support staff agreed with him: "We have all had considerable and varied experiences, but in our several careers, we have never met a man like Walter White who under an outward and charming manner has succeeded within a short time in alienating and antagonizing everyone of his co-workers, including all the clerks in the office." In Du Bois's telling, this protest got White's attention. White begged the board not to fire him, vowed to stop being obnoxious, won a reprieve, waged a charm offensive, and played for the long term, methodically firing Pickens, Bagnall, and Seligmann, even though they recanted. Du Bois claimed to see it coming: "I did not trust Walter White. Any employee who opposed him soon lost his job; but White never appeared as the cause."[118]

This rendering got some of the facts right, although Du Bois still did not bother to acknowledge that he wrongly dragged the clerical workers into it, jeopardizing their jobs without their consent; moreover, his account overpersonalized what happened. Du Bois and White might have worked together tolerably well had the Depression not hit the NAACP so hard. As it was, the NAACP's membership plunged from over ninety thousand in the late 1920s to twenty thousand in 1930, and the organization nearly folded, ending the year 1931 with a twelve-thousand-dollar deficit plus a fifteen-hundred-dollar *Crisis* deficit. A week before Du Bois urged the board to fire White, the NAACP eliminated key staff positions, imposed a 10 percent salary reduction, and turned business affairs of the magazine over to the association. Three days later Johnson submitted his resignation, joining Charles Spurgeon Johnson as a literature professor at Fisk and leaving Du Bois to fight with White.[119]

The *Crisis* had begun to fade long before the stock market crashed. In 1919 sales peaked at one hundred thousand; by 1924 sales were down to forty thousand. Every issue was much like the preceding one, and Ovington told Du Bois that the magazine was too drab and predictable. The covers and art, she judged, were "wretched," the staff was top heavy and too expensive, Du Bois was busy doing other things, and the magazine did not publish articles based on deep research. In some ways, Ovington observed, *Crisis* had become less interesting than its new rival, *Opportunity*, published by the Urban League. Charles Spurgeon Johnson, the Urban League's research director, who later became the first Afro-American president of Fisk University, was the guiding light at *Opportunity*. He boosted the careers of many Harlem Renaissance writers, especially Alain Locke. Du Bois chafed at Ovington's unfavorable comparison to two upstarts that did not compare to him. Johnson was too conservative for Du Bois, and by the mid-1920s Du Bois openly disliked Locke, who reeked of fussy, aesthetic, depoliticized self-regard. Though Du Bois respected Locke's intellectual creativity and depth, he judged that Locke's "New Negro" did not rage for social justice. Too much Locke would "turn the Negro renaissance into decadence," fixated on "pretty things" and the plaudits of frivolous white socialites. Du Bois had no intention of making *Crisis* more like Locke, catching "the passing fancy of the really unimportant critics and publishers." He preferred the way he already did things, publishing justice-centered propaganda infused by art and literature, not art for art's sake. If this was a rut, the NAACP was still lucky to have him.[120]

The *Crisis* stuck to its sameness, publishing serious work that mattered, and continued to fade. The next time that Ovington tried, in a long memo, to get her friend to change course, it was December 1930 and the magazine was barely hanging on. Ovington, as usual, had the job of telling Du Bois things that almost no one else could tell him. *Crisis*, she wrote, had once been more important than the NAACP, but that time had long passed. The organization, though embattled financially, had become very important. The magazine, also embattled financially, had become, well, less important: "It is not as unique as it once was. Much of its news is of the character of the news carried by the weekly papers." *Crisis* still produced "useful, interesting work," she assured, but it was no longer "as essential to Negro progress and to radical Negro thought as it once was" and it relied on support from the financially reeling NAACP. Ovington told Du Bois it was obvious where this story was heading. Sooner or later he was going to lose control of the magazine. Even if *Crisis* survived as an NAACP publication, it would not be the independent vehicle it had been and Du Bois would not enjoy keeping it going. She advised him to cut a new deal while it was still up to him—let go of editing the magazine, take a reduced salary as a part-time staffer, write occasional pieces for *Crisis*, lecture to the branches, and turn a corner.[121]

Du Bois replied that he recognized Ovington's intention of looking out for him. Nonetheless, "not for a moment" would he consider such a move: "Either *The Crisis* is necessary to the work of the NAACP or it is not." If it was not, he wanted the NAACP to do the letting go, letting him keep the magazine on an independent basis. "I will consider no other proposition nor will I work with the NAACP under any other conditions." That was not going to happen, however. *Crisis* still mattered to the NAACP, although the association could not afford it as it was. The organization wanted to keep the magazine at a reduced cost, which it did, with White at the helm, delicately dancing with Du Bois after Du Bois tried to terminate White.[122]

The ascension of White revived the perennial question of whether the NAACP was black enough. R. L. Vann, owner and editor of the influential *Pittsburgh Courier*, pressed Du Bois on the question, albeit somewhat indirectly. Moorfield Storey had died in 1929 and was succeeded as president by Joel Spingarn. Now White was replacing Johnson. Vann did not say outright that White was too white. He knew that the NAACP rested on White's shoulders; moreover, Du Bois had blistered the Garvey movement for making a big deal about degrees of darkness. White *was* too white, however, for this issue not to be talked about in local branches, and Spingarn was in a different category.

Vann protested that the NAACP should not have elected a white Jew to its presidency: "How can we expect Negroes ever to learn to follow Negro leadership if Du Bois is going to follow white leadership? Personally, I think the election of a white president will destroy some of the confidence we have labored to build up." Vann appreciated that Spingarn helped to keep the NAACP afloat, "but I can't appreciate his desire to be president as a reward for his financial help." For that matter, he even liked Spingarn, and he recognized that "Spingarn cannot help that he is a Jew." Nevertheless, Vann admonished that Christians were averse "to non-Christian leadership" and that having a Jewish president would hurt the cause. The NAACP, a civil rights organization, was sadly failing to cultivate Afro-American leaders. Vann urged it was either right or wrong to advocate black leadership; Du Bois could not have it both ways. Du Bois replied that the presidency was an honorary position and the executive secretary was the position that mattered. He had things to say about that position but preferred not to say them in a letter, offering to "go over the situation" with Vann in person.[123]

The situation was grim for Du Bois, although White paused before cutting the magazine's budget. White asked Charles Russell how to improve *Crisis*. Russell told him that readers needed humor and color to get through hard times; the magazine's unrelenting seriousness was too severe even for activists. That was a nonstarter for Du Bois, who was not running the magazine to amuse people. White, in crisis mode, focused on the NAACP's legal operation, which was financed by the Garland Fund, which suffered a two-thirds drop in value when the stock market crashed. That shredded the ambitious legal plan for the NAACP devised by White, Johnson, Spingarn, and Storey. White went all out in response, ramping up his already legendary schmoozing and fund-raising operation. He shook down his downtown friends for survival money. He hired Wilkins to replace him as assistant secretary. And he turned the NAACP into a top-down enterprise focused on litigation and lobbying.[124]

In 1931 White started down this road by appropriating the other half of a Rosenwald Fund subsidy that the NAACP had previously split with *Crisis*. Du Bois had helped to win the Rosenwald money; now White was taking it. This was the trigger for the staff revolt that Du Bois organized. For a while the stress was severe at the NAACP. Ovington sided with White against Du Bois, contending that White was indispensable to the NAACP's survival. She resigned as chair of the board to take over the vacant position of treasurer, which forced Spingarn, reluctantly, to add board chair to his duties as president. Spingarn and the board admonished White to play better with others. White promised to do so; the cagey Wilkins got back in White's favor; the others were pushed out, one by one; and White prevailed. In almost every way the NAACP got bigger, more aggressive, more effective, and more important on White's watch. Attorneys Thurgood Marshall and Charles H. Houston became household names, arguing civil rights cases in federal courts. By 1945 the NAACP had 571 branches in forty-one states and the District of Columbia, and it had won twenty-one of its twenty-three cases in the U.S. Supreme Court. The *Crisis* took a backseat to the NAACP's legal activism, but Wilkins kept it going as an effective flagship for the organization. Powell called it "the most sanely radical magazine in America."[125]

Three things made the situation intolerable for Du Bois. He couldn't stand White, who, as Ovington noted, did not take advice from underlings or even the board chair. Second, *Crisis* was imperiled by its inability to pay for itself. Spingarn, seeking a face-saving exit for Du Bois, wrote a confidential letter to John Hope in October 1932, asking him to invite Du Bois to teach at Atlanta University. Hope promptly invited Du Bois to be a guest professor in the spring semester of 1933. This initiative set in motion Du Bois's escape, although he was bitter when he headed for Atlanta in January, still determined to prevent White and Wilkins from retaining the magazine. Third, Du Bois never believed that the issue of the color line reduced to the battle against discrimination. The NAACP did not say, Du Bois observed, "nor even contemplate, what path Negroes would follow when they once became Americans who suffered no discrimination." In the early 1930s, living amid the carnage of the Depression, Du Bois resolved that he needed to deal with bigger things than the NAACP's relentless focus on lynching, the Fourteenth Amendment, and the Fifteenth Amendment.[126]

In 1926 Du Bois visited the Soviet Union and felt his vague, mild, somewhat condescending sympathy for the Russian Revolution turn into fervent conviction. A Soviet agent paid for the trip, on the condition that Du Bois would travel freely and decide for himself what he saw. He got there at the high point of the New Economic Policy (NEP) of Vladimir Lenin and Nikolai Bukharin, which the Tenth Party Congress adopted in 1921. The NEP generated capital for the "commanding heights" of the Soviet economy—public utilities, heavy industry, and transportation—by allowing private businesses to hire up to twelve workers and take profits. Du Bois caught the Soviet experiment in a hopeful, relatively prosperous moment, meeting hardworking officials and buoyant workers who talked about building a new civilization. He admitted straightaway, "I know nothing of political prisoners, secret police and underground propaganda." Neither did he know of the political crisis brewing between Communist Party general secretary Joseph Stalin and the "United Opposition" headed by Bolshevik hero Leon Trotsky and Leningrad party leader Grigori Zinoviev. The hopeful Russians that Du Bois met in Moscow, Nijni Novgorod, Kiev, and Leningrad enthralled him. Sitting in Revolution Square opposite the Second House of the Moscow Soviets, he wrote that he felt "astonishment and wonder" at the achievements of the Soviet revolution: "I may be partially deceived and half-informed. But if what I have seen with my eyes and heard with my ears in Russia is Bolshevism, I am a Bolshevik."[127]

Then Wall Street crashed spectacularly and Du Bois, already a Socialist, recalibrated the importance of Socialism to him and what he should think about Communism and Marxism. "The Negro and Communism," a longish piece for *Crisis*, appeared in September 1931. "Marxism and the Negro Problem," equally programmatic with a whiff of manifesto, appeared in May 1933, near the end of his days at *Crisis*. The sequence mattered because Du Bois overflowed with thoughts and feelings about Communism before he studied Marx in depth. The first article said that the white proletariat had to make the first step toward the emancipation of colored labor. The second article said that the Great Depression was so awful it might change everything, though redemption was not happening.[128]

"The Negro and Communism" appeared shortly after the NAACP and the American Communist Party clashed over the Scottsboro case. On March 25, 1931, nine black teenage boys were accused of forcing a group of white males off a freight train between Chattanooga and Memphis, Tennessee. A posse arrested the youths in Paint Rock, Alabama, where two white girls surprisingly turned out to be in their company. The girls accused the boys of rape, and the National Guard prevented an immediate lynching. The case was rushed to trial in Scottsboro, Alabama, where three all-white juries convicted eight of the defendants, two of whom were thirteen years old, and the youths were sentenced to be executed in short order. The NAACP and the International Labor Defense (ILD, the legal arm of the Communist Party) intervened, calling for a stay of execution and a retrial. There was plenty of confusion and blundering in the succeeding weeks as the NAACP and ILD competed for influence, each side accused the other of bad faith, the NAACP reeled from its financial crisis, and the ILD won over the parents of the defendants. Eventually the case was tried three times, with guilty verdicts each time, although charges were dropped for four of the defendants. "Scottsboro" was already a symbol of legal lynching when Du Bois wrote in September; later it took on mythic proportions.[129]

Du Bois excoriated the American Communist Party for jeopardizing the lives of the defendants to score some points against capitalism and the capitalist

NAACP. The Communists had a dogma about what it meant to be allied with capitalists, and they were willing to lie in defense of their dogma. In Du Bois's telling, this was a case of stupidity, dogmatism, and mendacity folding together. The ILD actually believed it was doing the youthful defendants a favor by maligning the NAACP and providing legal representation. This absurd belief rested on the equally absurd Communist dogma that black America's petit bourgeois minority dominated its "helpless black proletariat" by groveling to white profiteers. Du Bois called the latter idea "simply a fantastic falsehood." The notion that Afro-Americans could be dominated purely with capitalist ideas died with Washington, he chided. The Communist Party was overdue to acquire some nonsimplistic ideas about race, culture, and democratic politics.[130]

Du Bois and Ovington had long sparred over the intellectual deficiencies of Communists. Ovington had long-standing friendships with Communists; for her, "Workers of the world, unite!" was the essence of radicalism. She worried that Du Bois had not moved past his early, snotty reaction to the Bolshevik Revolution. In "The Negro and Communism," however, Du Bois said that Communism was powered by the mighty truth that capitalism was inherently predatory and unsustainable. He added that capitalist civilization rested on "the slavery and semi-slavery of the colored world." Until the person of color became free and self-determining, he argued, "white capital will use the profit derived from his degradation to keep white labor in chains." The Marxist dream of a united proletariat was, indeed, the answer. But white labor had to take the "first step toward the emancipation of colored labor."[131]

Two years later Du Bois judged that even global economic catastrophe had not broken the grip of racial prejudice. Thus, with regret, he felt compelled to reverse his previous conclusion. "Marxism and the Negro Problem" was more ambitious, reflecting Du Bois's recent grappling with Marx's *Capital*. Du Bois offered a primer on Marxist theory—labor theory of value; capital as machines, materials, and wages paid for labor; surplus value; the exploitation of laborers; and the inevitability of socialist revolution. He acknowledged that serious debates existed about each of these arguments and their relationships to each other. Still, writing in 1933, it was hard to avoid the verdict that labor, not gambling, was the foundation of value, that "business acumen" was a euphemism for exploitation, and that something was radically wrong "with an industrial system that turns out simultaneously paupers and millionaires and sets a world starving because it has too much food." The Great Depression was a textbook Marxian crisis of exploitation and overproduction. By then Du Bois had developed a deep admiration of Marx, "a colossal genius of infinite sacrifice and monumental industry, and with a mind of extraordinary logical keenness and grasp." He especially admired Marx's decoding of capitalist boom-and-bust cycles; Du Bois observed that Marx drew on his "extraordinary, thoroughgoing personal knowledge of industrial conditions" across Europe and elsewhere. Marx explained nineteenth-century capitalism better than any other theorist, and Marxist theory offered the best explanation of why capitalist civilization collapsed in 1929.[132]

Except that Marxist theory and strategy did not apply straightaway to the problem of the color line. Du Bois put it sharply: "Colored labor has no common ground with white labor." No white proletariat anywhere, he observed, sought to make people of color equal to it economically, politically, and socially. The Socialist Party in the United States was clear and brave about Socialism, but vague and tongue-tied about the rights of blacks. Marxist theory offered a "true diagnosis of the situation in Europe in the middle of the 19th century," but it had to be "modified" to apply to the United States of the past or present, or anywhere else that the color line mattered. In the United States, Du Bois explained, "the Negro is exploited to a degree that means poverty, crime, delinquency, and indigence." This exploitation came from white capitalists and the white proletariat, not from a virtually nonexistent black capitalist class. The white proletariat and the white capitalist class were equally hostile to blacks. On other occasions Du Bois clarified that actually, the white proletariat was worse, because a significant segment of the white capitalist class had a history of promoting black progress, which was not true of poor whites. The American Federation of Labor, for example, under William Green and Matthew Woll, had a record of determined and vicious opposition to African Americans. To most white unionists, African Americans were as subservient to their interests as the white unionists were subservient to the interests of capital. Afro-Americans had been left with no choice. They built survival organizations protecting them from both white enemies, and they cut deals with the handful of white capitalists and professional-class liberals that had a conscience about white racism.[133]

Du Bois had not given up hope that the Great Depression, having leveled so much in mighty catastrophe, might open the door to global revolution. America's fantastic industrial machine teetered on ruination. The trade unions representing skilled labor were "double-tongued and helpless." Unskilled white labor was too frightened by competition from blacks to unite with them; "it only begs a dole." American Socialists had a good economic program but no courage about racial justice, and they lacked a popular following. The Communists, to their distinct credit, tried to break down barriers between whites and blacks, but that ensured that nobody listened to the Communists. Du Bois cried out:

"There is not at present the slightest indication that a Marxian revolution based on a united class-conscious proletariat is anywhere on the American far horizon." All he could do was hope that "black workers alone," the only true believers in political and economic democracy, might "in time make the workers of the world effective dictators of civilization."[134]

For Du Bois, that was an argument against the draining and perhaps futile politics of racial integration, the only kind the NAACP practiced. If there was a way forward, it had to be through black-controlled institutions, schools, and businesses—a black cooperative economy modeled on nineteenth-century utopian Socialism, perhaps linked with friendly Socialist or Communist Parties. It surprised Du Bois to end up with a solution that barely existed in American society, although the seeds of this outcome were scattered throughout his work.

Plotting his exit from the NAACP, Du Bois declared that there was such a thing as good racial segregation. Racial discrimination was always repugnant, he assured, but he had nothing against segregated black schools or neighborhoods, as long as the schools and neighborhoods did not cheat blacks of their rights. In fact, black Americans were most successful when they operated in black-controlled enterprises: "The advance of the colored people has been mainly in the lines where they themselves working by and for themselves, have accomplished the greatest advance." Du Bois proposed that the NAACP should fight against discrimination and for black-controlled economic cooperation, not against segregation per se. The NAACP itself depended on the existence and support of twenty thousand segregated black churches. White replied that the NAACP had always categorically opposed segregation and it should not change its position. "Separate but equal" did not exist in American society, he argued. Neither was it anything to which Americans should aspire. Black-only clubs, churches, and schools were reactive responses to white racism. Segregation enabled white Americans to discriminate against black Americans, and it had no history not linked with racial discrimination: "Negroes and all other groups must without compromise and without cessation oppose in every possible fashion any attempt to impose from without the establishment of pales and ghettoes."[135]

This dispute was misleading on both sides. White knew that the argument was not really about "from without," and Du Bois knew that white America used every form of segregation as a point of discriminatory attack. This was an argument about the value of integrationist liberalism and Du Bois's resort to utopian black Socialism. Functionally, it gave him a rationale for leaving the NAACP. Du Bois, heightening the desperation factor, described black Socialism as an idea lacking an American history, brushing off Peter Clark, George

Washington Woodbey, George W. Slater Jr., Hubert Henry Harrison, George Frazier Miller, A. Philip Randolph, Chandler Owen, and the tiny organizations to which they belonged. Clark, America's first black Socialist, was an activist in the Cincinnati chapter of the Socialist Labor Party in the late 1870s. Harrison and Owen had preceded Du Bois into the secular, black-identified, Socialist political wilderness that he was about to enter, and Miller wrote for the *Messenger* during Randolph's early radical phase.

But there was a stream of black Socialist thought and activism that prefigured Du Bois's Socialist turn without giving up on Socialist universalism. Randolph upheld it in the union movement. More often, black Socialism was religious and espoused by ministers—the left flank of the black social gospel. Ransom and his followers in the AME Church had the most influence, through the *A.M.E. Church Review*. Miller and Bagnall were in it, but as Episcopal clerics. Mordecai Johnson was a leading black Baptist Socialist before and after he became president of Howard University in 1926. Much of the remaining black Christian Socialist following was Baptist and poor. It had no publishing houses, but it packed lectures and street rallies. It had a marginal role in the Socialist Party and the Industrial Workers of the World (IWW), especially in the western states. It lived in segregated social space without much choice in the matter. And its champion was Woodbey.

GEORGE WASHINGTON WOODBEY AND CHRISTIAN SOCIALISM

George Washington Woodbey preached Christian Socialism to audiences Ransom and Du Bois mostly did not reach. He was a pioneer of the black social gospel and a product of the Socialist and Christian Socialist movements of his time who stressed that he had no original ideas. He got his ideas from the Bible, Marx, Edward Bellamy, Eugene Debs, and the Christian Socialists, but Woodbey did not talk about these sources, except for an occasional reference to Marx and except for the Bible. Claiming originality would have undermined his purpose, for Woodbey contended that Christian Socialism was not new. It was merely a new name for the Golden Rule and the teaching of the Bible about God's identification with the oppressed.

He was born a slave in Johnson County, Tennessee, in 1854. Nothing is known of Woodbey's early life except that he studied for two terms in a common school and was otherwise self-educated. At nineteen he married Annie R. Goodin of Kansas, with whom he had five children. The following year Woodbey was ordained to the Baptist ministry in Emporia, Kansas. In the 1880s he worked in mines and factories in Kansas and Missouri, was active in Republican politics in both states, and ministered to several Baptist congregations. Later he moved to Nebraska and joined the Prohibition Party, where his speaking skills and activist temperament lifted him to a prominent party role. In 1896 Woodbey ran for lieutenant governor of Nebraska and for Congress on the Prohibition ticket. That year marked a turning point in his ideological development. Bellamy's science fiction novel, *Looking Backward* (1888), enthralled Woodbey with its vision of a Socialist America, circa 2000, in which all means of production were nationally owned, social goods were distributed equally to all citizens, everyone could eat at public kitchens, and all people retired at age forty-five with full benefits. That led Woodbey to a Socialist weekly published in Girard, Kansas, *Appeal to Reason*, which he devoured, though he hedged politically, joining the Populist Party.[136]

The presidential election of 1900 completed Woodbey's ideological turn. He started the campaign as a supporter of William Jennings Bryan on the Populist and Democratic tickets, giving speeches for Bryan on behalf of the Nebraska Democratic Party. Debs, however, came to Omaha, campaigning on the Social Democracy of America ticket. Upon hearing Debs speak, Woodbey had the conviction of hearing the real thing, although he still had qualms about throwing away his vote. For a while he gave campaign speeches for Bryan that made Bryan sound like Debs, but the Democrats stopped asking for his help and Woodbey decided they were right: He had become a Socialist. Resigning his pulpit, Woodbey announced that he would devote the rest of his life to the Socialist movement. He got a movement going in Omaha, speaking every night in the streets and parks. A Nebraska comrade later told Socialist organizer A. W. Ricker, "Omaha had never had the crowds that attended Woodbey's meetings."[137]

In the spring of 1902 Woodbey visited his mother in San Diego and spoke every night in the streets and lecture halls. The Socialist Party, formed in 1901 by leaders of the Socialist Labor Party and the three-year-old Social Democracy of America, sponsored some of his speeches. Often Woodbey held forth on a soapbox. San Diego was not a likely place for him to land, as it had a small and mostly contented working class and no large industries. The area's ideal climate attracted tourists and professionals, causing IWW martyr-bard Joe Hill to remark that San Diego was "not worth a whoop in Hell from a rebel's point of view." Downtown San Diego, however, had a tradition of street oratory smacking of Hyde Park, London, which hooked Woodbey. He told crowds he had come to see his mother, but, being "anxious to be free," he felt impelled to work for the cause constantly. The *Los Angeles Socialist* reported: "Comrade Woodbey is great and is a favorite with all classes. He has had very respectable audiences both on the streets and in the halls. He likes to speak on the street and it is the general verdict that he has done more good for the cause than any of our most eloquent speakers who have preceded him. He is full of resources and never repeats his speeches, but gives them something new every night." Woodbey passed a hat for contributions and branched out to Los Angeles, where the Northern Restaurant and Southern Hotel refused to accommodate him after he turned out to be black. He told audiences of his welcome to the city, which set off successful boycotts of both establishments.[138]

Back in San Diego, Mount Zion Baptist Church called Woodbey to be its pastor, where he settled in. He drew large crowds to the church, won election to the state executive board of the Socialist Party, and lectured across the state, winning accolades as "The Great Negro Socialist Orator." Posters heralded his appearances: "The well-known Socialist Lecturer. Quaint, Direct, Forceful. Has spoken to great audiences in all parts of the United States." That was slightly exaggerated geographically, but Woodbey worked hard at expanding his audience. In 1903 he packed a lecture hall in Los Angeles to assess Washington's "Capitalist Argument for the Negro." Woodbey lauded Washington's gentlemanly dignity and educational accomplishments, but panned, "He has all the ability necessary to make a good servant of capitalism by educating other servants for capitalism." Tuskegee, Woodbey explained, was in the business of pitting black workers against white workers, which lowered wages for all laborers and their families. Washington tried to make capitalism the basis of unity between white capitalists and black workers, failing to comprehend that capitalism was inherently predatory and divisive, never the basis of unity: "There is no race division industrially, but an ever-growing antagonism between the exploiting capitalists black or white, and the exploited workers, black or white." The "only solution to the race problem," Woodbey urged, was for people of all races to share the benefits of production.[139]

Woodbey's soapbox speaking made him a frequent target of police. He was thrown in jail several times and occasionally hospitalized after a police beating. The police in San Diego, Los Angeles, and San Francisco were especially thuggish. After he became an author and sold booklets on the streets, the beatings got worse. Woodbey was persistent and unbowed. In 1905 a San Diego police officer clubbed Woodbey on a street corner and Woodbey led a group of protesters to a police station. The group tried to lodge a complaint, but the offending officer intervened, screaming racial epithets at Woodbey and throwing him bodily out of the station house. Woodbey pressed the charge in court, where every witness testified that Woodbey had done nothing wrong, but an all-white, middle-class jury ruled for the police. Back on his soapbox, Woodbey urged victims of police brutality to fight for their rights in court, even if they were certain to lose. He also published the names of the jurors in his case, urging decent citizens to shun them.[140]

Woodbey's audiences were racially mixed, mostly working class with a sprinkling of middle-class activists and professionals, and appreciative. Every week listeners told him they had never understood Socialist ideas until they heard his lucid, compelling speeches. Often they asked for a written version, which yielded his first book, *What to Do and How to Do It; or, Socialism Versus Capitalism* (1903). A. W. Ricker, upon visiting Socialist publisher Julius A. Wayland in Girard, Kansas, read the forty-page book aloud to Wayland, who published it as the August 1903 issue of *Wayland's Monthly*. Ricker declared in *Appeal to Reason* that Woodbey's book compared favorably to Robert Blatchford's Socialist classic *Merrie England* and that all locals should encourage people to read it, "Negroes especially." Woodbey began with a two-sentence dedication. The first sentence paraphrased the title; the second was poignant and self-referential: "By one who was once a chattel slave freed by the proclamation and wishes to be free from the slavery of capitalism."[141]

What to Do was framed as a dialogue between Woodbey and his mother. She pitched half-incredulous questions and he gave straightforward answers. Had he given up the Bible and the ministry to go into politics? No, Socialism had brought him to a deeper Christian faith, making the Bible come alive to him. More than ever he grasped what the Bible said about God giving the earth to human beings as a home; God overthrowing the Egyptian slave masters and delivering the Hebrews from oppression; God prescribing a government of the people administered by judges, which they replaced with a monarchy; God repeatedly forbidding usury; and God prescribing a Jubilee law preventing the making of public debts. Woodbey's mother replied that a lot of his Socialist friends didn't believe in God or the Bible. He replied that he knew a lot of atheist Republicans when he worked for the Republican Party. Woodbey would not repudiate Socialist friends with whom he disagreed about God and eternity: "Whoever is willing to make things better here, which the Bible teaches is essential to the hereafter, I will join hands with as far as we can go."[142]

Woodbey told his mother that Socialists wanted four things. They wanted all people to share the land equally, "because the earth is our home and no one can live without it." They wanted all workers to own the tools with which they worked, "from a spade to a large factory." They wanted all people to own the common forms of transport, especially railroads and ships. And they wanted working people to make the laws governing industry by direct vote. His mother wondered what would happen to private property under this system. Woodbey replied that anything produced would be justly distributed as private property to those that produced it. The crucial thing was to socialize the process by which wealth was produced, making every American an equal shareholder in the wealth of the United States.[143]

Getting control of the government, Woodbey believed, would be harder than making Socialism work, but he thought that both were sure to occur. Sooner or later the overwhelming majority of workers would give themselves equality by voting for it. Socialists would be elected to city and county offices, then to state offices, and finally to federal offices. Gradually they would gain control of the government. Socialism was no more radical than the golden rule or social justice, Woodbey argued; in fact, it was merely another name for these things. Public education, a Socialist idea, was long considered anti-American and impossibly radical. Public industry would be similar, moving swiftly from being dangerous to being sensible and decent. As soon as Socialists gained control of the government, they would take possession of the means of production and distribution by acts of legislation, replacing capitalist enterprises with public ownership, which most people would like much better.

Woodbey's mother worried that if Socialists took over the government and the economy, wealthy people would start a civil war. He replied that capitalism was too much like the old slave system to find enough mercenaries to fight its battles. The slaveholders did not dare to arm the slaves when their system was attacked, and they could not accommodate the slaves without undoing the system. Capitalism had a bad case of the latter problem, Woodbey believed. Admittedly, capitalists had the law on their side, because they made the laws. But as soon as Socialists got elected and changed the laws, it would be game over for the capitalists.

Not many people of Woodbey's age had a mother who survived slavery and was still alive in 1903. He went on longer than usual when she asked how women would fare under Socialism. Women had it worse than men under capitalism, Woodbey acknowledged; Socialism offered a better life for men and a much better life for women. In a Socialist order, every woman would have her own income, just like the men. Women who did society's most important work—raising children—would not have to labor anywhere else. Woodbey stressed that capitalism emptied the working-class home of its nurturing mothers, but under Socialism, women and their families would be lifted to the valued status they deserved. Unmarried women would be able to work in industry or have a profession. The only women who might not like Socialism were the "idle parasites" under capitalism that lived off the spoils of unearned wealth. They would have to learn how to contribute something useful to society. Socialism, Woodbey observed, advocated "absolute equality of the sexes before the law," as stated in the Socialist Party platform. Capitalism exploited women and allowed society to discriminate against them, but under Socialism, women would be equal to men at the ballot box and everywhere else.[144]

Socialism was starting to sound pretty good to Woodbey's mother, but would it not require a great deal of government and a great many laws? Woodbey's answer revealed that he was a Marxist utopian all the way down when it came to Socialist government. Like most orthodox Marxists he called his position "scientific Socialism." Once the people collectively owned the land, the factories, and the means of transportation, he argued, government would not be necessary and only a few laws would be needed. Capitalism had to be regulated by representative government to make it minimally tolerable, and it relied on bosses to hold workers in line. Capitalism operated on the basis of compete or die, but under Socialism this logic would be abolished, so regulation and representative government would not be necessary. The people would make their own laws by voting directly for or against them, and they would not need to be bossed by anyone, since people worked effectively when the firm belonged to them. Plus, everyone hated to be bossed. Crime would disappear, too, because crime was a response to hunger and being humiliated. Woodbey figured that most people under Socialism would choose to live in towns, because towns were more conducive than rural areas or cities for neighborliness and community. In any case, the governance of towns and cities would be left to the direct vote of the people, just like in the larger industries.[145]

According to Woodbey, he convinced his mother that Socialism was the best option for African Americans and all others. He rushed past her questions about religion, however, explaining that getting into that would require another book. A year later he published a sequel, *The Bible and Socialism* (1904), this time responding to the queries of his mother's pastor. The pastor contended that Christianity was a religion, Socialism was a type of politics, and religion had to be separated from politics. Moreover, Woodbey's hero, Karl Marx, was no Christian—far from it. Woodbey replied that the Bible lacks any distinction between religion and politics and that Marx, "that wonderful man," caught the justice spirit of the Bible better than any modern thinker or minister. God delivering the Hebrews from slavery was "religion" and "politics" mixed together, Woodbey argued. After the Hebrews were liberated from Egyptian rule, they formed a state, replete with laws and politics, about all of which the Bible depicts God as having remarkably detailed prescriptions: "God is there represented as giving the Jews a regular system of government, touching every phase of human life, too numerous to mention. Indeed, I know of no relation of one man to another that is not touched upon in the Law of Moses."[146]

The Bible is loaded with normative ethical statements bearing on politics, Woodbey stressed. More precisely, the Bible is loaded with Socialism. Woodbey marshaled biblical texts opposing rent, interest, profits, love of money, and the exploitation of the poor. Rent is a violation of the fundamental biblical principle that the earth was given to all of humankind as a home. To violate the law of common ownership is to commit sin. Socialism, Woodbey argued, was a modern political expression of the biblical right to cooperative ownership and control of the land. In the Bible, the land belonged to God and the Israelites were tenants upon it. In modern capitalism, a handful of "cunning" types stole possession of the earth to live off the labor of others. Woodbey contended that only Socialism came close to the biblical law suspending agricultural work in the seventh year and canceling all debts in the Jubilee fiftieth year (although Woodbey conflated the Jubilee with the seventh-year Sabbath). In biblical times, the aim of the Jubilee was to prevent huge debts from accumulating "for parasites to live upon from age to age, as they do today."[147]

Woodbey read the 25th chapter of Leviticus as a manifesto for the "principle of universal brotherhood," the fundamental principle of Socialism. Verse 35 commanded that if any of the Israelites' kin fell into difficulty, the Israelites were obligated to support them, treating the dependents as resident aliens. Woodbey universalized "kin" as "brother," preaching that God cared about all people, not just Hebrews. Verse 36 prohibited taking interest in advance or in any way making a profit off one's charity to the poor. To fear God was to take care of the poor and vulnerable without reward, another verse that Woodbey universalized. Verse 37 said the same thing more specifically, forbidding Israelites from lending money at interest taken in advance or exacting a profit from providing food to the needy. Woodbey explained that the Bible taught a Socialist ethic in a pre-Socialist age; thus, it focused on the ethics of charity from the standpoint of social justice: "As the ultimate end, which is Socialism, was yet in the distant future, temporary relief for the brother or stranger fallen into decay is taught. But the Bible, no more than the Socialists, holds out charity as a solution of economic difficulties."[148]

Isaiah 24 was another staple of Woodbey's street preaching. Verse 5 pictured the earth lying polluted from the ravages of its inhabitants, who broke God's laws, violated the statutes, and broke the everlasting covenant. To Woodbey, this text was mostly about economic injustice—the defilement of creation by economic greed: "Socialism, or opposition to usury, has always been the relation that should be between man and man; but government has always been left to the rich, who profited through usury at the expense of the poor producer of wealth." The solution was to get the power of government into the hands of the producers, who would change the laws to gain for themselves the value of all they produced. Socialism was a bountiful vision of everyone becoming a producer, Woodbey urged. It was not about socializing poverty; it was about all people flourishing and thereby producing wealth: "Of course, the producer has the power to take over the industries now, but has yet to be convinced of it."[149]

Woodbey's ministerial interlocutor asked how he understood the teaching of Jesus, especially about patriotism and nonresistance. Woodbey replied that Christ's example was the best interpretive key to what he meant. He condemned the rich with unsparing scorn and drove the business vendors out of the temple with a whip, so "love your enemies" and "turn the other cheek" did not call his followers to be passive, cowardly, or oblivious. Woodbey claimed that Jesus, living under the Roman Empire, took the same position "that every good Socialist takes." He abided by the laws of the land until the laws could be changed. Woodbey's exegesis of the "Caesar's coin" story in Matthew and its Synoptic parallels took this plodding line, failing to notice the difference between Roman and Jewish coins in the story, the role of the spies, and Jesus's cagey non-answer in front of a crowd that believed it owed nothing to Caesar. In the story, some shady interrogators posing as pious Jews tried to trap Jesus with a question about paying taxes. He asked for a denarius, a coin minted by Rome with Caesar's image, and they whipped one out—something that no righteous Jew would have done. Jesus discredited the interrogators before moving to his shape-shifting answer, laced with irony, "Render to Caesar the things that are Caesar's, and to God the things that are God's." According to Woodbey, however, "render unto Caesar" was as straightforward as it sounded: Jesus told his followers to pay their taxes to the Roman government. For Woodbey, every problem text folded into a coming Socialist solution: "Like us Socialists, he meant, pay your tax and wait for better things, to be brought about by teaching the people."[150]

The war question was the last to arise before Woodbey pressed the pastor for a verdict. The key to "love your enemies" was the biblical doctrine of universal brotherhood, Woodbey argued. Socialism carried out the moral command by fashioning a politics of the biblical doctrine. What could be more loving than to treat one's enemy as a brother and an equal? The pastor countered that God commanded the Israelites to kill their enemies. Woodbey replied that as long as "robber empires" existed, war would curse the earth, and the only way that oppressed people could overthrow an empire was to take up arms. Socialists believed that war was an outgrowth of unjust economic conditions, Woodbey explained. The way to abolish war was to unite the workers of the world against economic tyranny.

That set up Woodbey's altar call. He cited Psalm 72:4, which commended those who defended the cause of the poor, brought deliverance to the needy, and crushed the oppressor. Woodbey urged the pastor, "Go preach the first part of that text to the needy children of the poor in the factories, and apply the latter part to their oppressors or get out of the pulpit and make way for someone who will do it." Did the pastor hear the cry of the poor for deliverance from their oppression? Did he believe that God called him to defend the poor and afflicted and bring justice to the land? Too many ministers preached only about getting to heaven after one died, Woodbey admonished. They ignored that the Bible resounds with admonition to pour oneself out for the poor and oppressed. Woodbey challenged the minister to preach the biblical call to social justice and to wear proudly the accusation that would come from doing so—that he was a Socialist Christian. *The Bible and Socialism* ended with the minister vowing to do so.[151]

Woodbey knew from his lecture crowds that there was an audience for his message. Getting that audience to join the Socialist Party, however, was a heavy lift. The party was founded in July 1901 as a merger of Debs's Social Democrats and most of the Socialist Labor Party led by Morris Hillquit and Max Hayes, although Daniel De Leon's sectarian faction of the latter group refused to join. From the beginning the party had three factions on the race issue: a flank led by Milwaukee journalist Victor Berger that didn't want black members; a majority led by Debs that advocated color-blind equality and inclusion; and a flank that wanted the party to make an issue of racial justice. These positions were aired at the party's founding convention in Indianapolis. For twenty years the Socialist movements represented at the convention had advocated equality "without distinction of color, race, sex or creed." This was the baseline for the new organization, a formulation already bordering on Socialist cliché that rejected all distinctions except class and, arguably, nation. Most American Socialists assumed a cultural version of white supremacy, but they affirmed the traditional European Socialist position that color-blind equality was a fundamental principle of justice. The issue at the party's founding convention was whether the party should issue a resolution about the special suffering of African Americans, which included references to lynching, wage discrimination, and disenfranchisement.[152]

Hillquit led the opposition to a special resolution, contending that the Socialist Party could not single out blacks, Jews, Germans, or any other racial or ethnic group without contradicting the party's commitment to color-blind equality. Two of the three Afro-American delegates at the convention—John H.

Adams of Brazil, Indiana, and Edward D. McKay of Richmond, Indiana—initially supported this position, but the other black delegate, William Costley of San Francisco, contended that the Socialist movement had a legacy of evasion to overcome on this issue. Costley urged that if Socialists did not name and condemn the distinct forms of suffering imposed on black Americans, it was pointless to expect blacks to join the Socialist Party. Several party leaders agreed—labor leaders Max Hayes (printers' union), John Collins (machinists' union), and William Hamilton (United Mine Workers), social gospeler George Herron, and the party's future secretary, William Mailley. Herron declared dramatically that he would rather lose every vote in the South than see the Socialist Party evade the race issue. Hamilton wanted the party to play a vanguard role in the trade-union movement, making unionism a force for racial justice. Adams, a coal miner, changed his position on the resolution, urging delegates to seize the moment. Opponents implored that the new party would get nowhere in the South if it forthrightly advocated black equality. The wrangling over that warning produced a strong resolution with two missing planks. The Socialist Party officially condemned "color prejudice and race hatred," affirmed the equality of white and black workers, invited blacks to join the Socialist movement, and did not mention lynching or segregation.[153]

The party's racial-justice wing hoped it had made a breakthrough. *Appeal to Reason* and other Socialist papers hailed the resolution as the strongest pro-black statement ever issued by an American political party, and the Socialist Party distributed the resolution as a leaflet. There was some reaction in the black press, all related to the steel strike of 1901, which reignited an old debate about whether African Americans should be strikebreakers. The *Colored American* upheld the Booker tradition, urging its readers to "side with the capitalists" in the steel strike. Eloquently, the *Colored American* pleaded that the black strikebreaker did not relish his role and did not wish to undermine the just demands of white workers:

> It is not that he is the servant of those who would grind the poor to powder. He is not the tool of soulless operators. It's because the white labor organizations refuse to make common cause with him and decline to give him the opportunity that is rightfully his to provide for his family. It is because his sympathy is alienated by treatment that drives him to the capitalist in self-defense. The corporation offers bread. The labor unions turn him away with a stone. Who can blame the Negro for thanking the Almighty for the situation that grants him what the unions deny, and establishes his power as a labor factor among those who think more of quality of servance than of the color of the servant?[154]

Charles L. Wood of Washington, Iowa, a white Socialist, replied that the Socialist Party had recently made an important statement on this matter. Wood confessed that the record of U.S. American trade unions on racial justice was "shameful in the extreme, and without cause." He did not blame African Americans for loathing trade unions. Still, he asked them not to give up on unionism and not to kid themselves that they had friends in the capitalist class. The capitalists sought to completely subjugate the poor and working classes, Wood contended. At the moment they used black workers as "tools" toward this end, but once they succeeded, they would subject blacks to merciless and defenseless tyranny. Wood urged that Socialists were the only party that treated the black American as "a fellow being and a brother." He added that the union movement was changing, though he gave no specifics. The United Mine Workers opposed racism, and some union leaders, notably Collins, were trying to eliminate the racist policies of their organizations. Meanwhile, Debs and other Socialists were organizing what became (in 1905) the Industrial Workers of the World—"one big union" that organized all workers regardless of nationality, craft, race, or gender.[155]

The Socialist Party never attracted many African Americans, as it never overcame its structural and historic impediments to doing so, and much of its internal debate over the issue would have repelled African Americans who read it. *International Socialist Review* (*ISR*), a monthly magazine owned by Charles H. Kerr, published numerous articles on this issue. Other leading Socialist publications—the *Worker, Appeal to Reason, Chicago Socialist, Seattle Socialist,* and the *Social Democratic Herald*—battled over the issue, often recycling debates from *ISR*. The nakedly white supremacist faction (Berger, William Noyes, H. Gaylord Wilshire) contended that blacks were inferior and not worth harming the movement over them. The racial justice faction (Collins, Hamilton, Herron, Costley, Quaker Socialist Caroline H. Pemberton) implored the movement not to sell its soul for a few southern chapters. The color-blind equality faction (Debs, Hillquit, the later Hayes) pleaded to stop litigating this hopelessly divisive issue that undermined the movement's influence with trade unions.

Debs was capable of blunt statements smacking of racial justice solidarity. In 1903, writing in *International Socialist Review,* he declared, "The history of the Negro in the United States is a history of crime without a parallel." White America, Debs observed, "stole him from his native land and for two centuries and a half robbed him of the fruit of his labor, kept him in beastly ignorance and subjected him to the brutal domination of the lash." But two paragraphs later Debs denied that this history of oppression made any difference to what mattered. The issue of social equality was a "pure fraud" that masked the real issue, he contended: "There never was any social inferiority that was not the shriveled fruit of economic inequality. The Negro, given economic freedom, will not ask the white man any social favors; and the burning question of 'social equality' will disappear like mist before the sunrise." To Debs, the class struggle was everything, and it had no color. On the one hand, he allowed, "my heart goes to the Negro and I make no apology to any white man for it." Whenever he looked upon a brutalized black American, "I feel a burning sense of guilt for his intellectual poverty and moral debasement that makes me blush for the unspeakable crimes committed by my own race." Debs wanted to believe that blacks would catch up with whites, achieving equality, although he had doubts that it was possible, as he viewed most blacks as low-performing victims. In any case, the other hand prevailed: "We have nothing special to offer the Negro, and we cannot make separate appeals to all the races." No matter how badly he felt about the savageries inflicted on the basis of race, not class, Debs stuck to Socialist salvation as the solution to everything: "The capitalists, white, black and other shades, are on one side, and the workers, white, black and all other colors, on the other side."[156]

The party's openly racist wing pushed back. A self-identified "staunch member of the Socialist Party" wrote to correct Debs, informing him that Thomas Dixon was the nation's leading authority on the race issue; Debs needed to read *The Leopard's Spots*. In the meantime, Debs needed to stop spewing nonsense about political equality for Afro-Americans, because political equality would lead to social equality and a hellish race war. Debs rubbed his eyes that this guy claimed to be a comrade. Had he read the Socialist Party's resolution on the race issue? Debs reprinted the entire text, six paragraphs long, highlighting the part that assured "our Negro fellow worker of our sympathy with him in his subjection to lawlessness and oppression." He stressed that Socialists repudiated everything that divided workers along lines of race, nationality, creed, or sex. You cannot be a Socialist and a racial bigot, Debs admonished: "I say that the Socialist Party would be false to its historic mission, violate the fundamental principles of Socialism, deny its philosophy and repudiate its own teachings if, on account of race considerations, it sought to exclude any human being from political equality and economic freedom." He put it stronger, declaring that the Socialist movement would "forfeit its very life" if it sold out the rights of blacks, "for it would soon be scorned and deserted as a thing unclean, leaving but a stench in the nostrils of honest men." Debs wanted the Socialist movement to be like him: committed to color-blind justice and not inclined to talk about it, as race was divisive and secondary, an epiphenomenon of economic oppression charged with toxic feelings.[157]

That was the mainstream position in the Socialist Party when it convened in 1904 in Chicago, where Woodbey was the only African American among 175 delegates representing thirty-three states and territories. The largest delegations were from California, Illinois, Massachusetts, Missouri, New York, and Wisconsin. Eight states—Alabama, Idaho, Indian Territory (Oklahoma), Louisiana, Mississippi, New Hampshire, Oregon, and Tennessee—each had a single delegate. Woodbey spoke twice, defending a delegate who worked for the state government of Indiana (he noted that German Socialists boasted about comrades in the German army) and defending the national secretary's salary. The color-blind faction got its way throughout the convention, as nobody said anything about race or even the fact that Woodbey was the only black delegate.[158]

Four years later, at another convention in Chicago, he was still the only black delegate, but this time Woodbey put race on the agenda. Woodbey spoke four times at the 1908 convention, taking bold positions on socialization and immigration. The party was burgeoning in 1908. Local chapters were growing, Debs routinely drew enormous crowds, he had won 402,000 votes in the 1904 presidential election (3 percent of the total), and American Socialists cheered at Social Democratic victories in Europe. Woodbey declared that soon American Socialists would have a victory to deal with in some large city. What did they propose to do upon taking power? Did they plan to make nice with the capitalist class? Would they compensate private corporations that they took over? Woodbey called for swift and decisive action. Any Socialist mayor, upon taking office, had to take possession as fast as possible, refusing to pay a cent of compensation: "I take the ground that you have already paid for these franchises—already paid more than they are worth, and we are simply proposing to take possession of what we have already paid for." He was for socializing "everything in sight," and as fast as possible. He also wanted to build new cooperative enterprises, following the example of the Socialist municipal governments in Germany, France, England, Holland, Denmark, Norway, and Sweden. It was not enough to socialize existing enterprises, Woodbey urged: "We can't afford to wait for the alleviation of the suffering of the people. We must do it as fast as we can get in charge."[159]

Immigration was the other hot issue. In 1907 the Socialist International debated immigration at its congress in Stuttgart, Germany. The American delegation was bitterly divided on this issue, as Hillquit, a Latvian-born New York attorney and party leader, led the effort to commit the Socialist International to a restrictive policy. Hillquit wanted to ban immigrants judged to be incapable of being educated to the class struggle. This proposal was hotly debated and overwhelmingly defeated. Of the twenty-three Socialist parties at the Congress, Hillquit's position won votes only from delegates representing South Africa, Australia, and the United States. The Socialist International declared its opposition to immigration restrictions on national, racial, or ethnic groups, and the American Socialists brought the issue to their convention of 1908.[160]

Victor Berger, Ernest Untermann, and most of the California delegation pushed hard to exclude Asian immigrants. All denied any racist motivation. Berger and Untermann contended that Asian immigrants were economically and psychologically backward and that too many had already entered California, driving down wages. Berger warned that if the Socialist Party supported admission for Chinese, Japanese, and Korean immigrants, America's (white) workers would rightly conclude that the Socialist Party took no interest in helping them.[161]

Woodbey led the fight for Socialist universality. Not only did he oppose immigration restrictions on Asians, he declared; he opposed all immigration restrictions period: "I am in favor of throwing the entire world open to the inhabitants of the world." Many delegates erupted in agreement, applauding Socialism. Woodbey continued: "There are no foreigners, and cannot be, unless some person came down from Mars, or Jupiter, or some place. I stand on the declaration of Thomas Paine when he said, 'The world is my country.'" Woodbey found it terribly strange that some American Socialists, having descended from European immigrants or, like Berger, themselves came from Europe, denied the same right to Asians. With cutting understatement he added, "So far as making this a mere matter of race, I disagree decidedly." A committee on the issue called for a new committee to study the issue. Woodbey replied that Socialists should not need committees for things like this. Concerning Berger and Untermann, he took the high road, declining to say that racism was obviously at play. Socialism was against nationalism and racism, he argued, so how could immigration be an issue at a Socialist convention? What was there to discuss? Woodbey allowed that the argument about driving down wages was a serious matter, but here Socialists needed to face up to reality. This problem was unavoidable as long as capitalism existed anywhere. Under capitalism, either the laborer moved to the job or the job moved to the laborer. If American workers did not produce things as cheaply as workers in Asia did, the capitalist class would move the means of production to Asia. Instead of betraying Socialism by keeping Asians out of America, Woodbey urged, it was better to fight for Socialism—the Brotherhood of Man—everywhere.[162]

The Socialist Party kept studying the issue, debating it at its conventions of 1910 and 1912. By then Berger was the first Socialist in the U.S. House of

Representatives, having been elected in 1910 to the first of his five terms in Congress representing Milwaukee. Formally, the Socialist Party kept faith with the Socialist International and "solidarity forever," opposing immigration restrictions, although many members disagreed without apology, citing Berger as a symbol of Socialist success. The party's determination not to talk about race impaired its ability to discuss why the immigration issue was so unsettling. Woodbey's leadership on the immigration issue threatened, but did not break, the party's decorum. Only once at the 1908 convention did anyone mention the race of the party's only black delegate. Ellis Jones of Ohio, nominating Woodbey as a candidate for vice president, urged the delegates to make a statement about their commitment to racial justice. Instead the Socialists chose Ben Hanford, a New York printer who had run with Debs in 1904. After the 1908 convention the party sent Woodbey on a lecture tour of northern cities, where he stumped for Debs and distributed a pamphlet titled "Why the Negro Should Vote the Socialist Ticket."[163]

Although Woodbey had spoken to black audiences for years, this pamphlet was the first thing he wrote specifically for them. It was the most concise statement of his political message that he ever wrote. Whatever belongs to the public belongs by right to all citizens collectively, he argued. Americans accepted that public streets, schools, and libraries belonged to them collectively. Socialism was about extending the same principle to land, mines, factories, shops, and railroads. Under a Socialist order, Woodbey explained, "when we build a railroad, it will belong not to some Vanderbilt or Gould, but to the people. And when we ride on that railroad, or use it, we will not have to pay a profit to the capitalist." The great objective was to turn all workplaces into public property. Once the public owned and democratically controlled the factories and railroads, everybody would have a job and nobody would suffer in poverty. Woodbey implored that everything depended upon working people putting aside their prejudices to work together for the common good: "We poor whites and blacks have fought each other long enough, and while we have fought, the capitalists have been taking everything from both of us."[164]

Woodbey invited readers to consider the many things they could see but not have. These things would still exist under Socialism, but with the difference that ordinary people would be able to have them: "You will have a chance to get them and not have to worry about how you will live any more than you need to worry now whether you can walk on the street from this meeting." The Socialist Party stood for the abolition of poverty, he stressed. This was its fundamental identity, just like the Republican Party once stood for the abolition of slavery. Woodbey recognized that for most Americans, Socialism seemed too radical.

He countered that the basic idea was not difficult or far out. Essentially it was to run railroads and mines like the post office. Everybody would have a job, and if they produced too much, work hours would be cut back, yielding more leisure time. Putting it this way, Woodbey realized, made Socialism seem prosaic, even boring. But it was more important to make Socialism not seem scary to Americans, and abolishing poverty would not be a prosaic achievement.[165]

The election of 1908, however, bruised the hopes of Socialists, as Debs barely improved on his 1904 total, winning 420,000 votes, despite attracting huge crowds and running against two flawed candidates. Woodbey worked hard for the party during the next electoral cycle, speaking constantly. By then he was free to speak across the country, as his congregation in San Diego tired of Socialist sermons. A parishioner later recalled that Woodbey "loosened up his flock with the Bible," but always "finished his sermon with an oration on Socialism." Woodbey apparently stayed on good terms with Mount Zion Church after giving up his salary, remaining on the church's staff while he devoted himself full-time to Socialist agitation, during the electoral cycle in which Debs more than doubled his following. In 1909 Woodbey urged that agitation was the first step toward converting America to Socialism. Millions of people had to imagine the cooperative commonwealth before it could be built. Socialism was "a fire in the bones of its converts and must flash out." Woodbey got some of his roughest treatment from police during this period, yet he sensed that Socialism was acquiring a new legitimacy in America. For one thing, it got easier to attract a crowd in previously unwelcoming places. It helped, he believed, that Socialist parties gained power in Europe, causing even individualistic Americans to be curious about it.[166]

Woodbey spoke the same language about "new abolition" and "new emancipation" that the NAACP liberals used, but he insisted that emancipation had to cut deeper and wider, liberating the vast masses of the poor from poverty. America was supposed to be a democracy, but Congress and the courts defended the right of individual capitalists to own what the public needed. To Woodbey, there was little difference between the capitalist and slaveholder uses of government. Both relied on government to protect their ostensible rights to dominate people lacking effective rights. When Woodbey told the story of slavery and abolitionist rebellion, he stressed that blacks were enslaved because a profit could be made from their labor, not because they were black. The new abolition boosted the poor of all colors and benefited nearly all people: "The workers of all colors now find themselves in need of another emancipation, from a condition of wage slavery which as completely robs them of the hundreds of millions of wealth produced by their labor as did chattel slavery." Woodbey put it as emphatically and categorically as Debs: Socialism was the only solution to the race problem. When workers attained control of the economy, "the race problem will be settled forever."[167]

Most of the Socialist Party leadership held back from the IWW when it was founded in 1905, fearing that it was too radical and that Daniel De Leon, a leading player in the founding, was an incorrigible divider. Woodbey took the Debs view that the dream of "one big union" was too precious not to try. This dream went back to the Knights of Labor of the 1870s and 1880s, which welcomed all workers excluding capitalists, lawyers, gamblers, and drunkards, pioneering the solidarity slogan as its motto: "An injury to one is the concern of all." The Knights had nearly one million members by 1886, but the organization was poorly managed and fell apart. The IWW "Wobblies" were the successors to the Knights and, in 1905, a radical alternative to the American Federation of Labor (AFL) led by Samuel Gompers. At the founding convention of the IWW in Chicago, Debs represented the left wing of the Socialist Party, along with Big Bill Haywood and *International Socialist Review* editor A. M. Simons. Other founders of the Wobblies included De Leon, trade unionist Mother Jones, and anarchist Lucy Parsons. The Wobblies were too unruly for much of the Socialist Party mainstream, including Socialist leaders holding stakes in the AFL. Some Socialists had fantasies about taking over the AFL, while others liked the place at the table they already held. Nearly all of them distrusted De Leon, a dogmatic sectarian who talked about "indoctrinating" workers.[168]

Debs couldn't stand De Leon either, but he was incredulous that much of the Socialist Party took no interest in building one big radical union. Berger, as editor of the *Social Democratic Herald,* filled the paper with denunciations of the IWW. Debs asked Berger how it could be that his paper had become "the official organ and special champion" of the sellout American Federation of Labor. For that matter, "Since when is it a condition of membership in the Socialist Party that one must belong to the AF of L?" The IWW offered Socialists an opportunity to redeem the dream of a revolutionary union—a movement to overthrow capitalism not divided by race, ethnicity, sex, craft, or nation. Berger epitomized the gas and water Socialists that wore the tag "Sewer Socialist" as a badge of honor and wanted to keep their privileged roles in the existing union movement. Debs had long held his nose at this type; now he put it sharply. The AFL was a "rotten" organization, he fumed, "but it is good enough for them, in fact just what they want, for a rotten labor movement is their salvation." Elsewhere he issued an either/or: "The choice is between the AF of L and capitalism on the one side and the Industrial Workers and Socialism on the other. How can a Socialist hesitate in his choice for an instant?"[169]

Woodbey had the same question for more reasons. Berger touted his ability to achieve progressive reforms by forging alliances with liberals, but Debs and Woodbey took no interest in reform movements to achieve limited objectives. Debs and Woodbey were the same kind of Socialist. The IWW was supposed to be a radical trade union, engaged in collective bargaining, and the Socialist Party was supposed to run for office, taking over the government. Even more than Debs, Woodbey pioneered the fight for free speech at the street level, which the Wobblies soon made famous. In 1908 Woodbey played a leading role in the Socialist Party's defiance of a San Francisco ordinance forbidding street meetings for nonreligious groups. Speakers were arrested and dragged off to jail, outstripping the city's capacity to jail and prosecute them. Woodbey told a reporter, "The police can't stop us. They can and do arrest us when we speak, but they can't stem the tide that has been started no more than they can the ocean. The more they ill treat us, the more Socialists there are." Liberals and labor groups flocked to the Socialists' defense, and the city council repealed the ordinance. Back on his soapbox, Woodbey told audiences that he knew how Wendell Phillips and Frederick Douglass felt: "The agitation is now going for the new emancipation, and the agitators are equally hated and despised."[170]

But the Wobblies veered away from collective bargaining and electoral politics. In the early going, they were strong in the western states, where the Western Federation of Miners belonged to the IWW. The Wobblies worked hard at organizing lumber workers and migratory harvesters. They became proficient at street theater, winning victories in municipal battles by filling jails, crowding court dockets, and draining city budgets. They clashed with governments at the city, state, and federal levels, garnering sensational publicity, which reinforced their proclivity for protest politics. Wobbly leaders Haywood, Elizabeth Gurley Flynn, and Frank Little personified the IWW's trademark blend of violent rhetoric, proud rebelliousness, physical courage, and commitment to nonviolent resistance. Debating their ideology, they settled on anarcho-syndicalism, contending that trade unions themselves should run the country. Then Haywood was imprisoned for fifteen months and the Wobblies lost the Western Federation of Miners.

Upon losing their anchor in ordinary trade unionism, the Wobblies tacked further into anarcho-syndicalist political nowhere. They spurned collective bargaining and dropped electoral politics, leaving Debs behind. Haywood urged that electoral politics was a waste of time for radicals. In 1908 the IWW dropped its last mention of electoral political action from the group's constitution and Debs quietly let his dues expire. In the past, when breaking from the Brotherhood of Locomotive Firemen or Social Democracy of America, Debs had felt obliged to issue a public statement. This was standard procedure on the left, a contribution to the quest for correct ideology and strategy. This time Debs issued no statement, still in love with the idea of the IWW and prizing his friendships there, especially with Haywood, who remained a Socialist Party leader. Debs could not bring himself to publicly criticize the IWW, but he could not abide its reckless romantic radicalism, which spurned the two pillars of radical politics. There was no substitute for a militant unionism that took up the grubby tasks of collective bargaining and there was no substitute for a militant Socialist Party that tried to convert ordinary Americans to Socialism.[71]

The issue of race was always there in Socialist debates about how to build a better radical movement. Debs and Haywood wanted to build a Socialist movement, nation, and world in which race did not matter. But the small organizations they formed were too foreign to black Americans to attract many members. The Socialists paid at both ends for taking an antiracist position that they tried not to talk about. Their vision of a color-blind world made no existential sense to people oppressed by racism. Moreover, the Socialists were stuck with the contradiction that their positions on gender, ethnicity, and race were decades ahead of the American population from which they sought votes. The Wobblies, seeing the contradiction, opted out of electoral politics, but the IWW fared only slightly better, in a few locales, at winning black supporters.

The Socialist Party advocated equal civil and political rights for men and women, in line with the policies of the Socialist International established at the founding conference of the Second International in 1889. Here there was a Marxist tradition to draw upon, beginning with Friedrich Engels's critique of the exploitation of women in *The Origin of the Family, Private, Property, and the State*. Debs was a stout defender of women's rights, boasting that the Socialist movement was the first to "pledge itself unqualifiedly" to abolish sexual discrimination in all areas bearing on "the rights, privileges and opportunities of civic and social life." The Socialist Party welcomed women into its ranks and established a Woman's National Committee comprised entirely of women. With greater angst the party also endorsed open immigration, holding off the Berger faction that paraded its white supremacism. The Socialist Party opposed xenophobia and anti-Semitism strongly enough to be stigmatized chiefly on this count. It welcomed large numbers of Jews, Slavs, and Italians to its Anglo-Saxon and German base, defying accusations that doing so made it anti-American. Berger, a Jewish immigrant from Nieder-Rehbach, Austria-Hungary, symbolized to many Americans that Socialism was foreign and Jewish, never mind that he zealously accommodated racial prejudices. Here again the party mainstream reflected the solidarity ethic of the Second International, and it had a quotable exemplar in Debs, who contended that any policy to exclude a specific racial or ethnic group was anathema.[172]

To be sure, the Socialist Party was not as feminist as its official position, and it struggled mightily with its ethnic inclusivity. The party of Debs said the same thing to women that it said to blacks: Socialism was the answer, with no special favors to anyone. Even the party's leading female activists, Kate Richards O'Hare and Lena Morrow Lewis, took this answer as axiomatic. But the Socialist Party did better with female and ethnic constituencies than it did with African Americans, because women and the new immigrants formed organizations demanding a place for themselves in the party and blacks did not. The Woman's National Committee developed organizations at the city and state levels that recruited women to the party and provided women-only spaces for them. These organizations revived numerous locals during the years that the party experienced its strongest growth. The new immigrants similarly formed semiautonomous organizations through which they related to the party and acted in it. By 1912, when Debs won nine hundred thousand votes, there were Finnish, Bohemian, Hungarian, Italian, Jewish, Polish, Scandinavian, South Slav, German, Slovak, and Polish federations in the Socialist Party, all carrying forward the languages and cultural traditions of European Socialism.[173]

Nothing comparable to these networks and federations existed within the black community that Socialist organizers might have tapped. There were no long-standing fraternal orders or cultural organizations in African American life that Socialist organizers might have converted to Socialist politics. To say the same thing from the other end, there was no black organization to join when an African American joined the Socialist Party. The Socialist Party had no organizational voice that spoke to black Americans. Although it welcomed black members, the party made no special efforts to recruit them, it did not assign organizers to black communities, and it published almost no literature specifically referring to racial justice. All it had was Woodbey's speaking tours and occasionally the speaking engagements of a Woodbey protégé such as George Slater Jr. Woodbey and Slater had come from the only black institution holding the potential to spark a movement demanding a new economic system—the church. But even Woodbey lost his congregation for talking too much about Socialism, and Slater was not as accomplished as Woodbey.[174]

In his later life Woodbey helped the Socialists and Wobblies work together, finding solidarity in protest, not ideology. In 1912 the IWW staged a fateful free-speech fight in San Diego after the Wobblies organized workers neglected by the AFL, and streetcar-franchise owner John Spreckels urged the city to abolish all speaking on soapbox row. The fight began immediately after the city banned all street speaking, even revival preaching, in January 1912. The Wobblies and the California Free Speech League spearheaded a resistance campaign joined by Socialists, Single Taxers, AFL unionists, and church groups. They filled the jails with speakers, the police were ferociously brutal, and local vigilantes were allowed to seize prisoners from the jails. The seized prisoners were escorted across the county line and warned not to return; those that returned got savage beatings. Woodbey was beaten several times at speaking events and in jail. The Free Speech League patrolled his home with armed guards to protect him from being killed. After four months of this battle, legendary anarchist Emma Goldman came to San Diego to give a speech, accompanied by her partner Ben Reitman. Reitman was captured, tortured with a lighted cigar, sexually assaulted, and tarred, while Goldman fled to Los Angeles. That was an omen of how this fight would end. The vigilante tactics defeated the Wobblies, convincing some to give up on nonviolent resistance. By the fall of 1912 soapbox row had been abandoned, and the Wobblies waited two years to return.[175]

Woodbey persisted to the end of his days, that we know of, speaking for the Socialist Party, running in 1914 as the party's candidate for state treasurer, and still listed as a pastor at Mount Zion Church. Philip S. Foner, the only scholar to give Woodbey his due, came up with nothing about Woodbey's last days after years of trying. We know nothing of his life after 1915. That year Woodbey published his last article, fittingly titled "Why the Socialists Must Reach the Churches with Their Message." American Socialists were never going to get anywhere if they did not reach the millions of working people who belonged to churches, Woodbey declared. Too many comrades tried to do it by attacking Christianity. Woodbey lamented that he had to spend much of his career in damage-control mode. It was self-destructive, plus factually wrong, for Socialists to claim that Socialism and Christianity were incompatible. Woodbey countered, "The Bible, in every line of it, is with the poor as against their oppressors." Everywhere that he had gone, Woodbey had to contend with a stupid debate between atheist Socialists and anti-Socialist Christians in which both sides failed or refused to see the social justice perspective of biblical faith.[176]

Woodbey had no solution except to bravely give witness, speaking as simply and clearly as he could, hoping to be heard. All he could do was preach the next sermon and head to the next town. He did not talk about things that distracted from the simple aim of converting his audiences to Christian Socialism. He did not cite Du Bois or any Christian Socialist to seal his points. In his later work he did not cite any authors, even Marx. The only authority to which he appealed was the Bible. To the extent that he had a model, it was Debs, but Woodbey was an accomplished speaker and political activist before Debs converted him to

Socialism. Woodbey did not reflect on himself or the structural obstacles to success, at least in public. He did not believe that he had failed. He knew that Socialism was new and growing and that he could not have worked harder to spread it.

Hubert Henry Harrison, born in Concordia, Danish West Indies (later St. Croix, U.S. Virgin Islands) had an early career as a soapbox speaker for the Socialist Party in Harlem before he struck out on his own, frustrated by the party's racial blinders and Marxist dogmatism. In his early career Harrison carried on Woodbey's work, striking with the Wobblies and silk workers in Paterson, New Jersey, in 1912–1913. He organized for the Socialist Party in Harlem until he got fed up with being paid less and treated worse than other organizers. In 1917 Harrison founded a race-first Socialist organization, the Liberty League of Afro-Americans, forging alliances with A. Philip Randolph and Chandler Owen. Upon launching the Liberty League, Harrison provided an audience for Garvey, whom he soon turned against, and edited the *Negro World*, espousing a blend of black nationalism and Socialist universalism that anticipated Du Bois's trajectory. In his later career Harrison specialized in Woodbey-like soapbox performances at Wall Street and Madison Square, holding forth on a wider range of subjects than Woodbey would have considered appropriate. Throughout his career Harrison wrote for radical publications such as the *New York Call*, *Modern Quarterly*, *International Socialist Review*, and the *Masses*.[177]

Harrison was more reflective than Woodbey about the work they shared. In 1911 he mused in the *Call* that interracial interactions were often awkwardly self-conscious. How should one act upon encountering "strange people"? Barbarians of every color treated the other as inferior, Harrison noted. Garden-variety racists acted on their prejudices, with or without acknowledgment. The "truly civilized" treated others frankly as human beings with no special self-consciousness about doing so. Harrison offered a gentle word of counsel to white Socialists. Often they told him, "I have always been friendly with colored people." Sometimes they claimed, "I have never felt any prejudice against Negroes." Du Bois, noting that whites often introduced themselves in this way, did not pause over their implicit plea, "Please do not assume that I am a racist." Harrison did pause, acknowledging that petitions of this sort often carried good intentions and some were even true. But they were "wholly unnecessary," he said, plus embarrassing: "If your heart be in the right place, and this is assumed at the start, it will appear in your actions. No special kindness and no condescension is either needed or expected. Treat them simply as human beings, as if you had never looked at the color of their faces. It is wonderful but true that what people will be to you depends very largely upon what you are to them."[178]

He tried in that spirit to help white Socialists grasp the reality and significance of the color line. Often they told him, "Socialism is the same for all people—women, Finns, Negroes and all." Harrison agreed, with a caveat: "But the minds of all these are not the same and are not to be approached in the same way." Black Americans lived behind the color line, he explained, "where none of these social movements have come to him." The few efforts to reach African Americans where they lived "broke down as soon as they had to cross the color line." This history made black Americans more difficult to reach with the Socialist message than was the case with women or Finns. It was "really a special work" to make Socialism make sense to blacks. Harrison told a story about distributing Slater's pamphlet, *The Colored Man's Case as Socialism Sees It*, in New York. It was hard to get street crowds to read anything, but the title of Slater's pamphlet broke through: "We would take one of these pamphlets and hold it so that the title showed plainly and walk up to a colored man with it. As soon as his eyes fell on the words, 'Colored Man's Case,' his attention was arrested." Harrison found that even Republican and Democratic Party hacks were eager to read Slater's pamphlet, based on the title alone. After all, they had to figure out how to appeal to the "strange people" on the other side of the color line.[179]

White and black Socialists had to acquire "special equipment" for this work, Harrison urged: "One must know the people, their history, their manner of life, and modes of thinking and feeling. You have to know the psychology of the Negro, for if you don't you will fail to attract or impress him. You will fail to make him think—and feel. For many of your arguments must be addressed to his heart as well as to his head. This is more true of him than of most other American groups." The Socialists had to try harder, giving higher priority to enlisting black members, which began with hiring black organizers. Debs told reporters that the Socialists had three or four paid black national organizers, but Harrison could think of only one, Woodbey. Woodbey had been "very effective," Harrison acknowledged, but he was only one person and could cover only so much territory. The party needed a bunch of Woodbeys, and it needed to try harder in Afro-American communities whether or not it found successors to Woodbey. Harrison had a parting question: "Does the Socialist Party feel that it needs the Negroes as much as the Negro needs Socialism?" If Socialist leaders believed they could overthrow capitalism "with one part of the proletariat against us," they needed to say so. Harrison could not believe they believed that, even though their actions said so. The Socialist project could not succeed if it left the black proletariat behind, he urged. Surely they agreed on that: "Let us act, then, in the light of this knowledge and add to the strength of the organized, all inclusive class conscious working class movement."[180]

As it was, the white Socialists remained clueless about black communities and only half-interested in organizing within them. Slater won a following through his columns in the *Chicago Daily Socialist*, popularizing the concept that Socialists were "the New Abolitionists." He told readers that he had lurched from one political project to another, briefly holding out for Teddy Roosevelt trust-busting, until he heard Woodbey speak in 1908. He lauded Woodbey for converting him to the "purity, simplicity, and justice" of Christian Socialism, which held "the solution of the more serious phases of the so-called race problem." Debs, in turn, praised Slater as "a fine example of the educated, wide-awake teacher, of his race, whose whole heart is in the work and who ought to be encouraged in every possible way to spread the light among the masses." But Slater did not acquire Woodbey's command of his subject nor command lecture audiences in Woodbey's fashion, and he fixated on proving that Abraham Lincoln was a Socialist. He never criticized the Socialist Party for its failings in black communities, which won him plaudits from white Socialist leaders but no progress on what mattered.[181]

Slater spent the years 1912–1919 serving as pastor of Bethel African Church in Clinton, Iowa, writing and speaking in forums sponsored by the Christian Socialist Fellowship and its magazine, the *Christian Socialist*. In 1913 he summarized his career as Woodbey's protégé, speaking as one who, like Woodbey, had worked "not a little among my people." Slater had three conclusions: (1) black Americans were "very much prejudiced against the word Socialism"; (2) blacks were "quite susceptible to the doctrines of the Cooperative Commonwealth"; (3) blacks readily took an interest in the cooperative commonwealth as soon as someone explained it clearly. Like Woodbey, Slater had a preacher's relationship to his audience and a preacher's concept of activism: Keep the faith and deliver the next sermon. He kept telling himself that Afro-Americans simply needed more exposure to the vision of a cooperative commonwealth.[182]

But that did not happen after Woodbey and Slater were gone, for reasons that Harrison grasped. The Socialists were already perceived as being dangerously pro-Negro politically, even as they tried not to talk about race and made little effort to acquire black members. Organizing African Americans sank to a lower priority after World War I traumatized and divided the party, eventually rendering it a shattered wreck, with Debs consigned to a federal prison in Atlanta for opposing the war. The Baptist preachers of Socialist universality moved as far as possible from the ecclesiastical separatism of Burroughs and Morris, and they stifled a sneer at the civil rights liberalism of Powell and the NAACP, which did important work but never got to the root problem. Woodbey did not say that Afro-Americans needed to build up their own organizations before they could make an impact on the political left. He could not say that, since he preached the Debsian gospel that Socialism was the solution to every social problem. It must have occurred to him, however, noticing the advantages that the cultural federations and women's groups had over him, that going for the ultimate global solution without a home of one's own had taken him to a lonely place. Du Bois warded off a similar loneliness while opting for Socialist salvation.

7

RESISTANCE AND ANTICIPATION

This book ends with the last important founder and a strong anticipation of the explosion to come. The early black social gospel leaders did not build a movement, they did not take over the churches, they made little impact on the Socialist movement, and they provided only modest ballast for the NAACP. But they started something new. They fought to abolish Jim Crow, lynching, and economic injustice. They established that progressive theology could be combined with social justice politics in a black church context. They built up black Christian communities and urged them to welcome the migrant stranger. They refuted the racist culture that demeaned their human dignity and equality. They paved the way for something stupendous. And they legitimized what they started, sometimes achieving national influence as leaders in the ecclesiastical realm, scholarship, business, journalism, academic administration, or social activism, or, in the case of Richard R. Wright Jr., all six.

The leading black social gospelers of the 1920s — Ransom, Burroughs, Powell, and Wright, plus upcoming Mordecai Johnson — had national ministries and were religious intellectuals. But Ransom, Burroughs, and Powell lacked the requisite training and interest to be scholars. They exercised their influence in and through religious communities and the outreach ministries of the church. The academy was not in play for them as a site of discourse and influence. For them, the available public audiences were the churches and the reading and lecture-going general black public, although Powell did a bit of teaching at Colgate University and Union Theological Seminary.

The pioneer of the rise of the academics was Wright, although he too spent most of his career in the public and ecclesiastical ministries of the church. In Wright's time a surge of social gospel leaders earned graduate degrees in the social sciences or theology or both. They included Johnson, George Edmund Haynes, Monroe Work, Vernon Johns, Kelly Miller, James Farmer Sr., Benjamin E. Mays, and Howard Thurman. These religious intellectuals shared with Du Bois life stories of advancement through academic achievement and public intellectual scholarship. Many of them produced works of theological and sociological scholarship that supported the new abolition. They refused to give up on the black churches, even as a rising tide of black intellectuals contended that black churches were hopelessly self-centered, provincial, insular, anti-intellectual, and conservative.[1]

Many intellectual stars of the Harlem Renaissance and Howard University rendered the latter judgment, notably Countee Cullen, E. Franklin Frazier, and Rayford W. Logan.[2] The social gospelers countered that Christian faith, critical rationality, and civil rights advocacy went together, or at least needed to do so. They drew on their training in white universities to make this argument, which slowed the growth of the black social gospel. Every black social gospeler experienced this double bind. To stick with old-style black church religion was provincial and conservative; to drink deeply from progressive white culture was to risk losing one's religious home. Du Bois was not very helpful in this regard, because he spurned churchgoing religion—for himself—shortly after he learned about Hegel and biblical criticism.

In white social gospel circles, religious leaders took for granted their responsibility and ability to address audiences in the church, academy, and general public. Even the stalwarts of the radical, anti-imperial, Socialist wing of the white social gospel—Harry Ward, George Coe, Vida Scudder, Kirby Page—assumed that their mission was to transform American society and culture in the light of normative Christian values. This presumption reigned in white Protestant ethics long after American Catholics belatedly produced their own tradition of social Christianity and long after Reinhold Niebuhr ended the reign of social gospel idealism in the leading seminaries and divinity schools. White American Protestantism, in its social gospel and Niebuhrian versions, comfortably referred to American society as "we," carrying on the custodial presumptions of what came to be called the "mainline" Protestant churches.[3]

The black intellectuals trained in Progressive Era theology and sociology could not assume access to the academy or general public, and some had uneasy relationships with their religious communities. Their expertise about Afro-American life was of little interest to the white public, and their expertise about anything else was of no interest to the white public. Under this circumstance, the black social gospel was remarkably successful at producing intellectual leaders and public intellectuals, especially in the social sciences. They got their academic bearings by fusing sociology, social ethics, and social gospel theology, in the manner taught at the University of Chicago, Union Theological Seminary, Boston University, Harvard University, Rochester Theological Seminary, Oberlin College, Howard University, Morehouse College, and other bellwether academic institutions. They had bigger problems to address than their personal double binds. They believed in the power of the gospel to change individuals and society. They believed in the power of the new social sciences to refute the racist culture of denigration. And they believed that social science combined with prophetic religion had a chance to build a commonwealth of freedom in American society and the world.

Some belonged to the generation succeeding Ransom and Du Bois and are thus, for me, subjects of a book to come. But this book ends with the last important black social gospeler of the Ransom and Du Bois generation—Richard R. Wright Jr. In his long and extraordinary career, Wright epitomized a mainstream version of the black social gospel in the AME Church as a minister, theologian, sociologist, church newspaper editor, social activist, real estate baron, banker, and bishop. He epitomized the civil rights intellectual that grew up in the South, earned graduate degrees in the North, fused the social sciences to the social gospel, and enlisted the church in the civil rights and ecumenical movements.

When Wright described himself he played up his affinities with Du Bois as a sociological scholar of black urban life and an advocate of black self-determination. He called Du Bois "my hero of many years." He appropriated the veil image, calling it "the black curtain." He experienced the controversy over higher education before Du Bois pressed it against Washington. He used his professional training in sociology as a tool for black progress. And he followed Du Bois into the Niagara Movement and the NAACP.[4]

But Wright also differed from Du Bois in important ways. Wright was a stalwart ally of the poor southern blacks who poured into the North in search of a better life. He refuted the stereotypes about black life that Du Bois sometimes recycled. Though Wright had a brief career as an academic, he answered to higher callings in the church and society. He advocated self-help and economic development with Booker-like fervor, practicing what he preached. He achieved greater success in business than any black social gospel leader. And he ascended to a bishop's chair, exuding an unabashed love of the AME Church despite hating its church politics. Wright wanted desperately to shred the black curtain, even as he prized the walled-off spiritual home that supported him in fighting it.

RICHARD R. WRIGHT JR. AND THE BLACK CURTAIN

By upbringing, Wright inherited Afro-Saxon religion, and by education, he came into liberal theology and the social gospel. He grew up in the shadow of a formidable father, eventually earning no entry in the *Dictionary of American Negro Biography*, where his father got two pages. During the period that liberal theology and the social gospel took over the elite seminaries and divinity schools, Wright earned graduate degrees and transmitted social gospel progressivism to the AME Church. Throughout his career, even as a bishop, he had to bear lecture introductions that mistakenly referenced aspects of his father's biography. He claimed not to mind, but he usually reminded audiences that he was the first Wright and the first black American to earn a Ph.D. in sociology.[5]

He was born in Cuthbert, Georgia, in 1878. Wright's mother, Lydia, was a high-achieving student from a prosperous family when she married fellow Atlanta University student Richard R. Wright Sr. in 1876. Her husband was valedictorian of Atlanta University's first collegiate class that year, having already lived a dramatic story. Richard R. Wright Sr. was sold at an auction in Dalton, Georgia, in 1859 when he was approximately three years old. After the Civil War he followed Sherman's army on the march from Atlanta to the sea, settling in Cuthbert in 1866 along with his mother and two siblings. The American Missionary Association, however, established the Storrs School in a freight car in Atlanta, so Wright's mother hauled the children back to Atlanta, over three hundred miles, where young Wright met Union Army general Oliver O. Howard, head of the Freedmen's Bureau. Howard had lost an arm in the war, and he spoke at Storrs with feeling. He asked the children if they had a message for their friends up North. There was a brief silence, until young Wright spoke up: "Massa, tell them we are rising." Howard was so touched by this statement that he told the story everywhere he went. "We are rising" became the motto of the Freedmen's Bureau and the theme of countless sermons and addresses. It was immortalized in Quaker abolitionist John Greenleaf Whittier's poem, "Howard at Atlanta," and a century later Richard R. Wright Jr. had to explain to audiences that this story was about his father, not him, as he was not around for the Civil War.[6]

Richard R. Wright Sr. went on to become a prominent educator, editor, Republican activist, and eventually a banker. He studied at Atlanta University during its hopeful founding, before hostile white neighbors segregated everything. In 1878, when his son Richard was born, the elder Wright organized the Georgia State Teachers Association, served as its first president, launched a newspaper, the *Weekly Journal of Progress*, and served as principal of an

American Missionary Association school in Cuthbert, Howard Normal School. The following year he plunged into Republican politics and the Kansas migration movement, representing Georgia blacks at the First National Conference of Colored Men of the United States, in Nashville, Tennessee. A year later he founded Georgia's first public high school for blacks, Ware High School in Augusta. In 1891, after a stormy debate in the state legislature about higher education for blacks, Wright was appointed founding president of Georgia State College of Industry for Colored Youth, in Savannah. There he presided for thirty years, while accepting from President McKinley an appointment as paymaster in the U.S. Army with the rank of major.[7]

Richard Wright Jr. thus grew up in Augusta and Savannah, acquiring his education in segregated communities where his father was revered. He avoided white people and deferred to them whenever he could not avoid them. He lived in neighborhoods that the city government ignored, where blacks policed themselves and put out their own fires. Neighbors told Wright that God had cursed the black race, whites were created to rule over blacks, and the Bible was clear on this subject. As far as he could tell, nobody held a different view.

Wright's Afro-Saxon parents treasured their connection to Atlanta University, in their telling an oasis of New England Puritanism. They attended the AME Church but spurned its revivalism, telling their children that God wanted them to be good, not emotional. Whippings were commonplace at home and at school, although Wright got few at school. In every way he strove to make his parents proud of him, embracing their plan for him: Excel at school, be a good Christian, earn a college degree at Atlanta University, and aim for a graduate degree up North, preferably at Harvard or Yale. John Hope was a role model, having grown up in Augusta and graduated from Brown University. William Scarborough was a role model from the elder Wright's generation, having written a Greek textbook, which defied prevailing dogmas about the capabilities of Afro-Americans. Wright acquired another role model during his college sophomore year, when his father told him that somebody named William E. Burghardt Du Bois would soon complete a Ph.D. at Harvard.

The state legislature of Georgia, however, disrupted the family plan by cutting off funding for Atlanta University. The state punished university officials for admitting white students and teaching classical languages to black students, which threw the state out of compliance with the Morrill Act, creating a dilemma for Georgia politicians. They were against higher learning for blacks but very keen to get land grant money from the federal government. That led to the founding of Georgia State College in 1891, where Wright's father taught Latin and Greek in addition to running the school. The following year Wright enrolled as a student, taking courses in carpentry, blacksmithing, and brick-laying, while argument raged over the right of blacks to learn academic subjects. As the son of a Latin and Greek professor, Wright puzzled over the notion that African Americans could not learn Latin or Greek. The state education commission came out against classics and higher mathematics for blacks, throwing Georgia State College into a crisis. Wright watched his father beg students not to leave the college. The elder Wright and his faculty colleagues saved the school by teaching classics as extracurricular activities in their homes. Ultimately they prevailed in court, restoring an academic component at the college, where Wright graduated in 1898. Higher education, as a justice issue, was deeply personal to Wright.[8]

He absorbed his father's Republicanism as a youth, learning that Democrats wanted to put African Americans back into slavery. There was no talk of economic issues until Booker Washington became famous; politics was exclusively about politics. Religion weighed more heavily on Wright. In his community there were only two categories religiously—sinners and Christians. Methodists said there was such a thing as backsliding, and Baptists said that no truly converted person fell away from the faith. They agreed, however, that to be saved, one had to be born again. Even Wright's Puritan parents believed that. For two years Wright attended every revival that came along, approaching the mourners' bench at Methodist revivals and the anxious seat at Baptist revivals, unsuccessfully. Something prevented him from feeling saved. Repeatedly he confessed his sins and gave himself to God but failed to come through, feeling nothing. Preachers told him that he held back something in his heart. Wright fretted over this situation until the age of twelve, when he broke through at a revival in Augusta. He ran home joyously to tell his mother, who declared that God had answered her prayer. Young people usually skipped school for several days after getting saved, emoting joyously. Wright went to school the next day, winning the prize that he wanted—his father's commendation for upholding his duties. Wright Senior added that now his son had a duty to bring his sibling brothers and sisters to Christ.[9]

Having been raised to leave the South, Wright was vaguely aware that he was sheltered by segregation and privilege. Shortly after graduating from Georgia State College, he headed for the University of Chicago Divinity School. Wright had never had a real conversation with a white person or ventured into the North. It struck him, crossing into Indiana, that nearly everybody was white and that people on the train did not speak to each other. In Georgia everybody greeted everybody else, bantering politely. Here there was silence that felt unfriendly. Wright saw something that astonished him—work crews made up of white laborers. He had not imagined that whites anywhere labored with pick and shovel, acting like African Americans, doing manual labor with no blacks to help them: "The whole situation seemed unnatural; I felt that there must be a mistake."[10]

In Chicago he found his way to the university, where a white janitor insisted incredibly that he was "Dan," not "Mister Dan," and that Wright was the mister, being a university student. Wright later recalled, "Was it not a strange world after all!" When classes began Wright discovered that the divinity school had about thirty black students, including John Hope. That was misleading, however, as most were teachers or professors who studied at Chicago during the summer quarter. The rest of the year, the divinity school had three black students and twenty-three hundred white students. Wright befriended Monroe Work, an Afro-American student from Kansas twelve years older than Wright, who moved into Divinity Hall at the same time as Wright. Work was there to study at Chicago Theological Seminary, a nearby Congregational seminary closely associated with the University of Chicago Divinity School and sociology department. Wright also tried to befriend a black student from Augusta, but inadvertently chased him away. The student was passing for white and promptly left the divinity school.[11]

Chicago, at every turn, was a culture shock for Wright. He exulted with amazement at being asked to teach Greek to white students, making the highest wage (fifty cents per hour) he had ever received. He blanched at being encouraged to disagree with white classmates but tried to do it. According to Wright, during the nine quarters of study for his first degree at the divinity school, he met only one person, a student, who exhibited any racial prejudice toward him. Had he sought much of a social life in Hyde Park, he would have encountered more racism. As it was he studied hard; worked as a waiter, janitor, and tutor; and assured his parents emphatically that things were much better for African Americans in the North, at least in educated circles. By then his father had a new title and position by which Wright and everyone else subsequently called him: "the Major."

At Chicago Wright worked mostly under three professors: William Rainey Harper, Ernest DeWitt Burton, and Shailer Mathews. Harper was the university's founding president and an accomplished Old Testament scholar; Burton was a prominent New Testament scholar, who later became the university's third president. Wright marveled at their vast knowledge and the fact that he was comfortable with them. Harper and Burton taught Wright the higher critical approach to the Bible, which troubled him. How could he be a minister after learning to deconstruct the literary history of the biblical text? For a while Wright despaired that divinity school was destroying his faith. Mathews, who later moved from New Testament to theology, became the special teacher in Wright's life by befriending him, training him in modern scholarship, and assuring him that neither of them had lost his Christian faith. Mathews told Wright that Christianity had no future if it did not face up to modern science and historical criticism. Learning modern theology was an act of faithfulness to the gospel, as the church needed ministers who understood modern thought.

"I loved Mathews," Wright later recalled. "He was a friend; he never talked down to me. He just seemed to have a special interest in me." Wright ate meals with Mathews and surprised himself by not feeling awkward or self-conscious. He puzzled that Mathews, despite coming from New England and knowing few African Americans, seemed to have no racial bias. Wright was "thrilled" by Mathews's rendering of the social gospel. Mathews had compelling, scholarly, and assuring answers to Wright's questions, always taking the questions seriously. At the time, Mathews was struggling to decide what he believed about the trend in German scholarship emphasizing the apocalyptic mentality of early Christianity. Years later, knowing how this debate turned out, Wright allowed that Mathews may have exaggerated the social ethical side of Jesus's teaching during the period that Wright studied under him. Nonetheless, Mathews had a detailed grasp of modern scholarship and a buoyant faith: "He wrought a revolution in my thinking. . . . He was introducing me to a concept of Jesus for which I had been for years searching unconsciously."[12]

Mathews taught Wright to see religion through the second commandment—neighbor love—and the love ethic of Jesus. Wright later recalled that he had no concept of social Christianity or social anything before he entered divinity school: "Brought up as I had been, with a theology which took little account of social conditions and concerned itself chiefly with 'getting to heaven,' I found in the social gospel a more satisfying meaning and purpose for Christianity than ever before. The more I studied the Bible, and indeed the history of my own church, the more enthusiastic I became about the social gospel." Social Christianity was not a throwback to works righteousness, Wright reasoned. It was "the necessary outflow of the spirit of Jesus." The black church at its best advocated the social ethical core of the gospel. Even in its provincial and otherworldly forms it gave witness to the gospel principle of human equality under God. For Wright, the social gospel recovered the relevance of the kingdom social ethic of Jesus for the modern world: "For me there was little else for the church to do than to make practical its belief in God and brotherhood, and to help build a Christian society on earth."[13]

Wright shared this conviction with Work, who quickly made a decision about his vocational path, which Wright pondered and resisted. Work had gotten a late start in higher education. His parents had moved from Cairo, Illinois, to Sumner County, Kansas, to take advantage of the Homestead Act, becoming independent farmers. Work wanted to attend high school, but his older siblings moved away, leaving him to care for his aging parents and the family farm. He was twenty-three years old before he began high school, in Arkansas City in 1889. Work struggled at first, but a supportive high school principal, David Ross Boyd (later the University of Oklahoma's first president), helped him to push through; along the way, Work discovered his talent for mathematics. Work later ministered at an AME Church in Wellington, Kansas, which didn't work out, as he had a stolid personality that made him a boring preacher. The congregation fired him, Work went back to farming for a while, and he took a job delivering cattle to Chicago's meatpacking companies, which at least got him to Chicago and thinking again about higher education. Work reasoned that if he earned a seminary degree, he might be able to reenter the ministry as an intellectual preacher. On that basis he enrolled at Chicago Theological Seminary in the summer of 1898.[14]

Chicago Theological Seminary shared with the University of Chicago a historic commitment to sociology as a discipline. The university was a Baptist institution founded in 1892 in the spirit of Harper's liberal Christian modernism. At its founding, the university also founded the nation's first independent sociology department, chaired by Albion W. Small, a Baptist minister and longtime friend of Mathews. Meanwhile Chicago Theological Seminary founded the nation's first seminary department of Christian sociology, also in 1892. Graham Taylor, an indefatigable social activist and settlement movement pioneer, had the founding role for sociology at the seminary. Small, Taylor, and Mathews blended a sociohistorical version of sociological positivism with social gospel theology. Through them, the departments of sociology at both institutions and the divinity school worked closely together, and Taylor subsequently taught for three years in the university sociology department.[15]

Work had barely begun studying at the seminary when Taylor convinced him that sociology was more interesting and relevant than theology. Work majored in Christian sociology, earning a bachelor of divinity degree in 1901. Then he enrolled in the sociology department at the university, earning a master's degree in 1903. At the university Work studied under Small and William I. Thomas, adopting Thomas's research agenda in folk psychology. It helped that Thomas had influenced Du Bois just before Du Bois versus Washington became the issue. Work published his first article—on black crime in Chicago—and aligned himself with Du Bois. Later he developed an equally close collegial relationship with Washington. Work began his sociological career at Georgia State College, teaching under Wright's father. Later he became a charter member of the Niagara Movement, founded the department of records and research at Tuskegee Institute, compiled annual encyclopedias of the black experience, and compiled a massive bibliography of references to blacks.[16]

Work had a laundry business, which Wright helped him maintain; he took Wright to Ransom's Institutional Church, and he was a peer model for Wright. In 1900 Wright served as Ransom's student assistant, getting his first taste of social gospel ministry. Work and Wright toured black churches together and attended parties at the homes of prominent Chicago blacks, showing off their learning as requested. But Wright resisted the decision that Work had already made, lifting sociology over theology. Wright wanted to be a theologian who used sociology, not the other way around. He majored in biblical theology and minored in sociology, although he wrote his bachelor of divinity thesis on the industrial conditions of African Americans in Chicago. Wright dreamed of studying theology and biblical criticism at Edinburgh. Mathews, however, told him not to settle for Scotland, as Germany had the greatest scholars. Specifically, Berlin had the greatest scholars, Adolf von Harnack and Bernhard Weiss. That settled the issue for Wright. In 1901 he completed his divinity degree at Chicago and joined the faculty at Payne Theological Seminary (Wilberforce), where he taught Hebrew and Greek for two years, all the while preparing for Germany by learning German.[17]

Payne Seminary was depressing for Wright, because his students did not learn Hebrew. For them it was enough to fake Hebrew and Greek so they could impress their congregations. Wright allowed that his own Hebrew was still meager, but at least he worked at it. He pleaded with officials at Wilberforce to end the sham of teaching Hebrew, to no avail. He also made lifelong friends at Payne and Wilberforce, with students who were close to his age. By 1903 he was ready for Berlin, where he studied under Weiss, Julius Kaftan, and Otto Pfleiderer. Wright absorbed Weiss's "wonderful power and keen insight," Kaftan's systematic rendering of Ritschlian school theology, and Pfleiderer's insightful lectures on Pauline theology. All were impressive, but nobody compared to Harnack, whose commanding lectures on early Christianity attracted huge audiences and who welcomed Wright to his home for meals. In Wright's telling, Harnack was unfailingly gracious and friendly toward him. More important, Harnack was like Mathews in combining personal kindness and reverence with a critical approach to theological scholarship. That was the ideal, Wright decided. If he was going to be a theologian, he wanted to be like Mathews and Harnack.[18]

Wright had the Du Bois experience of feeling liberated in Germany. He later recalled that studying in Germany "was epoch-making in my life." Growing up in the South, he had acquired a slew of deferential habits, never asserting himself with white people. Even in Chicago he evaded questions and routinely deferred to whites, by then unconsciously. In Germany the students teased him into consciousness, making him recognize his habits. He tried to explain how he had gotten this way, which helped him realize how much he still deferred. German women invited him out for dates, something unthinkable in America. Wright, feeling chastened and liberated at the same time, let go of obsequious habits, declining to speak English. He also resolved to marry his love interest, Lottie Crogman, when he returned to the United States, although that took six years to happen. Crogman taught Latin and Greek at her alma mater, Clark College in Atlanta, where her father, William Henry Crogman, taught classics and in 1903 became president. For Wright, Germany was a turning point: "I forgot American prejudice, for even the Americans in Germany treated me as a human being."[19]

Returning to Chicago, Wright wrote a master's thesis on the historicity of the New Testament book of Acts, expecting to go on for a doctorate in New Testament. But friends at Institutional Church wanted him to join them after Ransom was booted out, which got Wright thinking about ministry. He told Bishop Shaffer that he would accept a call anywhere in Chicago. Shaffer had just gotten rid of Ransom, but he did not hold Ransom against Wright. He sent Wright to a storefront church on West Eighteenth Street, Trinity Mission Church, where Wright launched a Ransom-style social ministry modeled on Institutional Church. The church's neighborhood was a bleak area rife with prostitution and gambling. Wright's building was a shambles, nobody came to his first service, there were troublesome renters upstairs, and the church owed back rent. There he changed his mind about what to do with his life.

Wright had barely arrived at Trinity Church when he began to map out his location, charting an area four blocks long in each direction. At first he just wanted to understand what he was dealing with. On some streets, over half the buildings were prostitution houses, and many others were saloons or gambling joints. The best-paying jobs in his neighborhood, Wright found, revolved around prostitution, gambling, and the saloon business. But the majority of his neighbors worked as maids, waiters, handymen, and domestic servants—people who were "just poor and made great effort to be decent." Many were recent immigrants from Mississippi, Tennessee, and Kentucky. The better-off black churches had already moved out, but some of Chicago's richest families and white congregations remained in Wright's neighborhood, holding on to grand

buildings. Wright reached out to his "decent" neighbors and welcomed whom-
ever walked in. He charted the area in great detail and befriended Jane Addams,
Mary McDowell, and Celia Parker Wooley, who told him he was on the right
track. He showed his chart to civic leaders, who found it fascinating. He worked
hard to build up the church and succeeded for a while, even though congregants told him that he was not much of a preacher. Good preachers got the
crowd to shout and emote; Wright gave earnest sermons featuring biblical exposition and no dramatics.[20]

Wright had almost no previous experience with people at the low end of the
economic scale. Having been raised for Harvard or Yale, he knew that he was
very good at school. His ministry at Trinity Church taught him something
else—he was good at organizing things, and he had the requisite feeling for
ministering to the poor and hurting. He built up the church by preaching a
simple gospel of personal redemption, later recalling that he learned "for the
first time in my life what a lost soul is, and the necessity of God's love in the
human heart and the community's life." The church outgrew its storefront
space, so Wright bought the entire building, enlisting Mathews's lawyer as a
cosigner. Conducting a house-to-house canvass, Wright shuddered at seeing
children taking care of children, so he opened a nursery on the second floor,
the neighborhood's greatest need. He also launched a women's club, a men's
association, a bathhouse, and a correspondence bureau, concentrating on the
needs of illiterate migrants. He asked Shaffer and other AME colleagues to
support the mission but was turned down, a fateful blow. Wright's ministry at
Trinity Church lasted less than a year, and he was forced to shut it down, a sad
ending he obscured in his glowing account of this episode. His conviction that
AME churches had to overcome their mixture of ambivalence and hostility
toward southern migrants took root during his brief run at the mission. Years
later, Wright reflected that his greatest convert in Chicago was him. At Trinity
he experienced "the practical value of the redemptive love of Jesus" like never
before. He found his vocation by confronting "the degradation of humanity in
the uphill fight against social conditions."[21]

It helped that he met Du Bois in the summer of 1905, although Wright gave
a confusing account of what happened. In Wright's telling, he met many
up-and-comers at the Sunday Club at Ransom's church, the club divided
sharply over *The Souls of Black Folk*, Wright was deeply involved in the discussion, Ransom and the group invited Du Bois to Chicago, and Du Bois came for
three days of discussion. On the third day Du Bois convened a meeting with
Wright and others at Charles Bentley's home, which launched the Niagara
Movement. This account got most of the facts right, but it confusedly folded

Wright's description of meeting Du Bois into his account of working under Ransom at Institutional Church. That forced readers to sort out the chronology on their own: Wright worked for Ransom in 1900–1901; the book came out in 1903, shortly before Wright left for Germany; the Sunday Club debate was still brewing when Wright returned from Germany; the invitation to Du Bois must have gone out in 1904, before Ransom left Chicago that year; and the visit occurred in 1905. Although Wright wobbled a bit in telling the story, he was clear about the key thing: From the beginning of the controversy with Washington, Wright considered himself a camp follower of Du Bois, because Du Bois championed black dignity, ability, and freedom. For the rest of his life Wright regretted that he missed the Niagara Conference for lack of bus fare. He attended subsequent Niagara meetings and followed Du Bois into the NAACP.[22]

Wright was already reconsidering his priorities when Du Bois came to Chicago. Higher criticism played little role in his mission church ministry, but sociology played a central role. Academically, sociology had loomed large for him during his studies at Chicago. Now he rethought his vocation: "Now I saw plainly that the church must devote more time to the social without of course neglecting the theological." Albion Small, preaching on John 10:10, interpreted Christ's "more abundant life" to include physical health, education, wages, artistic appreciation, and leisure enjoyment, not only spiritual health. Listening to Small, Wright had a convicting moment: "Now that my work every day put me right up against practical social problems, I decided to devote more time to the study of that side of church work."[23]

In 1905 he wrote an article on the Teamsters' strike for *Charities Magazine*. A former Chicago classmate, Frances Keller, noticing the article, told Wright that the University of Pennsylvania had a fellowship in sociology for someone to carry on Du Bois's work on blacks in Philadelphia. Wright applied and was accepted, arriving in Philadelphia in September, where he spent two years as a research fellow and twenty-five years as a church leader and social gospel sociologist.[24]

The fellowship was linked to the Eighth Ward Social Settlement headed by Frances P. Bartholomew, which Wright joined, although he lived around the corner, as the settlement residents were white women. There he became involved in reform movements to improve social conditions. W. W. Frazier, a sugar magnate, funded the settlement and Wright's fellowship. A kindly paternalist, Frazier could turn morose when sugar was down. Settlement staffers waited until sugar was up before pitching proposals to him. Wright dreamed of a building-and-loan association that helped black neighbors buy homes. He pitched the idea to Frazier, who went along despite believing that the Eighth

Ward Settlement Building and Loan Association would not succeed. Wright made sure it succeeded by serving as the bank's president from 1906 to 1918. On Frazier's insistence, Wright hired no lawyers in the early years, accepting Frazier's verdict that lawyers were parasites who dreamed up ways to drain their clients. If he followed the rules, Wright reasoned, thinking like Frazier and the Major, he should not need any lawyers. Wright's success at growing the bank gave him cachet with white and black civic leaders. He played a leading role in a new organization that dealt with workplace issues, the Industrial Improvement Work, funded by the Armstrong Association of Philadelphia, although his boss at Armstrong did not like Wright's banking venture. This group later became the first affiliated unit of the National Urban League. Meanwhile Wright helped to conduct one of the nation's first large urban surveys, the Pittsburgh Survey; he worked with Du Bois and Work to study economic conditions in Lowndes County, Alabama; and in 1908 he studied Afro-American church communities across the northern United States for the U.S. Census Bureau.[25]

By then Wright was enrolled in Penn's doctoral program in sociology, where he had a complicated friendship with his academic advisor, sociologist Carl Kelsey. Kelsey was from Iowa, had written a dissertation on black farmers, and was the department's expert on all things black American, despite lacking personal relationships with any black Americans. Politically, he was a right-leaning paternalist in the mode of General Armstrong and Lyman Abbott, though lacking their suave manners, owing to his humble background. Kelsey and Wright had the same argument repeatedly. Kelsey would expound on African American life, drawing on his vast knowledge of social surveys, and Wright would tell him that he did not understand what it was like to be black in America.

This argument came to a head when Kelsey taught a course titled "the American Negro." Wright cringed with embarrassment as his teacher delivered patronizing howlers about helping African Americans improve themselves. Kelsey, however, wanted to be a good teacher, and he noticed that Wright was not the only one who cringed. He and Wright struck a deal. Kelsey gave lecture previews to Wright, who identified the worst parts. In Kelsey's telling, Wright helpfully eliminated "emotional areas." In Wright's telling, he eliminated "areas of ignorance and prejudice." Kelsey never grasped the difference, despite his vast learning. But Wright appreciated that Kelsey befriended and supported him, pushed Wright to work hard, and modeled scholarly industry. Wright conducted extensive house-to-house canvasses during his years of study under Kelsey, compiling the database for his dissertation, *The Negro in Pennsylvania: A Study in Economic History*, which he published in 1912.[26]

Wright had a more strained relationship with a similar authority figure during the same period. Carl E. Grammer was rector of St. Stephen's Episcopal Church in Philadelphia and president of the Armstrong Association. He was the epitome of paternalistic charity: Eager to find jobs for African Americans, as long as they did not compete with white labor; effusive about helping blacks improve themselves, as long as they knew their place and did not press for equality; and irritated by anything that liberated black Americans from dependence on white charity. Otherwise, as Wright later recalled, Grammer was "a very charming Southern gentleman." Grammer hated Wright's community bank and the fact that he devoted a great deal of time to it. Grammer was sure the bank would fail, which would bring discredit on the Armstrong Association. He and Wright clashed over Wright's proclivity to eat meals with whites and Wright's tendency to undermine Grammer's stereotypes with factual data. Wright and Grammer gave speeches to civic groups about supporting the Armstrong Association. Grammer beseeched civic leaders to take pity on their backward black neighbors. Wright countered that "the Negro problem" was mainly a problem of white prejudice and the best solution to it was to abolish segregation. Wright later recalled, "I showed impatience when he spoke authoritatively to white groups about things of which he was almost totally ignorant." This was not a good fund-raising operation. Wright ministered briefly to a congregation in Conshohocken, and in 1909 he won the editorship of the *Christian Recorder,* so he resigned from the Armstrong Association. Years later he recalled gratefully that the organization changed its line after it became a branch of the Urban League.[27]

The things that Grammer did not know, however, were hard to find anywhere, even in black newspapers. Wright grieved that white newspapers reported extensively on black crime, ignoring all other aspects of Afro-American existence. Other venues were not much better. Even the best sociological treatment of black life, Du Bois's *Philadelphia Negro,* perpetuated stereotypes of black criminality and immorality. Moreover, institutions that might have touted their roles in black progress did not bother to do so. Wright asked Penn, Temple University, and the Institute of Fine Arts (Philadelphia) for data about their African American graduates. All replied that they had no such records. Wright was incredulous; his circle of friends included two blacks with Ph.D.'s from Penn (Pezavia O'Connell and Louis B. Moore) and a famous local physician with an M.D. from Penn, Nathan F. Mossell, who founded Philadelphia's Douglass Hospital. The art institute apparently did not know or care that one of its black graduates, painter Henry O. Tanner, was renowned in Europe. Wright vowed that somebody had to counter the flood of racist propaganda with counternarratives of black achievement. It was the same conviction that spurred

William Simmons to write *Men of Mark*. But Simmons wrote Victorian literary prose about heroic individuals, putting himself in their contexts and taking sides with them. Wright believed that sociology was more effective, depicting social realities that only needed to be seen to change the picture.

He poured out social gospel sociology, writing articles on education, labor, crime, and institutions, contending that Afro-Americans were more literate than any immigrant group in America, contrary to convention. Wright argued that blacks were relegated overwhelmingly to service work and menial labor because of racism, not because they made little effort to educate themselves. In 1909 he published a handbook on self-help in black education, took over as acting manager of the A.M.E. Book Concern, and doubled down as acting editor of the AME Church's newspaper, the *Christian Recorder*. Howard University called, offering a position in sociology. Wright could picture himself teaching under Kelly Miller, but he declined, preferring to influence the AME Church through its publications. Building a black public through the church was more important than reaching a handful of sociology students. The following year, 1910, he compiled a directory of black institutions in Philadelphia. By the time Wright completed his doctorate in 1911, he had rescued the church's publishing house and its newspaper from financial oblivion. But he had to fight to keep his base of power in the AME Church.[28]

The Book Concern of the AME Church was the nation's oldest incorporated black business enterprise, having been established in 1816. Church factions treated it as a spoil of victory in church politics; thus, the firm had no history of professional management. In 1908 the Book Concern went bankrupt, which shut down the *Christian Recorder*. Wright was hired to revive both enterprises. He cleaned up the Book Concern's managerial practices, wiped out his personal savings to pay off a lawsuit that would have forced liquidation proceedings, published a successful hymnal, and turned the publishing house and newspaper into profitable enterprises. Fortunately, he was oblivious to the pertinent church politics; otherwise he would not have bothered. Wright did not realize that he had won the job as a compromise between northern and southern factions that intended to brush him aside. Had he realized it, he would have taken the job at Howard and become an academic. He might have left the AME ministry, disgusted that everything in the AME Church was political. As it was, he backed into power as an emergency manager and saved the publishing house and newspaper—which immediately turned his two positions into political plums.

Wright flushed with indignation as bishops told him to step aside for a favorite nephew, son, or crony. Defying the bishops, he ran against them at the

General Conference of 1911 and won reelection as editor of the *Christian Recorder*. A southern machine opponent, however, J. I. Lowe, was elected business manager of the publishing house, despite knowing almost nothing about business, publishing, or accounting. For four years Wright submitted to Lowe's censorship and watched Lowe destroy the gains that Wright had made. By 1916 the Book Concern was bankrupt again and the General Conference asked Wright to save it again. This time he paid off every bond reaching back to 1895, rendering the Book Concern free of debt for the first time in its history. In 1919 Wright burned a ten-thousand-dollar mortgage with theatrical flair. Meanwhile, the newspaper, boasting four thousand subscribers when Wright took over, had twelve thousand by 1920.[29]

In the early going, Wright's rivals warned that he was too young and academic to run the publishing house or edit the newspaper. His organizational prowess put a stop to complaints about his youth and degrees, but the same people protested after he livened up the paper with cheeky headlines plus stories about Afro-American achievements. One way or another, Wright's critics felt that he upstaged or embarrassed them. Wright pushed on, trusting that most subscribers would appreciate a job well done. Hundreds of his subscribers could barely read, he reflected, yet they bought the *Christian Recorder* and *A.M.E. Church Review* out of loyalty to the Book Concern. Wright made the church's publications more interesting, informative, and financially solvent. In his telling, his number-one objective for the newspaper was to promote the spiritual and social ethical ideals of Christianity. Number two was to promote the AME Church by publicizing its work. Number three was to cultivate habits of reading and critical reflection among ministers and the laity.

Wright worried that many ministers did not know much theology or history. He established a weekly forum titled "The School Master" to address the problem. Every week he selected a book in theology, church history, or black history that ministers needed to know about but that many were unlikely to understand if they tried to read it. Wright provided questions and answers pertinent to each book. Methodist theologian John Miley's two-volume work, *Systematic Theology*, got special attention, as Wright offered more than four hundred questions and answers. Gradually Wright won over most readers to his idea of what the *Christian Recorder* should be, fending off his chief detractors— campaigners for a bishop's chair, who thought the paper should serve their ambitions. Wright cut them off by disallowing campaign articles until a year before the General Conference and by disallowing pictures of candidates at all times. He also abolished the timeworn practice of accepting one-dollar bribes from candidates.[30]

Though caustic about church politics, Wright otherwise loved the AME Church. He edited the *Christian Recorder* from 1909 to 1936 and doubled as editor of the Book Concern for seven years (1909 to 1912 and 1916 to 1920). His success at banking helped to finance his success as a publisher. Wright believed deeply that ministers should not drink and that African Americans needed to acquire greater business sense, but he was not one to preach "be like me" with an accusatory tone. Most Afro-Americans heard enough moral condemnation without hearing more of it from him. It surprised Wright to learn, very late in life, that Ransom resented his gibes about drinking; Wright thought he had found the right tone of avuncular teasing. When Wright turned serious, he stressed that African American life was healthier and more productive than the stereotypes about it. Most depictions of black life were shamefully one-sided and bigoted, he protested. The book that established his national reputation as a social scientist and church leader, *The Negro in Pennsylvania*, said it emphatically, backed by evidence from Wright's database.

The Negro in Pennsylvania offered no introduction to Wright's subject or argument. The book plunged straight into a capsule account of black American history in Pennsylvania before the Civil War, made an argument about the impact of the Civil War on black immigration to Pennsylvania, and turned swiftly to Wright's chief concern, the present condition of Afro-Americans in Pennsylvania. In Wright's telling, before the Civil War the "native Negroes" of Pennsylvania were "made of a desirable sort" and the immigrants from the South, though generally less desirable, included many of the South's "best" blacks. The educated, usually freeborn and light-colored blacks from Charleston, South Carolina, were prominent in the latter group. Daniel Payne was one of them, and many were skilled at mechanics. The immigrants from the West Indies too were nearly always skilled in a craft. Wright explained that the Civil War dramatically changed this picture. The end of slavery opened opportunities for the more industrious Afro-Americans in the South, who tended to stay there, and many able northern blacks headed to the South. The blacks that came north after the war, Wright stressed, were not the "intelligent and skilled" ones. Pennsylvania's black population soared by 175 percent between 1860 and 1900, mostly in Philadelphia and Pittsburgh, from 56,900 to 156,800. The increase was due almost solely to immigration, and it brought the direct ravages of slavery.[31]

Then a greater migration began. Wright realized that the current boom was too immediate for him to gauge, but he quantified why people left the South. In a survey of 512 Afro-Americans in Philadelphia, 42 percent said they left for higher wages, 8 percent said they left for higher wages and either protection or a geographical change, 11 percent said they sought better conditions, 13 percent came with their parents or guardian, 10 percent wanted to make a change, 4 percent were tired of the South, and no other reason reached 2 percent. More males than females moved for higher wages alone (by 5 percent), and more females than males came with a parent or guardian (by 6 percent). The dominance of the economic motive seemed off-kilter to Wright, since African Americans had more opportunities in the South with much less competition. To be sure, he acknowledged, northern jobs paid better, sometimes much better. Still, Wright emphasized that blacks possessing the education and/or skills to land a decent job in the South usually stayed there. The new migrants came with little education and no skills, in hopes of making a better living, to cities in which competition for working-class jobs was fierce and racial discrimination was pervasive. That was the key to everything else in this picture.[32]

In the South, African Americans monopolized certain kinds of labor. In the North they competed against "the world's best and most aggressive workmen," confronting higher standards in virtually every line of work, plus racist trade unions. In the South, Wright observed, blacks were excluded from most professions, except ministry and teaching, the lowest paid professions. In the North blacks had more opportunities to become professionals, with fair to middling results thus far. Wright counted 411 black clergy in Pennsylvania, 91 blacks in show business, 20 dentists, 24 lawyers, 258 musicians and music teachers, 12 government officials, 60 physicians and surgeons, 222 teachers and professors, and 114 in miscellaneous professions. Though he had no survey data about intelligence levels, he dispensed knowing opinions about it. Black America had some highly intelligent ministers, Wright assured, and overall, the clergy were "considerably superior" in intelligence to ministers of past generations. Still, he judged that the average intelligence of Afro-American ministers was "somewhat lower" than all other professionals. Black physicians were at the top and black ministers at the bottom, in intelligence and remuneration.[33]

Black lawyers did not make much money, either, so there weren't many of them. Wright explained that few Afro-Americans used lawyers and few white Americans would consider hiring a black lawyer. In American courtrooms the opposing lawyers were white, the judges were white, and the juries were white. The fix was in against black lawyers, but Wright highlighted that new lines of business enterprise were opening to African Americans, notably real estate and insurance. Philadelphia and Pittsburgh had thirty-seven black real estate dealers. Wright suggested there was ample room for more, based on the surmise that the immigration boom from the South would continue. That was an augur of Wright's future.[34]

The Negro in Pennsylvania praised the church as the most important moral influence and institution in black life, although Wright qualified the praise with social gospel criticism. Too many African American ministers still conveyed that religion was only about "feeling good," he admonished: "The Negroes' religion is largely personal; they seek chiefly for communion with God; they like to 'talk with God,' 'to feel His spirit.'" Black church prayers were overwhelmingly about confessing personal sins, expressing humility, and begging God's forgiveness, and they "nearly always end with fervent expressions anticipatory of the glories of heaven and the joys of the after-life." Wright lamented that it was hard to get black ministers and laity to relate their faith to social justice issues. On the other hand, he stressed something that Du Bois–like critics of the church insufficiently credited—that black Christians responded to the gospel through constant acts of charity: "It is quite difficult for anyone who has not kept in very close touch with the Negro church to realize the amount of casual charity done by Negro church members." Critics that did not go to church did not see the good things, so who were they to say? Black churches were filled with people that gave "part of their last dollar" to the church and the poor, Wright observed. They gave spontaneously after working twelve-hour days in exhausting jobs. Wright hoped for less spontaneity and more coordination with "organized charity."[35]

Carefully he worked his way to the issue of black criminality, on which Du Bois had expounded profusely. Not enough was known to say very much with authority, Wright said. Since the evidence at hand was meager, all one could do was indicate "mere tendencies." Culling the existing data, Wright concluded that it was "extremely difficult" to make racial comparisons in this area. Proportionally, Afro-Americans were arrested and convicted twice as often as white Americans. Blacks constituted 5 percent of the Pennsylvania population and accounted for 10 percent of the arrests. But these rates had not changed since Reconstruction, when it was obvious why blacks had higher rates. Wright put it emphatically: "The excess of criminality merely indicates what the excess of illiteracy indicates, namely, a lower social efficiency." When one compared poor blacks to poor whites, the criminality difference disappeared. African Americans belonging to "the higher economic group" were almost never arrested: "The criminal Negroes come from a very different group altogether." The leading crime problem in the black communities of Philadelphia and Pittsburgh, Wright showed, was stealing, followed by fighting and disorderly conduct. These were the crimes of poor people lacking resources and opportunity: "Fighting is everywhere the unintelligent man's way of settling a dispute and is resorted to quite frequently by the Negro who has not yet learned the lesson of self-control or the value of arbitration."[36]

Poverty was the key to criminality, regardless of race. Wright judged that Du Bois, describing the Seventh Ward of Philadelphia, introduced the right categories for the overwhelming majority: 9 percent were very poor, 10 percent were poor, and 48 percent were fair, as in, "fairly poor." If the white Americans that brayed about black crime actually cared about it, Wright suggested, they would stop excluding blacks from economic opportunity, if only out of self-interest. Wright tried to be philosophical about the difficulties of getting white Americans to recognize the real race problem in America—their own racism. Every great civilization trained its children to believe in their superiority, he noted. The Greeks divided the world into Greeks and barbarians, the Romans divided it into Romans and plebeians, and the Hebrews divided it into God's chosen people and the gentiles. In 1911, Germans and Americans were both outspoken in believing that their nation was the greatest in the world.

This proclivity of the strong fell hard on submerged peoples. Wright observed that white Americans fumbled the racial justice issue even when they tried to do something about it. When they talked about black Americans, they almost never knew what they were talking about: "White men do not associate with the best Negroes; they rarely enter their homes; they are excluded from their social circles; they cannot become members of their churches; they are seldom business partners and they cannot know the inside life of the higher group of Negroes. On the other hand, they are often benefactors of the poorer Negroes; they meet the criminal Negro in the court, the pauper at the poorhouse; they have the servant in their kitchen, and they read the newspapers in which are sensational reports of Negro crimes, written by reporters, most of them who never saw the inside of the homes of the well-to-do Negro." The so-called "race problem," Wright believed, was hopeless if the Talented Tenth could not break into the everyday racist consciousness of privileged whites. White southerners were right when they said that liberal white northerners knew nothing about blacks. Wright mused that it was getting awfully late to change this situation, because African Americans no longer revealed their souls to white people. On second thought, he could not speak for blacks everywhere in America, but he knew for sure that "that time has passed in Pennsylvania." Northern blacks, whether "intelligent or ignorant," no longer trusted any white American with their inner feelings.[37]

That got Wright rolling on a splurge of candor. Every attempt to define the race problem as a problem of black ignorance, crime, inefficiency, or inferiority masked the true problem, he believed: "The 'Negro Problem'—that condition which is peculiar to Negroes, and common to them—is rather found in the attitude of the white race toward the Negro; an attitude of a majority which seeks to shut out a minority from the enjoyment of the whole social and economic life." The problem was a trade union movement that excluded African Americans. It was a public high school that refused to hire a black graduate of Harvard or Cornell as a teacher. It was a college that refused to hire a black doctoral graduate of Harvard or Cornell. It got worse as one moved up the ladder of achievement. Wright put it sharply—the real Negro problem fell hardest on the highest achieving blacks: "The discriminations against Negroes increase with increasing intelligence, benefit and efficiency, on the part of the Negroes, and increased competition." At the low end of the social scale, Wright contended, race hardly mattered: "In the economically and intellectually lowest stratum—that of the pauper and criminal—there is but little race problem." Paupers and criminals, whether black or white, shared pretty much the same living quarters and problems, "often in close association." Racism only started to matter at the level of the working poor, and it got more insidious as blacks moved up the economic ladder, contrary to convention.[38]

Wright got more declarative at the end because he had reached the book's conclusion, where he dispensed with graphs. Here he spoke on the authority of personal experience. Most Afro-Americans could not imagine what it felt like to be a professional sociologist and still be invisible, at best, to white America. It galled Wright that his achievements merely provided more occasions for him to be pushed aside by white society, and for him to be conscious of it. The problem was terribly personal but also political, because the only solution was for white liberals and high-achieving types like Wright and Du Bois to work together to overthrow American segregation. Only middle-class blacks would form organizations to battle for their rights, and they had to have white liberal support to get anywhere. The churches, Wright believed, had an indispensable role to play in this struggle. However, they had no chance of playing the leading role, because white Americans liked their lily-white churches, few black Americans had any desire to enter white churches, and black ministers had a vested interest in maintaining this divide. Wright affirmed the positive side of religious segregation: "The separation has done much to develop leadership among the Negroes." Thus he followed Du Bois from the Niagara Movement to the NAACP and urged church members to join the NAACP. There was no alternative to cutting a deal with white liberals. Wright joined the NAACP's Committee of Forty and helped to organize the NAACP's 1913 annual conference in Philadelphia.[39]

Militant civil rights liberalism, a national strategy yoking two middle-class elites, was the answer to the race problem. Wright exhorted, "The aim of our nation is the common weal; is equal opportunity as far as possible. Race, nationality, or religion should not interfere with American economic progress. The greatest need of the Negro is economic freedom, economic justice. This is all the best Negroes of this State ask. And it is indeed a high platform upon which to stand. It is not a bid for charity; it is not a bid for hostility. It is only to be permitted to enter American rivalry, to go down if incompetent, to die out if weak, to go up if capable." The "best" African Americans pleaded only for fairness and decency—profound yet simple things, as these were "the common ground of political economy and the teaching of Jesus."[40]

Another major test of decency, however, was ongoing when Wright published *The Negro in Pennsylvania*. He had long believed that northern churches and city governments were failing to decently welcome poor migrants pouring in from the South. He said it repeatedly before he became editor of the *Christian Recorder*. He said it more ambivalently in *The Negro in Pennsylvania* and in his early years at the *Christian Recorder*, where he had audience issues and his own tenuous standing to negotiate.[41]

In 1916 Wright said it boldly, after the Great Migration got bigger and he was firmly in control at the *Christian Recorder*. The southern migration, he declared, had become a mass movement, the biggest change in Afro-American life since Emancipation. And the churches were stuck in a mixture of hostility and ambivalence toward it. Wright called for an "ecumenical council of dark skinned Christians" to discuss this momentous development. Confronted with the influx of poor southerners, churches that had resisted the social gospel until now were overdue to rethink their social ethic and their institutional priorities. Wright grieved that many Northern AME ministers were still imploring poor blacks to stay in the South. Some were debating whether northern blacks could afford to be hospitable. He told them they should extend arms of welcome "to every Negro who desires to come." This was a rock-bottom issue of Christian charity, hospitality, and justice, Wright urged. It was also the Northern AME Church's best chance to be revitalized by an infusion of newcomers: "Get these Negroes in your churches, make them welcome; don't turn up your noses and let the saloon man and his gambler do all the welcoming. Help them buy homes, encourage them to send for their families and to put their children in school. Welcome them, welcome them; yes bid them thrice welcome."[42]

Wright and Ransom used their bully pulpits at the *Christian Recorder* and the *A.M.E. Church Review* to make that case. They built up a social gospel constituency in the AME Church by doing so, giving rise to sermons in which the North became the latter-day Promised Land for Afro-Americans, often with echoes of the Underground Railroad. AME minister J. W. Rankin preached this sermon in 1917, describing the southern migrants as modern-day Israelites. In 1920 the *Christian Recorder* enthused that the AME General Conference of that year in St. Louis devoted more attention than previously to urban issues and the labor problem.[43]

But the Promised Land sermon did not prevail in the AME Church, nor did the modest hospitality version of it preached by Wright and Ransom. Most of the AME Church remained ambivalent, at best, toward the new migrants through the 1920s and 1930s. The Ransom-Wright line on civil rights liberalism proved to be more amenable to respectable churchgoers than did the Ransom-Wright line on welcoming the poor southern stranger. This palpable reserve, sometimes crossing into aversion, cost the denomination dearly. Ransom, Wright, and other reformers contended that the pressures brought on by migration offered the church an opportunity and a challenge to operate more democratically, allowing individual congregations to determine their own responses to local circumstances. AME bishops and officials were not interested in democratizing power. They tightened their bureaucratic control of the denomination, prompting one of the church's lodestar congregations, Bethel AME Church in Chicago, to break away from the denomination in 1920. Losing Bethel cut Ransom deeply and alarmed progressives into mobilizing for an ironic objective. To democratize the church, they had to become bishops. Eventually some of them succeeded, but in the meantime, the black denomination with the strongest abolitionist identity lost a historic opportunity to revitalize itself. Chicago was the key battleground, where progressives fought and lost repeatedly. Religious historian Wallace D. Best puts it aptly, observing that the battle over ecclesiastical control led to "a further fragmentation of AME power, a significant loss in numbers, and a further fraying of its cultural and religious significance." Many progressives concluded that they had to look beyond the church to attain democratic moral agency.[44]

POLITICS, BUSINESS, AND RELIGION

That heightened the question of ordinary politics. Wright and Ransom struggled with the question for most of their careers, long after they opted for the power and survival work of the episcopacy. Was it possible to stand for civil rights, welcoming the stranger, and economic justice without getting snared in the draining and perhaps futile work of electoral politics? If politics was unavoidable to some degree, at what point was it possible to hold back from it? For Wright, NAACP activism was a given. Beyond that, ambiguity prevailed for many years. He got his early understanding of things political from his father, who explained that blacks and southern Democrats had the same economic interests, but blacks had to vote Republican because Democrats cared about holding down blacks more than they cared about anything else. Until Wright studied at Chicago, he had never heard a political speech not devoted to race. In 1900 he cast his first vote, for McKinley. In 1904 he was in Europe, but would have voted for Roosevelt. In 1908 he voted for Bryan as the lesser of two evils. In the next election cycle he visited Wilson at Princeton University, who promised that he would be fair to black Americans, but Wright opted for Roosevelt's Bull Moose ticket. In 1916 he voted for Wilson, still hoping that Wilson would redeem his promise. As late as 1918, Wright held back from plunging into local politics. The Republican machine controlled the black vote in Philly, and Wright reasoned that he had better things to do in education, religion, journalism, and business.

But in 1918 a white police officer, angry with a black arrestee who had tried to run away, walked the prisoner to a police station and shot him dead on the step. Wright organized a group of protesters consisting mostly of ministers. Surely the chief of police was against cold-blooded murder? The chief launched a tirade against the ministers, telling them to tell poor African Americans to stop coming north. Wright replied that if the ministers could not get any redress from the police, they would take the issue to the polls. The chief laughed them out of the room, and Wright launched an organization called the Colored Protective Association. The group published a newspaper and swelled to ten thousand black and white members demanding equal treatment for Afro-Americans in the criminal courts. The offending police officer was suspended and tried but not convicted, outraging the protest movement.

Movement leadership caused Wright to expand his personal network, finding unexpected allies. He had an idea for Du Bois—writing a book (originally, with Emmett Scott) on black Americans in the war—which could not happen without Wright's network. Wright got an ally in the White House to help send Du Bois to the Paris Peace Conference, and he got a Philadelphia publisher, John C. Winston, to publish the book. His friendship with Winston led to further projects, as Winston was involved in the city's new charter to elect a mayor and city council in 1919. Wright plunged into local electoral politics, bringing the Colored Protective Association with him. The group helped to elect a reform mayor, J. Hampton Moore, who appointed African Americans to city jobs and briefly enticed Wright to serve as organizer of social work in the welfare department. Wright soon pulled back from holding a municipal government office, but he remained a player in local politics, mostly in connection to his rapidly expanding business interests in the black community.[45]

Meanwhile Wright grew into the sage role at the *Christian Recorder*, dispensing advice about marriage, courtship, mothers, education, leadership, finance, wills, and real estate for his national audience, plus commentary on church politics and the national political situation. There were many exhortations concerning education and leadership, such as, "The hope of our race is in the educated class," and "The need of the church today is a leadership which will cement the church." Wright lamented that every AME district was a little denomination unto itself, resulting in "18 little churches." Most of his sermonizing called readers to be strong, ethical, and industrious: "'I can' and 'I will' ought to be the motto of every man. 'I can't' is the thought of a child and a weakling." Wright admonished congregations to stop exaggerating how bad things were under the former pastor; gossiping about ministers was never good for the moral health of a congregation. Church people talked a lot about sensational preachers, usually to commend a spellbinder or to say that spellbinders got too much attention; Wright asserted that "all great preachers are sensational" because they conveyed a tremendous message, not because they made congregations shout and carry on. After women won the vote, Wright counseled that the church had to become more relevant: "So long as women were kept out of business and politics they had only the interests of the home and the church. Now their interests are many and if the church does not minister to these increased interests the women will be found less in the church than they are today. The church must measure up to the demands of this new condition."[46]

On things political Wright supported the NAACP and lamented that most church people opted out of civil rights politics. In 1921 he warned that the Klan was making a comeback, "spreading everywhere" in former southern strongholds and in many new northern ones. (The Klan peaked in New York State from 1920 to 1925 and fell off sharply afterward.) Wright urged that the NAACP needed far more support from black and white churches to fight off the Klan. Moreover, the cause of civil rights relied too much on the NAACP to lead the way: "It is almost impossible to understand the lethargy of colored men and women as to the rights of their people. They seem asleep to the situation." Later that year President Harding opined that black men should become the best possible black men, not the best possible imitation of white men: "The racial amalgamation should not be." Wright caught the sly casuistry of this statement, noting that it was Booker Washington all over again in style and substance. Wright did not dispute the existence of "natural lines" of racial demarcation — "There is a 'consciousness of kind' among different groups. This has been and always will be. Two can be different without being inferior." But Harding's formulation put a new mask on the old lie that blacks were "separate but equal" in American society. Wright protested that Afro-Americans had hoped for something better than a sly version of why they needed to accept their subordinate status.[47]

As a dutiful father of three children, Wright interfered when necessary on their behalf, confronting public school teachers that expected little from black students. On one occasion he found his oldest child, Ruth, at age nine, staring at herself in front of a mirror, squeezing her nose and rubbing her cheeks. Ruth asked, "Daddy, am I a Negro?" Wright pretended not to understand the question. Ruth explained that her teacher said that a Negro was "an ugly black person with thick lips, broad nose, and sloping forehead and a ring in his nose—a savage." Wright asked where the teacher got such nonsense. Ruth said it was a quote from her geography textbook. That week Wright blasted the book furiously in an editorial, calling it a terrible crime that hurt innocent children. He protested to the authors, who surprised Wright by asking him to rewrite the offending sentence for the next edition. They had merely recycled a statement from the book's original edition without giving any thought to it. This statement had appeared in several editions and nobody had complained, notwithstanding that Philadelphia had African American teachers that used the book.

When Ruth got to high school, Wright relived a familiar controversy. Ruth's advisor told her that taking Latin was "absolutely out of the question" and so was college. Ruth had to take home economics, something she could use. The advisor did not bother to review Ruth's academic record. She was black, so what else could matter? Lottie Crogman Wright intervened this time, telling the advisor that both of Ruth's grandfathers had taught Latin and Greek, both of Ruth's parents had taught Latin and Greek, and nobody in her family had been a domestic servant for three generations. The advisor absorbed this unimaginable information and apologized. She and Lottie Wright became friends, and Ruth Wright went on to a Ph.D. at Penn.[48]

These stories had Wright's trademark blend of family pride, repugnance at racism, and optimism. He was fond of saying that he was a radical in his early career, but got more conservative without changing. In his telling, hardly anyone espoused the new abolition when he started, but it became increasingly mainstream with each decade. In his early career Wright doubted that he should marry and have children, because he expected to be persecuted for his social gospel radicalism: "In the face of lynching, riots, political intimidation and industrial exploitation, I felt I, who opposed these, must suffer. I could picture myself driven about from place to place, jailed, tortured, lynched and my family suffering because of the gospel I preached. The suffering was, I thought, just too much to force them to share." Surely, if he followed the way of Jesus in racist America, he was better off not subjecting a wife and children to his Christian martyrdom. Teaching at Payne Seminary shook loose some of Wright's martyr complex, as people asked him constantly why he was unmarried. He hinted that he might have dated more at Wilberforce had Du Bois not set an embarrassing precedent there by marrying one of his students. As it was, Wright dated the daughter of his father's friend and later resolved, in Germany, to marry her, but took six years to do it. By the time Wright was ready to marry Lottie, he was more respectable than he had expected to be, at the mere beginning of his success as a banker, editor, publisher, sociologist, minister, real estate baron, and bishop.[49]

Wright's business acumen evoked awe from ministers and church audiences, sometimes too much for his comfort. He wanted African Americans to become more skilled and confident in this area, making his success less unusual. Whenever he warmed to this subject he stressed that he simply followed his father's maxims: "Be thrifty"; "Work hard"; "Maintain impeccable accounts"; "Stay out of debt"; and "Give something to get something." The depression of 1913–1914 hit Philadelphia hard, causing Wright to branch into real estate. Plus he had been puzzling anyway over what else he should do to practice what he preached—welcoming the migrant stranger. He responded by studying real estate at Penn's School of Finance, learning the business. He bought hundreds of houses, up to eighty at once, buying wholesale and selling retail. He found that many homeowners had trouble understanding mortgages, taxes, insurance, and the like, so he handled the payment schedules for clients. By 1920 Wright had a growing real estate empire in Philadelphia. That year the Wright family dramatically upped its stake in the banking business.

This development had a backstory in the family's debate over North versus South. In Wright's early career, his siblings teased him about living in the culturally impoverished section of the nation. Then the trickle of relatives to the North commenced, beginning with Wright's sister Lillian, who moved to Philadelphia in 1909 to live with him and to be his secretary. Two brothers and two brothers-in-law, all seeking higher education in Philadelphia, subsequently came to live with Wright, as did Wright's sister Essie and her children. The Major, ensconced in his presidency at Georgia State College, had no intention of leaving the South. Then an incident at Citizens and Southern Bank in Savannah sundered his southern identity.

Wright's twenty-nine-year-old sister Julia, a teacher, made a withdrawal at Citizens and Southern, where she had held an account for many years. A young white teller addressed her as "Julia." She asked the teller to call her "Miss Wright." He cursed her, charged out of the bank cage, kicked her, and tried to slap her, shouting, "I am a white man and I call no nigger, 'Miss.'" Julia Wright told her father, who protested to the bank's president, a longtime friend. The banker replied that nothing could be done; if he fired or reprimanded the teller, white Savannah would punish the bank. Wright's father got the same reply from other prominent whites he counted as friends. No one was willing to speak up for a distinguished black friend or his daughter. A lawyer told him to forget about pressing an assault case, which would only inflame the city, heap ridicule on educated Afro-Americans, and ruin the career of Julia Wright's lawyer. The Major bitterly absorbed that his thirty years of dedicated service to the community counted for nothing. His eldest son urged him to move to Philadelphia to start a bank.⁵⁰

The Wrights launched Citizens and Southern Bank (Philadelphia) in September 1920. Wright put up $11,200 and served as secretary-treasurer; his father put up $5,600 and served as president; the initial capital base was $125,000. It took two years to sell the stock, and the bank became an incorporated trust company in 1924, just in time to survive the fall of a private black bank, Brown and Stevens. The Wrights benefited from their reputations for honesty and thrift. They also benefited from the demise of Brown and Stevens, once the threat of panic had subsided. Slowly the bank became an important player in the black community, providing jobs above the status of janitor and providing mortgages for people who could not get them elsewhere. The Major had a slogan—"Security before profits"—and the patience it demanded, building the business on small loans and persistently developing security for them. By the early 1930s the bank was strong enough to survive the crashing and carnage of the Depression. Wright and the Major worked closely together, running a tight ship and avoiding risky investments. Together they worked around Wright's four years as president of Wilberforce University (1932–1936), his election as bishop in 1936, and his four-year term as bishop of South Africa (1936–1940). In the 1930s the bank increasingly attracted white customers, and by 1947, when the Major died, it was at the height of its success. One measure of its success was that nearly all Philadelphia banks had Afro-American clerks by the mid-1940s.⁵¹

The Wrights struggled to keep Citizens and Southern going after the Major died. Wright's brother E. C. Wright took over as president; a close family friend and Baptist pastor, W. C. Williamson, succeeded him in 1952; two years later Wright took over the presidency to shore up confidence in the bank and to hold off hostile political pressure. Even for Wright, however, it proved to be overtaxing to run a bank while serving as bishop of New York, New Jersey, New England, and Bermuda. Wright did it for two years and then retired from banking. Citizens and Southern had gradually integrated, starting with a few stock sales to white buyers, hiring a few white professional staff, electing a few whites to the board of directors, and eventually selling a majority of the stock to a group of white and black supporters. In his last years Wright remained on the board of directors while taking pride in having cofounded the nation's most thoroughly integrated bank. Reflecting on his life, Wright modestly described his banking career as "a little business experience," noting that it took place "on the fringe of business, in the area of America's small businesses, strictly behind the color curtain." Having devoted his entire career to building up the intellectual and organizational capital of the black community, Wright was long on "race pride and religious emotion." He stressed, however, that these two things were "no substitute for thorough training, character, experience, and capital."[52]

For most of his life Wright was a nominal Republican, like the Major. He complained about Republicans and usually voted for them, often with bitter regrets that there was no real choice for blacks. In the 1930s Wright made the leap to national politics, in the other party. It began with his vote for Franklin Roosevelt in 1932. Wright had long liked FDR but did not campaign for him. Then he moved to Wilberforce to assume its presidency, where Wright became friends with Ohio Democratic governor Martin L. Davey. Davey's friendship and his support of Wilberforce helped Wright make the adjustment to calling himself a Democrat, a statement that caught in his throat.

The New Deal turned Wright into a partisan, say-it-publicly Democrat, countering Ralph Bunche's influential left critique. Bunche, a political scientist at Howard University, made his early renown by blasting the early New Deal as a retrograde political development that strengthened white supremacy. The Agricultural Adjustment Act, he noted, forced many sharecroppers off the land without compensation, and the National Recovery Act provided legal cover for the racially discriminatory practices of labor unions. Wright weighed these objections against the broader effects of the New Deal in providing emergency relief, jobs, and social insurance, lifting millions of working-class people. He played a leadership role in Eleanor Roosevelt's Good Neighbor League, mobilizing support among political independents and wavering black Republicans for New Deal reforms. He gave speeches for the president in 1936 at campaign venues across the country, filling large auditoriums. One was a packed house at Madison Square Garden, where Wright read a special message from FDR on "the second emancipation." Church and civic groups across the nation gathered to hear this national radio address. Wright also wrote a pamphlet for the Democratic National Committee, *Why the Colored Voters Should Help Re-elect Franklin D. Roosevelt*, which reached a circulation of one million copies. After Roosevelt was reelected, Wright headed for South Africa as the AME Church's newest bishop. Arriving at his cabin, he found hundreds of congratulatory letters and telegrams, including a bouquet of orchids from Franklin and Eleanor Roosevelt.[53]

Wright should have been elected a bishop in 1932, but Ransom ginned up the disastrous campaign against Bishop Jones, which killed Wright's candidacy. Then Ransom persuaded Wright to save Wilberforce. By 1936 Wright had rescued Wilberforce and the General Conference was determined to reward him. He took a huge lead on the first ballot, among thirty-six candidates, and was elected on the third ballot. Opponents protested that Wright had a Ph.D. and he would surely give the best pastorates to fellow Ph.D.'s. Wright noted that the entire AME ministry had three Ph.D.'s and that laity and younger clergy did not make this argument. His opposition came from older clergy who had long felt shown up by him. The church sent him to South Africa, its Fifteenth Episcopal District, where his African constituents insisted that he travel first-class. Lottie Wright later recounted, "To us it was a matter of indifference; to them a matter of pride. So here we were, in luxury we had not wished."[54]

Wright preached an antiwar sermon as the ship sailed toward Cherbourg, France. War against Germany could be avoided if the Christian nations followed Jesus, he urged. Most of the passengers were Germans, who received the sermon warmly. According to the Wrights, everyone treated both of them with friendliness and respect. Lottie Wright recalled, "There was kindness, politeness, and service in the atmosphere. The fact that we were colored seemed not to matter. . . . The organization aboard an ocean liner is marvelous, as it must be. Everything goes off with the smoothness and accuracy of clockwork." Besides enthusing at pleasant, well-heeled company and the efficiency of ocean liners, Lottie exulted at having uninterrupted time with her busy husband, something that had never happened previously: "I felt a sort of new romance." From France they sailed to Southampton, England, and then to Capetown, where they were greeted by a service of praise music. Some singers had traveled hundreds of miles for the occasion. South African black Methodists, it turned out, loved to hear the story of how they joined the AME Church. Wright obliged them often during his three years there.[55]

This story began in 1892, when Mangena Mokone, a member of the Sotho tribe, established the Ethiopian Church of South Africa. Mokone had been a Wesleyan minister, but he led a group out of the Wesleyan Church as a protest against its Eurocentric racism. The Ethiopian Church grew slowly, attracting church leaders from the Sotho, Zulu, and Xhosa tribes. Meanwhile in 1893 a white American brought a concert group from South Africa to Chicago to sing at the World's Fair. The singers disbanded on tour, finding themselves abandoned in Cleveland, where they found their way to Allen Chapel AME Church.

There they met Ransom, who advised them to go to Wilberforce, where Bishop Arnett and university president S. T. Mitchell took them in. Six of the singers became scholarship students at Wilberforce. One of them, Charlotte Manye, living in Arnett's home, wrote to her sister using Arnett's official stationery, which had Bishop Turner's name at the top. Manye was Mokone's niece. Reading the letter, Mokone was intrigued to learn of this African Methodist church in the United States. He wrote to Turner for information about it, and soon the two church leaders were plotting a merger.[56]

The Ethiopian Church announced in March 1896 that it planned to unite, if possible, with the AME Church. Three months later, at a special session of the North Georgia annual conference, Turner received Ethiopian Church representative James M. Dwane and (through him) the entire Ethiopian Church into the AME Church, setting off a controversy about the reach of Turner's authority. In 1898 Turner made a triumphant visit to South Africa, drawing huge crowds in Capetown, Johannesburg, and Pretoria. South Africans had never seen a black bishop, and Turner's blunt outspokenness delighted them. Using the same controversial methods he had employed during Reconstruction in Georgia, Turner organized an annual conference and ordained many ministers. He also appointed a vicar bishop, something that did not exist in the AME Church. Turner was assailed for forging ahead on his own (lack of) legal authority, but AME Christianity took hold in South Africa. By the time Wright arrived there in 1936, ten AME bishops had preceded him.[57]

South Africa, Wright soon judged, was more like the United States than he had expected, only better. Race was not as rigidly binary in South Africa. Intermarriage was widespread, as pre-apartheid South Africa had no laws against it. Wright had trouble sorting out European whites, colored, and native blacks from each other, noting that Europeans and colored persons often looked much alike and that the South African Bantu were not as dark as many black Americans. All of this made cultural signals hard to read, for him. South Africa in the 1930s did not consign blacks to separate treatment on streetcars, buses, taxis, parks, or public places in general. Wright attended public lectures and concerts without incident and was generally struck by the courtesy shown to him. Overall he found less racial prejudice in Capetown than he experienced in U.S. American border states and the Deep South. He also witnessed, however, the rise of the Nationalist Party and was repulsed by its aggressive racism. This was worse than standard Deep South racism, he judged. American racists felt compelled to believe in "separate but equal," or at least say they did. Daniel Malan's Nationalist Party advocated a vicious system of apartheid with no recognition of equality of any kind.[58]

The Wrights journeyed through Swaziland, Basutoland, Bechuanaland, Northern and Southern Rhodesia, the Belgian Congo, and Portuguese East Africa, planting churches and making new friends. They helped to build fifty churches, notably in Capetown, Benoni, Bloemhof, Kensington, and Kliptown. They exulted at being set free from church politics. Lottie Wright was emphatic on this theme, marveling that church politics was almost nonexistent in South Africa—"The ministers and missionaries are free to carry on their kingdom-building without its blighting influence." In 1938 Wright returned briefly to the United States to attend a bishops' meeting and paid a visit to FDR, who inquired about South Africa. Wright told him the Dutch were the worst racists he had ever met; "they beat our Southerners." Roosevelt smiled, but Wright added anxiously, remembering the president's Dutch heritage, "I mean the South African Dutch." Returning to South Africa, Wright watched the Nationalists grow stronger, on their way to taking over after World War II. Otherwise he accentuated the positive about his years there, noting that the same sermons he gave in America about working hard, getting educated, living ethically, pulling together, and acquiring business skills applied as relevantly in South Africa.[59]

By December 1939 Wright was anxious to get home, expecting that America would soon be involved in World War II. He tried to book first-class passage out of Capetown, imploring a tourist agency every day, without success. Finally he cabled the White House that he was stranded, which quickly yielded first-class tickets. Wright returned to the United States in January 1940, in time to help FDR again, although he did not campaign as aggressively this time, since he was now a bishop and Roosevelt was in no danger of losing to Wendell Willkie. Wright wrote another pamphlet for the presidential campaign, *Why the Negro Vote Should Go to President Roosevelt.* There was no reason to regret having voted for Roosevelt in 1936, Wright argued. Every plank of the New Deal helped to build a more decent society. Under Roosevelt black Americans were part of a coalition including labor unions, city machines, white ethnics, and rural white southerners that benefited working-class people. Under Roosevelt blacks had their best representation ever in an administration, through the forty-five-member "Black Cabinet" (the Federal Council of Negro Affairs) headed by Mary McLeod Bethune. Wright appreciated that the Black Cabinet of policy advisors had a hand in shaping New Deal programs; thus he gave a pass to FDR on his passive approach to segregation. The NAACP was marching through the courts, and Wright undoubtedly reasoned, like some who said it openly, that Roosevelt's Supreme Court appointees would eventually make a difference. In any case, Wright enthused that black Americans finally had a president who cared about them. For the rest of his life, Wright stuck with the Democrats. In

1958 he urged Vice President Richard Nixon to prove that he wanted black votes by supporting the voting rights of southern blacks. Nixon was cautious and passive, however, and Wright gave up on him.[60]

In his later career Wright followed Ransom to the Thirteenth Episcopal District in Kentucky and Tennessee, served as an interim president for a year at Wilberforce, and subsequently served Episcopal districts in Georgia, the West Indies, South America, New York, New Jersey, New England, Bermuda, Mississippi, and Louisiana. He founded the R. R. Wright Jr. School of Religion at Wilberforce and was appointed historiographer of the AME Church—achievements that brought him special satisfaction, as Wright spent much of his career battling factional opponents and was delighted to leave an institutional legacy. In later life he regretted that he never got around to writing on theoretical subjects. In fact, he regretted it throughout his career. Wright wanted to write constructively about theology, social theory, and social ethics, but the burdens of church work and running businesses restricted most of his writing to journalism. It was hard to justify, or even imagine, confining himself to a scholarly project. His most widely circulated publication, aside from his pamphlets for FDR, was a pamphlet for the AME Church showing that black Americans gave one and a half cents per dollar to the church. Many ministers in the 1940s waved this pamphlet aloft while preaching stewardship sermons.[61]

One book, however, Wright tellingly kept writing. He first published *Outline of the Teaching of Jesus* in 1902, as a response to a classroom controversy at Wilberforce. He published five revised editions over the next forty-four years, periodically updating and sharpening the exposition. In every edition he declared that Jesus was the center of Christian faith and the source of Christian doctrine. Wright had little interest in formal theology, but he had a consuming interest in the theology of Jesus. To him it was axiomatic that the life and teaching of Jesus was "the basis of any true Christian theology." The life and teaching of Jesus centered on the kingdom of God, Wright taught, and the kingdom was radically expansive, bringing God into everything. The kingdom could be entered, as Jesus taught in Matthew 19:23 and Mark 9:47. Human beings were to seek it, as Jesus taught in Matthew 6:33 and Luke 12:31. The kingdom was a "religious and social order or society" that people joined under the rule of God. It was something "within" and/or "among" human subjects (Luke 17:21), though Wright preferred the social rendering. It started small, like a mustard seed, but grew into the greatest thing in the world, the moral and spiritual commonwealth of the divine ruler. Wright put it in classic social gospel terms: "The Kingdom is an order which Jesus came to set up here on earth, not political, but moral and spiritual, the members of which are in reality seeking the perfect life of love."[62]

Wright pressed hard on the themes that everyone is invited into the kingdom of God (John 6:37 and Matthew 11:28) and that nothing in the world is more important than to join it. Positively, "to become a member of this Kingdom is the greatest thing in the world." In the divine kingdom all people are brothers and sisters, and the rule of the family is the golden rule: "Jesus would have us begin with a loving heart, a recognition of the Fatherhood of God; and then He would have each child of God put himself in the place of the other person, and ask himself, 'How would I like to have him treat me if I were in his place?' and then act."[63]

When lightning struck in Montgomery, Alabama, in December 1955 and a young Baptist minister galvanized a protest movement that seemed to come from nowhere, Wright cheered with appreciation, but not with close acquaintance. Ecclesiastical supervision consumed his later career, attending to geographically disparate Episcopal districts. He was self-conscious about seeming old-fashioned to the youthful black social gospelers that swelled the Southern Christian Leadership Conference and the Student Nonviolent Coordinating Committee. He had more friends in the legally oriented northern civil rights movement clustered around the NAACP and New York than in the youthful, street-oriented, mostly Baptist, church-based southern movement. And sometimes he said things about race that only old-timers like him, among civil rights leaders, would still say.

Wright rejoiced that black Americans, in the 1960s, increasingly exuded that "black is beautiful." He glowed with pride when he heard white men praise the beauty of black women. But it bruised him to hear the word "Negro" derided by young black activists and to catch their lack of recognition of what race leaders like him had accomplished. Moreover, like Walter White in his last years, Wright dreamed of a world in which racial color did not exist. White, near the end of a life in which he had bravely campaigned against lynching and built the NAACP into a civil rights powerhouse, ended his autobiography with the despairing suggestion that bleaching might cure racism better than anything else. If black Americans were to suddenly turn white, he fantasized, white Americans would have to relinquish their idiotic belief that one race was smarter and morally superior to others. White, at least, ended with a poignant line: "I am white and I am black, and know that there is no difference."[64]

Wright, nearly twenty years later, took a ludicrous next step, urging medical scientists to develop a pill that turned black skin to white. Individually, Wright wanted blacks to have the option of becoming white, if that proved to be scientifically possible. On a larger scale, he reasoned, the white pill held the promise of relieving "us all from the hates, frustrations, and anxieties we have because of our fear of color." Wright acknowledged that, logically, a pill to turn everybody black might achieve the same thing. But he was trying to be realistic. White Americans would never take a black pill. Wright was also trying to be even-handed, counting himself in the group that needed to be liberated from racism, although he chose a desperately perverse way of saying it. In the same year, 1965, that Malcolm X was assassinated, that President Lyndon Johnson signed the Voting Rights Act, and that Los Angeles exploded, Wright said he would support almost anything to relieve the world of the racism and violence that had been inflicted on him and that ravaged the world still.[65]

This breathtaking conclusion confessed something that must have burned in Wright for years, demanding to be confessed. Every black minister knew, from ministering to others, about the battle against despair that lay behind Wright's conclusion. Some fought off, in themselves, the internalized abuse and self-hatred that yielded Wright's call for a white pill. Throughout his career Wright insisted that racism fell hardest on the high achievers. Blacks at the low end, he claimed, barely knew that racism hurt them. Blacks at his end knew more than they could stand. It made them sick and often ruined their lives. Wright revealed the depth of his trauma by ending his autobiography on this note. For his entire career Wright radiated equanimity, maturity, integrity, high intelligence, and accomplishment. Everyone said it, even people that resented his politics or theology. He was usually the sanest and most competent person in the room. He gave no sign of being a tortured soul, and he never said that he was. But he ended his memoir with an absurd proposal that could only have been a reflection of decades of well-masked trauma. He made himself readily forgotten by doing so, a symbol of the generation that resisted racism too quietly and politely, wounded in a way that made others look away.

But Wright deserved not to be forgotten. He resisted with courage and dignity. He was surpassed by very few of his time in enlisting the church in the struggle to abolish racist ordering. He bore a heavy burden of moral responsibility for decades, making it possible for others who suffered less to surpass him. In many ways he epitomized the class biases of what Evelyn Brooks Higginbotham aptly called "the politics of respectability," but he stoutly opposed bourgeois denigrations of the poor migrants from the South. His accomplishments in numerous fields set the gold standard for many, providing a rare example of combined excellence in sociology, business, journalism, and ministry. Above all, Wright shredded racist denigrations of black ability. At the end of his life he told a newspaper reporter, "There will always be differences in people, but they won't be weighted down by myths." That was the signature achievement of his generation, he rightly believed—to shred the myths of black inferiority that fueled every aspect of America's racial caste system.[66]

THE CROSS, THE LYNCHING TREE, AND
THE NEW ABOLITION

The first and second generations of black social gospel leaders refused to be denigrated. They rebelled against the regime of segregation and persecution imposed upon them. They applied the rhetoric of the old abolition to the new tyranny of Jim Crow, appealing always to the bedrock Christian doctrine that every human being bears the image and Spirit of God. They held fast to Jesus, especially Jesus on the cross, and the hope of the kingdom coming. And some of them lived to see their successors carry out the new abolition.

The black social gospel had all the standard tropes of the white social gospel, even the progress motif and even a variation on Manifest Destiny. It preached equality, democracy, peacemaking, and Jesus loving all the little children. It taught that God favors the oppressed and excluded. It taught that "Thy kingdom come" was the great and ignored center of Jesus's teaching and that Christians are called to build up the kingdom of God. It puzzled that the church claimed the Christian name for centuries while ignoring the biblical ethic of justice. It proclaimed that the salvation of Christ offers deliverance from the bondage of selfishness and will-to-power. It affirmed that missionary zeal is a measure of one's devotion to Christ and the good. It employed "Christianizing" and "democratizing" as interchangeable terms and called for a new age of the Spirit that would unleash the spiritual power of Christ-following idealism.

But one thing mattered more than anything else in black social gospel testimony and worship: the cross of Jesus. The black social gospel shared this emphasis with nearly every Afro-American denomination. White social gospel theology sometimes featured the cross and sometimes pushed it to the margin, but this was not an optional matter in the black church. Here the only option was whether the cross should be rendered doctrinally. Black social gospel ministers often preached the cross of Jesus in the manner of liberal theology, emphasizing moral and spiritual influence, where Jesus exemplified a religious ideal by suffering for others. Following Western tradition, they did not fold the cross into an Eastern Orthodox deification theology, although they sometimes recycled the ancient categories of Eastern and Western ransom theory, in which Jesus died to break the power of Satan over human destiny. Sometimes they vaguely or explicitly espoused a "satisfaction" theory of atonement, that Jesus died to appease the wrath of the Father, rescuing sinners by suffering in their place, or that Jesus died to satisfy the demands of divine moral order, not to appease God's wrath.[67]

Ransom, Powell, Wright, and others influenced by liberal theology usually steered clear of the magical thinking and vengeful deity assumed by the objective theories, and they recognized the pitfall of (subjective) moral influence theory—that interpreting it as an ethical absolute underwrote an ethic of martyrdom that sanctified suffering. Black social gospel leaders inveighed against passivity and defeatism wherever they encountered it in their congregations and communities. They called black Americans to rebel against the oppression and exclusion inflicted on them, usually avoiding any suggestion that the gospel inscribed an ethic of martyrdom. Holding fast to Jesus had nothing to do with accepting racial subjugation as God's will.

This, however, was a slippery problem of theology, ethics, and communication, for every atonement theory is shot through with the idea of redemptive suffering, and the only Western atonement theory that does not offend modern rational consciousness—moral influence doctrine—actually heightens the problem of sacrificial appropriation. All atonement doctrines turn the gospel of Jesus into a rational concept that is explained by a theory of salvation-via-sacrifice. Moral influence theory perpetuates the logic of surrogate sacrifice and heightens its danger of masochistic appropriation. If Jesus exemplified a religious ideal by suffering and dying for others, the gospel becomes a message of self-sacrifice and love perfectionism. Every black minister standing before a congregation had to feel the danger of the cross to the well-being of every listener. Powell, expounding on the "meekness" and self-sacrificial love of Jesus, had to trust that he would be heard in the way that he meant, not in the way of capitulation that it meant to many others.[68]

Yet nothing came close to the cross of Jesus as a subject of black church preaching and worship. Black churches reverberated with hymns, gospel songs, spirituals, prayers, testimonies, and sermons about the crucifixion of Jesus and being with him at the cross. In the testimonies of these religious communities, and in the theology and preaching of nearly every black social gospel thinker, Jesus was a friend of oppressed people who knew about their suffering. Jesus achieved salvation for "the least of these" through his solidarity with them, even unto death. African American Christians, like Jesus, did not deserve to suffer. But keeping faith in Jesus was the one thing that African American Christians possessed that white America could not control or take from them.

For black Christians, merely knowing that Jesus suffered as they did gave them faith that God was with them, even if they ended up, like Jesus, tortured to death on a tree. Liberation theologian James Cone, in *The Cross and the Lynching Tree*, luminously explains: "The more black people struggled against white supremacy, the more they found in the cross the spiritual power to resist the violence they so often suffered." The crucifixion of Jesus placed God among a persecuted, tyrannized, tortured, and crucified people. White communities lynched Afro-Americans in nearly every state of the United States. Lynching, as Cone remarks, was a "ritual celebration of white supremacy," suitable for family gatherings and sometimes drawing enormous crowds. Black Americans, like Jesus, were stripped, paraded, mocked, whipped, spat upon, and tortured to death. Just as Jesus was a victim of mob hysteria and imperial violence, Afro-Americans were victims of mob hysteria and white supremacy. The cross and the lynching tree both struck terror in the heart of the subject community. Terrorism was the point in both cases—terrorizing to enforce obedience and conformity.[69]

Black Christians did not emphasize the cross because they enjoyed suffering or gloried in it or sanctified it. They sang of Jesus because he endured what they suffered. Womanist theologian Shawn Copeland puts it vividly: "The enslaved Africans sang because they saw on the rugged wooden planks One who had endured what was their daily portion. The cross was treasured because it enthroned the One who went all the way with them and for them." To the slaves, as for their descendants in the black churches, the cross represented a victory over the powers of death, a "triumph over evil in this world." Cone adds: "The cross is the burden we must bear in order to attain freedom. . . . One has to have a powerful religious imagination to see redemption in the cross, to discover life in death and hope in tragedy."[70]

Martin Luther King Jr. had a religious imagination of this kind, conveying the terrible, sublime, redemptive power of the cross without trying to explain it in a theory. So did the early social gospel ministers who blazed a path to King, especially Ransom and Powell. They let the spiritual power of the cross do its work without enveloping it in a required doctrine. Powell took this tack even in his revival sermons. Admittedly, precious few ministers of any race or denomination condemned lynching from the pulpit or drew out the connection between lynching and the cross. Quincy Ewing was a rare exception among white social gospel leaders, preaching in Louisiana and Mississippi that lynching was outright murder condemned by God. Northern white social gospelers rarely mentioned this epidemic of social evil, despite their comparative safety. The clergy failed to say what Billie Holiday conveyed in her incomparable song "Strange Fruit"— that the lynching tree *was* the cross in the United States of America.[71]

Ransom, a brave exception, compelled his audiences to grasp that lynching was not merely a "national crime," an epidemic of mob violence, or even an alarming measure of racial antipathy. The plague of lynching said something profound about the kind of Christianity that existed in America and the kind of civilization that America was becoming. How it started was no mystery, Ransom observed. The former slaveholding states went on a lynching rampage to repress former slaves and their children. To justify their barbarities, the lynch mobs described black men as monsters that menaced the safety of white women. The lynch mobs and their allies in the press were so successful at stunting the conscience of the nation that a human being could be burned to death at the stake in Pennsylvania or Georgia without evoking a horrified reaction, "while the pulpit, which should be the first to lead in an attempt to purge the nation of this foul blot, is, for the most part, silent."[72]

Ransom implored black Americans to stop cowering and capitulating: "Negroes themselves are largely to blame for the contempt in which they are held and the impunity with which their liberties and their lives may be invaded. Sheriffs, mayors, courts, governors, will not take seriously into account the interest of a people who have lost or surrendered the right to retaliate or call them to account at the ballot box." As long as the lynch mobs did not fear being gunned down by armed black Americans, Ransom warned, they were sure to continue "their wild brutalities." Ransom refused to apologize for asserting the right of blacks to self-defense, which every other group in America took for granted. As for the ballot box, the Fifteenth Amendment no longer existed for most black Americans, and anyone who called for its reinstatement was branded "a fanatic" and "an enemy of both races." Ransom struggled to fathom how any minimally decent person could invoke the slogan about allowing the South to handle "the Negro problem" that only the South understood. In the gospel spirit of "but I say unto you," Ransom reversed the regnant shibboleth of his time.[73]

He replied, "Leave the Southern white people to us." African Americans had lived among white southerners for two and a half centuries, Ransom explained: "We both know and understand them. We have nursed their children, built their homes, and for more than two hundred years we have fed and clothed them. When they took up arms to destroy the Union in order to bind us in perpetual chains, we did not fire their cities with the torch, nor rise in violence against them, but protected their property, their helpless women and children. Leave them to us." Black Americans, despite their background in southern slavery and feudalism, were imbued with democratic ideals:

> We are Americans filled with the spirit of the twentieth century. Leave them
> to us, and we will make the free public school universal throughout the
> South and open alike to all, without regard to race, creed or color. We will
> make free speech as safe in Mississippi as it is in Massachusetts; we will abol-
> ish lynching and usher in a reign of law, of courts and juries, instead of the
> shotgun, the faggot and the mob. We will abolish peonage, elevate and pro-
> tect labor and make capital secure. Leave them to us; our chivalry shall know

no color line, but our womanhood shall be protected and defended, and our citizens, regardless of race or color, shall be permitted to participate in the government under which we live.[74]

If it were up to black Americans, Ransom concluded, Jim Crow would be abolished and all venues of public life would be "open alike to all without respect to race or color." The tests of recognition and distinction in American society would be "intelligence, character and worth," not anything bound up with race: "Thus as North and South divided over the Negro, so would the Negro unite them in the only bond of union that can stand the test of time — fraternity, justice and righteousness."[75]

It was no small thing to infuse a national denomination and give ballast to a fledgling national civil rights movement with this religious and radical democratic vision of deliverance. Ransom acquired less company than he sought in struggling for the new abolition, and the early black social gospelers were soon forgotten. But they helped to build a counterpublic and a civil rights movement. They planted the social gospel in the mainstream of the black Methodist and black Baptist churches. They refuted the white denigration of black ability and the assurances of white and black critics that there was no such thing as radical black Christianity. And they inspired a stream of successors who carried out America's greatest liberation movement.

NOTES

Where more than one edition of a work is cited, page numbers are for the most recent edition of that work.

CHAPTER 1. RECOVERING THE BLACK SOCIAL GOSPEL

1. For earlier versions of arguments that I make in this chapter about the rise and varieties of the social gospel, see Gary Dorrien, *Social Ethics in the Making: Interpreting an American Tradition* (Oxford: Wiley-Blackwell, 2009).

2. On the concept of a black counterpublic, see The Black Public Sphere Collective, ed., *The Black Public Sphere: A Public Culture Book* (Chicago: University of Chicago Press, 1995); John Brenkman, "Race Publics," *Transition* 66 (1995): 4–36; Michael C. Dawson, *Black Visions: The Roots of Contemporary African-American Political Ideologies* (Chicago: University of Chicago Press, 2001), 25–30. On the counterpublic idea, see Nancy Fraser, "Rethinking the Public Sphere: A Contribution to the Critique of Actually Existing Democracy," in *Habermas and the Public Sphere*, ed. Craig Calhoun (Cambridge, MA: MIT Press, 1992), 109–142.

3. See Booker T. Washington, *Up from Slavery* (1st ed., 1901; repr., New York: W. W. Norton, 1996); Richard R. Wright Jr., *The Bishops of the African Methodist Episcopal Church* (Nashville, TN: AME Sunday School Union, 1963), 173–178, 191–192; E. C. Morris, *Sermons, Addresses and Reminiscences* (Nashville, TN: National Baptist Publishing Board, 1901); August Meier, *Negro Thought in America, 1880–1915* (1st ed., 1963; repr., Ann Arbor: University of Michigan Press, 1988), 218–224; Emma Lou Thornbrough, "Booker T. Washington as Seen by His White Contemporaries," *Journal of Negro History* 53 (August 1968): 160–182; Ray Stannard Baker, *Following the Color Line: American Negro Citizenship in the Progressive Era* (1st ed., 1908; repr., New York: Harper & Row, 1964).

4. See Alexander Crummell, *The Future of Africa: Being Addresses, Sermons, Etc., Delivered in the Republic of Liberia* (New York: Charles Scribner, 1862); Crummell, *Africa and America: Addresses and Discourses* (Springfield, MA: Wiley, 1891);

525

Crummell, *Destiny and Race: Selected Writings, 1848–1898*, ed. Wilson Jeremiah
Moses (Amherst: University of Massachusetts Press, 1992); Sutton E. Griggs, *Imperium
in Imperio: A Study of the Negro Race Problem* (1st ed., 1899; repr., New York: Arno,
1969); Griggs, *Pointing the Way* (1st ed., 1908; reprint, New York: AMS Press, 1974);
William H. Ferris, *The African Abroad; or, His Evolution in Western Civilization,
Tracing His Development Under Caucasian Mileau*, 2 vols. (New Haven, CT: Tuttle,
Morehouse and Taylor, 1913); Wilson Jeremiah Moses, *The Golden Age of Black
Nationalism, 1850–1925* (New York: Oxford University Press, 1978); Wilson Jeremiah
Moses, ed., *Classical Black Nationalism: From the American Revolution to Marcus
Garvey* (New York: New York University Press, 1996); Eddie S. Glaude Jr., *Is It Nation
Time? Contemporary Essays on Black Power and Black Nationalism* (Chicago:
University of Chicago Press, 2002).

5. James R. L. Diggs to W. E. B. Du Bois, November 12, 1906, W. E. B. Du Bois Papers
and Special Collections, University of Massachusetts, Amherst, MA, quote; George
Frazier Miller, "The Social Value of the Undercultured," *Messenger* 10 (October 1919):
24–31; Francis J. Grimké, "The Anglo-American Pulpit and Southern Outrages,"
Independent 45 (May 11, 1893): 644; Grimké, *The Works of Francis J. Grimké*, 4 vols., ed.
Carter G. Woodson (Washington, DC: Associated Publishers, 1942), 1: 379–380; Elliot
Rudwick, "The Niagara Movement," *Journal of Negro History* 42 (1957): 177–200;
Angela Jones, *African American Civil Rights: Early Activism and the Niagara Movement*
(Santa Barbara, CA: Praeger, 2011), 215–234; Kami Fletcher, *The Niagara Movement:
The Black Protest Reborn* (Charleston, SC: VDM Verlag, 2008); Clarence Taylor, *The
Black Churches of Brooklyn* (New York: Columbia University Press, 1994), 121–123;
John Brown Childs, "Concepts of Culture in Afro-American Political Thought, 1890–
1920," *Social Text* 4 (Autumn 1981): 28–43; George Freeman Bragg, *History of the Afro-
American Group of the Episcopal Church* (Baltimore, MD: Church Advocate, 1922).

6. "An Aggregation of Soreheads," *New York Age*, August 16, 1906; George E. Haynes, *The
Trend of the Races* (New York: Council of Women for Home Missions and Missionary
Education Movement, 1922); Kelly Miller, *Race Adjustment: Essays on the Negro in
America* (New York: Neale Publishing, 1909); Monroe N. Work, "Self-Help Among
the Negroes," *Survey*, August 7, 1909, 616–618; "Against Race Prejudice: The Rev. W.
H. Brooks, Colored, Denounces Party Discrimination Against His People," *New York
Times*, October 18, 1897; Henry Hugh Proctor, *Between Black and White:
Autobiographical Sketches* (Boston: Pilgrim Press, 1925); Proctor, "From Cabin to
Pulpit—Life Sketch," *American Missionary* 56 (June 1902): 291–295; Levi J. Coppin,
Unwritten History: An Autobiography (Philadelphia: A.M.E. Book Concern, 1922);
Mary Church Terrell, *A Colored Woman in a White World* (Washington, DC:
Ransdell, 1940); J. W. E. Bowen, "Apology for Higher Education of the Negro,"
Methodist Review (1897); Carter G. Woodson, *The History of the Negro Church*
(Washington, DC: Associated Publishers, 1921), 191–201; Wallace D. Best, *Passionately
Human, No Less Divine: Religion and Culture in Black Chicago, 1915–1952* (Princeton,
NJ: Princeton University Press, 2005), 13–33.

7. Philip S. Foner, ed., *Black Socialist Preacher: The Teachings of Reverend George
Washington Woodbey and His Disciple, Reverend G. W. Slater, Jr.* (San Francisco:

Synthesis Publications, 1983); George Frazier Miller, *Socialism and Its Ethical Basis* (Brooklyn, NY: Hannibal Forum, 1911); Robert W. Bagnall, "The Three False Gods of Civilization," *Messenger* 5 (August 1923): 789–791; "Robert Bagnall with NAACP," *Messenger* 3 (March 1921): 196; Jervis Anderson, *A. Philip Randolph* (New York: Harcourt Brace Jovanovich, 1973), 86–87; David Fort Godshalk, *Veiled Visions: The 1906 Atlanta Race Riot and the Reshaping of American Race Relations* (Chapel Hill: University of North Carolina Press, 2005), 69–74.

8. For classic interpretations of the social gospel as a white phenomenon reacting to industrialization, see Arthur M. Schlesinger Sr., "A Critical Period in American Religion, 1875–1900," Massachusetts Historical Society, *Proceedings* 64 (June 1932): 523–547; Charles Howard Hopkins, *The Rise of the Social Gospel in American Protestantism, 1865–1915* (New Haven, CT: Yale University Press, 1940); Henry May, *Protestant Churches and Industrial America* (New York: Harper & Brothers, 1949); Aaron I. Abell, *The Urban Impact on American Protestantism, 1865–1900* (Cambridge, MA: Harvard University Press, 1943); and Donald K. Gorrell, *The Age of Social Responsibility: The Social Gospel in the Progressive Era, 1900–1920* (Macon, GA: Mercer University Press, 1988). For influential renderings of the convention, often relying on the above sources, that the white social gospel ignored racial justice issues, see Sidney E. Ahlstrom, *A Religious History of the American People* (New Haven, CT: Yale University Press, 1972), 691; Peter J. Frederick, *Knights of the Golden Rule: The Intellectual as Christian Social Reformer in the 1890s* (Lexington: University Press of Kentucky, 1976), 24; George Frederickson, *The Black Image in the White Mind: The Debate on Afro-American Character and Destiny, 1817–1914* (New York: Harper & Row, 1971), 302–304; Thomas F. Gossett, *Race: The History of an Idea in America* (New York: Schocken, 1963), 172–179; Rayford W. Logan, *The Negro in American Life and Thought: The Nadir, 1877–1901*, rev. ed., Logan, *The Betrayal of the Negro: From Rutherford B. Hayes to Woodrow Wilson* (New York: Collier Books, 1965), 165–167; Martin E. Marty, *Righteous Empire: The Protestant Experience in America* (New York: Harper & Row, 1970), 206; Robert Moats Miller, *American Protestantism and Social Issues, 1919–1939* (Chapel Hill: University of North Carolina Press, 1958), 9–10; David M. Reimers, *White Protestantism and the Negro* (New York: Oxford University Press, 1963), 53–54; Leonard I. Sweet, *Black Images of White America* (New York: W. W. Norton, 1976), 177; Preston N. Williams, "The Social Gospel and Race Relations: A Case Study of a Social Movement," in *Toward a Discipline of Social Ethics: Essays in Honor of Walter George Muelder*, ed. Paul Deats Jr. (Boston: Boston University Press, 1972), 232–255. Two scholars wrote breakthrough texts on the white social gospel movement's engagement with racial justice issues: Ralph E. Luker, *The Social Gospel in Black and White: American Racial Reform, 1885–1912* (Chapel Hill: University of North Carolina Press, 1991); and Ronald C. White Jr., *Liberty and Justice for All: Racial Reform and the Social Gospel (1877–1925)* (Louisville, KY: Westminster John Knox Press, 1990).

9. See E. Franklin Frazier, *Black Bourgeoisie* (New York: Free Press, 1962); Rayford W. Logan, *Howard University: The First Hundred Years, 1867–1967* (New York: New York University Press, 1969); Zachery R. Williams, *In Search of the Talented Tenth: Howard*

University Public Intellectuals and the Dilemmas of Race, 1926–1970 (Columbia: University of Missouri Press, 2009); Kenneth Robert Janken, *Rayford W. Logan and the Dilemma of the African American Intellectual* (Amherst: University of Massachusetts Press, 1993); Anthony Platt, *E. Franklin Frazier Reconsidered* (New Brunswick, NJ: Rutgers University Press, 1991).

10. See Taylor Branch, *Parting the Waters: America in the King Years, 1954–63* (New York: Touchstone, 1988); David J. Garrow, *Bearing the Cross: Martin Luther King Jr. and the Southern Christian Leadership Conference* (New York: Quill, 1986); Charles Marsh, *The Beloved Community: How Faith Shapes Social Justice, from the Civil Rights Movement to Today* (New York: Basic Books, 2005); David L. Chappell, *A Stone of Hope: Prophetic Religion and the Death of Jim Crow* (Chapel Hill: University of North Carolina Press, 2004); Lewis V. Baldwin, *There Is a Balm in Gilead: The Cultural Roots of Martin Luther King, Jr.* (Minneapolis, MN: Fortress Press, 1991); Johnny E. Williams, *African American Religion and the Civil Rights Movement in Arkansas* (Jackson: University of Mississippi Press, 2003); Aldon D. Morris, *The Origins of the Civil Rights Movement: Black Communities Organizing for Change* (New York: Free Press, 1984). For recent works arguing that most of the literature on the civil rights movement overemphasizes religion and King, see Jones, *African American Civil Rights*, 149–172, and T. V. Reed, *The Art of Protest: Culture and Activism from the Civil Rights Movement to the Streets of Seattle* (Minneapolis: University of Minnesota Press, 2005).

11. Woodson, *The History of the Negro Church*; Benjamin E. Mays and Joseph W. Nicholson, *The Negro's Church* (New York: Institute of Social and Religious Research, 1933).

12. See David W. Wills, "An Enduring Distance: Black Americans and the Establishment," in *Between the Times: The Travail of the Protestant Establishment in America, 1900–1960*, ed. William R. Hutchison (Cambridge: Cambridge University Press, 1990), 168–188; Moses N. Moore Jr., "From Atlanta to Brooklyn: The Social Gospel Ministry and Legacy of Henry H. Proctor," *Union Seminary Quarterly Review* 62 (2010): 52–69; Egbert Ethelred Brown, "Building the Church of Tomorrow," sermon preached at Harlem Unitarian Church, 1938, Egbert Ethelred Brown Papers, Schomburg Center for Research in Black Culture, New York, NY; Brown, "The Religion of the Negro," *New York Amsterdam News*, January 2, 1926; Juan M. Floyd-Thomas, *The Origins of Black Humanism in America: Reverend Ethelred Brown and the Unitarian Church* (New York: Palgrave Macmillan, 2008); Mark D. Morrison-Reed, *Black Pioneers in a White Denomination* (Boston: Skinner House Books, 1994).

13. On the politics of respectability, see Evelyn Brooks Higginbotham, *Righteous Discontent: The Women's Movement in the Black Baptist Church, 1880–1920* (Cambridge, MA: Harvard University Press, 1993), 185–229; Kevin Gaines, *Uplifting the Race: Black Leadership, Politics, and Culture in the Twentieth Century* (Chapel Hill: University of North Carolina Press, 1996), 31–78; Walter Earl Fluker, "Recognition, Respectability, and Loyalty: Black Churches and the Quest for Civility," in *New Day Begun: African American Churches and Civic Culture in Post-Civil Rights America*, ed. Drew Smith (Durham, NC: Duke University Press, 2003), 120–124.

14. Miller, *Race Adjustment*, 13–29; Adam Clayton Powell Sr., *Riots and Ruins* (New York: Richard R. Smith, 1945), 150.

15. Gayraud S. Wilmore, *Black Religion and Black Radicalism: An Interpretation of the Religious History of African Americans* (New York: Doubleday, 1973; 3rd ed., Maryknoll, NY: Orbis Books, 1998), quotes, ix, 197.

16. Ibid., 149–153, "without," 300; Cedric J. Robinson, *Black Marxism: The Making of the Black Radical Tradition* (1st ed., 1983; repr., Chapel Hill: University of North Carolina Press, 2000); James H. Cone, *A Black Theology of Liberation* (1st ed., 1970; repr., Maryknoll, NY: Orbis, 1990); Cone, *Martin & Malcolm & America: A Dream or a Nightmare?* (Maryknoll, NY: Orbis, 1991); Henry McNeal Turner, "The Races Must Separate," in *The Possibilities of the Negro—In Symposium*, ed. Willis B. Parks (Atlanta: Franklin, 1904), 91–92; C. L. R. James, *The C. L. R. James Reader*, ed. Anna Grimshaw (Oxford: Blackwell, 1993); Richard Wright, *Native Son* (New York: Harper & Brothers, 1940).

17. See Henry McNeal Turner, "The Colored National Emigration Association," *Voice of the People*, September 1903, in Turner, *Respect Black: The Writings and Speeches of Henry McNeal Turner*, ed. Edwin S. Redkey (New York: Arno, 1971), 194–195; Turner, "The Afro-American Future," *Twentieth Century Negro Literature*, ed. D. W. Culp (Philadelphia: J. L. Nichols, 1902), 42–45.

18. W. E. B. Du Bois, *Dusk of Dawn: An Essay Toward an Autobiography of a Race Concept* (New York: Harcourt, Brace & World, 1940), "vaster," xxx; Du Bois, "The Talented Tenth," in *The Negro Problem: A Series of Articles by Representative Negroes of To-day* (1903; repr., New York: AMS, 1970, "The Negro," 33; Lawrie Balfour, *Democracy's Reconstruction: Thinking Politically with W. E. B. Du Bois* (New York: Oxford University Press, 2011), 71–75, "mere," 75; Nahum D. Chandler, "The Figure of W. E. B. Du Bois as a Problem for Thought," *CR: The New Centennial Review* 6 (2007): 46–47.

19. Booker T. Washington, "A Sunday Evening Talk: The Kingdom of God," in *The Booker T. Washington Papers*, 14 vols., ed. Louis R. Harlan, Raymond W. Smock, and Geraldine McTighe (Urbana: University of Illinois Press, 1972–1989), 9: 87–90; Washington, "The Colored Ministry: Its Defects and Needs," *Christian Union* 42 (August 14, 1890): 199–200; Washington, "The Golden Rule in Atlanta," *Outlook* 84 (December 15, 1906): 913–916; Washington, *The Story of My Life and Work* (1st ed., 1900; repr., New York: Barnes & Noble, 2008), 67–75; Lyman Abbott, "Booker T. Washington on Our Racial Problem," *Outlook* 64 (January 6, 1900): 14–17; Abbott, "The Basis of Anglo-Saxon Understanding," *North American Review* 166 (May 1898): 513–521; J. W. E. Bowen, "Why?," *Christian Educator* 4 (October 1892): 3; Frank T. Bayley, "Address of the Reverend Frank T. Bayley," *American Missionary* 47 (December 1893): 437–438; W. E. C. Wright, "The New Negro," *American Missionary* 47 (January 1894): 10; Emma Lou Thornbrough, "Booker T. Washington as Seen by His White Contemporaries," *Journal of Negro History* 53 (August 1968): 160–182; Editorial, "Colony Notes," *Social Gospel* 2 (March 1898): 21–22; Samuel H. Comings, "Some Educational Plans," *Social Gospel* 3 (April 1898): 10; James Dombrowski, *The Early Days of Christian Socialism in America* (New York: Columbia University Press, 1936), 132–170; Ralph Albertson, "The Christian Commonwealth in Georgia," *Georgia*

Historical Quarterly 29 (September 1945): 125–142; John O. Fish, "The Christian Commonwealth: A Georgia Experiment, 1896–1900," *Georgia Historical Quarterly* 57 (Summer 1972): 213–226.

20. Washington Gladden, "Some Impressions Gained During a Visit to the Southern United States," sermon, May 31, 1903, Washington Gladden Papers, Ohio Historical Society, Columbus, OH; see Gary Dorrien, *The Making of American Liberal Theology: Imagining Progressive Religion, 1805–1900* (Louisville, KY: Westminster John Knox Press, 2001), 262–334.

21. See Lawrence Goodwyn, *The Populist Moment: A Short History of the Agrarian Revolt in America* (New York: Oxford University Press, 1978); Connie Lester, *Up from the Mudsills of Hell: The Farmers' Alliance, Populism, and Progressive Agriculture in Tennessee, 1870–1915* (Athens: University of Georgia Press, 2006); Paula Giddings, *When and Where I Enter: The Impact of Black Women on Race and Sex in America* (New York: HarperCollins, 1984), 79; W. J. Cash, *The Mind of the South* (New York: Knopf, 1941), 86–87; C. Vann Woodward, "Tom Watson and the Negro in Agrarian Politics," *Journal of Southern History* 4 (February 1938): 14–33; Woodward, *Tom Watson: Agrarian Rebel* (New York: Macmillan, 1938), 379–380.

22. On the Great Migration, see Nicholas Lemann, *The Promised Land: The Great Black Migration and How It Changed America* (New York: Knopf, 1991); Carol Marks, *Farewell—We're Good and Gone: The Great Black Migration* (Bloomington: Indiana University Press, 1989); James R. Grossman, *Land of Hope: Chicago, Black Southerners, and the Great Migration* (Chicago: University of Chicago Press, 1989); Milton C. Sernett, *Bound for the Promised Land: African American Religion and the Great Migration* (Durham, NC: Duke University Press, 1997).

23. George Freeman Bragg, *Afro-American Church Work and Workers* (Baltimore, MD: Church Advocate, 1904); Bragg, *History of the Afro-American Group of the Episcopal Church*, 26–291; Proctor, *Between Black and White*, 105–114; Woodson, *History of the Negro Church*, 191–201; Best, *Passionately Human, No Less Divine*, 13–93; Higginbotham, *Righteous Discontent*, 171–177.

24. Taylor, *Black Churches of Brooklyn*, 28–29; "Constitution and By-Laws of the Brooklyn Literary Union," *New York Age*, September 26, 1891.

25. See Washington Gladden, *Applied Christianity: Moral Aspects of Social Questions* (Boston: Houghton, Mifflin, 1886); Gladden, *Present Day Theology* (Columbus, OH: McClelland, 1913); Richard T. Ely, *Social Aspects of Christianity* (New York: Thomas Y. Crowell, 1889); Charles M. Sheldon, *In His Steps* (1897; repr., New York: Grosset & Dunlap, 1935).

26. W. E. B. Du Bois, "The Future of Wilberforce University," *Journal of Negro Education* 9 (October 1940), "childish" and "a miserable," 564–565; Du Bois, *Darkwater: Voices from Within the Veil* (New York: Harcourt, Brace, 1920; repr., Mineola, NY: Dover, 1999), "Credo," 1–2, "The Second Coming," 60–62, "Jesus Christ in Texas," 70–77, "A Hymn to the Peoples," 161–162; Du Bois, "Untitled," in *Creative Writings by W. E. B. Du Bois*, ed. Herbert Aptheker (Millwood, NY: Kraus-Thomson, 1985), "the tattered," 41; Jonathon S. Kahn, *Divine Discontent: The Religious Imagination of W. E. B. Du Bois* (New York: Oxford University Press, 2009), 3–8.

27. Kahn, *Divine Discontent*, "At these," 7; Edward J. Blum, *W. E. B. Du Bois: American Prophet* (Philadelphia: University of Pennsylvania Press, 2007), "Du Bois was," 10; Du Bois, "The Future of Wilberforce University," "Christianity," 565.

28. W. E. B. Du Bois, *The Souls of Black Folk* (Chicago: A. C. McClurg, 1903; repr., New York: Dover, 1994), 31–32.

29. See Reinhold Niebuhr, *Moral Man and Immoral Society: A Study in Ethics and Politics* (New York: Scribner's, 1932).

30. Reinhold Niebuhr, *The Children of Light and the Children of Darkness* (New York: Scribner's, 1944; repr., Chicago: University of Chicago Press, 2011); Gary Dorrien, *Economy, Difference, Empire: Social Ethics for Social Justice* (New York: Columbia University Press, 2010), 46–65.

31. See Howard Thurman, "Let Ministers Be Christians!" *Student Challenge*, January 1925, 1, 14; Thurman, "The Perils of Immature Piety," *Student Volunteer Movement Bulletin*, May 1925, 110–113; Benjamin E. Mays, "Democratizing and Christianizing America in This Generation," *Journal of Negro Education* 14 (Fall 1945): 527–534; James L. Roark, "American Black Leaders: The Response to Colonialism and the Cold War, 1943–1953," *African Historical Studies* 4 (1971): 253–270.

32. See Clayborne Carson, "Martin Luther King Jr. and the African-American Social Gospel," in *African American Religious Thought: An Anthology*, ed. Cornel West and Eddie S. Glaude Jr. (Louisville, KY: Westminster John Knox Press, 2003), 696–714; Calvin S. Morris, *Reverdy C. Ransom: Black Advocate of the Social Gospel* (Lanham, MD: University Press of America, 1990); Anthony B. Pinn, *ed., Making the Gospel Plain: The Writings of Reverdy C. Ransom* (Harrisburg, PA: Trinity, 1999); Pinn, *The African American Religious Experience in America* (Westport, CT: Greenwood, 2005); Luker, *Social Gospel in Black and White*; Walter E. Fluker, *They Looked for a City: A Comparative Analysis of the Ideal of Community in the Thought of Howard Thurman and Martin Luther King Jr.* (Lanham, MD: University Press of America, 1989); Quinton H. Dixie and Peter Eisenstadt, *Visions of a Better World: Howard Thurman's Pilgrimage to India and the Origins of African American Nonviolence* (Boston: Beacon Press, 2011).

33. Jones, *African American Civil Rights*, 2–3, 150–155, "spotlight," 3; Shawn Leigh Alexander, *An Army of Lions: The Civil Rights Struggle Before the NAACP* (Philadelphia: University of Pennsylvania Press, 2012), "Du Bois has," xiii; see Benjamin R. Justesen, *Broken Brotherhood: The Rise and Fall of the National Afro-American Council* (Southern Illinois University Press, 2008).

34. W. E. B. Du Bois, *The Philadelphia Negro: A Social Study* (Philadelphia: University of Pennsylvania Press, 1899, repr., 1996), 388.

35. Hazel B. Carby, *Race Men* (Cambridge, MA: Harvard University Press, 1998), "complete," 10; see Patricia Morton, *Disfigured Images: The Historical Assault on Afro-American Women* (New York: Greenwood, 1991), 58–59; Gaines, *Uplifting the Race*, 152–178; Brenda Gayle Plummer, *Rising Wind: Black Americans and U.S. Foreign Affairs, 1935–1960* (Chapel Hill: University of North Carolina Press, 1996), 135–136; Balfour, *Democracy's Reconstruction*, 98–111; Farah Jasmine Griffin, "Black Feminists and Du Bois: Respectability, Protection and Beyond," *Annals of the American Academy*

of Political and Social Science 568 (March 2000): 28–40; Joy James, *Transcending the Talented Tenth: Black Leaders and American Intellectuals* (New York: Routledge, 1997).

36. Cheryl Townsend Gilkes, "The Margin as the Center of a Theory of History: African-American Women, Social Change, and the Sociology of W. E. B. Du Bois," in *W. E. B. Du Bois on Race and Culture*, ed. Bernard W. Bell, Emily R. Grosholz, and James B. Stewart (New York: Routledge, 1996), "self-consciously," 134; Du Bois, *Darkwater*, 104.

37. Terrell, *Colored Woman in a White World*, 185–193; Mary Church Terrell, "First Presidential Address to the National Association of Colored Women," in *Quest for Equality: The Life and Writings of Mary Eliza Church Terrell, 1863–1954*, ed. Beverly Washington Jones (Brooklyn, NY: Carlson Publishing, 1990), 133–138; Higginbotham, *Righteous Discontent*, 150–184; Floris Barnett Cash, *African American Women and Social Action: The Clubwomen and Volunteerism from Jim Crow to the New Deal, 1896–1926* (Westport, CT: Greenwood, 2001); Deborah Gray White, *Too Heavy a Load: Black Women in Defense of Themselves, 1894–1994* (New York: W. W. Norton, 1999); Karen J. Blair, *The Clubwoman as Feminist: True Womanhood Redefined, 1868–1914* (New York: Holmes and Meier, 1980).

38. Charles Fox Parham, a white minister under whom Seymour studied briefly in Houston, is often credited as the founder of the Pentecostal movement, usually on the claim that he was the first to identify speaking in tongues with the baptism of the Holy Spirit. But Pentecostalism did not spread immediately to fifty nations because of a theological formulation. It was Seymour's three-year revival at Azusa Street Mission in Los Angeles that gave birth to modern Pentecostalism. See Charles Edwin Jones, *A Guide to the Study of the Holiness Movement* (Metuchen, NJ: Scarecrow, 1974); Phoebe Palmer, *The Way of Holiness* (New York: G. Lane and C. B. Tippett, 1845); William J. Seymour, *Doctrine and Discipline of the Azusa Street Apostolic Faith Mission of Los Angeles* (Los Angeles: William J. Seymour, 1915); Donald S. Metz, *Speaking in Tongues: An Analysis* (Kansas City, MO: Nazarene Publishing House, 1964); Vinson Synan, *The Holiness-Pentecostal Movement* (Grand Rapids, MI: Eerdmans, 1971); James R. Goff, *Fields White Unto Harvest: Charles F. Parham and the Missionary Origins of Pentecostalism* (Fayetteville: University of Arkansas Press, 1988); Iain MacRobert, *The Black Roots and White Racism of Early Pentecostalism in the USA* (Basingstoke, UK: Macmillan, 1988).

39. Melville Herskovits, *The Myth of the Negro Past* (Boston: Beacon Press, 1941), 211–217; James S. Tinney, "William J. Seymour: Father of Modern-Day Pentecostalism," in *Black Apostles: Afro-American Clergy Confront the Twentieth Century*, ed. Randall K. Burkett and Richard Newman (Boston: G. K. Hall, 1978), 213–222; Iain MacRobert, "The Black Roots of Pentecostalism," in *African-American Religion: Interpretive Essays in History and Culture*, ed. Timothy E. Fulop and Albert J. Raboteau (New York: Routledge, 1997), 297–307.

40. Du Bois, *Souls of Black Folk*, 116; James Farmer, *Lay Bare the Heart: An Autobiography of the Civil Rights Movement* (1985; repr., Fort Worth: Texas Christian University Press, 1986), quotes, 33; Cheryl Townsend Gilkes, *"If It Wasn't for the Women . . ."*

Black Women's Experience and Womanist Culture in Church and Community
(Maryknoll, NY: Orbis Books, 2001), 76–91, "overwhelmingly," 77; Best, *Passionately
Human, No Less Divine*, 159–180; Zora Neale Hurston, *The Sanctified Church*
(Berkeley, CA: Turtle Press, 1981).

41. Barbara Dianne Savage, *Your Spirits Walk Beside Us: The Politics of Black Religion*
(Cambridge, MA: Harvard University Press, 2008), quote, 23; see Woodson, *History of
the Negro Church*; Mays and Nicholson, *Negro's Church*; W. E. B. Du Bois, ed., *The
Negro Church* (Atlanta: Atlanta University Press, 1903).

42. Carter G. Woodson, "A United Negro Church," *New York Age*, August 15, 1931, 9;
Woodson, "Difficulties in Way of the United Church," *New York Age*, August 21, 1931,
9; Woodson, "The Union of Churches Considered Utopian," *New York Age*, September
5, 1931, 9; Woodson, "Superfluous Negro Preachers Prevent the Union of the
Churches," *New York Age*, October 10, 1931, 9; Jacqueline Giggin, *Carter G. Woodson:
A Life in Black History* (Baton Rouge: Louisiana State University Press, 1993), quote,
142; Savage, *Your Spirits Walk Beside Us*, "I find," 47–48.

43. W. E. B. Du Bois, "Careers Open to College-bred Negroes," in *Writings by W. E. B.
Du Bois in Non-Periodical Literature Edited by Others*, ed. Herbert Aptheker
(Millwood, NY: Kraus-Thomson, 1982), "divine," 9; Du Bois, *Prayers for Dark People*,
ed. Herbert Aptheker (Amherst: University of Massachusetts Press, 1980), "whether
they were," x; see David Levering Lewis, *W. E. B. Du Bois: Biography of a Race,
1868–1919* (New York: Henry Holt, 1993), 49–50, 65–66, 198; Arnold Rampersad, *The
Art and Imagination of W. E. B. Du Bois* (Cambridge, MA: Harvard University Press,
1976), 19–20, 85–86; Blum, *W. E. B. Du Bois*, 5–19, 163–180; Kahn, *Divine Discontent*,
10–47; Manning Marable, "The Black Faith of W. E. B. Du Bois: Sociocultural and
Political Dimensions of Black Religion," *Southern Quarterly* 23 (Spring 1985): 14–15;
Paul C. Taylor, "What's the Use of Calling Du Bois a Pragmatist?" *Metaphilosophy* 35
(January 2004): 99–114; Eddie S. Glaude Jr., *In a Shade of Blue: Pragmatism and the
Politics of Black America* (Chicago: University of Chicago Press, 2007), 3.

44. W. E. B. Du Bois, "Segregation," *Crisis* 41 (January 1934): 20; Du Bois, "Postscript,"
Crisis 41 (May 1934): 149; Du Bois, "Postscript," *Crisis* 41 (April 1934): 115–117.

45. Henry Louis Gates Jr., Introduction to Bantam reprint edition of W. E. B. Du Bois,
The Souls of Black Folk (New York: Bantam, 1989), xvii–xviii; Gates, *The Signifying
Monkey: A Theory of African-American Literary Criticism* (New York: Oxford University
Press, 1988), "the Afro-American's," 207; Balfour, *Democracy's Reconstruction*, 73–74;
Robert Gooding-Williams, *In the Shadow of Du Bois: Afro-American Political Thought
in America* (Cambridge, MA: Harvard University Press, 2009), 66–129; Gooding-
Williams, "Philosophy of History and Social Critique in *The Souls of Black Folk*,"
Social Science Information 26 (1987): 106–108; Joel Williamson, *The Crucible of Race:
Black-White Relations in the American South Since Emancipation* (New York: Oxford
University Press, 1984), 402–409; Cornel West, *Prophesy Deliverance! An Afro-American
Revolutionary Christianity* (Philadelphia: Westminster Press, 1982), 30–31; Lawrence
D. Bobo, "Reclaiming a Du Boisian Perspective on Racial Attitudes," *ANNALS of the
American Academy of Political and Social Science* 568 (March 2000): 186–202; Adolph
L. Reed Jr., *W. E. B. Du Bois and American Political Thought: Fabianism and the*

Color Line (New York: Oxford University Press, 1997), 107–125; Ernest Allen Jr., "Du Boisian Double Consciousness: The Unsustainable Argument," *Massachusetts Review* 43 (2002), "double," 217; Eboni Marshall Turman, *Toward a Womanist Ethic of Incarnation* (New York: Palgrave Macmillan, 2013); Paul Gilroy, *The Black Atlantic: Modernity and Double Consciousness* (Cambridge, MA: Harvard University Press, 1993), 111–145; Gilroy, *Against Race: Imagining Political Culture Beyond the Color Line* (Cambridge, MA: Harvard University Press, 2000), 51–52; see Shamoon Zamir, *Dark Voices: W. E. B. Du Bois and American Thought, 1883–1903* (Chicago: University of Chicago Press, 1995); Thomas F. Slaughter Jr., "Epidermalizing the World: A Basic Mode of Being Black," in *Philosophy Born of Struggle: Anthology of Afro-American Philosophy from 1917,* ed. Leonard Harris (Dubuque, IA: Kendall-Hunt, 1983), 283–284.

46. Peter J. Paris, *The Social Teaching of the Black Churches* (Philadelphia: Fortress Press, 1985).

CHAPTER 2. APOSTLES OF NEW ABOLITION

1. W. E. B. Du Bois, ed., *The Negro Church* (Atlanta: Atlanta University Press, 1903; rev. ed., ed. Alton B. Pollard III, Eugene, OR: Cascade Books, 2011), quotes, 162; Richard Allen, *The Life, Experience, and Gospel Labors of the Right Reverend Richard Allen* (Nashville, TN: Abingdon, 1983), 15–26.

2. Jarena Lee, *The Life and Religious Experience of Jarena Lee, A Colored Lady, Giving an Account of Her Call to Preach the Gospel,* 1836, repr. in *Sisters of the Spirit: Three Black Women's Autobiographies of the Nineteenth Century,* ed. William L. Andrews (Bloomington: Indiana University Press, 1986); Carol V. R. George, *Segregated Sabbaths: Richard Allen and the Emergence of Black Independent Churches, 1760–1840* (New York: Oxford University Press, 1973), 21–55, 63–183; Carter G. Woodson, *The History of the Negro Church* (Washington, DC: Associated Publishers, 1921), 54–56; C. Eric Lincoln and Lawrence H. Mamiya, *The Black Church in the African American Experience* (Durham, NC: Duke University Press, 1990), 51–52; Du Bois, *Negro Church,* 166, 169; Daniel A. Payne, *History of the African Methodist Episcopal Church* (Nashville, TN: AME Sunday School Union, 1891; repr., New York: Johnson Reprint, 1968), 313–408; Gary B. Nash, *The Struggle for Freedom: A History of African Americans* (Boston: Prentice-Hall, 2011), 156–157.

3. Mungo M. Ponton, *The Life and Times of Henry M. Turner* (Atlanta: A. B. Caldwell, 1917; repr., New York: Negro Universities Press, 1970), 33; Stephen Ward Angell, *Bishop Henry McNeal Turner and African-American Religion in the South* (Knoxville: University of Tennessee Press, 1992), 7; Reverdy Ransom, "Bishop Henry McNeal Turner," *A.M.E. Church Review* 32 (July 1915): 45–46. No evidence has been uncovered that confirms the royal bloodline story, but Ponton treated it as historical fact, reflecting Turner's view of it.

4. William J. Simmons, *Men of Mark: Eminent, Progressive, and Rising* (Cleveland: Rewell, 1887; repr., New York: Arno, 1968), 805–807; Ponton, *Life and Times of Henry M. Turner,* 34; Angell, *Bishop Henry McNeal Turner,* 8–13.

5. Ponton, *Life and Times of Henry M. Turner*, 34–35; Angell, *Bishop Henry McNeal Turner*, 20–24; Simmons, *Men of Mark*, 807; J. Minton Batten, "Henry M. Turner, Negro Bishop Extraordinary," *Church History* 7 (1938): 231–233.

6. Henry McNeal Turner, Journal entry, December 15, 1860, in *An African American Pastor Before and During the American Civil War, Volume One: The Literary Archive of Henry McNeal Turner*, ed. Andre E. Johnson (Lewiston, NY: Edwin Mellen Press, 2010), "with facility," 3; Turner, Journal entry, December 12, 1862, ibid., "very much," 4; Turner, "Emancipation Day," January 1, 1913, in Turner, *The Negro in Slavery, War, and Peace* (Philadelphia: A.M.E. Book Concern, 1913), reprinted in Turner, *Respect Black: The Writings and Speeches of Henry McNeal Turner*, ed. Edwin S. Redkey (New York: Arno, 1971), 1–4; Angell, *Bishop Henry McNeal Turner*, 25–30; Alexander W. Wayman, *My Recollections of African M. E. Ministers; or, Forty Years' Experience in the African Methodist Episcopal Church* (Philadelphia: A.M.E. Book Rooms, 1881), 71–75; Ponton, *Life and Times of Henry M. Turner*, 35–36.

7. Henry McNeal Turner, "The Colored Men and the Draft," *Christian Recorder*, August 23, 1863, in *An African American Pastor*, "We must," 30; Turner, "Washington Correspondence," *Christian Recorder*, October 4, 1862, ibid., "Mr. Lincoln," 112; Turner, "Emancipation Day," "Such," 3.

8. Henry Ward Beecher, "Against a Compromise of Principle," Thanksgiving Day Address of 1860, in Beecher, *Freedom and War: Discourses on Topics Suggested by the Times* (Boston: Ticknor and Fields, 1863), 28–56, "a rotten," 40; Beecher, "The Battle Set in Array," April 14, 1861, ibid., 84–110, "I hold," 95; see Horace Bushnell, *Reverses Needed, A Discourse Delivered on the Sunday after the Disaster of Bull Run, in the North Church, Hartford* (Hartford: L. E. Hunt, 1861); Bushnell, *The Vicarious Sacrifice, Grounded in Principles of Universal Obligation* (New York: Charles Scribner, 1866); Mark A. Noll, *The Civil War as a Theological Crisis* (Chapel Hill: University of North Carolina Press, 2006); David B. Chesebrough, ed., *"God Ordained This War": Sermons on the Sectional Crisis, 1830–1865* (Columbia: University of South Carolina Press, 1991).

9. Henry McNeal Turner to the Editor, *Washington Post*, February 2, 1895, "race love"; Petition to the U.S. House of Representatives and Senate, April 1862, in *Free At Last: A Documentary History of Slavery, Freedom, and the Civil War*, ed. Ira Berlin, Barbara J. Fields, Steven F. Miller, Joseph P. Reidy, and Leslie S. Rowland (New York: New Press, 1992), 38–41, quotes, 40; Alexander Crummell, *The Future of Africa: Being Addresses, Sermons, Etc., Delivered in the Republic of Liberia* (New York: Charles Scribner, 1862), 70–72; James Redpath, *Guide to Hayti* (Boston: Haytian Bureau of Emigration, 1861); see Redpath, *The Public Life of Capt. John Brown* (Boston: Thayer and Eldridge, 1860); John R. McKivigan, "James Redpath and Black Reaction to the Haitian Emigration Bureau," *Mid-America* 69 (October 1987): 139–153; McKivigan, *Forgotten Firebrand: James Redpath and the Making of Nineteenth-Century America* (New York: Cornell University Press, 2008).

10. Henry McNeal Turner, "Washington Correspondence," *Christian Recorder*, August 30, 1862, "compulsory" and "that it was"; Turner, "Washington Correspondence: Republican Form of Government," *Christian Recorder*, October 3, 1863, "For every";

Turner, "Washington Correspondence," *Christian Recorder*, August 8, 1862; Turner, "Washington Correspondence," *Christian Recorder*, April 11, 1863; Turner, "From Chaplain Turner," *Christian Recorder*, June 25, 1864; Turner, "A Very Important Letter," *Christian Recorder*, July 9, 1864; Angell, *Bishop Henry McNeal Turner*, 47–48; *An African American Pastor*, 96–97; Frederick Bancroft, *The Colonization of American Negroes, 1801–1865* (Norman: University of Oklahoma Press, 1957), 192–258.

11. Turner, "The Colored Men and the Draft," quotes, 30, 31.

12. Angell, *Bishop Henry McNeal Turner*, 52–59; Ponton, *Life and Times of Henry M. Turner*, 51–56; Edwin Redkey, "'Rocked in the Cradle of Consternation': A Black Chaplain in the Union Army Reports on the Struggle to Take Fort Fisher, North Carolina, in the Winter of 1864–1865," *American Heritage* 31 (December 1980): 70–79.

13. Lincoln and Mamiya, *Black Church*, 56–58; Woodson, *History of the Negro Church*, 57–60; William J. Walls, *The African Methodist Episcopal Zion Church: Reality of the Black Church* (Charlotte, NC: AME Zion, 1974), 39–52; David Henry Bradley, *History of the AME Zion Church* (Nashville, TN: Parthenon, 1970).

14. Henry McNeal Turner, "Emancipation Day Celebration Address," January 1, 1866, in Augusta *Colored American*, January 13, 1866, in Turner, *Celebration of the First Anniversary of Freedom* (Augusta: Georgia Union League, 1866), quotes, 12, 14, and in Turner, *Respect Black*, 4–12; see Andre E. Johnson, *The Forgotten Prophet: Bishop Henry McNeal Turner and the African American Prophetic Tradition* (Lanham, MD: Lexington Books, 2012), 46; Woodson, *History of the Negro Church*, 133–138; Angell, *Bishop Henry McNeal Turner*, 64–69; Ponton, *Life and Times of Henry M. Turner*, 66–67.

15. Walter L. Fleming, *Documentary History of Reconstruction: Political, Military, Social, Religious, Educational, and Industrial*, 2 vols. (Cleveland: A. H. Clark, 1906–1907), quote, 2: 13–14; Steven Hahn, *A Nation under Our Feet: Black Political Struggles in the Rural South from Slavery to the Great Migration* (Cambridge, MA: Harvard University Press, 2003), 185–186; Leon F. Litwick, *Been in the Storm So Long: The Aftermath of Slavery* (New York: Knopf, 1979), 78–92; Michael W. Fitzgerald, *The Union League Movement in the Deep South: Politics and Agricultural Change during Reconstruction* (Baton Rouge: Louisiana State University Press, 2000).

16. Henry McNeal Turner, Speech in Columbia, South Carolina, April 1867, in Johnson, *Forgotten Prophet*, "The interests," 50; Turner, Speech to the Georgia Annual Conference, 1871, in Ponton, *Life and Times of Henry M. Turner*, 67–72, and in Turner, *Respect Black*, 29–32, "My labors" and "I have," 31.

17. See John Hope Franklin, *Reconstruction after the Civil War* (Chicago: University of Chicago Press, 1961; 2nd ed., 1994), 129–130; Eric Foner, *Reconstruction: America's Unfinished Revolution, 1863–1877* (New York: Harper & Row, 1988), 346–348.

18. Franklin, *Reconstruction after the Civil War*, 92; W. E. B. Du Bois, *Black Reconstruction in America, 1860–1880* (1st ed., 1935; repr., New York: Free Press, 1992), 499.

19. Henry McNeal Turner, "Speech on the Eligibility of Colored Members to Seats in the Georgia Legislature," September 3, 1868, in Turner, *Respect Black*, 14–28, quotes, 15, 16–17. This speech, often titled "I Claim the Rights of a Man," is also reprinted in *Lift Every Voice and Sing: African American Oratory, 1787–1900*, ed. Philip Foner

and Robert J. Branham (Tuscaloosa: University of Alabama Press, 1998) and other anthologies.

20. Turner, "Speech on the Eligibility," quotes, 17, 20, 25.

21. Ibid., quotes, 25.

22. Angell, *Bishop Henry McNeal Turner*, 89–91, "we should," 90, "I have," 91; Franklin, *Reconstruction after the Civil War*, 131; Johnson, *Forgotten Prophet*, 59. Macon, Georgia's *American Union* published the Klan letter and Turner's response in its issue of February 26, 1869.

23. Angell, *Bishop Henry McNeal Turner*, 94–95; E. Merton Coulter, "Henry M. Turner: Georgia Negro Preacher-Politician During the Reconstruction Era," *Georgia Historical Quarterly* 48 (December 1964), 374–410; Edmund L. Drago, *Black Politicians and Reconstruction in Georgia: A Splendid Failure* (Baton Rouge: Louisiana State University Press, 1982), 66–67.

24. Angell, *Bishop Henry McNeal Turner*, 95–96; Payne, *History of the African Methodist Episcopal Church*, 470–471.

25. Franklin, *Reconstruction after the Civil War*, 132–135, quote, 134; Vernon Lane Wharton, "The Negro and Politics, 1870–1875," in *Reconstruction: An Anthology of Revisionist Writings*, ed. Kenneth M. Stampp and Leon F. Litwack (Baton Rouge: Louisiana State University Press, 1969), 338–369.

26. E. Franklin Frazier, *The Negro Church in America* / C. Eric Lincoln, *The Black Church Since Frazier* (New York: Schocken Books, 1988), 48; Samuel D. Smith, *The Negro Congress, 1870–1901* (Chapel Hill: University of North Carolina Press, 1940), 8; Peggy Lamson, "Richard Harvey Cain," *Dictionary of American Negro Biography*, ed. Rayford W. Logan and Michael R. Winston (New York: W. W. Norton, 1982), 84–85; Donald L. Singer, "Hiram Rhoades Revels," *Dictionary of American Negro Biography*, 523–524; Turner, Speech to the Georgia Annual Conference, quote, 30.

27. See James M. Washington, *Frustrated Fellowship: The Black Baptist Quest for Social Power* (Macon, GA: Mercer University Press, 1986), 112–122; Angell, *Bishop Henry McNeal Turner*, 103; Charles H. Phillips, *History of the Colored Methodist Church in America* (Jackson, TN: CME Church, 1898).

28. Henry McNeal Turner to the American Colonization Society, April 1875, *African Repository and Colonial Journal* 51 (April 1875), quotes, 39, in Turner, *Respect Black*, 42.

29. Turner to the American Colonization Society, July 1876, *African Repository and Colonial Journal* 52 (July 1876), quotes, 83, 84, 85–86, in Turner, *Respect Black*, 42–44.

30. Henry McNeal Turner, *The Negro in All Ages, A Lecture Delivered in the Second Baptist Church of Savannah, Ga., April 8th, 1873* (Savannah, GA: D. G. Patton, 1873), quote, 29; Turner, "Emigration of the Colored People of the United States," Speech to the Colored National Convention, May 6, 1879, in Turner, *Emigration of the Colored People of the United States: Is It Expedient? If so Where To?* (Philadelphia: AME Publishing House, 1879).

31. Benjamin T. Tanner, Editor's Column, *Christian Recorder*, December 17, 1874; Tanner, "Bishop Turner on the Advisory Committee," *Christian Recorder*, January 4,

1883; Tanner, "Bishop Turner's Reply," *Christian Recorder*, February 2, 1883; see Tanner, *An Apology for African Methodism* (Baltimore, MD, 1867).

32. Henry McNeal Turner to the Editor, *Christian Recorder*, March 30, 1876; Turner to the Editor, *Christian Recorder*, December 8, 1881, in Turner, *Respect Black*, quotes, 50–51; Gilbert Anthony Williams, *The Christian Recorder, Newspaper of the African Methodist Episcopal Church* (Jefferson, NC: McFarland, 1996), 91–100.

33. Angell, *Bishop Henry McNeal Turner*, 128–132, "slaughtered," 130, from *Christian Recorder*, March 22, 1877; Franklin, *Reconstruction after the Civil War*, 211–219; Foner, *Reconstruction*, 564–601.

34. Henry McNeal Turner to the Editor, *Christian Recorder*, March 25, 1880, in Turner, *Respect Black*, 49.

35. Daniel A. Payne, "Some Thoughts about the Past, the Present and the Future of the African M. E. Church," *A.M.E. Church Review* 1 (January 1884): 4; Payne, *Recollections of Seventy Years* (Nashville, TN: AME Sunday School Union, 1888), 261–262; Angell, *Bishop Henry McNeal Turner*, 146–155, quotes, 152; Joseph H. Morgan, *Morgan's History of the New Jersey Conference of the AME Church, from 1872 to 1887* (Camden, NJ: S. Chew, 1887), 123–124.

36. Payne, "Some Thoughts about the Past, the Present and the Future of the African M. E. Church," 5–8; Payne, *History of the African Methodist Episcopal Church*, quote, 448; Charles Spencer Smith, *A History of the African Methodist Episcopal Church* (Philadelphia: A.M.E. Book Concern, 1922), 351–368.

37. Henry McNeal Turner to the Editor, *Christian Recorder*, February 22, 1883, in Turner, *Respect Black*, quotes, 54, 56.

38. Henry McNeal Turner to the Editor, *Christian Recorder*, June 21, 1883, in Turner, *Respect Black*, "The truth," "The whole," and "all the," 57; Turner to the Editor, February 22, 1883, "All this."

39. Henry McNeal Turner to the Editor, *Christian Recorder*, January 25, 1883, in Turner, *Respect Black*, "We must" and "black men," 53; Turner to the Editor, February 22, 1883, "This has" and "our best," 55.

40. Henry McNeal Turner interview with the *St. Louis Globe-Democrat*, reprinted in the *Christian Recorder*, November 8, 1883, in Turner, *Respect Black*, 60–61.

41. Henry McNeal Turner, Open Letter to B. K. Sampson, November 6, 1883, in *Christian Recorder*, December 13, 1883, in Turner, *Respect Black*, 61–63, "farce" and "no moderate," 62; Turner to the Editor, *Voice*, January 4, 1889, in *Respect Black*, "molehill" and "wicked," 66, 68. Turner subsequently republished the latter letter as a pamphlet titled "The Barbarous Decision of the Supreme Court Declaring the Civil Rights Act Unconstitutional," 1893.

42. Henry McNeal Turner, "The Democratic Return to Power—Its Effects," *A.M.E. Church Review* 1 (January 1885): 246–248, in Turner, *Respect Black*, 70–72; Calvin Chase, Editorial, *Washington Bee*, May 9, 1885.

43. Turner, "The Democratic Return to Power," 247; Joel Williamson, *The Crucible of Race: Black-White Relations in the American South Since Emancipation* (New York: Oxford University Press, 1984), 112; Angell, *Bishop Henry McNeil Turner*, 170; James M. McPherson, *The Negro's Civil War* (New York: Pantheon, 1965), 196–199.

James Monroe Trotter fought with the 55th Massachusetts Regiment in the Civil War, worked for the Boston Post Office after the war, was outraged when Hayes terminated Reconstruction, and joined the Democratic Party in 1883.

44. Bess Beatty, *A Revolution Gone Backward: Black Response to National Politics, 1876–1896* (New York: Greenwood, 1987), "wails," 109; Henry McNeal Turner to the Editor, *Christian Recorder*, February 14, 1889; Williamson, *Crucible of Race*, 112–113; Angell, *Bishop Henry McNeal Turner*, 170–171; [Ida B. Wells], "Iola on Discrimination," *New York Freedman*, January 15, 1887; Howard N. Rabinowitz, *Race Relations in the Urban South, 1865–1890* (New York: Oxford University Press, 1978), 195.

45. Lyman Abbott, *Reminiscences* (Boston: Houghton Mifflin, 1915), 95–105; Abbott, *The Rights of Man: A Study in Twentieth Century Problems* (Boston: Houghton, Mifflin, 1901), 218–242; Francis Greenwood Peabody, *Education for Life: The Story of Hampton Institute* (Garden City: Doubleday, Page, 1918); Edgar Gardner Murphy, *Problems of the Present South* (New York: Macmillan, 1904); Murphy, *The Basis of Ascendancy: A Discussion of Certain Principles of Public Policy Involved in the Development of the Southern States* (New York: Longmans, Green, 1908).

46. "The Lake Mohonk Conference on the Negro Question," *Christian Union* 41 (June 12, 1890): 830; Lyman Abbott, "Remarks on 'How Can Northern and Southern Christians Best Co-operate for the Moral and Spiritual Elevation of the Negroes?,'" in *Second Mohonk Conference on the Negro Question*, ed. Isabel C. Barrows (Boston: George H. Ellis, 1891), 69–70.

47. Henry L. Morehouse, "The Talented Tenth," *Independent*, April 23, 1896; James McPherson, *The Abolitionist Legacy: From Reconstruction to the NAACP* (Princeton, NJ: Princeton University Press, 1975), 222.

48. Amory H. Bradford, *My Brother* (Boston: Pilgrim, 1910); Charles Cuthbert Hall, *Christian Belief Interpreted by Christian Experience* (Chicago: University of Chicago Press, 1905); Henry Churchill King, *Theology and the Social Consciousness* (New York: Macmillan, 1902); Charles J. Ryder, "Fifty Years of the American Missionary Association," *New England Magazine* 15 (October 1896): 231–232; Joe M. Richardson, *Christian Reconstruction: The American Missionary Association and Southern Blacks, 1861–1890* (Athens: University of Georgia Press, 1986), 65–91.

49. Joseph Cook, "Fraudulent Elections, South and North: Possible Future of Political Corruption," *Our Day* 6 (August 1890): 124–137; Cook, "Unsolved Southern Problems," *Our Day* 8 (July 1891): 30–41; Cook, "New Black Codes at the South," *Our Day* 12 (July 1893): 47, 53; Cook, *The Three Despised Races in the United States; or, The Chinaman, the Indian, and the Freedman* (New York: American Missionary Association, 1878); Editorial, "The Worship of Booker T. Washington," *Independent* 50 (December 8, 1898): 1708–1709.

50. Atticus Greene Haygood, *Our Brother in Black, His Freedom and His Future* (New York: Phillips, 1881); Quincey Ewing, "The Heart of the Race Problem," *Atlantic Monthly*, March 1909, 389–397; George Washington Cable, "The Freedman's Case in Equity," *Century Magazine* 29 (January 1885): 409–416; Cable, "The Silent South," *Century Magazine* 30 (September 1885): 674–691; Cable, *The Negro Question: A Selection of Writings on Civil Rights in the South by George W. Cable*, ed. Arlin Turner

(Garden City, NY: Doubleday, 1958); Williamson, *Crucible of Race*, 88–107; Arlin Turner, *George W. Cable: A Biography* (Durham, NC: Duke University Press, 1956), 3–34.

51. Otto H. Olsen, *Carpetbagger's Crusade: The Life of Albion Winegar Tourgée* (Baltimore, MD: Johns Hopkins University Press, 1965), 10–19; Theodore L. Gross, *Albion W. Tourgée* (New York: Twayne, 1963), 20–24.

52. Harlan Paul Douglass, *Christian Reconstruction in the South* (Boston: Pilgrim, 1909); Algernon S. Crapsey, "The Duty of the White Man of the North to the Black Man of the South," in *How to Solve the Race Problem: The Proceedings of the Washington Conference on the Race Problem in the United States under the Auspices of the National Sociological Society* (Washington, DC: R. Beresford, 1904), 238–239; Charles B. Spahr, *America's Working People* (New York: Longmans, Green, 1900); John Haynes Holmes, *The Disfranchisement of Negroes* (New York: NAACP, 1910); George A. Gates, *Personality: The Ultimate Fact of Philosophy and Life* (Grinnell: Iowa College, 1889); Edward A. Steiner, *On the Trail of the Immigrant* (New York: Fleming H. Revell, 1906); George Herron, *The New Redemption* (New York: T. Y. Crowell, 1893); Herron, *The Christian Society* (Chicago: Fleming H. Revell, 1894); Herron, *The Christian State: A Political Vision of Christ* (New York: T. Y. Crowell, 1895).

53. Albion W. Tourgée, "Shall White Minorities Rule?" *Forum* 7 (April 1889): 144–155; Tourgée, "The Right to Vote," *Forum* 9 (March 1890): 78–92; Lawrence J. Friedman, *The White Savage: Racial Fantasies in the Postbellum South* (Englewood Cliffs, NJ: Prentice-Hall, 1970), Cable quote, 105; Editorial, "Passage of the Lodge Election Bill," *Independent* 42 (July 10, 1890), "As between," 959; Editorial, "Southern Congressional Elections," *Independent* 41 (September 12, 1889): 1178–1179; Editorial, "Vital Points of Expert Opinion," *Our Day* 5 (May 1890): 435–438; Ralph E. Luker, *The Social Gospel in Black and White: American Racial Reform, 1885–1912* (Chapel Hill: University of North Carolina Press, 1991), 75–76; Richard E. Welch Jr., "The Federal Elections Bill of 1890: Post-scripts and Prelude," *Journal of American History* 52 (1965): 511–526.

54. Editorial, "Editorial Notes," *Independent* 43 (June 18, 1891): 911; McPherson, *Abolitionist Legacy*, 134–137; W. S. Scarborough, "The Political Necessity of a Federal Election Law," *Our Day* 6 (July 6, 1890): 25–33; Michael Perman, *Struggle for Mastery: Disfranchisement in the South, 1888–1908* (Chapel Hill: University of North Carolina Press, 2001).

55. See Robert L. Factor, *The Black Response to America: Men, Ideals, and Organization, from Frederick Douglass to the NAACP* (Reading, MA: Addison-Wesley, 1970), 117–120; Shawn Leigh Alexander, *An Army of Lions: The Civil Rights Struggle Before the NAACP* (Philadelphia: University of Pennsylvania Press, 2012), 7–8.

56. Henry McNeal Turner to the Editor, *Christian Recorder*, August 28, 1890, in Turner, *Respect Black*, quotes, 81–82; Luker, *Social Gospel in Black and White*, 76; Scarborough, "The Political Necessity of a Federal Election Law," 30–33.

57. Albion Tourgée, *A Fool's Errand, by One of the Fools* (New York: J. B. Ford, 1879); Tourgée, *Bricks Without Straw* (New York: Fords, Howard, & Hulbert, 1880); Tourgée, *An Appeal to Caesar* (New York: Fords, Howard, & Hulbert, 1884); Tourgée, *Pactolus*

Prime (New York: Fords, Howard, & Hulbert, 1890); Tourgée, *Murvale Eastman: Christian Socialist* (New York: Fords, Howard, & Hulbert, 1890).

58. Isabel C. Barrows, ed., *First Mohonk Conference on the Negro Question* (Boston: G. H. Ellis, 1890), Hayes quote, 9, Tourgée quotes, 13, 108, 110; Tourgée's speech, "The Negro's View of the Race Problem," reprinted in *Undaunted Radical: The Selected Writings and Speeches of Albion W. Tourgée*, ed. Mark Elliott and John David Smith (Baton Rouge: Louisiana State University Press, 2010), 152–170; see White Jr., *Liberty and Justice for All*, 8–9.

59. Albion W. Tourgée, "Brief of Plaintiff in Error" (1895), and "Oral Argument of A. W. Tourgée" (1896), in *Undaunted Radical*, 296–327, 328–339; C. Vann Woodward, "The Birth of Jim Crow," *American Heritage* 15 (April 1964): 100–102; Olsen, *Carpetbagger's Crusade*, 319–330; Otto Olsen, ed., *The Thin Disguise: Turning Point in Negro History, Plessy v. Ferguson: A Documentary History* (New York: Humanities, 1967); Luker, *Social Gospel in Black and White*, 87–88.

60. Otto Olsen, "Introduction," *The Thin Disguise*, 25–27; Luker, *Social Gospel in Black and White*, 88.

61. Rayford Logan, *The Negro in American Life and Thought: The Nadir, 1877–1901* (New York: Dial, 1954), 2nd ed., *The Betrayal of the Negro: From Rutherford B. Hayes to Woodrow Wilson* (New York: Collier, 1965); see Belle Kearney, "The South and Woman Suffrage," in *Up from the Pedestal: Selected Writings in the History of American Feminism*, ed. Aileen Kraditor (Chicago: Quadrangle, 1970), 262–265; Anna Howard Shaw, *The Story of a Pioneer* (New York: Harper & Brothers, 1915), 307–314.

62. Stephen W. Angell, "Bishop Turner's Advocacy of Women's Leadership in the AME Church," in *A Liberated Past: Explorations in AME Church History*, ed. Dennis Dickerson (Nashville, TN: AME Sunday School Union, 2003); Angell, *Bishop Henry McNeal Turner*, 181–184; John M. Brown and Jabez B. Campbell, "The Ordination of Women: What Is the Authority for It?" *A.M.E. Church Review* 2 (April 1886): 351–361; Susan Hill Lindley, *"You Have Stepped Out of Your Place": A History of Women and Religion in America* (Louisville, KY: Westminster John Knox Press, 1996), 180–181.

63. Henry McNeal Turner to the Editor, November 21, 1891, *Christian Recorder*, in Turner, *Respect Black*, "God save," 115; Turner to the Editor, November 29, 1891, ibid., "Liberia is," 117, "the lowest," 118; Turner to the Editor, December 4, 1891, ibid., "Oh!," "moneyed," and "She is," 121–122; see Edwin S. Redkey, *Black Exodus: Black Nationalist and Back-to-Africa Movements, 1890–1910* (New Haven: Yale University Press, 1969), 44–45.

64. Henry McNeal Turner to the Editor, December 5, 1891, *Christian Recorder*, in Turner, *Respect Black*, "If we," 125.

65. Henry McNeal Turner to the Editor, December 9, 1891, *Christian Recorder*, in Turner, *Respect Black*, quotes, 131–132.

66. Henry McNeal Turner to the Editor, Indianapolis *Freeman*, March 26, 1892, in Turner, *Respect Black*, 135–137, quotes, 136, 137.

67. Henry McNeal Turner, "Negro Convention Speech: Emigration of Justice," *Voice of Missions*, December 1, 1893; reprinted in Turner, *Respect Black*, 146–159, "Some of you" and "I have seen," 158; Redkey, *Black Exodus*, 183–192.

68. Angell, *Bishop Henry McNeal Turner*, "any preacher," 200; Turner, "What the Future A.M.E. Church Will Do," *Voice of Missions*, May 1894.

69. John William Colenso, *St. Paul's Epistle to the Romans, Newly Translated and Explained from a Missionary Point of View* (New York: D. Appleton, 1863); Colenso, *The Pentateuch and Book of Joshua Critically Examined* (London: Longman, Green, Longman, Roberts, and Green, 1862), 84; Colenso, *Lectures on the Pentateuch and the Moabite Stone* (London: Longmans, Green, 1873).

70. Alexander McCaul, *An Examination of Bp. Colenso's Difficulties with Regard to the Pentateuch, and Some Reasons for Believing in Its Authenticity and Divine Origin* (London: Rivingtons, 1863); Victor Shea and William Whitla, "Essays and Reviews and Bishop Colenso's 'Great Scandal,'" in *Essays and Reviews: The 1860 Text and Its Reading*, ed. Shea and Whitla (Charlottesville: University of Virginia Press, 2000), 847–856.

71. Henry McNeal Turner to the Editor, *Christian Recorder*, October 10, 1863, "The bold"; Turner to the Editor, *Christian Recorder*, November 1, 1863, "With the"; Turner to the Editor, *Christian Recorder*, November 7, 1863; Turner, *Voice of Missions*, December 1897, "The Bible," cited in Angell, *Bishop Henry McNeal Turner*, 255; Turner, Editorial, *Voice of Missions*, June 1898; Turner, *An African American Pastor*, 42–52.

72. Elizabeth Cady Stanton, ed., *The Woman's Bible, Part 1, Comments on Genesis, Exodus, Leviticus, Numbers and Deuteronomy* (New York: European Publishing, 1895); *The Woman's Bible, Part 2, Comments on the Old and New Testaments from Joshua to Revelation* (New York: European Publishing, 1898); Henry McNeal Turner, *Voice of Missions*, August 1899, cited in Angell, *Bishop Henry McNeal Turner*, 256.

73. Editorial, *Atlanta Constitution*, September 2, 1895; Henry Lyman Morehouse, *Baptist Home Mission Monthly* 17 (November 1895): 413–414; Henry McNeal Turner, "God is a Negro," *Voice of Missions*, February 1898, in Turner, *Respect Black*, quotes, 176–177.

74. Payne, *History of the African Methodist Episcopal Church*, 484–491; Walter L. Williams, *Black America and the Evangelization of Africa* (Madison: University of Wisconsin Press, 1982), 46–47; Angell, *Bishop Henry McNeal Turner*, 176, 216.

75. Angell, *Bishop Henry McNeal Turner*, 221–224; Williams, *Black America and the Evangelization of Africa*, 114–116; Hollis R. Lynch, *Selected Letters of Edward Wilmot Blyden* (Millwood, NY: KTO Press, 1978), 446–448; Henry McNeal Turner, Editorial, *Voice of Missions*, February 1896.

76. Turner, "Emancipation Day Celebration Address," January 1, 1866; Turner to the Editor, *Christian Recorder*, February 22, 1883, "I do not," 55; Henry McNeal Turner, "The American Negro and the Fatherland," in *Africa and the American Negro: Addresses and Proceedings of the Congress on Africa*, ed. J. W. E. Bowen (Atlanta: Franklin, 1896), 195–198; Turner, Editorial, *Voice of Missions*, August 1895; Williams, *Black America and the Evangelization of Africa*, 101; George Washington Williams, *History of the Negro Race in America from 1619 to 1880* (New York: G. P. Putnam's, 1882).

77. Williams, *Black America and the Evangelization of Africa*, 165–188; Lynch, *Selected Letters of Edward Wilmot Blyden*, 447; Angell, *Bishop Henry McNeal Turner*, 223–224.

78. Henry McNeal Turner, "The Colored National Emigration Association," *Voice of the People*, September 1903, in Turner, *Respect Black*, "We very much," 194–195; Angell, *Bishop Henry McNeal Turner*, "did little," 242.

79. Henry McNeal Turner to Booker T. Washington, 1901, in *The Booker T. Washington Papers*, 14 vols., ed. Louis R. Harlan, Raymond W. Smock, and Geraldine McTighe (Urbana: University of Illinois Press, 1972–1989), "You are," 6: 287; Turner, Editorial, *Voice of the People*, September 1903, "worth" and "Anything"; Redkey, *Black Exodus*, 277; Angell, *Bishop Henry McNeal Turner*, 240.

80. Alexander Crummell to John E. Bruce, November 26, 1895, in Crummell, *Destiny and Race: Selected Writings, 1840–1898*, ed. Wilson Jeremiah Moses (Amherst: University of Massachusetts Press, 1992), "truculent," 86; Henry McNeal Turner, Letter from Sierra Leone, *Voice of Missions*, April 1893, in Turner, *Respect Black*, "the only," 140; Turner, "Negroes Get Guns," *Voice of Missions*, March–May, 1897; Turner, "The Negro Should Not Enter the Army," *Voice of Missions*, May 1899; Turner, "McKinley, The God of Fool Negroes, Re-elected," *Voice of Missions*, December 1900; Turner, "The Afro-American Future," *Twentieth Century Negro Literature*, ed. D. W. Culp (Philadelphia: J. L. Nichols, 1902), 42–45, "I see," 44–45; Turner, "The Life of Rev. W. J. Simmons, A.B., A.M., D.D.," in Simmons, *Men of Mark*, "The Indian," 61.

81. Henry McNeal Turner, "Bishop H. M. Turner Upon the Anniversary of His Wife's Death," *Christian Recorder*, July 31, 1890, "the babes"; Angell, *Bishop Henry McNeal Turner*, 39, 284; Johnson, *Forgotten Prophet*, 25; Ponton, *Life and Times of Henry M. Turner*, "hungered" and "was more," 77, "regarded," 85.

82. Payne, *History of the African Methodist Episcopal Church*, "self-denial," 470–471; Ponton, *Life and Times of Henry M. Turner*, "But out," 87.

83. Henry McNeal Turner to the Editor, *Christian Recorder*, October 11, 1883, quotes; Angell, *Bishop Henry McNeal Turner*, 262.

84. Ponton, *Life and Times of Henry M. Turner*, Ponton quote, 47–48; tributes of Bowen and Walters to Turner in Ponton, ibid., 164, 160.

85. Angell, *Bishop Henry McNeal Turner*, 245–246.

86. John Hope Franklin, *From Slavery to Freedom: A History of American Negroes* (1947; 2nd ed., New York: Knopf, 1956), 287, 306, 314; Logan, *Betrayal of the Negro*, 289; Vincent Harding, *There Is a River: The Black Struggle for Freedom in America* (New York: Harcourt Brace Jovanovich, 1981), 176; Benjamin Quarles, *The Negro in the Making of America* (New York: Collier, 1964); James M. McPherson, *The Struggle for Equality: Abolitionists and the Negro in the Civil War and Reconstruction* (Princeton, NJ: Princeton University Press, 1964); McPherson, *Abolitionist Legacy*, 288; Frazier, *Negro Church in America*, 47; Woodson, *History of the Negro Church*, "one of the," 164; Lincoln and Mamiya, *Black Church in the African American Experience*, 177.

87. "Bishop Turner's Twenty-Fifth Anniversary," *A.M.E. Church Review* 22 (July 1905): 1–7; book version, *Bishop Turner's Quarto-Centennial* (n.p., 1905); cited in Ponton, *Life and Times of Henry M. Turner*, quotes, 78–79.

88. George W. Forbes, "Bishop Turner, the Grandest Old Roman of Them All," *A.M.E. Church Review* 32 (July 1915): 63–64; Ponton, *Life and Times of Henry M. Turner*, quotes, 80–81.

89. Ponton, *Life and Times of Henry M. Turner*, Flipper quote, 142; Henry McNeal Turner, "The Presidential Election," *Voice of Missions*, October 1896, in Turner, *Respect Black*, Turner quote, 175; Angell, *Bishop Henry McNeal Turner*, 272.

90. Henry Lincoln Johnson, "Bishop Turner Dead," *Atlanta Independent*, May 15, 1915, Johnson quote, 1; Ponton, *Life and Times of Henry M. Turner*, Holsey quotes, 155, 156–157.

91. Richard R. Wright Jr., "Bishop Henry McNeal Turner," *Christian Recorder*, July 18, 1915, "but his"; Richard R. Wright Jr., *The Bishops of the African Methodist Episcopal Church* (Nashville, TN: AME Sunday School Union, 1963), "commanding," 340; Booker T. Washington quoted in Ponton, *Life and Times of Henry M. Turner*, 153–154; Tanner cited in Wright, *Bishops*, 339; W. E. B. Du Bois, "Henry McNeal Turner," *Crisis* 10 (July 1915), "a man" and "In a sense," 130; Du Bois, *Dusk of Dawn: An Essay Toward an Autobiography of a Race Concept* (New York: Harcourt, Brace & World, 1940), "prouder" and "the crazy," 195.

92. Reverdy Ransom, "Bishop Henry McNeal Turner," *A.M.E. Church Review* 32 (July 1915): 45–46.

93. Ida B. Wells, *Crusade for Justice: The Autobiography of Ida B. Wells*, ed. Alfreda M. Duster (Chicago: University of Chicago Press, 1970), 7–9; Paula J. Giddings, *Ida: A Sword Among Lions* (New York: HarperCollins, 2008), 15–19; Vernon Lane Wharton, *The Negro in Mississippi, 1865–1890* (Chapel Hill: University of North Carolina Press, 1947), 27–28, 144–145; Hodding Carter, "A Proud Struggle for Grace: Holly Springs, Mississippi," in *A Vanishing America: The Life and Times of the Small Town*, ed. Thomas C. Wheeler (New York: Holt, Rinehart and Winston, 1964), 65–67.

94. Wells, *Crusade for Justice*, 9–10, quotes, 4, 22; Linda O. McMurry, *To Keep the Waters Troubled: The Life of Ida B. Wells* (New York: Oxford University Press, 1998), 12–13; Fitzgerald, *The Union League Movement in the Deep South*, 60–74; Litwick, *Been in the Storm So Long*, 165–224; Giddings, *Ida*, 24–26; Ruth Watkins, "Reconstruction in Marshall County," *Publications of the Mississippi Historical Society* 12 (1912): 155–213. Shaw University was established in 1866 and chartered in 1870. In 1882 it was renamed Rust University, and in 1915 it was renamed Rust College.

95. Wells, *Crusade for Justice*, 8–10, quote, 21; Miriam DeCosta-Willis, ed., *The Memphis Diary of Ida B. Wells* (Boston: Beacon Press, 1995), entry of June 12, 1886, 77–78.

96. McMurry, *To Keep the Waters*, 14–15; Giddings, *Ida*, 32–35; Wells, *Crusade for Justice*, 10; Gerard M. Capers Jr., *The Biography of a River Town: Memphis, Its Heroic Age* (Chapel Hill: University of North Carolina Press, 1939), 191; J. M. Keating, *A History of the Yellow Fever* (Memphis, TN: Howard Association, 1879), 101–110.

97. Wells, *Crusade for Justice*, 11–14.

98. Ibid., 15–17; *Memphis Diary*, entry of June 12, 1886, "My own," 78; James West Davidson, *"They Say": Ida B. Wells and the Reconstruction of Race* (New York: Oxford University Press, 2009), 48–53; Giddings, *Ida*, 11–13, 37–38; T. Thomas Fortune, "Ida B. Wells, A.M.," in *Women of Distinction, Remarkable in Works and Invincible in Character*, ed. Lawson A. Scruggs (Raleigh, NC: L. A. Scruggs, 1893), 33–39.

99. *Memphis Diary*, entry of April 3, 1885, "A tried," 57; Wells, *Crusade for Justice*, 18–21, "None," 21; "A Darky Damsel Obtains a Verdict for Damages Against the Chesapeake and Ohio Railroad—What It Cost to Put a Colored School-Teacher in a Smoking Car," *Memphis Daily Appeal*, December 25, 1884; *Chesapeake & Ohio & Southwestern Railroad Company v. Wells, Tennessee Reports*, "We think," 615, cited in Wells, *Crusade for Justice*, 20; Giddings, *Ida*, 62–68.

100. Wells, *Crusade for Justice*, "The bishops," "needed," and "I had," 22; *Memphis Diary*, entry of December 29, 1885, quotes, 24; Davidson, *"They Say,"* 58–59.

101. Wells, *Crusade for Justice*, "confinement," 31; McMurry, *To Keep the Waters*, "she hated," 77; Ida B. Wells, "Functions of Leadership," *Living Way*, September 12, 1885, in *Memphis Diary*, "Tell me," 179.

102. Ida B. Wells, "Woman's Mission," *New York Freeman*, December 26, 1885, in *Memphis Diary*, quotes, 181.

103. *Memphis Diary*, entry of February 8, 1886, diary quotes, 41; Louis M. Brown, *Washington Bee*, December 11, 1885, in Indianapolis *Freeman*, December 11, 1885, cited in Giddings, *Ida*, 87, and DeCosta-Willis, *Memphis Diary*, 35; McMurry, *To Keep the Waters*, 56–61; Davidson, *"They Say,"* 85–96.

104. W. Calvin Chase, editorial, *Washington Bee*, January 23, 1886, cited in *Memphis Diary*, 35, and Giddings, *Ida*, 89; *Memphis Diary*, entry of January 28, 1886, "He is," 36; see T. Thomas Fortune, *T. Thomas Fortune the Afro-American Agitator: A Collection of Writings, 1880–1928*, ed. Shawn Leigh Alexander (Gainesville: University of Florida Press, 2008); Emma Lou Thornbrough, *T. Thomas Fortune: Militant Journalist* (Chicago: University of Chicago Press, 1972).

105. *Memphis Diary*, entry of April 11, 1886, "I don't," 59–60; Wells, *Crusade for Justice*, 24.

106. *Memphis Diary*, entry of September 4, 1886, 102.

107. Wells articles in *Christian Index*, March 10, April 21, May 12, and June 9, 1888, cited in Giddings, *Ida*, quotes, 151.

108. Wells article in *Christian Index*, March 2, 1889, cited in Giddings, *Ida*, quotes, 152, 153.

109. Ann Alexander, "John R. Mitchell, Jr.," in Logan and Winston, *Dictionary of American Negro Biography*, "Don't," 444; I. Garland Penn, *The Afro-American Press and Its Editors* (Springfield, MA: Wiley, 1891), "had no," 186; Giddings, *Ida*, 153.

110. Ida B. Wells to Booker T. Washington, November 30, 1890, in *Booker T. Washington Papers*, quotes, 3: 108; Wells, *Crusade for Justice*, 41.

111. Giddings, *Ida*, "steely," 167; Wells, *Crusade for Justice*, remaining quotes, 37.

112. McMurry, *To Keep the Waters*, 130–135; Wells, *Crusade for Justice*, 48–51, "Tell my people," 51; Giddings, *Ida*, 177–187; Davidson, *"They Say,"* 124–145.

113. Wells, *Crusade for Justice*, quotes, 51, 52.

114. C. H. J. Taylor, editorial, Kansas *American Citizen*, March 25, 1892, and Ferdinand Barrett, Chicago *Conservator*, March 29, 1892, cited in Giddings, *Ida*, 194; Wells, *Crusade for Justice*, "Every," 55.

115. Davidson, *"They Say,"* 149–150; McMurry, *To Keep the Waters*, 141–142; Wells, *Crusade for Justice*, 53–54.

116. [Edward Ward Carmack], "More Rapes, More Lynchings," *Memphis Commercial*, May 17, 1892, and [Ida B. Wells], editorial, *Free Speech and Headlight*, May 21, 1892,

reprinted in Wells, *Southern Horrors: Lynch Law in All Its Phases* (New York: New York Age, 1892), 13, 3. This pamphlet, *Southern Horrors*, was based on Wells's seven-column front-page article, "The Truth About Lynching," *New York Age*, June 25, 1892.

117. Wells, *Crusade for Justice*, "who fulfilled," 59; Giddings, *Ida*, "Few meetings," 209; *Commercial* and *Scimitar* quotes in Wells, *Southern Horrors*, 3.

118. Wells, *Crusade for Justice*, "Having," 69; Wells, *Southern Horrors*, "There are," 4.

119. Wells, *Southern Horrors*, quotes, 7, 8, 17.

120. Ibid., 8, 6, 20.

121. Ibid., 8.

122. Ibid., i.

123. Wells, *Crusade for Justice*, quotes, 79, 80.

124. Wells, *Southern Horrors*, quotes, ii.

125. Frederick Douglass, "Lynch Law in the South," *North American Review* 155 (July 1892), quote, 23; see Douglass, Autobiographies: *Narrative of the Life of Frederick Douglass, An American Slave* (1845), *My Bondage and My Freedom* (1855), and *Life and Times of Frederick Douglass* (1893), ed. Henry Louis Gates Jr. (New York: Library of America, 1994).

126. Wells, *Crusade for Justice*, 72–73.

127. [Edward Carmack], editorial, *Memphis Commercial*, December 15, 1892, in Giddings, *Ida*, 245.

128. Mary Church Terrell, *A Colored Woman in a White World* (Washington, DC: Ransdell, 1940); Anna Julia Cooper, *A Voice from the South* (Xenia, OH: Aldine, 1892; repr., New York: Oxford University Press, 1988); Gayraud S. Wilmore, *Black Religion and Black Radicalism: An Interpretation of the Religious History of African Americans* (3rd ed., Maryknoll, NY: Orbis Books, 1998), 261–266; Wells, *Crusade for Justice*, quotes, 83; see Paula Giddings, *When and Where I Enter: The Impact of Black Women on Race and Sex in America* (New York: HarperCollins, 1984), 20–21.

129. Wells, *Crusade for Justice*, "seemed," 86; Ida B. Wells, "Lynch Law in All Its Phases," *Our Day* 11 (May 1893): 341–347, repr. in Mildred Thompson, *Ida B. Wells-Barnett: An Exploratory Study of An American Black Woman, 1893–1930* (Brooklyn, NY: Carlson, 1990), "strong," 185.

130. James E. Cutler, *Lynch Law; An Investigation into the History of Lynching in the United States* (New York: Longmans, Green, 1905); Ida B. Wells, "Lynch Law in America," in Thompson, *Ida B. Wells-Barnett*, 239–240; Giddings, *Ida*, 2.

131. Ida B. Wells, *A Red Record* (pamphlet, 1895), repr. in Ida B. Wells-Barnett, *On Lynchings* (Amherst, NY: Humanity Books, 2002), quote, 92.

132. Ibid., quotes, 99, 94.

133. Indianapolis *Freeman*, June 8, 1893; *Memphis Appeal-Avalanche*, April 23, 1893; Taylor cited in Giddings, *Ida*, 268, 295.

134. See Wells, *Crusade for Justice*, 111–112; McMurry, *To Keep the Waters*, "mesmerized," 73; James F. Findlay Jr., *Dwight L. Moody: American Evangelist* (Chicago: University of Chicago Press, 1969), 278–281; William G. McLoughlin, *Modern Revivalism* (New York: Ronald Press, 1959), 3–64; Lyle W. Dorsett, *A Passion for Souls: The Life of*

D. L. Moody (Chicago: Moody, 1997); Gary Dorrien, *The Remaking of Evangelical Theology* (Louisville, KY: Westminster John Knox Press, 1998), 13–15.

135. Atticus Greene Haygood, *Our Brother in Black: His Freedom and His Future* (New York: Phillips and Hunt, 1881); Haygood, *Pleas for Progress* (Nashville, TN: ME Church, South, 1889); Williamson, *Crucible of Race*, 88–90; Luker, *Social Gospel in Black and White*, 20–23; Harold W. Mann, *Atticus Greene Haygood: Methodist Bishop, Editor, and Educator* (Athens: University of Georgia Press, 1965), 27–42.

136. Atticus Greene Haygood, "Governor Altgeld's Crime," *Independent* 45 (July 20, 1893): 969–970.

137. Atticus Greene Haygood, "The Black Shadow in the South," *Forum* 16 (October 1893): 167–175, quote, 174.

138. Wells, *Red Record*, quote, 62; see Wells, "Lynch Law in All Its Phases," 343–344.

139. Carolyn De Swarte Gifford and Amy R. Slagell, eds., *Let Something Good Be Said: Speeches and Writings of Frances E. Willard* (Urbana: University of Illinois Press, 2007); Gifford, "'The Woman's Cause is Man's'? Frances Willard and the Social Gospel," in Gifford and Wendy J. Deichmann Edwards, *Gender and the Social Gospel* (Urbana: University of Illinois Press, 2003), 21–34; Ruth Bordin, *Frances Willard: A Biography* (Chapel Hill, NC: University of North Carolina Press, 1986).

140. Interview with Frances Willard, *Voice*, October 1890; reprinted in Wells, *On Lynchings*, 132–133.

141. Speech of Elizabeth Cady Stanton, May 9, 1869, *History of Woman Suffrage*, ed. Elizabeth Cady Stanton, Susan B. Anthony, Matilda Joslyn Gage, et al., 6 vols. (New York: Fowler and Wells, 1881–1886), 2: 353.

142. Wells, *Crusade for Justice*, 133–152, "They have," 151; Giddings, *Ida*, 185.

143. Wells, *Crusade for Justice*, 125–169; Giddings, *Ida*, 291–310; McMurry, *To Keep the Waters*, 207–214.

144. Lady Henry Somerset, "White and Black in America: An Interview with Miss Willard," *Westminster Gazette*, May 21, 1894, repr. in Wells, *Crusade for Justice*, 204–208, quotes, 205, 208.

145. Ida B. Wells to the Editor, *Westminster Gazette*, May 22, 1894, repr. in Wells, *On Lynchings*, quotes, 134–135, and Wells, *Crusade for Justice*, 208–209.

146. Editorial, *Christian Recorder*, August 2, 1894, quote; Wells, *Crusade for Justice*, 210–217; Giddings, *Ida*, 311–312.

147. Ida B. Wells, Indianapolis *Freeman*, July 21, 1894, cited in Giddings, *Ida*, 312.

148. Editorial, *New York Times*, August 2, 1894; Wells, *Crusade for Justice*, 220–223, quotes, 222–223; Giddings, *Ida*, 318–319.

149. Frances Willard, Address to Women's Christian Temperance Union, November 16, 1894, *Inter Ocean*, November 17, 1894, in Giddings, *Ida*, 334.

150. *Cleveland Gazette*, November 24, 1894; Reverdy C. Ransom, *The Pilgrimage of Harriet Ransom's Son* (Nashville, TN: AME Sunday School Union, 1948), quotes, 77; Giddings, *Ida*, 335.

151. Wells, *Crusade for Justice*, 231.

152. Ibid., quotes, 238; Giddings, *Ida*, 340–341.

153. Wells, *Crusade for Justice*, quotes, 251, 242; Giddings, *Ida*, 346.

154. McMurry, *To Keep the Waters*, quotes, 245; Beverly Washington Jones, "The Women's Club Movement," in *Quest for Equality: Life and Writings of Mary Eliza Church Terrell, 1863–1954*, ed. Beverly Washington Jones (Brooklyn, NY: Carlson, 1990), 19.

155. Elizabeth L. Davis, *Lifting As They Climb* (Chicago: Race Relations Press, 1933), "immorality of," 18; Jones, "The Women's Club Movement," 19–20; Terrell, *Colored Woman in a White World*, 185–188; Wells, *Crusade for Justice*, 243–244; Giddings, *Ida*, 359–367.

156. Mary Church Terrell, "First Presidential Address to the National Association of Colored Women," September 15, 1897, in *Quest for Equality*, quotes, 134, 136, 137, 138.

157. Terrell, *Colored Woman in a White World*, 185–193; see Mary Church Terrell, "The Duty of the National Association of Colored Women to the Race," *A.M.E. Church Review* 16 (January 1900): 340–354; Giddings, *When and Where I Enter*, 106.

158. See Giddings, *When and Where I Enter*, 95–117; Terrell, *Colored Woman in a White World*, 234–236; Terrell, "Lynching from a Negro's Point of View," *North American Review* 178 (June 1904): 853–868; Terrell, "The Disbanding of the Colored Soldiers," *Voice of the Negro*, December 1906, 554–558.

159. Thornbrough, *T. Thomas Fortune*, "Let us," 106; Shawn Leigh Alexander, *An Army of Lions: The Civil Rights Struggle Before the NAACP* (Philadelphia: University of Pennsylvania Press, 2012), "You must," 7.

160. Alexander, *An Army of Lions*, 8–60, quotes, 12, 50; Thornbrough, *T. Thomas Fortune*, 105–119.

161. Emma Lou Thornbrough, "The National Afro-American League, 1887–1908," *Journal of Southern History* 27 (November 1961): 494–512; Alexander Walters, *My Life and Work* (New York: Fleming H. Revell, 1917), 96–105; Cyrus Field Adams, *The National Afro-American Council, Organized 1898* (Washington, DC: Cyrus F. Adams, 1902), 26–29; Herbert Shapiro, *White Violence and Black Response: From Reconstruction to Montgomery* (Amherst: University of Massachusetts Press, 1988), 89–90; Willard B. Gatewood Jr., *Black Americans and the White Man's Burden, 1898–1903* (Urbana: University of Illinois Press, 1975), 31–33.

162. Alexander, *An Army of Lions*, 179–219; Thornbrough, "The National Afro-American League," 499–510; Giddings, *Ida*, 436–438; Adams, *National Afro-American Council*, 28–29.

163. Wells, *Crusade for Justice*, 250–251; Giddings, *Ida*, 359–367.

164. Wells, *Crusade for Justice*, 255.

165. Walter White, *Rope and Faggot: A Biography of Judge Lynch* (New York: Knopf, 1929); Arthur Raper, *The Tragedy of Lynching* (Chapel Hill: University of North Carolina Press, 1933).

CHAPTER 3. THE CRUCIBLE

1. Booker T. Washington, *Up from Slavery* (New York: Doubleday, Page, 1901; Norton Critical Edition, New York: W. W. Norton, 1996), quotes, 7, 10; Jacqueline James, "Uncle Tom? Not Booker T.," *American Heritage* 19 (August 1968): 96–97; Louis R.

Harlan, *Booker T. Washington: The Making of a Black Leader, 1856–1901* (New York: Oxford University Press, 1972), 3–15.

2. Booker T. Washington, *The Story of My Life and Work* (New York: Doubleday, Page, 1900; repr., New York: Barnes and Noble, 2008), quotes, 6; Harlan, *Booker T. Washington: The Making of a Black Leader,* 16–17; see Robert T. Norrell, *Up from History: The Life of Booker T. Washington* (Cambridge, MA: Harvard University Press, 2009), 19.

3. Washington, *Up from Slavery,* quotes, 12, 13, 14; see Harlan, *Booker T. Washington: The Making of a Black Leader,* 12–13.

4. Washington, *Up from Slavery,* quotes, 7, 12, 14; on the Lost Cause, see Charles Reagan Wilson, *Baptized in Blood: The Religion of the Lost Cause, 1865–1920* (Athens: University of Georgia Press, 1980); Gaines M. Foster, *Ghosts of the Confederacy: Defeat, the Lost Cause, and the Emergence of the New South* (New York: Oxford University Press, 1987); Tony Horowitz, *Confederate in the Attic: Dispatches from the Unfinished Civil War* (New York: Pantheon, 1998); W. Scott Poole, *Never Surrender: Confederate Memory and Conservatism in the South Carolina Upcountry* (Athens: University of Georgia Press, 2004).

5. Washington, *Up from Slavery,* quote, 24.

6. Ibid., 16–26; Washington, *Story of My Life and Work,* 8–13; Harlan, *Booker T. Washington: The Making of a Black Leader,* 40–42.

7. Washington, *Up from Slavery,* 39–40; Harlan, *Booker T. Washington: The Making of a Black Leader,* "To clean," 47; see Norrell, *Up from History,* 27–30.

8. Robert Francis Engs, *Educating the Disfranchised and Disinherited: Samuel Chapman Armstrong and Hampton Institute, 1839–1893* (Knoxville: University of Tennessee Press, 1999); James D. Anderson, *The Education of Blacks in the South, 1860–1935* (Chapel Hill: University of North Carolina Press, 1988), 33–75; Francis Greenwood Peabody, *Education for Life: The Story of the Hampton Institute* (Garden City, NY: Doubleday, Page, 1919); Edith Armstrong Talbot, *Samuel Chapman Armstrong: A Biographical Study* (New York: Doubleday, Page, 1904); Philip Whitwell Wilson, *An Unofficial Statesman—Robert C. Ogden* (New York: Doubleday, Page, 1924); Norrell, *Up from History,* 31–32; James M. McPherson, *The Abolitionist Legacy: From Reconstruction to the NAACP* (Princeton, NJ: Princeton University Press, 1975), 187–188.

9. Washington, *Up from Slavery,* quote, 28; Harlan, *Booker T. Washington: The Making of a Black Leader,* 56.

10. Washington, *Up from Slavery,* quote, 31; see "General Armstrong," *Christian Union* 47 (May 20, 1893): 960; "In Memory of General Armstrong," *Christian Union* 47 (June 10, 1893): 1130; Nathalie Lord, "Booker Washington's School Days at Hampton," *Southern Workman* 31 (May 1902): 255–259. W. J. Cash later epitomized the tradition of schoolmarm ridicule: "Generally horsefaced, bespectacled, and spare of frame, she was, of course, no proper intellectual, but at best a comic character, at worst a dangerous fool, playing with explosive forces which she did not understand." Cash, *The Mind of the South* (New York: Knopf, 1941; repr., New York: Vintage, 1991), 137.

11. Washington, *Up from Slavery*, 33–45; Washington, *Story of My Life and Work*, 15–26; Harlan, *Booker T. Washington: The Making of a Black Leader*, 74–76.

12. Washington, *Up from Slavery*, "over one," 47; Booker T. Washington, "Incidents of Indian Life at Hampton," *Southern Workman* 9 (December 1880), "to the" and "without," 125, cited in Harlan, *Booker T. Washington: The Making of a Black Leader*, 105.

13. Washington, *Up from Slavery*, "No white," 48; Booker T. Washington, "Incidents of Indian Life at Hampton," *Southern Workman* 10 (May 1881), "His long," 55, cited in Harlan, *Booker T. Washington: The Making of a Black Leader*, 107; see Washington, "Incidents of Indian Life at Hampton," *Southern Workman* 10 (April 1881): 43.

14. Samuel Chapman Armstrong to George Washington Campbell and Other Trustees of Tuskegee Normal School, May 31, 1881, in *The Booker T. Washington Papers*, 14 vols., ed. Louis R. Harlan, Raymond W. Smock, and Geraldine McTighe (Urbana: University of Illinois Press, 1972–1989), quote, 2: 127; Washington, *Up from Slavery*, 51–52; Norrell, *Up from History*, 40; Harlan, *Booker T. Washington: The Making of a Black Leader*, 110–113.

15. Norrell, *Up from History*, 57–59; *Tuskegee News*, August 31, 1882, cited ibid., 59; see William Warren Rogers and Robert David Ward, *August Reckoning: Jack Turner and Racism in Post-Civil War Alabama* (Baton Rouge: Louisiana State University Press, 1973).

16. Washington, *Up from Slavery*, 51–87; Norrell, *Up from History*, 61–69; Harlan, *Booker T. Washington: The Making of a Black Leader*, 120–127; Booker T. Washington, *The Story of the Negro: The Rise of the Race from Slavery*, 2 vols. (New York: Doubleday, Page, 1909).

17. William Hooper Councill to Booker T. Washington, September 3, 1887, in *Booker T. Washington Papers*, 2: 382–384; Ralph E. Luker, *The Social Gospel in Black and White: American Racial Reform, 1885–1912* (Chapel Hill: University of North Carolina Press, 1991), 135; Harlan, *Booker T. Washington: The Making of a Black Leader*, 168–170.

18. Booker T. Washington to Samuel Chapman Armstrong, May 18, 1889, in *Booker T. Washington Papers*, quote, 2: 531–532; Washington to Armstrong, August 13, 1889, in *Booker T. Washington Papers*, 3: 4; Norrell, *Up from History*, 91.

19. Margaret James Murray to Booker T. Washington, October 26, 1891, in *Booker T. Washington Papers*, 3: 174–175; Murray to Washington, November 1, 1891, ibid., 3: 177–178; Harlan, *Booker T. Washington: The Making of a Black Leader*, 176–190; Norrell, *Up from History*, 100–101.

20. Harlan, *Booker T. Washington: The Making of a Black Leader*, Blackwell quote, 233, henhouse quote, 124; Booker T. Washington, "A Speech before the Boston Unitarian Club, 1888," in *Booker T. Washington Papers*, 2: 503. Washington recycled the "called to preach" story in *Up from Slavery*, 61.

21. Booker T. Washington, "The Colored Ministry: Its Defects and Needs," *Christian Union* 42 (August 14, 1890): 199–200; Harlan, *Booker T. Washington: The Making of a Black Leader*, 194.

22. Booker T. Washington to the *Christian Union*, November 22, 1890; Washington, *Up from Slavery*, "Every association," 105; "Announcement of the Opening of Phelps Hall Bible School," in *Booker T. Washington Papers*, 2: 271–272; Daniel A. Payne to Booker

T. Washington, November 3, 1890, published in Indianapolis *Freeman*, November 29, 1890, cited in Harlan, *Booker T. Washington: The Making of a Black Leader*, 195; "The Bible School at Tuskegee," *Outlook* 47 (March 18, 1893): 505; Norrell, *Up from History*, 109–110; Luker, *Social Gospel in Black and White*, 134.

23. Frederick Douglass, "Self-Made Men," 1872 version, www.monadnock.net/douglass/self-made-men.html; see Douglass, *Life and Times of Frederick Douglass*, in *Frederick Douglass: Autobiographies* (New York: Library of America, 1994), 814–815.

24. Booker T. Washington, *My Larger Education; Being Chapters from My Experience* (Garden City, NY: Doubleday, Page, 1911), quotes, 106–107; Norrell, *Up from History*, 94–95; Harlan, *Booker T. Washington: The Making of a Black Leader*, 272–287.

25. On lynching as evidence of black progress, see Booker T. Washington, *Black-Belt Diamonds: Gems from the Speeches, Addresses and Talks to Students* (New York: Fortune and Scott, 1898), 72.

26. Washington, *Up from Slavery*, 89–94; Walter Cooper, *The Cotton States and International Exposition and South, Illustrated. Including the Official History of the Exposition* (Atlanta: Illustrator, 1896), 23–24; Harlan, *Booker T. Washington: The Making of a Black Leader*, 205–209; Russell Duncan, *Entrepreneur for Equality: Governor Rufus Bullock, Commerce, and Race in Post-Civil War Georgia* (Athens: University of Georgia Press, 1994).

27. Editorial, Chicago *Inter Ocean*, August 24, 1895, "the late"; Harlan, *Booker T. Washington: The Making of a Black Leader*, "What's that," 216; Washington, *Up from Slavery*, "I am" and "this was," 7, 98.

28. See C. Vann Woodward, *The Strange Career of Jim Crow* (1st ed., 1955; New York: Oxford University Press, 2002), 67–109; Rayford Logan, *The Negro in American Life and Thought: The Nadir, 1877–1910* (New York: Dial Press, 1954), 242–275; Norrell, *Up from History*, 117–118; George M. Frederickson, *The Black Image in the White Mind: The Debate on Afro-American Character and Destiny, 1817–1914* (New York: Harper & Row, 1971), 198–227, 256–282.

29. Stetson Kennedy, *Jim Crow Guide: The Way It Was* (Boca Raton: Florida Atlantic University Press, 1959); Woodward, *Strange Career of Jim Crow*, 97–109.

30. Washington, *Up from Slavery*, 99. Washington's Atlanta Exposition Speech is repr. in *Up from Slavery*, 98–102, and in *Negro Protest Thought in the Twentieth Century*, ed. Francis L. Broderick and August Meier (Indianapolis: Bobbs-Merrill, 1965), 3–8.

31. Washington, Atlanta Exposition Speech, *Up from Slavery*, 100.

32. Ibid.

33. Ibid., 101.

34. Cooper, *Cotton States*, Speer quote, 104; Editorial, "Editorial Notes," *Independent* 47 (September 26, 1895), "fit," 1297; Harlan, *Booker T. Washington: The Making of a Black Leader*, 219–223; Norrell, *Up from History*, 126–127; Howell and *Transcript* quotes cited in Washington, *Up from Slavery*, 102–103.

35. Booker T. Washington, New York *World*, September 20, 1895, "I seemed"; Mary E. Stearns to Booker T. Washington, September 19, 1895, "Your address," cited in Harlan, *Booker T. Washington: The Making of a Black Leader*, 221; John Wesley Edward Bowen to Washington, November 12, 1895, in *Booker T. Washington Papers*, "love," 4: 78;

W. E. B. Du Bois to Booker T. Washington, September 24, 1895, in *The Correspondence of W. E. B. Du Bois*, 3 vols., ed. Herbert Aptheker (Amherst: University of Massachusetts Press, 1973–1978), "Let me," 1: 39; Du Bois, *Dusk of Dawn: An Essay toward an Autobiography of a Race Concept* (New York: Harcourt, Brace & World, 1940; repr., New Brunswick, NJ: Transaction, 2009), 55; W. E. B. Du Bois, *The Autobiography of W. E. B. Du Bois* (New York: International, 1968), "statesmanlike" and "equal," 246.

36. [W. Calvin Chase], editorial, *Washington Bee*, November 2, 1895; George N. Smith, *Voice of Missions*, December 1895, cited in Philip S. Foner, ed., "Is Booker T. Washington's Idea Correct?" *Journal of Negro History* 55 (September 1967): 288; Atlanta *Advocate* statement in *Cleveland Gazette*, November 2, 1895, citations in Harlan, *Booker T. Washington: The Making of a Black Leader*, 226–227; Norrell, *Up from History*, 134; Henry McNeal Turner, *Voice of Missions*, October 1895, repr. in Turner, *Respect Black: The Writings and Speeches of Henry McNeal Turner*, ed. Edwin S. Redkey (New York: Arno, 1971), 165–166; Edwin S. Redkey, *Black Nationalist and Back-to-Africa Movements, 1890–1910* (New Haven, CT: Yale University Press, 1970), 231; Redkey, "Bishop Turner's African Dream," *Journal of American History* 54 (September 1967): 288.

37. Editorial, "The Worship of Booker T. Washington," *Independent* 50 (December 8, 1898), "the worship," "gave," and "sensible," 1708–1709; Booker T. Washington to Francis J. Grimké, May 8, 1898, in *The Works of Francis J. Grimké*, ed. Carter G. Woodson (Washington, DC: Associated Publishers, 1942), 4: 51; Washington, *My Larger Education*, 106–107; Washington, *Up from Slavery*, 98, 103; John Graham Brooks, *An American Citizen: The Life of William Henry Baldwin, Jr.* (Boston: Houghton Mifflin, 1910), 244–245); Norrell, *Up from History*, 156.

38. August Meier, *Negro Thought in America, 1880–1915* (Ann Arbor: University of Michigan Press, 1963), 95–96; Luker, *Social Gospel in Black and White*, 22–23; Dieter Jedan, "Theory and Practice: Johann Heinrich Pestalozzi," *Vitae Scholasticae* 9 (1990): 115–132; Charles Spencer Smith, *A History of the African Methodist Episcopal Church, 1856–1922* (Philadelphia: A.M.E. Book Concern, 1922), "Nothing," 174.

39. Emmett J. Scott and Lyman Beecher Stowe, *Booker T. Washington, Builder of a Civilization* (Garden City, NY: Doubleday, Page, 1916), 312–313; Harlan, *Booker T. Washington: The Making of a Black Leader*, quotes, 231.

40. Booker T. Washington, "An Address to the National Peace Jubilee, October 16, 1898," in *Booker T. Washington Papers*, 4: 490–493.

41. Editorial, *Atlanta Constitution*, October 18, 1898; Booker T. Washington to the editor, *Birmingham Age-Herald*, November 13, 1898; Harlan, *Booker T. Washington: The Making of a Black Leader*, 236–237; Norrell, *Up from History*, 164–165.

42. Woodward, *Strange Career*, 82–86; Woodward, *Origins of the New South, 1877–1913* (1951; 2nd ed., Baton Rouge: Louisiana State University Press, 1971), 321–349.

43. Vardaman quote, *Atlanta Constitution*, April 30, 1899; Tillman quote, *Nashville American*, May 4, 1900, cited in Norrell, *Up from History*, 179, 193; see Albert D. Kirwan, *Revolt of the Rednecks: Mississippi Politics, 1876–1925* (Lexington: University of Kentucky Press, 1951), 145–147; James D. Anderson, *The Education of Blacks in the South, 1860–1935* (Chapel Hill: University of North Carolina Press, 1988), 96;

J. Morgan Kousser, *The Shaping of Southern Politics: Suffrage Restrictions and the Shaping of the One-Party South, 1880–1910* (New Haven, CT: Yale University Press, 1974), 145–170; Ray Stannard Baker, *Following the Color Line: American Negro Citizenship in the Progressive Era* (1st ed., 1908: repr., New York: Harper & Row, 1964), 241.

44. See Louis R. Harlan, "The Secret Life of Booker T. Washington," in *Booker T. Washington in Perspective: Essays of Louis R. Harlan*, ed. Raymond Smock (Jackson: University of Mississippi Press, 1988), 112–115; *Race Problems of the South: Report of the Proceedings of the First Annual Conference Held under the Auspices of the Southern Society for Promotion of the Study of Race Conditions* (Richmond, VA: B.F. Johnson, 1900); Edgar Gardner Murphy, *Problems of the Present South: A Discussion of the Educational, Industrial, and Political Issues in the Southern States* (New York: Macmillan, 1904); Murphy, *The Basis of Ascendancy: A Discussion of Certain Principles of Public Policy Involved in the Development of the Southern States* (New York: Longmans, Green, 1908).

45. Booker T. Washington, *The Future of the American Negro* (Boston: Small, Maynard, 1899), 201–244.

46. Ibid., 209–230.

47. Ibid., 241, 244.

48. Norrell, *Up from History*, 203–208, quote, 203; Woodward, *Strange Career*, 82–89; Horace Mann Bond, *Negro Education in Alabama: A Study in Cotton and Steel* (1939; repr., New York: Octagon, 1969), 185–191.

49. Charles Carroll, *The Negro a Beast . . . or . . . In the Image of God: The Reasoner of the Age, the Revelator of the Century! The Bible as It Is! The Negro and His Relation to the Human Family!* (St. Louis, MO: American Book and Bible House, 1900); William P. Calhoun, *The Caucasian and the Negro in the United States. They Must Separate. If Not, Then Extermination. A Proposed Solution: Colonization* (Columbia, SC: R. L. Bryan, 1902).

50. John David Smith, *Black Judas: William Hannibal Thomas and The American Negro* (Athens: University of Georgia Press, 2000), 2–19.

51. William Hannibal Thomas, *The American Negro: What He Was, What He Is, and What He May Become* (New York: Macmillan, 1901), quotes, x, xi, xxiii, 117, 212; see Thomas, "Shall Negroes Become Landowners?" *A.M.E. Church Review* 3 (July 1887): 481–491; Thomas, "Til Another King Arose, Which Knew Not Joseph," *A.M.E. Church Review* 5 (October 1888): 332–343.

52. Reverdy Ransom, "Noted Here and There within the Sphere," *A.M.E. Church Review* 30 (April 1914): 355; Alexander Walters, "Negro Progress," *Independent* 53 (March 21, 1901): 651–652; Richard R. Wright Jr., review of *The American Negro*, by William H. Thomas, *American Journal of Sociology* 6 (May 1901): 849–852; Silas Xavier Floyd, *Life of Charles T. Walker* (New York: National Baptist Publishing Board, 1902), 143; Jenkin Lloyd Jones, "The Souls of Black Folk," *Unity* 51 (May 7, 1903): 148; "The American Negro," *Independent* 53 (February 14, 1901): 393; Edgar Gardner Murphy, "Thomas on Negroes," *New York Times*, February 24, 1901; Luker, *Social Gospel in Black and White*, 294–295.

53. Smith, *Black Judas*, 192–195; John R. Commons, "The Negro," *Chautauquan* 38 (November 1903): 234; review of *The American Negro*, by William H. Thomas, *Outlook* 67 (January 26, 1901): 229.

54. [Booker T. Washington], review of *The American Negro*, by William H. Thomas, *Outlook* 67 (March 30, 1901), in *Papers of Booker T. Washington*, 6: 69–75; Smith, *Black Judas*, 196–197.

55. Washington, *Story of My Life and Work*, 178, 176, 179, 180.

56. Washington, *Up from Slavery*, 40; Lyman Abbott to Booker T. Washington, December 9, 1899, in *Booker T. Washington Papers*, 5: 288–289; Abbott to Washington, October 1, 1900, ibid., 5: 646; Washington to Abbott, October 8, 1900, ibid., 5: 653–654; Sidonie Smith, "Casting Down," in *Where I'm Bound: Patterns of Slavery and Freedom in Black American Autobiography* (Westport, CT: Greenwood, 1974), 30–44, repr. in Norton Critical Edition of *Up from Slavery*, 219–228; review of *Up from Slavery*, by Booker T. Washington, *Southern Workman* 30 (August 1901): 749–750; review of ibid., *Independent* 53 (April 4, 1901): 787; James M. Cox, "Autobiography and Washington," *Sewanee Review* 85 (Spring 1977), in Norton Critical Edition of *Up from Slavery*, 228–239; Norrell, *Up from History*, 216–217.

57. Louis R. Harlan, *Booker T. Washington: The Wizard of Tuskegee* (New York: Oxford University Press, 1983), 130–134, quote, 133.

58. Review of *Up from Slavery*, by Booker T. Washington, *Nation*, April 4, 1901, 281–282; William Dean Howells, "An Exemplary Citizen," *North American Review* 173 (August 1901): 282–284.

59. W. E. B. Du Bois to Booker T. Washington, July 27, 1894, in *Correspondence of W. E. B. Du Bois*, 1: 37; Washington to Du Bois, July 15, 1902, ibid., 1: 46; David Levering Lewis, *W. E. B. Du Bois: Biography of a Race, 1868–1919* (New York: Henry Holt, 1993), 230–235.

60. Booker T. Washington to W. E. B. Du Bois, March 11, 1900, *in Correspondence of W. E. B. Du Bois*, 1: 44; Lewis, *W. E. B. Du Bois: Biography of a Race*, 235–237.

61. W. E. B. Du Bois, "The Evolution of Negro Leadership," *The Dial*, July 16, 1901, 53–55. This review of *Up from Slavery* is also repr. as "A Book Review by William Edward Burghardt De Bois" in *Booker T. Washington Papers*, 176–177.

62. Du Bois, *Dusk of Dawn*, quotes, 303.

63. Ibid., 8–19, "because it was," xxix; W. E. B. Du Bois, *Darkwater: Voices from Within the Veil* (New York: Harcourt, Brace, 1920; repr., Mineola, NY: Dover Publications, 1999), remaining quotes, 3, 4; Du Bois, *Autobiography of W. E. B. Du Bois*, 61–77.

64. Du Bois, *Darkwater*, quotes, 4, 5; see W. E. B. Du Bois to his mother, July 21, 1883, in *Correspondence of W. E. B. Du Bois*, 1: 3–4.

65. Du Bois, *Darkwater*, 6; Du Bois, *Dusk of Dawn*, 12, 108–109; Du Bois, *Autobiography of W. E. B. Du Bois*, 62, 72; "W. E. B. Du Bois Interview with William T. Ingersoll, May 1960, Columbia University Oral History Project, in Lewis, *W. E. B. Du Bois: Biography of a Race*, 27.

66. Du Bois, *Darkwater*, quotes, 5; Du Bois, *Autobiography of W. E. B. Du Bois*, 73–74.

67. Du Bois, *Darkwater*, 6.

68. Du Bois, *Dusk of Dawn*, "a boy's" and "property," 13; W. E. B. Du Bois, *The Souls of Black Folk* (Chicago: A. C. McClurg, 1903; repr., New York: Dover, 1994), "Then it dawned," 2; Du Bois, *Autobiography of W. E. B. Du Bois*, "began to feel," 83.

69. Du Bois, *Dusk of Dawn*, "I did not" and "in this way," 15, 16; Du Bois, *Darkwater*, "very much," 6; Lewis, *W. E. B. Du Bois: Biography of a Race*, 35; Du Bois, *Autobiography of W. E. B. Du Bois*, "but I was," 99.

70. Du Bois, *Darkwater*, "my first," "Now it was," and "a mighty," 7; Du Bois, *Dusk of Dawn*, "thoroughly," "habit," "but here," and "slavery," 18, 19, 22, 23; Du Bois, *Autobiography of W. E. B. Du Bois*, "half-guilty," 102; W. E. B. Du Bois to the Reverend Scudder, February 3, 1886, in *Correspondence of W. E. B. Du Bois*, 1: 5.

71. Thomas C. Holt, "The Political Uses of Alienation: W. E. B. Du Bois on Politics, Race, and Culture, 1903–1940," *American Quarterly* 42 (June 1990): 307; Arnold Rampersad, "Biography, Autobiography, and Afro-American Culture," *Yale Review* 73 (Autumn 1983): 12; Lawrie Balfour, *Democracy's Reconstruction: Thinking Politically With W. E. B. Du Bois* (New York: Oxford University Press, 2011), 76–77; see Rampersad, *The Art and Imagination of W. E. B. Du Bois* (1st ed., 1976; repr., New York: Schocken, 1990).

72. Henry Allen Bullock, *A History of Negro Education in the South: From 1619 to the Present* (New York: Praeger, 1969), 25–52; Jacqueline Jones, *Soldiers of Light and Love: Northern Teachers and Georgia Blacks, 1865–1873* (Athens: University of Georgia Press, 1992), 135–137; Joe M. Richardson, *Christian Reconstruction: The American Missionary Association and Southern Blacks, 1861–1890* (Athens: University of Georgia Press, 1986), 40–44; Richardson, *A History of Fisk University, 1865–1946* (Tuscaloosa: University of Alabama Press, 1980), 6–21; Carter G. Woodson, *The Miseducation of the Negro* (1933; repr., New York: AMS Press, 1977); Lewis, *W. E. B. Du Bois: Biography of a Race*, 56–58.

73. Du Bois, *Autobiography of W. E. B. Du Bois*, "sons, daughters," 108; Du Bois, *Darkwater*, "I willed" and "under," 8.

74. W. E. B. Du Bois, "My Evolving Program for Negro Freedom," in *What the Negro Wants*, ed. Rayford W. Logan (Chapel Hill: University of North Carolina Press, 1944), "a world," 37; Du Bois, "The Religion of the American Negro," *New World* 9 (December 1900), "A sort of," 614–615; Du Bois, *Dusk of Dawn*, "marching," 32–33; Du Bois, *Autobiography of W. E. B. Du Bois*, 109, 126; W. E. B. Du Bois to the Harvard College Admissions Office, October 29, 1887, in *Correspondence of W. E. B. Du Bois*, 1: 6; George Frederick Wright, *The Logic of Christian Evidences* (Andover, MA: Warren F. Draper, 1880); Rampersad, *Art and Imagination*, 22; see Gary Dorrien, *The Making of American Liberal Theology: Imagining Progressive Religion, 1805–1900* (Louisville, KY: Westminster John Knox Press, 2001), 349–365.

75. Du Bois, *Darkwater*, quotes, 8; Du Bois, *Dusk of Dawn*, 37–40; Du Bois, *Autobiography of W. E. B. Du Bois*, 132–153; Du Bois, "My Evolving Program," 40.

76. Francis Greenwood Peabody, *The Approach to the Social Question* (New York: Macmillan, 1909); David B. Potts, "Social Ethics at Harvard, 1881–1931: A Study in Academic Activism," in *Social Sciences at Harvard, 1860–1920: From Inculcation to the Open Mind*, ed. Paul Buck (Cambridge, MA: Harvard University Press, 1965), 94–96;

Gary Dorrien, *Social Ethics in the Making: Interpreting an American Tradition* (Oxford: Wiley-Blackwell, 2009), 15–20.

77. Du Bois, *Darkwater*, quotes, 8; see Thomas Babington Macaulay, *Critical Historical Essays* (London: J. M. Dent, 1907); Macaulay, *History of England*, 5 vols. (London: Macmillan, 1913); Albert Bushnell Hart, *The Southern South* (New York: D. Appleton, 1910); Rampersad, *Art and Imagination*, 32–33.

78. Du Bois, *Darkwater*, "No thought," 8.

79. Ibid., "I went" and "I wonder," 8, 9; W. E. B. Du Bois to Rutherford B. Hayes, April 3, 1891, in *Correspondence of W. E. B. Du Bois*, "you ought," "almost," and "but I never," 1: 13–14; Du Bois, *Dusk of Dawn*, 42–48; Lewis, *W. E. B. Du Bois: Biography of a Race*, 112–113; Du Bois, *Autobiography of W. E. B. Du Bois*, 150–153.

80. Du Bois, *Darkwater*, "I dreamed," 9; Du Bois, *Autobiography of W. E. B. Du Bois*, "I was just," 157; Lewis, *W. E. B. Du Bois: Biography of a Race*, "These are," 135; W. E. B. Du Bois to Rutherford B. Hayes, April 3, 1892, in *Correspondence of W. E. B. Du Bois*, 1: 16–17; Du Bois to D. C. Gilman, October 28, 1892, ibid., 1: 20–21; Du Bois, *Dusk of Dawn*, 42–48.

81. Lewis, *W. E. B. Du Bois: Biography of a Race*, "I rejoice" and "life-ruin," 134, 135; Du Bois, *Darkwater*, "suddenly," 9; W. E. B. Du Bois to John F. Slater Fund Trustees, March 10, 1893, in *Correspondence of W. E. B. Du Bois*, 1: 23–25; D. C. Gilman to Du Bois, April 13, 1894, ibid., 1: 29; Du Bois, *Dusk of Dawn*, 42–48.

82. Richard R. Wright Jr., *Bishops of the African Methodist Episcopal Church* (Nashville, TN: AME Sunday School Union, 1963), 287; Horace Talbert, *Sons of Allen: Together with a Sketch of the Rise and Progress of Wilberforce University* (Xenia, OH: Aldine, 1906), 266–268; Carter G. Woodson, *History of the Negro Church* (Washington, DC: Associated Publishers, 1921), 181; Daniel A. Payne, *Recollections of Seventy Years* (Nashville, TN: AME Sunday School Union, 1888).

83. Du Bois, *Darkwater*, "I had," "my first," and "For the," 10; Du Bois, *Autobiography of W. E. B. Du Bois*, "I was," 188; Du Bois, *Dusk of Dawn*, 50–65.

84. W. E. B. Du Bois, *The Suppression of the African Slave Trade to the United States of America, 1638–1870* (New York: Longman, Green, 1896; repr., ed. Herbert Aptheker, Millwood, NY: Kraus-Thomson, 1973); Lewis, *W. E. B. Du Bois: Biography of a Race*, 155–157; Philip D. Curtin, *The Atlantic Slave Trade: A Census* (Madison: University of Wisconsin Press, 1969), 65–77; J. E. Inikori, "Measuring the Atlantic Slave Trade: An Assessment of Curtin and Antsey," *Journal of African History* 17 (1976): 197–223.

85. Du Bois, *Souls of Black Folk*, 133–140, quotes, 133–134.

86. Crummell, "Africa and Her People: Lecture Notes," in Alexander Crummell, *Destiny and Race: Selected Writings, 1840–1898* (Amherst: University of Massachusetts Press, 1992), quotes, 65, 66; Wilson Jeremiah Moses, *Alexander Crummell: A Study of Civilization and Discontent* (New York: Oxford University Press, 1989), 11–20; Moses, *The Golden Age of Black Nationalism, 1850–1925* (New York: Oxford University Press, 1978), 62–64; Kathleen O'Mara Wahle, "Alexander Crummell: Black Evangelist and Pan-Negro Nationalist," *Phylon* 29 (1968): 388–395; Gregory Rigsby, *Alexander Crummell: Pioneer in Nineteenth-Century Pan-African Thought* (Westport, CT: Greenwood, 1987).

87. Alexander Crummell, *Africa and America: Addresses and Discourses* (Springfield, MA: Wiley, 1891), 272–305, quotes, 305; Crummell, *Jubilate: 1844–1894, The Shades and the Lights of a Fifty Years' Ministry* (Washington, DC: R. L. Pendleton, 1894), 5–25, in Crummell, *Destiny and Race*, 31–44; Moses, *Alexander Crummell*, 26–38.

88. Alexander Crummell to John Jay, August 2, 1850, "the last," in Moses, *Alexander Crummell*, 67; Crummell, *Jubilate*, "brilliant," 40.

89. Alexander Crummell, "The Relations and Duty of Free Colored Men in America to Africa," in Crummell, *The Future of Africa: Being Addresses, Sermons, Etc., Delivered in the Republic of Liberia* (New York: Charles Scribner, 1862), 215–220, "Darkness," 220; Crummell, *Jubilate*, 40; Moses, *Golden Age of Black Nationalism*, 67; Wilson Jeremiah Moses, "Introduction," in Crummell, *Destiny and Race*, "brooding," 5, "vituperative" and "combative," 11, "needlessly," 9; Alexander Crummell to P. P. Irving, January 10, 1856, in Moses, *Alexander Crummell*, "poor benighted" and "with rare," 92, "a perfect," 32; see Luckson Ejofodomi, *The Missionary Career of Alexander Crummell in Liberia, 1853–1873* (Ann Arbor, MI: University Microfilms, 1974); Sterling Stuckey, *The Ideological Origins of Black Nationalism* (Boston: Beacon Press, 1972), 9–11.

90. Alexander Crummell to Julian Hare, January 3, 1872, "newspapers," in Moses, *Alexander Crummell*, 193; Alexander Crummell, "Our National Mistakes and the Remedy for Them" (1870), in Crummell, *Africa and America*, "ignored" and "All," 165, 185; see Crummell, "Report from Caldwell, Liberia, on a Journey through the Dey and Vai Countries," in Crummell, *Destiny and Race*, 75–80; Moses, *Golden Age of Black Nationalism*, 69.

91. Alexander Crummell, "The Social Principle Among a People, and Its Bearing on Their Progress and Development," Thanksgiving Day sermon, 1875, in Crummell, *The Greatness of Christ and Other Sermons* (New York: Thomas Whittaker, 1882), 285–311, and Crummell, *Destiny and Race*, 254–268, quotes, 257, 259, 264.

92. Crummell, "The Black Woman of the South: Her Neglects and Her Needs" (1883), in Crummell, *Destiny and Race*, 211–223, "a merciful," "a prostrate," and "still," 212, 215; Crummell, "The Negro as a Source of Conservative Power," in Crummell, *Destiny and Race*, 235–244, "perfectly" and "ready," 237.

93. Crummell, *Africa and America*, iv; Alexander Crummell, "The Need of New Ideas and New Motives for a New Era" (1885), in Crummell, *Africa and America*, 24–36; Crummell, "The Discipline of Freedom," in Crummell, *Destiny and Race*, 245–253; Crummell, "Industrial Education: How to Apply the Unclaimed Bounty" (1880), in Destiny and Race, 206–210; Moses, *Golden Age of Black Nationalism*, 71; Moses, *Alexander Crummell*, 226–227.

94. Alexander Crummell, "The Destined Superiority of the Negro" (1877), in Crummell, *Destiny and Race*, 194–205, quotes, 195, 203.

95. Alexander Crummell, "Civilization the Primal Need of the Race" (1898), *American Negro Academy Occasional Papers* 3 (Washington, DC: American Negro Academy, 1898), quotes, 3, 5; Moses, *Golden Age of Black Nationalism*, 73–74.

96. Crummell, *Greatness of Christ and Other Sermons*, 1–13.

97. Ibid., 12.

98. Ibid., 17–18.

99. Crummell, *Jubilate*, quote, 20; Du Bois, *Souls of Black Folk*, 137–140.

100. Du Bois to Washington, September 24, 1895, in *Correspondence of W. E. B. Du Bois*, "phenomenal," 1: 39; Du Bois, *Darkwater*, "slip," 11; Du Bois, *Dusk of Dawn*, 50–65.

101. Dorrien, *Social Ethics in the Making*, 168–185; Du Bois, *Dusk of Dawn*, quote, 58; Lewis, *W. E. B. Du Bois: Biography of a Race*, quote, 187–88; C. C. Harrison to Whom It May Concern, August 15, 1896, in *Correspondence of W. E. B. Du Bois*, 1: 40; see E. Digby Baltzell, *Puritan Boston and Quaker Philadelphia: Two Protestant Ethics and the Spirit of Class Authority and Leadership* (New York: Free Press, 1979), 370–377; Roger Lane, *Roots of Violence in Black Philadelphia, 1860–1900* (Cambridge, MA: Harvard University Press, 1986), 13–14.

102. Du Bois, *Darkwater*, "They had," 11; Charles Booth, *Life and Labour of the People in London* (London: Macmillan, 1897); Jane Addams, *Hull House Maps and Papers, by Residents of Hull House* (Boston: Crowell, 1895); W. E. B. Du Bois, *The Philadelphia Negro: A Social Study* (Philadelphia: University of Pennsylvania Press, 1899; repr., New York: Oxford University Press, 2007), quotes, 4, 249, 387; W. E. B. Du Bois to Carroll D. Wright, May 5, 1897, in *Correspondence of W. E. B. Du Bois*, 1: 41–43; see Lane, *Roots of Violence*, 148; *W. E. B. Du Bois on Sociology and the Black Community*, ed. Dan S. Green and Edwin D. Driver (Chicago: University of Chicago Press, 1978), 39.

103. Du Bois, *Philadelphia Negro*, 328, 330, 326.

104. Ibid., 311, 315, 351.

105. Ibid., 97, 390, 394, 395.

106. Ibid., 389, 316.

107. Review of *The Philadelphia Negro*, by W. E. B. Du Bois, *Nation*, October 26, 1899, 310; *Literary Digest* 19 (December 16, 1899): 732; *Outlook* 63 (1899): 647–648; in Lewis, *W. E. B. Du Bois: Biography of a Race*, 207; Du Bois, *Darkwater*, "Nobody," 11.

108. E. Franklin Frazier, *Black Bourgeoisie* (New York: Free Press, 1957); Frazier, *The Negro Family in the United States* (Chicago: University of Chicago Press, 1939); Du Bois, *Darkwater*, "hot," 11; see George E. Haynes, *The Negro at Work in New York City* (New York: Columbia University Press, 1912); Carter G. Woodson, *The Negro Professional Man and the Community* (Washington, DC: Association for the Study of Negro Life and History, 1934); St. Clair Drake and Horace R. Cayton, *Black Metropolis: A Study of Negro Life in a Northern City* (1945; repr., New York: Harper & Row, 1962); John H. Bracey Jr., August Meier, and Elliott Rudwick, eds., *Black Matriarchy: Myth or Reality?* (Belmont, CA: Wadsworth, 1971).

109. Du Bois, *Darkwater*, 11–12.

110. G. W. F. Hegel, *Phenomenology of Spirit*, trans. A. V. Miller (Oxford: Clarendon Press, 1977), #178–196, 111–119; Gary Dorrien, *Kantian Reason and Hegelian Spirit: The Idealistic Logic of Modern Theology* (Oxford: Wiley-Blackwell, 2012), 185–191.

111. W. E. B. Du Bois, "Strivings of the Negro People," *Atlantic Monthly* 80 (August 1897): 194–198, rev. vers., "Of Our Spiritual Strivings," in Du Bois, *Souls of Black Folk*, 1–7, quotes, 1, 2; Du Bois, *Philadelphia Negro*, 397; see Bliss Perry to W. E. B. Du Bois, June 28, 1902, in *Correspondence of W. E. B. Du Bois*, 1: 47. For works that

attribute a strong Hegelian influence on Du Bois, see Joel Williamson, *The Crucible of Race: Black-White Relations in the American South Since Emancipation* (New York: Oxford University Press, 1984), 402–413; Paul Gilroy, *The Black Atlantic: Modernity and Double Consciousness* (Cambridge, MA: Harvard University Press, 1993), 134–135; Robert Gooding-Williams, "Philosophy of History and Social Critique in *The Souls of Black Folk*," *Social Science Information* 26 (1987): 106–108; and Jacqueline Stevens, "Beyond Tocqueville, Please!" *American Political Science Review* 89 (December 1995): 987–990. For works contending that Du Bois was influenced by Emerson and/or Herder, see Rampersad, *Art and Imagination*, 74–75; Cornel West, *The American Evasion of Philosophy: A Genealogy of Pragmatism* (Madison: University of Wisconsin Press, 1989), 142–143.

112. Ralph Waldo Emerson, "The Transcendentalist," Emerson, *Nature, Addresses, and Lectures*, ed. Robert E. Spiller and Alfred R. Ferguson (Cambridge, MA: Harvard University Press, 1979), 201–216; Du Bois, "Strivings of the Negro People," in *The Souls of Black Folk*, 2, 3.

113. Du Bois, "Strivings of the Negro People," in *The Souls of Black Folk*, 2, 7.

114. W. E. B. Du Bois, "The Conservation of Races," Address to the American Negro Academy, March 5, 1897, *Occasional Papers* 2 (Washington, DC: American Negro Academy, 1897), repr. in Du Bois, *Pamphlets and Leaflets*, ed. Herbert Aptheker (White Plains, NY: Kraus-Thomson, 1986), and Du Bois, *W. E. B. Du Bois: A Reader*, ed. David Levering Lewis (New York: Henry Holt, 1995), 20–27, quotes, 21.

115. Du Bois, "The Conservation of Races," in *W. E. B. Du Bois: A Reader*, 21–22.

116. Ibid., 24, 25, 26.

117. Ibid., 26, 27.

118. Moses, *Alexander Crummell*, 265; Lewis, *W. E. B. Du Bois: Biography of a Race*, 173.

119. Herbert Spencer, *First Principles* (New York: D. Appleton, 1864); Spencer, *The Principles of Sociology*, 3 vols. (New York: D. Appleton, 1876–1897); Richard Hofstadter, *Social Darwinism in American Thought* (Boston: Beacon Press, 1955), 31–50; George W. Stocking Jr., *Race, Culture, and Evolution: Essays in the History of Anthropology* (Chicago: University of Chicago Press, 1968), 234–269; Stephen Jay Gould, *Ontogeny and Phylogeny* (Cambridge, MA: Harvard University Press, 1977); Charles Darwin, *The Descent of Man* (New York: John Murray, 1874), 166–168.

120. Ernst Haeckel, *The History of Creation*, 2 vols. (1876; 6th ed., New York: D. Appleton, 1914), quote, 2: 249; Robert J. Richards, *The Tragic Sense of Life: Ernst Haeckel and the Struggle over Evolutionary Thought* (Chicago: University of Chicago Press, 2008), 255–261.

121. Du Bois, *Dusk of Dawn*, "actual," 51; Du Bois, "The Conservation of Races," in *Pamphlets and Leaflets*, "same," 10.

122. Albion W. Small, *An Introduction to the Study of Society* (New York: American Book, 1894); Thomas F. Gossett, *Race: The History of an Idea in America* (New York: Schocken, 1965), 54–83; George M. Frederickson, *Race: A Short History* (Princeton, NJ: Princeton University Press), 51–75; M. K. Richardson and G. Keuck, "Haeckel's ABC of Evolution and Development," *Biological Reviews* 77 (2002): 495–528. Small founded *The American Journal of Sociology* in 1895.

123. Moses, *Golden Age of Black Nationalism*, 132–138, quotes, 135, 133.

124. Anthony Appiah, "The Uncompleted Argument: Du Bois and the Illusion of Race," *Critical Inquiry* 12 (Autumn 1985): 21–37, quotes, 23, 25.

125. Williamson, *Crucible of Race*, 397–405, quote, 405.

126. William I. Thomas, "The Scope and Method of Folk Psychology," *American Journal of Sociology* 1 (January 1896): 438–440, "artificial," 439; Du Bois, "The Conservation of Races," *Pamphlets and Leaflets*, "sociological," 10; Adolph L. Reed Jr., *W. E. B. Du Bois and American Political Thought: Fabianism and the Color Line* (New York: Oxford University Press, 1997), 121–122.

127. Gunnar Myrdal, *An American Dilemma: The Negro Problem and Modern Democracy*, 2 vols. (1st ed., 1944; repr., New York: Harper & Row, 1962), "dual," 2: 809; Carol B. Stack, *All Our Kin: Strategies for Survival in a Black Community* (New York: Harper & Row, 1974), "conflicting," 26–27; Robert Gooding-Williams, *In the Shadow of Du Bois: Afro-American Political Thought in America* (Cambridge, MA: Harvard University Press, 2009), 66–129; Henry Louis Gates Jr., Introduction to W. E. B. Du Bois, *The Souls of Black Folk* (New York: Bantam, 1989), "Du Bois,"' xviii; Cornel West, *Prophesy Deliverance! An Afro-American Revolutionary Christianity* (Philadelphia: Westminster, 1982), 30–31.

128. Lawrence D. Bobo, "Reclaiming a Du Boisian Perspective on Racial Attitudes," *ANNALS of the American Academy of Political and Social Science* 568 (March 2000): 186–202; Reed, *W. E. B. Du Bois and American Political Thought*, 120–125; Ernest Allen Jr., "Du Boisian Double Consciousness: The Unsustainable Argument," *Massachusetts Review* 43 (2002): 216–217.

129. Manning Marable, *W. E. B. Du Bois: Black Radical Democrat* (Boulder, CO: Paradigm, 2005), 36–37; Houston A. Baker Jr., "Caliban's Triple Play," in *"Race," Writing, and Difference*, ed. Henry Louis Gates Jr. (Chicago: University of Chicago Press, 1986), 381–395; Baker, "There Is No More Beautiful Way: Theory and the Poetics of Afro-American Woman's Writing," in *Afro-American Literary Study in the 1990s*, ed. Baker and Patricia Redmond (Chicago: University of Chicago Press, 1989), "a field," 150.

130. Gilroy, *Black Atlantic*, 111–145; Gilroy, *Against Race: Imagining Political Culture Beyond the Color Line* (Cambridge, MA: Harvard University Press, 2000), "embeddedness," 52; Gilroy, *Darker than Blue: On the Moral Economies of Black Atlantic Culture* (Cambridge, MA: Harvard University Press, 2010), 152–155; Gilroy, *Postcolonial Melancholy* (New York: Columbia University Press, 2005), 33–38; see Francis L. Broderick, *W. E. B. Du Bois: Negro Leader in a Time of Crisis* (Stanford, CA: Stanford University Press, 1959), 53; Rampersad, *Art and Imagination of W. E. B. Du Bois*, 61; Reed, *W. E. B. Du Bois and American Political Thought*, 132–160; Houston A. Baker Jr., *Blues, Ideology, and Afro-American Literature: A Vernacular Theory* (Chicago: University of Chicago Press, 1984); Henry Louis Gates Jr., *Loose Canons: Notes on the Culture Wars* (New York: Oxford University Press, 1992), 43–69.

131. Du Bois, *Dusk of Dawn*, "provided," 98–99, "Facing" and "a changing," 51.

132. Clarence Bacote, *The Story of Atlanta University: A Century of Service, 1865–1965* (Atlanta, GA: Atlanta University, 1969), 9–15; George A. Towns, "Phylon Profile, XVI:

Horace Bumstead, Atlanta University President (1888–1907)," *Phylon* 9 (1948): 109–114; Lewis, *W. E. B. Du Bois: Biography of a Race*, 214–215.

133. Towns, "Phylon Profile, XVI: Horace Bumstead, Atlanta University President," state government quote, 112; Atticus G. Haygood, "Changing for the Wrong Thing," *Wesleyan Christian Advocate*, August 17, 1887; Williamson, *Crucible of Race*, 90; Du Bois, *Autobiography of W. E. B. Du Bois*, "conditions" and "indications," 210.

134. Du Bois, *Dusk of Dawn*, quote, 67; Du Bois, *Autobiography of W. E. B. Du Bois*, 222.

135. Du Bois, *Souls of Black Folk*, 127–131; W. E. B. Du Bois, "I Bury My Wife," *Chicago Globe*, July 15, 1950, repr. in Du Bois, *W. E. B. Du Bois: A Reader*, quote, 143.

136. Edgar Gardner Murphy to Booker T. Washington, January 31, 1903, in *Booker T. Washington Papers*, 7: 17.

137. Owen Charles Mathurin, *Henry Sylvester Williams and the Origins of the Pan-African Movement, 1869–1911* (Westport, CT: Greenwood Press, 1976), 42–45; Imanuel Geiss, *The Pan-African Movement: A History of Pan-Africanism in America, Europe and Africa* (New York: Africana, 1974), 5–7; Booker T. Washington, "To the Editor," Indianapolis *Freeman*, August 12, 1899, 1, in *Booker T. Washington Papers*, 5: 154–155; W. E. B. Du Bois, *The World and Africa* (1st ed. 1947; repr., Millwood, NY: Kraus-Thomson, 1976), 2–3.

138. Mathurin, *Henry Sylvester Williams and the Origins*, 43–44; Alexander Walters, *My Life and Work* (New York: Fleming H. Revell, 1917), 253–254; Lewis, *W. E. B. Du Bois: Biography of a Race*, 249; Anna Julia Cooper, *A Voice from the South* (Xenia, OH: Aldine, 1892; repr., New York: Oxford University Press, 1988).

139. Walters, *My Life and Work*, quotes, 261, 257; Geiss, *Pan-African Movement*, 6–7.

140. Du Bois did not refer to Williams until 1945, when he mentioned an unnamed "West Indian barrister" in his article, "Revival of Pan-Africanism," *Chicago Defender*, September 29, 1945; Mathurin, *Henry Sylvester Williams and the Origins*, 74–75.

141. W. E. B. Du Bois, "To the Nations of the World," in Du Bois, *Writings in Non-Periodical Literature*, ed. Herbert Aptheker (Millwood, NY: Kraus-Thomson, 1982), 11–12, quotes, 11; also reprinted in Walters, *My Life and Work*, 257–260; Lewis, *W. E. B. Du Bois: Biography of a Race*, 250.

142. Du Bois, "To the Nations of the World," 11–12.

143. Ibid., 12.

144. See Ridgely Torrence, *The Story of John Hope* (1st ed., 1948; repr., New York: Arno, 1969); Jacqueline A. Rouse, *Lugenia Burns Hope: Black Southern Reformer* (London: University of Georgia Press, 1989); Lewis, *W. E. B. Du Bois: Biography of a Race*, 252–254.

145. Du Bois, *Autobiography of W. E. B. Du Bois*, 213–216, quote, 241; Du Bois, *Dusk of Dawn*, 71–76.

146. W. E. B. Du Bois, "The Storm and Stress in the Black World," review of *The American Negro*, by William Hannibal Thomas, *The Dial* 30 (April 16, 1901): 262–264; Du Bois, *Dusk of Dawn*, quote, 80. The five previously unpublished chapters in *The Souls of Black Folk* were titled "Of the Wings of Atalanta," "Of the Passing of the First-Born," "Of Alexander Crummell," "Of the Coming of John," and "The Sorrow Songs."

147. Theodore Roosevelt to Albion Tourgeé, November 8, 1908, in Joseph B. Bishop, *Theodore Roosevelt and His Time, Shown in His Own Letters,* 2 vols. (New York: Scribner's, 1920), 1: 166; H. W. Brands, *TR: The Last Romantic* (New York: Basic Books, 1997), 422; Harlan, *Booker T. Washington: The Making of a Black Leader,* 312–313; Norrell, *Up from History,* 243–244.

148. "Roosevelt Dines a Darkey," *Richmond Dispatch,* October 18, 1901; Willard B. Gatewood Jr., *Theodore Roosevelt and the Art of Controversy: Episodes of the White House Years* (Baton Rouge: Louisiana State University Press, 1970), "A Rank" and "Our," 36; "Both Politically and Socially, President Roosevelt Proposes to Coddle Descendants of Ham," *Atlanta Constitution,* October 18, 1901; Clarence Lusane, *The Black History of the White House* (San Francisco: City Lights Publishers, 2013), "The most," 254; Dewey W. Grantham Jr., "Dinner at the White House: Theodore Roosevelt, Booker T. Washington, and the South," *Tennessee Historical Quarterly* 18 (June 1958): 115–118; Edmund Morris, *Theodore Rex* (New York: Modern Library, 2002), 54–55.

149. Grantham Jr., "Dinner at the White House," 116–118; Morris, *Theodore Rex,* 55; Norrell, *Up from History,* "that white woman," "White men," and "might now," 248; Brands, *TR: The Last Romantic,* "vigor," 423.

150. Grantham Jr., "Dinner at the White House," 117–118; Morris, *Theodore Rex,* "the action," 55; Norrell, *Up from History,* 246, "President Roosevelt," 248; William F. Holmes, *The White Chief: James Kimble Vardaman* (Baton Rouge: Louisiana State University Press, 1970), 99; Brands, *TR: The Last Romantic,* 423.

151. Brands, *TR: The Last Romantic,* "the idiot" and "just as," 323; Roosevelt to Tourgeé, November 8, 1908; *Dallas Morning News,* October 13, 1904, Davis quotes, cited in Norrell, *Up from History,* 307.

152. Thomas E. Dixon Jr., *The Life Worth Living: A Personal Experience* (New York: Doubleday, Page, 1914), 8–15; Raymond Allen Cook, *Fire From the Flint: The Amazing Careers of Thomas Dixon* (Winston-Salem, NC: John F. Blair, 1968); H. Shelton Smith, *In His Image, But . . . Racism in Southern Religion, 1780–1910* (Durham, NC: Duke University Press, 1972), 275–276; Williamson, *Crucible of Race,* 140–176.

153. Thomas E. Dixon Jr., *The Leopard's Spots: A Romance of the White Man's Burden, 1865–1900* (New York: Doubleday, Page, 1902); Dixon, *Dixon's Sermons* (New York: F. L. Bussey, 1899); Dixon, *Life Worth Living,* 15–22; Smith, *In His Image, But,* 276; Harriet Beecher Stowe, *Uncle Tom's Cabin; or, Life Among the Lowly* (1852; New York: Barnes & Noble, 1995); Thomas F. Gossett, *Uncle Tom's Cabin and American Culture* (Dallas: Southern Methodist University Press, 1985); Williamson, *Crucible of Race,* 158; George M. Fredrickson, *The Black Image in the White Mind: The Debate on Afro-American Character and Destiny, 1817–1914* (New York: Harper & Row, 1971), 280–281; Luker, *Social Gospel in Black and White,* 296–297; Willie Lee Rose, "Race and Region in American Historical Fiction: Four Episodes in Popular Culture," in *Region, Race, and Reconstruction: Essays in Honor of C. Vann Woodward,* ed. J. Morgan Kousser and James M. McPherson (New York: Oxford University Press, 1982), 113–139.

154. Dixon, *Leopard's Spots,* 122–128, 231–263, 382–383, 451–460, quotes, 198, 242, 442.

155. Thomas E. Dixon Jr., *The Clansman: An Historical Romance of the Ku Klux Klan* (New York: Doubleday, Page, 1905); see Dixon, *The Sins of the Father: A Romance of the South* (New York: Appleton, 1912).

156. Dixon, *Leopard's Spots*, 149, 211, 239, 270, 379; Dixon, *Clansman*, 215–220, 248–251, 304; "The Negro a Menace Says Thomas Dixon," *New York Times*, June 9, 1903, "You can't" quote; Luker, *Social Gospel in Black and White*, 296–298; Dixon, "Booker T. Washington and the Negro: Some Dangerous Aspects of the Work of Tuskegee," *Saturday Evening Post*, August 19, 1905; see Smith, *In His Image, But*, 275–276; Dixon, *The Failure of Protestantism in New York and Its Causes* (New York: Victor O. A. Strauss, 1896).

157. Booker T. Washington to Theodore Roosevelt, in *Booker T. Washington Papers* 6: 274; Norrell, *Up from History*, Vardaman quote, 256.

158. Du Bois, *Souls of Black Folk*, "The problem" quote, v, 9.

159. Ibid., 26.

160. Ibid., 26, 27.

161. Ibid., 30.

162. Ibid., 31.

163. Ibid., 31–32.

164. Ibid., 33, 35.

165. Ibid., quotes, 102–103; see C. Vann Woodward, *Origins of the New South, 1877–1913* (1951; repr., Baton Rouge: Louisiana State University Press, 1971); George M. Frederickson, "C. Vann Woodward and Southern History," in Frederickson, *The Arrogance of Race: Historical Perspectives on Slavery, Racism, and Social Inequality* (Hanover, NH: University Press of New England, 1988), 142–153; Lewis, *W. E. B. Du Bois: Biography of a Race*, 284–285.

166. Du Bois, *Souls of Black Folk*, quotes, 65, 50.

167. Ibid., "dollars," 50; W. E. B. Du Bois, "The Talented Tenth," in *The Negro Problem: A Series of Articles by Representative American Negroes of Today* (New York: James Pott, 1903), 33–75, repr. in W. E. B. Du Bois, *Writings by W. E. B. Du Bois in Non-Periodical Literature*, 17–29, quotes, 17, 20.

168. Du Bois, *Souls of Black Folk*, 67.

169. Reviews of *The Souls of Black Folk*, by W. E. B. Du Bois, Louisville *Courier-Journal*, June 13, 1903; *Nashville American*, September 26, 1903; *Christian Advocate*, July 16, 1903; *New York Times*, April 25, 1903; see citations in Herbert Aptheker, Introduction to Du Bois, *The Souls of Black Folk*, 1953 McClurg ed. (repr., Millwood, NY: Kraus-Thomson, 1973), 16–18.

170. Reviews of *The Souls of Black Folk*, by W. E. B. Du Bois, *Keystone*, July, 1903; *Houston Chronicle*, August 15, 1903; Aptheker, Introduction, 18.

171. Review of *The Souls of Black Folk*, by W. E. B. Du Bois, *Louisville Post*, May 2, 1903.

172. John Spencer Bassett, "Stirring Up the Fires of Race Antipathy," *South Atlantic Quarterly* 2 (October 1903): 297–305; Bassett, "Two Negro Leaders," *Southern Atlantic Quarterly* 2 (July 1903), repr. in W. E. B. Du Bois, *The Souls of Black Folk*, Norton Critical Edition, ed. Henry Louis Gates Jr. and Terri Hume Oliver (New York: W. W. Norton, 1999), 230–234, quotes, 234; see Williamson, *Crucible of Race*, 261–267.

173. Reviews of *The Souls of Black Folk*, by W. E. B. Du Bois, Wendell Phillips Dabney, in Ohio *Enterprise* (undated clipping in Du Bois papers, probably May 1903); in *Christian Recorder*, July 23, 1903; in Boston *Guardian* (n.d., 2003); in *Dallas Express* (undated clipping in Du Bois papers, 1903); citations in Aptheker, Introduction, 15–16.

174. Reviews of *The Souls of Black Folk*, by W. E. B. Du Bois, in *Detroit Informer* (n.d., 1903); in *Progressive American* (n.d., 1903, cited in McClurg brochure, 4th printing of *The Souls of Black Folk*); cited in Aptheker, Introduction, 16; John Daniels, *Alexander's Magazine* 1 (September 15, 1903): 10–11, repr. in Norton Critical Edition of *The Souls of Black Folk*, 234–235.

175. Review of *The Souls of Black Folk*, by W. E. B. Du Bois, *Literary Digest*, July 11, 1903; "The Black Man's Soul," *Collier's Weekly*, August 29, 1903, 6; review of *The Souls of Black Folk*, *Collier's Weekly*, September 19, 1903; cited in Aptheker, Introduction, 18, 23.

176. Review of *The Souls of Black Folk*, by W. E. B. Du Bois, Elia W. Peattie, *Chicago Tribune*, May 22, 1903.

177. Reviews of *The Souls of Black Folk*, in *New York Evening Post*, June 12, 1903, and in *Nation*, June 11, 1903, repr. in Norton Critical Edition, *Souls of Black Folk*, 227–230, quotes, 227, 228, 229.

178. "The Souls of Black Folk," *Independent* 55 (May 28, 1903): 1273–1274; review of *The Souls of Black Folk*, by W. E. B. Du Bois, *Congregationalist*, June 27, 1903; [Jenkin Lloyd Jones], "The Souls of Black Folk," *Unity* 51 (May 7, 1903): 148–149.

179. [Lyman Abbott], "Two Typical Leaders," *Outlook* 74 (May 23, 1903), quotes, 214–215; review of *The Souls of Black Folk*, by W. E. B. Du Bois, *Outlook* 74 (July 11, 1903).

180. Washington Gladden, "Some Impressions Gained during a Visit to the Southern United States," sermon, May 31, 1903, Washington Gladden Papers, Ohio Historical Society, Columbus, Ohio.

181. Ibid.

182. Washington Gladden, *The Negro's Southern Neighbors and His Northern Friends* (New York: Congregational Rooms, [1903]), "for no unnatural fusion" and "perfect equality"; Gladden, "Sociological Aspects of A.M.A. Work," *Congregationalist* 81 (October 29, 1896): 646–649; Gladden, "The Negro Crisis: Is the Separation of the Two Races to Become Necessary?" *American Magazine* 63 (January, 1907): 296–301; Gladden, *Recollections*, 366–376; Gladden, "The Anti-Papal Panic," *Harper's Weekly* 59 (July 18, 1914), "bitter and violent," 55; see Dorn, *Washington Gladden*, 293–302; Luker, *Social Gospel in Black and White*, 211–216.

183. William H. Ferris, *The African Abroad; or His Evolution in Western Civilization Tracing His Development Under Caucasian Milieu*, 2 vols. (New Haven, CT: Morehouse and Taylor, 1913), 1: 273, 276.

184. Washington Gladden, "Some Impressions Gained during a Visit to the Southern United States,"' "I fear"; Gladden, "Even These Least," sermon, January 9, 1916, Gladden Papers; Gladden, *Recollections*, "it is . . . moral universe," 375–376; see Luker *Social Gospel in Black and White*, 215–216.

185. Du Bois, *Dusk of Dawn*, "because," xxix; Du Bois, *Autobiography of W. E. B. Du Bois*, "Had it," 155.

CHAPTER 4. IN THE SPIRIT OF NIAGARA

1. W. E. B. Du Bois, *Darkwater: Voices from Within the Veil* (New York: Harcourt, Brace, 1920; repr., New York: Dover, 1999), quote, 12. Francis L. Broderick points to Du Bois's dead end but overlooks that Du Bois briefly alluded to it in acknowledging that "to the cold hard stare of the world" the Niagara Movement "seemed merely the envy of fools against a great man, Booker Washington" (*Darkwater*, 12). Broderick, *W. E. B. Du Bois: Negro Leader in a Time of Crisis* (Stanford, CA: Stanford University Press, 1959), 89.

2. *New York Times*, April 15, 1903, Robert J. Norrell, *Up from History: The Life of Booker T. Washington* (Cambridge, MA: Harvard University Press, 2009), Cleveland quotes, 274, and David Levering Lewis, *W. E. B. Du Bois: Biography of a Race, 1868–1919* (New York: Henry Holt, 1993), Murphy quote, 298.

3. Gordon Macdonald to editor of *Washington Post*, April 28, 1903, in *The Booker T. Washington Papers*, 14 vols., ed. Louis R. Harlan, Raymond W. Smock, and Geraldine McTighe (Urbana: University of Illinois Press, 1972–1989), 7: 132–135; [William Monroe Trotter], Editorial, *Boston Guardian*, April 25, 1903; Norrell, *Up from History*, 276.

4. See Bruce D. Dickson Jr., *Archibald Grimké: Portrait of a Black Independent* (Baton Rouge: Louisiana State University Press, 1993); Mark Perry, *Lift Up Thy Voice: The Grimké Family's Journey from Slaveholders to Civil Rights Leaders* (New York: Viking, 2001); Archibald H. Grimké, "Modern Industrialism and the Negroes of the United States," pamphlet (Washington, DC: American Negro Academy, 1908).

5. [William Monroe Trotter], "Why Be Silent?" *Boston Guardian*, December 20, 1902, "throw off"; [Trotter], "Some Real Tuskegee Gems," *Boston Guardian*, April 4, 1903, "claptrap"; [Trotter], Editorial, Boston *Guardian*, June 13, 1903, "Tuskegee."

6. Stephen R. Fox, *The Guardian of Boston: William Monroe Trotter* (New York: Atheneum, 1970), 32–42, 50–52, 95–100, "shot," 39; "An Account of the Boston Riot in the *Boston Globe*, July 31, 1903," in *Booker T. Washington Papers*, 7: 229–240; Louis R. Harlan, *Booker T. Washington: The Wizard of Tuskegee* (New York: Oxford University Press, 1983), 44–46; Norrell, *Up from History*, 282–283; Eliot Rudwick, "Race Leadership Struggle: Background of the Boston Riot of 1903," *Journal of Negro Education* 31 (1962): 16–24.

7. Fox, *Guardian of Boston*, quote, 38; Norrell, *Up from History*, 289–290; W. E. B. Du Bois, *Dusk of Dawn: An Essay Toward an Autobiography of a Race Concept* (New York: Harcourt, Brace & World, 1940; repr., New Brunswick, NJ: Transaction Publishers, 1984), 87; Du Bois, *The Autobiography of W. E. B. Du Bois* (New York: International Publishers, 1968), 248.

8. Kelly Miller, "Washington's Policy," *Boston Evening Transcript*, September 18–19, 1903, repr. in Hugh Hawkins, ed., *Booker T. Washington and His Critics* (Lexington, MA: D. C. Heath, 1974), 87–94, quotes, 89, 92.

9. Booker T. Washington to Robert C. Ogden, October 20, 1903, in *Booker T. Washington Papers*, 7: 298; Kelly Miller to Emmett Scott, September 24, 1903, ibid., 7: 292; Lewis, *W. E. B. Du Bois: Biography of a Race*, 302–303; Harlan, *Booker T. Washington: The Wizard of Tuskegee*, 50.

10. Harlan, *Booker T. Washington: The Wizard of Tuskegee*, "the weighty," 70; Booker T. Washington to W. E. B. Du Bois, November 8, 1903, in *Correspondence of W. E. B. Du Bois*, 3 vols., ed. Herbert Aptheker (Amherst: University of Massachusetts Press, 1973–1978), 1: 53–54; "An Extract from the Proceedings of the Washington Conference of the National Sociological Society, November 10, 1903," in *Booker T. Washington Papers*, 7: 325, 340–342, "We eat," 341; Booker T. Washington to William Henry Baldwin, October 26, 1903, ibid., 7: 339–340.

11. Booker T. Washington to William Henry Baldwin, January 22, 1904, in *Booker T. Washington Papers*, 7: 409–411, "either," 411; Booker T. Washington to Robert Russa Moton, January 22, 1904, ibid., 7: 407; Norrell, *Up from History*, 294–295; Lewis, *W. E. B. Du Bois: Biography of a Race*, 306–308.

12. Charles Anderson to Booker T. Washington, January 26, 1904, in *Booker T. Washington Papers*, quotes, 7: 413–414; Du Bois, *Dusk of Dawn*, 78–79; Du Bois, *Autobiography of W. E. B. Du Bois*, 243.

13. W. E. B. Du Bois, "The Parting of the Ways," *World Today* 6 (April 1904): 521–523, in Du Bois, *W. E. B. Du Bois: A Reader*, ed. David Levering Lewis (New York: Henry Holt, 1995), 529–532, quotes, 329.

14. Ibid.

15. Ibid., 330.

16. Ibid., 330–331, 332.

17. Kelly Miller to W. E. B. Du Bois, April 23, 1904, and W. E. B. Du Bois to Archibald Grimké and Kelly Miller, March 21, 1905, in Lewis, *W. E. B. Du Bois: Biography of a Race*, 311, and Harlan, *Booker T. Washington: The Wizard of Tuskegee*, 80.

18. W. E. B. Du Bois, "Credo," *Independent* 57 (October 6, 1904): 787; repr. in Du Bois, *Darkwater*, 1–2, and Du Bois, *W. E. B. Du Bois: A Reader*, 105–106.

19. Francis J. Grimké to W. E. B. Du Bois, January 7, 1905, in *Correspondence of W. E. B. Du Bois*, 1: 91; see Jonathan M. Hansen, *The Lost Promise of Patriotism: Debating American Identity, 1890–1920* (Chicago: University of Chicago Press, 2003), 104–105; Herbert Shapiro, *White Violence and Black Response: From Reconstruction to Montgomery* (Amherst: University of Massachusetts Press, 1988), 127–128.

20. "John Wesley Edward Bowen," *Dictionary of American Negro Biography*, ed. Rayford W. Logan and Michael R. Winston (New York: W. W. Norton, 1982); Rufus Burrow Jr., "The Personalism of John Wesley Edward Bowen," *Journal of Negro History* 82 (Spring 1997): 244–256.

21. Jesse Max Barber, "What Is a Good Negro?" *Voice of the Negro* 1 (December 1904): 618; Booker T. Washington to John Wesley Edward Bowen, December 27, 1904, in *Booker T. Washington Papers*, 8: 167–168; W. E. B. Du Bois, "Debit and Credit, The American Negro in the Year of Grace Nineteen Hundred and Four," *Voice of the Negro* 2 (January 1905): 677; August Meier, "Booker T. Washington and the Negro Press: With Special Reference to the *Colored American Magazine*," *Journal of Negro History* 28 (January 1953): 67–90; Norrell, *Up from History*, 316.

22. Meier, "Booker T. Washington and the Negro Press, 78–87; Louis R. Harlan, "Booker T. Washington and the *Voice of the Negro*, 1904–1907," *Journal of Southern History* 45 (February 1979): 45–62; Norrell, *Up from History*, 316–319.

23. William Hayes Ward to W. E. B. Du Bois, February 18, 1905, in *Correspondence of W. E. B. Du Bois*, 1: 96; Du Bois to Ward, March 10, 1905, ibid., "sold out," 96; Oswald Garrison Villard to W. E. B. Du Bois, February 7, 1905, ibid., "positive," 1: 97; W. E. B. Du Bois to William Monroe Trotter, March 15, 1905, ibid., "every," 1: 97–98; Trotter to Du Bois, March 18, 1905, ibid., 1: 98; Du Bois to Villard, March 24, 1905, ibid., 1: 98–102; Villard to Du Bois, April 18, 1905, ibid., "any essential," 1: 102–103; Du Bois to Villard, April 20, 1905, ibid., "general," 1: 103–104; Meier, "Booker T. Washington and the Negro Press," 78–87; Du Bois, *Autobiography of W. E. B. Du Bois*, "All this," 247.

24. Isaac Max Rubinow to W. E. B. Du Bois, November 10, 1904, in *Correspondence of W. E. B. Du Bois*, 1: 81–82; Du Bois to Rubinow, November 17, 1904, ibid., 82.

25. [S. Becker von Grabil], *Letters from Tuskegee, Being the Confessions of a Yankee* (Montgomery, AL: Roberts & Son, 1905); C. Vann Woodward, *Tom Watson: Agrarian Rebel* (New York: Macmillan, 1938), "What a blessed" and "What does," 380; Norrell, *Up from History*, 313–324.

26. Thomas E. Dixon Jr., *The Clansman: An Historical Romance of the Ku Klux Klan* (New York: Doubleday, Page, 1905); Dixon, "Booker T. Washington and the Negro: Some Dangerous Aspects of the Work of Tuskegee," *Saturday Evening Post*, August 19, 1905.

27. Norrell, *Up from History*, 325–327, quote, 326.

28. Editorial, "The Significance of the Niagara Movement," *Voice of the Negro* 2 (September 1905): 600; Angela Jones, *African American Civil Rights: Early Activism and the Niagara Movement* (Santa Barbara, CA: Praeger, 2011), 215–233; Lewis, *W. E. B. Du Bois: Biography of a Race*, 316–318; Harlan, *Booker T. Washington: The Wizard of Tuskegee*, 87; Du Bois, *Autobiography of W. E. B. Du Bois*, 248–249.

29. Niagara Movement, Declaration of Principles, 1905, www.yale.edu/glc/archive/1152.htm.

30. Ibid.

31. Ibid.

32. Harlan, "Booker T. Washington and the *Voice of the Negro*, 1904–1907," 47–52; Lewis, *W. E. B. Du Bois: Biography of a Race*, 316–318; Harlan, *Booker T. Washington: The Wizard of Tuskegee*, 87; Emma L. Thornbrough, "Booker T. Washington as Seen by His White Contemporaries," *Journal of Negro History* 53 (April 1968): 161–182.

33. Jesse Max Barber, "The Twenty-fifth Anniversary of Tuskegee Institute," *Voice of the Negro*, May 1906," in *Booker T. Washington Papers*, 9: 15–24; Lewis, *W. E. B. Du Bois: Biography of a Race*, 319; Harlan, *Booker T. Washington: The Wizard of Tuskegee*, 104–105; Norrell, *Up from History*, 337; August Meier, *Negro Thought in America, 1880–1915: Racial Ideologies in the Age of Booker T. Washington* (Ann Arbor: University of Michigan Press, 1963), 180–185.

34. W. E. B. Du Bois, *The Philadelphia Negro: A Social Study* (Philadelphia: University of Pennsylvania Press, 1899; repr., New York: Oxford University Press, 2007), 197–207; Du Bois, *The Souls of Black Folk* (Chicago: A. C. McClurg, 1903; repr., New York: Dover, 1994), quotes, 159.

35. W. E. B. Du Bois, "Address to the Country," 1906, repr. in Du Bois, *W. E. B. Du Bois: A Reader*, 367–369, quotes, 367.

36. Ibid., quotes, 368.

37. Ibid., quotes, 369.

38. John D. Weaver, *The Senator and the Sharecropper's Son: Exoneration of the Brownsville Soldiers* (College Station, TX: Texas A&M University Press, 1997), quote, 109; Weaver, *The Brownsville Raid* (New York: W. W. Norton, 1970); Harlan, *Booker T. Washington: The Wizard of Tuskegee*, 309; H. W. Brands, *TR: The Last Romantic* (New York: Basic Books, 1997), 587–588; Norrell, *Up from History*, 345–347; Edmund Morris, *Theodore Rex* (New York: Modern Library, 2001), 453–455.

39. Booker T. Washington to Theodore Roosevelt, November 2, 1906, in *Booker T. Washington Papers*, 9: 113; Booker T. Washington to Charles Anderson, November 7, 1906, ibid., 9: 118; Brands, *TR: The Last Romantic*, 588; Norrell, *Up from History*, 347; Morris, *Theodore Rex*, 465.

40. Emma Lou Thornbrough, *T. Thomas Fortune: Militant Journalist* (Chicago: University of Chicago Press, 1972), "carrying," 282; Norrell, *Up from History*, 347; Weaver, *Senator and the Sharecropper's Son*, "not a particle," 107; Louis N. Wynne, "Brownsville: The Reaction of the Negro Press," *Phylon*, Spring 1972, 154–155; W. E. B. Du Bois, "Brownsville," *Horizon* 1 (June 1907), *Christian Register* citation, 7; Morris, *Theodore Rex*, 588; James A. Tinsley, "Roosevelt, Foraker, and the Brownsville Affray," *Journal of Negro History* 41 (1956): 43–46.

41. Theodore Roosevelt to S. McBee, November 27, 1906, "I have been," in Brands, *TR: The Last Romantic*, 588; Theodore Roosevelt to Ray Stannard Baker, March 39, 1907, "the colored people," in Norrell, *Up from History*, 355; Roosevelt to Baker, March 30, 1907, "I had never," in Brands, *TR: The Last Romantic*, 589; Theodore Roosevelt, Address to Congress, *New York Times*, December 5, 1906, "the negro." In the 1970s the federal government changed the dishonorable discharges against the soldiers to honorable. John Weaver's book *The Brownsville Raid* played a decisive role in the decision. By then only one of the soldiers involved was still alive.

42. Booker T. Washington to Charles William Anderson, November 7, 1906, in *Booker T. Washington Papers*, 9: 118–119; Thomas T. Fortune to Booker T. Washington, December 8, 1906, ibid., 9: 156–158; W. E. B. Du Bois, "Hearken, Theodore Roosevelt," *The Horizon: A Journal of the Color Line* 1 (March 1907): 3–10.

43. W. E. B. Du Bois, "A Litany of Atlanta," *Independent* 61 (October 11, 1906): 856–868, in Du Bois, *W. E. B. Du Bois: A Reader*, 441–444, quote, 442, 443; see David Fort Godshalk, *Veiled Visions: The 1906 Atlanta Race Riot and the Reshaping of American Race Relations* (Chapel Hill: University of North Carolina Press, 2005), 8–25; Harlan, *Booker T. Washington: The Wizard of Tuskegee*, 309; Ray Stannard Baker, *Following the Color Line: American Negro Citizenship in the Progressive Era* (New York: Harper Torchbooks, 1964), 9–25; Charles Crowe, "Racial Massacre in Atlanta, September 22, 1906," *Journal of Negro History* 54 (April 1969): 150–175.

44. Fortune to Washington, December 8, 1906, in *Booker T. Washington Papers*, 9: 156–158; Harlan, *Booker T. Washington: The Wizard of Tuskegee*, 320–321; *New York Times*, December 16, 1906, "The awful," in Norrell, *Up from History*, 350; *Booker T. Washington Papers* 9: "enshrined," 333.

45. Alexander Walters, "Address Before the Afro-American Council, October 11, 1906," in *Booker T. Washington Papers* 9: 94–96; Booker T. Washington to Charles W. Anderson, November 7, 1906, ibid., 9: 119.

46. W. E. B. Du Bois, "The Lash," *Horizon* 1 (May 1907): 3–10, "Arch-Temptor," 4.

47. W. E. B. Du Bois, "Subscription," *Horizon* 1 (January 1907), "the bravest" and "militant," 2–3; Du Bois, "Books," *Horizon* 1 (April 1907): 3–9; Du Bois, "Books and Papers," *Horizon* 3 (January 1908): 1–5, "digester," "Encourager," "hodge-podge," and "wobbly," 2; Du Bois, "Roosevelt," *Horizon* 1 (January 1907): 2–10, "most," 8.

48. W. E. B. Du Bois, "Socialist of the Path," *Horizon* 1 (February 1907), "a socialist" and "can and ought," 3–4; Du Bois, "Negro and Socialism," *Horizon* 1 (February 1907), "the one great," 4; see Du Bois, *Selections from the Horizon*, ed. Herbert Aptheker (White Plains, NY: Kraus-Thomson, 1985), 5–7; Du Bois, "The President and the Soldiers," *Voice of the Negro* 3 (December 1906): 552–553; Du Bois, "Hearken, Theodore Roosevelt," *Horizon* 1 (March 1907): 3–4; Mary White Ovington to Du Bois, June 10, 1904, in *Correspondence of W. E. B. Du Bois*, 1: 76–77; Ovington, *Half a Man: The Status of the Negro in New York* (New York: Longmans, Green, 1911); Ovington, *The Walls Came Tumbling Down* (New York: Harcourt, Brace, 1947), 13–54; Ray Stannard Baker, *Following the Color Line: An Account of Negro Citizenship in the American Democracy* (New York: Doubleday, Page, 1908).

49. W. E. B. Du Bois, "To Black Voters," *Horizon* 3 (February 1908): 17–20, " 'tis," 17; Du Bois, "Bryan," *Horizon* 3 (March 1908), 7–8; "Taft," *Horizon* 3 (April 1908), "we are sentenced," 7; Du Bois, "The Negro Vote," *Horizon* 4 (September 1908): 1–9.

50. W. E. B. Du Bois, "Union," *Horizon* 3 (June 1908): 2–5; Du Bois, *John Brown* (1909; repr., New York: International Publishers, 1962); Frederick L. McGhee, Charles E. Bentley, Gertrude W. Morgan, William Henderson, and W. E. B. Du Bois, "Niagara Movement," *Horizon* 4 (September 1908): 1–2; Jones, *African American Civil Rights*, 21–29.

51. William H. Ferris to *New York Age*, November 14, 1907; Fox, *Guardian of Boston*, 108–114, 139–141, quote, 140; Meier, *Negro Thought in America*, 180–185; see Ferris, *The African Abroad: Or, His Evolution in Western Civilization*, 2 vols. (New Haven, CT: Tuttle, Morehouse & Taylor, 1913).

52. W. E. B. Du Bois, "Well-Wisher," *Horizon* 3 (May 1908): 1–3.

53. Albert Bushnell Hart to W. E. B. Du Bois, April 24, 1905, and Du Bois to Hart, October 9, 1905, in *Correspondence of W. E. B. Du Bois*, 1: 110–111.

54. W. E. B. Du Bois, "Reconstruction and Its Benefits," *American Historical Review* 15 (July 1910): 781–799; Du Bois, *Black Reconstruction in America, 1860–1880* (1935; repr., New York: Free Press, 1998); see David Levering Lewis, Introduction to *Black Reconstruction in America*, vii–xvii; William Archibald Dunning, *Reconstruction, Political and Economic, 1865–1877* (New York: Harper & Brothers, 1907); Walter L. Fleming, *Civil War and Reconstruction in Alabama* (New York: Columbia University Press, 1905); Claude Bowers, *The Tragic Era: The Revolution after Lincoln* (Cambridge, MA: Houghton Mifflin, 1929); Howard K. Beale, "On Rewriting Reconstruction," *American Historical Review* 45 (July 1940): 802–827; Eric Foner, "Reconstruction Revisited," *Reviews in American History* 10 (December 1982): 82–100.

55. W. E. B. Du Bois to J. Franklin Jameson, June 2, 1910, *in Correspondence of W. E. B. Du Bois*, 1: 171.

56. J. Franklin Jameson to W. E. B. Du Bois, June 10, 1910, in *Correspondence of W. E. B. Du Bois*, 1: 171–172; Du Bois to Jameson, June 13, 1910, ibid., 172; Jameson to Du Bois, June 22, 1910, Du Bois Papers, quotes in Lewis, *W. E. B. Du Bois: Biography of a Race*, 385.

57. W. E. B. Du Bois to J. Franklin Jameson, July 5, 1910, in *Correspondence of W. E. B. Du Bois*, 1: 172.

58. Graham Taylor, "The Race Riot in Lincoln's City," *Charities and the Commons* 20 (August 29, 1908): 627–628; see Gary Dorrien, *Social Ethics in the Making: Interpreting an American Tradition* (Oxford: Wiley-Blackwell, 2009), 49.

59. William English Walling, "The Race War in the North," *Independent* 63 (September 3, 1908): 529–534, quotes, 531, 534; see Walling, *Socialism As It Is: A Survey of the World-wide Revolutionary Movement* (New York: Macmillan, 1912); Walling, *The Larger Aspects of Socialism* (New York: Macmillan, 1913).

60. Oswald Garrison Villard to Hugh Gordon, September 19, 1906, Oswald Garrison Villard Papers, Houghton Library, Harvard University, Box 1460; Mary White Ovington, "Reminiscences," *Baltimore Afro-American*, November 26, 1932, 24–26, repr. as "The NAACP Begins," in Ovington, *Black and White Sit Down Together: The Reminiscences of an NAACP Founder* (New York: Feminist Press, 1995), 56–60; Ovington, *Walls Came Tumbling Down*, 103–104; James M. McPherson, *The Abolitionist Legacy: From Reconstruction to the NAACP* (Princeton, NJ: Princeton University Press, 1975), 372–376; Patricia Sullivan, *Lift Every Voice: The NAACP and the Making of the Civil Rights Movement* (New York: New Press 2009), 4–5.

61. Oswald Garrison Villard, *Fighting Years: Memoirs of a Liberal Editor* (New York: Harcourt, Brace, 1939), "no greater" 92, "an unselfishness"; Mary White Ovington, *How the National Association for the Advancement of Colored People Began*, pamphlet (New York: NAACP, 1914), "This government," 1; Charles Flint Kellogg, *NAACP: A History of the National Association for the Advancement of Colored People* (Baltimore. Johns Hopkins University Press, 1967), 11–13; Villard, "The Call," Appendix A in Kellogg, *NAACP*, 298; Ovington, *Walls Came Tumbling Down*, 100–107; Carolyn Wedin, *Inheritors of the Spirit: Mary White Ovington and the Founding of the NAACP* (New York: Wiley, 1998), 106–107; August Meier and John H. Bracey Jr., "The NAACP as a Reform Movement, 1900–1965: 'To Reach the Conscience of America,'" *Journal of Southern History* 49 (February 1993): 3–30; see Langston Hughes, *Fight for Freedom: The Story of the NAACP* (New York: Norton, 1962).

62. W. E. B. Du Bois, "National Committee on the Negro," in Du Bois, *Writings by W. E. B. Du Bois in Periodicals Edited by Others*, ed. Herbert Aptheker (Millwood, NY: Kraus-Thomson, 1982), "darker," 399; Du Bois, "National Negro Conference," *Survey*, June 12, 1909, in *Documentary History of the Negro People in the United States*, 2 vols., ed. Herbert Aptheker (New York: Citadel Press, 1969), 2: 924; Du Bois, *Autobiography of W. E. B. Du Bois*, "Scientists," 254; *New York Times*, June 2, 1909, 9; Kellogg, *NAACP*, 12–13; Fox, *Guardian of Boston*, 122–123; Ovington, *How the National*

Association for the Advancement of Colored People Began, 1–3; Ovington, *Walls Came Tumbling Down*, 104–106.

63. William H. Ward, "Address of William Hayes Ward," in *Proceedings of the National Negro Conference, 1909* (1909; repr., New York: Arno, 1969), 9–13; Livingston Farrand, "Race Differentiation—Race Characteristics," ibid., 14–21; Burt G. Wilder, "The Brain of the American Negro," ibid., 22–66; Edwin R. A. Seligman, "Address of Edwin R. A. Seligman," ibid., 67–70; see Frederick L. Hoffmann, *Race Traits and Tendencies of the American Negro* (New York: American Economic Association, 1896).

64. Celia Parker Woolley, "Race Reconciliation," in *Proceedings of the National Negro Conference, 1909*, 74–78; W. E. B. Du Bois, "Politics and Industry," ibid., 79–88; William L. Bulkley, "Race Prejudice as Viewed from an Economic Standpoint," ibid., 89–97; William English Walling, "The Negro and the South," ibid., 98–109; Ovington, *Walls Came Tumbling Down*, "unspeakable," 46.

65. Charles W. Anderson to Booker T. Washington, May 31, 1909, in *Booker T. Washington Papers*, 10: 127; "Discussion," in *Proceedings of the National Negro Conference, 1909*, 110–120, "launched," 119; Elliott M. Rudwick, "The National Negro Committee Conference of 1909," *Phylon Quarterly* 18 (4th qtr., 1957): 413–419; Ida B. Wells, *Crusade for Justice: The Autobiography of Ida B. Wells*, ed. Alfreda M. Duster (Chicago: University of Chicago Press, 1970), 323; Wedin, *Inheritors of the Spirit*, 109; Lewis, *W. E. B. Du Bois: Biography of a Race*, 392–393; Paula J. Giddings, *Ida: A Sword Among Lions* (New York: HarperCollins, 2008), 474.

66. Ida B. Wells-Barnett, "Lynching Our National Crime," in *Proceedings of the National Negro Conference, 1909*, 174–179; Mary White Ovington, "The Beginnings of the NAACP," *Crisis* 32 (June 1926), quotes, 77; W. E. B. Du Bois, "National Committee on the Negro," *Survey* 22 (June 12, 1909): 401–407, Du Bois quote, 402, in *A Documentary History of the Negro People in the United States*, 926–930; Rudwick, "The National Negro Committee Conference of 1909," 415–416.

67. Oswald Garrison Villard to Francis Garrison, June 4, 1909, Villard Papers, Box 1460. See Kellogg, *NAACP*, 22; Giddings, *Ida*, 476; and Lewis, *W. E. B. Du Bois: Biography of a Race*, 395.

68. "Resolutions," in *Proceedings of the National Negro Conference, 1909*, 223–224; Du Bois, "National Committee on the Negro," quote, 402; Ovington, "The NAACP Begins," "namby" and "cranks," 59; Ovington, *Walls Came Tumbling Down*, 106; Ovington, "The Beginnings of the NAACP," 77; Mary White Ovington to Oswald Garrison Villard, June 2, 1909, Villard Papers, Box 1460.

69. Du Bois, "National Committee on the Negro," 402.

70. Wells, *Crusade for Justice*, quotes, 324–325; Ovington, *Walls Came Tumbling Down*, 106.

71. Wells, *Crusade for Justice*, 325; Ovington, "The NAACP Begins," quotes, 60.

72. Wells, *Crusade for Justice*, 325–326.

73. Ovington, *Walls Came Tumbling Down*, "fitted," 60; Ovington, "The NAACP Begins," "a great," 60; W. E. B. Du Bois, "National Negro Conference," *Horizon* 5 (November 1909): 2–3.

74. "The Committee of Forty," Appendix B, Kellogg, *NAACP*, 300–301; Lewis, *W. E. B. Du Bois: Biography of a Race*, 399; William English Walling to W. E. B. Du Bois, June 8, 1909, in *Correspondence of W. E. B. Du Bois*, 1: 147–150.

75. Ellis Paxson Oberholtzer to W. E. B. Du Bois, November 11, 1903, in *Correspondence of W. E. B. Du Bois*, 1: 61–62; Du Bois to Oberholtzer, November 18, 1903, ibid., 62; Oberholtzer to Du Bois, January 25, 1904, ibid., 63–64; Du Bois to Oberholtzer, January 30, 1904, ibid., 64; Oberholtzer to Du Bois, February 3, 1904, ibid., 64; Du Bois to Oberholtzer, undated, ibid., 64–65; Oberholtzer to Du Bois, February 16, 1904, ibid., 65.

76. W. E. B. Du Bois, *John Brown* (1st ed., 1909; repr., Armonk, NY: M. E. Sharpe, 1997), quote, 201; see Keith E. Byerman, *Seizing the Word: History, Art, and Self in the Work of W. E. B. Du Bois* (Athens: University of Georgia Press, 1994), 162–178; Lawrie Balfour, *Democracy's Reconstruction: Thinking Politically with W. E. B. Du Bois* (New York: Oxford University Press, 2011), 47–70; Arnold Rampersad, *The Art and Imagination of W. E. B. Du Bois* (1st ed., 1976; repr., New York: Schocken Books, 1990), 112–113; Richard O. Boyer, *The Legend of John Brown: A Biography and History* (New York: Knopf, 1973); David S. Reynolds, *John Brown, Abolitionist: The Man Who Killed Slavery, Sparked the Civil War, and Seeded Civil Rights* (New York: Knopf, 2005).

77. W. E. B. Du Bois to the Editor of *Nation*, November 6, 1909, in *Correspondence of W. E. B. Du Bois*, 1: 154–155; P. E. Moore to W. E. B. Du Bois, November 12, 1909, ibid., 1: 155–157; Du Bois to Moore, November 15, 1909, ibid., "but savagely," 1: 157.

78. Oswald Garrison Villard to W. E. B. Du Bois, November 26, 1909, in *Correspondence of W. E. B. Du Bois*, 1: 158–159; Du Bois to Villard, December 1, 1909, ibid., "I complain," 1: 164.

79. John Hope to W. E. B. Du Bois, January 17, 1910, in *Correspondence of W. E. B. Du Bois*, 1: 164–167, quotes, 165, 166.

80. Ibid., 166–167.

81. W. E. B. Du Bois to John Hope, January 22, 1910, in *Correspondence of W. E. B. Du Bois*, 1: 167.

82. William English Walling, "The Founding of the NAACP," *Crisis* 36 (July 1919): 226; Francis Garrison to Oswald Garrison Villard, November 23, 1909, and Villard to Garrison, December 7, 1909, Villard Papers, Box 1460; Mary White Ovington, "Beginnings of the NAACP," *Crisis*, June 1926, quotes, 77; Wedin, *Inheritors of the Spirit*, 112; Lewis, *W. E. B. Du Bois: Biography of a Race*, 405; Kellogg, *NAACP*, 37–42.

83. Kellogg, *NAACP*, 38–45, 90; Ovington, *Black and White*, 67; William B. Hixson Jr., *Moorfield Storey and the Abolitionist Tradition* (New York: Oxford University Press, 1972).

84. William English Walling to W. E. B. Du Bois, June 8, 1910, in *Correspondence of W. E. B. Du Bois*, 1: 169–170; Du Bois to Walling, June 13, 1910, ibid., 170.

85. Du Bois, *Dusk of Dawn*, "I don't," 225; Kellogg, *NAACP*, 52–54; Ovington, *Black and White*, 66–67; Lewis, *W. E. B. Du Bois: Biography of a Race*, 409.

86. *Crisis: A Record of the Darker Races* 1 (November 1910); Mary Dunlop Maclean, "African Civilization," *Crisis* 1 (March 1911): 23–25; Kellogg, *NAACP*, 52–54; Ovington,

Black and White, 66–67; Lewis, *W. E. B. Du Bois: Biography of a Race*, 411; Mary White Ovington, "Mary Dunlop Maclean," *Crisis* 4 (August 1912): 184–185.

87. W. E. B. Du Bois, "Segregation," *Crisis* 1 (November 1910), "Separate," 10.

88. W. E. B. Du Bois, "A Winter Pilgrimage," *Crisis* 2 (January 1911), "the race," "half forgotten," and "on sacred," 15; Du Bois, "Violations of Property Rights," *Crisis* 2 (May 1911): 28–32, "simply," 30; see Du Bois, "I Go A-Talking," *Crisis* 6 (July 1913): 130–132.

89. Du Bois, "Violations of Property Rights," quotes, 32; W. E. B. Du Bois, "Starvation and Prejudice," *Crisis* 2 (June 1911): 62–64; Du Bois, "Triumph," *Crisis* 2 (September 1911): 195.

90. W. E. B. Du Bois, "The Second Birthday," *Crisis* 5 (November 1912), "fit," 27; Jesse Max Barber to Du Bois, March 2, 1912, in *Correspondence of W. E. B. Du Bois*, 1: 176–177; Du Bois, *Dusk of Dawn*, "The Crisis came," 226; Du Bois, "Editing *The Crisis*," March 1951, in *The Crisis Reader: Stories, Poetry, and Essays from the NAACP's Crisis Magazine* (New York: Modern Library, 1999), "blazing," xxviii; Sullivan, *Lift Every Voice*, 23.

91. Kellogg, *NAACP*, 98; Elliott M. Rudwick, *W. E. B. Du Bois: Propagandist of the Negro Protest* (New York: Atheneum, 1968), 168–171; Lewis, *W. E. B. Du Bois: Biography of a Race*, "Harvardized," 416; W. E. B. Du Bois, "Lynching," *Crisis* 7 (March 1914): 239.

92. W. E. B. Du Bois, "The Negro Church," *Crisis* 4 (May 1912): 24–25, 28–33, "instilled," 24; Du Bois, "Editing *The Crisis*," "talked turkey," xxviii.

93. Du Bois, "The Negro Church," 24–25.

94. W. E. B. Du Bois, "The New Wilberforce," *Crisis* 8 (August 1914): 191–194; W. S. Scarborough to Oswald Garrison Villard, September 8, 1914, and Villard to Scarborough, September 10, 1914, Villard Papers, Box 1463; Kellogg, *NAACP*, 99–100.

95. W. E. B. Du Bois, *The Quest of the Silver Fleece: A Novel* (1911; repr., New York: Harlem Moon, 2004); Lewis, *W. E. B. Du Bois: Biography of a Race*, 449; Irene Diggs, "Du Bois and Women: A Short History of Black Women, 1910–1934," *Current Bibliography on African Affairs* 7 (Summer 1974): 260–279.

96. W. E. B. Du Bois, "The Black Mother," *Crisis* 5 (December 1912), 21. The Mammy statue movement was widely noted in the black press, notably the Nashville *National Baptist Union-Review*, May 4, 1923; the Jackson, Tennessee, *Christian Index*, February 22, 1923; and the *New York Age*, January 6, 1923; see Marilyn Kern-Foxworth, *Aunt Jemima, Uncle Ben, and Rastus: Blacks in Advertising Yesterday, Today, and Tomorrow* (Westport, CT: Praeger, 1994), 88, and Emilie M. Townes, *Womanist Ethics and the Cultural Production of Evil* (New York: Palgrave Macmillan, 2006), 36.

97. W. E. B. Du Bois, "Hail Columbia!" *Crisis* 5 (April 1913): 289–290; see Du Bois, "Forward Backward," *Crisis* 2 (October 1911): 243–244; Du Bois, "Votes for Women," *Crisis* 4 (September 1912): 234.

98. W. E. B. Du Bois, "Woman Suffrage," *Crisis* 9 (April 1915): 284–285; see Du Bois, "Woman Suffrage," *Crisis* 11 (November 1915): 29–30; Kelly Miller, "The Risk of Woman Suffrage," *Crisis* 11 (November 1915): 37–38.

99. See Lewis, *W. E. B. Du Bois: Biography of a Race*, 463–465.

100. Du Bois, *Darkwater,* 100.

101. See Eugene Debs, "The Negro in the Class Struggle," *International Socialist Review,* November 1903, and Debs, "The Negro and His Nemesis," *International Socialist Review,* January 1904, in Debs, *Writings and Speeches of Eugene V. Debs,* ed. Joseph M. Bernstein (New York: Hermitage Press, 1948), 63–66, 66–73; Nick Salvatore, *Eugene V. Debs: Citizen and Socialist* (Urbana: University of Illinois Press, 1982), 225–230.

102. W. E. B. Du Bois, "The Last Word in Politics," *Crisis* 5 (November 1912), "manly" and "The Negro," 29; Du Bois, "Socialism and the Negro Problem," *New Review* 1 (February 1, 1913): 138–141, remaining quotes, 139; W. E. B. Du Bois to Carolina M. Dexter, November 6, 1812, in *Correspondence of W. E. B. Du Bois,* 1: 180.

103. Du Bois, "The Last Word in Politics," quote, 29; Du Bois, *Dusk of Dawn,* 233–234; Lewis, *W. E. B. Du Bois: Biography of a Race,* 422; Kellogg, *NAACP,* 155.

104. W. E. B. Du Bois, "Politics," *Crisis* 4 (August 1912): 180–181, quote, 181; see Du Bois, "The Election," *Crisis* 5 (December 1912): 75; Du Bois, *Dusk of Dawn,* 234–235.

105. W. E. B. Du Bois, "Another Open Letter to Woodrow Wilson," *Crisis* 6 (September 1913): 232–236; see Du Bois, "An Open Letter to Woodrow Wilson," *Crisis* 5 (March 1913): 236–237.

106. Du Bois, "Another Open Letter to Woodrow Wilson," quotes, 235–236; Oswald Garrison Villard to Woodrow Wilson, September 18, 1913, and Wilson to Villard, September 22, 1913, Villard Papers, Box 1463.

107. Du Bois, "Editing *The Crisis,*" quote, xxix.

108. W. E. B. Du Bois to Oswald Garrison Villard, March 18, 1913, in *Correspondence of W. E. B. Du Bois,* 1: 181; Du Bois, *Dusk of Dawn,* 240–241; Kellogg, *NAACP,* 93–95; Sullivan, *Lift Every Voice,* 35–48.

109. W. E. B. Du Bois, "Intermarriage," *Crisis* 5 (February 1913): 180–181; Kellogg, *NAACP,* 93–110; Lewis, *W. E. B. Du Bois: Biography of a Race,* 474–477; Ovington, *Black and White,* 67; Thomas Lee Philpott, *The Slum and the Ghetto: Neighborhood Deterioration and Middle-Class Reform, Chicago, 1880–1930* (New York: Oxford University Press, 1978), 299–300.

110. W. E. B. Du Bois to Mary White Ovington, April 9, 1914, in *Correspondence of W. E. B. Du Bois,* 1: 188–191.

111. Joel E. Spingarn to Mary White Ovington, November 5, 1914, and Ovington to Spingarn, November 8, 1914, in Lewis, *W. E. B. Du Bois: Biography of a Race,* 495–496.

112. Mary White Ovington to W. E. B. Du Bois, April 11, 1914, *in Correspondence of W. E. B. Du Bois,* 1: 191–193, quote, 192.

113. Ibid., 192–193. The hog reference echoed Du Bois's statement in *Crisis* in September 1913: "It takes extraordinary training, gift, and opportunity to make the average white man anything but an overbearing hog."

114. Joel Williamson, *The Crucible of Race: Black-White Relations in the American South Since Emancipation* (New York: Oxford University Press, 1984), Wilson quote, 176; Everett Carter, "Cultural History Written with Lightning: The Significance of the *Birth of a Nation,*" *American Quarterly* 12 (1960), Dixon quote, 347; Kellogg, *NAACP,* 165–187; W. E. B. Du Bois, "The Clansman," *Crisis* 10 (May 1915): 33; Du

Bois, "The Lynching Industry," *Crisis* 9 (February 1915): 198; Du Bois, "The Waco Horror," *Crisis* 12 (June 1916); Du Bois, "William Monroe Trotter," *Crisis* 9 (December 1914):, 82; Du Bois, "Mr. Trotter and Mr. Wilson," *Crisis* 9 (January 1915): 119–127; see Lewis, *W. E. B. Du Bois: Biography of a Race*, 506, 514; Thomas Cripps, *Slow Fade to Black: The Negro in American Film* (New York: Oxford University Press, 1977), 45–52; Villard, *Fighting Years: Memoirs of a Liberal Editor*, 239–240; Fox, *Guardian of Boston*, 170–175.

115. W. E. B. Du Bois, "We Come of Age," *Crisis* 11 (December 1915): 25–28; Du Bois, "The Drama Among Black Folk," *Crisis* 12 (August 1916): 169–173; Kellogg, *NAACP*, 117–137, 165–187.

116. Joel E. Spingarn to W. E. B. Du Bois, October 24, 1914, in *Correspondence of W. E. B. Du Bois*, 1: 200–202, quotes, 201, 202.

117. Ibid., 202.

118. W. E. B. Du Bois to Joel E. Spingarn, October 28, 1914, *in Correspondence of W. E. B. Du Bois*, 1: 203–207, quotes, 203, 204.

119. Ibid., 204, 206.

120. Ibid., 207.

121. Du Bois, *Dusk of Dawn*, quote, 241; Norrell, *Up from History*, 394; Harlan, *Booker T. Washington: Wizard of Tuskegee*, 369–378.

122. Harlan, *Booker T. Washington: Wizard of Tuskegee*, 382–401; Norrell, *Up from History*, 395–397, quote, 395.

123. Harlan, *Booker T. Washington: Wizard of Tuskegee*, 379–382; Norrell, *Up from History*, 393–395; Lewis, *W. E. B. Du Bois: Biography of a Race*, 433–434; Kellogg, *NAACP*, 80–83.

124. Oswald Garrison Villard to Robert Russa Moton, April 5, 1911, in *Booker T. Washington Papers*, 11: 83; W. E. B. Du Bois, "Starvation and Prejudice," *Crisis* 2 (June 1911): 62–64, quote, 64.

125. Fox, *Guardian of Boston*, 134.

126. Booker T. Washington to Francis J. Grimké and Archibald H. Grimké, April 6, 1911, in Norrell, *Up from History*, 399; Harlan, *Booker T. Washington: Wizard of Tuskegee*, 400–404.

127. W. E. B. Du Bois, "Booker T. Washington," *Crisis* 11 (December 1915): 82.

128. Ibid., 243–245, quote, 244; W. E. B. Du Bois, *The Amenia Conference, An Historic Gathering*, pamphlet repr. in Du Bois, *Pamphlets and Leaflets by W. E. B. Du Bois*, 210–216; Du Bois, "An Open Letter to Robert Russa Moton," *Crisis* 12 (July 1916): 136–137; Lewis, *W. E. B. Du Bois: Biography of a Race*, 518–519.

129. James Weldon Johnson, *Along This Way: The Autobiography of James Weldon Johnson* (New York: Viking, 1933), 204–208; Johnson, *The Autobiography of an Ex-Coloured Man* (1st ed., 1912; repr., New York: Hill and Wang, 1960); Rudolph P. Byrd, ed., *The Essential Writings of James Weldon Johnson* (New York: Modern Library, 2008); Sullivan, *Lift Every Voice*, 58–77; Ovington, *Walls Came Tumbling Down*, quote, 167.

130. W. E. B. Du Bois, "The Negro Party," *Crisis* 12 (October 1916): 268–269; Du Bois to Woodrow Wilson, October 10, 1916, in *Correspondence of W. E. B. Du Bois*, 1: 217–218;

J. Tumulty to Du Bois, October 17, 1916, ibid., 218–219; Du Bois, "Mexico," *Crisis* 8 (June 1914): 79; Du Bois, "Hayti," *Crisis* 10 (October 1915), "SHAME," 291.

131. W. E. B. Du Bois, "The African Roots of the War," *Atlantic Monthly* 115 (May 1915): 707–714, quotes, 708; see Adam Hochschild, *King Leopold's Ghost: A Story of Greed, Terror, and Heroism in Colonial Africa* (Boston: Houghton Mifflin, 1998); Robert T. Edgerton, *The Troubled Heart of Africa* (New York: St. Martin's, 2002).

132. Du Bois, "The African Roots of the War," 708–709.

133. John A. Hobson, *Imperialism* (1902; repr., London: Allen and Unwin, 1948), quotes, 35, 72.

134. Du Bois, "The African Roots of the War," 709–710.

135. Ibid.

136. Ibid., 710–711.

137. Ibid., 711–712.

138. Ibid., 712–713.

139. W. E. B. Du Bois, "Ireland," *Crisis* 12 (August 1916), "no human" and "foolishness," 166–167; Du Bois, "The Battle of Europe," *Crisis* 12 (September 1916), "brown," 216–217; Du Bois, "The World Last Month," *Crisis* 13 (January 1917), "a chance," 111.

140. B. Joyce Ross, *J. E. Spingarn and the Rise of the NAACP, 1911–1939* (New York: Atheneum, 1972), 90–93; Du Bois, *Dusk of Dawn*, 255.

141. W. E. B. Du Bois, "The Perpetual Dilemma," *Crisis* 13 (April 1917), "because," "damnable," and "We must," 270–271; Fox, *Guardian of Boston*, "a rank" and "betrayed," 219; Du Bois, "Officers," *Crisis* 14 (June 1917), "We have," 60; Du Bois, *Dusk of Dawn*, "The war," 250.

142. Du Bois, *Dusk of Dawn*, 250–252; W. E. B. Du Bois to NAACP Board of Directors, July 2, 1918, in *Correspondence of W. E. B. Du Bois*, 1: 227–228.

143. Du Bois, *Dusk of Dawn*, 252–253.

144. W. E. B. Du Bois, "Close Ranks," *Crisis* 16 (July 1918), quotes, 111; Du Bois, *Dusk of Dawn*, 253–254; Lewis, *W. E. B. Du Bois: Biography of a Race*, 555–556.

145. Du Bois, *Dusk of Dawn*, 254; Lewis, *W. E. B. Du Bois: Biography of a Race*, 556–557; "Dr. Du Bois Draws Fire," *Pittsburgh Courier*, July 20, 1918; Byron Gunner to W. E. B. Du Bois, July 25, 1918, in *Correspondence of W. E. B. Du Bois*, 1: 228; Du Bois to Gunner, August 10, 1918, ibid., 228.

146. W. E. B. Du Bois, "A Philosophy in Time of War," *Crisis* 16 (August 1918), "Our country" and "The war," 164–165; Du Bois, "Our Special Grievances," *Crisis* 16 (September 1918): 216–217; Du Bois to L. M. Hershaw, August 5, 1918, in *Correspondence of W. E. B. Du Bois*, 1: 229; Du Bois, *Dusk of Dawn*, "Fortunately," 257; "Perhaps," 255.

147. J. P. Tumulty to W. E. B. Du Bois, November 29, 1918, in *Correspondence of W. E. B. Du Bois*, 1: 232; W. E. B. Du Bois, "My Mission," *Crisis* 18 (May 1919), 7–9.

148. W. E. B. Du Bois, "Letters from Dr. Du Bois," *Crisis* 17 (February 1919), quotes, 168–169; Lewis, *W. E. B. Du Bois: Biography of a Race*, 565.

149. F. P. Schoonmaker to Intelligence Officers, January 1, 1919, in *Correspondence of W. E. B. Du Bois*, 1: 232; W. E. B. Du Bois, "For What?" *Crisis* 17 (April 1919), "the Thing," 268; Du Bois, "Vive la France!" *Crisis* 17 (March 1919): 215–216.

150. W. E. B. Du Bois, *The World and Africa: An Inquiry into the Part Which Africa Has Played in World History* (New York: International Publishers, 1965), "Don't," 10; Janet G. Vaillant, *Black, French, and African: A Life of Leopold Sedar Senghor* (Cambridge, MA: Harvard University Press, 1990), 46–47; Michael Crowder, *West Africa Under Colonial Rule* (Evanston, IL: Northwestern University Press, 1968), 264–265; Manning Marable, *W. E. B. Du Bois: Black Radical Democrat* (1986; rev. ed., Boulder, CO: Paradigm, 2005), 101; C. L. R. James, *The Future in the Present: Selected Writings* (Westport, CT: Lawrence Hill, 1980), 207; Lewis, *W. E. B. Du Bois: Biography of a Race,* 567; George Padmore, *Pan-Africanism or Communism* (Garden City, NY: Anchor Books, 1972), 98.

151. Walter Lippmann to W. E. B. Du Bois, February 20, 1919, in *Correspondence of W. E. B. Du Bois,* 1: 233; Du Bois, *World and Africa,* 10; Padmore, *Pan-Africanism or Communism,* 99–100; Marable, *W. E. B. Du Bois,* 101–102.

152. Du Bois, *World and Africa,* Congress quotes, 11–12; W. E. B. Du Bois, "The Pan-African Congress," *Crisis* 17 (April 1919): 271–274; Du Bois, "The Pan-African Movement," in *History of the Pan-African Congress,* ed. George Padmore (Manchester, UK: Pan-African Federation, n.d.), 13–17; Kwame Nkrumah, *Africa Must Unite* (New York: International, 1970), Nkrumah quote, 103; Marable, *W. E. B. Du Bois,* 102.

153. W. E. B. Du Bois, "Documents of the War," *Crisis* 18 (May 1919): 198–199; Du Bois, "The Black Man in the Revolution of 1914–1918," *Crisis* 17 (March 1919): 218–223; Du Bois, "An Essay Toward a History of the Black Man in the Great War," *Crisis* 18 (June 1919): 63–87; Lewis, *W. E. B. Du Bois: Biography of a Race,* "First," 572; Du Bois, "Robert Russa Moton," *Crisis* 18 (May 1919): 9–10; Du Bois, "Our Success and Failure," *Crisis* 18 (July 1919), "If," 129–130; Emmett J. Scott, *Scott's Official History of the American Negro in the World War* (Chicago: Homewood, 1919).

154. Lewis, *W. E. B. Du Bois: Biography of a Race,* 574; "Du Bois Draws Fire," Pittsburgh *Courier,* July 20, 1919; "Scott Answers Dr. Du Bois," Boston *Chronicle,* May 24, 1919; W. E. B. Du Bois, "Returning Soldiers," *Crisis* 18 (May 1919), "This is," 13–14.

155. W. E. B. Du Bois, "Let Us Reason Together," *Crisis* 18 (September 1919), "When the," 231; James F. Byrnes, Statement of August 1919, in *W. E. B. Du Bois,* ed. William M. Tuttle Jr. (Englewood Cliffs, NJ: Prentice-Hall, 1973), 124–125, in Marable, *W. E. B. Du Bois,* 103; Du Bois, "The Black Majority," *Crisis* 18 (September 1919): 232–233; Du Bois, "Byrnes," *Crisis* 18 (September 1919): 284–285.

156. W. E. B. Du Bois, "The Religion of Jesus Christ," *Horizon* 5 (March 1910): 4–5.

157. W. E. B. Du Bois, review of *The History of the Negro Church,* by Carter G. Woodson, Indianapolis *Freeman,* October 4, 1922, quotes, 92–93.

158. W. E. B. Du Bois, "The Joy of Living," in *Writings in Periodicals Edited by Others,* ed. Herbert Aptheker, 4 vols. (Millwood, NY: Kraus-Thomson, 1982), 219; see Jonathon S. Kahn, *Divine Discontent: The Religious Imagination of W. E. B. Du Bois* (New York: Oxford University Press, 2009), 7–19; Edward J. Blum, *W. E. B. Du Bois: American Prophet* (Philadelphia: University of Pennsylvania Press, 2007), 181–210.

CHAPTER 5. NEW ABOLITION BISHOPS

1. Reverdy C. Ransom, *The Pilgrimage of Harriet Ransom's Son* (Nashville, TN: AME Sunday School Union, 1949), 15–20, quote, 15. Ransom's third wife, Georgia Teal Ransom, told Calvin S. Morris in a 1979 interview that Ransom resented the assumption that his father was white. Calvin S. Morris, *Reverdy C. Ransom: Black Advocate of the Social Gospel* (Lanham, MD: University Press of America, 1990), 22.

2. Ransom, *Pilgrimage*, quote, 19; Richard R. Wright Jr., *The Bishops of the African Methodist Episcopal Church* (Nashville, TN: AME Sunday School Union, 1963), 287; Alexander Keyssar, *The Right to Vote: The Contested History of Democracy in the United States* (New York: Basic Books, 2000), 52. This section on Ransom adapts material from Gary Dorrien, *Social Ethics in the Making: Interpreting an American Tradition* (Oxford: Wiley-Blackwell, 2009), 147–160.

3. Ransom, *Pilgrimage*, quotes, 22, 23.

4. Ibid., quote, 24.

5. Ibid, quotes, 26, 26–27.

6. Horace Talbert, *Sons of Allen: Together with a Sketch of the Rise and Progress of Wilberforce University* (Xenia, OH: Aldine Press, 1906), 266–268; John Hope Franklin and Alfred A. Moss Jr., *From Slavery to Freedom: A History of Negro Americans*, 6th ed. (New York: Knopf, 1988), 150; Carter G. Woodson, *History of the Negro Church* (Washington, DC: Associated Publishers, 1921), 181.

7. Payne, *Recollections of Seventy Years*, 248–257, "an incurable," "most ridiculous," and "cornfield," 254–255; Josephus R. Coan, *Daniel Alexander Payne: Christian Educator* (Philadelphia: A.M.E. Book Concern, 1935); David Wills, "Reverdy C. Ransom: The Making of an AME Bishop," in *Black Apostles: Afro-American Clergy Confront the Twentieth Century*, ed. Richard Newman and Randall K. Burkett (Boston: G. K. Hall, 1978), 181–212, repr. in Anthony B. Pinn, ed., *Making the Gospel Plain: The Writings of Bishop Reverdy C. Ransom* (Harrisburg, PA: Trinity, 1999), 9–43; Ransom, *Pilgrimage*, "praying school" and "Racial self-confidence," 31; Wright, *Bishops*, "little more," 81; Reverdy C. Ransom, *School Days at Wilberforce* (Springfield, OH: New Era, 1890), 20–40; Hallie Q. Brown, *Pen Pictures of Pioneers of Wilberforce* (Xenia, OH: Aldine, 1937); Annetta L. Gomez-Jefferson, *The Sage of Tawawa: Reverdy Cassius Ransom, 1861–1959* (Kent, OH: Kent State University Press, 2002), 12.

8. Ransom, *Pilgrimage*, quote, 33; Ransom, *School Days*, 18–19; Gomez-Jefferson, *Sage of Tawawa*, 14.

9. Ransom, *School Days*, quote, 19; Ransom, *Pilgrimage*, 32–34, 39.

10. Ransom, *School Days*, 37–42; Ransom, *Pilgrimage*, 37–38, quote, 38. On Oberlin, see Gary Dorrien, *The Making of American Liberal Theology: Idealism, Realism, and Modernity, 1900–1950* (Louisville, KY: Westminster John Knox Press, 2003), 62–65.

11. Ransom, *Pilgrimage*, 37–38, quotes, 38–39, 41–42; John G. Brown, "Wilberforce University: Twenty-Third Commencement Exercises—A Brilliant Closing," *Christian Recorder* 24 (July 8, 1886): 1; Reverdy C. Ransom, "Why This Haste?" *Christian Recorder* 28 (August 28, 1890): 1; Gomez-Jefferson, *Sage of Tawawa*, 23; Will, "Reverdy C. Ransom," 20–21.

12. Daniel A. Payne, "Some Thoughts about the Past, Present and Future of the African M.E. Church," *A.M.E. Church Review* 1 (January 1884): 5–8; Payne, *History of the African Methodist Episcopal Church*, 439–474; Payne and Charles Spencer Smith, *A History of the African Methodist Episcopal Church, Chronicling the Principal Events in the Advance of the African Methodist Episcopal Church from 1856 to 1922* (Philadelphia: A.M.E. Book Concern, 1922; New York: Johnson Reprint, 1968); Will, "Reverdy C. Ransom," 16.

13. Ransom, *Pilgrimage*, quotes, 47, 50; see Reverdy C. Ransom, "Too Cultured for His Flock," *Christian Recorder* 24 (November 18, 1886): 2.

14. Reverdy C. Ransom, "Dr. C. S. Smith's Version of the Apostles' Creed," *Christian Recorder* 28 (April 24, 1890), quotes, 1; Ransom, *Pilgrimage*, "carpets" and "mar," 55; Ransom, *School Days*, 25–35.

15. Reverdy C. Ransom, "Out of the Midnight Sky: A Thanksgiving Address," November 30, 1893, Cleveland, OH, in Pinn, *Making the Gospel Plain*, 59–67, quotes, 61, 64, 65.

16. Ibid., quotes, 65, 66.

17. Reverdy C. Ransom, "Lions by the Way," in *Disadvantages and Opportunities of the Colored Youth* (Cleveland: Thomas and Mattill, 1894), in Pinn, *Making the Gospel Plain*, 67–74, quote, 69.

18. Ibid., "No matter," 71; Ransom, *Pilgrimage*, "Every two or three," 20; Reverdy C. Ransom, "Confessions of a Bishop," *Ebony* 5 (March 1950): "a serious," 73.

19. Ransom, "Race Soil," in *Disadvantages and Opportunities of the Colored Youth*, quote, 13; Reverdy Ransom, "The Industrial and Social Conditions of the Negro," Thanksgiving sermon, Bethel AME Church, Chicago, November 26, 1896, Rembert E. Stokes Learning Resources Center, Stokes Library, Wilberforce University, Wilberforce, OH.

20. See George Herron, *The Larger Christ* (Chicago: Fleming H. Revell, 1891); Herron, *The New Redemption: A Call to the Church to Reconstruct Society According to the Gospel of Christ* (Boston: Thomas Y. Crowell, 1893); Herron, *The Christian State: A Political Vision of Christ* (Boston: Thomas Y. Crowell, 1895); Herron, *Between Caesar and Jesus* (Boston: Thomas Y. Crowell, 1899); Morris, *Reverdy C. Ransom*, 42; David A. Gerber, *Black Ohio and the Color Line* (Urbana: University of Illinois Press, 1976), 345–370; August Meier, *Negro Thought in America, 1880–1915: Racial Ideologies in the Age of Booker T. Washington* (Ann Arbor: University of Michigan Press, 1988), 51, 71. Ransom's library at Tawawa Chimney Corners in Wilberforce was stocked with Herron's writings, including a lined copy of *Between Caesar and Jesus*.

21. Ransom, *Pilgrimage*, 65–77; Will, "Reverdy C. Ransom," 32–33; Wright, *Bishops*, 82.

22. Ransom, *Pilgrimage*, 81–85, quote, 82; Wright, *Bishops*, 287; Carol Marks, *Farewell— We're Good and Gone: The Great Black Migration* (Bloomington: Indiana University Press, 1989); James R. Grossman, *Land of Hope: Chicago, Black Southerners, and the Great Migration* (Chicago: University of Chicago Press, 1989); Nicholas Lemann, *The Promised Land: The Great Black Migration and How It Changed America* (New York: Knopf, 1991); Wallace D. Best, *Passionately Human, No Less Divine: Religion and Culture in Black Chicago, 1915–1952* (Princeton, NJ: Princeton University Press, 2005).

23. Ransom, "The Industrial and Social Conditions of the Negro"; see St. Claire Drake and Horace Clayton, *Black Metropolis: A Study of Negro Life in a Northern City* (New York: Harcourt, Brace, 1945), 12–19; Allan H. Spear, *Black Chicago: The Making of a Negro Ghetto*, 1890–1920 (Chicago: University of Chicago Press, 1967), 2–24.

24. Ransom, "The Industrial and Social Conditions of the Negro."

25. Ransom, *Pilgrimage*, quotes, 92; Reverdy C. Ransom, "Heredity and Environment," Address to the Literacy Congress, Indianapolis, IN, 1898, in Ransom, *The Spirit of Freedom and Justice: Orations and Speeches* (Nashville, TN: AME Sunday School Union, 1926), 161–163.

26. Louis Harlan, *Booker T. Washington: The Making of a Black Leader, 1856–1901* (New York: Oxford University Press, 1972), 263–266; Wills, "Reverdy C. Ransom," 181–212.

27. Wills, "Reverdy C. Ransom," quote, 199; Reverdy C. Ransom, "Chicago Honored by the Race," *Christian Recorder*, September 7, 1899, 1, 6; Ransom, *Pilgrimage*, 84–85; Morris, *Reverdy C. Ransom*, 134–138; Harlan, *Booker T. Washington: The Making of a Black Leader*, 263–266.

28. Wills, "Reverdy C. Ransom," quotes, 200; "The Afro-American Quarrel, Booker T. Washington Defines His Attitude for His Critics," *New York Times*, August 21, 1899; Reverdy C. Ransom to the Editor, Chicago *Inter Ocean*, August 25, 1899; Emma Lou Thornbrough, *T. Thomas Fortune: Militant Journalist* (Chicago: University of Chicago Press, 1972), 191; Shawn Leigh Alexander, *An Army of Lions: The Civil Rights Struggle Before the NAACP* (Philadelphia: University of Pennsylvania Press, 2012), 122–126; Reverdy C. Ransom to Booker T. Washington, August 31, 1899, in *The Booker T. Washington Papers*, ed. Louis R. Harlan, Raymond W. Smock, and Geraldine McTighe (Urbana: University of Illinois Press, 1972–1989); Harlan, *Booker T. Washington: The Making of a Black Leader*, 264–265.

29. Wright, *Bishops*, quote, 289; see Irving Stone, *Clarence Darrow for the Defense* (New York: Doubleday, 1941), 96–101, 471; Ransom, *Pilgrimage*, 86, 114.

30. Reverdy C. Ransom, "The Negro and Socialism," *A.M.E. Church Review* 13 (1896–1897), in Pinn, *Making the Gospel Plain*, 183–189, quotes, 187, 189; George W. Woodbey, *Black Socialist Preacher*, ed. Philip S. Foner (San Francisco: Synthesis, 1983), 282–289.

31. Reverdy C. Ransom, "Deborah and Jael," sermon to the I.B.W. Woman's Club, at Bethel AME Church, Chicago, June 6, 1897 (Chicago: Crystal Print, n.d.), in Pinn, *Making the Gospel Plain*, 75–85, quotes, 77, 80.

32. Reverdy C. Ransom, "Thanksgiving Address, 1904," Address delivered in Bethel AME Church, New Bedford, MA, in Pinn, *Making the Gospel Plain*, 85–91, quotes, 89, 91; Ransom, *Pilgrimage*, 85–86.

33. Reverdy C. Ransom, *First Quadrennial Report of the Pastor and Warden of the Institutional Church to the Twenty-Second General Conference*, Quinn Chapel AME Church, 1904; Ransom, *Pilgrimage*, 111–112; Gomez-Jefferson, *Sage of Tawawa*, 66–67.

34. Ransom, *Pilgrimage*, 88, 103–118; Reverdy C. Ransom to Claude A. Barnett, May 14, 1945, in Morris, *Reverdy C. Ransom*, quote, 112.

35. Ransom, *Pilgrimage*, 111–112.

36. Ibid., 93–97, quotes, 94.

37. Editorial, "The Policy Swindle," *Chicago Tribune*, May 4, 1903; Ransom, *Pilgrimage*, quotes, 123, 125–126.

38. Reverdy C. Ransom, sermon of August 2, 1903, Institutional Church and Settlement House, Chicago, *Literary Digest* 27 (1903): 188, in Wills, "Reverdy C. Ransom," 36; "The Opposition to Booker T. Washington," *Literary Digest* 27 (August 15, 1903): 188–189; W. E. B. Du Bois, *Dusk of Dawn* (1940; repr., New York: Schocken Books, 1970), 86–88.

39. Ransom, *Pilgrimage*, "You are" and "to any," 135; Richard R. Wright Jr., *Eighty-seven Years behind the Black Curtain: An Autobiography* (Philadelphia: Rare Book, 1965), "a regular," 148.

40. Ransom, *Pilgrimage*, 143–148, quote, 143.

41. See John Daniels, *In Freedom's Birthplace: A Study of Boston Negroes* (New York: Houghton Mifflin, 1914), 1–59; James Brewer Stewart, *Wendell Phillips: Liberty's Hero* (Baton Rouge: Louisiana State University Press, 1986).

42. Ransom, *Pilgrimage*, 149–151; Gomez-Jefferson, *Sage of Tawawa*, 76–77.

43. Reverdy C. Ransom, "How Should the Christian State Deal with the Race Problem?" Speech to the National Reform Convention, October 3, 1905, in Ransom, *Spirit of Freedom and Justice*, 16–25, quotes, 16, 17, 22.

44. Emma S. Ransom, "The Home-Made Girl," Address to the Convention of the Northeastern Federation of Women's Clubs, August 11, 1905, pamphlet, 1–8, quotes, 1, 6, 8, in Gomez-Jefferson, *Sage of Tawawa*, 78–79.

45. Reverdy C. Ransom, "William Lloyd Garrison," Address to the Centennial Celebration of the Birth of William Lloyd Garrison, Faneuil Hall, November 11, 1905, in Ransom, *Spirit of Freedom and Justice*, 5–14, quotes, 13–14.

46. *Boston Evening Transcript* and *Boston Herald* reviews, December 12, 1905, in Ransom, *Pilgrimage*, 169–171; Meier, *Negro Thought in America*, 182.

47. Reverdy C. Ransom, "The Spirit of John Brown," Address delivered at the Second Annual Meeting of the Niagara Movement, Harper's Ferry, West Virginia, August 17, 1906, in Ransom, *Spirit of Freedom and Justice*, 16–25, quotes, 17, 19.

48. Ibid., quotes, 20, 21, 23.

49. Ibid., quotes, 23, 24.

50. J. Max Barber, "The Niagara Movement at Harper's Ferry," *Voice of the Negro*, October 1906, 408; W. E. B. Du Bois, "A Word," August 29, 1935, Foreword to Reverdy C. Ransom, *The Negro: The Hope or the Despair of Christianity* (Boston: Ruth Hill, 1935).

51. "Boston Pastor is Ejected from Car," *Boston Herald*, May 29, 1906; Ransom, *Pilgrimage*, 174–178.

52. Ransom, *Pilgrimage*, quotes, 177.

53. Ibid., quotes, 178, 180; "Forced Him from the Car: Newport Men Handled a High Degree Frenchman; They Felt so Certain that he was a Mulatto that They Took a Very Forcible Hand," Knoxville *Journal and Tribune*, May 28, 1906.

54. Booker T. Washington to T. Thomas Fortune, June 19, 1906, in *Booker T. Washington Papers*, "The scoundrels," 9: 34; Fortune, "Running Amok in Boston," *New York Age*, July 2, 1906, "Everyone" and "Why"; "Rev. R. C. Ransom Twice Thrown Out," *Boston Daily Globe*, May 29, 1906.

55. "Ejected Colored Minister: Boston Friends Aroused at Action of Pullman Company," *Boston Post*, May 29, 1906, "aroused"; George W. Forbes to Editor, *Boston Guardian*, 1906, repr. in Ransom, *Pilgrimage*, 185; Henry McNeal Turner, "The Trial and Acquittal of Dr. Ransom," 1906, in Ransom, *Pilgrimage*, 187–189, quote, 188.

56. Turner, "The Trial and Acquittal of Dr. Ransom," quotes, 187, 189.

57. H. M. Turner to R. C. Ransom, May 7, 1907, in Ransom, *Pilgrimage*, "This is not," 200; Ransom, *Pilgrimage*, "No minister," 199.

58. Seth M. Scheiner, *Negro Mecca: History of the Negro in New York City, 1865–1920* (New York: New York University Press, 1965), 15–22; David Levering Lewis, *When Harlem Was in Vogue* (New York: Oxford University Press, 1981), 22–29; Ransom, *Pilgrimage*, 202.

59. "Welcome to Rev. Ransom," *New York Age*, August 15, 1907, "vigorously"; Ransom, *Pilgrimage*, 203–208; James Weldon Johnson, *Black Manhattan* (repr., Salem, NH: Ayer, 1988), 128–132; Gomez-Jefferson, *Sage of Tawawa*, 96–97.

60. Reverdy C. Ransom, "Concerning the Editorship of the *Christian Recorder*," *Voice of Missions*, February 1907, 2; "Almost a Riot and in a Church," *Cleveland Gazette*, October 17, 1908.

61. Ransom, *Pilgrimage*, 223–225, quote, 225; "Many Express Faith in their Leader," *New York Age*, March 30, 1911.

62. Reverdy C. Ransom, "Wendell Phillips: Centennial Oration," Address delivered November 29, 1911, Plymouth Church, Brooklyn, New York, in Pinn, *Making the Gospel Plain*, 123–134, quotes, 126; Ransom, *Pilgrimage*, 215–216, 221–225.

63. Ransom, *Pilgrimage*, 173–192, quotes, 183, 184.

64. Wright, *Bishops*, "There is also," 290; Reverdy C. Ransom, "Editorial, the Federal Council," *A.M.E. Church Review* 33 (January 1917), "peace and harmony" and "It did not," 159–160; see Morris, *Reverdy C. Ransom*, 60.

65. Reverdy C. Ransom, "Thanksgiving Sermon: The American Tower of Babel or the Confusion of Tongues," Bethel AME Church, New York, November 25, 1909, in Ransom, *Spirit of Freedom and Justice*, 62–70, quotes, 70.

66. Reverdy C. Ransom, "Charles Sumner: A Plea for the Civil and Political Rights of Negro Americans," Boston Centennial Oration, January 6, 1911, at Park Street Church, Boston, in Pinn, *Making the Gospel Plain*, 112–122, quotes, 117.

67. Reverdy C. Ransom, "The National Republican Convention: Remarks at Bethel AME Church, Chicago, June 17, 1912," in Ransom, *Spirit of Freedom and Justice*, 98–103, quotes, 99.

68. Reverdy C. Ransom, "The Mission of the Religious Press: Speech to the General Conference of the AME Church, Kansas City, MO, May 16, 1912," in Ransom, *Spirit of Freedom and Justice*, 88–97, quotes, 92, 97.

69. William Seraile, *Fire in His Heart: Bishop Benjamin Tucker Tanner and the AME Church* (Knoxville: University of Tennessee Press, 1998), 100–102; Reverdy C. Ransom, "Our Church Competitor," *A.M.E. Church Review* 29 (July 1912): 81; Ransom, *Pilgrimage*, 226–227; W. E. B. Du Bois to Reverdy C. Ransom, April 27, 1912, in Gomez-Jefferson, *Sage of Tawawa*, 117.

70. Reverdy C. Ransom, "The *Review* in Philadelphia," *A.M.E. Church Review* 29 (July 1912): 83.

71. Reverdy C. Ransom, "Editorial, The Editor's Chair," *A.M.E. Church Review* 36 (April 1920): 507–508; Ransom, "Editorial, The Preacher-Editor," *A.M.E. Church Review* 29 (July 1912): 81; Ransom, "The Mission of the Religious Press," 94–97; Morris, *Reverdy C. Ransom*, 60–61.

72. Ransom, "The National Republican Convention," 176–177.

73. Reverdy C. Ransom, "Hunting Big Game Out of Africa," *A.M.E. Church Review* 29 (October 1912), "monstrous," 141–142; Ransom, "The National Republican Convention," "the Democratic," 177; Ransom, "The Negro's Political Conscience," *A.M.E. Church Review* 29 (July 1912): 84–85.

74. Booker T. Washington, "Industrial Education and Negro Progress," *A.M.E. Church Review* 29 (January 1913): 226–228; Reverdy C. Ransom, "The New Emancipation," *A.M.E. Church Review* 29 (January 1913): 260–264, quote, 263–264.

75. Reverdy C. Ransom, "The Editor's Vision and Task in New York's Black Tenderloin," *A.M.E. Church Review* 30 (October 1913): 149–151.

76. Ransom, *Pilgrimage*, 231–232.

77. Ransom, "The Editor's Vision and Task in New York's Black Tenderloin," 150–151; see Reverdy C. Ransom, "A Black Soul Among Prophets," *A.M.E. Church Review* 30 (October 1913): 151–153.

78. Stephen R. Fox, *The Guardian of Boston: William Monroe Trotter* (New York: Atheneum, 1970), quotes, 180, 181; John Milton Cooper Jr., *The Warrior and the Priest: Woodrow Wilson and Theodore Roosevelt* (Cambridge, MA: Harvard University Press, 1983), 274; Ray Stannard Baker, ed., *Woodrow Wilson: Life and Letters*, 8 vols. (Garden City, NY: Doubleday, 1927–1939), 5: 141; W. E. B. Du Bois, "William Monroe Trotter," *Crisis* 9 (December 1914): 82.

79. Du Bois, "William Monroe Trotter," quotes, 82; W. E. B. Du Bois, "Mr. Trotter and Mr. Wilson," *Crisis* 9 (January 1915): 119–127.

80. Reverdy C. Ransom, "The Ape That Speaks Like a Man," *A.M.E. Church Review* 31 (January 1915): 306–307.

81. Reverdy C. Ransom, "Race Pride," in Pinn, *Making the Gospel Plain*, 181–182.

82. Reverdy C. Ransom, "News Item," *A.M.E. Church Review* 31 (April 1915): 407–408.

83. Reverdy C. Ransom, "Bishop Henry McNeal Turner," *A.M.E. Church Review* 32 (July 1915), "broad culture," 46–47; Ransom, "The Passing of a New Age," *A.M.E. Church Review* 32 (January 1916), "great," "the mightiest," "the high," and "new," 208–209.

84. Reverdy C. Ransom, "The Old Black Mule," *A.M.E. Church Review* 33 (October 1916): 98–99.

85. Reverdy C. Ransom, "One Country One Flag," *A.M.E. Church Review* 33 (April 1917), quote, 241–242; Ransom, "Close Ranks," *A.M.E. Church Review* 35 (October 1918): 113–114.

86. Ransom, "Close Ranks," 113–114; *Journal of Proceedings of the Twenty-Sixth Quadrennial Session of the General Conference of the AME Church*, St. Louis, MO, May 3–16, 1920, 117–120; Reverdy C. Ransom, "The Coming Vision," Address to the AME General Conference of 1920, *A.M.E. Church Review* 37 (January 1921): 135–139, quotes, 135.

87. Ransom, *Pilgrimage*, quotes, 234.
88. Ibid., quotes, 235.
89. "Negro Dark Horse in Congress Race," *New York Evening Post*, February 27, 1918; "Hayes Asks About Negro's Nomination," *New York Journal*, February 28, 1918; "Colored Bolt Threatens Hulbert," *New* York *Sun*, February 27, 1918; "Place on Ballot is Denied Ransom," *New York Times*, March 2, 1918; "Justice Strikes Name of Negro from Ballot," *New York American*, March 2, 1918; Ransom, *Pilgrimage*, 236–252.
90. Reverdy C. Ransom, "The General Conference of 1920," A.M.E. *Church Review* 37 (July 1920): 36–37; Ransom, *Pilgrimage*, 261–262, quotes, 262; Wright, *Bishops*, 102–103, 236–238, 344–345; Annetta L. Gomez-Jefferson, *In Darkness with God: The Life of Joseph Gomez, a Bishop in the African Methodist Episcopal Church* (Kent, OH: Kent State University Press, 1998), 77–79.
91. Reverdy C. Ransom, "Has the AME Church Forgotten Its Mission?" *A.M.E. Church Review* 36 (October 1919), quotes, 369, 370; Ransom, "The Coming Vision," 136–138; *Journal of Proceedings of the Twenty-Sixth Quadrennial Session of the General Conference of the AME Church*, 53–54; Ransom, "A Step Toward Denominational Union," A.M.E. *Church Review* 29 (July 1912): 85; Ransom, "Organic Union," A.M.E. *Church Review* 37 (January 1921): 155–156.
92. See Rupert Lewis, *Marcus Garvey: Anti-Colonial Champion* (Trenton, NJ: Africa World, 1988); Judith Stein, *The World of Marcus Garvey: Race and Class in Modern Society* (Baton Rouge: Louisiana State University Press, 1986); E. David Cronon, *Black Moses: The Story of Marcus Garvey and the Universal Negro Improvement Association* (Madison: University of Wisconsin Press, 1955); Tony Martin, *Race First: The Ideological and Organizational Struggle of Marcus Garvey and the Universal Negro Improvement Association* (Westport, CT: Greenwood Press, 1976).
93. Marcus Garvey, "The West Indies in the Mirror of Truth," *Champion Magazine*, January 1917, repr. in *Selected Writings and Speeches of Marcus Garvey*, ed. Bob Blaisdell (Mineola, NY: Dover), 14–16; Garvey, "A Journey of Self-Discovery," *Current History*, September 1963, repr. in *Marcus Garvey and the Vision of Africa, ed.* John Henrik Clarke (New York: Vintage Books, 1974), 71–81; Stein, *World of Marcus Garvey*, 43–44; Richard B. Moore, "Harrison, Hubert Henry," in *Dictionary of American Negro Biography*, ed. Rayford W. Logan and Michael R. Winston (New York: W. W. Norton, 1982), 292–293.
94. Robert A. Hill, *The Crusader: A Facsimile of the Periodical* (New York: Garland Publishing, 1987), 3 vols., quote, 1: 52; in David Levering Lewis, *W. E. B. Du Bois: The Fight for Equality and the American Century, 1919–1963* (New York: Henry Holt & Co., 2000), 57; Stein, *World of Marcus Garvey*, 62; W. Burghardt Turner and Joyce Moore Turner, eds., *Richard B. Moore, Caribbean Militant in Harlem, Collected Writings, 1920–1972* (Bloomington: University of Indiana Press, 1980), 30–31.
95. Charles Mowbray White, "Interview with W. E. B. Du Bois," *The Marcus Garvey and Universal Negro Improvement Association Papers*, ed. Robert A. Hill, 9 vols. (Berkeley: University of California Press, 1983–2000), "the lowest," 2: 620; W. E. B. Du Bois, "The Rise of the West Indian," *Crisis* 21 (September 1920), "rise of," 214.
96. Du Bois, "The Rise of the West Indian," 214–215.

97. Marcus Garvey, "The Negro's Greatest Enemy," *Current History*, September 1923, in *Marcus Garvey and Universal Negro Improvement Association Papers*, "The weaker," 1: 3; Robert A. Hill, "Retreat from Radicalism," *Marcus Garvey and Universal Negro Improvement Association Papers*, "over the," 1: lxxviii; Garvey, "Leadership," Speech at Liberty Hall, New York City, July 23, 1921, in *Selected Writings and Speeches of Marcus Garvey*, 37–44;

98. Manifesto: "Declaration of the Rights of the Negro Peoples of the World," International Convention of the Negroes of the World, New York City, August 31, 1920, in *Selected Writings and Speeches of Marcus Garvey*, 16–24, quotes, 18, 20, 21, 23.

99. Reverdy C. Ransom, "Back to Africa, A Militant Call," *A.M.E. Church Review* 37 (October 1920), quotes, 88–89.

100. W. E. B. Du Bois, "The Social Equality of Whites and Blacks," *Crisis* 21 (November 1920), quote, 16.

101. Ibid., 16–17.

102. W. E. B. Du Bois, "Marcus Garvey," *Crisis* 21 (December 1920): 58–59.

103. W. E. B. Du Bois, "Marcus Garvey," *Crisis* 21 (January 1921): 114–115.

104. W. E. B. Du Bois, "The Black Star Line," *Crisis* 24 (September 1922), quote, 210; Du Bois, "The U.N.I.A.," *Crisis* 25 (January 1923): 120–122; Lewis, *W. E. B. Du Bois: The Fight for Equality and the American Century*, 80–81; Marcus Garvey, "An Appeal to the Soul of White America," October 2, 1923, speech in *Marcus Garvey and Universal Negro Improvement Association Papers*, 5: 464–468; "Hon. Marcus Garvey Tells of Interview with the Ku Klux Klan," Liberty Hall, New York City, July 9, 1922, in *Selected Writings and Speeches of Marcus Garvey*, 74–82.

105. Marcus Garvey, "The Negro's Greatest Enemy," New York *World*, August 5, 1923; Garvey, "The Negro's Greatest Enemy," *Current History Magazine*, September 1923; "Garvey Found Guilty," Pittsburgh *Courier*, June 23, 1923, in *Marcus Garvey and Universal Negro Improvement Association Papers*, 5: 376–377; Garvey, "First Speech after Release from the Tombs," September 11, 1923, in *Selected Writings and Speeches of Marcus Garvey*, 150–154; Robert W. Bagnall, "The Madness of Marcus Garvey," *Messenger*, March 1923, 638–648, quotes, 638, 648.

106. W. E. B. Du Bois, "A Lunatic or a Traitor," *Crisis* 28 (May 1924), quotes, 8, 9.

107. Ibid., 9.

108. George W. Forbes, "Garvey Plight—The Pity of It All," *A.M.E. Church Review* 40 (July 1923): 49–50.

109. Ira May Reynolds to W. E. B. Du Bois, July 5, 1923, in *Correspondence of W. E. B. Du Bois*, volume 1: *Selections, 1877–1934*, ed. Herbert Aptheker (Amherst: University of Massachusetts Press, 1973), 271–272.

110. W. E. B. Du Bois, "Brothers, Come North," *Crisis* 19 (January 1920): 105–106; Du Bois, "Dives, Mob and Scab, Limited," *Crisis* 19 (March 1920): 235–236; Du Bois, "The Class Struggle," *Crisis* 22 (June 1921): 55–56; Du Bois, "Americanization," *Crisis* 24 (August 1924): 154.

111. W. E. B. Du Bois, *Darkwater: Voices from Within the Veil* (New York: Harcourt, Brace, 1920), quotes, 69; Du Bois, "The Negro and Labor," *Crisis* 25 (April 1923): 248–249; Lewis, *W. E. B. Du Bois: The Fight for Equality and the American Century*,

96–97; see Theodore Allen, *The Invention of the White Race* (London: Verso, 1994); Noel Ignatiev, *How the Irish Became White* (New York: Routledge, 1995); Matthew Frye Jacobson, *Whiteness of a Different Color: European Immigrants and the Alchemy of Race* (Cambridge, MA: Harvard University Press, 1998); Toni Morrison, *Playing in the Dark: Whiteness and the Literary Imagination* (Cambridge, MA: Harvard University Press, 1992); David Roediger, *The Wages of Whiteness: Race and the Making of the American Working Class* (London: Verso, 1991).

112. David Levering Lewis, *The Portable Harlem Renaissance* (New York: Viking, 1994), quote, xv; see Wilson Jeremiah Moses, "The Lost World of the Negro, 1895–1919: Black Literary and Intellectual Life before the Renaissance," *Black American Literature Forum* 21 (1987): 61–65.

113. W. E. B. Du Bois, *The Quest of the Silver Fleece: A Novel* (1911; repr., New York: Harlem Moon, 2004); James Weldon Johnson, *The Autobiography of an Ex-Colored Man* (1912; repr., New York: Penguin Books, 1990); David Levering Lewis, *When Harlem Was in Vogue* (New York: Oxford University Press, 1989), 86.

114. James Weldon Johnson, ed., *The Book of American Negro Poetry* (1922; repr., New York: Harcourt Brace Jovanovich, 1969), quote, 9; see Lewis, *When Harlem*, 86–87; Carolyn Wedin Sylvander, *Jessie Redmon Fauset: Black American Writer* (Troy, NY: Whitson Publishing, 1981).

115. W. E. B. Du Bois, "The Negro Mind Reaches Out," in *The New Negro*, ed. Alaine Locke (New York: Albert & Charles Boni, 1925; repr., New York: Simon and Schuster, 1992), 385–414, quotes, 385–386.

116. Edward F. McSweeney, Foreword to W. E. B. Du Bois, *The Gift of Black Folk: The Negro in the Making of America* (Boston: Stratford, 1924; repr., New York: Garden City, NY: Square One Publishers, 2009), ix–x; Josiah Royce, *Race Questions, Provincialism, and Other American Problems* (New York: Macmillan, 1908); Waldo Frank, *Our America* (New York: Boni and Liveright, 1919); Horace Kallen, *Culture and Democracy in the United States* (New York: Boni and Liveright, 1924); Randolph Bourne, *War and the Intellectuals*, ed. Carl Resek (New York: Harper Torchbooks, 1964); Edward Abrahams, *The Lyrical Left: Randolph Bourne, Alfred Stieglitz, and the Origins of Cultural Radicalism in America* (Charlottesville: University of Virginia Press, 1986); Casey Nelson Blake, *Beloved Community: The Cultural Criticism of Randolph Bourne, Van Wyck Brooks, Waldo Frank, and Lewis Mumford* (Chapel Hill: University of North Carolina Press, 1990).

117. Du Bois, *Gift of Black Folk*, quotes, 135, 136.

118. Ibid., quotes, 144, 151.

119. Ibid., quote, 154–155; see Melville J. Herskovits, *The Myth of the Negro Past* (1941; repr., Boston: Beacon Press, 1990); E. Franklin Frazier, *The Negro Family in the United States* (Chicago: University of Chicago Press, 1939); Joseph E. Holloway, ed., *Africanisms in American Culture* (Bloomington: Indiana University Press, 1990).

120. Du Bois, *Gift of Black Folk*, 161.

121. Reverdy C. Ransom, "Future Influence of Negro Scholarship in America," Address to Kappa Alpha Psi, December 27, 1925, in Ransom, *Spirit of Freedom and Justice*, quote, 167.

122. Ransom, "Future Influence of Negro Scholarship in America," 167, 165.

123. Ibid., quotes, 165.

124. Ibid., quotes, 168.

125. Reverdy C. Ransom, "The New Negro," in Ransom, *Spirit of Freedom and Justice*, 71.

126. Reverdy C. Ransom, "Reply to Prof. William Starr Myers," in Ransom, *Spirit of Freedom and Justice*, 158–159.

127. Reverdy C. Ransom, "The Paraclete of God the Only Hope for Brotherhood and Peace," in Pinn, *Making the Gospel Plain*, 166–170, quote, 169.

128. Ibid.

129. Ransom, *Pilgrimage*, quotes, 261, 264; Wright, *Bishops*, 287–292; Gomez-Jefferson, *Sage of Tawawa*, 174.

130. Ransom, *Pilgrimage*, 303–319; George A. Singleton, *The Romance of African Methodism* (New York: Exposition, 1952), 86–88, 162–182; Morris, *Reverdy C. Ransom*, 60–63; Wright, *Eighty-Seven Years*, 219–222; Will, "Reverdy C. Ransom," 41–42; Wright, *Bishops*, 291–292.

131. Reverdy C. Ransom, "A Teaching Church," *A.M.E. Church Review* 38 (April 1922), "a church," 198–199; Ransom, "Shall We Have Eighteen Ecclesiastical Principalities or a Connectional Church?" *Southern Christian Recorder*, December 16, 1926; Gomez-Jefferson, *Sage of Tawawa*, 180.

132. Reverdy C. Ransom, "The Cross and the Dollar Sign," *Southern Christian Recorder*, March 24, 1927; Richard R. Wright Jr., "The View from Look Out Mountain," *Christian Recorder*, May 5, 1927; Ransom, "As Seen Through Editor Wright's Dark Thunder Clouds," *Christian Recorder*, May 5, 1927; Singleton, *Romance of African Methodism*, 162–167; Gomez-Jefferson, *Sage of Tawawa*, 180–184; *Journal of the Twenty-Eighth Quadrennial Session of the General Conference of the AME Church*, May 7–23, 1928, 119–120.

133. Ransom, *Pilgrimage*, quotes, 268, 269; Singleton, *Romance of African Methodism*, 168.

134. *Journal of the Twenty-Eighth Quadrennial Session of the General Conference of the AME Church*, 156–157; Reverdy C. Ransom, "Ecumenical, What? Ecumenicity, Where? The Shame of Negro Methodism," *Christian Recorder*, August 9, 1951, quote.

135. Alexander Walters, *My Life and Work* (New York: Fleming H. Revell, 1917), quote, 23.

136. Ibid., "I was very," 30; William J. Simmons, *Men of Mark: Eminent, Progressive and Rising* (Cleveland: George M. Rewell, 1887), "I was born," 221.

137. Walters, *My Life and Work*, quote, 46.

138. Ibid., quote, 47; George M. Miller, "The Social Mission of Bishop Alexander Walters," in *Black Apostles*, 248; Simmons, *Men of Mark*, 222; Julia A. J. Foote, *A Brand Plucked from the Fire: An Autobiographical Sketch* (Cleveland: W. F. Schneider, 1879); *Sisters of the Spirit: Three Black Women's Autobiographies of the Nineteenth Century*, ed. William L. Andrews (Bloomington: Indiana University Press, 1986).

139. Simmons, *Men of Mark*, 222.

140. Walters, *My Life and Work*, quote, 85.

141. *New York Age*, August 22, 1891, in Shawn Leigh Alexander, *An Army of Lions: The Civil Rights Struggle Before the NAACP* (Philadelphia: University of Pennsylvania Press, 2012), 48.

142. "The Christian Endeavor Story," christianendeavor.com/history; "International Society of Christian Endeavor," *Encyclopedia Britannica*, www.britannica.com/EBchecked/topic/291269/International-Society-of-Christian-Endeavor.

143. Alexander Walters, Address to the World's Christian Endeavor Convention, London, England, 1890, in Walters, *My Life and Work*, quotes, 222, 224.

144. Ibid., quotes, 226, 231, 232.

145. Alexander Walters, "The Responsibility of the Afro-American in America," Address to the National Convention of the Christian Endeavor Society, United States, July 11, 1895, Boston, MA, in Walters, *My Life and Work*, 200–201.

146. Ibid., quote, 205.

147. Ibid., quotes, 209.

148. Ibid., 213.

149. Alexander Walters to the *New York Age*, March 10, 1898, in Walters, *My Life and Work*, 98.

150. Objects of the Afro-American Council, December 29, 1898, in Walters, *My Life and Work*, 113.

151. Alexander Walters, Address to the Afro-American Council Convention, December 29, 1898, Metropolitan Baptist Church, Washington, DC, in Walters, *My Life and Work*, quotes, 115, 127.

152. Ibid., quotes, 127, 131.

153. Alexander Walters, Address to the New Jersey Methodist Conference, Jersey City, New Jersey, May 8, 1899, in Alexander, *An Army of Lions*, 110–111.

154. Ibid., 111.

155. Alexander, *An Army of Lions*, "in a crusade," 111; John Edward Bruce, Introduction to Walters, *My Life and Work*, "big-hearted," 14.

156. W. Calvin Chase, *Washington Bee*, April 15, 1899, "erratic"; John E. Bruce, *Colored American*, June 3, 1899, "Pray," in Alexander, *An Army of Lions*, 115; William Seraile, *Bruce Grit: The Black Nationalist Writings of John Edward Bruce* (Knoxville: University of Tennessee Press, 2003), 102–103.

157. W. Calvin Chase, *Washington Bee*, November 4, 1899, "a strong" and "The preacher"; John E. Bruce, *Colored American*, November 11, 1899, in Alexander, *An Army of Lions*, 130–131; August Meier, "The Negro and the Democratic Party, 1875–1915," *Phylon* 17 (Summer 1956): 173–191.

158. Benjamin R. Justesen, *George Henry White: An Even Chance in the Race of Life* (Baton Rouge: Louisiana State University Press, 2001), 274–279; Ida B. Wells-Barnett, "Lynch Law in America," *Arena* 23 (January 1900): 15–24; Alexander, *An Army of Lions*, 139.

159. Alexander Walters to Booker T. Washington, August 14, 1900, in *Booker T. Washington Papers*, quote, 5: 593; Ida B. Wells-Barnett, *Mob Rule in New Orleans: Robert Charles and His Fight to the Death*, in Wells-Barnett, *Southern Horrors and Other Writings: The Anti-Lynching Campaign of Ida B. Wells, 1882–1900*, ed. Jacqueline Jones Royster (New York: Bedford, 1997), 158–208.

160. Alexander, *An Army of Lions*, quotes, 151, 155.

161. Ida B. Wells-Barnett, "National Afro-American Council," *Howard's American Magazine* 6 (May 1901): 415–418.

162. William Monroe Trotter, "The Afro-American Council," July 26, 1902, in Chicago *Broad Ax*, July 26, 1902; Emmett Scott to Booker T. Washington, July 17, 1902, in *Papers of Booker T. Washington*, quote, 6: 497; Paula J. Giddings, *Ida: A Sword Among Lions* (New York: HarperCollins, 2008), 438; Alexander, *An Army of Lions*, 192–236; Emma Lou Thornbrough, *T. Thomas Fortune: Militant Journalist* (Chicago: University of Chicago Press, 1972), 228–229.

163. Walters's speech in Richmond quoted in *Cleveland Gazette*, December 20, 1902, in Alexander, *An Army of Lions*, 197.

164. Frederick McGhee to the Editor, *Washington Bee*, August 12, 1905; George Mason Miller, "'A This Worldly Mission': The Life and Career of Alexander Walters (1858– 1917)" (Ph.D. diss., State University of New York at Stony Brook, 1984), 258–259; Alexander, *An Army of Lions*, 250.

165. Ida B. Wells-Barnett to the Editor, *New York Age*, August 31, 1905; Ida B. Wells, *Crusade for Justice: The Autobiography of Ida B. Wells*, ed. Alfreda M. Duster (Chicago: University of Chicago Press, 1970), "a man," 298; Giddings, *Ida*, 438–439; Alexander, *An Army of Lions*, 251.

166. August Meier and Elliott Rudwick, "Negro Boycotts of Segregated Streetcars in Florida, 1901–1905," *South Atlantic Quarterly* 64 (Autumn 1970): 525–533; Harry Smith, *Cleveland Gazette*, August 12, 1905; Alexander, *An Army of Lions*, 248–260; W. E. B. Du Bois, "Growth of the Niagara Movement," *Voice of the Negro* 3 (January 1906): 43; Du Bois, "Union," *Horizon* 3 (June 1908), "essentially," 7.

167. Alexander Walters, "The Afro-American Council and Its Work," *Colored American Magazine* 11 (September 1906), quotes, 205.

168. Ibid., quotes, 206, 207.

169. Ibid., quotes, 207, 208, 209.

170. Ibid., quote, 210.

171. Ibid.

172. Miller, "'A This Worldly Mission,'" "The object," 269; *New York Times*, October 10, 1906, "We may."

173. Alexander, *An Army of Lions*, quotes, 288–289, 290; Miller, "'A This Worldly Mission,'" 275–276.

174. Miller, "'A This Worldly Mission,'" 298–305.

175. Fox, *Guardian of Boston*, 162–163; Miller, "'A This Worldly Mission,'" 305–306; Alexander, *An Army of Lions*, 293–294; Du Bois, "Union," 7.

176. Bishop Alexander Walters, "Civil and Political Status of the Negro," in *Proceedings of the National Negro Conference, 1909* (1909: repr., New York: Arno, 1969), 167–173.

177. "Bishop Alexander Walters, President of the National Colored Democratic League," *Broad Ax*, October 12, 1912; Kellogg, *NAACP*, 74; Walters, *My Life and Work*, quotes, 184, 185.

178. Woodrow Wilson to Alexander Walters, October 16, 1912, in Walters, *My Life and Work*, 195.

179. Woodrow Wilson to Oswald Garrison Villard, August 29, 1913, Oswald Garrison Villard Papers, Box 1463; Kellogg, *NAACP*, 163–166, quote, 163.

180. Josephus Daniels, "Diary," April 11, 1913, in Arthur S. Link, *Wilson: The New Freedom*, 2 vols. (Princeton, NJ: Princeton University Press, 1956), quote, 2: 247; Walters, *My Life and Work*, 195–197; Alexander, *An Army of Lions*, xiii; Kathleen Long Wolgemuth, "Woodrow Wilson's Appointment Policy and the Negro," *Journal of Southern History* 24 (November 1948): 457–471.

181. Walters, *My Life and Work*, quotes, 195–196, 178.

182. Alexander Walters, Address to the United World Society of Christian Endeavor, 1915, in Walters, *My Life and Work*, quotes, 238, 239.

183. Ibid., quotes, 241, 243.

184. Ibid., quotes, 243, 244.

185. Reverdy C. Ransom, "Bishop Alexander Walters," *A.M.E. Church Review* 33 (April 1917).

186. Ransom, *Pilgrimage*, quotes, 270, 271; Gomez-Jefferson, *Sage of Tawawa*, 189; William S. Pollitzer, *The Gullah People and Their African Heritage* (Athens, GA: University of Georgia Press, 1999), 149.

187. Ransom, *Pilgrimage*, 271.

188. "Crispus Attucks, a Negro, the First to Die for American Independence: An Address," Address to the Metropolitan Opera House, Philadelphia, PA, March 6, 1930, in Ransom, *Negro*, quotes, 79, 85.

189. Wright, *Bishops*, 242–243; Ransom, *Pilgrimage*, 271–274, quotes, 274; *Journal of Proceedings of the Twenty-Ninth Quadrennial Session of the General Conference of the AME Church*, May 2–16, 1932, Cleveland, OH; "Battle of Laymen Goes to Committee," *Cleveland News*, May 4, 1932; Gomez-Jefferson, *Sage of Tawawa*, 191.

190. Wright, *Eighty-seven Years*, "a home-loving" and "led lewd," 220, "than any one," 221; Wright, *Bishops*, "but their," 243. Howard D. Gregg, in his authorized history of the AME Church, confirmed Wright's account, but added concerning Wright's strategic absence from the Jones proceeding: "Politics, a plague on our house, seemingly has been and continues to be one of our major afflictions." Howard D. Gregg, *History of the African Methodist Episcopal Church* (Nashville, TN: AME Sunday School Union, 1980), 325.

191. Ransom, *Pilgrimage*, 277–278; Wright, *Eighty-seven Years*, quote, 222.

192. Frederick A. McGinnis, *A History and An Interpretation of Wilberforce University* (Blanchester, OH: Brown, 1941), 55–79; Gomez-Jefferson, *Sage of Tawawa*, 194; "The Wilberforce Dilemma: A Critical and Objective Evaluation of Dr. Wesley's Administration," *Wilberforce University Bulletin* 32 (January 1948), 7–8.

193. W. E. B. Du Bois to Charles W. Wesley, June 1932, quotes; and Wesley to Reverdy C. Ransom, June 11, 1932, Ransom Papers, Wilberforce University.

194. Ransom, *Pilgrimage*, "This was," 279; Wright, *Eighty-seven Years*, 28–49; Gregg, *History of the African Methodist Episcopal Church*, 326–327.

195. Wright, *Eighty-seven Years*, 180–185; Ransom, *Pilgrimage*, "To Dr. Wright," 279; Gregg, *History of the African Methodist Episcopal Church*, 328–331.

196. Reverdy C. Ransom, "The Negro, The Hope or the Despair of Christianity," Address to the World Fellowship of Faiths, Second Parliament of Religions, Chicago, IL, 1933, in Ransom, *Negro*, 1–7, quote, 5.

197. Ransom, "The Race Problem in a Christian State," Address to the Women's International League and Fellowship of Faith, Dayton, Ohio, February 15, 1935, in Ransom, *Negro*, 64–77, "We hear," 72–73.

198. Reverdy C. Ransom, "The Pulpit and the American Negro," in Ransom, *Negro*, 41–47, quotes, 44–45.

199. Reverdy C. Ransom, "Why Vote for Roosevelt?" *Crisis* 39 (November 1932), quotes, 343; Ransom, "The Negroes' Bewildering Political Predicament," Address at Douglas High School, Cleveland, Ohio, November 3, 1934, Ransom Papers, Wilberforce University.

200. Ransom, "The Negro, the Hope or the Despair of Christianity," 2–3.

201. Ibid., quotes, 3, 6.

202. Reverdy C. Ransom, "The Future of the Negro in the United States," in Ransom, *Negro*, 88–98, quotes, 95, 96.

203. Richard R. Wright Jr., Preface to Ransom, *Negro*, "and he is," n.p.; Reverdy C. Ransom, "The Church That Shall Survive," sermon to the AME General Conference, New York, May 6, 1936, in Singleton, *Romance of African Methodism*, 146–156, and Pinn, *Making the Gospel Plain*, 152–161, quote, 158.

204. "The Wilberforce Dilemma: A Critical and Objective Evaluation of Dr. Wesley's Administration," 6–21; "Wilberforce Trustees Vacate Presidency," *The Cleveland Call and Post*, June 13, 1942; "Dean Wesley Named Wilberforce Head," *The Cleveland Call and Post*, June 13, 1942; Gomez-Jefferson, *Sage of Tawawa*, 219–222, 228–230; Ransom, *Pilgrimage*, 281–284.

205. Gomez-Jefferson, *Sage of Tawawa*, 230–237; Ransom, *Pilgrimage*, 283–286; "The Wilberforce Dilemma," 21–27.

206. Reverdy C. Ransom to Richard R. Wright Jr., July 16, 1951, in Gomez-Jefferson, *Sage of Tawawa*, 261.

207. Gomez-Jefferson, *Sage of Tawawa*, quotes, 261, xv.

208. Joseph Gomez, "Reverdy Cassius Ransom: Prevailer Extraordinary," in Gomez-Jefferson, *Sage of Tawawa*, 275; W. E. B. Du Bois, "A Tribute to Reverdy Cassius Ransom," *A.M.E. Church Review* 75 (April–June 1959), in Pinn, *Making the Gospel Plain*, xvii–xix, quotes, xix.

209. Morris, *Reverdy C. Ransom*; Pinn, *Making the Gospel Plain*.

210. Reverdy C. Ransom, "Editorial, Segregation," *A.M.E. Church Review* 29 (January 1913): 229–230.

211. Ransom, *Negro*, quote, i; see Reverdy C. Ransom, "President Wilson, Trotter, and the American People," *A.M.E. Church Review* 31 (January 1915), 309–318.

212. Ransom, *Negro*, quote, i.

CHAPTER 6. SEPARATISM, INTEGRATION, SOCIALISM

1. See Clarence C. Goen, *Revivalism and Separatism in New England, 1740–1800: Strict Congregationalists and Separate Baptists in the Great Awakening* (New Haven, CT: Yale University Press, 1962); Nathan O. Hatch, *The Democratization of American Christianity* (New Haven, CT: Yale University Press, 1989), 67–122; Sydney E.

Ahlstrom, *A Religious History of the American People* (New Haven, CT: Yale University Press, 1972), 435–454; David W. Bebbington, *Baptists Through the Centuries: A History of a Global People* (Waco, TX: Baylor University Press, 2012); Jon Butler, *Awash in a Sea of Faith: Christianizing the American People* (Cambridge, MA: Harvard University Press, 1990), 164–193, 257–288.

2. Lewis G. Jordan, *Negro Baptist History, USA* (Nashville, TN: Sunday School Publishing Board, National Baptist Convention, 1930), 255–265; Carter G. Woodson, *History of the Negro Church* (Washington, DC: Associated Publishers, 1921), 138–141; James Melvin Washington, *Frustrated Fellowship: The Black Baptist Quest for Social Power* (Macon, GA: Mercer University Press, 1986), 23–185; Walter L. Williams, *Black Americans and the Evangelization of Africa, 1877–1900* (Madison: University of Wisconsin Press, 1982).

3. Henry McNeal Turner, "Introduction, Accompanied by a Sketch of the Life of Rev. W. J. Simmons, A.B., A.M., D.D.," in William J. Simmons, *Men of Mark: Eminent, Progressive and Rising* (Cleveland: George M. Revell, 1887), 5–7; Albert W. Pegues, *Our Baptist Ministers and Schools* (Springfield, MA: Wiley, 1892), 61–62; Arnold H. Taylor, "William J. Simmons," *Dictionary of American Negro Biography*, ed. Rayford W. Logan and Michael R. Winston (New York: W.W. Norton, 1982), 556–557.

4. Turner, "Introduction," 8; Pegues, *Our Baptist Ministers and Schools*, 61.

5. Lawrence H. Williams, *Black Higher Education in Kentucky, 1879–1930* (Lewistown, NY: Edwin Mellen, 1987), 28–29; Evelyn Brooks Higginbotham, *Righteous Discontent: The Women's Movement in the Black Baptist Church, 1880–1920* (Cambridge, MA: Harvard University Press, 1993), 59–60.

6. William J. Simmons, "Industrial Education," 1886, in Turner, "Introduction," quote, 6; Simmons, "History of the School at Louisville, Chap. 1," *Home Mission Echo*, May 1885, 3–4; James L. Diggs, "State University, Louisville, Ky.," *Colored American Magazine*, May 1908, 312–314.

7. Higginbotham, *Righteous Discontent*, 60–61; William J. Simmons, "Schools," *Baptist Home Missions Monthly* 5 (November 1883): 247; Mary V. Cook, "The Work for Baptist Women," in *The Negro Baptist Pulpit*, ed. Edward M. Brawley (Philadelphia: American Baptist Publication Society, 1890), 279–280.

8. William J. Simmons, editorial, *American Baptist*, April 5, 1886; Jordan, *Negro Baptist History, USA*, 260–263; Higginbotham, *Righteous Discontent*, 64.

9. William J. Simmons, Address to the American National Baptist Convention, 1887, ANBC *Journal and Lectures*, in Washington, *Frustrated Fellowship*, 142–143.

10. Turner, "Introduction," quote, 9–10.

11. William J. Simmons, Speech to the Kentucky Legislature, Representing the State Convention of Colored Men of Kentucky, 1886, in Turner, "Introduction," quotes, 11, 12.

12. William J. Simmons, Address to the Lexington Emancipation Celebration, Lexington, Kentucky, January 1, 1887, in Turner, "Introduction," 16–17.

13. Ida B. Wells, *Crusade for Justice: The Autobiography of Ida B. Wells*, ed. Alfreda M. Duster (Chicago: University of Chicago Press, 1970), "truly," 31; Simmons, *Men of Mark*, "I wish," 2.

14. Simmons, *Men of Mark*, quotes, 3.

15. Turner, "Introduction," quotes, 9, 15, 16, 19.

16. American National Baptist Convention, 1887, *Journal and Lectures*, quote, 2:67, in Washington, *Frustrated Fellowship*, 160.

17. Lemuel Call Barnes, *Pioneers of Light: The First Century of the American Baptist Publication Society, 1824–1924* (Philadelphia: American Baptist Publication Society, 1925), 131–142; Washington, *Frustrated Fellowship*, 160–166.

18. *National Baptist*, June 5, 1890, in Washington, *Frustrated Fellowship*, quote, 168.

19. See James M. McPherson, *The Abolitionist Legacy: From Reconstruction to the NAACP* (Princeton, NJ: Princeton University Press, 1975), 284–287; Vincent P. Franklin, *Black Self-Determination: A Cultural History of the Faith of the Fathers* (Westport, CT: Lawrence Hill, 1984), 161–176; Leroy Fitts, *A History of Black Baptists* (Nashville, TN: Broadman, 1985), 73–84; Washington, *Frustrated Fellowship*, 159–185; Williams, *Black Higher Education*, 131–137; Higginbotham, *Righteous Discontent*, 64–67.

20. Charles E. Becker, Address to the South Carolina Baptist Convention, December 1882, *Independent*, January 11, 1883, in McPherson, *Abolitionist Legacy*, 285–286, quote, 285.

21. William J. Simmons, *People's Advocate*, July 28, 1883; Charles L. Purce, *Home Missions Monthly*, 10 (December 1888): 348, in McPherson, *Abolitionist Legacy*, quotes, 285, 286.

22. Washington, *Frustrated Fellowship*, 171–173; McPherson, *Abolitionist Legacy*, 286–287.

23. Obituary for William J. Simmons, *New York Age*, November 8, 1890, "a calamity"; Washington, *Frustrated Fellowship*, "one of" and "should," 173; Pegues, *Our Baptist Ministers*, 78–82; Taylor, "William J. Simmons," 556; Edward M. Brawley, ed. *The Negro Baptist Pulpit* (Philadelphia: American Baptist Publication Society, 1890), 292–299.

24. Henry Lyman Morehouse, Address to the Founding Convention of the National Baptist Convention, September 1895, *Baptist Home Mission Monthly* 17 (November 1895), quote, 413–414.

25. *National Baptist Magazine* 3 (January 1896), Johnson quotes, 16, 17, and *National Baptist Magazine* 4 (October 1896), Love quote, 261, in Washington, *Frustrated Fellowship*, 189–190, 191; see Miles Mark Fisher, *A Short History of the Baptist Denomination* (Nashville, TN: Sunday School Publishing Board, 1933), 109–113.

26. Pegues, *Our Baptist Ministers*, 353–357.

27. E. C. Morris, "The Demand for a Negro Baptist Publishing House," Address to the American National Baptist Convention, Washington, DC, 1893, in Morris, *Sermons, Addresses and Reminiscences and Important Correspondence* (Nashville, TN: National Baptist Publishing Board, 1901), quotes, 57, 58, 59, 60.

28. J. H. Frank, chair, Report of the Committee on the Publishing House, American National Baptist Convention, Washington, DC, 1893, in Morris, *Sermons, Addresses and Reminiscences*, 60–63, quote, 61; Fitts, *History of Black Baptists*, 130–151.

29. E. C. Morris, "President's Address to the National Baptist Convention," Nashville, TN, September 1899, in Morris, *Sermons, Addresses and Reminiscences*, quotes, 107.

30. Ibid., quotes, 108.
31. Ibid., quotes, 111–112.
32. Ibid., quotes, 112–113.
33. Ibid., quote, 116–117.
34. Ibid., quotes, 117.
35. Ibid., quotes, 122.
36. Higginbotham, *Righteous Discontent*, 160; Jordon, *Negro Baptist History*, 260–261; Virginia Broughton, *Twenty Years' Experience of a Missionary* (Chicago: Pony, 1907), 102.
37. L. H. Hammond, *In the Vanguard of a Race* (New York: Council of Women for Home Missions and Missionary Education Movement, 1922), "I would," 48–49; Earl L. Harrison, *The Dream and the Dreamer* (Washington, DC: Nannie H. Burroughs Literature Foundation, 1956), "It came," 10; Evelyn Brooks Barnett [Higginbotham], "Nannie Burroughs and the Education of Black Women," in *The Afro-American Woman: Struggles and Images*, ed. Sharon Harley and Rosalyn Terborg-Penn (Port Washington, NY: Kennikat, 1978), 97–108; Barnett [Higginbotham], "Nannie Burroughs," *Dictionary of American Negro Biography*, 81–82; Sharon Harley, "Nannie Helen Burroughs: 'The Black Goddess of Liberty,'" *Journal of Negro History* 81 (Winter-Autumn, 1996): 62–71.
38. *Journal of the Twentieth Annual Session of the National Baptist Convention, Held in Richmond, Virginia, September 12–17, 1900* (Nashville, TN: National Baptist Publishing Board, 1900), 10; Higginbotham, *Righteous Discontent*, 150.
39. Higginbotham, *Righteous Discontent*, 138–139.
40. Nannie H. Burroughs, "No Color But Character," *Voice of the Negro*, July 1904, quotes, 277.
41. Ibid., quotes, 278.
42. Ibid., 278–279.
43. Ibid., 279.
44. Barnett, "Nannie Burroughs and the Education of Black Women," 98–99; "Baptists May Oust Nannie H. Burroughs," *Chicago Defender*, September 9, 1939; Barbara Dianne Savage, *Your Spirits Walk Beside Us: The Politics of Black Religion* (Cambridge, MA: Harvard University Press, 2008), 166.
45. Nannie H. Burroughs, "Chips from Our Woodpile," *National Baptist Union-Review*, August 8, 1903, quotes; Higginbotham, *Righteous Discontent*, 211, 290; Barnett, "Nannie Burroughs and the Education of Black Women," 101.
46. Nannie H. Burroughs, Address to the Ninth Annual Session of the Women's Convention, 1909, in Higginbotham, *Righteous Discontent*, 213; Harley, "Nannie Helen Burroughs: 'The Black Goddess of Liberty,'" quotes, 65.
47. Higginbotham, *Righteous Discontent*, "The politics," 221; Nannie H. Burroughs, Annual Report to the Women's Convention of 1912, National Baptist Convention, *Twelfth Annual Session of the Women's Convention 1912*, 40–41, in Higginbotham, *Righteous Discontent*, 172; Carole Marks, *Farewell—We're Good and Gone: The Great Black Migration* (Bloomington: Indiana University Press, 1989), 145–147; Florette Henri, *Black Migration: Movement North, 1900–1920* (Garden City, NY: Anchor, 1975), 50–65.

48. Woodson, *History of the Negro Church*, 191–201; Higginbotham, *Righteous Discontent*, 171–177; Evelyn Brooks Higginbotham, "From Strength to Strength: The History of Shiloh Baptist Church of Washington DC, 1863–1988," in *From Strength to Strength: A Journey of Faith, 1873–1988*, ed. Madlyn Calbert (Washington, DC: Shiloh Baptist Church, 1989), 44–57; Wallace D. Best, *Passionately Human, No Less Divine: Religion and Culture in Black Chicago, 1915–1952* (Princeton, NJ: Princeton University Press, 2005), 13–93.

49. Nannie H. Burroughs, Annual Report to the Women's Convention of 1914, National Baptist Convention, *Fourteenth Annual Assembly of the Women's Convention, 1914*, quotes, 169–171, in Higginbotham, *Righteous Discontent*, 175–176.

50. *Fifteenth Annual Report of the Executive Board and Corresponding Secretary of the Women's Convention, 1915*, National Baptist Convention, quote, 37, in Higginbotham, *Righteous Discontent*, 208.

51. Barnett, "Nannie Burroughs and the Education of Black Women," 101; Higginbotham, *Righteous Discontent*, 183.

52. Barnett, "Nannie Burroughs and the Education of Black Women," 101–102.

53. Nannie H. Burroughs, "With All Thy Getting," *Southern Workman*, July 1927, quotes, 299.

54. Ibid., 300.

55. Ibid., 301.

56. "Conduct in Public Places," *Journal of the Tenth Annual Session of the Women's Convention, Held in New Orleans, Louisiana, September 14–19, 1910* (Nashville, TN: National Baptist Publishing Board, 1910), 35, in Higginbotham, *Righteous Discontent*, 193.

57. Floyd Calvin, "That's Nannie Burroughs' Job, and She Does It," *Pittsburgh Courier*, June 8, 1929, "We specialize"; Nannie H. Burroughs, "Nannie Burroughs Says the Doctor Is Tired, Fought a Good Fight, but Did Not Keep the Faith on the Segregation Issue," *Baltimore Afro-American*, April 28, 1934, "close."

58. Nannie H. Burroughs, "What Must the Negro Do to Be Saved?" *Louisiana Weekly*, December 23, 1933, in *Black Women in White America: A Documentary History*, ed. Gerder Lerner (New York: Vintage, 1992), quotes, 551–552; Burroughs, "Unload Uncle Toms," *Los Angeles Weekly*, December 23, 1933; Burroughs, "Fighting Woman Educator Tells What Race Needs," *Pittsburgh Courier*, December 23, 1933.

59. Nannie H. Burroughs, "Says Manhood, Patriotism, Religion Going Out of Style Among Negroes," *Pittsburgh Courier*, March 12, 1932.

60. Nannie H. Burroughs, "Up from the Depths," Lecture to the Alumni Association of Howe Institute, January 25, 1954, in Roy L. Hill, *Rhetoric of Racial Hope* (Brockport, NY: McDaniel, 1976), "The same thing," 50; Burroughs, "What Must the Negro Do to Be Saved?" "When we," "as a," "The Negro," and "The men," 553.

61. Burroughs, "Up from the Depths," 50–51.

62. Nannie H. Burroughs, *Annual Report of Miss Nannie H. Burroughs*, Memphis, Tennessee, September 10, 1942, in Savage, *Your Spirits Walk Beside Us*, "Our real" and "complete," 185; Burroughs, "Up from the Depths," "great," "They know," "wonderful," "I am," and "Yes," 51–52.

63. Savage, *Your Spirits Walk Beside Us,* quote, 187.

64. Nannie H. Burroughs, "Leaders or Followers," *Pittsburgh Courier,* December 10, 1932, "I am"; Burroughs, *Annual Report of the Corresponding Secretary of the Woman's Convention Auxiliary to the National Baptist Convention,* Memphis, Tennessee, September 5–10, 1933, "So far as," "army," and "in our hearts," 20–21; Burroughs, *Annual Report of Miss Nannie H. Burroughs,* Oklahoma City, Oklahoma, September 5–9, 1934, "waiting," 18, in Savage, *Your Spirits Walk Beside Us,* 167, 172.

65. Nannie H. Burroughs, "Declaration of 1776 Is Cause of Harlem Riot," *Baltimore Afro-American,* April 13, 1935, in *Black Women in White America,* 408–409.

66. See Burroughs, "Nannie Burroughs Says the Doctor Is Tired"; Savage, *Your Spirits Walk Beside Us,* 175–178; Paul Harvey, *Redeeming the South: Religious Cultures and Racial Identities among Southern Baptists, 1865–1925* (Chapel Hill: University of North Carolina Press, 1997).

67. Era Bell Thompson, "A Message from a Mahogany Blond," *Negro Digest,* July 1950, 33.

68. National Baptist Convention, *Journal of the Eighth Annual Assembly of the Women's Convention, September 16–21, 1908* (Nashville, TN: National Baptist Publishing Board, 1909), 243, in Higginbotham, *Righteous Discontent,* 209.

69. Adam Clayton Powell Sr., *Against the Tide: An Autobiography* (New York: Richard R. Smith, 1938), 6–7; Adam Clayton Powell Jr., *Adam by Adam* (New York: Dial Press, 1971), 2–10, quotes, 2; Samuel D. Proctor, "Adam Clayton Powell, Sr.," *Dictionary of American Negro Biography,* 501–502; Edward L. Queen II, "Adam Clayton Powell, Sr.," *The Encyclopedia of American Religious History,* ed. Edward L. Queen II, Stephen R. Prothero, and Gardiner H. Shattuck Jr., 2 vols. (New York: Facts on File, 1996), 2: 517–518; Ben Richardson, *Great American Negroes* (New York: Thomas Y. Crowell, 1956), 201–203; "Dr. A. C. Powell, Sr., Minister, 88, Dead," *New York Times,* June 13, 1953, 15; "Thousands Mourn Rev. Powell's Death," *New York Amsterdam News,* June 20, 1953, 1.

70. Powell, *Against the Tide,* quotes, 13, 14; "Negro Solon's Destiny Took Shape in W. Va.," *Charleston Gazette,* April 3, 1959, in Adam Clayton Powell Sr. Collection, Schomburg Center for Research in Black Culture, New York Public Library, New York, NY.

71. Powell, *Against the Tide,* quotes, 22–23, 26–27; Miles Mark Fisher, *Virginia Union and Some of Her Achievements—25th Anniversary, 1899–1924* (Richmond: Brown, 1924).

72. Adam Clayton Powell Sr., *A Souvenir of the Immanuel Baptist Church—Its Pastors and Members* (New Haven, CT: Clarence H. Ryder, 1895), 38; Samuel J. Harris, *The Self-Revelation of God* (New York: George P. Putnam's Sons, 1887); Harris, *The Philosophical Basis of Theism* (New York: Scribner's, 1898); Harris, *God, the Creator and Lord of All* (New York: Scribner's, 1896); Ralph Garlin Clingan, *Against Cheap Grace in a World Come of Age: An Intellectual Biography of Clayton Powell, 1865–1953* (New York: Peter Lang, 2002), 18–19.

73. Adam Clayton Powell Sr., "The Religion of Frederick Douglass," *Colored American,* April 1902; Powell, *Souvenir of the Immanuel Baptist Church,* 38–40; Benjamin Kidd, *Social Evolution* (New York: George P. Putnam's Sons, 1892); Powell, *Against the Tide,* "On my," 45; Powell Jr., *Adam by Adam,* "He was," 7; Robert Austin Warner, *New*

Haven Negroes: A Social History (New Haven, CT: Yale University Press, 1940), 170; John William Kinney, "Adam Clayton Powell, Sr. and Adam Clayton Powell, Jr.: A Historical Exposition and Theological Analysis" (Ph.D. diss., 1979, Columbia University, New York, NY), 25–26.

74. Adam Clayton Powell Sr., *Palestine and Saints in Caesar's Household* (New York: Richard B. Smith, 1939), "among the," 95; Powell, *Against the Tide*, "A manly," 48; "too full" and "I needed," 45; Powell Jr., *Adam by Adam*, "His wanderlust," 7; Powell, "A Plea for Strong Manhood," in Powell, *Palestine and Saints*, 184–185; "Abyssinian Baptist Church," *New York Age*, December 3, 1908, 3; William H. Ferris, *The African Abroad; or, His Evolution in Western Civilization, Tracing His Development Under Caucasian Mileau*, 2 vols. (New Haven, CT: Tuttle, Morehouse and Taylor Press, 1913).

75. Adam Clayton Powell Sr., *Upon This Rock* (New York: Abyssinian Baptist Church, 1949), 2–6; Queen, "Adam Clayton Powell, Sr.," 517; Powell, *Against the Tide*, 56–57; William Welty, "Black Shepherds: A Study of the Leading Negro Churchmen in New York City, 1900–1940" (Ph.D. diss., New York University, 1969), 16–18.

76. Powell, *Upon This Rock*, 9–10; Powell, *Against the Tide*, 50–53; Welty, "Black Shepherds," 18–19.

77. Adam Clayton Powell Sr., "A Graceless Church, *New York Age*, September 21, 1911, 2.

78. Powell, *Against the Tide*, 57, 58.

79. Adam Clayton Powell Sr., "The Significance of the Hour," in Powell, *Palestine and Saints*, quotes, 98, 99, 107.

80. Adam Clayton Powell Sr., "The Source of All Power," in Powell, *Palestine and Saints*, "the rubbish" and "with a heart," 145; Powell, *Against the Tide*, "If you," Blessed," 63, 66; Powell, "The Significance of the Hour," "Christians," 104.

81. Adam Clayton Powell Sr., *Riots and Ruins* (New York: Richard R. Smith, 1945), quote, 150; Warner, *New Haven Negroes*, 287–288; August Meier, *Negro Thought in America, 1880–1915* (Ann Arbor: University of Michigan Press, 1963), 218–224; Guichard Parris and Lester Brooks, *Blacks in the City: A History of the National Urban League* (Boston: Little, Brown, 1971), 37–38; George E. Haynes, *The Trend of the Races* (New York: Council of Women for Home Missions and Missionary Education, 1922).

82. Powell, *Riots and Ruins*, 150.

83. Powell, *Upon This Rock*, 15–16; Powell, *Against the Tide*, 68–71, quotes, 71; Gilbert Osafsky, *Harlem: The Making of a Ghetto* (New York: Harper & Row, 1966), 112–117; Roi Ottley and William Weatherby, eds., *The Negro in New York: An Informal Social History, 1626–1940* (New York: Praeger, 1967), 182–187; Kinney, "Adam Clayton Powell, Sr. and Adam Clayton Powell, Jr.," 79–80; Welty, "Black Shepherds," 142–144; Claude McKay, *Harlem: Negro Metropolis* (New York: Harcourt Brace Jovanovich, 1940), 143–180; Truman Hughes Talley, "Marcus Garvey: The Negro Moses?" *World's Work* 41 (December 1920): 165–166; Lawrence Rushing, "The Racial Identity of Adam Clayton Powell, Jr: A Case Study in Racial Ambivalence and Redefinition," *Afro-Americans in New York Life and History* 34 (January 2010); Powell Jr., *Adam by Adam*, 22–28; Edmund D. Cronon, *Black Moses* (Madison: University of Wisconsin Press, 1955), 178–182.

84. "Tells Negroes to Wage Bloodless War," *New York Age*, March 29, 1917, quotes, 1; Kinney, "Adam Clayton Powell, Sr. and Adam Clayton Powell, Jr.," 64; Miles Mark Fisher, "The Negro Church and the World War," *Journal of Religion* 5 (September 1925): 483–499.

85. Adam Clayton Powell Sr., *Patriotism and the Negro* (New York: Beehive, 1918), self-published and unpaged.

86. "Nearly Ten Thousand Take Part in Big Silent Protest Parade," *New York Age*, August 2, 1917, 1; "League of Darker Peoples Sees Light," *New York Age*, January 11, 1919; "Church Makes Fine Showing," *New York Age*, May 18, 1918, 1; John Hope Franklin, *From Slavery to Freedom: A History of Negro Americans* (New York: Vintage, 1969), 474–475; Kinney, "Adam Clayton Powell, Sr. and Adam Clayton Powell, Jr.," 68–71.

87. "Another Downtown Church Plans to Move to Harlem," *New York Age*, April 10, 1920, 1; "Abyssinian Baptist Church Pays $15,000 for Lots," *New York Age*, April 17, 1920; Powell, *Against the Tide*, quotes, 74, 77; Powell, *Upon This Rock*, 20; "Abyssinian Baptist Church Shocked and Surprised When Rev. A. Clayton Powell Reads Resignation Sunday," *New York Age*, December 17, 1921, 1.

88. Powell, *Against the Tide*, 82.

89. Adam Clayton Powell Sr., "Why the New York Negroes Should Oppose the Liquor Traffic," *New York Age*, April 13, 1916, 8; Powell to the *New York Age*, October 7, 1922, "Ministers Approve Campaign of the *Age* Against Bootleggers," *New York Age*, October 7, 1922, 1; Powell, *Upon This Rock*, 85–100; Charles Flint Kelley, *NAACP: A History of the National Association for the Advancement of Colored People, 1909–1920* (Baltimore, MD: Johns Hopkins University Press, 1967), 61; Powell, *Against the Tide*, 180–181; "Garvey Followers Engage in Violent Demonstration," *New York Age*, August 28, 1922, 1; Kinney, "Adam Clayton Powell, Sr. and Adam Clayton Powell, Jr.," 94–105; Welty, "Black Shepherds," 151–157; Powell Jr., *Adam by Adam*, 52.

90. Powell, *Against the Tide*, quotes, 181.

91. Powell, *Against the Tide*, "I am," "pernicious," and "in the struggle," 182–183; Powell, *Riots and Ruins*, "If the" and "The Negro," 71; Adam Clayton Powell Sr., "The Plea of the Self-Respecting Negro—'Not Charity But Chance,'" *Negro Baptist History, USA: 1750–1930*, ed. Lewis G. Jordon (Nashville, TN: National Baptist Convention Board, 1930), 306–310.

92. Powell, *Against the Tide*, "Race prejudice" and "My race," 187; "We eat" and "show off," 173.

93. Powell, *Patriotism and the Negro*, n.p.; Powell, "The Value of an Ideal," in Powell, *Palestine and Saints*, "the only," 152; Powell, "The Fool's Motto," in Powell, *Palestine and Saints*, 168; "American Religion Is an Abomination with God," *New York Age*, May 14, 1914; see Ruth Zerner, "Dietrich Bonhoeffer's American Experiences: People, Letters, and Papers from Union Seminary," *Union Seminary Quarterly Review* 31 (Summer 1976): 276; Reggie L. Williams, *Bonhoeffer's Black Jesus: Harlem Renaissance Theology and an Ethic of Resistance* (Waco, TX: Baylor University Press, 2014), 77–106.

94. Powell, *Against the Tide*, 208–209.

95. Powell to the *New York Age*, October 7, 1922, "Ministers Approve of the Campaign of the *Age* Against Bootleggers," "two or three," 1; E. Franklin Frazier, *The Negro Church in America* (New York: Schocken Books, 1963), 49–56; Gayraud Wilmore, *Black Religion and Black Radicalism: An Interpretation of the Religious History of African Americans* (Maryknoll, NY: Orbis Books, 1998), 190–194.

96. "Dr. A. C. Powell Scores Pulpit Evils," *New York Age*, November 16, 1929, "abnormal," "rotten," and "I do not," 1; Adam Clayton Powell Sr., "Lifting Up a Standard for the People," sermon at Abyssinian Church, November 3, 1929, Powell Papers, Schomburg Center; Powell, *Against the Tide*, "the evils" and "These sins," 212, 216; Powell, "A Plea for Strong Manhood," "the ethical," 189; "Churches Prefer Rotten Pastors Says Dr. Powell," Baltimore *Afro-American*, November 23, 1929, 1.

97. Powell, "A Plea for Strong Manhood," quotes, 185–186, 190.

98. Adam Clayton Powell Sr., "The Silent Church," *New York Amsterdam News*, February 16, 1935, "feeding," 1; Powell, "A Hungry God," *Watchman-Examiner*, December 5, 1930; Powell, "Clergy Can Relieve Present Distress," *Baltimore Afro-American*, December 20, 1930, 1; "Dr. A. Clayton Powell Starts Drive Among Abyssinian Church Members to Relieve Unemployment Situation," *New York Age*, December 6, 1930, 1; Powell, *Upon This Rock*, 42–44.

99. Powell, *Against the Tide*, quotes, 220, 234, 237, 240–241; "Baptist Ministers Strike Back at Powell," Baltimore *Afro-American*, December 27, 1930, 1; "Baptist Pastors Clash on Charity Aid," *New York Age*, January 3, 1931, 3; "NY City Ministers Resent Attack by Rev. A. Clayton Powell," *Pittsburgh Courier*, January 17, 1931, 1; Williams, *Bonhoeffer's Black Jesus*, 101–102.

100. Adam Clayton Powell Sr., "H. L. Mencken Finds Flowers in a Dunghill," *Opportunity: A Journal of Negro Life* 9 (March 1931), "a negation," 72; H. L. Mencken, "Dunghill Varieties of Christianity," *Opportunity*, February 1931; Powell, *Against the Tide*, 249–250.

101. Powell, "H. L. Mencken Finds Flowers in a Dunghill," quotes, 73–74; Powell, *Against the Tide*, 253.

102. Adam Clayton Powell Sr., "The Negro's Enrichment of the Church of Today," *Watchman-Examiner* 25 (July 22, 1937): 842–843, in Powell, *Against the Tide*, 271–273.

103. Ibid., 273.

104. Powell, "A Hungry God," quote; see John Howard Johnson, "Don't Buy Where You Can't Work," *Harlem, the War and Other Addresses* (New York: W. Malliet, 1942), 61–68; Welty, "Black Shepherds," 300–301; Kinney, "Adam Clayton Powell, Sr. and Adam Clayton Powell, Jr.," 176–177.

105. Powell, *Against the Tide*, "Preach with," 290; Powell Jr., *Adam by Adam*, "When my father," 49.

106. Powell, *Riots and Ruins*, 17.

107. Winifred Rauschenbusch, *How to Prevent a Race Riot in Your Home Town* (New York: Committee Against Racial Discrimination, American Civil Liberties Union, 1943), cited in Powell, *Riots and Ruins*, 18.

108. Powell, *Riots and Ruins*, 36.

109. Ibid., 38, 39.

110. Ibid., 52, 53.

111. Ibid., quotes, 53, 62.
112. Ibid., quote, 141; Powell Jr., *Adam by Adam*, 10–11; see Adam Clayton Powell Jr., *Marching Blacks* (New York: Dial Press, 1945); Charles V. Hamilton, *Adam Clayton Powell, Jr.: The Political Biography of an American Dilemma* (New York: Macmillan, 1991); Neil Hickey and Ed Edwin, *Adam Clayton Powell and the Politics of Race* (New York: Fleet, 1965).
113. Powell, *Riots and Ruins*, quotes, 65, 74.
114. Ibid., quote, 134.
115. Ibid., 148.
116. Walter White, *A Man Called White: The Autobiography of Walter White* (New York: Viking, 1948), 3–43; Kenneth Robert Janken, *White: The Biography of Walter White, Mr. NAACP* (New York: New Press, 2003), 1–28; Edward E. Waldron, *Walter White and the Harlem Renaissance* (Port Washington, NY: Kennikat, 1978).
117. Walter White, *Rope and Faggot: A Biography of Judge Lynch* (New York: Knopf, 1929), "It is" and "no especial," 41, 46; White, *Man Called White*, 44–59; Janken, *White*, 29–87; Mary White Ovington, *The Walls Came Tumbling Down* (New York: Harcourt, Brace, 1947), "knew when," 177; Ovington, *Portraits in Color* (1st ed., 1927; repr., New York: Viking, 1971) "always," 17; Carolyn Wedin, *Inheritors of the Spirit: Mary White Ovington and the Founding of the NAACP* (New York: John Wiley, 1998), 171–198. In 1938 White had to make peace with the National Baptist Convention after the NAACP got caught in a dispute between Burroughs and NAACP's national field secretary William Pickens, on one side, and NBC leaders on the other. Russell Barbour, editor of the *National Baptist Voice*, blasted the NAACP, which got White's panicked attention. See William Pickens, "Pickens Says She's Bigger than 'A Baptist Member,'" *Pittsburgh Courier*, October 22, 1938; Russell Conwell Barbour, "NAACP Leader Insults Baptist Leaders: Three Million Baptists Resent Such Policy; Will Have Nothing to Do with Organization," *National Baptist Voice*, November 12, 1938; Savage, *Your Spirits Walk Beside Us*, 180–181.
118. W. E. B. Du Bois, *Autobiography of W. E. B. Du Bois* (New York: International, 1968), "his attitude" and "I did not," 293, 294; Wedin, *Inheritors of the Spirit*, "We have all," 255.
119. B. Joyce Ross, *J. E. Spingarn and the Rise of the NAACP, 1911–1939* (New York: Atheneum, 1972), 142–145; Wedin, *Inheritors of the Spirit*, 252; Ovington, *Walls Came Tumbling Down*, 180–220; David Levering Lewis, *W.E.B. Du Bois: The Fight for Equality and the American Century, 1919–1963* (New York: Henry Holt, 2000), 292–293.
120. Mary White Ovington, "The State of *The Crisis*," May 1924, in Lewis, *W.E.B. Du Bois: The Fight for Equality*, "wretched," 155, and Wedin, *Inheritors of the Spirit*, 245; David Levering Lewis, *When Harlem Was in Vogue* (New York: Knopf, 1981), 141–149; W. E. B. Du Bois, "The New Negro," *Crisis* 31 (January 1926), "turn," "pretty," and "the passing," 140–141; Alain Locke, "The New Negro," and Charles S. Johnson, "The New Frontage on American Life," in *The New Negro*, ed. Alain Locke (New York: Albert & Charles Boni, 1925; repr., New York: Simon & Schuster, 1992), 3–16, 278–298. Though Du Bois's memorial statements were sometimes devastating, he praised Locke after Locke died in 1954, commending Locke's "severe logic, his

penetrating analysis, [and] his wide reading. . . . Alain Locke stood singular in a stupid land as a rare soul." W. E. B. Du Bois, "The Passing of Alain Leroy Locke," *Phylon* 15 (1954): 251–252.

121. Mary White Ovington to W. E. B. Du Bois, December 20, 1930, in *Correspondence of W.E.B. Du Bois*, 3 vols., ed. Herbert Aptheker (Amherst: University of Massachusetts Press, 1973), 1: 430–431.

122. W.E.B. Du Bois to Mary White Ovington, December 24, 1930, ibid., 431.

123. R. L. Vann to W. E. B. Du Bois, December 26, 1930, ibid., 431–432; Du Bois to Vann, December 29, 1930, ibid., 432–433.

124. Ross, *J. E. Spingarn and the Rise of the NAACP, 1911–1939*, 142–145; Lewis, *W.E.B. Du Bois: The Fight for Equality*, 292–295; Du Bois, *Autobiography of W. E. B. Du Bois*, 294.

125. Powell, *Riots and Ruins*, quote, 45; see W. E. B. Du Bois, "Our Program," *Crisis* 37 (May 1930): 174.

126. Du Bois, *Autobiography of W. E. B. Du Bois*, quote, 297; see W. E. B. Du Bois, "The Negro Bourgeoisie," *Crisis* 38 (September 1931): 314.

127. W. E. B. Du Bois, "Russia, 1926," *Crisis* 33 (November 1926), quotes, 7–8; see Du Bois, "My Recent Journey," *Crisis* 33 (December 1926): 66; Du Bois, "Judging Russia," *Crisis* 33 (February 1927): 189–190; Du Bois, "As the Crow Flies," *Crisis* 35 (May 1928): 149.

128. W. E. B. Du Bois, "The Negro and Communism," *Crisis* 38 (September 1931): 313–315, 318, 320; Du Bois, "Marxism and the Negro Problem," *Crisis* 40 (May 1933): 103–104.

129. James R. Acker, *Scottsboro and Its Legacy: The Cases that Challenged American Legal and Social Justice* (New York: Praeger, 2007); Dan T. Carter, *Scottsboro: A Tragedy of the American South* (Baton Rouge: Louisiana State University Press, 1979); James Haskins, *The Scottsboro Boys* (New York: Henry Holt, 1994).

130. Du Bois, "The Negro and Communism," quotes, 318, 320; Du Bois, "Negro Editors on Communism," *Crisis* 39 (June 1932): 190–191.

131. Du Bois, "The Negro and Communism," 319–320.

132. W. E. B. Du Bois, "Marxism and the Negro Problem," *Crisis* 40 (May 1933), quotes, 103–104; see Du Bois, "Communist Strategy," *Crisis* 38 (September 1931): 313–314; Du Bois, "Our Class Struggle," *Crisis* 40 (July 1933): 164–165.

133. Du Bois, "Marxism and the Negro Problem," quotes, 104, 118.

134. Ibid., quotes, 118; see W. E. B. Du Bois, "Cooperation and Communism—The Education of the Proletariat—Cooperatives in Various Lands," *Pittsburgh Courier*, August 11, 1937, 11.

135. W. E. B. Du Bois, "Segregation," *Crisis* 41 (January 1934), "The advance," 20; Walter F. White, "Segregation—A Symposium," *Crisis* 41 (March 1934), "Negroes and," 80–81; see Du Bois, "Will the Church Remove the Color Line?" *Christian Century*, December 9, 1931, 1554–1556; Du Bois, "Postscript," *Crisis* 41 (May 1934): 149; Du Bois, "Postscript," *Crisis* 41 (April 1934): 182–184.

136. "George Washington Woodbey," *Who's Who of the Colored Race*, ed. Frank Lincoln Mather (Chicago: Memento Edition, Half-Century Anniversary of Negro Freedom

in U.S., 1915), 290–291; Edward Bellamy, *Looking Backward: 2000–1887* (Boston: Houghton Mifflin, 1888); Philip S. Foner, *American Socialism and Black Americans: From the Age of Jackson to World War II* (Westport, CT: Greenwood Press, 1977), 45–60, 151–152; Foner, "Reverend George Washington Woodbey: Early Twentieth Century California Black Socialist," *Journal of Negro History* 61 (April 1976): 136–157.

137. A. W. Ricker, *Appeal to Reason*, October 31, 1903, in Foner, *American Socialism and Black Americans*, 152.

138. Joe Hill to E. W. Vanderleith, n.d., in Melvyn Dubofsky, *We Shall Be All: A History of the Industrial Workers of the World* (New York: Quadrangle, 1969), "not worth," 190; *Los Angeles Socialist*, July 12, 1902, in Foner, *American Socialism and Black Americans*, "anxious" and "Comrade," 153.

139. *Common Sense*, October 27, 1906, "The well-known," and *Los Angeles Socialist*, May 2, 1903, "He has" and "There is," in Foner, *American Socialism and Black Americans*, 153–154.

140. "Battery Charge," *San Diegan-Sun*, July 11, 1905, in Foner, *American Socialism and Black Americans*, 154.

141. A. W. Ricker, *Appeal to Reason*, October 31, 1903; George Washington Woodbey, *What to Do and How to Do It; or, Socialism Versus Capitalism* (1903), repr. in George W. Woodbey, *Black Socialist Preacher*, ed. Philip S. Foner (San Francisco: Synthesis Publications, 1983), quote, 40.

142. Woodbey, *What to Do and How to Do It*, quote, 43.

143. Ibid., quotes, 48.

144. Ibid., 79–80.

145. Ibid., 82–83.

146. George Washington Woodbey, *The Bible and Socialism* (1904), in Woodbey, *Black Socialist Preacher*, quotes, 91, 92.

147. Ibid., 102.

148. Ibid., 105.

149. Ibid., 117.

150. Ibid., 133.

151. Ibid., 145.

152. Morris Hillquit, *History of Socialism in the United States* (New York: Russell and Russell, 1910), 310–312; "Comrade Debs is Pleased," *Worker*, August 11, 1901; Eugene V. Debs, "The Socialist Movement in America," *Social Democratic Herald*, April 26, 1902; James Weinstein, *The Decline of Socialism in America, 1912–1925* (New York: Vintage Books, 1969); Ira Kipnis, *The American Socialist Movement, 1897–1912* (New York: Columbia University Press, 1952), 105–106.

153. Charles H. Vail, "The Negro Problem," *International Socialist Review* 1 (February 1901): 464–470; "The Negro Resolution," *International Socialist Review* 5 (January 1905), "color prejudice," 192–193; Foner, *American Socialism and Black Americans*, 94–98; Sally M. Miller, "The Socialist Party and the Negro, 1901–1920," *Journal of Negro History* 56 (July 1971): 220–229; Howard H. Quint, *The Forging of American Socialism: Origins of the Modern Movement* (Columbia: University of South Carolina Press, 1953), 42–43; James Dombrowski, *The Early Days of Christian Socialism in*

America (New York: Columbia University Press, 1936), 187–190; Laurence R. Moore, "Flawed Fraternity: American Socialist Response to the Negro, 1901–1912," *Historian* 32 (November 1969): 1–18.

154. Editorial, *Colored American*, August 18, 1901, quotes; see Foner, *American Socialism and Black Americans*, 100; *Appeal to Reason*, August 17, 1901.

155. Charles L. Wood to *Colored American*, September 14, 1901, September 28, 1901, and October 26, 1901, in Foner, *American Socialism and Black Americans*, 101–102.

156. Eugene V. Debs, "The Negro in the Class Struggle," *International Socialist Review*, November 1903, in Debs, *Writings and Speeches of Eugene V. Debs*, ed. Joseph M. Bernstein (New York: Hermitage Press, 1948), quotes, 64, 65, 66.

157. Eugene V. Debs, "The Negro and His Nemesis," *International Socialist Review*, January 1904, in *Writings and Speeches of Eugene V. Debs*, quotes, 68, 69.

158. "1904 Socialist Party Convention," *International Socialist Review* 4 (May 1904): 686–687.

159. *Proceedings, National Convention of the Socialist Party, Chicago, Illinois, May 10–17, 1908*, Chicago, 1908, quotes, 208–209, in George W. Woodbey, "Remarks of Rev. Woodbey at the 1908 Socialist Party Convention," in Woodbey, *Black Socialist Preacher*, 243.

160. Morris Hillquit, "Immigration in the United States," *International Socialist Review* 8 (August 1907): 65–75; Sally M. Miller, "For White Men Only: The Socialist Party of America and Issues of Gender, Ethnicity and Race," *Journal of the Gilded Age and Progressive Era* 2 (July 2003): 295; Victor Berger, "The Misfortunes of the Negroes," *Social Democratic Herald*, May 31, 1902.

161. Socialist Party, *Proceedings, National Convention of the Socialist Party, Chicago, Illinois, May 10–17, 1908*, Chicago, 1908, 106–121; Cameron H. King Jr., "Asiatic Exclusion," *International Socialist Review* 8 (May 1908): 61–69; Bruce Rogers, "Our Asiatic Fellows," *International Socialist Review* 15 (April 1915): 626; Miller, "For White Men Only," 295–296; Kipnis, *American Socialist Movement*, 279–288.

162. *Proceedings, National Convention of the Socialist Party, Chicago, Illinois, May 10–17, 1908*, Chicago, 1908, quotes, 106; Woodbey, "Remarks of Rev. Woodbey at the 1908 Socialist Party Convention," in Woodbey, *Black Socialist Preacher*, 244.

163. Sally M. Miller, *Victor L. Berger and the Promise of Constructive Socialism, 1910–1920* (Westport, CT: Greenwood, 1973); Marvin Wachman, *History of the Social Democratic Party of Milwaukee, 1897–1910* (Urbana: University of Illinois Press, 1945); Victor L. Berger, *Voice and Pen of Victor L. Berger: Congressional Speeches and Editorials* (Milwaukee: Milwaukee Leader, 1929).

164. George W. Woodbey, "Why the Negro Should Vote the Socialist Ticket," Socialist Party leaflet, 1908, in Woodbey, *Black Socialist Preacher*, 252–253.

165. Ibid., 254.

166. George W. Woodbey, "Socialist Agitation," *Chicago Daily Socialist*, January 3, 1909, in Woodbey, *Black Socialist Preacher*, "a fire," 245; Foner, *American Socialism and Black Americans*, "loosened," 170.

167. George W. Woodbey, "The New Emancipation," *Chicago Daily Socialist*, January 18, 1909, in Woodbey, *Black Socialist Preacher*, 245–246.

168. Dubofsky, *We Shall Be All*, 91–109; Ray Ginger, *The Bending Cross: A Biography of Eugene Victor Debs* (New Brunswick, NJ: Rutgers University Press, 1949), 238–244; A. M. Simons, "IWW," *International Socialist Review* 6 (August 1905): 76–77.

169. Eugene V. Debs, letter to the *Social Democratic Herald*, in Ginger, *Bending Cross*, "the official," "Since when," and "rotten . . . but it," 240; Debs, "The Coming Labor Union," *Miners' Magazine* 7 (October 26, 1905), "The choice," 13; Victor L. Berger, *Berger's Broadsides* (Milwaukee: Social-Democratic Publishing, 1912); Miller, *Victor L. Berger and the Promise of Constructive Socialism*, 21–37; Elmer A. Beck, *The Sewer Socialists: A History of the Socialist Party of Wisconsin, 1897–1940*, 2 vols. (Fennimore, WI: Westburg, 1982).

170. *Chicago Daily Socialist*, May 11, 1908, "The police," in Foner, *American Socialism and Black Americans*, 169–170; Woodbey, "The New Emancipation," "The agitation," 249.

171. Dubofsky, *We Shall Be All*, 120–170; Ginger, *Bending Cross*, 253–258.

172. Albert S. Lindemann, *A History of European Socialism* (New Haven, CT: Yale University Press, 1983), 133–184; Friedrich Engels, *The Origin of the Family, Private Property, and the State* (New York: International Publishers, 1942); August Bebel, *Woman under Socialism* (New York: New York Labor News, 1904); Eugene V. Debs, "Enfranchisement of Women," *Progressive Woman* 22 (March 1909), "pledge" and "the rights," 5; Debs, "A Letter from Debs on Immigration," *International Socialist Review* 11 (July 1910): 17; Miller, "For White Men Only," 284.

173. Mary Jo Buhle, *Women and American Socialism, 1870–1920* (Urbana: University of Illinois Press, 1981), 145–175; Sally M. Miller, "Other Socialists: Native-Born and Immigrant Women in the Socialist Party of America, 1901–1917," *Labor History* 24 (Winter 1983): 84–102; Miller, "For White Men Only," 288–291; Kate Richards O'Hare, "'Nigger' Equality," in *Kate Richards O'Hare: Selected Writings and Speeches*, ed. Philip S. Foner and Sally M. Miller (Baton Rouge: Louisiana State University Press, 1982), 44–89; Charles Leinenweber, "The American Socialist Party and 'New' Immigrants," *Science and Society* 32 (Winter 1968): 2–25; Kipnis, *American Socialist Movement, 1897–1912*, 272–288.

174. Mark Naison, *Communists in Harlem During the Depression* (Urbana: University of Illinois Press, 1983), 4; Miller, "For White Men Only," 297–298; George W. Slater Jr., "Negroes Becoming Socialists," *Chicago Daily Socialist*, September 15, 1908; Slater, "Booker T. Washington's Error," *Chicago Daily Socialist*, September 22, 1908, in Woodbey, *Black Socialist Preacher*, 299–301, 302–304.

175. Grace L. Miller, "The IWW Free Speech Fight: San Diego, 1912," *Southern California Quarterly* 54 (1972): 211–238; Dubofsky, *We Shall Be All*, 189–197; Foner, *American Socialism and Black Americans*, 171–172; Rosalie Shanks, "The IWW Free Speech Movement: San Diego, 1912," *Journal of San Diego History* 19 (Winter 1973): 25–33.

176. George W. Woodbey, "Why the Socialists Must Reach the Churches with Their Message," *Christian Socialist*, February 1915, in Woodbey, *Black Socialist Preacher*, quote, 261. For brief accounts of Woodbey's career, see Robert H. Craig, *Religion and Radical Politics: An Alternative Christian Tradition in the United States* (Philadelphia: Temple University Press, 1992), 116–120; Allen Dwight Callahan, "Remembering

Nehemiah: A Note on Biblical Theology," in *Black Zion: African American Religious Encounters with Zionism*, ed. Yvonne Chireau and Nathaniel Deutsch (New York: Oxford University Press, 2000), 161–162; Juan M. Floyd-Thomas, *The Origins of Black Humanism in America: Reverend Ethelred Brown and the Unitarian Church* (New York: Palgrave Macmillan, 2008), 105–106; Winston A. James, "Being Black and Red in Jim Crow America: Notes on the Ideology and Travails of Afro-America's Socialist Pioneers, 1877–1930," *Souls* 1 (Fall 1999): 47–48.

177. Jeffrey B. Perry, *Hubert Henry Harrison: The Voice of Harlem Radicalism, 1882–1918* (New York: Columbia University Press, 2008); Richard B. Moore, "Harrison, Hubert Henry," in *Dictionary of American Negro Biography*, 292–293.

178. Hubert Henry Harrison, "How to Do It—And How Not," *New York Call*, December 16, 1911, in Harrison, *A Hubert Harrison Reader*, ed. Jeffrey B. Perry (Middletown, CT: Wesleyan University Press, 2001), quotes, 60.

179. Ibid., quotes, 61.

180. Ibid., 61–62.

181. George W. Slater Jr., "The New Abolitionists," *Chicago Daily Socialist*, January 4, 1909; Slater, "How and Why I Became a Socialist," *Chicago Daily Socialist*, September 8, 1908, "purity" and "the solution," 298; Slater, "Abraham Lincoln a Socialist," *Chicago Daily Socialist*, October 6, 1908; Eugene Debs to *Chicago Daily Socialist*, January 4, 1909, "a fine," 336, in Woodbey, *Black Socialist Preacher*, 334–335, 296–298, 309–311, 336.

182. George W. Slater Jr., "The Negro and Socialism," *Christian Socialist*, July 1, 1913, in Woodbey, *Black Socialist Preacher*, 346.

CHAPTER 7. RESISTANCE AND ANTICIPATION

1. See George Edmund Haynes, *The Trend of the Races* (New York: Council of Women for Home Missions and Missionary Education, 1929); Haynes, *Negro Migration, 1916–1917* (Washington, DC: U.S. Department of Labor, 1918); Monroe N. Work, *The Negro Year Book for 1921–22* (Tuskegee, AL: Negro Year Book, Tuskegee Institute, 1923); Work, *A Bibliography of the Negro in Africa and America* (New York: H. W. Wilson, 1928); Richard I. McKinney, *Mordecai, The Man and His Message: The Story of Mordecai Wyatt Johnson* (Washington, DC: Howard University Press, 1997).

2. See Countee Cullen, *The Black Christ and Other Poems* (New York: Harper & Brothers, 1929); Cullen, *My Lives and How I Lost Them* (New York: Harper & Brothers, 1942); E. Franklin Frazier, *The Negro Church in America* (1st ed., 1964; repr., New York: Schocken Books, 1974); Zachery Williams, *In Search of the Talented Tenth: Howard University Public Intellectuals and the Dilemmas of Race, 1926–1970* (Columbia: University of Missouri Press, 2009); Rayford W. Logan, *Howard University: The First Hundred Years, 1867–1967* (New York: New York University Press, 1969).

3. See Gary Dorrien, *Soul in Society: The Making and Renewal of Social Christianity* (Minneapolis, MN: Fortress Press, 1995), 207–228; Dorrien, *Social Ethics in the Making: Interpreting an American Tradition* (Oxford: Wiley-Blackwell, 2010), 533–

534; Dorrien, *Economy, Difference, Empire: Social Ethics for Social Justice* (New York: Columbia University Press, 2010), 29–65.

4. Richard R. Wright Jr., *Eighty-seven Years behind the Black Curtain: An Autobiography* (Philadelphia: Rare Book, 1965), quote, 204.

5. James G. Spady, "Wright, Richard Robert, Sr.," in *Dictionary of American Negro Biography*, ed. Rayford W. Logan and Michael R. Winston (New York: W. W. Norton, 1982), 674–675; Richard R. Wright Jr., *The Bishops of the African Methodist Episcopal Church* (Nashville, TN: AME Sunday School Union, 1963), 371–377.

6. Wright, *Eighty-seven Years*, quote, 17; Elizabeth Ross Haynes, *The Black Boy of Atlanta* (Boston: House of Edinboro, 1952), 4–14; Wright, *Bishops*, 371; June O. Patton, "'And the Truth Shall Make You Free': Richard Robert Wright, Sr., Black Intellectual, and Iconoclast, 1877–1897," *Journal of Negro History* 81 (Winter-Autumn, 1996): 17–21.

7. Spady, "Wright, Richard Robert, Sr.," 674; Wright, *Eighty-seven Years*, 24–27, 69; Haynes, *Black Boy of Atlanta*, 10–35; Patton, "'And the Truth Shall Make You Free,'" 17–30.

8. Wright, *Eighty-seven Years*, 34–37.

9. Ibid., 70, 79–83.

10. Ibid., quote, 39.

11. Ibid., quote, 40; Linda O. McMurry, *Recorder of the Black Experience: A Biography of Monroe Nathan Work* (Baton Rouge: Louisiana State University Press, 1985), 22.

12. Wright, *Eighty-seven Years*, quotes, 43. At the time, Mathews was moving from a straightforward social gospel rendering of the teaching of Jesus to the eschatological interpretation promulgated by Johannes Weiss and other scholars in the German history-of-religions school. See Gary Dorrien, *The Making of American Liberal Theology: Idealism, Realism, and Modernity, 1900–1950* (Louisville, KY: Westminster John Knox Press, 2003), 185–199; Shailer Mathews, *The Social Teaching of Jesus: An Essay in Christian Sociology* (New York: Macmillan, 1897); Mathews, *The Messianic Hope in the New Testament* (Chicago: University of Chicago Press, 1905); Johannes Weiss, *Die Predigt Jesu von Reiche Gottes* (Göttingen: Vandenhoeck & Ruprecht, 1892); Ernst Issel, *Die Lehre vom Reiche Gottes im Neuen Testament* (Leiden: E. J. Brill, 1891).

13. Wright, *Eighty-seven Years*, quotes, 149.

14. Jessie P. Guzman, "Monroe Nathan Work and His Contributions," *Journal of Negro History* 34 (October 1949): 428–432; McMurry, *Recorder of the Black Experience*, 15–17.

15. Dorrien, *Social Ethics in the Making*, 41–45; Fred H. Matthews, *Quest for an American Sociology: Robert E. Park and the Chicago School* (Montreal: McGill-Queen's University Press, 1977), 88–96.

16. William I. Thomas, "The Scope and Method of Folk Psychology," *American Journal of Sociology* 1 (January 1896): 434–445; Monroe N. Work, "Crime Among the Negroes in Chicago," *American Journal of Sociology* 6 (September 1900): 204–223; Work, ed., *Negro Year Book: An Annual Encyclopedia of the Negro, 1912* (Nashville, TN: Sunday School Union 1912); Work, ed., *Negro Year Book: An Annual Encyclopedia of the*

Negro, 1937–1938 (Tuskegee, AL: Negro Year Book Publishing, Tuskegee Institute, 1938); Work, *A Bibliography of the Negro in Africa and America* (New York: H. W. Wilson, 1928).

17. Richard R. Wright Jr., "The Industrial Condition of Negroes in Chicago" (master's thesis, University of Chicago Divinity School, 1903); Wright, *Eighty-seven Years*, 43; Wright, review of *The American Negro*, by William Hannibal Thomas, *American Journal of Sociology* 6 (May 1901): 850–851; Monroe N. Work, interview by Lewis A. Jones, May 15, 1932, Jessie P. Guzman Papers, Tuskegee Institute Archives; Work, "Sociology in the Common Schools," *Proceedings of the American Sociological Society* 13 (December 1918): 95–97.

18. Wright, *Eighty-seven Years*, quote, 45; see Julius Kaftan, "Die Selbständigkeit des Christentums, *Zeitschrift für Theologie und Kirche* 6: 373–394; Otto Pfleiderer, *Die Entwicklung der protestantischen Theologie in Deutschland seit Kant und in Grossbritannien seit 1825* (Freiburg: J.C.B. Mohr, 1891); Pfleiderer, *The Influence of the Apostle Paul on the Development of Christianity*, trans. John F. Smith (New York: Scribner's, 1885); Adolf von Harnack, *History of Dogma* (1st German ed., 3 vols., 1885, 1887, 1889; 3rd German ed., English trans., 7 vols., trans Neil Buchanan (Eugene, OR: Wipf and Stock Publishers, 1997).

19. Wright, *Eighty-seven Years*, 46.

20. Ibid., quote, 104.

21. Ibid., quotes, 106, 47; Wright, *Bishops*, 303; Richard R. Wright Jr., "The Migration of Negroes to the North," *Annals of the Academy of Political and Social Science* 27 (May 1906): 97–108; Wallace D. Best, *Passionately Human, No Less Divine: Religion and Culture in Black Chicago, 1915–1952* (Princeton, NJ: Princeton University Press, 2005), 132.

22. Wright, *Eighty-seven Years*, 96.

23. Ibid., quotes, 114, 115; see Albion W. Small, *An Introduction to the Study of Society* (New York: American Book, 1894); Small, *General Sociology: An Exposition of the Main Development in Sociological Theory from Spencer to Ratzenhofer* (Chicago: University of Chicago Press, 1905); Small, *Between Eras from Capitalism to Democracy* (Kansas City, MO: Inter-Collegiate, 1913).

24. Richard R. Wright Jr., "The Negro in Times of Industrial Unrest," *Charities Magazine* 15 (October 7, 1905): 69–73; Wright, "Forty Years of Negro Progress," *Southern Workman* 36 (March 1907): 157.

25. Richard R. Wright Jr., "Recent Improvements in Housing Among Negroes in the North," *Southern Workman* 37 (November 1908): 601; Richard R. Wright Jr., "Social Work and the Influence of the Negro Church," *Annals of the American Academy of Political and Social Science* 30 (1907): 509–521; Wright, *A Study of the Industrial Conditions of the Negro Population of Pennsylvania* (Harrisburg, PA: Bureau of Industrial Statistics, 1914).

26. Richard R. Wright Jr., *The Negro in Pennsylvania: A Study in Economic History* (Philadelphia: African Methodist Episcopal Book Concern, 1912); Wright, *Eighty-seven Years*, quotes, 49; Wright "Housing and Sanitation in Relation to Mortality of Negroes," *Southern Workman* 35 (September 1906): 475.

27. Wright, *Eighty-seven Years*, quotes, 160, 161; Wright, *Bishops*, 372–373; Richard R. Wright Jr., "The Negro and Crime," *Southern Workman* 39 (March 1910): 137; Wright, "Home Ownership and Savings Among Negroes of Philadelphia," *Southern Workman* 36 (December 1907): 665.

28. Richard R. Wright Jr., *Self-Help in Negro Education* (Cheyney, PA: Committee of Twelve, 1909); Wright, *The Philadelphia Colored Directory: A Handbook of the Religious, Social, Political, Professional, Business and Other Activities of the Negroes of Philadelphia* (Philadelphia: Philadelphia Colored Directory, 1910); Wright, "Criminal Statistics," *Southern Workman* 40 (May 1911): 291; Wright, "The Negro in Unskilled Labor," *Annals of the American Academy of Political and Social Science* 49 (1913): 19–27; Wright, *The Negro Problem* (Philadelphia: A.M.E. Book Concern, 1911).

29. Wright, *Bishops*, 372; Wright, *Eighty-seven Years*, 169–173; Gilbert Anthony Williams, *The Christian Recorder, Newspaper of the African Methodist Episcopal Church* (Jefferson, NC: McFarland, 1996), 125–138.

30. Wright, *Bishops*, 372; Wright, *Eighty-seven Years*, 177–178; see John Miley, *Systematic Theology*, 2 vols. (New York: Hunt and Eaton, 1893).

31. Wright, *Negro in Pennsylvania*, quotes, 52, 53.

32. Ibid., 54–63.

33. Ibid., quotes, 70, 78.

34. Ibid., 80–83.

35. Ibid., 119.

36. Ibid., 140–159, quotes, 144, 158.

37. Ibid., 183.

38. Ibid., quotes, 186–187.

39. Ibid., quote, 167; Charles Flint Kellogg, *NAACP: A History of the National Association for the Advancement of Colored People, 1909–1920* (Baltimore, MD: Johns Hopkins University Press, 1967), 126.

40. Wright, *Negro in Pennsylvania*, 200–201.

41. Wright, "The Migration of Negroes to the North," 97–101; Richard R. Wright Jr., "Social Work and Social Science," *Charities* 30 (November 1907): 88; Wright, "The Negro in Times of Industrial Unrest," 69–72; Best, *Passionately Human*, 132–133.

42. Richard R. Wright Jr., "Should the Negroes Come North?" *Christian Recorder*, August 31, 1916.

43. Reverdy Ransom, "AME Churches Tell of Conditions," *Christian Recorder*, December 14, 1916; J. W. Rankin, "The Active Missionary Role," *Christian Recorder*, July 26, 1917; Milton C. Sernett, *Bound for the Promised Land: African American Religion and the Great Migration* (Durham, NC: Duke University Press, 1998); Best, *Passionately Human*, 134.

44. "Bethel Church Split," *Chicago Defender*, October 9, 1920; Best, *Passionately Human*, quote, 134.

45. Wright, *Eighty-seven Years*, 203–207. Du Bois omitted Wright from his account of his trip to the peace conference, and, thus, so did others. See W. E. B. Du Bois, *Dusk of Dawn: An Essay Toward an Autobiography of a Race Concept* (New York: Harcourt, Brace & World, 1940), 260–261; Du Bois, "Letter from Du Bois," *Crisis* 17 (February

1919): 163–166; David Levering Lewis, *W.E.B. Du Bois: Biography of a Race, 1868–1919* (New York: Henry Holt, 1993), 561–562.

46. Richard R. Wright Jr., "Editorial: Ministering to Our Expanding Life," *Christian Recorder* 68 (September 16, 1920), "The hope," 1; Wright, "Editorial: Leadership," *Christian Recorder* 70 (June 22, 1922), "The need" and "18," 1; Wright, "Editorial: The Mother's Edition," 70 (April 27, 1922), "'I can,'" 1; Wright, "Editorial: Sensational Preaching," *Christian Recorder* 69 (August 4, 1921), "all great," 1; Wright, "Editorial: He Found Us in a Very, Very Bad Shape," *Christian Recorder* 70 (September 21, 1922): 1; Wright, "Editorial: Women, Politics and the Church," *Christian Recorder* 68 (September 16, 1920), "So long," 1; Wright, "Editorial: Race Leadership," *Christian Recorder* 69 (April 14, 1921): 1; Wright, "Editorial: Training for Marriage," *Christian Recorder* 69 (November 3, 1921): 1; Wright, "Editorial: The Next Bishops' Council and the Crisis in African Methodism," *Christian Recorder* 70 (May 4, 1922); Wright, "Editorial: Children," *Christian Recorder* 70 (June 8, 1922): 1.

47. Richard R. Wright Jr., "Editorial: Ku Klux Klan in the North," *Christian Recorder* 68 (January 20, 1921), "spreading" and "It is," 1; Wright, "Editorial: President Harding on the Negro," *Christian Recorder* 69 (November 3, 1921), "The racial," 1, "natural" and "There is," 4; Wright, "Editorial: Georgia's Peonage Case," *Christian Recorder* 69 (April 14, 1921): 1.

48. Wright, *Eighty-seven Years*, 141–142.

49. Ibid., 131.

50. Ibid., 189–190.

51. Spady, "Richard Robert Wright, Sr.," 675; Wright, *Eighty-seven Years*, 190–195; Wright, *Bishops*, 373.

52. Wright, *Eighty-seven Years*, 198.

53. Richard R. Wright Jr., *Why the Colored Voters Should Help Re-elect Franklin D. Roosevelt* (New York: Democratic National Committee, 1936, Charles L. Blockson Afro-American Collection, Temple University, Philadelphia, PA); Wright, *Eighty-seven Years*, 210; Charlotte Crogman Wright, *Beneath the Southern Cross: The Story of an American Bishop's Wife in South Africa* (New York: Exposition, 1955), 13; see Jonathan S. Holloway, *Confronting the Veil: Abram Harris, Jr., E. Franklin Frazier, and Ralph Bunche, 1919–1941* (Chapel Hill: University of North Carolina Press, 2002).

54. Crogman Wright, *Beneath the Southern Cross*, quote, 14; Wright, *Eighty-seven Years*, 223–224.

55. Crogman Wright, *Beneath the Southern Cross*, 14–15.

56. L. L. Berry, *A Century of Missions of the African Methodist Episcopal Church, 1840–1940* (New York: AME Missionary Department, 1942), 74–76; Charles S. Smith, *A History of the African Methodist Episcopal Church* (Philadelphia: A.M.E. Book Concern, 1922), 182–183; F. M. Gow, et al., "Africa, South, the AME Church in," in *Encyclopedia of the African Methodist Episcopal Church*, ed. Richard R. Wright Jr. (Philadelphia: A.M.E. Book Concern, 1947), 318–324.

57. Henry McNeal Turner, "My Trip to South Africa," *A.M.E. Church Review* 15 (April 1899): 812; Smith, *History of the African Methodist Episcopal Church*, 183–190; Wright,

Eighty-seven Years, 227–228; Berry, *Century of Missions of the African Methodist Episcopal Church, 1840–1940*, 77–79.

58. Wright, *Eighty-seven Years*, 232–235.

59. Crogman Wright, *Beneath the Southern Cross*, quote, 127; Wright, *Eighty-seven Years*, quotes, 210.

60. Richard R. Wright Jr., *Why the Negro Vote Should Go to President Roosevelt* (Chicago: Democratic National Committee, 1940); Wright, *Eighty-seven Years*, 210–211; Nancy J. Weiss, *Farewell to the Party of Lincoln: Black Politics in the Age of FDR* (Princeton, NJ: Princeton University Press, 1983).

61. Richard R. Wright Jr., *What the Negro Gives His Church: Two Cents* (Philadelphia: A.M.E. Book Concern 1940); Wright, *Bishops*, 373–374.

62. Richard R. Wright Jr., *Outline of the Teaching of Jesus*, 1st ed., 1902; 6th ed. rev. (Nashville, TN: AME Sunday School Union, 1946), quotes, 9, 45, 46.

63. Ibid., quotes, 48, 95.

64. Walter White, *A Man Called White: The Autobiography of Walter White* (New York: Viking Penguin, 1948), 364–366, quote, 366.

65. Wright, *Eighty-seven Years*, 340.

66. Evelyn Brooks Higginbotham, *Righteous Discontent: The Women's Movement in the Black Baptist Church, 1880–1920* (Cambridge, MA: Harvard University Press, 1993), "the politics," 185; Walter Earl Fluker, "Recognition, Respectability, and Loyalty: Black Churches and the Quest for Civility," in *New Day Begun: African American Churches and Civic Culture in Post-Civil Rights America*, ed. Drew Smith (Durham, NC: Duke University Press, 2003), 121–122; Wright, "Social Work and the Influence of the Negro Church," 509–521; J. K. Anderson, "Negro Bishop Finds Hope in Racial Unrest," *Detroit Free Press*, June 22, 1963, "There will," cited in Kevin F. Modesto, " 'Won't Be Weighted Down': Richard R. Wright, Jr.'s Contributions to Social Work and Social Welfare," *Journal of Sociology and Social Welfare* 31 (June 2004): 87; see Terrell Dale Goddard, "The Black Social Gospel in Chicago, 1896–1906: The Ministries of Reverdy C. Ransom and Richard R. Wright, Jr.," *Journal of Negro History* 84 (Summer 1999): 227–246.

67. See Hastings Rashdall, *The Idea of Atonement in Christian Theology* (London: Macmillan, 1919); Gustaf Aulén, *Christus Victor: An Historical Study of the Three Main Types of the Idea of Atonement*, trans. A. G. Hebert (New York: Macmillan, 1931); Jürgen Moltmann, *The Crucified God: The Cross of Christ as the Foundation and Criticism of Christian Theology*, trans. R. A. Wilson and John Bowden (New York: Harper & Row, 1974).

68. See Rita Nakashima Brock and Rebecca Ann Parker, *Proverbs of Ashes: Violence, Redemptive Suffering, and the Search for What Saves Us* (Boston: Beacon Press, 2001); Jacquelyn Grant, "The Sin of Servanthood and the Deliverance of Discipleship," in *A Troubling in My Soul: Womanist Perspectives on Evil and Suffering*, ed. Emilie Townes (Maryknoll, NY: Orbis Books, 1993), 199–218; JoAnne M. Terrell, *Power in the Blood? The Cross in the African American Experience* (Maryknoll, NY: Orbis, 1998); Joanne Carlson Brown and Rebecca Ann Parker, "For God So Loved the World?" in *Christianity, Patriarchy and Abuse*, ed. Joanne Carlson Brown and Carole R. Bohn (New York: Pilgrim, 1989), 1–30.

69. James H. Cone, *The Cross and the Lynching Tree* (Maryknoll, NY: Orbis, 2011), quotes, 22, 9.

70. M. Shawn Copeland, "Wading through Many Sorrows: Toward a Theology of Suffering in Womanist Perspective," in *A Troubling in My Soul*, 109–129, "The enslaved," 120; Cone, *Cross and the Lynching Tree*, "The cross," 157–158.

71. Quincy Ewing, "The Heart of the Race Problem," *Atlantic Monthly*, March 1909, 389–397; Ewing, "The Beginning of the End," *Colored American Magazine*, October 1901, 471–478; David Margolick, *Strange Fruit: Billie Holliday, Café Society, and an Early Cry for Civil Rights* (Philadelphia: Running Press, 2000).

72. Reverdy C. Ransom, "Lynching and American Public Opinion," Appendix B in Calvin S. Morris, *Reverdy C. Ransom: Black Advocate of the Social Gospel* (Lanham, MD: University Press of America, 1990), 178–182, quotes, 179.

73. Ibid., 179, 181.

74. Ibid., 181.

75. Ibid., 181–182.

INDEX

Abbott, Lyman: assimilationist ideology and, 61; Du Bois criticized by, 217–218; paternalism of, 497; social gospel movement and, 18; Washington and, 137, 154, 156, 226; Wells and, 94

Abernathy, Ralph, 8

abolitionism: African emigration movement, 34–36; antislavery vs., 64; black social gospel and, 8–10; in Boston, 317; Crummell and, 170–179; Du Bois and, 229, 237; left-assimilationist ideology and, 62–68; social gospel and, 4–7; Turner and, 37–42. *See also* civil rights movement; new abolitionism

Aborigines Protection Society, 199

Abyssinian Baptist Church, Powell Sr. and, 428–447

accommodationist tradition: Du Bois's critique of, 158, 210–211, 227–233; Ransom's criticism of, 326; separatism movement, 401–403; Washington's belief in, 61, 131–132, 138–154

Adams, Cyrus Field, 370

Adams, John, 47, 317

Adams, John H., 466–467

Adams, John Quincy, 370

Adams, Lewis, 132–134

Adams, Samuel, 47

Addams, Jane: Burroughs and, 416–417; Du Bois and, 197; NAACP and, 250, 269, 272; pacifism of, 286; Ransom and, 311, 313, 391–392; settlement movement and, 20, 181–182; Wells-Barnett and, 123; Wright and, 494

Adkins, Joseph, 48

Africa: African American cultural influences from, 352; colonialism and Christianity in, 72–76; Crummell's views of, 170–179; Du Bois on imperialism in, 282–286; indenture system in, 199–200; Turner's trips to, 69–70. *See also* Pan-African movement

African American Civil Rights, 26

African Association, 199

African Civilization Society, 70

African Communities (Imperial) League, 340

African emigration movement: black radicalism and, 14–15; black social gospel and, 5–6, 12–13; Crummell and, 173–174; Du Bois's opposition to, 210; Garvey and, 192, 294, 340–358; Ransom's opposition to, 353–354; Turner's support for, 34–36, 39–42, 50–60, 70–84; Wells-Barnett's discussion of, 96–98

African Legions, 343

and, 84, 114–115, 122–123; on white
  nationalism, 153–154; Wright and, 492,
  494–495, 500, 513, 516
Ransom, Reverdy, Jr., 304
Ransom, Reverdy, III, 389
rape, lynching linked to, 98–100, 107–117.
  See also sexuality
Ratzel, Friedrich, 188
Rauschenbusch, Walter, 24–25, 444
Rauschenbusch, Winifred, 444
Reconstruction: black churches and, 51;
  black social gospel and, 2–5, 12–13, 19;
  Du Bois's research on, 211, 246–247;
  lynching during, 20; politics and, 53–60;
  Simmons and, 395–398; Southern black
  churches and, 42–51; Washington's
  attitude toward, 131, 133
Reconstruction Amendments. *See*
  Fifteenth Amendment; Fourteenth
  Amendment
Redpath, James, 40
"Red Summer" (1919), 293, 434
Reed, Adolph L., Jr., 32, 193–195
Reitman, Ben, 478
religious orthodoxy: Du Bois's criticism of,
  22–23, 31–33; Wright's exploration of,
  487–488, 506–518
Remond, Charles Lennox, 317
Rends, W. P., 426
Republican Party: African Americans
  and, 12; Arnett and, 307; black churches
  and, 51; Burroughs and, 422–423; Du
  Bois and, 244–248, 268–271; Powell Sr.
  and, 428, 438; Ransom's criticism of,
  320, 325, 328, 336, 386–387;
  Reconstruction-era politics and, 44–51,
  53–60, 64; Roosevelt and, 243–244;
  Walters and, 360, 365–368, 374–378;
  Washington and, 128–129; Wright Jr.
  and, 488, 506–507, 512; Wright Sr. and,
  487, 512
Revels, Hiram R., 50
Revels, Willis H., 37–38
Reynolds, Ira May, 347–348

Richards, William H., 233
Richmond Dispatch, 203
Richmond Institute, 62
Richmond News, 204
Richmond Planet, 94
Richmond Theological Institute, 402
Richmond Times, 203
Ricker, A. W., 459, 461
Ridgel, Alfred L., 5, 75–76
Robinson, Cedric J., 14
Rochester Theological Seminary, 485
Rockefeller, John D., 146
Rockefeller, John D., Jr., 435
Rogers, Henry H., 146
Roman, C. V., 329
Roman Catholic Church, 68
Roosevelt, Alice Lee, 203–205
Roosevelt, Edith, 203
Roosevelt, Eleanor, 446–447, 512
Roosevelt, Franklin D., 386–387, 422–423,
  512, 515
Roosevelt, Theodore: Fort Brown incident
  and, 238–240; Progressive Party and,
  268–269; racial policies of, 234, 242–244;
  Ransom and, 320, 325, 330; Walters and,
  371–372, 375; Washington and, 77–78,
  122, 202–208, 224, 226, 239–242; Wright
  and, 507
*Rope and Faggot: An Interview with Judge
  Lynch* (White), 123, 448–449
Rosenwald Fund, 452
Royall, John M., 337
Royce, Josiah, 165, 351
Roye, Edward James, 174–175
R. R. Wright Jr. School of Religion
  (Wilberforce), 516
Rubinow, Isaac Max, 231
Ruffin, Josephine St. Pierre, 27, 101–103,
  115, 117–118
Ruffner, Louis, 127–128
Ruffner, Viola (Knapp), 127–128, 130
Rush, Benjamin, 47
Russell, Charles Edward: *The Crisis* and,
  249, 252–254, 256, 262, 286, 294, 452;